Macworld®
ClarisWorks® 4
Bible

Macworld®
ClarisWorks® 4
Bible

by Steven A. Schwartz, Ph.D.

IDG Books Worldwide, Inc.
An International Data Group Company

Foster City, CA ♦ Chicago, IL ♦ Indianapolis, IN ♦ Braintree, MA ♦ Dallas, TX

Macworld® Press ClarisWorks 4 Bible
Published by
IDG Books Worldwide, Inc.
An International Data Group Company
Suite 400 919 E. Hillsdale Blvd.
Foster City, CA 94404

Library of Congress Catalog Card No.: 95-81539

ISBN: 1-56884-588-x

Printed in the United States of America

10 9 8 7 6 5 4 3 2 1

1B/QU/RS/ZV

Distributed in the United States by IDG Books Worldwide, Inc.

Distributed by Macmillan Canada for Canada; by Computer and Technical Books for the Caribbean Basin; by Contemporanea de Ediciones for Venezuela; by Distribuidora Cuspide for Argentina; by CITEC for Brazil; by Ediciones ZETA S.C.R. Ltda. for Peru; by Editorial Limusa SA for Mexico; by Transworld Publishers Limited in the United Kingdom and Europe; by Al-Maiman Publishers & Distributors for Saudi Arabia; by Simron Pty. Ltd. for South Africa; by IDG Communications (HK) Ltd. for Hong Kong; by Toppan Company Ltd. for Japan; by Addison Wesley Publishing Company for Korea; by Longman Singapore Publishers Ltd. for Singapore, Malaysia, Thailand, and Indonesia; by Unalis Corporation for Taiwan; by WS Computer Publishing Company, Inc. for the Philippines; by WoodsLane Pty. Ltd. for Australia; by WoodsLane Enterprises Ltd. for New Zealand.

For general information on IDG Books Worldwide's books in the U.S., please call our Consumer Customer Service department at 800-762-2974. For reseller information, including discounts and premium sales, please call our Reseller Customer Service department at 800-434-3422.

For information on where to purchase IDG Books Worldwide's books outside the U.S., contact IDG Books Worldwide at 415-655-3021 or fax 415-655-3295.

For information on translations, contact Marc Jeffrey Mikulich, Director, Foreign & Subsidiary Rights, at IDG Books Worldwide, 415-655-3018 or fax 415-655-3295.

For sales inquiries and special prices for bulk quantities, write to the address above or call IDG Books Worldwide at 415-655-3200.

For information on using IDG Books Worldwide's books in the classroom, or ordering examination copies, contact Jim Kelly at 800-434-2086.

For authorization to photocopy items for corporate, personal, or educational use, please contact Copyright Clearance Center, 222 Rosewood Drive, Danvers, MA 01923, or fax 508-750-4470.

 is a trademark under exclusive license to IDG Books Worldwide, Inc., from International Data Group, Inc.

About the Author

In 1978, Dr. Steven Schwartz bought his first microcomputer, a new Apple II+. Determined to find a way to make money with it, he began writing software reviews, BASIC programs, and user tips for *Nibble* magazine. Shortly thereafter, he was made a Contributing Editor.

Over the past 17 years, Steven has written hundreds of articles for more than a dozen computer magazines. He currently writes for *MacWorld* and *Multimedia World*. He was also a founding editor of *Software Digest*, as well as Business Editor for *MACazine*.

Steven is the author of more than 25 books. He has a Ph.D. in psychology and presently lives in the Arizona desert, where the wildlife — particularly the lizards — keeps him perpetually amused.

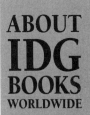

Welcome to the world of IDG Books Worldwide.

IDG Books Worldwide, Inc., is a subsidiary of International Data Group, the world's largest publisher of computer-related information and the leading global provider of information services on information technology. IDG was founded more than 25 years ago and now employs more than 7,700 people worldwide. IDG publishes more than 250 computer publications in 67 countries (see listing below). More than 70 million people read one or more IDG publications each month.

Launched in 1990, IDG Books Worldwide is today the #1 publisher of best-selling computer books in the United States. We are proud to have received 8 awards from the Computer Press Association in recognition of editorial excellence and three from Computer Currents' First Annual Readers' Choice Awards, and our best-selling ...*For Dummies*® series has more than 19 million copies in print with translations in 28 languages. IDG Books Worldwide, through a joint venture with IDG's Hi-Tech Beijing, became the first U.S. publisher to publish a computer book in the People's Republic of China. In record time, IDG Books Worldwide has become the first choice for millions of readers around the world who want to learn how to better manage their businesses.

Our mission is simple: Every one of our books is designed to bring extra value and skill-building instructions to the reader. Our books are written by experts who understand and care about our readers. The knowledge base of our editorial staff comes from years of experience in publishing, education, and journalism — experience which we use to produce books for the '90s. In short, we care about books, so we attract the best people. We devote special attention to details such as audience, interior design, use of icons, and illustrations. And because we use an efficient process of authoring, editing, and desktop publishing our books electronically, we can spend more time ensuring superior content and spend less time on the technicalities of making books.

You can count on our commitment to deliver high-quality books at competitive prices on topics you want to read about. At IDG Books Worldwide, we continue in the IDG tradition of delivering quality for more than 25 years. You'll find no better book on a subject than one from IDG Books Worldwide.

John J. Kilcullen

John Kilcullen
President and CEO
IDG Books Worldwide, Inc.

IDG Books Worldwide, Inc., is a subsidiary of International Data Group, the world's largest publisher of computer-related information and the leading global provider of information services on information technology. International Data Group publishes over 250 computer publications in 67 countries. Seventy million people read one or more International Data Group publications each month. International Data Group's publications include: **ARGENTINA:** Computerworld Argentina, GamePro, Infoworld, PC World Argentina; **AUSTRALIA:** Australian Macworld, Client/Server Journal, Computer Living, Computerworld, Digital News, Network World, PC World, Publishing Essentials, Reseller; **AUSTRIA:** Computerwelt, PC TEST; **BELARUS:** PC World Belarus; **BELGIUM:** Data News; **BRAZIL:** Annuário de Informática, Computerworld Brazil, Connections, Super Game Power, Macworld, PC World Brazil, Publish Brazil, SUPERGAME; **BULGARIA:** Computerworld Bulgaria, Networkworld/Bulgaria, PC & MacWorld Bulgaria; **CANADA:** CIO Canada, ComputerWorld Canada, InfoCanada, Network World Canada, Reseller World; **CHILE:** Computerworld Chile, GamePro, PC World Chile; **COLUMBIA:** Computerworld Colombia, GamePro, PC World Colombia; **COSTA RICA:** PC World Costa Rica/Nicaragua; **THE CZECH AND SLOVAK REPUBLICS:** Computerworld Czechoslovakia, Elektronika Czechoslovakia, PC World Czechoslovakia; **DENMARK:** Communications World, Computerworld Danmark, Macworld Danmark, PC World Danmark, PC World Danmark Supplements, TECH World; **DOMINICAN REPUBLIC:** PC World Republica Dominicana; **ECUADOR:** PC World Ecuador, GamePro; **EGYPT:** Computerworld Middle East, PC World Middle East; **EL SALVADOR:** PC World Centro America; **FINLAND:** MikroPC, Tietoverkko, Tietoviikko; **FRANCE:** Distributique, Golden, Info PC, Le Guide du Monde Informatique, Le Monde Informatique, Reseaux & Telecoms; **GERMANY:** Computer Business, Computerwoche, Computerwoche, Computerwoche Extra, Computerwoche Focus, Electronic Entertainment, GamePro, I/M Information Management, Macwelt, PC Welt; **GREECE:** GamePro, Macworld & Publish; **GUATEMALA:** PC World Centro America; **HONDURAS:** PC World Centro America; **HONG KONG:** Computerworld Hong Kong, PCWorld Hong Kong, Publish in Asia; **HUNGARY:** ABCD CD-ROM, Computerworld Szamitastechnika, PC & Mac World Hungary, PC-X Magazine; **INDIA:** Computerworld India, PC World India, Publish in Asia; **INDONESIA:** InfoKomputer PC World, Komputek Computerworld, Publish in Asia; **IRELAND:** ComputerScope, PC Live!; **ISRAEL:** PC World 32 BIT, People & Computers; **ITALY:** Computerworld Italia, Computerworld Italia Special Editions, Lotus Italia, Macworld Italia, Networking Italia, PC Shopping, PC World Italia, PC World/Walt Disney; **JAPAN:** Macworld Japan, Nikkei Personal Computing, SunWorld Japan, Windows World Japan; **KENYA:** East African Computer News; **KOREA:** Hi-Tech Information/Computerworld, Macworld Korea, PC World Korea; **MACEDONIA:** PC World Macedonia; **MALAYSIA:** Computerworld Malaysia, PC World Malaysia, Publish in Asia; **MEXICO:** Computerworld Mexico, GamePro, Macworld, PC World Mexico; **MYANMAR:** PC World Myanmar; **NETHERLANDS:** Computable, Computer! Totaal, LAN Magazine, Macworld, Net Magazine; **NEW ZEALAND:** Computer Buyer, Computerworld New Zealand, MTB, Network World, PC World New Zealand; **NICARAGUA:** PC World Costa Rica/Nicaragua; **NIGERIA:** PC World Africa; **NORWAY:** Computerworld Norge, Computerworld Privat, CW Rapport Klient/Tjener, CW Rapport Nettverk & Telecom, CW Rapport Offentlig Sektor, IDG's KURSGUIDE, Macworld Norge, Multimedia World, PC World Ekspress, PC World Nettverk, PC World Norge, PC World's Produktguide, Windows Spesial; **PAKISTAN:** Computerworld Pakistan, PC World Pakistan; **PANAMA:** GamePro, PC World Panama; **PARAGUAY:** PC World Paraguay; **P. R. OF CHINA:** China Computerworld, China Infoworld, Computer & Communication, Electronic Product World, Electronics Today, Game Camp, PC World China, Popular Computer Week, Software World, Telecom Product World; **PERU:** Computerworld Peru, GamePro, PC World Profesional Peru, PC World Peru; **POLAND:** Computerworld Poland, Computerworld Special Report, Macworld, Networld, PC World Komputer; **PHILIPPINES:** Computerworld Philippines, PC Digest, Publish in Asia; **PORTUGAL:** Cerebro/PC World, Correio Informático/Computerworld, Mac•In/PC•In Portugal; **PUERTO RICO:** PC World Puerto Rico; **ROMANIA:** Computerworld Romania, PC World Romania, Telecom Romania; **RUSSIA:** Computerworld Rossiya, Network World Russia, PC World Russia; **SINGAPORE:** Computerworld Singapore, PC World Singapore, Publish in Asia; **SLOVENIA:** MONITOR; **SOUTH AFRICA:** Computing S.A., Network World S.A., Software World; **SPAIN:** Computerworld España, COMUNICACIONES WORLD, Dealer World, Macworld España, PC World España; **SWEDEN:** CAP&Design, Computer Sweden, Corporate Computing, MacWorld, Maxi Data, MikroDatorn, Nätverk & Kommunikation, PC/Aktiv, PC World, Windows World; **SWITZERLAND:** Computerworld Schweiz, Macworld Schweiz, PCtip; **TAIWAN:** Computerworld Taiwan, Macworld Taiwan, PC World Taiwan, Publish Taiwan, Windows World; **THAILAND:** Thai Computerworld, Publish in Asia; **TURKEY:** Computerworld Monitör, MACWORLD Turkiye, PC WORLD Turkiye; **UKRAINE:** Computerworld Kiev, Computers & Software Magazine, PC World Ukraine; **UNITED KINGDOM:** Acorn User, Amiga Action, Amiga Computing, Amiga, AppletalK, CD Powerplay, CD-ROM Now, Computing, Connexion, GamePro, Lotus Magazine, Macaction, Macworld, Open Computing, Parents and Computers, PC Home, PC Works, The WEB; **UNITED STATES:** Cable in the Classroom, CD Review, CIO Magazine, Computerworld, Computerworld Client/Server Journal, Digital Video Magazine, DOS World, Electronic, InfoWorld, I-Way, Macworld, Maximize, MULTIMEDIA WORLD, Network World, PC World, PUBLISH, SWATPro Magazine, Video Event, WebMaster; **URUGUAY:** PC World Uruguay; **VENEZUELA:** Computerworld Venezuela, GamePro, PC World Venezuela; and **VIETNAM:** PC World Vietnam   10/17/95

Dedication

To Sheldon and Barbara Schwartz, the best parents anyone could wish for.

Acknowledgments

I am grateful to the many people who offered their encouragement and support for this updated edition of the book, including Jay Lee (Claris Corporation); Nancy Dunn, Ken Brown, and Kathi Duggan (IDG Books Worldwide); and Matt Wagner (Waterside Productions).

(The Publisher would like to give special thanks to Patrick J. McGovern, without whom this book would not have been possible.)

Credits

**Senior Vice President
and Group Publisher**
Brenda McLaughlin

Acquisitions Editor
Nancy E. Dunn

Brand Manager
Pradeepa Siva

Developmental Editor
Kenyon Brown

Editorial Assistant
Suki Gear

Production Director
Beth Jenkins

Production Assistant
Jacalyn L. Pennywell

**Supervisor of
Project Coordination**
Cindy L. Phipps

Supervisor of Page Layout
Kathie S. Schnorr

Production Systems Specialist
Steve Peake

Pre-Press Coordination
Tony Augsburger
Patricia R. Reynolds
Theresa Sánchez-Baker

Media/Archive Coordination
Leslie Popplewell
Kerri Cornell
Michael Wilkey

Project Editor
Kathryn Duggan

Technical Reviewer
Jay Lee

Associate Project Coordinator
Sherry Gomoll

Graphics Coordination
Shelley Lea
Gina Scorr
Carla Radzikinas

Production Staff
Todd Klemme
Drew R. Moore
Laura Puranen

Proofreaders
Jenny Kaufeld
Christine Meloy Beck
Gwenette Gaddis
Dwight Ramsey
Karl Saff
Robert Springer

Indexer
Sherry Massey

Book Design
Beth Jenkins
Shelley Lea

Contents at a Glance

Table of Contents

Part III: Integrating the ClarisWorks Environments 373

Introduction

About This Book

The *Macworld ClarisWorks 4.0 Bible* is a different kind of computer book. First, it's not a manual. Many people don't like computer manuals — perhaps because they feel obligated to read them from cover to cover to avoid missing something important or because manuals are designed to explain how features work rather than how to put a program to work for you. The *Macworld ClarisWorks 4.0 Bible* is not a book that you *have* to read. It's a book that you'll *want* to read — because it provides easy-to-find, easy-to-understand explanations of many of the common tasks for which you bought ClarisWorks in the first place. When you want to know how to use a particular program feature, you can use the Table of Contents or the Index to quickly identify the section of the book that you need to read.

Second, unlike many computer books, this one is *task oriented*. The reason most people buy computer books is not because they want to become an expert with a particular piece of software. Instead, they have a task that they want to accomplish. In addition to the step-by-step explanations of normal ClarisWorks procedures, the book also provides many worked-through task examples. Rather than spend your time reinventing the wheel, you can just follow the numbered steps to accomplish many common business and home-computing tasks.

Finally, the philosophy of this book — as well as the other books in the *Macworld Bible* series — is that you don't want or need a handful of books on a computer program; one should suffice. The *Macworld ClarisWorks 4.0 Bible* is an all-in-one book. Rarely will you be referred back to your manual or ClarisWorks Help. You can find almost anything you want to know about ClarisWorks 4.0 in this book.

What Is ClarisWorks?

ClarisWorks belongs to a class of programs known as *integrated software*. The idea behind integrated software is that — within a single box — you acquire a core set of programs that fulfill all your basic computing needs. The typical program components, or *modules*, are word processing, spreadsheet, database, graphics, and telecommunications. And the modules function together as a cohesive unit — more or less. I say "more or less" because the early integrated software packages (as well as many of the current ones) were often only a collection of programs. They frequently had little in common with each other beyond being in the same box. There may have been no way to share data between the modules or significant differences in the command structure in the different modules. Learning how to use one module may have taught you nothing about using the other modules.

As a class of software, integrated software was often viewed with disdain by computing purists. In order to squeeze the entire package into a reasonable amount of memory, the modules were often stripped down to bare-bones programs. "Big time" features — such as a spelling checker, thesaurus, character and paragraph styles, and advanced searching and sorting — were routinely missing. Thus, many users felt (rightfully so) that the integrated modules couldn't hold a candle to full-featured stand-alone programs.

Microsoft Works was the first major integrated package for the Macintosh. The Mac's native support for cut-and-paste made it relatively easy to merge data from different types of documents, enabling you to paste a graphic into a word processing file, for example. Although integration was considerably better than in the early programs, each Works module was essentially a stand-alone tool. To create a new spreadsheet that you wanted to incorporate into an annual report, you had to work in both the spreadsheet and word processing modules and then cut and paste the spreadsheet into the final document.

Why Choose ClarisWorks? _____

ClarisWorks has carried the integration concept forward to the next logical step. It, too, has separate components, but you can use features of the different components no matter what type of document you're currently working on. For example, although a word processing document is primarily composed of words, you can add a spreadsheet section to the document simply by selecting the spreadsheet tool and then drawing a frame, as shown in Figure INTRO-1.

While you are working in the spreadsheet frame, the menu bar and menu commands change to ones relevant to spreadsheets — hiding the irrelevant word processing commands. If you click in any part of the word processing text, the menus change back to ones appropriate for word processing. This tight integration between components makes ClarisWorks significantly easier and more convenient to use than its competitors. In fact, Claris prefers that the ClarisWorks components be referred to as *environments* — rather than modules — to emphasize the high level of integration between the different parts of the program.

**Figure
INTRO-1:**
A spreadsheet
frame within a
word process-
ing document

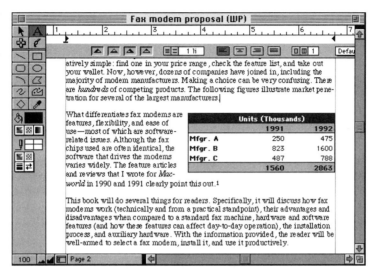

ClarisWorks has also made great strides toward including the "power features" that have traditionally been absent from integrated programs. For example

- ✦ The word processor includes a spelling checker, thesaurus, and outliner, as well as support for custom text and paragraph styles.

- ✦ The paint environment offers gradients, and the draw environment has advanced drawing tools.

- ✦ The spreadsheet includes charts, text wrap within cells, cell shading, and variable row heights and column widths, and it allows multiple fonts per worksheet.

- ✦ The communications environment provides standard file transfer protocols and support for the Communications Toolbox.

- ✦ The database offers pop-up menu, value list, check box, and radio button fields, and it enables you to create multiple custom layouts for each database file.

- ✦ The built-in macro recorder enables you to automate common or repetitive tasks with ease.

ClarisWorks provides solid integration with *other* programs, too. Numerous import and export filters that are included with ClarisWorks enable it to exchange data with many popular business programs, such as Microsoft Office. And with the System 7 feature called Publish & Subscribe, you can easily embed ClarisWorks documents (or portions of documents, such as a spreadsheet chart) in documents created in other programs. You may want to publish a ClarisWorks spreadsheet chart for inclusion in a desktop publishing layout, for example. When the underlying ClarisWorks documents change, you can set the desktop publishing program (in this case, the *subscriber*) to automatically replace the old chart with the new one. Publish & Subscribe works in the opposite direction, too. You can use it to embed non-ClarisWorks documents into ClarisWorks files and have them automatically update whenever changes are made to the external documents.

Finally, if your Mac is part of a network, you can take advantage of ClarisWorks' support for PowerTalk messaging, which enables you to easily create, send, and receive messages, as well as attached documents.

Who Should Use This Book _____

The *Macworld ClarisWorks 4.0 Bible* is for anyone who uses version 4.0 of ClarisWorks:

➥ If you're a beginning ClarisWorks user, detailed steps help you get up to speed quickly with common (and not-so-common) ClarisWorks features and procedures.

➥ If you're an intermediate or advanced ClarisWorks user — someone who wants only the ClarisWorks essentials but doesn't need much hand holding — the tips and insights in each chapter will help you get the most from ClarisWorks. You'll find Quick Tips sections, sidebars, and icons indicating the newest ClarisWorks features.

How This Book Is Organized _____

The *Macworld ClarisWorks 4.0 Bible* is made up of parts, chapters, and sections.

The Parts

This book is divided into five parts.

Part I: The Basics

This is a gentle introduction to performing basic ClarisWorks procedures, such as opening and saving documents, printing, and managing windows. It also lists the major features and enhancements that were introduced in ClarisWorks 4.0.

Part II: Using the ClarisWorks Environments

This part explains the workings of each of the six major ClarisWorks components (word processing, spreadsheet, database, draw, paint, and communications).

Part III: Integrating the ClarisWorks Environments

This part offers suggestions and examples for using elements of two or more environments in the same document (generating a mail merge and using spreadsheet frames to create word processing tables).

Part IV: Mastering ClarisWorks

This part covers material that helps you make more productive use of ClarisWorks. It isn't essential to learn about these features immediately, but you will want to tackle them after you're comfortable with the ClarisWorks basics.

Part V: Appendixes

This part includes three appendixes to aid you in your work:

- ◆ *Appendix A, "Installing ClarisWorks 4.0,"* provides information on how to install ClarisWorks. If you will be installing on any disk other than your start-up hard disk or are upgrading from a previous version of the program, reading this appendix is especially important.

- ◆ *Appendix B, "Spreadsheet and Database Functions,"* is a complete reference to the spreadsheet and database functions that are provided in ClarisWorks 4.0.

- ◆ *Appendix C, "Keyboard Shortcuts,"* lists the many keyboard shortcuts in ClarisWorks. If you're new to using a mouse or don't want to take your hands off the keyboard, you'll want to check out this appendix.

The Chapters

Each chapter of this book is organized around a major task you're likely to perform in ClarisWorks, such as working with the word processor, setting preferences, recording macros, and so on. When you need to perform a particular ClarisWorks task, scan the Table of Contents to locate the chapter that addresses your needs.

The Sections

Each chapter contains the following sections:

- *In This Chapter* provides a list of topics covered in the chapter.

- *Overview* provides an introduction to the chapter.

- *Steps* appear throughout each chapter. Each Steps section spells out the specific instructions necessary to accomplish a particular task.

- *Summary* lists the main points covered in the chapter. You can turn to the Summary section of any chapter to see whether it contains the information you need at the moment.

In addition to these sections, many of the chapters include the following:

- *Quick Tips* give useful tips about additional tasks that you can perform in the ClarisWorks environment or about the subject being discussed. You also can turn to this section for ideas on how to better use the features or the environment.

- *Moving On Up* provides you with information on upgrading from a ClarisWorks environment to a more advanced program.

Icons Used in This Book _____

Five icons are used in this book to highlight important information, new features, and ancillary material that may interest you:

 The New to Version 4.0 icon marks discussions of features that are found only in ClarisWorks 4.0.

 The Internet Connection icon highlights information about how you can use ClarisWorks 4.0 to prepare and translate HTML (HyperText Markup Language) documents for the World Wide Web.

 The Power Tip icon offers an insight into the feature or task being discussed, in many cases suggesting better or easier ways of accomplishing it.

 The By the Way icon identifies information and issues regarding a feature or topic, which might be of interest to you.

The Take Note icon provides additional information relevant to a particular feature or task.

 The Caution icon warns you about potentially dangerous situations — particularly those in which data may be lost.

How to Use This Book

Far be it from me to tell you how to read this book. Reading and learning styles are all very personal. When I get a new computer program, I frequently read the manual from cover to cover before even installing the software. Of course, I'll be flattered if you read the *Macworld ClarisWorks 4.0 Bible* the same way, but I'll be *surprised* if you do, too.

This book is written as a reference to "all things ClarisWorks." When you want to learn about the database environment, there's a specific chapter to which you can turn. If you just need to know how to use the spelling checker, you can flip to the Table of Contents or the Index and find the pages where the spelling checker is discussed. Most procedures are explained in step-by-step fashion, so you can quickly accomplish even the most complex tasks. You can read this book as you would a Stephen King novel (but with fewer surprises, and less snappy dialog and bloodletting), read just the chapters that interest you, or use it as a quick reference for when you need to learn about a particular feature or procedure.

For those who prefer a little more direction than "whatever works for you," I've included some guidelines in the following sections — arranged according to your level of ClarisWorks experience.

I do have one general suggestion: *If at all possible, read this book with ClarisWorks 4.0 on-screen.* Sure, you can read about editing a user dictionary for the spelling checker while relaxing in the tub, but — unless you have exceptional recall — what you read will be more meaningful if you're sitting in front of the computer.

For the New ClarisWorks User

Chapter 1, "ClarisWorks Essentials," is a must read for every ClarisWorks user. Many ClarisWorks tasks, such as arranging windows and printing, are not specific to any one environment. Rather than discuss them again in each of the environment chapters, I have included these procedures and features only in Chapter 1.

From that point on, you should pick a ClarisWorks environment — the word processor is a good place to start — and, with book in hand, work through the appropriate chapter in Part II. Each chapter in Part II explains the fundamentals for a single ClarisWorks environment. The really advanced stuff is in Part III, "Integrating the ClarisWorks Environments," and Part IV, "Mastering ClarisWorks." Although you'll eventually want to check out the material in those parts, too, you'll note that I've purposely separated the advanced matters from the basics in order to keep new users from being overwhelmed.

 Although this book discusses many of the basic concepts and procedures necessary for the beginning user to start working productively with ClarisWorks, it is *not* a substitute for the documentation that came with your Mac. As you work on the desktop and begin experimenting with ClarisWorks, you're bound to encounter additional Mac issues. When that happens — *and it will* — it's time to drag out the manuals for your Macintosh, peripherals (printers, modems, and so on), and system software, and see what you've missed. After you fill in the gaps in your Mac education, you'll feel more confident and comfortable tackling ClarisWorks and any other programs you eventually purchase.

For Those Who Have Upgraded from a Previous Version of ClarisWorks

If you're an experienced ClarisWorks 2.0, 2.1, or 3.0 user, the best place for you to start is in Chapter 2, "New Features in ClarisWorks 4.0." This chapter is a quick guide to the new features that you need to learn about in ClarisWorks 4.0, and it directs you to the chapters in which the features are discussed.

Before you jump ahead, however, be sure to at least skim through Chapter 1, "ClarisWorks Essentials." Although the basics of using the program haven't changed drastically, you need to be familiar with some new procedures and options.

The Basics

This section introduces you to
basic ClarisWorks procedures, such
as opening and saving documents,
printing, and managing windows.
It also discusses the major features
and enhancements that are included
in ClarisWorks 4.

ClarisWorks Essentials

In This Chapter

- Starting ClarisWorks
- Creating a new document
- Opening existing documents
- Saving documents
- Closing document windows
- Selecting and using tools
- Using the Shortcuts palette
- Creating and using frames
- Changing the display
- Printing
- Using the ClarisWorks help features
- Viewing the on-screen tour
- Quitting the program

Overview

Before you leap into ClarisWorks, you need to get some basics under your belt. If you're new to the Mac, this chapter is particularly helpful. Many of the procedures that it describes — such as starting the program, opening and saving documents, and printing — are applicable to almost any Mac program. Even if you consider yourself an experienced Mac user, you can benefit from at least skimming through this chapter. You may pick up a time-saving tip or two that improves your productivity with ClarisWorks.

Starting ClarisWorks _____

As with most Macintosh programs, you can start ClarisWorks in several ways. From the desktop, which is shown in Figure 1-1, you have two methods to choose from:

    ☞ Double-click the ClarisWorks 4.0 program icon.

    ☞ Click the ClarisWorks 4.0 program icon to select it and then choose Open from the File menu (or press ⌘-O).

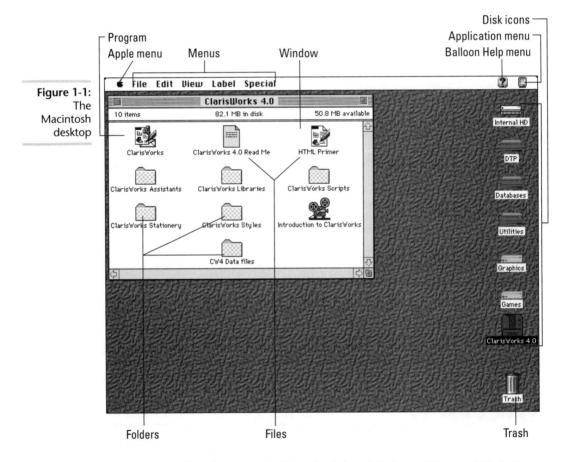

Figure 1-1:
The
Macintosh
desktop

The desktop shows icons for all mounted disks (both hard disks and floppy disks), the Trash, windows for open drives and folders, and icons for programs and data files.

The Balloon Help menu icon shown in Figure 2-1 is the one for System 7.5 and System 7.5.1. If you have System 7.0 or System 7.1, this icon is displayed as a cartoon balloon.

If you want to load a document (or perhaps several) as you launch the program, you can use one of the following methods:

- ☞ Double-click a ClarisWorks document icon.

- ☞ Select several ClarisWorks document icons (by Shift-clicking the icons or by drawing a selection rectangle around them) and then choose Open from the File menu (or press ⌘-O).

Whether you open documents from the desktop or load them from within ClarisWorks, you can open as many documents as memory allows.

Creating a New Document_____

Each time you start ClarisWorks, the program loads, and the New Document dialog box automatically opens so that you can create a new document.

 This is how the program works when you first install it. If you prefer, you can change ClarisWorks' start-up action so that it displays an Open file dialog box (so you can open an existing file) or no dialog box at all. To change the start-up action, see Chapter 11, "Setting Preferences."

Steps:	Creating a New Document at Start-Up
Step 1.	Load ClarisWorks. The New Document dialog box (shown in Figure 1-2) appears.
	If you have changed the "On startup, show" setting in the Preferences dialog box, as described in Chapter 11, you may see the Open file dialog box or no dialog box at all. In that case, you must choose New from the File menu to make the New Document dialog box appear.
Step 2.	To start with a blank document from any of the six ClarisWorks environments, select a document type from the scrolling list, and click OK.

Select a document type from this list

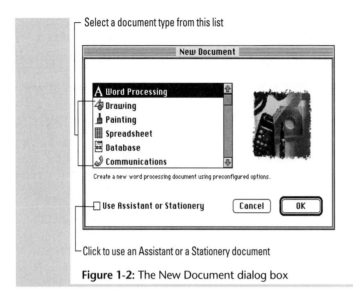

Figure 1-2: The New Document dialog box

New documents can also be based on *stationery files* (templates), or they can be created for you by some of the ClarisWorks Assistants.

Steps: Creating a New Document Using a Stationery File or an Assistant

Step 1.   Click the Use Assistant or Stationery check box, as shown in Figure 1-3.

Select a template or Assistant from this list

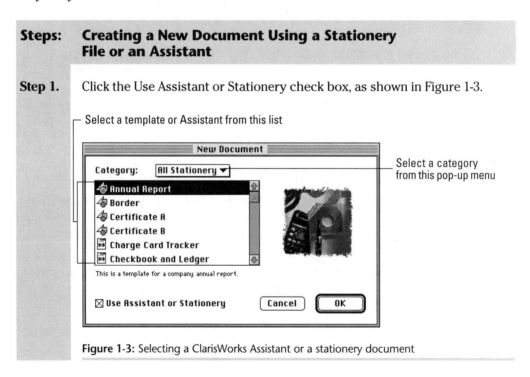

Figure 1-3: Selecting a ClarisWorks Assistant or a stationery document

Step 2. Select All Assistants, All Stationery, or a specific class of Assistants and Stationery from the Category pop-up menu.

Step 3. Choose a document from the scrolling list.

Step 4. Click OK.

For more information on working with stationery documents and Assistants, see Chapter 10.

If you have created a *default stationery document* for an environment (see "Using Stationery to Set New Environment Defaults" in Chapter 10), you see two different documents listed for that environment. For example, a default word processing stationery document is simply listed as Word Processing. The ClarisWorks standard document for that environment, on the other hand, is listed as Standard Word Processing. (In previous versions of ClarisWorks, default stationery documents were known as *options stationery documents*.)

If you want to open an existing document instead of creating a new one, click Cancel. Then choose Open from the File menu and select the document (following the steps described in "Opening Existing Documents," later in this chapter).

If you want to create a new document after the program has been running awhile, you can either choose New from the File menu or press ⌘-N. The New Document dialog box appears. Select a document type and then click OK.

You can create new documents or open existing documents at any time during a ClarisWorks session. The only limitation on the number of documents you can have open at the same time is the amount of memory available to ClarisWorks. See the Quick Tips at the end of this chapter for help with changing the memory allocation for ClarisWorks.

New documents are assigned a temporary name that consists of the word *Untitled,* a number that represents the number of documents created thus far in the session, and a pair of letters in parentheses that represents the document type. For example, *Untitled 4 (PT)* indicates that the document is a new Paint document that is the fourth new document created during the session.

Memory Versus Disk Space (Storage Capacity)

New users often confuse a Mac's storage capacity with the amount of memory in the machine. *Storage capacity* refers to a Mac's total disk space, calculated by adding the capacity of all attached hard disks. The Mac's *memory* (also called *RAM* or Random Access Memory) is used to run programs and desk accessories and to manipulate data. Unlike disk storage, the contents of RAM disappears whenever you quit from a program or shut down the Mac. Memory is for temporary storage; disks are for long-term storage. Thus, although you may have free disk space, this has no bearing on the amount of memory available for you to run programs like ClarisWorks.

Remember that new documents are not automatically saved to disk. If you neglect to save a new document (see "Saving Documents," later in this chapter), it disappears forever after you click its close box or quit the program. If a document is important to you, be sure to save early and save often. Note that if you attempt to close a new document without saving, ClarisWorks presents an alert box that offers an option to save the document.

Opening Existing Documents _____

As mentioned in "Starting ClarisWorks," earlier in this chapter, you can open existing ClarisWorks documents from the desktop by double-clicking them. Doing so simultaneously launches ClarisWorks and opens the selected document. After the program is running, you can open other ClarisWorks documents, as well as documents created in many other programs.

Opening ClarisWorks Documents from Within the Program

The following instructions describe how to open ClarisWorks documents when the program is running.

Steps: Opening ClarisWorks Documents from Within ClarisWorks

Step 1.   Choose the Open command from the File menu (or press ⌘-O). You see a
file dialog box like the one in Figure 1-4.

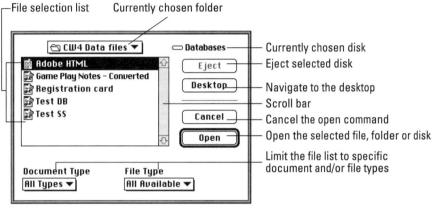

Figure 1-4: The Open dialog box

Step 2.   Using the mouse or arrow keys, select the particular file that you want to
open and either click Open or double-click the file name.

The ClarisWorks Open dialog box has a special pair of pop-up menus at the bottom.
You use the Document Type pop-up menu on the left to restrict the documents that
appear in the file list to a particular type, such as database files. If you have a large
number of files in a particular folder, using the Document Type pop-up menu can make
it simpler to find the file you want. If you don't feel like opening the menu, you can press
a Command-key equivalent to restrict the list to a single document type. Table 1-1
shows the Command-key equivalents.

To enter a Command-key equivalent, hold down the Command key (⌘) and
press the number, letter, or character that is to accompany it.

Table 1-1	
Document Type Command-key Equivalents	
Document Type	**Command-Key Equivalent**
All types	⌘-0
Word processing	⌘-1
Drawing	⌘-2
Painting	⌘-3
Spreadsheet	⌘-4
Database	⌘-5
Communications	⌘-6

You use the File Type pop-up menu on the right side of the Open dialog box to restrict the file list to only particular types of documents. You can specify whether you want to see regular ClarisWorks documents (ClarisWorks), ClarisWorks stationery documents (ClarisWorks Stationery), or all document types for which you have Claris translators (All Available). If you want to restrict the file list to just those documents from a particular program, such as Microsoft Word for Windows, you can select that document type in the File Type pop-up menu.

The Open dialog box (as shown in Figure 1-5) has a Preview option that enables you to see a thumbnail representation of any graphic document selected in the file list. The Preview option is presented only if Apple's QuickTime system software extension is currently loaded.

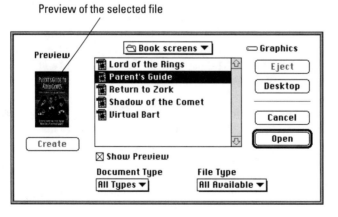

Figure 1-5: The modified Open dialog box (with QuickTime active)

By clicking the Show Preview check box, you instruct ClarisWorks to show a preview image for any graphic or movie file that has had a preview saved for it. If no preview is shown for a particular file, you can tell ClarisWorks to construct one by clicking the Create button. (Note that previews are available for some text files, too.)

Finally, if a preview is no longer correct for a file, the Create button changes to Update. Click it to create an updated preview for the file.

Opening Non-ClarisWorks Documents

Claris programs include a file translation system called the *XTND system*. Depending on which Claris translator files are in the Claris folder within the System Folder, the XTND system can interpret documents that were created by many other programs, such Microsoft Word, WriteNow, and Microsoft Excel. This capability is particularly useful if you have recently switched from another word processor, spreadsheet, or graphics program or if a friend has given you a document for which you don't have the creating program.

To open a non-ClarisWorks document from within ClarisWorks, choose Open from the File menu (or press ⌘-O). *Optional:* In the Open dialog box, click the Document Type pop-up menu and choose the type of file that you want to open (Word Processing, Drawing, Painting, Spreadsheet, Database, or Communications). Similarly, if you want to restrict the file list to a certain type of document (just GIF or MacPaint files, for example), you can choose a program or file type from the File Type pop-up menu. Navigate to the disk and folder where the document file is stored, and select the file that you want to open. If the file that you want does not appear in the file list, you do not have the translator that is needed to open the file. Click Open or double-click the file name to load the file and convert it to ClarisWorks format.

After you select the file, the Converting File dialog box appears. A progress thermometer shows how much of the conversion has been completed. You can click Cancel at any time during the conversion if you change your mind about loading the file. Otherwise, after the conversion is finished, ClarisWorks opens the document for you. The file is given a temporary name that consists of its original file name followed by - *Converted* and a pair of letters in parentheses that indicate the document type (such as *DB* for a database document).

The conversion process does nothing to the original file; ClarisWorks simply reads the file and makes a converted copy of it. The file that ClarisWorks creates is not automatically stored on your disk. If you neglect to save the converted file, it disappears at the end of the current session.

When you save a converted file, you have two options:

☞ Save it with a different name from that of the original file.

This option leaves the original file intact and creates a second file that is in ClarisWorks 4.0 format.

☞ Save it with the same name as that of the original file.

 The second option deletes the original file and replaces it with the new ClarisWorks-formatted file. Use this option only if you have no further use for the original document.

You also can use the *drag-and-drop* procedure to make ClarisWorks simultaneously launch and open a non-ClarisWorks document. To use the drag-and-drop technique to open a foreign file, on the desktop, click once to select the icon for the non-ClarisWorks document that you want to open. Drag the icon onto the ClarisWorks program icon.

If ClarisWorks is able to interpret the document that you've selected, the ClarisWorks icon turns dark, and the program launches and attempts to convert the document — just as it does when you open a foreign document from within ClarisWorks. If the document is not one of the types that ClarisWorks can read, the ClarisWorks icon doesn't become dark, and the program doesn't launch.

 This drag-and-drop procedure can be used with several files at once — even if the files were created in different programs.

 ClarisWorks 4.0 provides yet another means of converting foreign files to ClarisWorks format. Using the AppleScript named Convert Documents (found in the ClarisWorks Scripts folder inside the ClarisWorks 4.0 folder), you can convert large numbers of files *and save them* in one step.

To use this or any other AppleScript, you must have the AppleScript 1.1 extension (from Apple Computer) installed and active on your Macintosh. AppleScript is included with System 7.5 and System 7 Pro, although it can be purchased separately as well.

Steps:	Using the Convert Documents Script to Convert Foreign Files
Step 1.	On the desktop, Shift-click to select the icons for the non-ClarisWorks documents that you want to convert. Or, if you want to convert the contents of an entire folder, simply select the folder.
Step 2.	Drag the file icons or folder onto the Convert Documents script icon, shown in Figure 1-6.

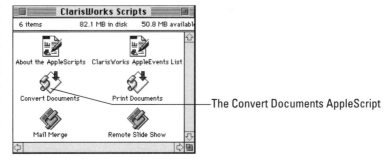

Figure 1-6:
The Convert
Documents
Apple Script
can be found
in the
ClarisWorks
Scripts folder.

—The Convert Documents AppleScript

Each foreign document is automatically opened in ClarisWorks, converted, and then saved as a new document in the same folder as the original document. A suffix of .cwk is appended to the name of the converted document. (Files that ClarisWorks is unable to convert are simply ignored by Convert Documents.)

For more information about the Convert Documents script, refer to the "About the AppleScripts" document in the ClarisWorks Scripts folder (located in the ClarisWorks 4.0 folder).

If you use the Convert Documents script often, you'll find it more convenient to make an *alias* of the icon and place it on your desktop. To make an alias, click once to select the Convert Documents icon, choose Make Alias from the Finder's File menu, and then drag the new alias icon onto the desktop. Since every System 7 alias works just like the original document or program that it represents, you can then drag your foreign files onto the alias to activate the Convert Documents script.

Opening Documents Created with an Earlier Version of ClarisWorks

One other type of conversion that many users are curious about is the manner in which ClarisWorks 4.0 handles documents created by earlier versions of ClarisWorks. You don't need to worry. When you open a file created with ClarisWorks 1.0, 2.0, 2.1, or 3.0, a dialog box appears that states: *This document was created by a previous version of ClarisWorks. A copy will be opened and '[v4.0]' will be added to the filename.* Note that this message says that a *copy* will be opened. As with XTND translations of foreign files, the original document is merely read into memory — not replaced on disk. If you want to make a permanent copy of the document in the current version's format, you need to use the Save or Save As command to save a new copy of the file.

ClarisWorks 4.0 documents cannot be read by earlier versions of the program. If some of your colleagues use previous versions of ClarisWorks, you'll be able to read their documents, but they will not be able to read yours. For now, the best solution when preparing a file for them is to use the Save As command to translate the file to a format that their version of ClarisWorks *can* read. A second approach is to save a copy of your word processing documents in ClarisWorks 1.0 format. All versions of ClarisWorks except 2.0 can read ClarisWorks 1.0 word processing documents.

Inserting Files and Graphics

The Insert command in the File menu lets you place the entire contents of a non-ClarisWorks file into a ClarisWorks document.

 If you need to use only *part* of a file (such as a single paragraph or a graphic), it may be faster to simply open the second file, copy the portion that you need, and then paste it into your document.

To Insert a file or graphic into a document, if you're working in a word processing document or frame, position the cursor where you want to place the insert; in other types of frames and documents, click where you want to place the insert. Choose Insert from the File menu. A standard file dialog box appears. If you want to restrict your choices to a particular file type, choose the type from the Show pop-up menu. Navigate to the drive and folder that contain the file. Select the file that you want to insert by clicking it and clicking Insert or by double-clicking the name of the file.

 Only file types that are supported for the current frame or document environment will appear in the Show pop-up menu. As always, the Show list is created from the Claris XTND translator files installed in the System Folder.

 In addition to opening graphic files directly as Draw or Paint documents, you can use the Library command to insert or drag any of the graphics, text items, or spreadsheet cells from ClarisWorks *libraries* into existing documents. See Chapter 20 for details about this hot new feature.

 You cannot use the Insert command to place a ClarisWorks 2.0, 2.1, 3.0, or 4.0 document into a ClarisWorks 4.0 document. However, all versions of ClarisWorks higher than 2.0 (2.1 and up) include an XTND filter for ClarisWorks 1.0 files, meaning you *can* insert ClarisWorks 1.0 word processing files into ClarisWorks 4.0 word processing documents or text frames. As a result, you can also insert a ClarisWorks 2.0, 2.1, 3.0, or 4.0 word processing document into a ClarisWorks 4.0 document by saving it as a ClarisWorks 1.0 file, as described in the following procedure.

Steps:	**Inserting a ClarisWorks Word Processing Document into Another ClarisWorks Document**

Step 1. Open the ClarisWorks 2.0 – 4.0 word processing document that you want to insert.

Step 2. Choose the Save As command from the File menu.

Step 3. Select the ClarisWorks 1.0 Text filter in the Save As pop-up menu, as shown in Figure 1-7.

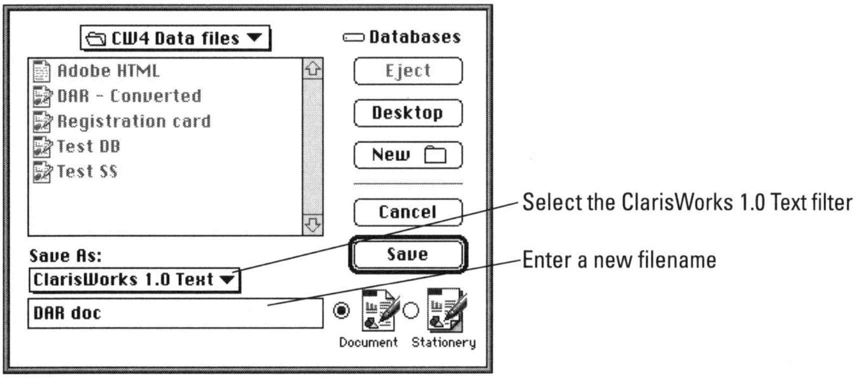

Figure 1-7: Saving a ClarisWorks word processing document as a ClarisWorks 1.0 file

Step 4. Enter a new name for the converted file in the text-edit box, and click the Save button. The document is saved as a ClarisWorks 1.0 text file.

Step 5. Position the cursor in the ClarisWorks 4.0 document where you want to insert the text, select Insert from the File menu, and choose the newly converted ClarisWorks 1.0 text file.

Saving Documents

To save a ClarisWorks document to disk, you use either the Save or the Save As command from the File menu. For new Mac owners, determining which of these commands is the correct one to use is often a major source of confusion. This section clears up the confusion once and for all.

Saving Existing Files

You use the Save command (⌘-S) to save existing files. If the file is already on disk, the Save command merely replaces the old copy of the file with the new copy. No dialog box appears.

Because the Save command automatically deletes the previous copy of the file, at times you may prefer to use the Save As command to save an existing file. The Save As command enables you to assign a new name to the file, as well as to specify a different location on disk in which to store it. You can use the Save As command when you want to keep multiple versions of a file instead of just replacing the old version, or when you want to save a document in a different format.

To use the Save As command to save an existing file, choose Save As from the File menu. The standard file dialog box appears. Navigate to the disk drive and folder where you want to save the file. If you want to create a new folder in which to store the file, click the New button. Type a name for the file. If you want to save the file as something other than a standard ClarisWorks file, use the Save As pop-up menu to choose a file type. Click a radio button to choose Document or Stationery. Choose Stationery if you want to save the document as a reusable template; otherwise, choose Document. Click the Save button (or press Return or Enter). If you change your mind and decide not to save the file, click Cancel.

If you are saving a file that already exists on disk and don't change the name from the one suggested, the program asks whether you want to replace the existing file. Click Replace if you want to replace the old file on disk with the new one. Click Cancel if you don't want to replace the old file. You can then specify a new name or location (a different disk or folder), or you can cancel the Save altogether.

The Replace dialog box appears whenever you choose the Save As command and try to save a file under its original name or under any other file name that's already in use.

Saving New Files

You can save new files by using either the Save or Save As command. After you select either command from the File menu, a standard file dialog box appears and gives you the opportunity to name the new file and specify a location on disk in which to store it. To avoid overwriting any files that are already on the disk, be sure to enter a name that is different from any existing file names.

If the file you want to save has never been saved before (that is, it's a new file) *and it's empty,* ClarisWorks *grays out* the Save command (makes it unselectable). Until at least one character has been typed into the document, the only save option presented is Save As.

ClarisWorks 4.0 enables you to save identifying information with any file by choosing the Document Summary Info command on the File menu. You can use the file's Document Summary Info dialog box to do the following:

☞ Provide a more elaborate title for a document

☞ Identify the author

☞ Specify a version number (to distinguish multiple revisions of a file, for example)

☞ Assign keywords that can be used to help identify the file's contents

☞ Specify a category and type descriptive text (to classify and explain the purpose of a stationery document when it appears in the New Document dialog box)

An example of a Document Summary is shown in Figure 1-8. Because this information is primarily for your benefit, you can enter as much or as little information as you like. If you later want to change some of the entries, just choose the Document Summary Info command again, make the changes, and then save the document again. (Document Summary Info also is discussed in Chapter 10.)

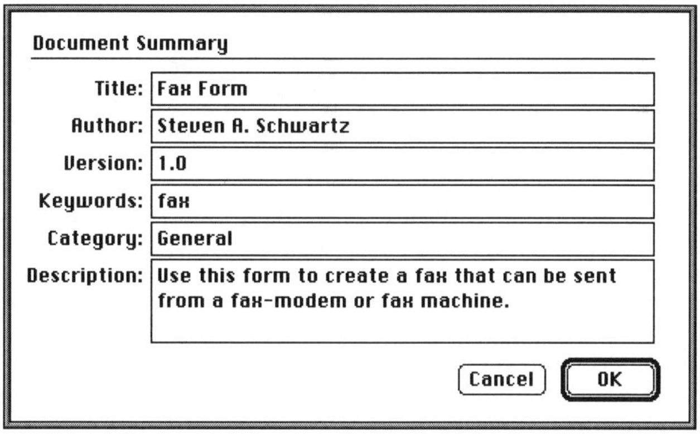

Figure 1-8:
The
Document
Summary
dialog box

> **Document Summary**
>
> Title: `Fax Form`
> Author: `Steven A. Schwartz`
> Version: `1.0`
> Keywords: `fax`
> Category: `General`
> Description: `Use this form to create a fax that can be sent from a fax-modem or fax machine.`
>
> [Cancel] [OK]

For all practical purposes, the Keywords section of the Document Summary dialog box is useless. The Find ClarisWorks Documents Assistant cannot search by keyword — the keywords can only be seen in the Document Summary Info dialog box (unlike the Description text, which sometimes can be seen in the Preview section of the Open dialog box). Save yourself some work; don't bother to enter keywords.

Save As Options

When you use the Save As command to save a file, a Save file dialog box appears, as shown in Figure 1-9. It looks a little different than the Save dialog box used by other programs. Using the radio buttons and the pop-up menu at the bottom of the dialog box, you can

ᴄ⊛ Select from several file format options by clicking the Save As pop-up menu.

ᴄ⊛ Save the file as either a document or a stationery file by clicking the appropriate radio button.

In most cases, you can leave the Save As pop-up menu alone. The default setting is ClarisWorks, which means that the file will be saved as a standard ClarisWorks file.

Figure 1-9:
The
ClarisWorks
4.0 Save As
dialog box

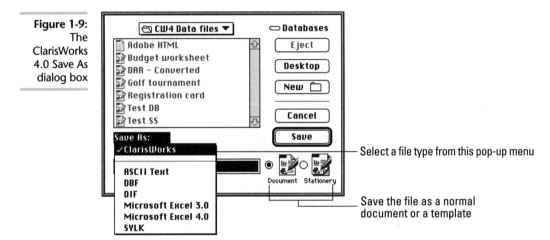

Select a file type from this pop-up menu

Save the file as a normal document or a template

Depending on the Claris XTND translators that have been installed, the Save As pop-up menu may have options for saving the document as a non-ClarisWorks file. You may want to save a spreadsheet in Microsoft Excel format, for example, if you plan to give it to a friend who uses Excel rather than ClarisWorks. Or, you may want to save Draw graphic files in PICT format so they can be opened by any draw program. Note that the file format options presented vary, depending on the ClarisWorks environment that you're in when you choose Save As. For example, if you're saving a spreadsheet, the Save As pop-up menu lists only spreadsheet formats.

When saving a document in a non-ClarisWorks format, it's a smart idea to save a copy of the file in ClarisWorks format, too, so that if you ever use the document in ClarisWorks again, you can work on the original rather than a translated copy of the file.

The pair of radio buttons in the lower-right corner of the dialog box enables you to save the file as a normal document or a *stationery file*. A stationery file is a template for frequently used documents, such as fax forms and memos. If you click the Stationery radio button, ClarisWorks automatically navigates to the ClarisWorks Stationery folder within the ClarisWorks 4.0 folder. You can later open any stationery document saved in this folder by clicking the Use Assistant or Stationery check box in the New Document dialog box. (Choose New from the File menu or press ⌘-N.) See Chapter 10 for additional information on working with stationery files.

 The Save As pop-up menu and the radio buttons work together. You must select a file format from the Save As pop-up menu *and* choose a file type by clicking the Document or Stationery radio button.

Closing Document Windows _____

Saving a document copies its contents to a file on disk. It does not close the document window. After you finish using a document, you can close its window by using one of the following methods:

- ☞ Click once in its close box (in the upper-left corner of the window, as shown in Figure 1-10).

- ☞ Choose Close from the File menu.

- ☞ Press ⌘-W.

Close box

Figure 1-10:
Click the
close box to
close a
window.

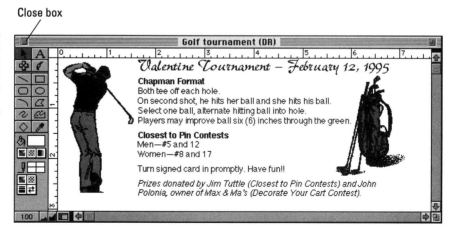

If the file has been saved, the window immediately closes. If changes have been made to the file, you are given a chance to save the file before ClarisWorks closes it.

You can close all of the document windows at one time by choosing Quit from the File menu (or by pressing ⌘-Q). If you have already saved all of the documents, ClarisWorks simply closes all windows and quits. If any documents have not been saved — new files or files you have changed — ClarisWorks gives you an opportunity to save them one by one.

 To close all document windows *without* quitting the program, hold down the Option key and do one of the following:

    ↪ Click in the close box for any window.

    ↪ Choose the Close command from the File menu.

As usual, if you haven't saved some documents, the program gives you an opportunity to save them or to cancel before their windows are closed. (This tip also works from the desktop and is a fast way to eliminate window clutter.)

Selecting and Using Tools_____

Along the left side of most document windows is the Tool panel. The tools enable you to create new frames (such as adding paint graphics or a spreadsheet to a word processing document); select drawing and painting tools; and set fill and pen colors, patterns, gradients, and line styles.

 If the tools aren't visible, choose Show Tools from the View menu. Other ways to show and hide the Tool panel are discussed later in this chapter in "Hiding and Showing Tools."

You can divide the objects in the Tool panel into the following categories, according to their functions: environment tools, drawing tools, painting tools, fill palettes, and pen palettes. The Tool panel has two different states: *basic* and *expanded* (see Figure 1-11). The *expanded Tool panel* adds painting tools to the basic panel, and it appears only when you are working on a paint document or have selected the Paintbrush tool to create a paint frame in a document of another type.

To create a new frame in the current document, click an environment tool: the *A* for a word processing frame, the plus symbol for a spreadsheet frame, or the paintbrush for a paint frame. To add a draw object to the document, click any of the draw icons. To work with colors, patterns, gradients, or line styles, click any of these tool icons at the bottom of the panel and select the option you prefer.

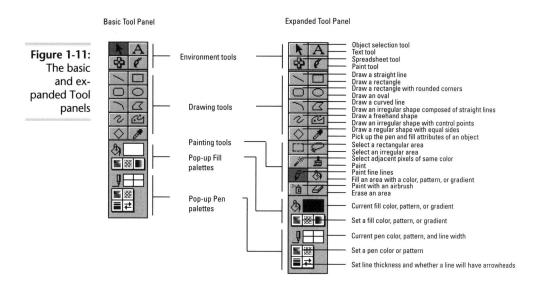

Figure 1-11:
The basic and expanded Tool panels

The color, pattern, line style, and arrow tools are *tear-off* palettes. If you use any of them frequently, you can keep them open and on-screen.

To tear off a palette, click the palette icon of interest. The panel drops down. While holding down the mouse button, drag the palette away from the Tool panel. Release the mouse button.

After you release the mouse button, the palette is in its own small window, where it's easily accessible (see Figure 1-12). To close a floating palette of this type, click its close box (in the upper-left corner). To temporarily shrink the palette and cause it to move to the upper-right corner of the document window, click the box in the palette's upper-right corner. To move the palette, click in its title bar and drag it to the desired position.

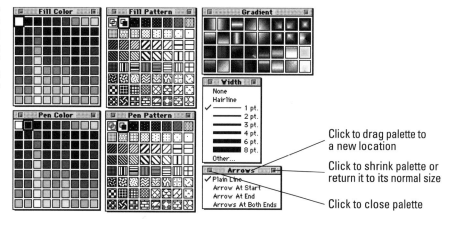

Figure 1-12:
The Tool panel's tear-off palettes

Option-clicking the close box for any tear-off palette simultaneously closes *all* open palettes. Similarly, Option-clicking in the grow/shrink box in the upper-right corner of a palette causes all palettes to grow or shrink.

ClarisWorks 4.0 makes extensive use of palettes. For instance, the Shortcuts palette and the stylesheet are also presented as floating windows with their own miniature title bars, close boxes, and grow/shrink boxes. In other Macintosh programs, such windows are commonly referred to as *windoids*. In this book, the terms *palette* and *windoid* are used interchangeably because every ClarisWorks palette is presented in a windoid.

Using the Shortcuts Palette _____

To save you the effort of needlessly pulling down menus to choose commands or of having to memorize Command-key equivalents, ClarisWorks provides a feature called the Shortcuts palette (see Figure 1-13). You can issue many common commands by simply clicking a button on the Shortcuts palette. To make the palette appear, choose Shortcuts from the File menu and then choose Show Shortcuts (or press Shift-⌘-X).

Figure 1-13:
The Shortcuts
palette

The contents of the palette change to match the environment or frame in which you are working. After you draw a spreadsheet frame, for example, the buttons change to become relevant to spreadsheet operations.

Like the graphic palettes, the Shortcuts palette floats above the current document. You can move, reduce, or close the palette by following the procedures discussed in the preceding section, "Selecting and Using Tools." You can even customize the Shortcuts palette by adding and removing buttons or assigning *macros* (user-created ClarisWorks scripts) to buttons. Chapter 12 discusses customizing the Shortcuts palette.

The Tile Windows command arranges document windows in a vertical stack, one above the other. Documents are full width, but their height is reduced, as shown in Figure 1-18. You can make any document active by simply clicking it.

Figure 1-18:
Tiled windows

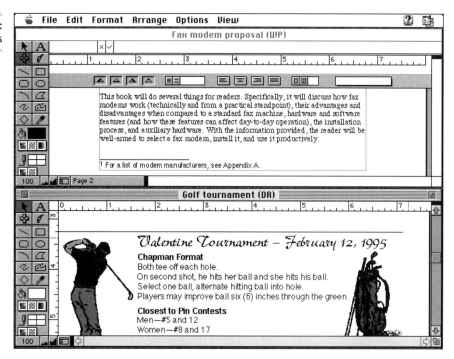

If you don't need to refer constantly to any of the other open documents, you can expand the current document so that it takes over the entire screen by clicking its zoom box (in the right corner of the document's title bar). When you're ready to switch to a different document window, click the current window's zoom box again to make it shrink to its original, tiled position.

The Stack Windows command arranges documents so that they cascade from the upper-left corner of the screen to the bottom right, as shown in Figure 1-19. Because a small portion of each document always shows, you can easily switch between documents by clicking the edge of the one you want to bring to the front.

Regardless of how you have your windows arranged, you can bring any window to the front and make it active by either clicking in that window or by choosing its name from the View menu. (All open documents are listed at the bottom of the View menu.)

Figure 1-19:
Stacked
windows

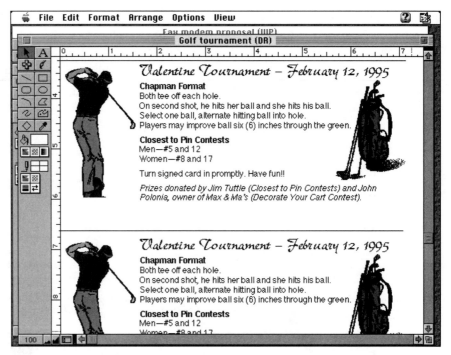

Splitting the Screen

ClarisWorks enables you to split any document horizontally and/or vertically into two or four panes (see Figure 1-20). In each pane, you can examine or edit a different part of the document. Each pane scrolls independently of other panes so that working on one part of the document while viewing another part of it is easy to do. Changes that you make in any pane are simultaneously recorded in all panes.

To split the screen, click the vertical or horizontal pane control and drag it to the spot where you want to divide the document. Release the mouse button. A pair of dividing lines marks the edge of each pane.

To remove a split pane, click the dividing line and drag it to the edge of the document window.

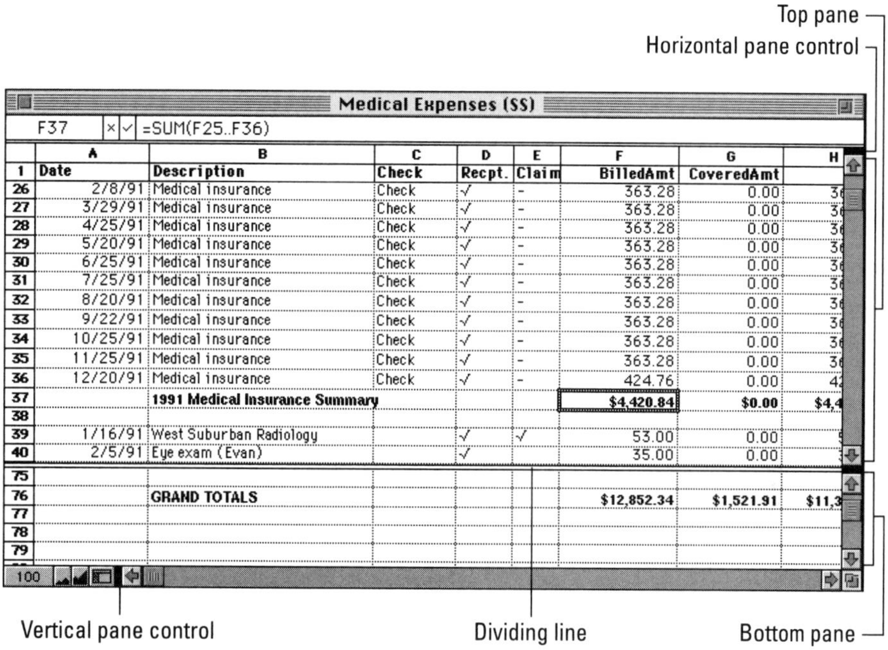

Top pane

Horizontal pane control

Figure 1-20:
A split screen

	A	B	C	D	E	F	G	H
	Date	Description	Check	Recpt.	Claim	BilledAmt	CoveredAmt	
26	2/8/91	Medical insurance	Check	√	–	363.28	0.00	36
27	3/29/91	Medical insurance	Check	√	–	363.28	0.00	36
28	4/25/91	Medical insurance	Check	√	–	363.28	0.00	36
29	5/20/91	Medical insurance	Check	√	–	363.28	0.00	36
30	6/25/91	Medical insurance	Check	√	–	363.28	0.00	36
31	7/25/91	Medical insurance	Check	√	–	363.28	0.00	36
32	8/20/91	Medical insurance	Check	√	–	363.28	0.00	36
33	9/22/91	Medical insurance	Check	√	–	363.28	0.00	36
34	10/25/91	Medical insurance	Check	√	–	363.28	0.00	36
35	11/25/91	Medical insurance	Check	√	–	363.28	0.00	36
36	12/20/91	Medical insurance	Check	√	–	424.76	0.00	42
37		1991 Medical Insurance Summary				$4,420.84	$0.00	$4,4
38								
39	1/16/91	West Suburban Radiology		√	√	53.00	0.00	5
40	2/5/91	Eye exam (Evan)		√		35.00	0.00	
75								
76		GRAND TOTALS				$12,852.34	$1,521.91	$11,3
77								
78								
79								

The cell reference shows F37, with formula =SUM(F25..F36), in the Medical Expenses (SS) window. The zoom box shows 100.

Vertical pane control

Dividing line

Bottom pane

Creating a New View of a Document

If you want to open two copies of the same document, choose New View from the View menu. Any changes that you make in one copy are instantly reflected in the other copy. To distinguish the copies, ClarisWorks appends a number at the end of each name in the title bar. If the original document is called Memo (WP), for example, you end up with two documents on-screen: Memo:1 (WP) and Memo:2 (WP).

What's the point of having multiple copies of the same document on-screen? Creating multiple views of a document has the following advantages:

⌒ It enables you to see a zoomed out view (the entire document) and a 100% view (the normal view) at the same time. Editing changes are reflected in both views so that you can see their effects.

⌒ If you have a spreadsheet frame in a word processing or database document, the only way to increase the number of rows and columns in the frame is by creating a new view of the frame (by using the Open Frame command).

⌒ In the database environment, you can use two views to look at the document in both Browse and Layout modes at the same time. As you make changes to the layout, you can instantly see how they will affect the formatting of the data.

Printing

The final step for most documents is creating a *printout* — a printed copy of the spread-sheet, memo, graphic image, or database report. To print a document, open or create a ClarisWorks document. Choose Print from the File menu. The Print dialog box appears on-screen. Select the print options you want to use for this printout. Click Print to send the print job to the printer.

The Print dialog box that you see depends on the printer that you select in the Chooser and the version of system software that is installed on the Mac. Figure 1-21 shows the LaserWriter 8 Print dialog box.

Figure 1-21:
The Print dialog box for Apple LaserWriters

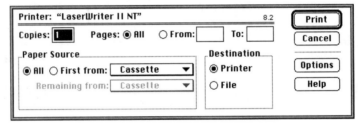

Printer: "LaserWriter II NT"   8.2

Copies: 1   Pages: ● All   ○ From: To:

Paper Source
● All ○ First from: Cassette ▾
    Remaining from: Cassette ▾

Destination
● Printer
○ File

[Print]
[Cancel]
[Options]
[Help]

Be sure that you have selected a printer in the Chooser desk accessory, particularly if you have more than one printing device. The printer that is currently selected receives the print job. Whenever you change the printer selection in the Chooser, you also should use the Page Setup command to make sure that the options are correct for the newly selected printer.

To select a printer, open the Chooser desk accessory (see Figure 1-22) by selecting it from the Apple menu. Click the appropriate Chooser icon in the left side of the window, and select the printer and other options in the right side of the window. (The printer must be turned on for its name to appear in the right side of the window.)

Using the ClarisWorks Help Features

The ClarisWorks Help System continues to evolve. First, it was a HyperCard stack (in ClarisWorks 2.0 and 2.1), then it was rewritten as a standalone application with its own unique interface (in ClarisWorks 3.0), and now it's a standard Windows-style Help application.

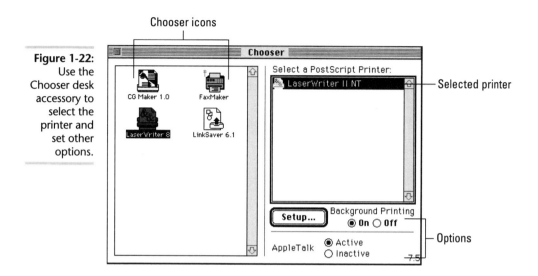

Chooser icons

Figure 1-22:
Use the
Chooser desk
accessory to
select the
printer and
set other
options.

Selected printer

Options

ClarisWorks 4.0 provides two ways for you to get help. In addition to QuickHelp (also known as the *ClarisWorks Help System*) for obtaining in-depth help, you can turn on Balloon Help to get assistance in identifying ClarisWorks' tools and controls.

Using QuickHelp, the ClarisWorks Help System

In early versions of ClarisWorks, all important program information could be found in the manual. Beginning with ClarisWorks 3, major portions of the manual were moved into the on-line help system. You'll now find that much of the program information is available *only* in QuickHelp, and the manual is more of an annotated index for the Help System.

QuickHelp is a separate program from ClarisWorks. Although you can request help from within ClarisWorks (which launches the QuickHelp program), QuickHelp can also be launched directly from the desktop — whether or not ClarisWorks is running.

When you're running ClarisWorks, you can invoke QuickHelp by doing any of the following:

- ∞ Choose the ClarisWorks Help Contents, Index, or How to Use Help command from the Balloon Help menu (see Figure 1-23).

- ∞ Press ⌘-?.

- ∞ Press the Help key (if you have an Apple Extended keyboard).

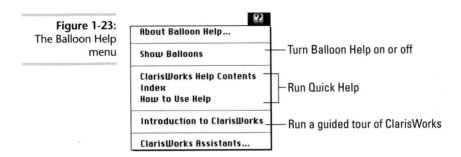

Figure 1-23:
The Balloon Help
menu

Help is not context-sensitive in ClarisWorks 4.0. However, the type of help information that is displayed, as well as the particular Help screen shown, can be controlled as follows:

- To reach the opening screen of the ClarisWorks Help System (see Figure 1-24), choose ClarisWorks Help Contents from the Balloon Help menu, press ⌘-?, or press the Help key (Apple Extended keyboards only). If ClarisWorks Help is already open, you can return to the opening screen by clicking the Contents button.

- To display an alphabetical list of help topics, choose Index from the Balloon Help menu or — after you have invoked Help — click the Index button (see Figure 1-24).

- To view a guided tour of ClarisWorks 4.0, choose Introduction to ClarisWorks from the Balloon Help menu or double-click the Introduction to ClarisWorks icon in the ClarisWorks 4.0 folder.

- For general information on using the ClarisWorks Help System, select How to Use Help from the Balloon Help menu or from the opening Help screen.

After QuickHelp opens, you can do any of the following:

- Display the opening Help screen by clicking the Contents button.

- Display the Help Index by clicking the Index button.

- Display the most recent Help screen viewed by clicking the Go Back button.

- Go to the next or previous Help screen that is related to the current topic by clicking the book page buttons.

- Search for help on a particular topic by typing an entry in the Keyword box. As you type, QuickHelp displays matching topic titles in the Help screen topic list. Press Enter to make QuickHelp display the selected help topic or index entry.

  You can also choose the Global Find (⌘-F) or Global Find Again (⌘-G) commands from the Find menu to perform general searches.

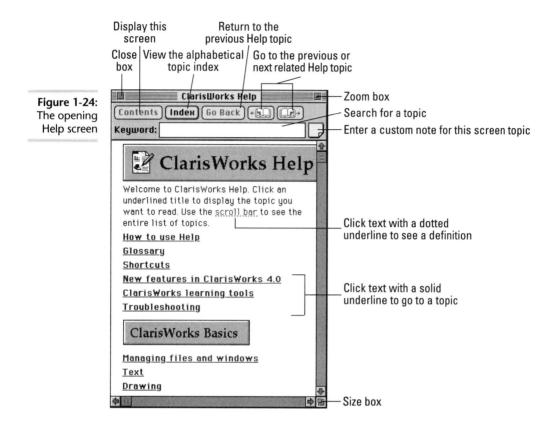

Figure 1-24:
The opening
Help screen

- Go directly to any topic of interest by clicking on text that contains a solid underline, or by selecting a topic from the Index and clicking Go To Topic. (If you want to view a help topic chosen with the latter method without closing the Index, click View Topic rather than Go To Topic.)

- View glossary definitions by clicking text that contains a dotted underline.

- Print the current help topic or all help topics by choosing Print or Print All Topics from the File menu.

- Copy the current help topic by choosing Copy Topic Text (for a copy of only the text) or Copy Topic as a Picture (to treat the topic as a graphic) from the Edit menu.

Copy Topic Text displays the entire text of the current topic in a new window. To copy the entire contents of the window to the clipboard, click Copy All Text. To copy only a portion of the text, highlight the desired text and click the Copy Selected Text button that appears.

Copy Topic as a Picture changes the entire topic to a PICT graphic and transfers it to the clipboard. Although you can no longer edit the text (as you can when using Copy Topic Text), this option includes all graphics that are part of the chosen help topic.

↝ Create bookmarks for help topics that are important to you.

To create a bookmark, choose Set Bookmark from the Bookmarks menu and either accept the suggested name or enter a new one in the Set Bookmark dialog box. Each bookmark's name is automatically added to the bottom of the Bookmarks menu.

To assign a Command-key equivalent with which a bookmark can be invoked, choose a number from the ⌘ Key pop-up menu. Up to ten bookmarks can be assigned Command keys.

To go to a bookmark, you can either select it from the Bookmarks menu or press its Command-key equivalent (if one was assigned).

To edit a bookmark, choose Edit Bookmarks from the Bookmarks menu, select the bookmark from the scrolling list, and click View Topic. (You can also use the Edit Bookmarks command to delete bookmarks.)

↝ Add sticky notes that further explain a help topic.

To create a note, drag a note icon from the top of the ClarisWorks Help window into the current topic and begin typing. The note expands as you type. Since wordwrap is not supported, however, you must end each line by pressing Return.

To reposition a note, move the cursor over the note until the cursor changes into a hand. Then drag the note to a new position.

To delete a note, drag it away from the Help window. When the cursor changes to a trash can, release the mouse button.

To show or hide all notes, choose Show Notes from the View menu.

One of the fastest ways to find help on a particular subject is to use the Index. The Index, shown in Figure 1-25, is an alphabetical list of all help topics. Scroll to the topic of interest, select it, and click Go To Topic. You can speed up the process by typing the first letter or two of the topic for which you're searching. The list automatically scrolls to the first topic that begins with the letter or letters you type.

 Help can remain on-screen while you continue to work on ClarisWorks documents. When you are through with QuickHelp, you can dismiss it by selecting Quit from the File menu.

For information on ClarisWorks Assistants (the last Balloon Help menu command), refer to Chapter 10.

Figure 1-25:
The Index
dialog box

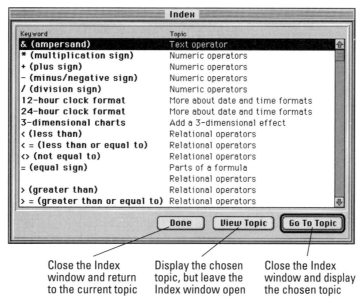

Close the Index
window and return
to the current topic

Display the chosen
topic, but leave the
Index window open

Close the Index
window and display
the chosen topic

Using Balloon Help

By choosing Show Balloons from the Balloon Help menu, you can get helpful information about ClarisWorks components. Whenever the pointer passes over an object that has a Balloon Help message attached to it, a cartoon-style thought balloon pops up, providing some general information about the object. Resizing controls, icons in the Tool panel, buttons in the Shortcuts palette, dialog box buttons, and parts of the document window are some of the items within ClarisWorks that have Help balloons. Figure 1-26 shows an example of a Help balloon.

Figure 1-26:
A Help balloon that tells about a ClarisWorks menu

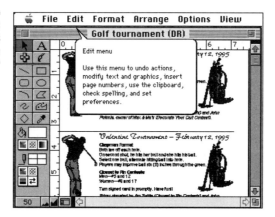

To turn on Balloon Help, click the balloon or question mark (?) icon in the upper-right corner of the screen. The Balloon Help menu appears. While holding down the mouse button, choose Show Balloons. Release the mouse button.

Now, whenever you point to a Balloon Help object, a balloon will appear. Because most people find the balloons distracting when they are attempting to work, you'll probably want to turn Balloon Help off after you find out what you need to know.

To turn off Balloon Help, click the balloon or question mark (?) icon in the upper-right corner of the screen. The Balloon Help menu appears. While holding down the mouse button, choose Hide Balloons. Release the mouse button.

Help balloons are always available for the buttons in the Shortcuts palette (as long as Automatic Icons is set as a Shortcuts preference). Just let the pointer rest on one of the buttons for a few seconds, and a Help balloon will pop up. (See Chapter 12 for more information on the Shortcuts palette and Chapter 11 for assistance in setting preferences.)

Viewing the On-Screen Tour _____

New ClarisWorks users can run an on-screen guided tour to get a quick overview of ClarisWorks 4.0's features and capabilities. More experienced users may want to refer to the tour the first time they explore an environment.

You can start the tour from within ClarisWorks 4.0 or run it from the desktop by using one of the following methods:

- ☞ *From the desktop.* Double-click the Introduction to ClarisWorks icon in your ClarisWorks 4.0 folder.

- ☞ *When ClarisWorks is running.* Choose Introduction to ClarisWorks from the Balloon Help menu.

To move from screen to screen within the tour, click the arrow buttons or choose a new topic from the Menu screen (see Figure 1-27). When you want to leave the tour, click the Exit button.

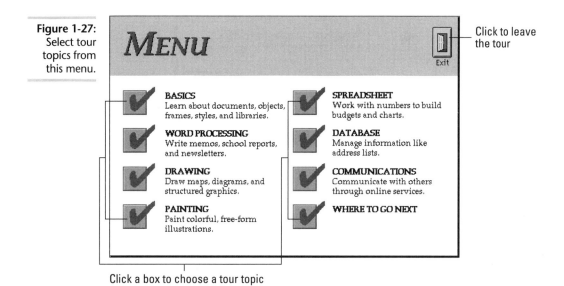

Figure 1-27:
Select tour
topics from
this menu.

Click to leave
the tour

Click a box to choose a tour topic

If you launch the tour from the desktop, you are returned to the desktop after you finish the tour. If you start the tour from within ClarisWorks, after you are done with the tour you are returned to whatever you were last doing in ClarisWorks.

Quitting the Program

After you finish using ClarisWorks, choose Quit from the File menu (or press ⌘-Q). If you have new documents open that have never been saved or documents with changes that haven't been saved, ClarisWorks gives you an opportunity to save the files before quitting (see Figure 1-28). If a file has never been saved (that is, it's a new file that you created in the current session) and you click the Save button in the Save Changes dialog box, ClarisWorks presents the standard Save As file dialog box (as described previously in this chapter in "Saving Documents"). If, on the other hand, the file *has* been saved before, clicking the Save button simply saves the new version of the file over the older one.

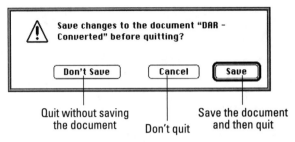

Figure 1-28:
The Save Changes
dialog box

A Save Changes dialog box appears for every unsaved open document. If you change your mind about quitting, click the Cancel button. The ClarisWorks session immediately picks up where you left off.

Clicking Don't Save tells ClarisWorks to close the document without saving it.

If you close a document using Don't Save, all changes since the most recent save are ignored; that is, they are not recorded on disk. If this is a new document and it has *never* been saved, the document itself is discarded. Be sure not to click Don't Save by mistake.

Quick Tips

The following tips contain some helpful hints to

- ☞ Ensure that you have enough memory for your ClarisWorks sessions
- ☞ Skip the New Document dialog box when you launch ClarisWorks
- ☞ Optimally shrink and expand windows
- ☞ Print from the desktop
- ☞ Compensate for not having a translator for a file that you want to open or insert
- ☞ Find misplaced ClarisWorks documents quickly

Changing the Memory Allocation for ClarisWorks

While running ClarisWorks, you may occasionally receive a message that there is insufficient memory to open a document or that a paint document will be opened in a reduced size. You can increase the memory available to ClarisWorks and your documents by using the following procedure.

Steps:	**Changing ClarisWorks' Memory Allocation**
Step 1.	Quit ClarisWorks by choosing Quit from the File menu (or pressing ⌘-Q). If any open documents are new or have been changed, you are given an opportunity to save them. You are then returned to the desktop.
Step 2.	Select the ClarisWorks icon by clicking it and then choose Get Info from the File menu (or press ⌘-I). You see an Info window similar to the one shown in Figure 1-29.

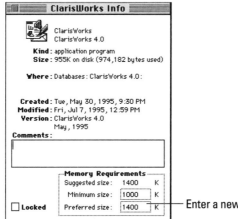

Figure 1-29: The ClarisWorks Info window

Step 3.	Type a larger number into the Preferred size box. (Increase the Suggested size by 25 to 50 percent to start. Later, as you determine the amount of memory that you require for a typical ClarisWorks session, you can fine-tune the memory allocation.)
Step 4.	Click the close box in the upper-left corner of the Info window to save the changes. The next time you run ClarisWorks, the additional memory will be available for your documents.

Skipping the New Document Dialog Box at Start-Up

If you want to skip the New Document dialog box that normally accompanies the program start-up, hold down the ⌘ key as you launch ClarisWorks. After the program loads, it immediately presents the Open dialog box, rather than the New Document dialog box.

 If you've changed the General preferences settings to make ClarisWorks present the Open dialog box rather than the New Document dialog box, holding down the Command key as you launch the program makes the New Document box appear instead.

An Alternative to Tiled and Stacked Windows

If tiled or stacked windows don't appeal to you, you can take more control over your document window arrangement by shrinking and expanding individual windows. To shrink and expand document windows, use the size box to shrink each document window to the smallest possible size. Manually arrange the document windows so that the title bar of each one is exposed. To make one of the documents active (so you can work with it), click once in its window. (When several windows are on-screen, the active window is the one with a series of horizontal lines in its title bar. The title bars for the other windows are blank.) Click the zoom box to expand the document to its full size.

When you're ready to switch to a different document, click the active document's zoom box again; it shrinks back to its reduced size and position. Then repeat Steps 3 and 4 for the next document that you want to use.

Printing ClarisWorks Files from the Desktop

If you aren't currently in ClarisWorks and just want to print an existing document without making changes to it, you can do so by using a special procedure. Go to the desktop and select the file or files that you want to print. Choose Print from the File menu or press ⌘-P. Instead of starting ClarisWorks in the usual way, choosing Print from the desktop loads the selected document into ClarisWorks and then immediately presents the Print dialog box. Select print options and then click Print. After the document has been printed, ClarisWorks automatically quits and you are returned to the desktop.

You can use this Print procedure with most programs. The only drawback is that if you change your mind about printing the document or decide that you need to make some changes before printing it, you need to restart the program and reload the documents.

File Conversion Tips

Although ClarisWorks can understand dozens of foreign file formats, there are formats that ClarisWorks *can't* read. What do you do if ClarisWorks doesn't have a translator for the foreign file that you want to open or insert? One solution is to use the originating program to save or export the file into a format that ClarisWorks *does* support.

Suppose, for example, that you have a word processing document that was created in Microsoft Word 6.0, a program that ClarisWorks 4.0 doesn't support. All that you have to do is open the file in Word 6.0 and then use the Options command from the Save As menu to save a new copy of the file in a format that ClarisWorks supports. Alternatively, if you don't have Word 6.0, see whether you have another program that understands Word 6 files. Then load the file into that particular program and save or export it to a format that ClarisWorks supports.

In general, when you create a file for export, you should select one of the more specific translators that ClarisWorks supports — that of a particular program, such as Excel, Word, MacWrite, or another popular program of the correct type. When ClarisWorks translates such files, it attempts to retain the proper formatting, margins, styles, formulas, and so on. The next best solution is translating the file to a general format, such as ASCII text or SYLK (spreadsheet). Although much of the original formatting will disappear, at least you can work with the basic text of the document and save some retyping time.

In the case of a word processing document, if you can't find a popular word processing format that's supported, see whether the program can create an *RTF* file (a Microsoft document format that has wide support in the computer industry). Unlike straight ASCII text, you'll find that much of the original formatting is retained.

Locating Misplaced ClarisWorks Documents

You're probably already familiar with the Find menu command that is built into Apple's system software. Simply put, this command enables you to search for files on the hard disk. All you have to know is part of the filename. To make it easy to locate files *without leaving ClarisWorks 4.0*, an Assistant called Find ClarisWorks Documents is provided.

Steps: Using the Find ClarisWorks Documents Assistant

Step 1. Choose ClarisWorks Assistants from the Balloon Help menu. The Select Assistant dialog box appears, as shown in Figure 1-30.

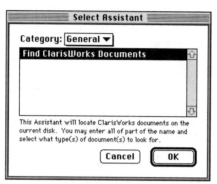

Figure 1-30: The Select Assistant dialog box

Step 2. Choose General as the Category, choose Find ClarisWorks Documents, and click OK. The Find Document Assistant dialog box appears, as shown in Figure 1-31.

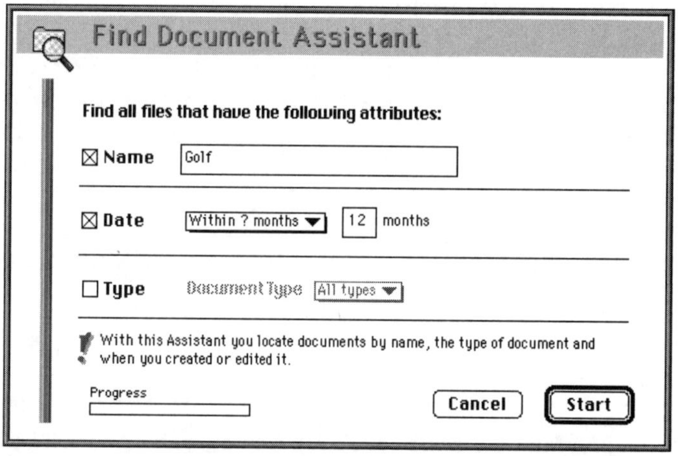

Figure 1-31: The Find Document Assistant dialog box

Step 3. Enter search instructions consisting of any combination of the file's name (or a part of its name), the file date or period that you want to consider, and the document type.

Step 4. Click Start to execute the search. The search progress is displayed in a new dialog box (see Figure 1-32).

Step 5. In the Documents Found box, highlight the file you want to load and click the Open button. If the desired file is not found, click Cancel.

The Find Document Assistant searches only the *active* hard disk — the one from which ClarisWorks is launched. If you have more than one hard disk, or the hard disk is partitioned into multiple volumes, the usefulness of this Assistant may be somewhat limited. You may be better off using the Apple Find utility or another third-party utility.

Pull down to view either File Information or
Location Information about a selected file

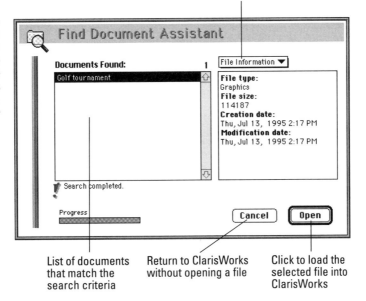

Figure 1-32:
Choose a
document to
open from the
Documents
Found list.

List of documents   Return to ClarisWorks   Click to load the
that match the   without opening a file   selected file into
search criteria   ClarisWorks

If you want to see *every* ClarisWorks document on the active drive, leave all the search criteria blank and unchecked.

■ ■

Summary

➺ You can launch ClarisWorks in several ways. It can open with a particular document on-screen (or several documents), to the New Document dialog box, or to the Open dialog box — depending on your needs for the session.

➺ To make finding a particular document easier, the ClarisWorks Open dialog boxes contain a Document Type pop-up menu that can restrict document choices to an environment of your choosing.

➺ Using the provided Claris Translator filters, ClarisWorks (and other Claris programs) can open or insert many types of non-ClarisWorks files.

➺ You use the Save command to quickly resave documents that are already stored on disk. You use the Save As command to save new files and multiple generations or backup copies of existing files.

➺ When you're through with a particular document, you can close its window by clicking its close box or by choosing Close from the File menu. You can simultaneously close all document windows by holding down the Option key while clicking any close box or choosing the Close command.

➺ You click icons in the Tool panel to add different environment frames to a document, to select drawing tools, and to specify colors, gradients, and patterns for objects. You can hide the Tool panel so that you can see larger areas of the document.

➺ The Shortcuts palette enables you to quickly execute common commands. Its contents change to match the current environment.

➺ You can integrate two or more environments in a single document by using frames.

➺ You can change the display for any document by hiding or showing tools, resizing the document window, and splitting the screen. If you're working with multiple documents, you can optimize their arrangement with the Tile Windows or Stack Windows commands in the View menu.

➺ You can print documents from within ClarisWorks or from the desktop.

➺ ClarisWorks offers two forms of program help: the ClarisWorks Help System (QuickHelp) and Balloon Help.

■ ■

New Features in ClarisWorks 4.0

In This Chapter

➡ A history of the changes introduced in ClarisWorks 2.1 and 3.0

➡ A summary of the new features in the ClarisWorks 4.0 spreadsheet, database, word processing, and draw environments, as well as some general enhancements

Overview

If you previously used an earlier version of ClarisWorks and have just upgraded to ClarisWorks 4.0, this chapter will acquaint you with the program's new features and enhancements. The description of each new feature is followed by a reference to the chapter in which it is fully discussed. Thus, this chapter leads you directly to the feature that you want to learn about next.

If you're still using any version of ClarisWorks prior to 4.0, you can contact Claris Corporation at 800-544-8554 or 408-727-8227 for upgrade information.

ClarisWorks Update History

Although ClarisWorks 4.0 is the latest version of the program, most of the major changes were introduced in ClarisWorks 2.0. Small improvements were added in versions 2.1, 3.0, and 4.0 but the basic program, the six environments, and the way things work have changed very little.

To make it easy to identify features that are new in ClarisWorks 4.0, you'll see New to Version 4 icons in the margins of this book. If you are upgrading from ClarisWorks 2.0 or 2.1, however, you may not recognize *other* features that — although not new in 4.0 — were new in ClarisWorks 2.1 and 3.0 (and hence are new to you). To bring you up to date, the following sections briefly discuss the changes that were introduced in ClarisWorks 2.1 and 3.0. The chapter concludes with a list of the new features in ClarisWorks 4.0, and provides references to the chapters in which the features are discussed. If you are upgrading from ClarisWorks 3.0, you can skip directly to this final section.

If this is your *first* version of ClarisWorks, you can skip this entire chapter. *Everything* is new to you!

New in ClarisWorks 2.1

In February 1994, Claris released ClarisWorks 2.1, which included not only a handful of changes that made ClarisWorks easier to use, but also two important new features:

- ↝ *Hyphenation.* A custom hyphenation dictionary enables you to set automatic hyphenation for any word processing document, database, or text frame. You also can enter discretionary hyphens (which appear only when a word is split across two lines), keep certain words from being hyphenated, and edit the hyphenation dictionary. Hyphenation is covered in Chapter 3.

- ↝ *PowerTalk electronic mail support.* As long as you have System 7.5, System 7 Pro, or a later version of the system software and you have the PowerTalk system software installed, you can add a mailer (an address header) to a ClarisWorks document, making the document a letter that you can send to other PowerTalk users. Documents sent via PowerTalk can include enclosures, such as other ClarisWorks documents. Chapter 19 discusses PowerTalk messaging.

New in ClarisWorks 3.0

Although the main purpose of ClarisWorks 3.0 was to bring the Windows version of the program up to par with the Macintosh version, a few significant features and enhancements were added to the Mac program:

- ↝ *Introduction to ClarisWorks.* New users of ClarisWorks will appreciate this guided tour of the program. Still available in ClarisWorks 4.0, you can run the tour as often as you like by selecting the option for it from the Balloon Help menu. The guided tour is discussed in Chapter 1.

- ❧ *Welcome screen*. Rather than assume that you always want to create a new document, the new Welcome screen enabled you to either create a new document, load an existing document, invoke a ClarisWorks Assistant, or view an on-screen tour of ClarisWorks. (The Welcome screen was removed in ClarisWorks 4.0.)

- ❧ *Assistants*. Assistants are built-in "experts" that make it simple to perform tasks such as formatting footnotes, creating mailing labels and envelopes, and designing newsletters and presentations. Assistants are discussed in Chapter 10.

- ❧ *Revised help system*. The help system was changed dramatically in ClarisWorks 3.0 and is discussed in Chapter 1.

- ❧ *Document Summary Info*. You can save identifying information with any file to show a more descriptive title, the name of the person who created the file, a version number, keywords, a category, and a description. You'll find an explanation of the Document Summary Info dialog box in Chapter 1.

- ❧ *Word count*. This feature provides an accurate count of the number of characters, words, lines, paragraphs, and pages in the current document. Counts in ClarisWorks 3.0, however, were always based on the entire contents of the document. In ClarisWorks 4.0, this feature also can perform a count on selected text. See Chapter 3 for more information.

- ❧ *Improved Save As and Open dialog boxes*. The new Save As dialog box makes it extremely simple to save any document as a stationery template. With Apple's QuickTime extension, the Open dialog box can show you a thumbnail preview of any graphic image or QuickTime movie before you open the file. These new features of the Save As and Open dialog boxes also appear in ClarisWorks 4.0. They are discussed in Chapter 1.

- ❧ *Automatic macros*. Certain macros can automatically play whenever you launch ClarisWorks, create a new document in a particular environment, or open a document in a particular environment. See Chapter 13 for a description of automatic macros.

- ❧ *Clip art*. To help you create more interesting, attractive documents, ClarisWorks 3.0 included 75 clip art images. In ClarisWorks 4.0, clip art images are now organized in libraries (discussed in Chapter 20).

- ❧ *MacWrite Pro file filter*. ClarisWorks 3.0 added a filter that can translate files created with MacWrite Pro.

New in ClarisWorks 4.0

As in most previous ClarisWorks updates, version 4.0 introduces a few big new features and a host of small tweaks, enhancements, and changes.

General Enhancements

- ❧ *Stylesheet palette.* ClarisWorks now has a Stylesheet palette that you can use to quickly format text, paragraphs, outlines, spreadsheet tables, and graphics. In addition to using the predefined styles, you also can create your own reusable styles. See Chapter 15 for details.

- ❧ *Libraries.* ClarisWorks 4.0 includes 20 ReadyArt libraries of clip art, each organized around a theme, such as education, flags, and foods. Any of the supplied images can be dragged and dropped into your documents. You also can create new libraries to store your own graphics, important text, spreadsheet formulas, and QuickTime movies. Libraries are discussed in Chapter 20.

- ❧ *New Assistants.* ClarisWorks Assistants make it simple to accomplish common personal and business tasks by guiding you through the process via a series of dialog boxes. ClarisWorks 4.0 adds three new Assistants for home finance, generating mailing labels, and creating certificates. Assistants are discussed generally in Chapter 10. You'll find additional information about the mailing label Assistant in Chapter 5.

 HTML translator and stationery. Since people are continually expressing interest in the Internet and the World Wide Web, ClarisWorks 4.0 can now create and translate HTML (HyperText Markup Language) documents that are used to present information and graphics on the Web. A stationery document with predefined HTML tag styles is also provided. For information on viewing, editing, and creating HTML documents, see Chapter 21.

- ❧ *Sample AppleScripts.* If you have Apple Computer's AppleScript software installed on your Mac, you can use the four sample AppleScripts to print batches of documents, translate groups of non-ClarisWorks documents to ClarisWorks format, run remote slide shows, or use FileMaker Pro data in a mail merge.

Spreadsheet Enhancements

- ❧ *Cell shading.* In previous versions of ClarisWorks, spreadsheet embellishments were largely limited to applying borders, choosing fonts, and adding a background color. ClarisWorks 4.0 enables you to apply colors and patterns to individual worksheet cells. See Chapter 4 for more information.

◦ *Fill Special command.* Spreadsheet users are familiar with the Fill Down and Fill Right commands (allowing you to create mathematical sequences or to number a series of rows, for example). Fill Special is a more powerful version of these two commands, making it easy to create a numerical sequence without having to figure out the formula or to label a series of cells with dates, times, month names, days, or quarters. The Fill Special command is discussed in Chapter 4.

Database Enhancements

◦ *New field types.* ClarisWorks 4.0 introduces seven new field types: name, pop-up menu, radio buttons, check box, serial number, value list, and record info. See Chapter 5 for a discussion of the new field types and the other changes to the database environment.

◦ *List mode.* In previous versions of ClarisWorks, all data entry, editing, and record viewing was done in Browse mode. By selecting list mode, any database can be viewed and worked with in a spreadsheetlike grid.

◦ *Named searches and sorts.* ClarisWorks enables you to save sort and find instructions for each database so they can easily be reexecuted whenever you like.

◦ *Report generator.* You also can save and reuse report-creation instructions (including the name of the layout to be used, the Sort and Find instructions, and whether or not the report should automatically be printed).

◦ *Mailing Label Assistant.* ClarisWorks 4.0 provides a new Assistant for easily creating mailing labels.

Word Processing Enhancements

◦ *Sections.* With more complex documents (such as books and reports), users can divide them into logical sections. Each section can have its own title page, as well as different headers and footers. Left- and right-facing pages are also supported. This and other changes to the word processing environment are discussed in Chapter 3.

◦ *Outlining.* In earlier versions of ClarisWorks, a word processing document could be displayed either in normal or in outline view. In ClarisWorks 4.0, outlining is fully integrated into the word processing environment — enabling you to create an outline within a regular word processing document.

◦ *Endnotes.* In previous versions of the program, only footnotes could be produced. With the new support for endnotes, users can now move all in-text citations to the end of the current document.

 ❧ *Selective word count.* In addition to being able to gather statistics for an entire document, ClarisWorks 4.0 can also create a report based on the current text selection.

 ❧ *Paragraph Styles menu.* Paragraph and outline formats can be chosen and applied from this pop-up menu in the ruler bar.

 ❧ *New font styles.* ClarisWorks 4.0 includes three new font styles: superior, inferior, and double underline.

 ❧ *On-screen mail merge preview.* When performing a mail merge, users can now preview how their documents will look and print using actual merge data.

Drawing Enhancements

 ❧ *Free rotation.* In previous versions of the program, draw objects could only be rotated in 90-degree increments. In ClarisWorks 4.0, objects can be rotated to any angle by using either the Free Rotation or Object Info command. See Chapter 6 for information on using these commands.

Using the ClarisWorks Environments

II

This section explains the workings of each of the six major ClarisWorks components: word processing, spreadsheet, database, drawing, painting, and communications. You learn the basics of using each component to help you perform routine tasks quickly and easily.

The Word Processing Environment

In This Chapter

- ➼ Creating word processing documents
- ➼ Text editing procedures
- ➼ Formatting words, paragraphs, sections, and documents
- ➼ Finding and replacing text
- ➼ Creating headers, footers, footnotes, and endnotes
- ➼ Using the spelling checker and thesaurus
- ➼ Performing a word count on a document or text selection
- ➼ Using auto-hyphenation
- ➼ Working with outlines
- ➼ Incorporating graphics in a word processing document
- ➼ Using Assistants to address envelopes, insert footnotes, and add tables

Overview

Everyone writes. And whether you're working on a letter, memo, fax, report, or the Great American Novel, a word processor is the ideal writing tool.

What Is a Word Processor?

A word processing program makes it easy for you to edit, reorganize, and polish your writing. Spelling checkers, thesauruses, and grammar checkers help you choose the best (and correct) words. Because you create documents on the Mac's screen, you can avoid paper waste by not printing until the document is exactly as you want it. Instead of making copies of documents for your files, you can simply save them on disk. If you ever need to refer to the original document again or want another printed copy, you just open the document in the word processor. Finally, you can store frequently used paragraphs on disk and reuse them whenever you like. You can copy and paste them into the document or save them as reusable stationery documents (as described in Chapter 10).

 As you read this chapter, keep in mind that everything in it applies to word processing *frames* as well as to documents. In addition, some of the features that you traditionally associate with word processing, such as the spelling checker and rulers, are also available in other ClarisWorks environments. This chapter includes a discussion of these features (because this is where you'd normally expect to read about them), and other chapters refer you back to this chapter as necessary.

Word Processing Essentials

The first step in using the word processor is to create a new word processing document. In ClarisWorks, you do these by choosing New from the File menu (or pressing ⌘-N) and selecting Word Processing in the scrolling list box. A blank document opens (see Figure 3-1) with the cursor positioned at the top of the page, ready for you to start entering text.

Text that you type, paste, or add with the Insert command always appears at the location of the cursor (which is also called the *text insertion point*). The insertion point is marked by a tiny vertical line. You can change the insertion point by moving the mouse and then clicking in a new location. To help you accurately position the text insertion point, ClarisWorks displays an *I-beam cursor* (shown in Figure 3-1) as you move the mouse over the page.

As you type, ClarisWorks automatically handles line ends by wrapping extra text to the next line. When you approach the end of a line, the word processor checks whether the word you are typing, plus the other words in the line, exceed the printable page width. If so, the last word is automatically moved or *wrapped* to the next line. Unlike with a typewriter, you don't have to press Return to start a new line in a word processing document. You just keep typing. In fact, the only times that you should press Return are to end a paragraph or to insert an extra blank line between paragraphs.

Text insertion point   I-beam cursor   Page guide   Ruler

Figure 3-1:
A new word
processing
document

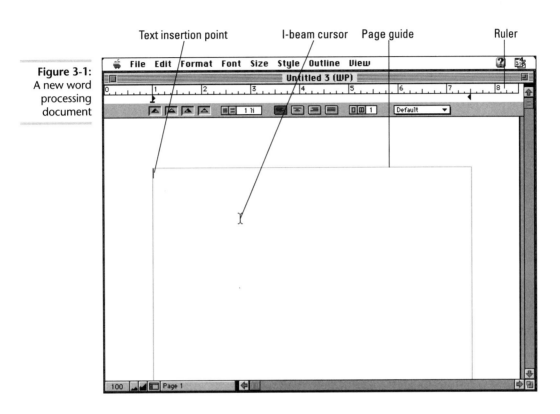

In addition to reformatting lines for you, the word processor features *automatic repagination*. As you insert, delete, or move text in the document, the program automatically adjusts the composition of the pages. Suppose, for example, that you add a couple of paragraphs to the middle of a report. If you are using a typewriter, you have to retype all the pages that follow the insertion. In the ClarisWorks word processor, however, any text following the two new paragraphs automatically shifts down, and the program forms new pages as required. Large deletions work the same way. When you delete, the word processor automatically closes up the space and repaginates the document.

Like all current word processing programs, the ClarisWorks word processor is *paragraph-oriented*. Tabs, indents, and text alignment options that you apply always affect an entire paragraph — not just the line where the text insertion point happens to be. When you press Return, a new paragraph is started, which — by default — contains the same settings as the previous paragraph. Because each paragraph is treated as a separate entity, you can change settings on a paragraph-by-paragraph basis.

You also can apply text-formatting options such as fonts, sizes, and styles to entire paragraphs or to selected text strings within a paragraph. With a typewriter, you have to change type balls or wheels to change the formatting. In the word processor, you simply select some text and then choose the appropriate text formatting commands from the Font, Size, and Style menus.

Navigation

ClarisWorks provides several ways to navigate through a document without changing the insertion point. If you're just reading a document on-screen or checking what was written on page 7, for example, you can use the techniques in Table 3-1 to move through the document. Again, when you are using these techniques, the text insertion point does not change.

Table 3-1 Navigational Techniques	
Navigation	*Key or Action*
Move up or down one line of text	Click the up- or down-arrow symbol on the scroll bar
Move up or down one screenful of text	Press the Page Up or Page Down key (Extended keyboard only) or click in the gray area of the vertical scroll bar
Move up or down to an approximate location	Drag the box in the vertical scroll bar to a new position
Move to the beginning or end of the document	Press the Home or End key (Extended keyboard only) or drag the box in the scroll bar to the top or bottom
Go to a specific page	Double-click in the page number area at the bottom of the document and type a page number in the dialog box that appears

Elementary Text Editing

Few of us are blessed with the ability to write precisely what we want the very first time. In fact, depending on the type and complexity of the document, we may actually spend more time editing than doing the initial writing. This section describes some essential techniques for text editing in the word processing environment.

Selecting Text

To manipulate text — to cut it, change the font or style, and so on — you first have to select it.

To select text, position the cursor where you want the selection to start and then either shift-click where you want it to end or drag to complete the selection. In addition to this basic text-selection technique, you can also use these shortcuts:

- To select a single *word*, double-click anywhere within the word.

- To select the *current line*, triple-click anywhere within the line.

- To select the *current paragraph*, quadruple-click anywhere within the paragraph.

- To select the *entire document*, choose Select All from the Edit menu (or press ⌘-A).

Inserting Text in a Word Processing Document or Frame

Whether you type text, paste it, or insert it with the Insert command, it is always entered at the text insertion point (described previously). You can enter new text into a word processing document or into a text frame.

Position the cursor over the spot where you want to insert the text and click the mouse button once, or use the arrow keys to move the cursor as described in Table 3-2. Type the text, paste it, or enter it with the Insert command from the File menu.

| **Table 3-2** | |
| **Insertion Point Navigational Shortcuts** | |
Cursor Movement	*Keystroke*
One character left or right	Left- or right-arrow key
One line up or down	Up- or down-arrow key
To the start or end of a line	⌘-left-arrow key or ⌘-right-arrow key
One word to the left or right	Option-left-arrow key or Option-right-arrow key
To the beginning or end of a paragraph	Option-up-arrow key or Option-down-arrow key
To the beginning or end of the document	⌘-up-arrow key or ⌘-down-arrow key
Continuous scrolling	Hold down the up- or down-arrow key

When you position the cursor, you need to place it immediately before, after, or within the current text of the document. In a new, blank document, for example, no matter where you click, the insertion point is set at the start of the first page. Similarly, even if you click several inches below the last paragraph in a partially written document, the insertion point is placed immediately following the last character of the document. If you want to start typing well below the current end of the document, you can press Return several times to add the necessary white space so that you can position the insertion point where you want it.

Deleting Text from a Word Processing Document or Frame

Nobody's perfect. Part of the writing process is deleting text — either character-by-character or entire text blocks.

To delete a character, position the cursor to the right of the character and press Delete or Backspace. Each keypress deletes one character to the left of the cursor. If you have an Extended keyboard, you can position the cursor to the left of the character that you want to delete and press the Del key. Each press of the Del key deletes one character to the right of the cursor.

To delete a text block, select the text and press Delete, Backspace, Clear, or Del, or choose Clear from the Edit menu. Each of these operations deletes the text selection without copying it to the Macintosh Clipboard. You can also choose Cut from the Edit menu (or press ⌘-X). This method simultaneously deletes the text selection and copies it to the Macintosh Clipboard. Use this approach when you want to paste the text elsewhere — either in the current document or in another one.

Copying and Reusing Text

The Copy command comes in handy when you have text strings or phrases that you want to use in several places in a document or copy to a different document. To copy text select the text to be copied, and choose Copy from the Edit menu (or press ⌘-C). A copy of the selected text is transferred to the Clipboard, and the text is immediately available for pasting. Until you copy or cut (⌘-X) something else to the Clipboard, you can paste the copied text repeatedly (⌘-V) in the current document as well as in other documents.

Moving Text in a Word Processing Document or Frame

In ClarisWorks, moving text is usually a two-step process: cut and then paste. You cut selected text from the document and then paste it in another position in the document. To move text by cutting and pasting, select the text to be moved. Choose the Cut command from the Edit menu (or press ⌘-X). The text is removed to the Clipboard. Move the text insertion point to the spot where you want to move the text. Choose the Paste command from the Edit menu (or press ⌘-V). The Paste command makes a copy of the text that is in the Clipboard and pastes it at the text insertion point.

ClarisWorks also provides a shortcut for directly moving a text selection to a new location without using the normal cut-and-paste routine. To use this method, select the text to be moved and hold down the ⌘ and Option keys while you use the mouse button to click the destination location in the document. The text is transferred from its original location to the destination.

Using the Macintosh Clipboard

Throughout this book, and in many other Macintosh books, magazines, and manuals, you see frequent references to the *Clipboard*. What is the Clipboard, and how does it work?

The Clipboard is a temporary storage area in Macintosh RAM (memory). The last object or text selection that you copied with the Copy command (⌘-C) or removed with the Cut command (⌘-X) is stored in the Clipboard. Each time you copy or cut a new object or text selection, the new object or text replaces the current contents of the Clipboard.

The beauty of the Clipboard is that whatever it currently contains is available for pasting with the Paste command (⌘-V). And not only can you paste the object or text into the current document, you also can paste it into other documents, even into documents in other programs. You can, for example, copy a name and address from a word processing document and paste it into an address book desk accessory (or vice versa).

The only things that clear the contents of the Clipboard are cutting or copying a new object or text selection and turning off the Mac. Otherwise, you can quit one program and start another, confident that the Clipboard's contents are still intact. (Note, however, that a few Mac programs create their own Clipboard — separate from the Mac's general Clipboard. Information that is copied or cut to a program-specific Clipboard may not be available for pasting in other programs. See your program manuals for details.)

Undoing Your Actions

While typing or editing a document, you'll probably make errors. You may find that you've typed a phrase in the wrong spot — perhaps in the middle of a word — or that you've chosen the wrong formatting command. You may be able to correct the damage by using the Undo command.

ClarisWorks keeps track of the last thing that you did to change the current document, such as cutting text, typing new text, or applying formatting to text. If the program can undo the last action, choosing the Undo command from the Edit menu (or pressing ⌘-Z) puts the document back to the condition it was in immediately before you performed the action. The wording of the Undo command changes to reflect the last action. If, for example, the last change that you made was a cut, the command reads *Undo Cut*.

After choosing Undo, you can still change your mind. The Undo menu command now reads *Redo command* (in this case, Redo Cut). Choose the Redo command, and the Undo is undone.

 Undo tracks only the last change that you made to the document. If you delete some text and then type new text, you cannot undo the deletion. For the Undo command to work, you have to catch the error immediately — before you make any other change to the document. Also, you cannot undo some actions. Saving a new version of a file over an existing file is one example. In those instances, the Undo command is grayed out and reads *Can't Undo.* Think carefully before you make major changes (and be sure to keep current backups).

If you've been experimenting with a document and want to undo *all* the changes you've made, choose the Revert command from the File menu. Revert replaces the document on-screen with a copy of the most recently saved version of the file. It's as though you closed the current document without saving it and then reloaded the original document from disk. Be careful when using Revert — you cannot undo it by using the Undo command. Also note that you can use Revert with *any* type of ClarisWorks document, not just with word processing files.

Formatting: Word Processing with Style

Formatting is what distinguishes an ordinary document from one with style. Sure, you can just pick a standard font (such as Times or Helvetica) and type the entire document, pausing only to press Return now and then to begin a new paragraph. But the word processor enables you to do much more. You can choose different fonts for headers and body text, apply italic to selected phrases to add emphasis, set left and right indents differently for different paragraphs, create hanging indents to format bulleted lists, and use tabs to align items in a list or columns of numbers. You learn to master these formatting commands, and others, in this section.

Within the word processing program, there are four classes:

- ∞ *Text formatting* is concerned with applying fonts, sizes, and styles to characters, words, phrases, sentences, and paragraphs.

- ∞ *Paragraph formatting* enables you to set tabs, indents, line spacing, and between-paragraph spacing for paragraphs.

- ∞ *Section formatting* enables you to divide a document into logical chunks (such as chapters) and specify whether a section begins with a title page, whether left- and right-hand headers and footers are different from each other, and whether page numbering should pick up where the last chapter ended or restart at a particular number. You can also set a different number of columns for text in different sections.

- ∞ *Document formatting* governs the look of the entire document. It includes setting margins, controlling the on-screen appearance of margins and page guides, setting a starting page number for the document, and specifying whether the document will have footnotes or endnotes.

ClarisWorks 4.0 has two new related features to help you consistently apply text and paragraph styles. They are stylesheets and the Paragraph Styles menu. Both are discussed briefly in this chapter. For additional information about stylesheets, see Chapter 15.

Formatting Words

Formatting words, as discussed here, refers to applying different fonts, sizes, and styles. Although you can apply these formats to individual characters within a document, you'll usually stick to formatting words and phrases.

Changing Fonts and Styles

Most people format correspondence and reports using a single font in a single size. When you want to make some text stand out (for example, by applying italic to emphasize a phrase or by changing the font to differentiate a header from body text), ClarisWorks enables you to apply different fonts, sizes, and styles.

To enter text in a document using a specific font, size, or style, position the text insertion point and choose from the font, size, or style menu before typing. To change existing text, select it and then choose a new font, size, or style from the corresponding menu.

Although each character can have only one font and size combination (Helvetica 12 point, for example), you can assign multiple styles to any text. To apply additional styles, select some text and then choose the Style commands that you want to apply to the text.

Styles that you can combine include the following:

- ⇨ **Bold** (⌘-B)
- ⇨ *Italic* (⌘-I)
- ⇨ <u>Underline</u> (⌘-U) or <u>Double Underline</u>
- ⇨ ~~Strike Thru~~
- ⇨ Outline
- ⇨ Shadow

In addition, you can do the following:

- ⇨ Apply a color to selected text by choosing a color from the Text Color pop-up menu in the Style menu.
- ⇨ Move letters in a text string closer together (Condense) or farther apart (Extend).
- ⇨ Format characters so that they appear higher (Superscript, Shift-⌘-+), lower (Subscript, Shift-⌘-), higher in a reduced size (Superior), or lower in a reduced size (Inferior) than the surrounding text.

 The following sets of styles are mutually exclusive: Condense and Extend; Underline and Double Underline; and Superscript, Subscript, Superior, and Inferior.

Removing Styles

Each Style command works as a toggle. To remove a single style from a text string, select the text and choose the Style command that you want to remove. This method of removing styles is particularly useful when a text string has several styles and you want to remove one or some of them but leave the other styles intact.

Choosing and Using Fonts

Regardless of the type of document that you're working on, you'll do well to restrict your use of fonts to a small number — perhaps two. (Too many fonts can make a document look like a ransom note.) Within a selected font (Helvetica or Times, for example), you can freely apply other typefaces and styles, such as italic, bold, and so on.

Fonts can be divided into two general types that are referred to as *serif* and *sans serif*. A serif font, such as Times, has angular points and lines (called *serifs*) at the base and top of each character. Serif fonts are designed to be easy on the eyes and are regularly used to format body text. Sans serif fonts, such as Helvetica, are essentially smooth (they have no serifs) and are often used as headings (*sans* means *no* or *without*).

If you're new at selecting and using fonts (as most of us are), try these suggestions as a starting point:

- For body text, choose a serif font (such as Times, Palatino, or Adobe Garamond).

- For heads, use a sans serif font (such as Helvetica Bold or Franklin Gothic).

You can instantly remove all styles (except color) from text by selecting the text and then choosing Plain Text (⌘-T) from the Style menu.

Formatting Paragraphs

The ClarisWorks word processor treats every paragraph as a distinct entity. If you like, you can give every paragraph different settings for tabs, indents, alignment, and the spacing between lines and between paragraphs. You can set these paragraph formatting options with the ruler or choose the Paragraph command from the Format menu.

 When you type new paragraphs, each time you press Return to end one paragraph and begin another, ClarisWorks automatically applies the format of the previous paragraph to the new paragraph. These formatting options remain in effect for additional paragraphs until you specifically change them.

Using the Ruler

The word processing ruler serves a greater function than simply showing the page width. By clicking and dragging, you can use the ruler to set most paragraph formatting options, as shown in Figure 3-2.

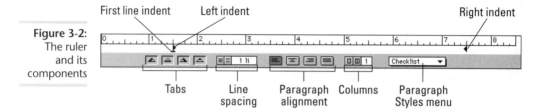

Figure 3-2:
The ruler
and its
components

First line indent   Left indent   Right indent

Tabs   Line   Paragraph   Columns   Paragraph
            spacing   alignment   Styles menu

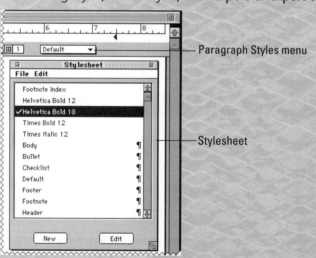

Custom Text Styles

As you work with the word processor, you may find that you frequently use some special text styles (12 point Helvetica Bold, for example). Text styles in the stylesheet are called *basic* styles. You can add custom text styles to the stylesheet, edit existing styles, delete styles, and import or export styles (enabling you to share styles between documents and users). In addition to text styles, the stylesheet can also contains paragraph and outline styles that you can use in word processing documents.

Paragraph Styles menu

Stylesheet

To apply a text style to selected text, click the name of the style in the Stylesheet palette. Paragraph styles can be selected from the Stylesheet palette or from the Paragraph Styles menu in the ruler bar. See Chapter 15 for information about using stylesheets in the word processor, as well as in other environments.

The options that you can set with the ruler include:

- Indents (left, right, and first)
- Tab stops (left, center, right, or decimal)
- Line spacing
- Paragraph alignment (left, center, right, or justified)
- Number of columns (described in "Working with columns" later in this chapter)
- Paragraph styles (described in "Custom Text Styles" and "Hanging Indents" in this chapter)

When you want to make minor changes to paragraph formatting, this visually-guided approach is easy to use. Just change ruler settings until the paragraph looks right. If the ruler isn't visible, choose Show Rulers from the View menu (or press Shift-⌘-U). To hide the ruler, choose Hide Rulers from the View menu (or press Shift-⌘-U).

Although most people prefer a ruler that measures in inches, you can change the measurement units, as well as specify the number of ruler divisions (up to 14). Examples of the different measurement units are shown in Figure 3-3.

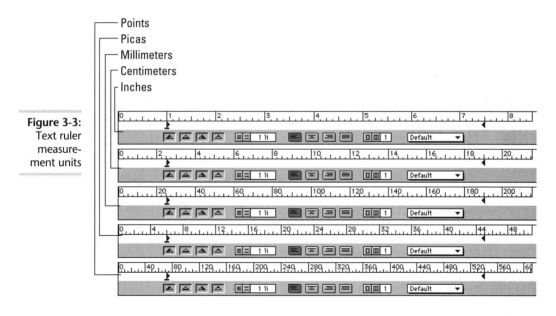

Figure 3-3:
Text ruler measurement units

Steps:	Setting Ruler Measurement Units and Divisions
Step 1.	Open an existing word processing document or create a new document.
Step 2.	Choose Rulers from the Format menu. The Rulers dialog box appears.
Step 3.	Select either the Text ruler or the Graphics ruler by clicking the appropriate radio button in the Ruler Type box.
	The Text ruler is a standard horizontal ruler that appears at the top of the page. Selecting the Graphics ruler creates a pair of rulers: a horizontal ruler across the top of the page and a vertical ruler down the left side of the page. Graphics rulers, however, are only aids for positioning; they do not contain the same controls that Text rulers have. Thus, Graphics rulers are not recommended for use with word processing documents.
Step 4.	Select a unit of measurement by clicking the appropriate radio button in the Units box.
Step 5.	Type a number in the Divisions text-edit box to indicate the number of minor divisions that you want in each segment of the ruler. You can specify a maximum of 512 divisions, although ClarisWorks can display only as many as 14 division marks on the ruler.
Step 6.	Click OK. A ruler appears with the units and divisions you specified.

ClarisWorks saves the ruler with the document. Note that every document can have a different type of ruler with different divisions.

If you find, for example, that you prefer a ruler with points as the units of measurement rather than inches, you may want to create a blank stationery document with that style of ruler. You also can make that style of ruler the default for all new word processing documents by including the ruler in a default stationery document. Chapter 10 includes instructions for creating both types of stationery files.

Indents

Indents are paragraph-specific settings that indicate how far in from the left or right margins the text should be positioned. In ClarisWorks, as in other word processors, you can set a first line indent so that the first line is treated differently from other lines in the paragraph. First line indents can be used to create *hanging indents*. Indents are useful for formatting bulleted lists, numbered lists, and quotations, as shown in Figure 3-4.

Figure 3-4:
Examples of
different
indents

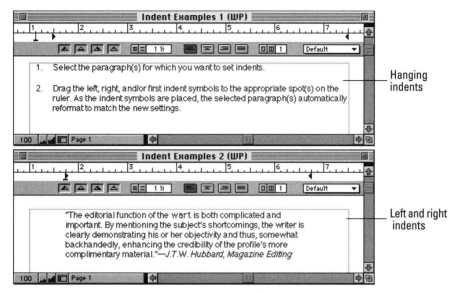

Hanging
indents

Left and right
indents

To set indents withthe ruler, select the paragraph or paragraphs for which you want to set the indents and drag the left, right, and/or first indent symbols to the appropriate locations on the ruler. As the indent symbols are placed, the selected paragraphs automatically reformat to match the new settings.

Hanging Indents

Hanging indents are frequently used in documents, particularly for formatting numbered lists and bulleted lists. (In a *hanging indent*, the first line begins farther to the left than the remaining lines.) To create a hanging indent, drag the left indent marker (the solid right-pointing triangle) on the ruler to the right. Its location marks the spot where the text will begin. Drag the first line marker (the inverted T symbol) to the desired position. Its location marks the spot where the numbers or bullets will appear. (If you want the numbers or bullets to be flush with the left margin, you don't need to change the position of the first line marker.) Refer to the ruler in the top half of Figure 3-6 for an example of a hanging indent.

Normally, when you attempt to drag the left indent marker, the first line marker also comes along for the ride. To move the left indent marker by itself (so you can easily create a hanging indent), hold down the Option key while you click and drag the left indent marker.

To form the hanging indent, start by typing the number or bullet symbol. Then press Tab and type the text of the step or point. If the text is longer than one line, the remaining text automatically wraps to the position of the left indent marker.

ClarisWorks 4.0 also contains predefined styles you can use to instantly format paragraphs to show bullets or sequential numbers. Select the paragraphs, and then choose Bullet or Number from the Paragraph Styles menu in the ruler bar or from the Stylesheet palette. Note, however, that you're stuck with the style of bullets or numbers that ClarisWorks provides. You cannot change the bullet character (using a Zapf Dingbat character, for example), nor can you change the font or style of the numbers.

Tab Stops

If you're familiar with a typewriter (I haven't touched one in more than 15 years), you already know about tabs. Tabs are used to align text in columns, to create tables, and to precisely position important text strings (enabling you to right-align a page number in a footer, for example). ClarisWorks offers four tab stop options: left, center, right, and decimal. Figure 3-5 shows examples of the four types of tab stops.

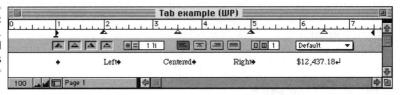

Figure 3-5:
Left, center, right, and decimal tabs

Tabs can be set in two ways: by dragging them onto the ruler and by typing their exact locations using the Tab command. After you set a tab, you can reposition it by simply dragging it to a new location on the ruler. You can remove a tab by dragging it off the ruler.

Steps:	Setting Tab Stops with the Tab Command
Step 1.	Select the paragraph or paragraphs for which you want to set tab stops.
Step 2.	Choose the Tab command from the Format menu. The Tab dialog box appears. (If the Tab dialog box covers any of the paragraphs that will be affected by the command, you can drag the dialog box to a different position.)

You can quickly summon the Tab dialog box by double-clicking any of the four tab icons at the bottom of the ruler bar.

Step 3. Choose the settings for the first tab stop that you want to set. Click the radio button for the Alignment desired, type a number in the Position text-edit box, and (optional) click a radio button to select a Fill pattern (also called a *leader*).

A leader is a character, such as a period, that fills the blank space leading up to the tab. Leader characters are particularly useful in formatting entries in a table of contents and separating invoice items from prices (for example, Jello.......$0.49).

Step 4. Click Apply to insert the new tab.

Step 5. Repeat Steps 3 and 4 for additional tabs that you want to set at this time.

Step 6. Click OK to accept the new tab settings or Cancel to revert to the original tab settings.

The Tab dialog box does not provide a method for *removing* tab stops. Regardless of how you set tabs, you have to remove them manually by dragging them off the ruler.

The decimal tab (the Align On option) is followed by a text-edit box. Although you normally set this tab to align on a decimal point (.), you can specify any character you like. You may, for example, want a column of numbers to align on the percent sign (%).

When you are creating a document, such as a résumé, that uses many different indentations, use tabs instead of spaces between items. Though it may look good on the screen, the printout may look quite different. Tabs are also much easier to adjust than spaces.

Line Spacing

Most documents are printed *single-spaced* (with no blank lines between lines of text). Occasionally, however, you need to alter the between-line spacing. High school and college homework, for example, often must be *double-spaced* (with one blank line between every pair of text lines). Manuscripts submitted to magazines and book publishers sometimes must be double-spaced as well — to make it easier for an editor to edit and write comments on the printed copy.

To set line spacing, select the paragraphs for which you want to set between-line spacing and in the ruler bar, click the line spacing icon on the left to decrease the between-line spacing or click the line spacing icon on the right to increase the between-line spacing. Line spacing always increases or decreases in half-line increments. Figure 3-6 shows examples of several of the most common settings for line spacing.

Like other ruler settings, line spacing can be different for every paragraph in a ClarisWorks word processing document. If you want to set line spacing for the entire document, choose Select All from the Edit menu (or press ⌘-A) and then select a line spacing option.

Line spacing also can be set using the Paragraph command (discussed later in this chapter).

Figure 3-6:
Some line
spacing
examples

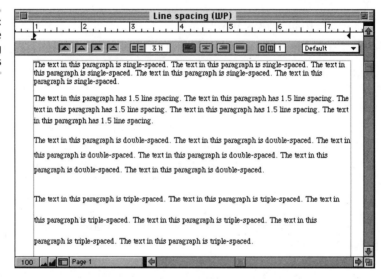

Paragraph Alignment

Most documents are *left-aligned* (flush with the left margin and with a ragged right margin). For those times when you need it, however, ClarisWorks also provides options for center-aligned, right-aligned, and justified paragraphs. Figure 3-7 shows examples of the four types of paragraph alignment.

Making a document title *center-aligned* centers it instantly on the page; you don't need to mess with tabs or the spacebar. You can use the *right-align* setting to position the current date in a letter.

Justified paragraphs are flush with both the left and right margins. ClarisWorks automatically adds extra space between words to make each line edge square with the margins. Magazine articles often have justified paragraphs.

To set paragraph alignment, select the paragraph or paragraphs for which you want to set an alignment and click one of the four paragraph alignment icons in the ruler bar. The chosen alignment is applied to the selected paragraphs.

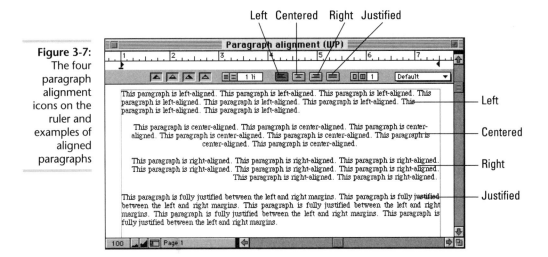

Figure 3-7:
The four
paragraph
alignment
icons on the
ruler and
examples of
aligned
paragraphs

Using the Copy Ruler and Apply Ruler Commands

After you set formatting options for a paragraph, you may want to repeat these settings in other paragraphs in the document. For example, when writing a report, you may create a paragraph format for long quotations. Manually recreating this format each time you have a new quote is time consuming and prone to error. To simplify the transfer of paragraph formats, ClarisWorks provides the Copy Ruler and Apply Ruler commands.

 The stylesheet is also particularly useful for storing and applying paragraph styles. See Chapter 15 for information about stylesheets.

To apply ruler settings to a new paragraph, move the cursor into the paragraph whose ruler settings you want to copy. Choose Copy Ruler from the Format menu (or press Shift-⌘-C). Move the cursor into the target paragraph. Alternatively, you can use normal text selection techniques to select several contiguous paragraphs to which you want to apply the ruler settings. Choose Apply Ruler from the Format menu (or press Shift-⌘-V). The ruler settings from the copied ruler are applied to the selected paragraph(s).

Note that the Apply Ruler command remains active (not gray) even after you paste the settings. You can continue to paste these settings into additional paragraphs until you quit ClarisWorks or issue a new Copy Ruler command.

 You also can use the Copy Ruler and Apply Ruler commands to transfer ruler settings between documents.

Using the Paragraph Command

Although the ruler is handy, you also can use the Paragraph command from the Format menu to set paragraph indents and line spacing directly. The advantages of using the Paragraph command over using the ruler include:

- ∞ The Paragraph command gives you improved precision in establishing settings.

- ∞ You can set several options in a single dialog box (as opposed to setting them one by one with the ruler).

- ∞ You can use any measurement system that you like — not just the one shown on the current ruler — for line and paragraph spacing.

- ∞ You can select outlining label formats for paragraphs — such as diamonds, check boxes, and Roman numerals — and choose a paragraph alignment.

- ∞ The only way to set spacing above and below a paragraph is with the Paragraph command.

 You can also summon the Paragraph dialog box by double-clicking any of the following elements on the ruler bar: the line-spacing indicator, the number of columns indicator, or the alignment icons.

Steps: **Choosing Paragraph Settings with the Paragraph Command**

Step 1. Select the paragraph or paragraphs for which you want to alter paragraph format settings and choose the Paragraph command from the Format menu. The Paragraph dialog box appears, as shown in Figure 3-8.

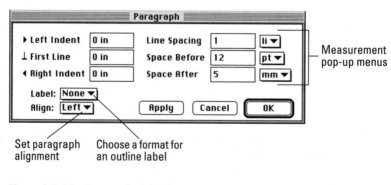

Figure 3-8: The Paragraph dialog box

Step 2. Type numbers in the text-edit boxes and choose options from the pop-up menus for the settings that you want to change. Here are some pointers:

- ↪ The Left indent, First line, and Right indent settings are preceded by their corresponding ruler symbols.

- ↪ The only measurement settings in the Paragraph dialog box that do not appear on the ruler are Space before and Space after. Fill in their boxes in the Paragraph dialog box to set the amount of blank space that you want to appear before or after the selected paragraphs.

- ↪ You can change the measurement system for Line spacing, Space before, or Space after by selecting an option from their respective pop-up menus. You can mix and match measurement systems, as previously illustrated in Figure 3-8.

- ↪ Paragraph alignment can be chosen from the Align pop-up menu. If the selected paragraphs are outline topics or subtopics, you can choose a new label format from the Label pop-up menu.

Step 3. Click Apply to apply the new settings to the selected paragraphs. (Apply is a tentative option. You can remove changes made with Apply by clicking Cancel; the formatting instantly reverts to the original settings.)

Step 4. Click OK to accept the paragraph formatting changes or Cancel to revert to the original settings.

If you routinely want each paragraph to automatically be separated from the next paragraph by one blank line, set Space after to **1 li**. With that setting, you don't have to press Return an extra time between paragraphs.

Formatting Sections

To enable you to create more complex and varied word processing documents, ClarisWorks 4.0 introduces the concept of *sections*. Each section of a word processing document can have a different title page, headers and footers, page numbering, and number of columns.

If you are writing a book, for example, you can define each chapter as a separate section and set the following options:

⌦ Each chapter begins on a right-hand page and is treated as a title page (with no headers or footers)

⌦ Page numbering is chapter-relative (that is, it restarts at 1, but is preceded by the chapter number and a dash, as in 5-1)

⌦ The left and right headers and/or footers are different from each other (the book title is in the header of all left pages and the chapter title is in the header of all right pages, for instance)

You must specify section options individually for each section in the document. To create a new section, move the insertion point to where you want the section to begin and choose Insert Section Break from the Format menu (or press Option-Enter).

To set options for a section, place the insertion point anywhere within the section and then choose Section from the Format menu. The Section dialog box appears in Figure 3-9, as shown.

Figure 3-9:
The Section
dialog box

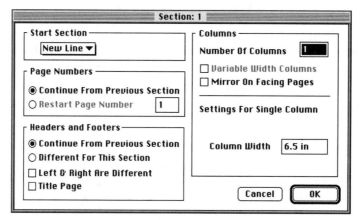

The meaning of each option in this dialog box is explained in the following sections. To remove a section break, position the text insertion point at the start of the section that follows the break and press Delete.

Many — perhaps most — documents have only *one* section. Nevertheless, you can still use the Section dialog box to specify page number, header/footer, and column settings (in this instance, for the entire document).

Start Section

Depending on your selection from the Start Section pop-up menu in the Section dialog box, the current section can begin on a New Line, New Page, New Left Page, or New Right Page. (Book chapters generally begin on a right-hand page, for example).

Page Numbers

To make page numbering pick up where the previous section left off, click the Continue From Previous Section radio button. If the last section ended on page 17, for example, this section would start with page 18.

If you want the page numbering in this section to start with some other number, click the Restart Page Number radio button and enter a page number in the text-edit box to the right of this option.

Headers and Footers

Click Continue From Previous Section if you want to use the same headers and footers that were used in the previous section; click Different For This Section if you want to specify new headers and/or footers. After making this choice, you can safely edit the headers and footers in the new section without changing the previous section's headers and footers.

If you want to have different headers/footers for left- and right-hand pages, click the Left & Right Are Different check box. This is a common practice in books and in lengthy reports.

When you click the Title Page check box, ClarisWorks treats the first page of the section as a title page. It eliminates the headers and footers for that page only. Normally, you do not want to display page numbers and date stamps (common items for a header or footer) on the first page of a chapter, for example. If the document doesn't have headers or footers, this setting is irrelevant.

Columns

ClarisWorks allows word processing documents and documents sections to have multiple columns. Newsletters, magazines, and church bulletins are often formatted with two or more columns, for example.

You can use the ruler bar to specify the number of columns for a section by clicking the Decrease-Columns and Increase-Columns controls (see Figure 3-10).

Decrease   Increase   Current number
Columns control   Columns control   of columns

Figure 3-10:
Setting the
number of
columns by
using the
ruler

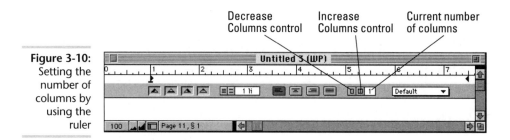

You can also manually adjust column widths and the space between columns. To manually adjust the widths of two adjacent columns, move the pointer into the space between a pair of columns and press Option. The pointer changes to a pair of arrows surrounding a hollow box. Press the mouse button and move the pointer to the left or right. As you move the pointer, the widths of the two columns change. Release the mouse button to set the new column widths. Using this procedure, the space between the columns does not change. You are merely allocating the combined widths of the two columns in a new way.

To manually change the space between two adjacent columns, move the pointer so that it touches the inside edge of a column and press Option. The pointer changes to a pair of arrows surrounding two vertical lines. Press the mouse button and move the pointer to the left or right. As you move the pointer, the width of the column that the pointer is touching and the space between the columns change. Release the mouse button to set the new column width and between-column spacing.

You can also use the Section command to set columns.

Steps:	Setting Multiple Columns with the Section Command

Step 1.   Position the text insertion point within the section you want to format. (If the document contains only one section, position the text insertion point anywhere in the document.)

Step 2.   Choose Section from the Format menu. The Section dialog box appears, as shown previously in Figure 3-9.

Step 3.   Type a number in the Number of Columns text-edit box.

Step 4.   If you want all columns to be the same width, leave the Variable Width Columns check box unchecked. The default Column Width and Space Between for that number of columns are shown at the bottom of the dialog box. As long as you don't exceed the page width, you can alter either or both of these numbers.

— or —

Step 4. If you want the columns to be different widths, click the Variable Width Columns check box. By default, all columns are set to the same width. To change the widths, select a column number (the columns are numbered from left to right) from the Settings for Column pop-up menu, and enter numbers for Space Before, Column Width, and Space After. Repeat this procedure for the remaining columns.

When you set two or more columns, the Columns portion of the Section dialog box changes depending on your choice of variable-width or equal-sized columns (as shown in Figure 3-11).

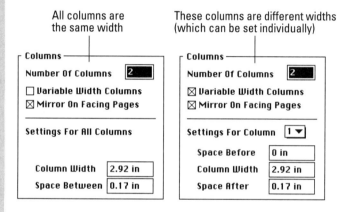

Figure 3-11: When equal-sized columns are selected, Column Width and Space Between is simultaneously set for all columns (left). With variable-width columns, the space before, column width, and space after can be set individually for each column (right).

Step 5. *Optional:* If the section has multiple variable-width columns and is to be printed like a book, you may want click the Mirror On Facing Pages check box.

For example, if the left-hand pages have a two-inch column near the outside margin and a four-inch column beside the inner margin (also called the *gutter*), right-hand pages would be mirrored; that is the four-inch column would still be beside the gutter and the two-inch column would be near the outer margin. If Mirror On Facing Pages was not checked, the four-inch column would always be on the right.

Step 6. Click OK to use the new column settings or Cancel to revert to the column settings that were in effect before you chose the Columns command. If you click OK, ClarisWorks automatically reformats the text to flow into the columns that you created.

If you enter an individual column width that is wider than the allowable maximum, the program displays an error message, and you have to enter a new width number. Similarly, if the combined width of all columns and the space between columns exceeds the page width, you are asked to enter new numbers.

Page and Column Breaks

One feature that ClarisWorks lacks is the capability to handle widows and orphans in text. A *widow* is a lone line of text that ends a page or column (the first or only line of a paragraph or a heading). An *orphan* is a lone line of text that starts a page or column (usually the final line of a paragraph). Widows and orphans make a document look unprofessional. To eliminate them, you can manually insert breaks as needed as the final editing step before printing the document.

To insert a page or column break, position the text insertion point at the beginning of the line that you want as the first line in the new page or column and choose Insert Page Break or Insert Column Break from the Format menu. The break appears, and the line of text is moved to the next page or column.

 ClarisWorks 4.0 also includes a handy way to insert page and column breaks. Simply press the Enter key. If the text-insertion point is in a single-column section, a page break is inserted. If the insertion point is in a multicolumn section, a column break is inserted.

If Show Invisible is on (that is, you have checked it in the Text preferences, have clicked its button on the Shortcuts palette, or have pressed ⌘-; [semicolon]), a break is indicated by a tiny downward- or upward-pointing arrow. You can remove a break by selecting the arrow and pressing Delete or Backspace. If the arrow is invisible, move the text insertion point to the start of the text line that begins the break and then press Delete.

Formatting Documents

Document formatting controls the overall appearance of each page — both on-screen and when printed. Document options include

- ⟳ Margins (top, bottom, left, and right)
- ⟳ Margin and page guides (shown or invisible)
- ⟳ On-screen page display (single pages or two pages side-by-side)
- ⟳ Starting page number
- ⟳ Footnotes and endnotes

You set document formatting options by choosing Document from the Format menu. The Document dialog box appears, as shown in Figure 3-12. Set options and click OK to put your choices into effect (or click Cancel if you change your mind).

Figure 3-12:
The Document
dialog box

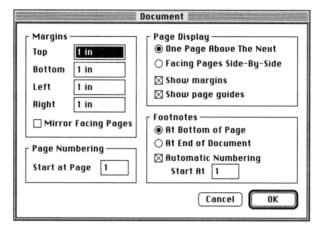

Note that several of the options (Margins, Footnotes, and Page Numbering) affect the way the document will print. The remaining settings (Page Display) affect only the document's appearance on-screen.

All settings in the Document dialog box affect only the active document. When you create a new document, you have to reset the Document options. Although you can't save these options as preferences, you can avoid the boring, repetitious task of resetting the options. Create a new blank document, set the document preferences, and then save the file as a default stationery document, as described in Chapter 10. New word processing files then use your preferred Document settings automatically. (You can use this same tactic for any ClarisWorks environment that you wish to standardize.)

Setting Margins

To change a margin setting in the Document dialog box, simply type a number in the appropriate margin text-edit box.

You'll note that the units of measurement for each margin setting match those of the ruler. If you want to specify a different measurement unit, choose the Rulers command to select the unit and *then* choose the Document command.

If you intend to have your document printed double-sided (as you would with a bound book, for example), click the check box for Mirror Facing Pages. The wording for the Left and Right margin settings changes to "Inside" and "Outside."

Number of Pages Displayed

By default, ClarisWorks is set to display every document one page at a time (One Page Above The Next). If you would rather see pages side by side, click the Facing Pages Side-By-Side radio button in the Document dialog box.

The Facing Pages Side-By-Side option is particularly useful if you have a monitor that has room to show two complete pages at the same time. Even if you have a small monitor (14 inch, for example), you can choose this option and then zoom the document to 50 percent to check its overall layout and design.

Show Margins and Show Page Guides

The setting for Show margins determines whether the body text will be separated from the edges of the page by white space (when Show margins is checked). Checking Show page guides causes the work area of the document to be outlined by a faint gray border. Having the page guides visible is particularly useful when you are working with headers and footers.

Start at Page

This option works in conjunction with the automatic page-numbering feature (Insert Page # in the Edit menu). You can specify a starting page number by entering a number in the text-edit box. Although you usually want page numbering to begin with 1 (the default), this feature can be useful. For example, if you are writing a book and you know that Chapter 1 ended on page 27, you can specify a starting page number of 28 for Chapter 2.

Footnotes and Endnotes

Important in-text notes can be displayed at the bottom of each page as *footnotes* or grouped together at the end of the document as *endnotes*. (The use of endnotes is a new feature introduced in ClarisWorks 4.0.) If you want footnotes, click the At Bottom of Page radio button; for endnotes, click At End of Document. (Of course, if you don't intend to insert footnotes in the document, your choice is irrelevant.)

When you check the Automatic Numbering check box, ClarisWorks automatically numbers footnotes and endnotes, beginning with the number entered in the Start At text-edit box. Leave this option unchecked if you want to manually number footnotes or endnotes, or if you want to use characters other than numbers, such as asterisks (*).

Advanced Editing Tools and Techniques

The features and editing techniques that are discussed in this section are non-essentials. Although you can initially do without them, you'll eventually find many of the following tools and techniques helpful in creating clean, attractive, readable documents:

- Finding and replacing text
- Headers and footers
- Footnotes and endnotes
- Inserting automatic date, time, and page numbers
- Using the spelling checker and thesaurus
- Performing a word count
- Using the hyphenation feature
- Creating outlines

Finding and Replacing Text

Like other word processing programs, the ClarisWorks word processing environment includes a set of Find/Change commands. Use Find to locate a particular section of a document quickly (where you talked about Social Security, for example). Use the Change option to replace one text string with another. Find/Change enables you to do the following:

- Find the next occurrence of a particular text string
- Find subsequent occurrences of the same text string
- Replace a found text string with another text string (or simultaneously replace all instances of one text string with another text string)
- Find a text string that matches the currently selected text in the document

Steps: Finding a Text String

Step 1.   Choose Find/Change from the Find/Change submenu of the Edit menu (or press ⌘-F). The Find/Change dialog box that is shown in Figure 3-13 appears.

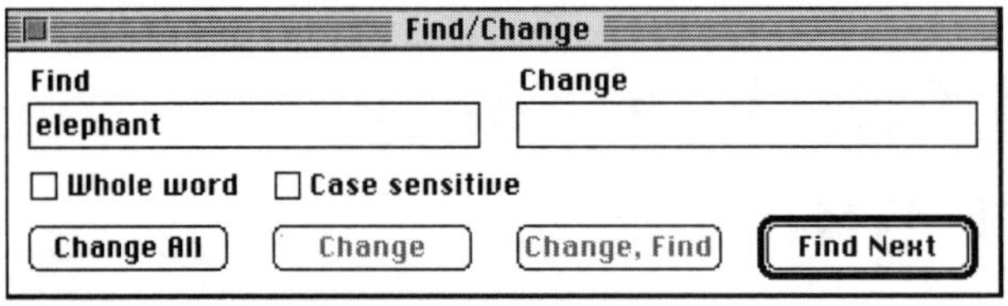

Figure 3-13: The Find/Change dialog box

Step 2.   In the Find text-edit box, type the text string for which you want to search (leave the Change text-edit box empty):

- *Whole word.* If you want to search only for complete words, click the Whole word check box. With Whole word checked, searching for *and* will find only *and* — not *sand* or *bandage*.

- *Case sensitive.* Click the Case sensitive check box if you want the case of each character in the Find string to be considered during the search. If you check this box, a search for *Young* would not match *young* or *YOUNG.* If you're unsure of the capitalization, you probably don't want to check Case sensitive.

Step 3.   Click the Find Next button (or press Return or Enter). The search commences downward from the current cursor position. Eventually, the search wraps around so that the whole document is searched — including text that is above the initial cursor position.

If the document contains a match, ClarisWorks highlights the first instance of the text string. If no match is found, a message to that effect appears.

Step 4.   If the found text is not the instance for which you are searching, click Find Next again. Each click restarts the search from the point of the last found text.

Step 5.   When you are finished, click the close box of the Find/Change dialog box.

You can repeat a search by choosing Find Again (⌘-E) from the Find/Change submenu of the Edit menu.

Sometimes the Find/Change dialog box obscures the found text. If necessary, you can move the dialog box to a different location by clicking its title bar, holding down the mouse button, and dragging.

You probably noticed that the Find/Change dialog box also contains a Change text-edit box. Text that you type into this box can replace instances of found text — either one match at a time (with your approval) or globally (automatically replacing all instances without one-by-one approval).

Steps:	**Finding and Changing Text**

Step 1. Choose Find/Change from the Find/Change pop-up menu of the Edit menu (or press ⌘-F). The Find/Change dialog box (previously shown in Figure 3-13) appears.

Step 2. In the Find text-edit box, enter the text string to be located, and in the Change text-edit box, enter a replacement text string.

Step 3. Set the Whole word and Case sensitive settings as desired:

- If you check Whole word, ClarisWorks will find only whole words that match the Find string.

- If you check Case sensitive, the program will locate only strings that have capitalization that is identical to the Find string's capitalization.

Step 4. To change all instances of the Find string to the Change string without prompting from the program, click Change All. A dialog box appears stating: *The Change All feature is not undoable.* Click OK to continue or click Cancel.

— or —

Step 4. To examine each Find result before you change the text, click Find Next. As text is found, click one of the following:

- Click Change to change only the current instance. Normally, you choose this option when you are ready to end the search (after you have found the single or final instance of text that you want to change). If you decide that you want to continue the search after you click Change, click Find Next.

- Click Change, Find to change the current instance and then find the next one.

- Click Find Next if the current instance is not one that you want to change.

Step 5. When you are finished, click the close box of the Find/Change dialog box.

On subsequent finds in this session, the Find/Change dialog box will contain the last set of Find/Change text strings and settings that you used.

Finding Special Characters

Occasionally, you may want to locate — and optionally replace — some special ClarisWorks characters, such as tabs, paragraph returns (end-of-paragraph markers), or automatic dates. To search for these characters or use them as replacements, enter the symbols shown in Table 3-3 in the Find or Change text-edit boxes of the Find/Change dialog box.

Table 3-3 Find/Change Symbols for Special Characters	
Search Character	**Characters to Type**
Space	Spacebar
Nonbreaking space	Option-spacebar
Tab	\t or ⌘-Tab
Discretionary hyphen	\- or ⌘- - (hyphen)
Paragraph return	\p or ⌘-Return
Line break (soft return)	\n or Shift-⌘-Return
Column break	\c or ⌘-Enter
Page break	\b or Shift-⌘-Enter
Section break	\- Option -6
Automatic date	\d
Fixed date	(Date)
Automatic time	\h
Fixed time	(Time)
Automatic page number	\#
Fixed page number	(Number)
Backslash	\\

Because the backslash character (\) is used to define many of the special characters in the table, you have to type a pair of backslashes (\\) to find a backslash that appears in the text.

Because the need to search for such characters or use them as replacements may not be readily apparent, consider the following examples:

- *Removing double spaces.* Modern typesetting conventions frown on double spaces between sentences. (I know that you were taught to use double spaces when you learned to type, but double spaces are not necessary when using a computer, a word processing program, and a high-quality printer.) Use the Find/Change command to substitute a single space for every instance of a double space. In addition to eliminating double spaces between sentences, you'll also get rid of extra spaces between words.

- *Substituting spaces for tabs in communications text.* Some information services and bulletin boards aren't prepared to handle tabs in text files. Search for the tab character (\t) and replace each instance with a fixed number of spaces (5 or 8, for example).

- *Eliminating extra space at the end of paragraphs.* Some of my publishers are sticklers for this one. Search for Space Return (\p) and replace with Return (\p).

- *Replacing automatic date and time with a fixed date or time.* Automatic dates or times (which you enter by choosing Insert Date or Insert Time from the Edit menu) change every time you open the document. These features are useful if you want to show a new date or time whenever you print the document. If you want to show when a document was written, on the other hand, you can replace the automatic date and time with a fixed date and time.

If you can't remember what to type when you want to execute a search for a particular character or if Table 3-3 isn't handy, you can copy the special characters in your document and then paste them into the Find/Change dialog box.

Steps: Copying and Pasting Special Characters

Step 1. Find an example of the character in your document.

To more easily find characters that are normally hidden, click the Show/Hide Invisibles button in the Shortcuts palette (Figure 3-14), choose Preferences from the Edit menu and check the Show Invisibles check box in the Text options, or press ⌘-; (semicolon).

Figure 3-14: The Show/Hide Invisibles button

Step 2.   Select the character and choose Copy from the Edit menu (or press ⌘-C).

Step 3.   Choose Find/Change from the Find/Change submenu of the Edit menu (or press ⌘-F). The Find/Change dialog box appears.

Step 4.   Press ⌘-V to paste the character into the Find or the Change text-edit box, as appropriate. When pasting into a Find/Change text-edit box, ClarisWorks automatically substitutes the correct symbols for the special character.

Creating Headers and Footers

Headers and footers can contain any text or graphics that you want to separate from the body of the document. Because they are printed on the top or bottom of every page, headers and footers are very useful for displaying document-identification text, such as the date, your name, a document filename, and the report title. You also can place logos and other graphics in headers and footers to save yourself the trouble of repeatedly pasting images onto every page of the document. Figure 3-15 shows a header and a footer for a typical letterhead.

Figure 3-15:
Examples of a
header and a
footer

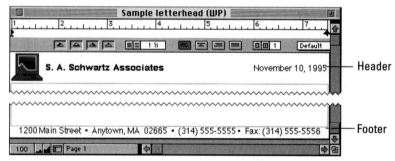

Page numbers are routinely placed in the header or footer. For page numbers that automatically change to reflect pagination changes in the text, see "Inserting Automatic Date, Time, and Page Numbers," later in this chapter.

To create a headerr footer, choose Insert Header or Insert Footer from the Format menu. A header or footer appears in the document, and the text insertion point moves into the header or footer area. You can then type the header or footer text.

As with other text, you can format header and footer text with different fonts, styles, sizes, and paragraph/ruler bar settings.

Unless you check the Show page guides check box in the Document dialog box (accessed by choosing the Document command in the Format menu), you may have a difficult time distinguishing the header and footer text from the body text. After you check Show page guides, faint gray outlines surround the header and footer.

If you later decide that you do not need a header or a footer, you can eliminate them by choosing Remove Header or Remove Footer from the Format menu. Doing so instantly deletes all text and graphics in the header or footer.

Remember, if a document is divided into sections, you can set different headers and footers for each section, if you like. Refer to "Formatting Document Sections," earlier in this chapter.

Footnotes and Endnotes

If you're working on a school report or a professional paper, you'll appreciate the ClarisWorks features for managing footnotes.

Steps:	**Inserting a Footnote**

Step 1. Position the text insertion point where you want the footnote to appear.

Step 2. Choose Insert Footnote from the Format menu (or press Shift-⌘-F).

Step 3. If you have checked Automatic Numbering in the Document dialog box (described earlier in this chapter), the next footnote number in sequence appears at the insertion point.

— or —

Step 3. If you have not checked Auto Number Footnotes, the Mark with dialog box appears, as shown in Figure 3-16. Type the character that you want to use to mark the footnote and click Enter. The character appears at the insertion point.

```
Mark with  [          ]
         [ Cancel ] [   OK   ]
```

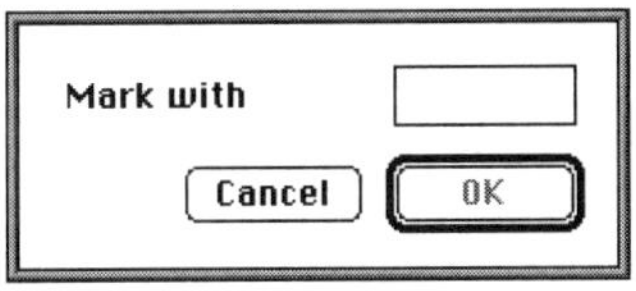

Figure 3-16: Use the Mark with dialog box to specify a special footnote character

After the program inserts the footnote mark, the cursor automatically moves into the footnote area at the bottom of the current page or at the end of the document (depending on whether footnotes or endnotes were chosen in the Document dialog box).

Step 4.   Type the footnote or endnote, and then press Enter or click in the body text area to continue working with the document. Figure 3-17 shows some examples of footnotes.

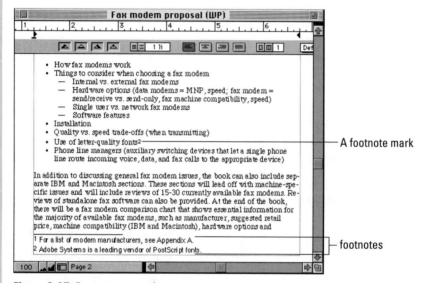

Figure 3-17: Footnote examples

If you decide to create your own footnote symbols instead of using a simple numbered sequence, you may want to consider the following characters (some of these symbols may appear as an empty square in the Mark with dialog box).

Character	Keystroke
*	Shift-8
†	Option-T
‡	Shift-Option-7

To remove a footnote or endnote, select the footnote/endnote number or symbol where it appears in the body text and then press Delete or Backspace. The program automatically removes the reference at the bottom of the page or the end of the document and renumbers the remaining footnotes/endnotes if necessary.

For more information about creating footnotes, see "Using the Word Processing Assistants," later in this chapter.

Inserting Automatic Date, Time, and Page Numbers

Whether for record keeping purposes or for use in headers and footers, you may want to date stamp or time stamp certain documents to show when you printed or last updated them. To insert the current date or time in a document, position the insertion point. Choose Insert Date or Insert Time from the Edit menu. The program inserts the current date or time for you.

The program takes the date and time from the Mac's clock. If the wrong date or time appears, you can correct it by entering the proper information in the General control panel. (In System 7.1 or higher, you can set this information in the Date & Time control panel.)

The format for dates is taken from the setting in the Text preferences. For information on setting preferences, see Chapter 11.

Dates or times that you insert in this manner automatically change to reflect the new date and time whenever you reopen the document. To permanently affix the current date or time in the document (so that it will not update), press Option as you choose Insert Date or Insert Time.

You use a similar command, Insert Page #, to add page numbers to documents. If you add them inside a header or footer, page numbering automatically carries through to every page in the document.

Steps:	Adding Page Numbers to a Document
Step 1.	Specify a starting page number in the Document or Section dialog box (access these dialog boxes by choosing Document or Section from the Format menu, as described earlier in this chapter).
Step 2.	If the document already contains a header or footer, skip to Step 3.
	— or —
Step 2.	If the document doesn't already contain a header or footer, choose Insert Header or Insert Footer from the Format menu.

Step 3. Position the text insertion point in the header or footer.

Step 4. Choose Insert Page # from the Edit menu.

The Insert Page Number dialog box appears, as shown in Figure 3-18.

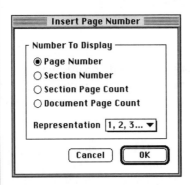

Figure 3-18: The Insert Page Number dialog box

Step 5. Select the desired options from the Insert Page Number dialog box as follows:

- To insert a page number, click the Page Number radio button.

- To insert the current section number, click the Section Number radio button.

- To insert the total number of pages in the current section, click the Section Page Count radio button.

- To insert the total number of pages in the document, click the Document Page Count radio button.

Step 6. Choose a format for the number from the Representation pop-up menu.

Step 7. Click OK to complete the command or click Cancel if you change your mind. ClarisWorks inserts the current page number and renumbers all pages in the document, beginning with the number specified in the Document or Section dialog box.

Page numbers inserted in this manner automatically change as the document changes (that is, as you add, delete, or move pages).

Remember that you can add formatting to header and footer text, just as you can to body text. For example, you can right- or center-justify page numbers by clicking the appropriate alignment icon below the ruler or by using tabs. (If the ruler isn't visible, choose Show Rulers from the View menu.) You also can apply different fonts or styles. After you apply formatting to an element of a header or footer, the program automatically repeats the formatting on every page.

Depending on the type of document that you're working on, plain numbers may look odd. You may prefer to precede each number with the word *Page,* for example. To do this, simply type **Page**, followed by a space, in front of where you have inserted or are about to insert the automatic page number.

To create chapter-relative or section-relative page numbers (Page 4 or A-1, for example) choose Section Number in the Insert Page Number dialog box. In the Section dialog box (choose Section from the Format menu), click the Restart Page Number radio button and enter **1** in the text-edit box (for the starting page number). Be sure to choose the same settings for each section in the document.

Using the Spelling Checker

The inclusion of a built-in spelling checker was one of the first great advancements in word processing. A spelling checker examines every word in a document and compares it to words found in its massive dictionary. The program then flags unknown words for you and gives you an opportunity to replace them — either by typing the replacement word or by selecting a word from a list of the most likely replacements. Now with only a modicum of effort, every man, woman, and child can produce correctly spelled letters, memos, and reports.

Checking Spelling

ClarisWorks provides two spell-checking options: Check the entire document or check only the currently selected text. Spell checking is available for all ClarisWorks documents that contain text except communications documents. To spell check a communications document, select the text, copy it to the Clipboard (⌘-C), paste it into a word processing document (⌘-V), and then invoke the spell checker.

You initiate spell checking by choosing the Writing Tools pop-up menu from the Edit menu and choosing either of the following options:

> ❧ *Check Document Spelling* (⌘-=). Select this option if you want to spell check the entire document. Note that when you choose the command, the position of the cursor doesn't matter. Spell checking automatically starts at the beginning of the document.

↺ *Check Selection Spelling* (Shift-⌘-Y). Select this option if you want to spell check only the currently selected text. Check Selection is particularly useful for checking a single word or just a paragraph or two that you've recently edited.

Regardless of which command you use to start the spelling checker, ClarisWorks displays the spelling checker's progress in the Spelling dialog box.

As the spelling checker examines the document or selection, it stops at each word that it doesn't find in its dictionary or in the user dictionary that you created. For each word, you can do the following:

↺ Correct the spelling by typing the proper word in the Word text-edit box and clicking Replace. (After making a manual correction in this fashion, you can click the Check button to make sure that the replacement you've typed is spelled correctly.)

↺ Select a replacement by double-clicking any of the words in the list box, by typing its Command-key equivalent (⌘-1, ⌘-2, and so on), or by highlighting the replacement and clicking the Replace button.

↺ Accept the spelling as correct by clicking Skip.

↺ Accept the spelling as correct and add it to the current user dictionary by clicking Learn.

↺ End the spell check by clicking Cancel.

You can click the tiny flag icon in the bottom-right corner of the dialog box to toggle between showing the potentially misspelled word in context and showing only the word itself.

As the spell check continues, ClarisWorks reports the number of words checked, as well as the number of questionable words found. After you deal with each questionable word, the spell checker progresses through the document (or selection) until it finds the next questionable word or the spell check is completed. When all words have been checked, the top button in the dialog box changes to read *Done.* Click Done to end the spell check.

 As good as spell checking is, it is not a substitute for proofreading. The ClarisWorks spelling checker does not flag duplicate words (*and and*), grammatical errors, or mistakes in punctuation. Nor will it find words that are spelled correctly but happen to be the wrong words (She *one* the game *to* many times.) If you need help in these areas, consider one of the many Macintosh grammar-checking programs, such as RightWriter (Que Software), Grammatik Mac (Reference Software International), or Sensible Grammar (Sensible Software).

Working with Dictionaries

At any given moment, you can have two dictionaries available for use with the spelling checker: a main dictionary and a user dictionary (one that you've created). When you spell check a document or selection, ClarisWorks automatically uses the words in both dictionaries.

ClarisWorks comes with a 100,000-word dictionary that it normally uses as the main dictionary, although replacement dictionaries (most notably for foreign languages) are also available from Claris.

The *user dictionary* contains a list of words that you want ClarisWorks to accept as correct, even though they are not in the main dictionary. Whenever you click Learn in the Spelling dialog box, the spell checker adds the current word that it is questioning to the active user dictionary. You also can add words manually by using the User Dictionary command from the Writing Tools submenu of the Edit menu. Examples of words that you may want to add to a user dictionary include proper nouns (such as product names and company names), technical terms, and current slang.

When you create multiple user dictionaries, keep in mind that only one of them can be active during a spell check. If the writing in any document covers several dictionary content areas, you have to check the document in multiple passes — one for each different user dictionary that you need. If this situation occurs frequently, you may be better off creating a single, composite user dictionary.

If you like, you can create several user dictionaries, each for a particular type of writing. If you write about computers, for example, you may want to create a separate user dictionary for computer terminology. If you write many interoffice memos, you may want a second user dictionary that includes the spelling of each employee's name.

Creating and Opening Dictionaries

The following instructions tell you how to open a different main, user, or thesaurus dictionary; create a new user dictionary; and how to not use any dictionary at all.

Steps:	Installing a Dictionary

Step 1. Choose Select Dictionaries from the Writing Tools submenu of the Edit menu. The Select Dictionary dialog box appears, as shown in Figure 3-19. (ClarisWorks automatically navigates to the Claris folder within the System Folder, where all dictionaries are stored.)

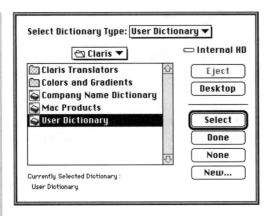

Figure 3-19: The Select Dictionary Type dialog box

Step 2.   Choose one of the dictionary types from the pop-up menu at the top of the dialog box (Main Dictionary, User Dictionary, Hyphenation Dictionary, or Thesaurus) to indicate the type of dictionary that you want to install. The name of the currently installed dictionary of the selected type appears at the bottom of the dialog box.

Step 3.   Select the new dictionary file and click Select.

Step 4.   Click Done to close the dialog box. The program now uses the new dictionary.

If you decide not to choose a new dictionary (because you intend to keep using the current one, for example), just click Done without choosing a dictionary. If you don't want to use a main dictionary, user dictionary, hyphenation dictionary, or thesaurus *at all*, select the appropriate dictionary type from the pop-up menu at the top of the Select Dictionary dialog box, click None, and then click Done to close the dialog box.

To create a new user dictionary, choose Select Dictionaries from the Writing Tools submenu of the Edit menu. The Select Dictionary dialog box appears, as previously shown in Figure 3-19. Choose User Dictionary from the pop-up menu at the top of the dialog box. The name of the currently installed user dictionary appears at the bottom of the dialog box. Click New. A Save dialog box appears. Type a filename for the new user dictionary. Click Save to create the new dictionary file or Cancel if you change your mind. After you create a new user dictionary in this fashion, ClarisWorks automatically puts it into use.

Dictionary Editing

As mentioned earlier, you can add words to the active user dictionary during a spell check by clicking the Learn button. Periodically, however, you may want to examine the complete contents of the user dictionary to see whether it contains incorrect entries or words that you no longer need. You also can add words while editing the dictionary.

Steps:	Editing a User Dictionary
Step 1.	If the appropriate user dictionary is not already open, choose Select Dictionaries from the Writing Tools submenu of the Edit menu. Select the user dictionary and click Open.
Step 2.	Choose Edit User Dictionary from the Writing Tools submenu of the Edit menu. The User Dictionary dialog box appears. The name of the current user dictionary is shown at the top of the dialog box.
Step 3.	Add or remove words from the dictionary. To add a new word, type the word in the Entry text-edit box and click Add. To remove a word, select the word and click Remove.
Step 4.	After you finish editing the dictionary, click OK to save the changes and return to the document (or click Cancel to ignore the changes).

Importing and Exporting User Dictionaries

The User Dictionary dialog box has two more commands — Import and Export — that make it easy to add entire word lists to a user dictionary or export the current dictionary to a text file. If you've already created a user dictionary in another word processing program, for example, you can import the words into a ClarisWorks dictionary without waiting for them to be individually flagged as questionable during a spelling check.

Steps:	Importing Words into a User Dictionary or Exporting a Word List
Step 1.	If the appropriate user dictionary is not already open, choose Select Dictionaries from the Writing Tools submenu of the Edit menu. Select the user dictionary and click Open.
Step 2.	Choose Edit User Dictionary from the Writing Tools submenu of the Edit menu. The User Dictionary dialog box appears. The name of the current user dictionary is at the top of the dialog box.

Step 3. To reveal the Import and Export buttons in the User Dictionary dialog box, click the small triangle beside "Text File." The dialog box expands, as shown in Figure 3-20.

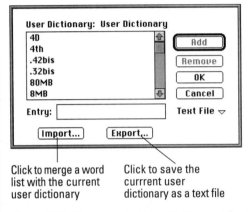

Click to merge a word list with the current user dictionary

Click to save the currrent user dictionary as a text file

Figure 3-20: The expanded User Dictionary dialog box contains Import and Export buttons.

Step 4. To import a word list, click Import. Choose a text file in the file dialog box, and then click Open. ClarisWorks compares every word in the document with the words in the current user and main dictionaries and then adds every new word to the user dictionary.

— or —

Step 4. To export a user dictionary to a text file, click Export. Navigate to the disk and folder where you want the exported text saved, enter a name for the new file, and click Save. ClarisWorks exports the entire contents of the user dictionary as a text file.

Using the Thesaurus

When you're stuck for a word or find yourself using the same pet phrase over and over again, you can turn to the Word Finder thesaurus for assistance. Because it contains more than 220,000 *synonyms* (words with the same or similar meanings), chances are excellent that you can find a new word or phrase that will add a little variety and style to your writing.

Steps: **Finding a Synonym**

Step 1. Invoke the thesaurus by choosing Thesaurus from the Writing Tools submenu of the Edit menu (or by pressing Shift-⌘-Z).

If you invoke the thesaurus while a word in the document is selected, the program displays synonyms for that word in the Word Finder Thesaurus dialog box (see Figure 3-21).

If no word is selected, the dialog box is initially blank. In the Find box, type the word for which you want to display synonyms and click Lookup.

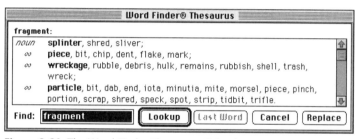

Figure 3-21: The Word Finder Thesaurus dialog box

Step 2. Scroll through the list of synonyms. If you find a word that you want to use, select it and click Replace (or double-click the word). The dialog box closes, and the word is inserted at the current cursor position in the document. (If a word was highlighted in the document, that word is replaced by the synonym.)

To exit from the thesaurus without replacing a word, click Cancel.

— or —

Step 2. If you don't see a synonym that you like, but you do see a word with a similar meaning, select it with the cursor. To see synonyms for that word, click Lookup. When you find a word that you like, click Replace.

To exit from the thesaurus without replacing a word, click Cancel.

If you want to re-examine other words that you've looked at during this thesaurus session, click Last Word. The Last Words dialog box appears. To recheck one of these words, select it and click Lookup. To return to the thesaurus as you left it, click Cancel.

Performing a Word Count

By selecting Word Count from the Writing Tools submenu of the Edit menu, you can get statistical information about the text in a document, including the number of characters, words, lines, paragraphs, pages, and sections. The Word Count feature is an enormous help to those who must write within a specific length limit (no more than 400 words, for example), as well as to writers who are paid by the word.

 When the Word Count dialog box appears, its statistics are based on the entire contents of the current document. Unlike ClarisWorks 3.0, version 4.0 can also provide a count for *selected* text. To obtain statistics on part of a document, select the text of interest, choose the Word Count command, and click the Count Selection check box in the Word Count dialog box. The statistics change to reflect only the current selection.

Using Hyphenation

Sometimes the traditional "ragged right" formatting used in documents is just too ragged. Hyphenation can work wonders to improve the appearance of documents.

To turn on auto-hyphenation for a document, select Auto Hyphenate from the Writing Tools submenu of the Edit menu or click the Auto Hyphenate button in the Shortcuts palette, as shown in Figure 3-22.

Figure 3-22:
The Auto Hyphenate button

— Auto Hyphenate

When auto-hyphenation is on, a check mark appears in front of the command. Selecting the command again turns auto-hyphenation off and removes the check mark.

After you turn on auto-hyphenation, ClarisWorks automatically examines line ends, consults its hyphenation dictionary, and then determines whether (and how) a word should be hyphenated.

Auto-hyphenation is document-specific; that is, turning on auto-hyphenation affects only the current document. If you want to make auto-hyphenation the default for all new word processing documents, you can do so by creating a default stationery document, as explained in the "Using Stationery to Set New Environment Defaults" section in Chapter 10.

 The Auto Hyphenate button is not a standard part of the ClarisWorks 4.0 Shortcuts palette. You must add the Auto Hyphenate button manually, as explained in the "Adding Buttons" section in Chapter 12.

Hyphenating a Word Your Way

Auto-hyphenation is an "all-or-nothing" affair — that is, it affects the entire document, section, or text frame.

If you decide that you don't want a particular word hyphenated, or if ClarisWorks fails to hyphenate a word because the word isn't in the hyphenation dictionary, you can edit the hyphenation dictionary.

 Only words of five or more letters can be added to the hyphenation dictionary.

Steps:	Editing a Hyphenation Dictionary

Step 1.	Choose Select Dictionaries from the Writing Tools submenu of the Edit menu. The Select Dictionary dialog box appears, as shown previously in Figure 3-19. By default, the dialog box opens to the Claris folder, where the various Claris dictionaries are stored.
Step 2.	Click the Select Dictionary pop-up menu and choose Hyphenation Dictionary.
Step 3.	If you're using the standard dictionary supplied with ClarisWorks 4.0, choose US English – Hyphenation, click Select, and click Done. If you want to use another hyphenation dictionary, select it instead.
Step 4.	Choose Edit Hyphenation Dictionary from the Writing Tools submenu of the Edit menu. The Hyphenation File dialog box appears.
Step 5.	Edit the hyphenation dictionary as desired: • To specify a word's hyphenation, type the word in the Entry text-edit box, inserting the appropriate hyphens. Then click Add.

- To prevent ClarisWorks from hyphenating a particular word, type the word in the Entry text-edit box without hyphens. Then click Add.

- To change the hyphenation for a word previously added to the hyphenation file, select the word and make the appropriate changes in the Entry text-edit box. Then click Replace.

- To remove a word previously added to the hyphenation file, select it and then click Remove.

Step 6. Click Done to accept the changes to the hyphenation file and return to your document; otherwise, click Cancel.

Even when auto-hyphenation is on, you can adjust a word's hyphenation by manually inserting regular and discretionary hyphens:

☞ To insert a *regular hyphen*, set the text insertion point where you want the hyphen to appear and then press the hyphen key (-).

A hyphen inserted in this manner will always show up at that spot in the word — regardless of where the word appears in the line. As a result, if the text is later edited or reformatted, regular hyphens can show up in the middle of a line. (If you ever see a word like *Mac-intosh* in the middle of a line, someone probably inserted a regular hyphen, edited the surrounding text, and then forgot to proofread the text.) You should insert a regular hyphen only if a word is *always* hyphenated, as in *money-changer*.

☞ To insert a *discretionary hyphen*, set the text insertion point where you want the hyphen to appear and then press ⌘-hyphen. Unlike regular hyphens, discretionary hyphens appear only when the word must be split between two lines; otherwise, they're invisible.

Installing a Different Hyphenation Dictionary

In the United States, ClarisWorks 4.0 is shipped with a U.S. English hyphenation dictionary. If you work in other languages, you can purchase other language-specific hyphenation dictionaries from Claris. To install a hyphenation dictionary, choose Select Dictionaries from the Writing Tools submenu of the Edit menu. The Select Dictionary dialog box appears, as shown previously in Figure 3-19. By default, the dialog box opens to the Claris folder, where the various Claris dictionaries are stored. Click the Select Dictionary pop-up menu and choose Hyphenation Dictionary. Select the hyphenation dictionary you want to use, click Select, and click Done. ClarisWorks installs the new hyphenation dictionary, which will be used for all documents until you choose a different dictionary.

Although most users associate hyphenation with word processing, don't forget that you can use it with database fields and text frames that are inserted into other types of documents, such as spreadsheets.

Working with Outlines

Think back to your high school days. Remember making outlines — those numbered lists that you used to arrange your thoughts for a paper or speech into a coherent, meaningful order? Well, many of us still use outlines, and ClarisWorks 4 makes outlining easier than ever.

The main headings in an outline are called *topics*. Subordinate headings are called *subtopics*. Each subtopic is a point or an idea that is related to the topic above it, as shown in Figure 3-23. A ClarisWorks outline can have up to 16 levels of subtopics.

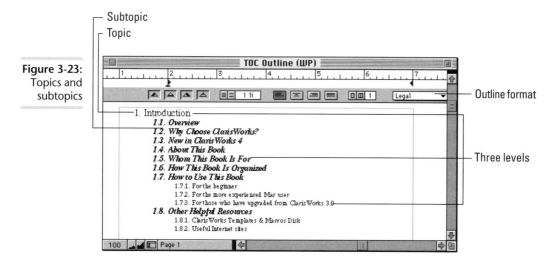

Figure 3-23: Topics and subtopics

In previous versions of ClarisWorks, the Outline View command worked as a toggle. Each time you chose the command, it toggled between an outline and a normal view of the current document. In ClarisWorks 4.0, outlining is now fully integrated with the word processing environment. An outline can now be a complete word processing document or simply incorporated as *part* of a word processing document or frame.

What defines a paragraph as being part of an outline — rather than normal word processing text — is that an *outline format* has been applied to it. When working in a word processing document or frame, you can choose from any of three predefined outline formats in the Paragraph Styles Menu (the pop-up menu in the ruler bar) or the Stylesheet palette (choose Show Styles from the View menu or press Shift-⌘-W). The predefined outline formats are Diamond, Harvard, and Legal. Each format includes style definitions for between five and twelve outline levels.

After choosing an outline format, you can immediately type your first topic. As you begin typing, a level 1 label automatically appears to the left, as shown in Figure 3-24. To create a new topic at the same level, press Return. To create a new topic to the left or the right of the current topic, choose New Topic Left or New Topic Right from the Outline menu (or press ⌘-L or ⌘-R).

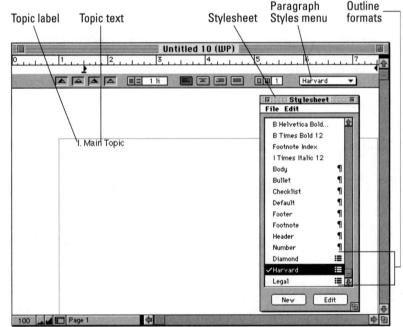

Figure 3-24: Outline formats can be chosen from the stylesheet or the Paragraph Styles Menu.

Each outline should have only *one* outline format (Diamond, Harvard, or Legal). If you select a topic in the middle of the outline and apply a different outline format to it, ClarisWorks can get very confused. It may treat the selected topic as a new outline (resulting in two topics labeled **1** and **I**, for example) or it may change the formatting and labels to something outlandish. To correct this problem, immediately choose Undo from the Edit menu or reapply the original outline style to the affected topics.

Outline Formats and Topic Labels

Every outline has a general format that you choose from the stylesheet or the Paragraph Styles menu. Although you are free to customize individual topics or subtopics (by changing their font or style, for example), an outline format specifies a default style for every new topic and subtopic that you create. Thus, you don't need to format individual topics and subtopics; their formatting is handled for you in the outline format definition.

If you want to get fancy, on the other hand, you can create a custom outline format or edit the formatting of the levels of an existing outline format (as explained later in "Custom Formats").

 To change from one outline format to another, select the entire outline and choose a new outline format (Diamond, Harvard, or Legal), as described previously.

As you work with outlines, you'll note that each predefined outline format has its own method of assigning *topic labels* (the symbol, letter, or number that precedes each topic and subtopic in the outline), as well as the particular font and style for each level. ClarisWorks has 12 different topic label formats, as shown in Figure 3-25. Although an outline format automatically assigns a topic label to every topic and subtopic, you can change any topic label.

Figure 3-25:
You can choose different topic labels in the Paragraph dialog box.

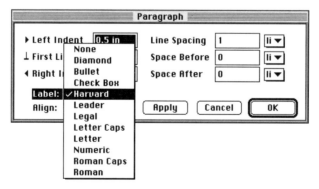

To change a topic label, select one or more contiguous topics or subtopics in the outline by clicking and dragging through them. Choose Paragraph from the Format menu. The Paragraph dialog box appears. Choose a label style from the Label pop-up menu, as shown previously in Figure 3-25. The label style is applied to the selected topics and subtopics. Click OK to accept the new topic label style. (If you wish, you can first click Apply to see how the new label looks.)

When changing topic labels, it's usually best to restrict changes to one level at a time. Remember that the Paragraph command also sets line indents for all selected paragraphs. If you select topics that span two or more levels and then choose a new topic label (as described previously), the indenting of *all* selected topics is changed to match the new setting.

As you work with outlines, you'll quickly discover that you cannot directly edit the topic labels (the numbers, letters, diamonds, and Roman numerals that precede each topic). These labels are governed by the level of each topic and are automatically handled for you by ClarisWorks. In fact, the formatting of each topic label is directly connected to the first character in the topic name. If you change the font, size, color, or style of the first character, the topic label instantly changes to match. Thus, formatting only the first word of a topic as italic, for example, will also change the topic label to italic. On the other hand, if you change the format of an entire topic — as you'd normally do when you want to reformat a level, for example — the fact that the label changes as well is probably just what you'd expect (and want).

Custom Outline Formats

For a quick-and-dirty outline, stick with the level definitions that ClarisWorks provides for the outline format that you've selected. For presentations or formal papers, on the other hand, you may well want to design your own format for the outline so that you can select the topic labels, indents, fonts, styles, and sizes for each level.

Although you can alter the appearance of any topic or subtopic in the outline manually (by selecting the text and changing its font or size, for example), a better way to make the appearance of the levels in the outline consistent is to create a custom format.

Regardless of which outline format you've chosen, you can make changes to the level formats, as described in the following steps.

Steps:	Creating a Custom Format
Step 1.	If the stylesheet isn't visible, choose Show Styles from the View menu (or press Shift-⌘-W).
Step 2.	In the Stylesheet palette, click the Edit button. The palette expands to show a Properties list. The pointer changes to the style-editing pointer — a shadow S.

Step 3. In the left side of the dialog box, click the triangle in front of the particular outline format that you want to change. The outline format is selected and expands to show all outline levels.

Step 4. Select the level that you want to change. The level's current properties are listed in the Properties window, as shown in Figure 3-26.

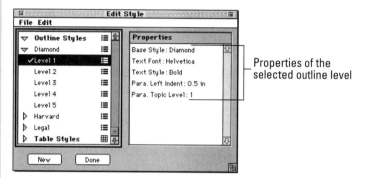

Figure 3-26: The expanded Stylesheet palette shows the properties of the selected level.

Step 5. Choose Paragraph from the Format menu. In the Paragraph dialog box that appears, you can change the line indents, line spacing, alignment, and label style of the new level format. (Note that several of these settings can also be selected by merely clicking icons in the ruler bar.)

Step 6. Change any Text settings that you want to alter for the level by choosing options from the Font, Size, and Style menus.

Step 7. When you finish making changes for one level, repeat steps 4 through 6 for each additional level you want to change. Click Done when you've made all necessary changes.

When you click Done, existing topics and subtopics for any changed levels are instantly updated to match the new styles. Any new topics and subtopics that you create for levels that you've just modified will have the attributes that you specified.

Using different text colors is an excellent way to differentiate levels. In a demonstration, for example, lecture items could all be one color, and points to be demonstrated could be formatted in another color.

For more information about creating and modifying styles (you may want to define *new* outline styles rather than edit the existing ones, for example), see Chapter 15.

Creating New Topics and Subtopics

Now that you know about the components of an outline and how to assign formats and labels to topics, you need to step back and examine the mechanics of entering outline topics and subtopics.

After you type a new topic, you can do the following:

- ∽ Create a new topic at the same level by pressing ⌘-Return or choosing New Topic from the Outline menu (these methods apply the default format for the level)

- ∽ Create a new topic at the same level with the same formatting as the previous topic by pressing Return

- ∽ Create a new topic below and to the right of the current topic (a subtopic) by pressing ⌘-R or choosing New Topic Right from the Outline menu

- ∽ Create a new topic below and to the left of the current one (at a higher level) by pressing ⌘-L or choosing New Topic Left from the Outline menu

Collapsing and Expanding

ClarisWorks enables you to expand and collapse the entire outline or just selected topics and subtopics. You may want to collapse the outline to show only one or two levels of topics so you can focus on the main points without the clutter of additional subtopics. Similarly, you may want to collapse only the levels below a particular topic or subtopic. When I'm working with a book outline, I often use this approach to show that a chapter has been completed.

Steps: Collapsing or Expanding the Outline

Step 1.   Select the topics and subtopics you want to collapse or expand.

To choose multiple topics, click in the first topic to set the text insertion point and then drag to choose the additional topics. Select all outline topics if you want to collapse or expand the entire outline.

Step 2.   Choose Collapse or Expand from the Outline menu. The selected portion of the outline collapses to show only the highest level or expands to show all subordinate levels, respectively.

— or—

Step 2. Press the Option key as you open the Outline menu, and choose Expand All or Collapse All. For each topic selected, ClarisWorks reveals (Expand All) or conceals (Collapse All) all the subtopics.

— or —

Step 2. Choose the Expand to command from the Outline menu. The Expand to dialog box appears.

In the text-edit box, type the number of outline levels that you want to display and then click OK. The selected portion of the outline changes to show only that number of levels. Enter **1**, for example, to display only the main topics for the selected portion of the outline. Type a larger number (the maximum is 16) to display all levels.

To collapse or expand a single topic and associated subtopics, select the topic you want to collapse or expand. Double-click the topic label, choose Collapse or Expand from the Outline menu, or press Ctrl-spacebar. If a topic cannot be collapsed or expanded, nothing happens. (For example, you cannot collapse the lowest level topic because it has no subtopics.)

Tips for Expanding and Collapsing

When a topic's subtopics have been collapsed, the topic label is usually underlined. In a diamond-format outline, however, collapsed subtopics are indicated by a gray diamond. Double-click it to reveal the subtopics that are hidden below.

Although check boxes are excellent for to-do lists, they pose a special problem when you expand or collapse levels. In a normal outline that uses diamond symbols, bullets, or numbers as topic labels, you can expand or collapse levels by double-clicking the label. (*Double-clicking* is much easier to remember than the keyboard shortcut — Ctrl-spacebar — and handier than pulling down the Outline menu.) Unfortunately, double-clicking in a check box merely toggles the check mark on and off. The trick to collapsing a check box level is to double-click *to the left of* the check box, rather than in it.

Rearranging Topics and Subtopics

One of the nice things about working with outlines in ClarisWorks 4.0 is the ease with which you can rearrange topics and subtopics. ClarisWorks provides a variety of features for rearranging topics, including dragging them to different levels and using keyboard or menu commands.

Moving Topics

By using the mouse, you can easily move a topic and its subtopics to a new position in the outline.

Steps:	Moving a Topic by Using the Mouse
Step 1.	Click the topic label to choose the topic and its associated subtopics. (If the topic has a check box label, click to the left of the check box.)
Step 2.	Click to the left of the selected topic and press the mouse button. As you drag up or down, the cursor changes to a double-headed arrow, with a tiny horizontal line that separates the arrowheads. A thick horizontal line (called the *insertion marker*) appears, showing where the selected topic will move (see Figure 3-27).

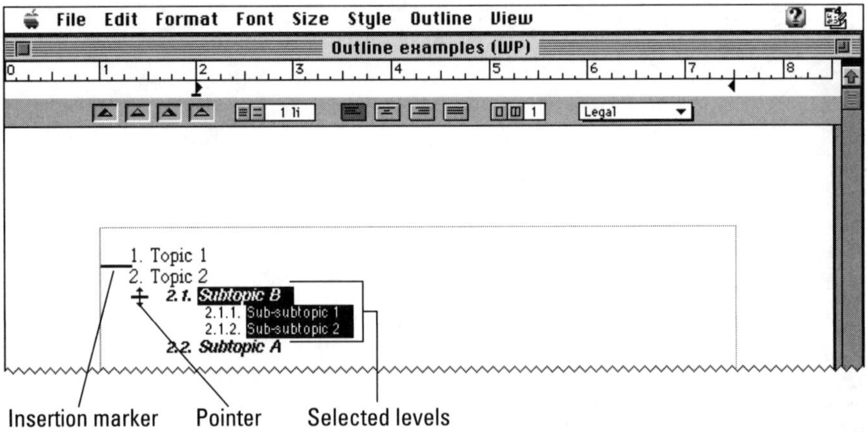

Figure 3-27: Moving a topic

Step 3.	When the insertion marker is in the location where you want to move the topic, release the mouse button. The topic and associated subtopics move to the new position, and the outline is re-labeled as necessary.

You can also use the Move Above (Ctrl-up arrow) or Move Below (Ctrl-down arrow) commands from the Outline menu to move a selected topic above or below adjacent topics while retaining the same level in the outline hierarchy.

If you want to move a topic up or down without also moving its subtopics, press the Option key when you choose the Move Above or Move Below command from the Outline menu (or press Option-Ctrl-up arrow or Option-Ctrl-down arrow). This will assign subtopics to the topic.

Raising or Lowering Topic Levels

Although you can use the mouse to move a topic anywhere in the outline, you cannot change a topic's level by moving it with the mouse. If a topic was at level 3 before the move, it will still be at level 3 after the move. To change a topic's level, you need to use the Move Left or Move Right command (or the keyboard equivalents).

To change a topic's level, select the topic whose level you want to change by clicking anywhere within its text. Choose Move Left (Shift-⌘-L or Ctrl-left arrow) or Move Right (Shift-⌘-R or Ctrl-right arrow) from the Outline menu. The selected topic and all associated subtopics are promoted or demoted one level in the outline hierarchy. If you want to promote or demote a topic without affecting its sub-topics, press Option when you choose the Move Left or Move Right command from the Outline menu (or press Option-Ctrl-left arrow or Option-Ctrl-right arrow). Repeat the previous step for each additional level that you want to promote or demote the selected items.

 You can also promote a topic and its associated subtopics by selecting it and then choosing Raise Topic from the Outline menu.

Deleting Topics

As you work, you may decide to delete some topics or levels in the outline. The procedure you use to do this depends on whether you want to delete a topic and its subtopics or just delete a single level in the outline without eliminating its subtopics.

To delete a single level, triple-click in the text of the level that you want to delete. The entire line of text is selected. If the topic contains more than one line, you have to quadruple-click to select it. You can also drag to select all the text in the level. Press Delete or Backspace. The line is eliminated. If the topic was one of several topics at the same level, the other topics below it move up and are renumbered, as necessary.

To delete a topic and associated subtopics, click the topic label. (If the topic has a check box label, click to the left of the check box.) The topic and all associated subtopics are selected. Press Delete or Backspace. The topic and its subtopics are eliminated. Labels for topics below the deleted topic are automatically renumbered, as necessary.

Concentrate on the Important Outline Commands

Because there are so many different commands for raising and lowering topics, moving topics, and creating new topics, you probably won't be able to remember them all unless you use them on almost a daily basis. Instead, you are better off doing the following:

- For reorganizing topics and subtopics, try the visual approach. Select the topic and subtopics that you want to move and drag them to where they should go.

- Expand and collapse topics by double-clicking their labels.

- Concentrate on remembering only the most important commands, and use the Outline menu to choose the others. The commands listed in the following table are the ones that you're likely to need most:

Procedure	Keystroke
New topic at the same level	⌘-Return
New topic at the same level with the same formatting	Return
New topic to the left	⌘-L
New topic to the right	⌘-R
Shift topic to the left	Shift-⌘-L
Shift topic to the right	Shift-⌘-R

Adding Graphics to Word Processing Documents _____

The selective use of graphics can go a long way toward enhancing a report or memo. For example, you can add a company logo to letterhead or presentation pages and embed spreadsheet charts in reports. ClarisWorks enables you to add graphics to a word processing document or frame in two ways: as free-floating *objects* or as *in-line graphics* (part of the text).

Because floating objects are not part of the text, you can move them wherever you like. And because they are objects, you can add a new background color, gradient, or bounding lines to them. Finally, you also can specify a text wrap for each object (none, regular, or irregular). Figure 3-28 shows examples of both types of graphics.

Outline Ideas

Although the outlines that you created in high school or college were usually designed to organize points for a paper or speech, there's no reason that you can't write the entire paper or speech with outline formatting. Why use an outline just for notes? After all, a topic doesn't have to be a point — it can just as easily be an entire paragraph.

Outline view is also excellent for creating presentations. You can use the diamond or bullet format to design standard text charts, or you can create a custom format, if you prefer. When you finish the charts, you can use a laser printer to print transparencies or handouts.

You also can use the ClarisWorks slide show feature to create an on-screen presentation. For an example of a slide show that is based on an outline, you can load one of the ClarisWorks sample files as follows:

1. Choose New from the File menu. The New Document dialog box appears.

2. Click the Use Assistant or Stationery check box.

3. Choose All Assistants from the Category pop-up menu, and then choose Presentation from the scrolling list.

4. Click OK. The Presentation Assistant appears.

5. Click Next several times to accept the default choices. After a few minutes, ClarisWorks generates a 4-page draw document.

6. Choose Slide Show from the View menu. The Slide Show dialog box appears.

7. Click Start. The slide show begins.

You advance through the three slides by clicking the mouse button. When you're through, press Q. Click Done or Cancel to return to the Outline view. (For more information about slide shows, see Chapter 16.)

Although a word processing document is normally used for outlines, you can also make an outline in a text frame. Insert a text frame into a slide show page, and you can quickly make a bulleted list or text chart.

In-line graphic   Object

Press the up-arrow key to move the cursor up to the previous line.

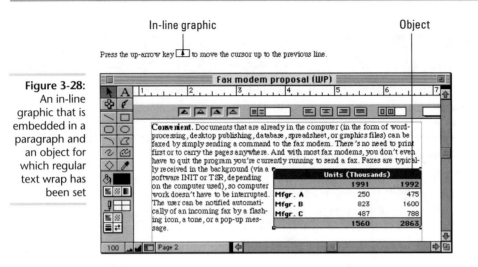

Figure 3-28:
An in-line graphic that is embedded in a paragraph and an object for which regular text wrap has been set

In-Line Graphics

An in-line graphic in a word processing document is treated exactly the same as text. For all practical purposes, you can think of it as just another character. As a result, if the graphic is in a paragraph by itself, you can use paragraph formatting commands to align the graphic to a tab stop or to center it, for example.

In most cases, the best place for an in-line graphic is in a paragraph by itself — without any surrounding text. An in-line graphic that is in the same line with text can cause serious problems with spacing between lines because line height is defined by the largest font or image in the line.

Steps:	**Adding an In-Line Graphic**
Step 1.	Set the text insertion point where you want to insert the graphic.
Step 2.	To insert a graphic from a file, choose Insert from the File menu and choose a graphic file to insert. The entire contents of the file appears at the text insertion point.

— or —

Step 2.	To insert a graphic from the Clipboard, select and copy the graphic (⌘-C) from a ClarisWorks paint or draw document, from within another graphics program, or from the Scrapbook. Within the ClarisWorks document, choose Paste from the Edit menu (or press ⌘-V). The graphic appears at the text insertion point.
Step 3.	*Optional:* Resize the graphic as needed by dragging its handle to a new position. You can maintain the original proportions by pressing Shift as you drag.

Graphic Objects

You can paste graphic objects into a document, insert them with the Insert command, create them from scratch with the drawing tools, or embed them in a Paint frame.

To paste a picture from the clipboard as a free-floating graphic in the ClarisWorks graphics environment, another graphics program, or in the Scrapbook desk accessory, select the picture. Choose Copy from the Edit menu (or press ⌘-C). A copy of the image is temporarily stored in the Clipboard. Select the pointer tool from the ClarisWorks Tool panel. (If the Tool panel isn't visible, click the Show/Hide Tools control at the bottom of the document window.) Selecting the pointer tool takes you out of word processing mode and instructs ClarisWorks to treat the graphic to be pasted as a free-floating object rather than as an in-line graphic. Choose Paste from the Edit menu (or press ⌘-V). The picture is pasted as an object that you can resize or move. After the picture is pasted, it should be surrounded by handles. If the handles are not visible, the picture has probably been pasted as an in-line graphic (part of the text), rather than as an object. Press Delete to remove the picture, and then go back to Step 3.

To insert a picture from a file as a free-floating graphic, select the pointer tool from the ClarisWorks Tool panel. (If the Tool panel isn't visible, click the Show/Hide Tools control at the bottom of the document window.) Selecting the pointer tool takes you out of word processing mode and instructs ClarisWorks to treat the graphic to be pasted as a free-floating object rather than as an in-line graphic. Choose Insert from the File menu. A standard file dialog box appears. Navigate to the proper drive and folder and choose the graphics file that you want to insert in the document. Click Insert. The program inserts the file in the document as an object that you can resize or move about. After the picture is pasted, it should be surrounded by handles. If the handles are not visible, the picture has probably been pasted as an in-line graphic (part of the text), rather than as an object. Press Delete once to remove the picture, and then go back to Step 1.

Chapter 6 discusses the details of creating a picture from scratch. In general, you select drawing tools from the Tool panel and drag to create different shapes.

ClarisWorks 4.0 also includes dozens of clip art images that you can place in your documents. To make them easier to work with, the graphics are organized in *libraries*. To insert any of these images into a word processing document, decide whether you want an in-line graphic or a floating graphic (by setting the text insertion point or by choosing the pointer tool), select a ReadyArt library from the Library submenu of the File menu, choose a graphic from the library palette, and click Use or drag it into your document. For more information about using, customizing, and creating ClarisWorks libraries, see Chapter 20.

Wrapping Text Around Graphic Objects

If you are going to surround the graphic object with text, you can specify how (or whether) the text should wrap around the object (see Figure 3-29). You can choose from the following text wrap options:

↬ *None*. The object obscures any text that it is covering. If you move the object to the back, the text appears over the object.

↬ *Regular*. An invisible rectangle is drawn around the object, and text wraps to the edges of the rectangle.

↬ *Irregular*. Text wraps as closely as possible to the original edges of the object.

You can also specify a text wrap for other objects, such as spreadsheet frames.

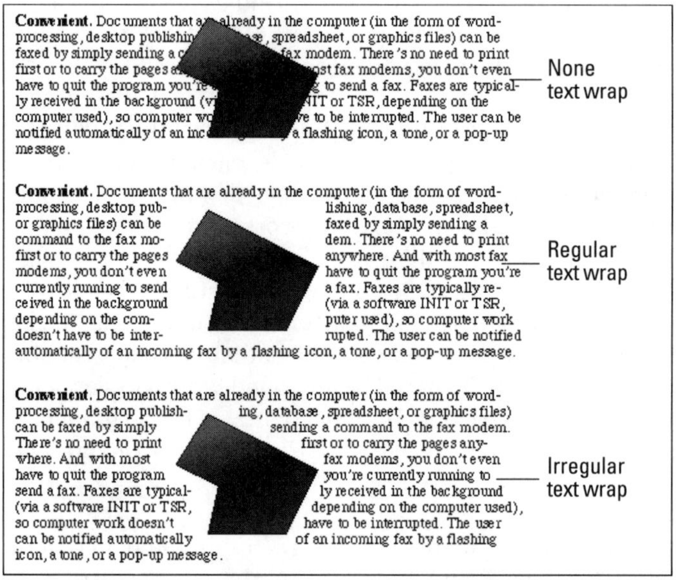

Figure 3-29:
Text wraps

Steps: Setting Text Wrap for an Object

Step 1.   Add a picture to the document by using one of the methods described previously. Note, however, that the object must be a floating object rather than an in-line object. (Remember that ClarisWorks *frames* can be objects, too.)

Step 2.   Select the picture. After you select it, handles appear around the object.

Step 3. Choose Text Wrap in the Options menu. The Text Wrap dialog box appears.

Step 4. Click the icon for None, Regular, or Irregular, depending on the type of text wrap you want.

Step 5. Click OK. The text wraps around the object in the manner that you specified.

When you try to do an irregular text wrap around an imported PICT image, the object often appears to be embedded in a large rectangle — regardless of the actual shape of the image. To get the wrap that you want, ungroup the object in ClarisWorks and then group it again (the Ungroup and Group commands are in the Arrange menu). The text should wrap correctly. (Note, however, that if the object really is surrounded by a rectangular box — as in the case of most scans, for example — this procedure may change nothing.)

Note that the only time this tip will work is if the graphic is a "draw" object, made up of QuickDraw shapes. If the image is a bitmap, then the handles will define the image area. A workaround to this is to insert the bitmap, draw a shape (using the polygon tool) around the text wrap area, assign the appropriate text wrap, and make the polygon transparent.

Layering Pictures and Text

Of course, text does not have to be wrapped around graphic objects. You can place a picture behind or in front of text by selecting the picture and choosing the Move Forward, Move to Front, Move Backward, or Move to Back command from the Arrange menu.

With Text Wrap set to None, you can make a graphic float on top of the document, hiding the text beneath it. And by using the Move to Back command, you can make text print over a graphic. This technique is useful for creating a letterhead watermark or a rubber stamp effect, as shown in Figure 3-30.

Objects that have been moved to the back of a word processing document usually work best if they are light-colored. Dark objects, or ones with dark areas, may make reading the overlaying text difficult or impossible.

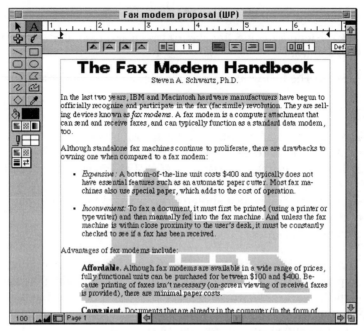

Figure 3-30:
A light gray
draw or paint
graphic can
make an
interesting
background for
a word
processing
document.

Using the Word Processing Assistants

When you're working in a word processing document or frame, you can select ClarisWorks Assistants from the Balloon Help menu to get help with three common tasks: addressing envelopes, inserting and formatting footnotes, and creating tables. After you select ClarisWorks Assistants, the Select Assistant dialog box appears, as shown in Figure 3-31.

Figure 3-31:
These ClarisWorks
Assistants are available in word
processing documents.

The following sections explain how to use the three Assistants.

Using the Address Envelope Assistant

The Address Envelope Assistant makes it easy to address and print envelopes from within ClarisWorks. To address an envelope in the document, select (highlight) the address of the individual or company to whom you want to send the letter. (You do not need to copy or cut the address to the Clipboard.) Choose ClarisWorks Assistants from the Balloon Help menu. In the Select Assistant dialog box, choose Address Envelope and click OK. The Assistant incorporates the highlighted address into a new word processing document that is formatted as a business envelope. If your envelopes do not include a preprinted return address, you can add one to the document now.

When you are ready to print, choose Page Setup from the File menu and make sure that the options are correct (envelopes are printed in landscape mode on most laser printers, for example), insert an envelope into the printer or its tray, and choose Print from the File menu (or press ⌘-P). If you have any problems, refer to the printer manual for the special options and procedures necessary when printing envelopes.

Using the Insert Footnote Assistant

Whether you are writing a college term paper, a professional article, or any other work in which you include footnotes, the Insert Footnote Assistant is an enormous help in ensuring that each footnote contains the necessary information. Unlike footnotes that you create manually with the Insert Footnote command in the Format menu (Shift-⌘-F), the Insert Footnote Assistant steps you through the process of composing the footnote and then formats it according to the footnote style you've chosen.

Steps:	Adding a Footnote with the Insert Footnote Assistant
Step 1.	In a word processing document, position the cursor where you want to insert the footnote.
Step 2.	Choose ClarisWorks Assistants from the Balloon Help menu.
Step 3.	In the Select Assistant dialog box, choose Insert Footnote and click OK. The Footnote Assistant dialog box appears, as shown in Figure 3-32.

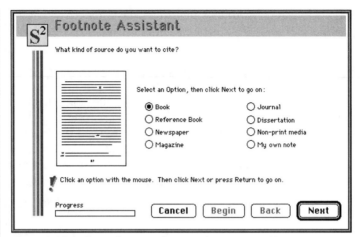

Figure 3-32: Indicate the type of source that you are citing.

Step 4. Click the radio button for the type of source you want to cite and then click Next.

Step 5. Another dialog box appears (such as the one in Figure 3-33), where you fill in the appropriate information for your source. The information requested varies with different types of sources. Any field that you leave blank is marked with a placeholder in the footnote that you can fill in later.

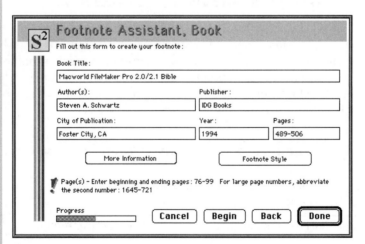

Figure 3-33: Fill in the blanks with your source information.

Step 6. *Optional:* Some source forms include a Footnote Style button that you click to select one of two footnote styles: Modern Language Association or *Chicago Manual of Style*. Click OK to continue. If you do not make a style selection, the Modern Language Association style is used.

Step 7. Click Done. The new footnote number is inserted at the cursor position, and the footnote is added to the bottom of the current page, as shown in Figure 3-34.

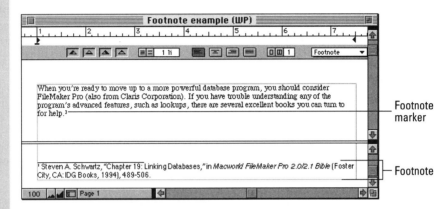

Footnote marker

Footnote

Figure 3-34: After adding a footnote with the Assistant, it automatically appears at the bottom of the current document page.

If you want *endnotes* in this document (notes that are grouped together at the end of the document) rather than *footnotes* (notes that appear at the bottom of the pages on which they are referenced), choose the Document command from the Format menu, click the At End of Document radio button (in the Footnotes section of the Document dialog box), and click OK. All footnotes — including those created by the Assistant — are moved to the last page of the document.

Although the Insert Footnote Assistant is also listed in the Select Assistant dialog box when you invoke this dialog box from a word processing *frame*, you can use this Assistant only in a word processing *document*. (An error message appears if you select the Assistant from a word processing frame.)

Using the Make Table Assistant

As shown in the "Down to Business" example at the end of this chapter, one of the easiest ways to add a table to a word processing document is by inserting a spreadsheet frame. By taking advantage of the Make Table Assistant, you can reduce much of the work required in designing a table.

Steps:	**Adding a Spreadsheet Table to a Document**
Step 1.	Decide whether you want the table to be a free-floating graphic or an in-line graphic (as described in "Adding Graphics to Word Processing Documents," earlier in this chapter). To create a floating table, click the pointer tool in the Tool panel. For an in-line graphic, position the text insertion point at the spot in the document where you want the table.
Step 2.	Choose ClarisWorks Assistants from the Balloon Help menu.
Step 3.	In the Select Assistant dialog box, choose Make Table and click OK. The opening dialog box appears (see Figure 3-35).
Step 4.	Click a radio button to indicate the type of column headings that the table will have and then click Next. If none of the numeric options is appropriate, click Custom.
Step 5.	Set additional headings and options by choosing from the pull-down menus in the dialog box that appears next (see Figure 3-36) and then click Next to continue. The options and their wording vary depending on the table headings chosen in the preceding dialog box. Check the Show Extra Category check box to add a blank column at the start of the table. (If you want to enter row headings manually as well, the extra blank column creates the necessary space for you to do so.)

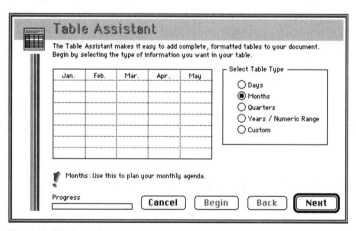

Figure 3-35: Set column headings in this dialog box.

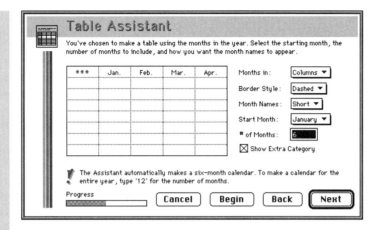

Figure 3-36: Set additional table options.

Step 6. In the final dialog box, set data formatting options. Click Create to generate the table. The table appears in the current document. (If the table is too large to fit within the margins of the document, you may have to adjust either its size or the number of rows or columns.)

In addition to helping you create tables in the word processing environment, the Make Table Assistant also can be invoked from a draw document or from Layout mode in a database.

Down to Business: An Improved Fax Form Template

Although ClarisWorks includes a fax form template (called Fax Cover Sheet), you may want to make your own.

My approach to faxing is to combine the cover page information with the body of the fax. As you can see in the finished fax form that is shown in Figure 3-37, the essential To:/From: information takes up less than a third of the page, leaving plenty of room for the fax message. If you use this form rather than a cover page, you can probably reduce most transmissions to a single page.

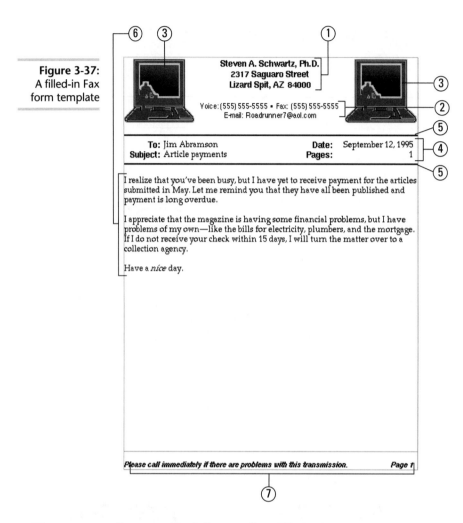

Figure 3-37:
A filled-in Fax
form template

This exercise illustrates the following ClarisWorks features:

- ☞ Placing and drawing graphics in a word processing document
- ☞ Locking graphic elements (so they cannot be moved or altered inadvertently)
- ☞ Using multiple fonts, styles, and sizes
- ☞ Paragraph formatting
- ☞ Creating a footer
- ☞ Automatic page numbering

☞ Using a spreadsheet frame as a table

☞ Changing spreadsheet column widths

☞ Pasting formulas

☞ Protecting spreadsheet cells

☞ Automatic date entry

Designing the Template

To create the template, begin by creating a new word processing document (choose the New command from the File menu or press ⌘-N). Then choose the Document command from the Format menu. In the Document dialog box that appears, set the Left and Right Margins to *1 in*. This setting ensures that you will not lose text from the sides of the document when you send it as a fax.

The key elements of the fax form are numbered in Figure 3-37. The discussion that follows refers to each element by number.

1: Name/Company Name/Return Address

Center your name, company name, and return address on the page. (Click the center alignment icon in the ruler bar to center text between the margins.) Use 12 point Helvetica Bold for the font.

2: Fax and Voice Phone Numbers

You center these lines as you centered the address information. The phone numbers and the electronic mail account information (America Online) are 10 point Helvetica.

You can replace the e-mail address with your electronic mail address (if you have one) or with other pertinent information, or you can simply delete it.

Finally, separate the last line of the phone number or electronic mail information from the body text below it. Although you can accomplish this task by pressing Return several times to insert blank lines, inserting them by setting Space after for the final line is preferable. To separate the return address text from the body text, position the text insertion point anywhere in the electronic mail text line. Choose the Paragraph command from the Format menu. The Paragraph dialog box appears. Set Space after to **5 li** and then click OK.

3: Logo or Graphic

I like to use graphics or logos in my faxes. The logos in Figure 3-37 are pasted onto the document as objects rather than as in-line graphics.

Steps:	Adding a Graphic to a Template
Step 1.	In the Scrapbook, a ClarisWorks library, or a graphics program (the ClarisWorks Draw environment, for example), select the image that you want to copy.
Step 2.	Choose Copy from the Edit menu (or press ⌘-C).
Step 3.	Return to the fax form in ClarisWorks and select the pointer tool from the Tool panel.
Step 4.	Choose Paste from the Edit menu (or press ⌘-V). The graphic appears on-screen, surrounded by handles to show that it is selected. (If the handles are not visible, the graphic has been pasted as in-line text rather than as an object. Press Delete to remove the image and return to Step 3.)
Step 5.	With the image still selected, drag it to the upper-left corner of the fax form. If the image is too large or too small, click its bottom right handle and, while pressing Shift, drag to resize the image. (Using Shift while resizing a graphic helps to maintain the same proportions.)
Step 6.	*Optional:* To make an exact copy of the graphic for use in the upper-right corner of the fax form, select the graphic and choose Copy from the Edit menu (or press ⌘-C).
	Choose Paste from the Edit menu (or press ⌘-V). A copy of the graphic is pasted directly on top of the original graphic.
	Select the new graphic and, while pressing Shift, drag it horizontally to the right edge of the fax form. (Pressing Shift while dragging an image assures that all movements are exactly horizontal or vertical and keeps the two graphics perfectly aligned.)

4: The Spreadsheet Table (Addressee Information)

The addressee information is a spreadsheet frame. Figure 3-38 shows what the spreadsheet frame looks like as you work with it.

Figure 3-38:
The spreadsheet
frame

	A	B	C	D
1	**To:**	Jim Abramson	**Date:**	September 12, 1995
2	**Subject:**	Article payments	**Pages:**	1

Steps: Creating the Addressee Table

Step 1. Click the spreadsheet tool in the Tool panel and draw the frame.

Step 2. In cells A1, A2, C1, and C2, enter the text strings as follows:

Cell	*Text*
A1	To:
A2	Subject:
C1	Date:
C2	Pages:

Format the four cells with 12 point Helvetica Bold and make them right-aligned. To set the font (Helvetica), style (Bold), and point size (12), select the cells and then choose the appropriate options from the Font, Style, and Size submenus of the Format menu. To set the alignment, choose Right from the Alignment submenu in the Format menu.

Step 3. Use a 12-point font (Helvetica, for example) and the General alignment (the default setting) for the remaining cells (B1, B2, D1, and D2). Set the font and point size for these cells by using the procedure described in Step 2.

Step 4. Add a formula to cell D1 that automatically inserts the current date by selecting the cell and then choosing Paste Function from the Edit menu. The Paste Function dialog box appears, as shown in Figure 3-39.

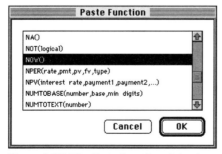

Figure 3-39: The Paste Function dialog box

Step 5. Select NOW() and click OK. The function appears in the entry bar at the top of the spreadsheet.

Step 6. Press Enter to enter the formula in the cell.

Step 7. To display cell D1 as a date, rather than as a numeric string, choose Number from the Format menu. The Format Number, Date, and Time dialog box appears, as shown in Figure 3-40.

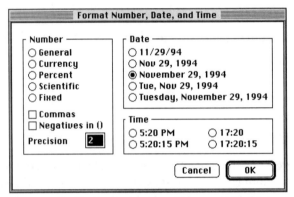

Figure 3-40: The Format Number, Date, and Time dialog box enables you to set numeric, date, and time formats for selected cells.

Step 8. Click a radio button for a date format and then click OK. Cell D1 is now formatted as a date.

Step 9. When you first created the spreadsheet frame, the column widths were all uniform. To change them to their final sizes, select a column, choose Column Width from the Format menu, and enter the width. Set the widths as follows:

Column Name	Width
A	56
B	212
C	46
D	120

Step 10. To get rid of the ugly grid lines and row/column labels, select any cell in the spreadsheet (which cell you select doesn't matter) and then choose Display from the Options menu. The Display dialog box appears.

Step 11. Remove all check marks from the check boxes and then click OK. If any unnecessary rows or columns are visible, drag one of the spreadsheet frame's handles to resize the frame.

Step 12. To prevent the formatting or formula from being changed inadvertently, select cells A1 and A2 and then choose Lock Cells from the Options menu (or press ⌘-H). Repeat this procedure for cells C1, C2, and D1.

Step 13. Drag the spreadsheet frame to its proper position on the fax form. When it is in position, choose Lock from the Arrange menu (or press ⌘-H). This procedure locks the frame into position and displays a gray handle on each corner of the table. (If you later need to change the position of the table, select it choose Unlock from the Arrange menu.)

5: The Horizontal Lines

A pair of thick horizontal lines separates the addressee information from the rest of the fax form. To create the lines, select the line tool from the Tool panel. Starting at the left margin, hold down Shift and drag until you reach the right margin. Then release the mouse button. With the newly drawn line still selected, choose 2 pt. from the line width palette in the Tool panel. To make a copy of the line, choose Copy from the Edit menu (or press ⌘-C). Then choose Paste from the Edit menu (or press ⌘-V). A new copy of the line is pasted directly on top of the original copy. (You could use the Duplicate command to make a copy of the line, but it would be pasted away from the original rather than on top of it.) Select the copy of the line and, while pressing Shift, drag the line down to the bottom of the spreadsheet table. Finally, to keep the two lines from ever shifting by mistake, select them both (click one and then Shift-click the other) and choose Lock from the Arrange menu.

6: The Body Text

Enter a dummy line of body text, such as *Message goes here*, so that you can set the paragraph format and choose a font for the fax text. Move the text insertion point to the end of the electronic mail line in the return address information, press Return, and type the dummy text. Choose a font for the body text from the Font menu and use it to format the dummy text line. Make sure that the font you choose is very legible so that the recipient's copy will be clear. Times is a good choice for the font.

Every paragraph of the body text uses the same font and paragraph format settings. To set the paragraph format, choose Paragraph from the Format menu. The Paragraph dialog box appears. Match the settings that appear on the screen, then click OK to accept the new settings.

 Be sure that Space After is set to **1 li**. Otherwise, the previous paragraph's setting (5 li) will be used for the body text, too.

7: The Footer

The footer repeats on every page of the fax, displaying a standard message and the page number for each page. To create the footer, choose Insert Footer from the Format menu. A blank area at the bottom of the page is now reserved for the footer. Press Return once to add a blank line at the top of the footer (to separate it from the body text). Set the font, style, and size as Helvetica, Bold and Italic, and 10 point, respectively. Type the following message: **Please call immediately if there are problems with this transmission.** Press Tab once and then type **Page**, followed by a space. Drag a right tab — the third tab icon — to the 7-inch mark on the ruler. Doing so causes the page number information to align with the right margin. To complete the footer, insert the automatic page number. With the text insertion point at the end of the footer text, choose Insert Page # from the Edit menu, click the Page Number radio button in the Insert Page Number dialog box, and click OK.

Because you want to have ready access to the template and ensure that you do not change it by mistake, save it as a stationery document.

Steps:	Saving the Template as a ClarisWorks Stationery Document
Step 1.	Choose Document Summary Info from the File menu. The Document Summary dialog box appears, as shown in Figure 3-41. By filling in the fields in this dialog box, you can make it easier to identify your template.
	Of particular importance are the Category and Description fields. The text entered for *Category* determines the group in which your template is listed when you use the New Document dialog box's Category pop-up menu. "General" is a good choice for the fax template's category.
	Text entered in *Description* appears beneath the stationery list when the template is highlighted. To remind yourself of what this template is for, you can enter a short description.
	Click OK when you have finished entering the information.

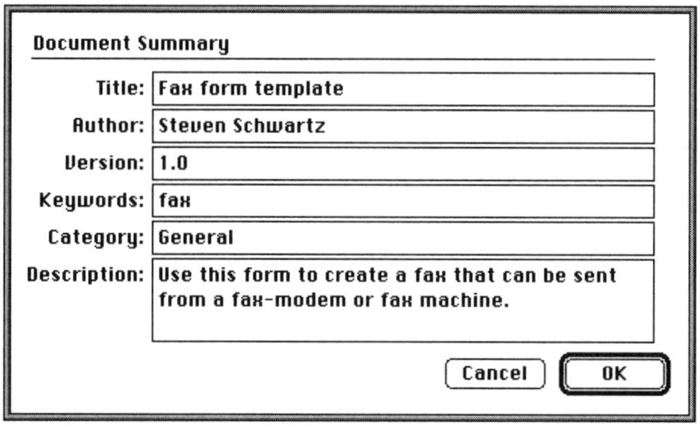

Document Summary

Title:	Fax form template
Author:	Steven Schwartz
Version:	1.0
Keywords:	fax
Category:	General
Description:	Use this form to create a fax that can be sent from a fax-modem or fax machine.

Cancel   OK

Figure 3-41: The Document Summary dialog box

Step 2. Choose Save As from the File menu. The standard Save file dialog box appears.

Step 3. Click the Stationery radio button. By default, ClarisWorks automatically selects the ClarisWorks Stationery folder. Saving the stationery document in the ClarisWorks Stationery folder will enable you to easily choose the template when creating new files.

Step 4. Enter a name for the document, such as **Fax Form Template**.

Step 5. Click Save.

To open this — or any other — stationery document in ClarisWorks 4.0, choose New Document from the File menu (or press ⌘-N), click the Use Assistant or Stationery radio button, select the correct file list by choosing from the Category pop-up menu, choose a stationery file, and click OK.

Using the Template

Now that you have created the fax form template, you need to know how to use it.

Steps:	**Creating a Fax**

Step 1. Choose New from the File menu. The New Document dialog box appears.

Step 2. Click the Use Assistant or Stationery radio button, select the correct file list by choosing from the Category pop-up menu, choose Fax Form Template, and click OK. An untitled copy of the Fax Form Template appears.

Step 3.   Fill in the address information. Begin by clicking to the right of the *To:* cell. Enter the name of the fax recipient and press Return. The cursor moves to the cell below, where you can now enter the subject of the fax.

Step 4.   Select the line of text that reads *Message goes here*, and type the body of the fax. You'll notice that each time you press Return to start a new paragraph, the program automatically inserts a blank line for you.

Step 5.   When you've completed the body text, select the spreadsheet cell to the right of *Pages:* and enter the total number of pages for the fax.

Step 6.   If you are going to transmit the fax on a standard fax machine, turn on the printer and choose Print from the File menu. The Print dialog box appears. Change settings as necessary (you can usually accept the default settings) and click OK. The fax prints.

— or —

Step 6.   If you are going to transmit the fax on your fax modem, select the Chooser desk accessory from the Apple menu. The Chooser dialog box appears. (The specific procedure for sending a document with your fax modem may differ, depending on the fax software installed on the Mac. See the software manual for exact instructions.)

Step 7.   Select the fax modem driver from the left side of the Chooser dialog box and click the close box to make that driver the current driver.

Step 8.   In ClarisWorks, choose Page Setup from the File menu and change settings as needed. Click OK to return to the document.

Step 9.   Choose Print from the File menu, change settings as necessary, specify a recipient for the fax, and click OK. The document is now translated into fax format and transmitted to the recipient.

Quick Tips

The following Quick Tips describe how to create glossary terms and suggest ways to improve the quality of your documents by using special papers.

A Do-It-Yourself Glossary

You may have noticed that the ClarisWorks word processor lacks a glossary feature. (A *glossary* enables you to easily insert frequently used terms and phrases into documents by simply selecting them from lists or by pressing hot keys.) However, with minimal effort, you can create glossary terms. Two approaches work fairly well: using the Find/Change command and using macros.

To use the Find/Change method, you define one or more abbreviations to represent a longer word or phrase, use them in the text, and then issue the Find/Change command to replace each abbreviation with the expanded phrase.

To create a glossary term with the find/change command, decide on a term or phrase for which you want to define an abbreviation. The phrase can contain up to 255 characters, including spaces. Pick an abbreviation for the phrase. Ideally, the abbreviation should not be a real word or a portion of a word. For example, you can use three asterisks (***) or a nonsense syllable (cpt). When typing the document, use the abbreviation, rather than the full word or phrase that it represents. After you finish typing the document, replace all abbreviations with the full word or phrase. Do so by choosing Find/Change from the Find/Change submenu of the Edit menu (or by pressing ⌘-F), entering the abbreviation in the Find box, entering the expanded word or phrase in the Change box, and clicking Change All.

Steps: Creating a Glossary Term Macro

Step 1. Open a new or existing word processing document.

Step 2. Choose Record Macros from the Shortcuts submenu of the File menu (or press Shift-⌘-J). The Record Macro dialog box appears, as shown in Figure 3-42.

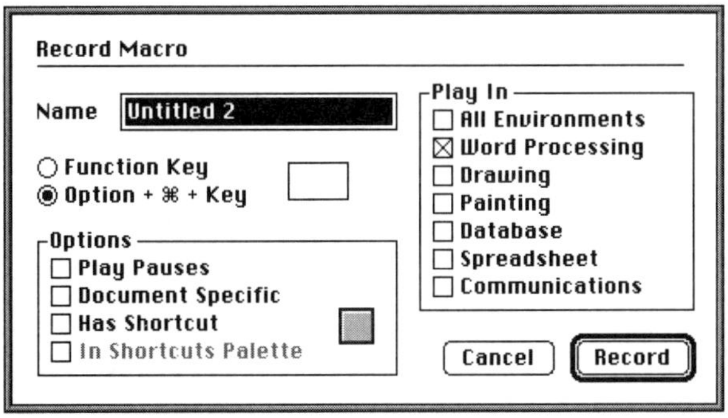

Record Macro

Name [Untitled 2]

○ Function Key
⦿ Option + ⌘ + Key [   ]

Options
☐ Play Pauses
☐ Document Specific
☐ Has Shortcut
☐ In Shortcuts Palette

Play In
☐ All Environments
☒ Word Processing
☐ Drawing
☐ Painting
☐ Database
☐ Spreadsheet
☐ Communications

[Cancel] [Record]

Figure 3-42: The Record Macro dialog box

Step 3. Enter a name for the macro and specify an Option-⌘ key or function key with which to execute the macro.

Step 4. Choose from the following options:

- If you don't intend to use the glossary term anywhere other than in the present document, click Document Specific. If you want the macro to be available in other documents, leave that check box blank.

- If you want to add the macro to the Shortcuts palette, click Has Shortcut and In Shortcuts Palette and then create an icon for the macro (as described in Chapter 13).

- If you want to use the glossary term in other environments (in addition to the word processing environment), click their Play In check boxes.

Step 5. Click Record. You are returned to the document, and the macro recorder starts.

Step 6. Type the term or phrase that you want to record. In most cases, you will probably want to end the macro term or phrase with a space (that is, you will type "ClarisWorks " rather than "ClarisWorks"). If you include a space at the end of the macro, you don't have to press the spacebar before you type the next word when you execute the macro.

Step 7. Choose Stop Recording from the Shortcuts submenu on the File menu (or press Shift-⌘-J).

Whenever you want to insert the new glossary term, simply press the Option-⌘ key or function key that you assigned to the macro or click its button on the Shortcuts palette.

Paper, Paper...Who's Got the Paper?

Letterhead and fan-fold computer paper do not meet every word processing need. Whether you just want to make a document look its best or you have something different in mind (such as a brochure, an imprinted postcard, or an award certificate), a special paper may be exactly what you need.

Unless you happen to have a heavy-duty stationery shop nearby, one of the best sources of specialty papers is Paper Direct (800-272-7377). Call and ask for a copy of the catalog. If you own a laser printer or a high-quality ink-jet printer, you'll be amazed at the printing capabilities you have but didn't know about.

Summary

→ Word processing text can contain any combination of fonts, sizes, and styles. You can apply multiple styles to the same text string. If you use certain text styles often, you can add their definitions to the stylesheet.

→ Paragraph formatting controls the look of a particular paragraph. It includes settings for tabs, indents, line spacing, and text alignment. You can set most paragraph options directly on the ruler or choose the Paragraph command from the Format menu.

→ ClarisWorks offers four kinds of tab stops: left, centered, right, and character. Character tab stops are frequently used to align a column of numbers on the decimal point. You can also specify a fill or leader character for tab stops.

→ The four alignment options enable you to create left-, right-, center-, or full-justified paragraphs.

→ Section commands are used to break a document into logical sections, such as book chapters. Each section can have a different number of columns, a separate title page, and different headers and footers from other sections.

→ Document commands enable you to see multiple pages of text on-screen at the same time, set margins, and choose footnotes or endnotes for the document.

→ If you want to lay out a newsletter or a magazine article, you can easily change to a multicolumn layout. You can use the Insert Break command to manually adjust page and column breaks and to avoid widows and orphans.

→ The Find/Change commands enable you to search for words and, optionally, to replace them with other words.

→ Headers and footers are sections that can appear on every page of a document. They are useful for displaying page numbers, a company logo, and so on.

→ ClarisWorks can automatically number and manage footnotes, or you can mark them with special characters that you have selected.

→ You can insert automatic dates, times, or page numbers into any document. Dates and times automatically update each time you open the document. Page numbers automatically adjust as the pagination for the document changes.

→ The spelling checker enables you to check the entire document or just the text that is currently selected. You can create user dictionaries that contain the spellings of words that are not in the main dictionary. The Word Finder thesaurus helps you find synonyms when you're stuck for the right word.

➥ Use the Word Count command if you need summary statistics on an entire document or selected text.

➥ ClarisWorks 4.0 has an auto-hyphenation feature that can dramatically improve the appearance of documents.

➥ Outlines can now be incorporated within a normal ClarisWorks word processing document. There are three general outline formats to choose from, as well as twelve styles of topic labels.

➥ You can add pictures to word processing documents as in-line graphics or as objects. ClarisWorks treats the former as text. The latter are free-floating, and you can position them next to, behind, or in front of text. You also can wrap text around graphics.

The Spreadsheet Environment

4

■ ■

In This Chapter

➦ Spreadsheet basics (selecting cells, entering and editing data, worksheet navigation)

➦ Formulas and functions

➦ Rearranging the worksheet (inserting and deleting cells, rows, and columns; moving cells; sorting; changing the size of the worksheet)

➦ Formatting cell contents and backgrounds

➦ Making charts

➦ Printing worksheets

➦ Other spreadsheet procedures and options, such as locking cells and titles, setting a default font, and choosing display options

■ ■

Overview _____

A spreadsheet program is like an electronic version of a bookkeeper's ledger page. A spreadsheet document (or *worksheet*) is a grid composed of numbered rows and lettered columns. You enter data into worksheet *cells* — the intersections of the rows and columns. The default size for a ClarisWorks worksheet is 500 rows by 40 columns. Figure 4-1 shows the components of a worksheet.

The power of the spreadsheet lies in its calculation capabilities. You can mathematically combine the contents of cells by creating *formulas* that add, subtract, divide, or multiply cells by each other or by constants. The ClarisWorks spreadsheet environment also offers a large number of mathematical, statistical, time, text, financial, and logical *functions* that enable you to perform complex calculations, such as determining the average of a group of numbers or computing a modified internal rate of return.

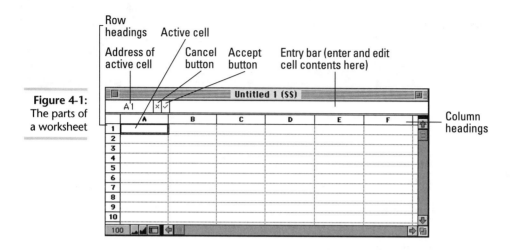

Figure 4-1:
The parts of
a worksheet

The spreadsheet is the ideal environment for data that requires calculations. As such, it is frequently used for accounting, bookkeeping, and record keeping. You can use the charting capabilities to summarize any portion of your data pictorially. And although the ClarisWorks spreadsheet does not contain the database commands that other spreadsheet programs offer, you can still keep simple lists in a worksheet and sort them as needed. You also can use worksheet frames as tables in other ClarisWorks environments.

 A *spreadsheet* is a type of program, or, in ClarisWorks, an environment. A *worksheet* is a spreadsheet document. These terms are sometimes used interchangeably when referring to the document.

Understanding Spreadsheet Basics

Worksheet cells are identified by the letter and number combination of the intersection of the cell's column and row. For example, the cell in the upper-left corner of every worksheet is A1 (column A, row 1). The current cell has a double border and is called the *active cell.* To make a different cell active, you can click it with the mouse, move to it by using the cursor keys, or choose the Go To Cell command (⌘-G) from the Options menu.

The letter and number combination for a cell is called its *cell address.* A cell address uniquely identifies every cell in the worksheet. You can use cell addresses in formulas. For example, to add the contents of cells A1 and B1 and display the result in cell C1, you enter this formula in C1: **=A1+B1.**

The equal sign (=) informs ClarisWorks that you are entering a formula.

You can use a combination of cell addresses and constants in formulas, as shown in the following formulas: =B3*15 and =(A17/5)+2.37.

You also can work with a rectangular group of cells that is known as a *range* (see Figure 5-2). You can include ranges in some types of formulas, such as =SUM(A1..A4), where A1..A4 is a range that represents the four cells from A1 to A4 (that is, A1, A2, A3, and A4). This formula adds the contents of the four cells. When you want to quickly apply a format (a font, style, size, or numeric format, for example) to a large number of cells by using a single command, you can select a range prior to issuing a formatting command.

To specify a range in a formula, you separate the upper-left and lower-right cells in the range (called *anchors* or *anchor cells*, as shown in Figure 4-2) with a pair of periods, as in =SUM(A1..A5).

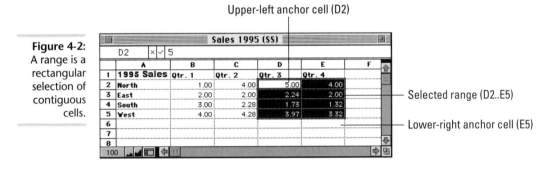

Figure 4-2: A range is a rectangular selection of contiguous cells.

Upper-left anchor cell (D2)

Selected range (D2..E5)

Lower-right anchor cell (E5)

Selecting Cells

Many actions in a spreadsheet program require that you preselect one or more cells and then choose the action that you want to perform on those cells. After you choose cells, you can apply formats to them, fill them to the right or down, clear them, create a chart based on the selected values, sort them, and so on.

You use the following methods to select cells:

- ✎ *To select a single cell,* click it. The cell is surrounded by a double border and becomes the active cell.

- ✎ *To select a cell range,* click to select the first cell and then drag the cursor or Shift-click to choose the remaining cells.

☞ *To select an entire row or column*, click the heading for that row or column or drag through the row or column.

☞ *To select the entire worksheet*, click the blank box above the *1* heading for row 1 or choose Select All from the Edit menu.

☞ *To select the active area of the worksheet* (the cell range that contains entries), press Option as you click the blank box above the *1* heading for row 1.

Cell Contents

Every cell can contain a text string, a number, or a formula. Numbers can be positive or negative, and you can type them directly (as in **43** and **–123.654**). You also can type directly any entry that begins with a letter (as in **Sam Jones** and **Social Security #123-45-6789**). As soon as you enter a space or other text character, that cell is treated as text.

To enter a formula, you must precede it with an equal sign (as in **= A5+B4**). If you want to treat a number as text, enter it as if it were a formula; that is, precede the number with an equal sign and enclose it in quotation marks (as in **="1996"**).

ClarisWorks treats cell data and the formatting that has been applied to the data as separate entities. If you delete the contents of a cell, the formatting remains. Understanding this concept is particularly important when you want to print a worksheet. The print range defaults to printing all cells that have data in them — which is interpreted by ClarisWorks to mean all cells that have data *or* formatting. For example, if you used the Select All command to apply a different font or size to all cells when you created the worksheet, every cell in the worksheet will be printed — resulting in pages and pages of blank printout.

Entering and Editing Data

To enter data into a cell select a cell. The cell is surrounded by a double border, showing that it is the active cell. Type the text, number, or formula that you want to enter into the cell. Whatever you type appears in the entry bar at the top of the document window. To accept the entry, press Return, Enter, Tab, or an arrow key, or click the Accept button (the √) in the entry bar. To cancel the entry, click the Cancel button (the X) in the entry bar or press Esc.

If you press any key other than Enter or Esc to conclude a cell entry, the cursor moves to an adjacent cell and makes that cell the active cell. The direction in which the cursor moves depends on the key you press, as described in Table 4-1.

Table 4-1
Spreadsheet Cursor Movement

Key/Button	Cursor Movement
Esc, Cancel button	Stays in the current cell and cancels the entry
Enter, Accept button	Stays in the current cell and accepts the entry
Return, down arrow (or Option-down arrow)	Moves to the cell below
Right-arrow (or Option-right arrow), Tab	Moves to the cell to the right
Left-arrow (or Option-left arrow), Shift-Tab	Moves to the cell to the left
Up-arrow (or Option-up arrow), Shift-Return	Moves to the cell above

 In ClarisWorks 4.0, the way that the arrow and Option-arrow keys work is determined by the setting chosen in spreadsheet preferences. One set of these key commands moves the cursor in the entry bar (when entering or editing cell data); the other set of key commands moves the cursor from the current cell to an adjacent cell. See Chapter 11 for details.

You can also edit or clear the cell contents. To edit the contents of a cell, click the cell that you want to edit. The contents of the active cell appear in the entry bar. In the entry bar, click to position the text insertion point. Use normal editing procedures to add or delete characters and to insert new cell references. (You are always in insertion mode when you are editing or entering text.) To move the cursor within an entry, press the left- or right-arrow key (or the Option-left arrow or Option-right arrow keys depending on the setting you've chosen for spreadsheet preferences). See Chapter 11 for details. To complete the entry, press Return, Enter, Tab, or an arrow key (or Option-arrow key); or click the Accept button.

Steps:	Clearing the Contents of a Cell or Range of Cells
Step 1.	Select the cell or cell range that you want to clear.
Step 2.	Choose Clear from the Edit menu or press the Clear key (if your keyboard has one). The cell contents, as well as any formats that were applied to the selected cells, are cleared.

— or —

Step 2. Choose Cut from the Edit menu (or press ⌘-X). The program copies the cell contents to the Clipboard and then clears the cells, as well as any formats that were applied to the selected cells.

— or —

Step 2. Press Delete. ClarisWorks clears the cell contents, but formats applied to the selected cells remain intact.

Entering Cell Names and Ranges by Pointing

To prevent inaccuracies when you enter or edit formulas, you can use the cursor to point to cell addresses and ranges instead of typing them. Suppose, for example, that you want to add the contents of cells A2 and A3. After selecting the destination cell (A4, for example), you would normally type the following formula: = **A2 + A3**. Or, you can accomplish the same task using the pointing method, as described in the following steps.

Using the Pointing Method to Add Two Cells:

Step 1. Select cell A4 and press = (the equal sign).

Step 2. Using the pointer, click cell A2, press + (the plus sign), and click cell A3. (Clicking a cell has exactly the same effect as typing its cell address.)

In fact, you can even skip entering the plus sign if you want to. If no symbol separates two selected cell addresses or ranges, ClarisWorks assumes that you want to add them, and it inserts the plus sign for you.

Pointing is particularly useful for selecting a range. To compute the sum of a particular range (A1 through A6, for example), you can type this formula: =**SUM(A1..A6)**. Or, you can accomplish the same thing using the pointing method, as described in the following steps.

Using the Pointing Method to Add a Range of Cells:

Step 1. Select the destination cell and press = (the equal sign).

Step 2. Choose Paste Function from the Edit menu, choose SUM, and click OK. The SUM function appears in the entry bar.

Step 3. Highlight the arguments in the SUM function and then use the pointer to highlight the desired range (A1 through A6, for example).

Step 4. Click the Accept button (or press Return, Enter, Tab, or an arrow key) to complete the entry.

Worksheet Navigation

The ClarisWorks spreadsheet environment offers a number of ways for you to move about the worksheet:

- ⮞ Use the horizontal or vertical scroll bars.

- ⮞ Press the Page Up or Page Down keys to move up or down one screen.

- ⮞ Press Home or End to move to the top or bottom of the worksheet.

- ⮞ Press Enter to make the worksheet scroll to display the active cell.

None of these commands changes the active cell. They are pure navigation commands. If you want to change your view of the worksheet and also change the active cell, do one of the following:

- ⮞ Choose Go To Cell (⌘-G) from the Options menu to go to a specific cell and make it active.

- ⮞ Press an arrow key, Tab, Return, Shift-Tab, or Shift-Return to move one cell in the appropriate direction (as described previously).

Formulas

Formulas are the raison d'être for spreadsheets. A formula can be as simple as adding the contents of two cells (for example, =A1+A2) or so complex that it contains several nested spreadsheet functions. As mentioned earlier in this chapter, you need to begin every formula with an equal sign (=).

Table 4-2 lists the numeric operators that you can use in formulas.

Table 4-2		
Numeric Operators in Formulas		
Symbol	*Meaning*	*Examples*
+	Addition	= A5+3
–	Subtraction or negative number	= B7–6; –15
*	Multiplication	= A2*A3
/	Division	= A7/3
^	Exponentiation (raise to the power of)	=A1^2

The ampersand (&) is the only text operator. You use it to *concatenate* (combine) pairs of text strings. For example, if A1 contains the word *Steve* and B1 contains *Schwartz,* you can place a formula in C1 that creates a full name, as in **=A1 & " " & B1** (that is, *Steve,* a space, and *Schwartz*). Note that you need to surround text constants in formulas, such as the space in the preceding example, with quotation marks.

Precedence in Formulas

When a formula contains multiple operators, the precedence of the operators determines the order in which the program performs calculations. Higher-precedence operations are performed before lower-precedence operations. If all operators have the same precedence level, the program evaluates the formula from left to right.

 You can use parentheses to change the precedence level. When you use parentheses, the program first performs calculations on the innermost set of parentheses.

The precedence levels for different operators are listed in Table 4-3.

Table 4-3
Precedence of Operators

Operator	Precedence Level
% (divide by 100)	7
^ (exponentiation)	6
+, − (sign)	5
*, / (multiplication, division)	4
+, − (addition, subtraction)	3
& (text concatenation)	2
=, >, >=, <, <=, <> (logical comparison)	1

The following examples explain how ClarisWorks evaluates different formulas:

➲ **=7+2–5**

The result is 4. Because addition and subtraction have the same precedence, the program evaluates the formula from left to right.

☞ **=5+4*3**

The result is 17. Because multiplication has a higher precedence than addition, the program evaluates 4*3 first and then adds 5 to produce the result.

☞ **=(5+4)*3**

The result is 27. The parentheses change the calculation order, forcing the program to evaluate 5+4 first and then multiply that result by 3.

☞ **=3+(2*(4+5))–5**

The result is 16. The program evaluates the contents of the innermost parentheses first, giving a result of 9. Then it evaluates the next set of parentheses, producing 18. Finally, because the formula contains no more parentheses and the remaining operators are the same precedence level, it evaluates the rest of the formula from left to right, giving a result of 16.

Using Functions in Formulas

ClarisWorks provides more than 100 built-in functions that you can use in formulas. Function categories include business and financial, numeric, statistical, text, trigonometric, logical, date/time, and information. For additional information on using the ClarisWorks database and spreadsheet functions, refer to Appendix B or ClarisWorks Help.

Steps: **Entering a Formula That Contains a Function**

Step 1. Select the cell in which you want to enter the formula.

Step 2. Type = (an equal sign).

Step 3. Choose Paste Function from the Edit menu. The Paste Function dialog box appears, as shown in Figure 4-3.

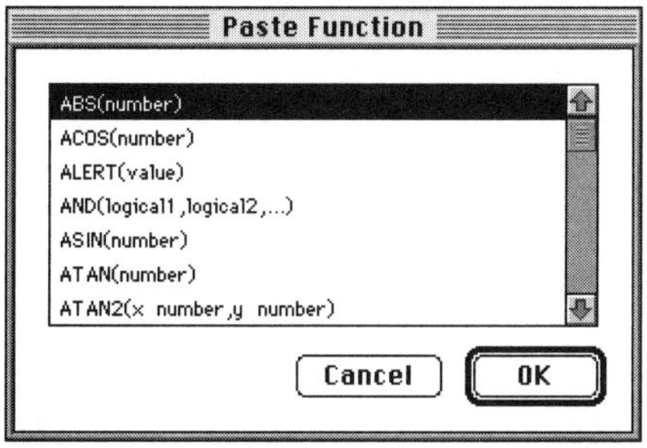

```
╔══════════ Paste Function ══════════╗
║ ┌─────────────────────────────┐ ▲  ║
║ │ ABS(number)                 │ ▓  ║
║ │ ACOS(number)                │    ║
║ │ ALERT(value)                │    ║
║ │ AND(logical1,logical2,...)  │    ║
║ │ ASIN(number)                │    ║
║ │ ATAN(number)                │    ║
║ │ ATAN2(x number,y number)    │ ▼  ║
║ └─────────────────────────────┘    ║
║              ┌────────┐ ┌────────┐  ║
║              │ Cancel │ │   OK   │  ║
║              └────────┘ └────────┘  ║
╚═════════════════════════════════════╝
```

Figure 4-3: The Paste Function dialog box

You can move quickly to any function in the list by pressing the letter key for the first letter in the function name.

Step 4. Choose a function from the scrolling list. (To choose a function, click OK or double-click the function name.) The function and its arguments appear at the text insertion point in the entry bar, as shown in Figure 4-4. The first argument is automatically selected for you.

Arguments to the SUM function

		Sales 1995 (SS)					
A	E6	× ✓	=SUM(number1,number2,...)				
	A	**B**	**C**	**D**	**E**	**F**	
1	1995 Sales	Qtr. 1	Qtr. 2	Qtr. 3	Qtr. 4		
2	North	2.35	5.35	5.00	4.00		
3	East	2.00	2.31	2.24	2.00		
4	South	3.00	2.28	1.73	1.32		
5	West	4.00	4.53	3.97	3.32		
6							
7							
8							
9							
10							
11							

Figure 4-4: Pasted functions include the arguments to the function (in this case, *number1,number2,...*).

Step 5. Replace the arguments in the function with real numbers and/or cell references.

Step 6. To add more functions to the formula, click in the entry bar to set the text insertion point and repeat Steps 3 through 5.

Step 7. Click the Accept button (or press Return, Enter, Tab, or an arrow key) to complete the entry.

You also can manually enter functions into formulas. Simply type the function and its arguments at the appropriate spot in the formula.

You can *nest* functions (have one function act on another one). An example is =DAYOFYEAR(NOW( )). The NOW( ) function returns a number from the system clock that represents this moment in time. The DAYOFYEAR function converts the number to the day of the current year. (For example, if today were August 30, 1995, the result would be 242.) Note that the inner function — NOW() — is surrounded by parentheses to set it apart from the outer function, DAYOFYEAR.

Absolute and Relative Cell References

When a formula in a cell refers to another cell or range of cells, it is called a *cell reference*. For example, you may have a formula in cell B1 that multiplies the contents of cell A1 by 0.15, as in =A1*0.15. If you copy cell B1 and then paste it into cell B2, the formula updates to read = A2*0.15. The cell that the formula refers to is no longer the original cell. The reason for the change is that the initial cell reference is a *relative reference*; that is, the reference is relative to the position of the active cell. ClarisWorks interprets the formula in B1 to mean: "Take the contents of the cell to my immediate left and multiply it by 0.15." No matter which cell you copy this formula to, ClarisWorks interprets it in the same manner.

Normally, a relative cell reference is what you want. When you copy a cell that contains a formula or apply Fill Down or Fill Right to a group of cells that begins with a cell containing a formula, you want the new cells to contain the same formula — but with the appropriate cell references. Occasionally, however, you may want the row or column reference to remain unchanged — pointing to the original row and/or column of the cell. Any reference that does not change when you copy the cell elsewhere is called an *absolute reference.*

Suppose cell A1 contains an estimate of inflation (.15, for example), and the range from A2 to A7 contains various expense figures, as shown in the figure. In cells B2 through B7, you want to calculate new expense figures after taking inflation into account. If you were using relative cell references, the formula in B2 would read =A2+(A1*A2). However, to keep the reference to cell A1 from changing when you copy or fill the formula in B2 to the remaining cells (B3 through B7), you need to make it into an absolute reference, as in =A2+(A1*A2). The *$* in front of the *A* makes the column reference absolute. The *$* in front of the *1* makes the row reference absolute. When you copy the new formula to cells B3 through B7, every instance refers directly to cell A1. The references to A2, on the other hand, are still relative and are updated to point to the correct relative cell.

☐	Inflation calc (SS)		☐
B5	×✓	=A5+(A1*A5)	
	A	**B**	**C**
1	0.15		
2	12	13.8	
3	134	154.1	
4	34	39.1	
5	24	27.6	
6	123	141.45	
7	27	31.05	
100			

Tip: When you enter a formula, you can automatically make a reference absolute by holding down Option and ⌘ when clicking the cell.

You also can create *mixed references*, in which the row reference is absolute and the column reference is relative (or vice versa), as in =B$1+7.

Circular references, on the other hand, are errors, and you should avoid them. They occur when two or more cells depend on the contents of each other. The following formulas contain circular references: A1=B3+7 and B3=A1/5. Because cells A1 and B3 are mutually dependent, the program cannot calculate the results. Cells that contain circular references are indicated by bullets that surround the cell contents, as in •8.75•.

Copying and Pasting Cells

One way to duplicate or move cells is to copy or cut the cells and then paste them into a new location. To copy and paste, you select the cells of interest, choose Copy from the Edit menu, select a destination, and then choose Paste from the Edit menu. When you copy a formula, the program reflects the new location by updating the cell references that the formula contains.

You cannot paste the copied contents of a single cell into more than one cell at a time. During a paste, the program automatically replicates the shape of the copied cell grouping. Thus, if you copy a single cell and select multiple cells for the paste, the data or formula is copied only to the first cell in the destination range. If you select a string of three cells when copying (A1 through A3, for example), regardless of the area selected for pasting, ClarisWorks fills the first cell of the destination range and the two cells immediately below it.

You also can paste formula results (or *values*), leaving the formulas behind. To paste values, select the cell or cells that you want to copy. Choose Copy from the Edit menu (or press ⌘-C). Select a destination. Choose Paste Special from the Edit menu. The Paste Special dialog box appears. Click the Values only radio button and click OK.

When pasting values only, the cell formatting from the copied cell is ignored. The pasted information is displayed in the worksheet's default font.

Filling Cells

ClarisWorks provides two commands for copying a formula into a series of cells quickly: Fill Down and Fill Right. (You also can use these commands to copy a single number or text string into a series of cells.) To fill cells down or to the right, select the source cell whose formula you want to copy. Drag the cursor or press Shift to se. additional cells to the right or below that will serve as the destination for the cop formula. Choose Fill Right (⌘-R) or Fill Down (⌘-D) from the Calculate menu, as appropriate. The program copies the formula into every selected cell to the right or below the source cell.

 In other spreadsheet programs, you can use Fill Right or Fill Down to conveniently number a series of cells, increasing each one by an increment of your choice. In ClarisWorks 4.0, you can achieve the same effect by using the Fill Special command. Fill Special can fill cells with a repeating pattern, as well as a series of dates or times.

Steps:	Filling Cells with a Special Sequence
Step 1.	Drag the pointer to select the cells you want to fill. The selected range must be contained within a single row or column; otherwise, the Fill Special command will be unselectable.
Step 2.	Choose Fill Special from the Calculate menu. The Fill Special dialog box appears (see Figure 4-5).
Step 3.	On the left side of the dialog box, click a radio button to indicate the type of data that the series will contain: numbers, times, dates, and so on.
Step 4.	Depending on the data type selected, either enter a starting number or select a start pattern (Quarter 1, Sunday, and so on).
Step 5.	Type or select an increment.
	Some sequences present additional increment options. Dates, for example, can be incremented by days, weeks, months, or years.
Step 6.	Select additional options, if any are shown.
Step 7.	Click OK.

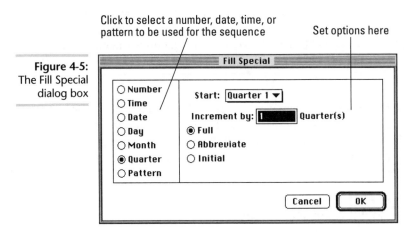

Click to select a number, date, time, or
pattern to be used for the sequence

Set options here

Figure 4-5:
The Fill Special
dialog box

 Rather than start with a blank range, you may prefer to enter the initial value in the range before choosing the Fill Special command. If the first cell contains a date, for example, ClarisWorks will try to select the proper sequence for you.

The Fill Special command can also be used to duplicate a pattern. Suppose, for example, that you have two column headers labeled Yes and No. If you need to repeat this same set of headers several times, just select the range to which the pattern is to be applied, choose the Fill Special command, click the Pattern radio button, and indicate the number of cells in the pattern (two, in this instance).

Rearranging the Worksheet _____

Creating a useful worksheet is an evolving process. The basic structure can change frequently. New rows and columns are inserted, ranges are moved, and columns are sorted as you determine the best way to display the data. ClarisWorks provides all the commands that are necessary to ensure that rearranging the worksheet is as easy and trouble free as possible.

Inserting and Deleting Cells, Columns, and Rows

Clearing the contents of a cell or range of cells has no other effect on the worksheet (unless formulas in other cells refer to the cleared cells). Sometimes, however, you may want to add one or more new cells, a new row, or a new column to a worksheet; or you may want to delete cells, rows, or columns.

When you add cells, you need to shift other cells below or to the right to make room for the new cells. (The shift is automatic if you insert entire rows or columns.) When you delete cells, you need to close up the hole that is left by the departing cells. (The shift is automatic if you delete entire rows or columns.)

Using the Insert Cells or Delete Cells command (described in the following steps) is much faster than the alternative: cutting, pasting, and otherwise manually rearranging the worksheet. You may find, for example, that you haven't left sufficient space at the top of a worksheet for a general label ("Budget Worksheet for Fall 1995") or other identifying information. You can use the Insert Cells command to easily insert a row or two.

Steps: Inserting New Cells

Step 1. Select the cell or range where you want to add the new cells.

Step 2. Choose Insert Cells from the Calculate menu (or press Shift-⌘-I). The Insert Cells dialog box appears, as shown in Figure 4-6.

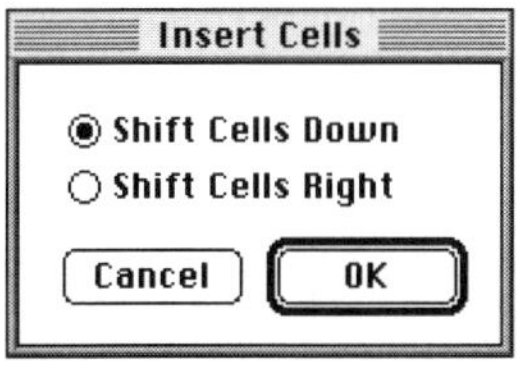

```
══════ Insert Cells ══════
  ◉ Shift Cells Down
  ○ Shift Cells Right
  ( Cancel )  (  OK  )
```

Figure 4-6: The Insert Cells dialog box

Step 3. Choose Shift Cells Down if you want the selected cells and all cells directly below the selection to move down.

— or —

Step 3. Choose Shift Cells Right if you want the selected cells and all cells directly to the right of the selection to move to the right.

Step 4. Click OK. The program inserts the new cell or cells and rearranges the worksheet as requested.

To insert new columns or rows, select the headings for the columns or rows where you want to insert the new columns or rows. Choose Insert Cells from the Calculate menu (or press Shift-⌘-I). New blank columns or rows are inserted in place of the selected columns or rows, and the originally selected columns or rows automatically shift to the right or down to make room.

Steps: **Deleting Cells**

Step 1. Select the cell or range that you want to delete.

Step 2. Choose Delete Cells from the Calculate menu (or press Shift-⌘-K). The Delete Cells dialog box appears, as shown in Figure 4-7.

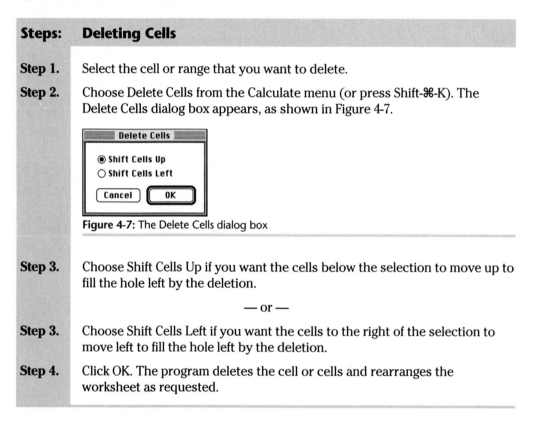

Figure 4-7: The Delete Cells dialog box

Step 3. Choose Shift Cells Up if you want the cells below the selection to move up to fill the hole left by the deletion.

— or —

Step 3. Choose Shift Cells Left if you want the cells to the right of the selection to move left to fill the hole left by the deletion.

Step 4. Click OK. The program deletes the cell or cells and rearranges the worksheet as requested.

To delete entire columns or rows, select one or more columns or rows to be deleted by clicking the column or row headings. Choose Delete Cells from the Calculate menu (or press Shift-⌘-K). The program removes the selected columns or rows, and the columns to the right or rows below automatically move to close the gap.

Moving Cells

When you use the cut-and-paste method to move cells from one worksheet location to another, the program updates the relative cell references that are contained within the moved cells so that they refer to the new locations. If you want the cell references to remain unchanged, use the Move command instead.

Suppose, for example, that cell A1 contains *10* and cell B1 contains the formula *=A1+5* (which evaluates as 15). If you use the Move command to move cell B1 to D10, the formula remains unchanged (=A1+5). On the other hand, if you cut cell B1 and paste it into D10, the formula reads *=C10+5* and evaluates incorrectly — assuming that you still wanted the cell to reflect the contents of cell A1 plus 5.

In this same example, if you want to move *both* cells A1 and B1, you can use either the Cut and Paste commands or Move. The result is the same. If a move contains all cells that are referred to by other cells in the move, the program updates the references, just as it does when you cut and paste.

Steps: **Moving Cell Contents**

Step 1. Select the cell or range that you want to move.

Step 2. Choose Move from the Calculate menu. The Move dialog box appears, as shown in Figure 4-8.

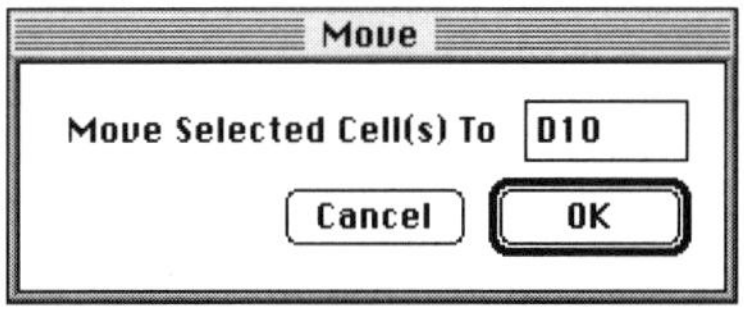

Move
Move Selected Cell(s) To D10
Cancel   OK

Figure 4-8: The Move dialog box

Step 3. Enter a destination cell address (the cell in the upper-left corner of the destination range) for the move.

Step 4. Click OK. The program moves the cell or range to the new location.

When executing a move or a paste, be sure that there is room at the destination for the moved or pasted cells. Existing data in the destination cells will be overwritten by the moved or pasted data. If you make this mistake, immediately choose Undo from the Edit menu.

You can accomplish a move quickly by pointing. Select the cell or range that you want to move. Then hold down the ⌘ and Option keys while you click the destination cell.

Sorting

ClarisWorks has flexible sorting options that enable you to perform one- to three-way ascending or descending sorts on columns (vertical) or rows (horizontal). At the simplest level, a sort can affect a single string of cells in a row or column. To perform this type of sort, you select the cells, issue the Sort command, select an *order key* (a cell within the string), choose ascending or descending order, and specify whether the sort is horizontal or vertical.

More common, however, is sorting a range of cells that consists of several columns and rows, based on the values in one or more of the columns or rows.

Steps: Performing a Sort

Step 1. Select the area of the worksheet that you want to sort.

Step 2. Choose Sort from the Calculate menu (or press ⌘-J). The Sort dialog box appears, as shown in Figure 4-9.

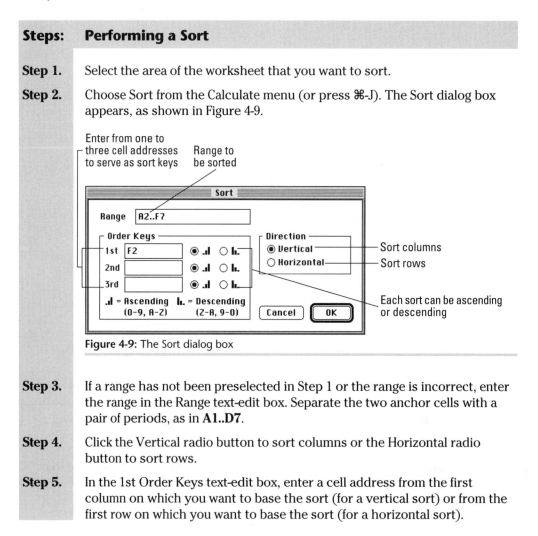

Figure 4-9: The Sort dialog box

Step 3. If a range has not been preselected in Step 1 or the range is incorrect, enter the range in the Range text-edit box. Separate the two anchor cells with a pair of periods, as in **A1..D7**.

Step 4. Click the Vertical radio button to sort columns or the Horizontal radio button to sort rows.

Step 5. In the 1st Order Keys text-edit box, enter a cell address from the first column on which you want to base the sort (for a vertical sort) or from the first row on which you want to base the sort (for a horizontal sort).

Step 6. If you want to perform additional sorts, enter a cell address for a second and third column or row on which you want to base the sort.

Step 7. For each order key, click a radio button to indicate whether you want to sort in *ascending order* (from A to Z and lowest to highest number) or *descending order* (from Z to A and highest to lowest number).

Step 8. Click OK. The program performs the requested sort or sorts.

When sorting on a single order key, the program sorts the selected range on the basis of the contents of the key's column (vertical sort) or row (horizontal sort).

When performing a multikey sort, the program sorts the selected range on the basis of the contents of the first key's column (vertical sort) or row (horizontal sort). It then re-sorts on the basis of the second key, where all *ties* (duplicate values) in the first key sort are reordered according to the second key. If you selected a third key, records that are still tied after the program sorts on the second key are reordered according to the third key.

As an example, Figure 4-10 shows a simple address database with fields in columns A through F (First Name, Last Name, Street, City, State, zip). Each row is a record.

To sort the data records by zip code, start by choosing Sort from the Command menu and specifying the data range — **A2..F7**, in this case. (Don't include the labels in row 1 as part of the sort, because you don't want them to change positions.) Enter a key (cell address) from the zip code field (**F2**, for example), and click the Ascending radio button.

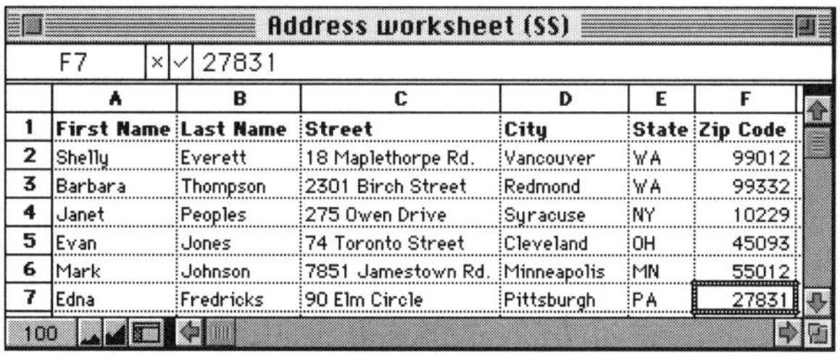

Figure 4-10:
The original address
worksheet

	A	B	C	D	E	F
1	First Name	Last Name	Street	City	State	Zip Code
2	Shelly	Everett	18 Maplethorpe Rd.	Vancouver	WA	99012
3	Barbara	Thompson	2301 Birch Street	Redmond	WA	99332
4	Janet	Peoples	275 Owen Drive	Syracuse	NY	10229
5	Evan	Jones	74 Toronto Street	Cleveland	OH	45093
6	Mark	Johnson	7851 Jamestown Rd.	Minneapolis	MN	55012
7	Edna	Fredricks	90 Elm Circle	Pittsburgh	PA	27831

Address worksheet (SS) — F7 27831

The result of the sort is shown in Figure 4-11. Because you are simultaneously sorting columns A through F, each entire *record* changes position — not just the zip code. If you had set the range as **F2..F7**, on the other hand, the program reorders only the zip codes — not the accompanying data in columns A through E.

Figure 4-12 shows the settings for and the results of a two-way sort of the same worksheet. The first sort is on State (column E), and the second sort is on Last Name (column B). When the program executes the sort instructions, it sorts the entire worksheet (A2..F7) alphabetically based on State. It then re-sorts any duplicate entries (*WA*, in this case) alphabetically according to the person's Last Name.

Figure 4-11:
The worksheet
reordered by zip code

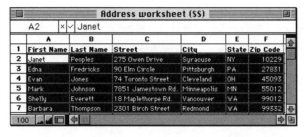

Figure 4-12:
A two-way sort on
the same data

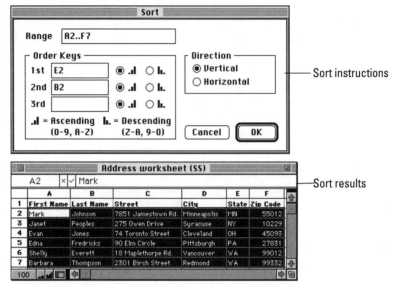

Sort instructions

Sort results

When performing a multiway sort, list the sort keys in order of decreasing importance.

If you make a mistake during a sort (specify the wrong range, sort in the wrong order, or sort rows instead of columns, for example), you can restore the data to its original condition by immediately choosing the Undo command from the Edit menu (⌘-Z). The Undo command should read *Undo Sort*.

If you've gone a few steps too far, you can choose the Revert command from the File menu to revert to the most recently saved version of the document.

Transposing a Range

Another way to rearrange information is to *transpose* it. Transposing a range swaps columns for rows and vice versa. Figure 4-13 shows a range before and after it has been transposed.

Figure 4-13:
Range A7..D10
contains trans-
posed information
from the range
A1..D4.

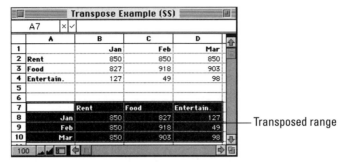

Transposed range

Steps: Transposing Information

Step 1. Select the area that you want to transpose.

Step 2. Choose Copy (⌘-C) or Cut (⌘-X) from the Edit menu to place a copy of the range on the Clipboard.

Step 3. Select a destination cell for the range.

Step 4. Choose Paste Special from the Edit menu. The Paste Special dialog box appears, as shown in Figure 4-14.

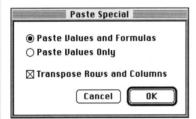

Figure 4-14: The Paste Special dialog box

Step 5. Click the Transpose Rows and Columns check box and then click OK. The range is transposed and pasted into place, starting at the chosen destination cell.

When you select a destination for the transposed range, be sure to leave yourself enough room in the cells to the right and below. The transposed range overwrites data that is in the cells that it covers. If you overwrite important data, immediately choose Undo from the Edit menu (⌘-Z) and select a different destination.

In some instances, the reason you want to transpose a range is because — after looking at the original data — it simply makes more sense to display it transposed. If within the range, the number of rows is the same as the number of columns (a 5 cell by 5 cell range, for example), you can safely paste the transposed data over the *original* range without fear of overwriting other cells in the worksheet.

Changing the Size of the Worksheet

When you create a ClarisWorks worksheet, it contains 40 columns and 500 rows. (A new spreadsheet frame in another ClarisWorks environment contains 10 columns and 50 rows.) Although these dimensions are adequate for most worksheets, you may occasionally find that you've run out of room. ClarisWorks enables you to increase or decrease the numbers of worksheet rows and/or columns as your needs change.

Steps: **Changing the Size of a Worksheet**

Step 1. Select Document from the Format menu. The Document dialog box appears, as shown in Figure 4-15.

Document

Margins

Top | 0.5 in
Bottom | 0.5 in
Left | 0.5 in
Right | 0.5 in

☐ Mirror Facing Pages

Page Display

☒ Show margins
☐ Show page guides

Size

Columns across | 40
Rows down | 500

Enter new numbers here to resize the worksheet

Page Numbering

Start at Page | 1

Cancel   OK

Figure 4-15: The Document dialog box

Step 2. To alter the size of the current worksheet, enter numbers in the Size section of the Document dialog box (Columns across and Rows down). To double the width of the worksheet, for example, type 80 in the Columns across text-edit box. (Remember, too, that you can also use this dialog box to *reduce* the size of a worksheet.)

Step 3. Click OK to close the dialog box. The worksheet is resized according to your specifications.

To reach the Document dialog box from a spreadsheet *frame,* on the other hand, you first have to open the frame to full size by choosing Open Frame from the View menu. Then choose the Document command from the Format menu.

Formatting Cells

As recently as a few years ago, worksheets were pretty drab. They were usually restricted to a single font in a single point size. Modern spreadsheet programs, such as the ClarisWorks spreadsheet environment, encourage you to be creative when you format worksheets. For example, you can

- Use multiple fonts, sizes, and styles
- Add color to text
- Surround cells with border lines
- Hide the cell gridlines or row and column headings
- Change the width and height of individual columns and rows

- Format cells with colors and patterns

Setting Cell Formats

ClarisWorks provides a host of methods for dressing up the contents of any cell:

- Assigning a font, size, and style
- Applying a color
- Setting an alignment (general, left, right, or center)
- Making text wrap in the cell if it is too wide to fit
- Assigning a number format for displaying numbers, dates, or times

To assign text formatting attributes to a cell, select a cell or range of cells. Choose options from any of the following submenus of the Format menu: Font, Size, Style, Text Color, or Alignment. The program applies the new settings to the entire contents of the selected cells.

The General Alignment option (the default) automatically left-aligns cells that contain text and right-aligns cells that contain numeric data.

If you set a large point size for a cell, ClarisWorks does not automatically adjust the row height to accommodate the largest font in the row. If you do not change the row height, some of the text may be clipped at the top. (Instructions for changing row heights are provided in "Making Cell Contents Fit" later in this chapter.)

Steps: Adding or Removing Cell Borders

Step 1. Select a cell or range of cells.

Step 2. Choose Borders from the Format menu. The Borders dialog box appears, as shown in Figure 4-16.

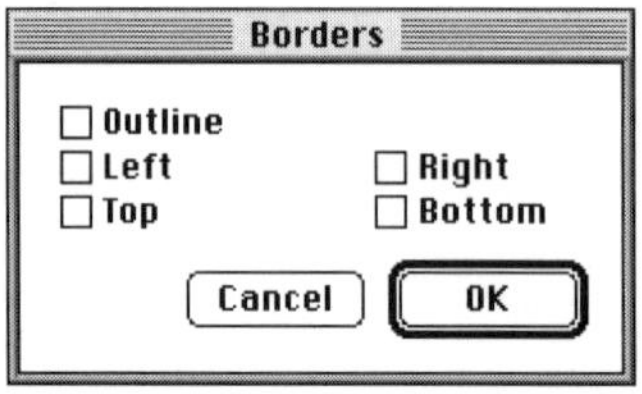

```
┌══════ Borders ══════┐
│  ☐ Outline          │
│  ☐ Left    ☐ Right  │
│  ☐ Top     ☐ Bottom │
│    ( Cancel ) ( OK ) │
└─────────────────────┘
```

Figure 4-16: The Borders dialog box

Step 3. Place check marks in the check boxes to indicate the sides on which the program should apply border lines. (Each check box works as a toggle.)

A dash in a check box means that some, but not all, of the selected cells have that particular border option set.

Removing a check mark clears the border on that side of the selected cell or cells.

Step 4. Click OK. The program applies the selected border options individually to every selected cell. The exception to this rule is the Outline option — if you checked this box in Step 3, an outline border appears around the *group* of cells that you selected, not around every individual cell.

Steps: Setting a Numeric Format

Step 1. Select a cell or range of cells.

Step 2. Choose Number from the Format menu (or press Shift-⌘-N). The Format Number, Date, and Time dialog box appears, as shown in Figure 4-17.

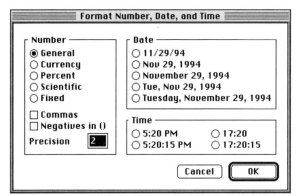

Figure 4-17: Use this dialog box to assign a number, date, or time format to any cell or range of cells.

You can directly summon the Format Number, Date and Time dialog box by double-clicking any cell.

Step 3. Set options and click OK to apply the options to the selected cell or cells.

In previous versions of ClarisWorks, you could add color to a worksheet in only two ways:

⌁ Assign a text color for selected cells.

⌁ Add a solid background color (only possible with a spreadsheet frame — not spreadsheet documents).

ClarisWorks 4.0 takes the next big step in providing the tools necessary for *spreadsheet publishing* — it enables you to apply colors and/or patterns to selected cells. These features can be used whether the worksheet is a document or a frame.

To assign a cell color or pattern, if the Tool panel is not visible, choose Show Tools from the View menu, press Shift-⌘-T, or click the Show/Hide Tools control at the bottom of the document window. Select the cell or range of cells that you want to format. Choose a fill color and/or fill pattern from the fill palettes. The color and/or pattern is applied to the selected cells.

Figure 4-18 shows a simple example of a colored, patterned worksheet range.

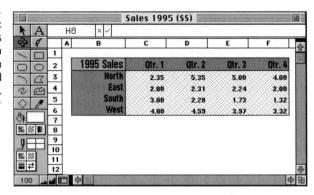

Figure 4-18:
A section of this worksheet has been embellished with solid and patterned colors.

If you'd like to dress up your worksheets but aren't into design, you can use one of the ClarisWorks predefined table styles in the Stylesheet palette.

To format cells with the stylesheet, if the Stylesheet palette is not visible, choose Show Styles from the View menu (or press Shift-⌘-W). The Stylesheet palette appears, listing the available tables styles. Select the range of cells that you want to format. (Table styles are meant to be applied to a range.) Click a table style in the Stylesheet palette. The style is applied to the selected range. To see the effect of the table style, click any cell outside of the original range.

If you don't like the effect of the current table style, either choose Undo from the Edit menu (it will say *Undo Format*) or select the same range again and choose another table style.

After applying a table style, some tweaking is often required, particularly with number formats, which are often defined as part of the style. For example, you may have to change a column of zip codes from currency format (as applied by the table style) to the more appropriate general format.

Also, although the Stylesheet palette initially shows seven table styles, ClarisWorks 4.0 contains more than two dozen table styles. To use the others, choose Import Styles from the Stylesheet palette's File menu, open the file named More Table Styles (located in the ClarisWorks Styles folder), and choose the additional styles you'd like to import.

To learn more about styles and using the Stylesheet palette, see Chapter 15.

Reusing Cell Formats

When you are formatting cells, ClarisWorks also provides a pair of commands that enable you to copy an existing cell format and apply it to other cells. To copy and paste cell formats, select a cell that contains the format options that you want to duplicate. Choose Copy Format from the Edit menu (or press Shift-⌘-C). All formatting in the cell is copied — including font, size, style, alignment, and color; number format; borders; and cell color and pattern. Select the cell or range to which you want to apply the format options. Choose Paste Format from the Edit menu (or press Shift-⌘-V). The program applies the formats to the target cell(s).

Making Cell Contents Fit

When you make an entry into a cell, sometimes it doesn't fit. If the cell contains text, it overflows into blank cells on the right, left, or both the right and the left (depending on the Alignment option that you choose for the original cell). If the cell next to the current cell is not empty, only as much of the text string as will fit in the current cell is displayed.

 If a *number* doesn't fit in its cell, the program converts it to scientific notation or displays it as a string of # symbols.

You can make text fit within a cell by applying the Wrap option from the Alignment submenu of the Format menu. Wrap works like the word wrap feature in a word processing program. (You may have to change the row height to see all of the wrapped text, however.)

In many cases, you may prefer to simply change the width of the column that contains the cell. ClarisWorks enables you to widen or narrow columns selectively. You also can change the height of rows.

Steps: Using the Row Height and Column Width Commands

Step 1. Select a cell or group of cells from the rows or columns whose height or width you want to change.

Step 2. Choose Row Height or Column Width from the Format menu. The Row height or Column width dialog box appears, as shown in Figure 4-19.

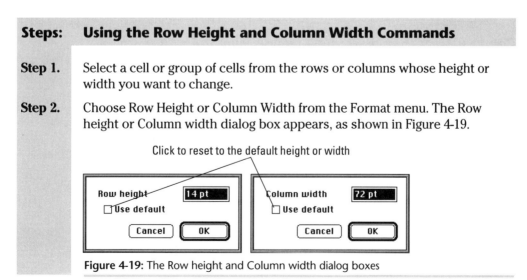

Figure 4-19: The Row height and Column width dialog boxes

Step 3. Type the number of points for the desired height or width. (One inch equals 72 points.) As an alternative, if you click the Use default check box, ClarisWorks enters the default height (14 points) or width (72 points).

Step 4. Click OK. The program applies the new height or width to the selected rows or columns.

You can also set row heights and column widths manually. Move the pointer into the heading area at the top or left side of the worksheet. Whenever the pointer is over the dividing line between a pair of rows or a pair of columns, it changes into a special cursor, as shown in Figure 4-20. Click and drag to change the width or height of a column or row.

Figure 4-20:
Manually
changing a
column width

	Checkbook (SS)	

This pointer appears when you manually change a column width

	A	B	C	D	E
1					Payment
2	Number	Date	Payee	Description	or Debit
3		6/19/93		Beginning balance	
4	127	6/20/93	Ace Hardware	Repair materials	12.75
5	128	6/20/93	Citizen's Electric	May electric bill	149.72
6		6/22/93		Salary	
7		6/28/93	Cash	ATM withdrawal	100.00
8	129	6/29/93	Federal Express	Shipping charges for May	127.49
9					

C4 ✕ ✓ Ace Hardware

100

Making Charts

Question of the Day: If a picture is worth a thousand words, how much data is a chart worth?

Charts and graphs provide a pictorial representation of data, making it easy to see significant trends, for example. ClarisWorks has the capability to produce bar, area, line, scatter, pie, pictogram, stacked bar, stacked area, X-Y line, X-Y scatter, hi-low, stacked pictogram, and combination charts.

As long as a chart is attached to a worksheet, changes that you make to the data are instantly reflected in the chart. If you copy a chart to another ClarisWorks document, however, the chart loses its link with the data. If the data changes, the chart remains the same. However, the link between the ClarisWorks document and the chart can be maintained by using Publish & Subscribe (as explained in Chapter 18).

Steps: Creating a Chart

Step 1.   Select the data range that you want to express as a chart.

If you also select the labels above and to the left of the data, they will appear in the chart and be used in the legend. Any text in the upper-left corner of the range becomes the chart title.

Step 2.   Choose Make Chart from the Options menu (or press ⌘-M). The Chart Options dialog box appears, as shown in Figure 4-21.

Step 3.   Select a chart type from the Gallery section of the dialog box.

Step 4.   *Optional:* Choose chart enhancements at the bottom of the dialog box by clicking in check boxes. The enhancements that are listed vary according to the type of chart that you select.

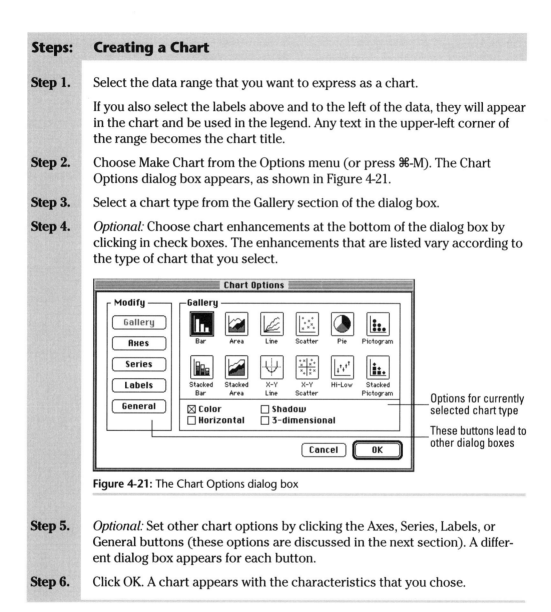

Figure 4-21: The Chart Options dialog box

Step 5.   *Optional:* Set other chart options by clicking the Axes, Series, Labels, or General buttons (these options are discussed in the next section). A different dialog box appears for each button.

Step 6.   Click OK. A chart appears with the characteristics that you chose.

Figure 4-22 shows the parts of a chart.

Figure 4-22:
Essential
chart
components

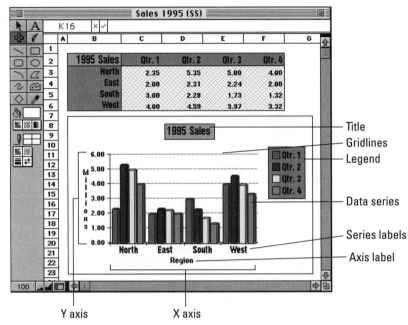

Chart Options

If a chart doesn't look exactly the way you want it to look, ClarisWorks provides plenty of options for changing it without starting over. The following sections discuss chart options according to the Chart Options dialog box that is displayed.

Gallery Options

ClarisWorks presents Gallery options (previously shown in Figure 4-21) whenever you issue the Make Chart or Modify Chart command. These options enable you to do the following:

- ✍ Select an initial chart type
- ✍ Change an existing chart to another chart type
- ✍ Set basic display options for the chart such as
    - color versus black & white
    - horizontal versus vertical
    - 2-dimensional versus 3-dimensional
    - whether shadows appear behind each plotted data series

The display options that are presented in the Chart dialog box vary according to the chart type chosen.

Axes Options

Axes options enable you to do the following:

- Add labels to the X (horizontal) and Y (vertical) axes
- Specify whether grid lines are displayed
- Set minimum, maximum, and/or step values for axis divisions
- Use a log scale
- Specify whether tick marks are shown and, if so, how they appear

You have to change the elements of each axis individually. Select an axis by clicking the X axis or Y axis radio button at the top of the Chart Options (Axes) dialog box. All other settings that you choose affect that axis only.

 The X axis is the horizontal axis, running along the bottom of the chart; the Y axis is the vertical axis, running along the left side of the axis. Pie charts do not have axes.

To change the color, pattern, or line width for an axis and its gridlines, select the axis on the chart and then modify it using the Tool panel. To alter the font attributes for the axis text, select the axis on the chart and then choose the appropriate attributes from the Format menu.

Series Options

You use the Series options to specify settings for one or all of the data series included in the current chart. You can label data points with their values and change the type of display for individual data series. The latter option enables you to create combination charts. For example, you can show one data series with bars and the second data series as a line.

Steps:	Specifying a Series Option
Step 1.	In the Edit series pop-up menu, choose All or the specific series that you want to change.
Step 2.	*Optional:* Choose a graph type for the series from the Display as pop-up menu.

Some graph types also enable you to pick a symbol to use for data points, as shown in Figure 4-23. To select a symbol for the data points for a particular series, choose a series from the Edit pop-up menu and then click a new symbol. To change a symbol's color, click the box to the right of the Symbol check box and select a color from the pop-up palette. To change the size of a symbol, enter a new number (in points) in the Size text-edit box. (One inch equals 72 points.)

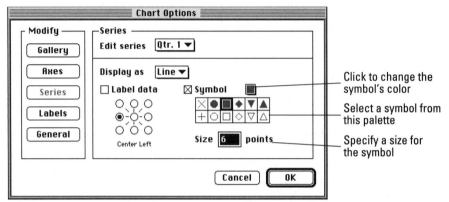

Figure 4-23: You use this dialog box to choose the shape, size, and color of the symbol for data points.

Other graph types, such as pie charts, offer different options, such as the ability to *explode* a slice (pull it away from the body of the pie).

Step 3. *Optional:* To label data points with their values, click the Label data check box. Click any of the nine radio buttons below the check box to indicate where the data label will appear in relation to each data point.

For some graph types, such as bar and pictogram, an example of a data label is shown in a Sample box.

Step 4. Click OK to put the new options into effect.

To change the color or pattern of any series, select its box in the chart legend and then select another color, pattern, or gradient from the Tool panel.

Labels Options

Use Labels options to specify settings for the chart title and legend. When adding or modifying a chart title, if a title was in the upper-left corner of the selected chart range, it appears in the Title text-edit box. You can change it in the spreadsheet or in the Chart Options (Labels) dialog box. If the chart has no title, you can create one in the dialog box. To display the title horizontally, check the Horizontal check box. To display the title vertically, remove the check mark. To add a drop shadow behind the chart title, check the Shadow check box. To specify a different location for the chart title, click one of the eight title placement radio buttons at the right of the Title text-edit box.

Text characteristics (such as the font and size), the background color, and the pattern for the title come directly from the formatting that you apply (or change) in the title's cell in the worksheet. You can change the title text either in the cell or in the Labels section of the Chart Options dialog box. To eliminate the title, delete it from the cell.

If a title did not come from the worksheet (that is, you created it in the Chart Options [Labels] dialog box), you can change the title's attributes by selecting it in the chart and then choosing options from the Format menu.

Regardless of where the title was created, you can alter its bounding box or background color and/or pattern by selecting the title in the chart and then choosing a pattern, gradient, background color, line width, or pen color from the Tool panel.

Labels in the legend are determined by the series labels at the left and top of the worksheet range that you specify when you create the chart. To change any of the labels, change the contents of the appropriate cells.

Steps:	Modifying the Legend
Step 1.	To change from the labels of one series to the labels of another series, click the General button in the Chart Options dialog box. Click the radio button for Series in Rows or Series in Columns to change the series used for the legend. (This action also changes the chart layout.)
Step 2.	To change the position of the legend relative to the chart, click one of the eight position radio buttons in the Chart Options (Labels) dialog box
Step 3.	Use the Horizontal check box in the Chart Options (Labels) dialog box to designate whether the legend elements are to be displayed in a vertical or horizontal list.
Step 4.	To place a shadow behind the legend box, click the Shadow check box.

Step 5. Some chart types, such as line graphs, use symbols to represent data points. If you want the symbols to be displayed in the legend, click the Use Symbols check box.

Step 6. To hide the legend, remove the check mark from the Legend check box.

You also can alter the legend's background and bounding box by selecting the legend in the chart and then choosing a pattern, gradient, background color, line width, or pen color from the Tool panel.

If you don't like the way that series names are displayed in the legend, you can select the legend in the chart and then choose new text attributes from the Format menu.

General Options

Use the General options to do the following:

- ∽ Change the data range for the chart
- ∽ Use numbers as axis labels
- ∽ Indicate whether the data series in the selected range is in rows or in columns

To specify a new chart range, type it into the Chart range text-edit box. Remember to separate the anchor points in the range with a pair of periods, as in **A1..D7.**

In most cases, you will use text from the worksheet as axis labels. If the first row or first column of the selected chart range contains numbers that you want to use as labels, click the (Use numbers as labels in) First row or First column check box, as appropriate.

To indicate whether the data series in the selected range is arranged in rows or in columns, click the (Series in) Rows or Columns check box, as appropriate. The labels that appear in the Series names list box represent the data that will be plotted.

Pictograms

Pictograms use pictures, rather than bars, lines, and so on, to represent data. Pictogram images can be a single image or a series of repeating images, one above the other. To use pictogram images in a chart, you do one of the following:

- ∽ Select Pictogram or Stacked Pictogram as the chart type.
- ∽ Set one or more of the series to display as pictograms in the Chart Options (Series) dialog box.

The default pictogram symbol is a large arrow, but you can provide your own symbols, as shown in Figure 4-24.

Figure 4-24:
A pictogram
with a repeating
custom symbol

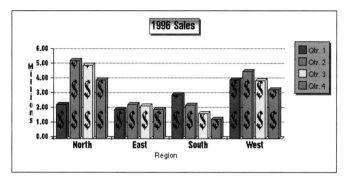

| Steps: | **Changing a Pictogram Symbol** |

Step 1. In the Scrapbook, a graphics program, or a ClarisWorks draw document, select the image that you want to use as a pictogram. (Claris recommends using a draw image rather than a paint picture.)

For example, you could use a large dollar sign ($) as a pictogram image for a financial chart.

Step 2. Choose Copy from the Edit menu to place a copy of the image on the Mac's Clipboard.

Step 3. In the Chart Options (Series) dialog box, choose All or a specific data series from the Edit series pop-up menu. (You can use the same image for all series or a different image for each series.) The current pictogram image appears in the Sample box.

Step 4. Click the Sample box. A dark border surrounds the box.

Step 5. Choose Paste from the Edit menu (or press ⌘-V). The image on the Clipboard replaces the one in the Sample box and is used for the selected series or all series, depending on the choice that you made in the Edit series pop-up menu.

Step 6. Click the Repeating check box to make a constant-size symbol repeat in each bar. If you want repeating symbols to overlap each other, enter a number in the % overlap text-edit box. Leave the Repeating check box blank if you want the symbol to be sized to match the height of the bar.

Step 7. If you want to use the same image for other data series, repeat Steps 3 through 6 as required.

To display only a pictogram symbol without the usual bounding box, click the box in the legend associated with that data series and then set the line width to None in the Tool panel.

Other Chart Changes and Embellishments

In addition to using the options in the Chart Options dialog boxes, you can use other methods to modify and embellish charts. After you create a chart, it acts like any other ClarisWorks object. When you first click a chart, handles appear at its corners. You can drag it to a new location or resize it by dragging a handle.

You can embellish the chart by adding text (as callouts, for example) and graphics. You can draw attention to an important element in the chart, such as an outstanding quarterly sales figure, by using the drawing tools to add an arrow pointing to the bar or data point. Finish off the effect by selecting the text tool to create a comment ("Best quarter since the company's inception!"), and then surround the comment with a colored box or oval.

Chart-Editing Shortcuts

So that you can avoid wading through dialog boxes and buttons, ClarisWorks provides several shortcuts that take you directly to the appropriate Chart Options dialog box:

- Double-click an open area of a chart to make the Chart Options (Gallery) dialog box appear. This action is equivalent to choosing Modify Chart from the Options menu. The Chart Options (Gallery) dialog box enables you to change the chart type or to set basic display options.

- Double-click the X or Y axis of a chart to make the Chart Options (Axis) dialog box appear.

- Double-click a chart symbol in the legend to make the Chart Options (Series) dialog box appear.

- Double-click the chart title (if the chart has a title) or a label in the legend to make the Chart Options (Labels) dialog box appear.

You also can add a background color for the chart, color the legend box, and change the line width or color of the box that encloses the chart by choosing options from the palettes in the Tool panel. Because a chart is just another object, to achieve an uncluttered look you can use the chart to hide the data used to create it. When you copy a chart into a word processing document, you can specify a text wrap for a more professional appearance.

 Remember that when a chart is simply pasted into a document, it loses its link with the worksheet in which it was created. You may prefer to add the worksheet to the document as a *table* and display only the chart portion.

Printing

ClarisWorks contains several features that apply only to printing worksheets. These features can be used to do the following:

- ☞ Add manual page breaks
- ☞ Specify a print range
- ☞ Decide whether to print or omit the cell grid, as well as the column and row headings

Adding Page Breaks

Although ClarisWorks automatically determines where page breaks occur based on full pages, you may want to force a page break at a strategic spot in the worksheet — usually to keep important information from being split across pages.

To insert a page break, select the cell that you want to print as the last item on a page and choose Add Page Break from the Options menu. Any cells to the right or below the selected cell will print on succeeding pages.

You can remove a manual page break by selecting the same cell and choosing Remove Page Break from the Options menu. To remove all manual page breaks simultaneously, choose Remove All Breaks from the Options menu.

 If you want to see how the worksheet will print (and where the page breaks will occur), choose Page View (Shift-⌘-P) from the View menu.

Specifying a Print Range

When the time comes to print the worksheet, ClarisWorks intelligently defaults to printing the entire active portion of the worksheet; that is, it prints all areas of the worksheet (beginning with cell A1) that contain data. You can also specify a different print range. Choose Set Print Range from the Options menu. A Print Range dialog box appears. Click the Print Cell Range radio button and type the specific range that you want to print. (Remember that a range consists of the upper-left cell coordinate and the lower-right cell coordinate, separated by a pair of periods.) Click OK to set the new range.

If you preselect a range by dragging and then go directly to the Print command, you do not have to use the Print Range command. The program automatically sets the Print Range to match the highlighted range.

Working with a Modified Print Dialog Box

When you choose Print from the File menu (or press ⌘-P), you'll notice that the Print dialog box has been modified slightly, as shown in Figure 4-25.

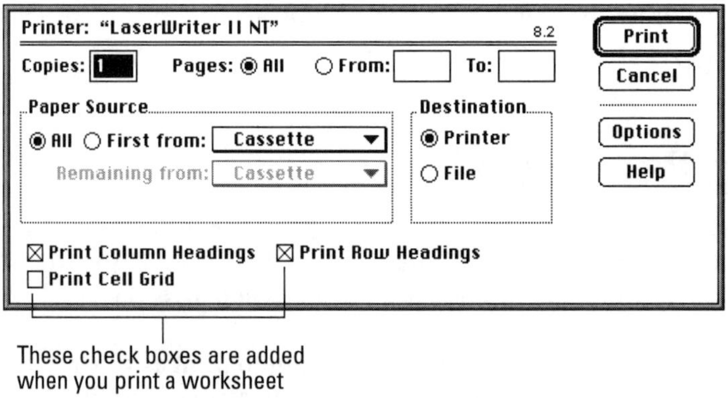

Figure 4-25:
When you print a worksheet, a modified Print dialog box appears.

```
Printer: "LaserWriter II NT"                          8.2        [ Print ]

Copies: [1  ]    Pages: ● All   ○ From: [    ]  To: [    ]      [ Cancel ]
─Paper Source───────────────────────    ─Destination──────
● All ○ First from: [ Cassette    ▼]     ● Printer           [ Options ]
      Remaining from: [ Cassette  ▼]     ○ File              [  Help   ]

        ⊠ Print Column Headings   ⊠ Print Row Headings
        ☐ Print Cell Grid
```

These check boxes are added when you print a worksheet

At the bottom of the dialog box is a series of check boxes that appears only when you are printing a worksheet. Depending on the boxes that are checked, you can print or omit column headings, row headings, and the cell grid. Initially, these settings match the options that you have chosen in the Display dialog box (which is discussed in "Changing Display Options" later in this chapter).

Other Procedures and Options _____

This section explains the remaining commands, procedures, and options that are available to you in the spreadsheet environment. (In short, other stuff.) Although you don't have to use any of these features (some you may *never* use), knowing that they're around is nice.

Automatic and Manual Recalculation

Normally, ClarisWorks recalculates the worksheet whenever it is necessary. If a cell contains a formula that refers to another cell (B17, for example) and you change the contents of that cell (B17), the program automatically recalculates the formula. In very large worksheets or on slow Macs, recalculation can be time-consuming. If you like, you can turn off the automatic recalculation by choosing Auto Calc from the Calculate menu and removing its check mark.

When Auto Calc is turned off, ClarisWorks recalculates the worksheet only when you choose Calculate Now from the Calculate menu (or press Shift-⌘-=).

 If you check Auto Calc, you *never* have to choose Calculate Now.

Locking Cells

Like any other computer document, a worksheet can be a fragile thing. If you make a wrong entry in a critical cell, many of the worksheet's underlying assumptions may become incorrect and lead you to wrong conclusions about the data or its summary figures. If you edit a formula and make a mistake, similar consequences can result. To prevent inadvertent changes of this sort, ClarisWorks enables you to protect selected cells by locking them. To lock a cell or range, select the cell or range that you want to protect. Choose Lock Cells from the Options menu (or press ⌘-H).

If you attempt to edit, delete, or move a locked cell, ClarisWorks displays an alert box with the message *Some cells are locked.* If a locked cell contains a formula, on the other hand, the calculation will still be recomputed as necessary.

To remove protection from a cell or range, select the cell or range and then choose Unlock Cells from the Options menu (or press Shift-⌘-H).

In previous versions of ClarisWorks, the Lock command was called Protect. If you protected an entire column of data (by clicking a column heading and choosing the Protect Cells command), you could still enter data into blank cells in the column. This is *not* the way that ClarisWorks 4.0's Lock Cells command works. Locked is locked. If you need to enter data into *any* cell that has been locked, you must first unlock that cell.

Locking Titles

Depending on the nature of the worksheet, locking row or column titles in place is sometimes useful. To lock titles, do one of the following:

☞ *To lock a set of row and column titles in place*, select the cell that intersects the row and column titles and choose Lock Title Position from the Options menu.

☞ *To lock a set of column titles in place*, select the entire bottom row of the titles (by clicking the row number heading) and choose Lock Title Position from the Options menu.

☞ *To lock a set of row titles in place*, select the entire right-most column of the titles (by clicking the column number heading) and choose Lock Title Position from the Options menu.

As you scroll the worksheet, the titles remain in view. Figure 4-26 shows a worksheet with column A and rows 1 and 2 locked in place.

Figure 4-26:
Solid lines, rather than the usual dotted gridlines, surround the cells in the locked rows (1 and 2) and column (A).

	A	B	C	D	E	F	G
1	**Expense Record**						
2		January	February	March	April	May	June
3	Auto						
4	Electricity						
5	Entertainment						
6	Gas						
7	Groceries						
8	Hobbies						
9	Insurance						
10	Medical						
11	Publications						
12	Rent						
13	Telephone						

Untitled 4 (SS) — B3

To unlock the titles (to choose a different set of locking titles, to edit a cell in the title region, or to remove the locking titles), choose Lock Title Position again.

Setting a Default Font

Normally, the default font for worksheets is 9-point Geneva. Unless you manually select another font for a cell, the program uses the default font for all formatting. To set a different default font for the current worksheet, choose Default Font from the Options menu. The Default Font dialog box appears. Select a new font from the list box (all fonts installed in the system are displayed in the list) and type a point size in the Size text-edit box. Click OK. All cells that have not had a different font or size manually applied to them change to the new default font and size. Cells that you have manually set to a specific font or size retain that font or size.

Changing Display Options

The Display command in the Options menu enables you to exert some control over the way ClarisWorks displays the current worksheet. For example, you may want to alter the display before printing a worksheet or using it as part of a presentation or slide show.

In the Display dialog box, checking or clearing a particular check box has the following effects:

- ✎ *Cell grid.* When this box is unchecked, ClarisWorks displays the worksheet without a cell grid.

- ✎ *Solid lines.* When this box is checked, the program displays the cell grid as solid lines. When it is unchecked (the default), a dotted cell grid is displayed.

- ✎ *Formulas.* When this box is checked, ClarisWorks displays formulas in cells, instead of displaying the results of the formulas. This option is useful for checking the accuracy of a worksheet.

- ✎ *Column headings.* When this box is unchecked, the program does not display column headings (letters).

- ✎ *Row headings.* When this box is unchecked, the program does not display row headings (numbers).

- ✎ *Mark circular refs.* When this box is checked, data in a cell that contains a circular reference is surrounded by bullet characters (•).

Down to Business: Creating a Check Register Worksheet

As an illustration of some of the ClarisWorks spreadsheet capabilities, you can create a worksheet that fulfills the reason that many new users say they bought their computer: to balance their checkbook. (Of course, when you think about it, paying several thousand dollars for slightly more capability than a hand calculator doesn't make a great deal of sense, does it?)

This worksheet is useful if you don't like to balance your checking account manually or if you want a clean printed copy of your checking activity. But because the worksheet duplicates the check register, you have to enter your checks and deposits twice — once in the check register and once in the worksheet.

In addition to duplicating a standard check register, the worksheet tosses in a few extra features:

- ∞ Separate Payee and Description columns, so that you can record to whom each check was made out as well as what it was for
- ∞ Automatic calculation of the balance
- ∞ Automatic calculation of the total of uncleared checks, withdrawals, and deposits (the uncleared total)

Creating the Worksheet

Figure 4-27 shows the worksheet with a half dozen sample entries. Use the following steps to create a working copy of the worksheet.

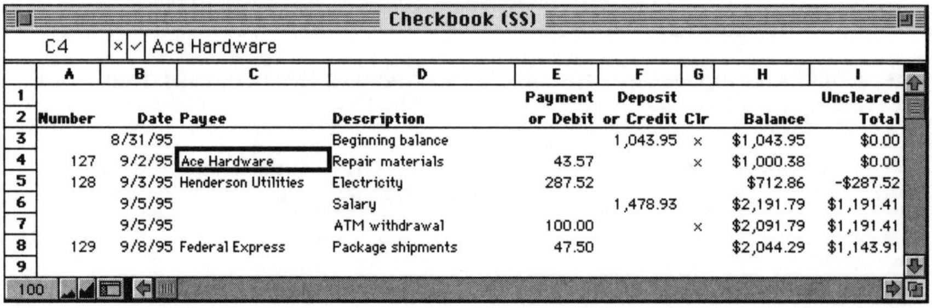

Figure 4-27:
The check
register
worksheet

	A	B	C	D	E	F	G	H	I
					Payment	Deposit			Uncleared
2	Number	Date	Payee	Description	or Debit	or Credit	Clr	Balance	Total
3		8/31/95		Beginning balance		1,043.95	×	$1,043.95	$0.00
4	127	9/2/95	Ace Hardware	Repair materials	43.57		×	$1,000.38	$0.00
5	128	9/3/95	Henderson Utilities	Electricity	287.52			$712.86	-$287.52
6		9/5/95		Salary		1,478.93		$2,191.79	$1,191.41
7		9/5/95		ATM withdrawal	100.00		×	$2,091.79	$1,191.41
8	129	9/8/95	Federal Express	Package shipments	47.50			$2,044.29	$1,143.91

Steps: **Laying Out the Worksheet**

Step 1. Create the column labels in rows 1 and 2.

All label text is 9-point Geneva bold. (All other text is 9-point Geneva.)

Step 2. Set the alignment for each column:

- Set columns A, B, E, F, H, and I as right-aligned (⌘-]).
- Set columns C and D as left-aligned (⌘-[).
- Set column G as center-aligned (⌘-\).

To set the alignment for a column, click a column heading to select the entire column, and then choose an option from the Alignment submenu of the Format menu.

Step 3. Use the Column Width command in the Format menu to set the column widths as follows:

- A (44)
- B (52)
- C (104)
- D (124)
- E and F (56)
- G (22)
- H and I (64)

Step 4. Add a bottom border to cells A2 through I2 by using the Borders command in the Format menu.

Step 5. Set the number formats for data in the worksheet as follows:

- A (Fixed with a Precision of 0 [zero])
- B (choose the first Date option)
- E and F (Fixed, Commas, Precision 2)
- H and I (Currency, Commas, Precision 2)

To set the number format for a column, click a column heading to select the entire column, choose an option from the Number submenu of the Format menu (or press Shift-⌘-N), and click OK.

Step 6. The record in row 3 is reserved for the beginning balance. For now, enter the following:

- Today's date in B3
- **Beginning balance** in D3
- **1000** in F3
- **=F3** in H3
- **0** in I3

You can change this information later to match your real beginning balance.

Step 7. Enter this formula into cell H4 to calculate the running balance (Balance):

```
=IF(B4<>"",H3-E4+F4,"")
```

After entering the formula, copy it to the remaining cells in column H by selecting cells H4 through H500 and choosing Fill Down (⌘-D) from the Calculate menu.

Step 8. Enter this formula into cell I4 to calculate the running total of uncleared checks, withdrawals, and deposits (Uncleared Total):

```
=IF(B4="","",IF(G4<>"x",I3-E4+F4,I3))
```

After entering the formula, copy it to the remaining cells in column I by selecting cells I4 through I500 and choosing Fill Down (⌘-D) from the Calculate menu.

Step 9. To keep the labels in rows 1 and 2 from scrolling off-screen as additional transactions are entered, make them into titles. Select row 2 by clicking the row heading (the number 2) and choose Lock Title Position from the Options menu.

After you lock the rows, you cannot edit any of the cells in rows 1 or 2. Later, if you need to make changes in either row, choose Lock Title Position again.

Step 10. *Optional:* Select columns H and I by clicking their headings and choose Lock Cells from the Options menu (or press ⌘-H) to keep the entries in these columns from being altered accidentally. (The entries in columns H and I are all calculated automatically, based on your transactions.)

Understanding the Formulas

The formulas are fairly complex, so they require further examination. The formula in H4 is as follows:

```
=IF(B4<>"",H3-E4+F4,"")
```

First, the formula checks cell B4 — the date for the current record — to see whether it is empty. If B4 contains something (a date, presumably), the first action is performed. That is, the formula takes the previous balance (H3), subtracts any payment entered for this record (E4), and adds any deposit entered for this record (F4). If, on the other hand, the date field is blank for the record, the second action is taken: the Balance entry is left blank. (You test for the existence of a date because every legitimate record should contain one. If no date is found, you assume that the record does not yet exist.)

This formula could have been written as =H3–E4+F4. When filled down to the remaining records, however, transactions that didn't exist yet would all display the current balance. Using this more complex approach to test whether a transaction exists produces a more attractive worksheet.

The formula in I4 is even more complex. It contains an IF function nested within another IF function:

```
=IF(B4="","",IF(G4<>"x",I3-E4+F4,I3))
```

The formula performs two actions. First, if the Date field is blank — IF(B4="" — it assumes that the record does not yet exist and leaves the Uncleared Total entry blank (just as the previous formula left the Balance entry blank). Because the first test has been met, the remainder of the formula is not evaluated.

On the other hand, if the Date field is *not* blank, the formula checks the Clr entry (G4) for the current record to see whether it contains an *x*. (You use an *x* to indicate that — according to the bank statement — a check, withdrawal, or deposit has cleared.) If an *x* is not found, the formula takes the previous Uncleared Total (I3), subtracts the current Payment from it (E4), and adds the current Deposit (F4). Thus, if an entry has not cleared, its payment or deposit is reflected in the Uncleared Total. If an *x* is found, on the other hand, the previous Uncleared Total in I3 is simply copied to the cell.

Using the Worksheet

The best time to begin using this worksheet is when you open a new account or immediately after you've received a bank statement and balanced your checkbook.

Begin by editing the first record (row 3). Replace the temporary date (B3) and balance (F3) with today's date and your balance. Placing the balance in F3 automatically copies it to the Balance column (H3). Because the beginning balance won't be part of a later reconciliation, type a lowercase *x* in the Clr column (G3) for the entry.

Now go back through your check register and, beginning in row 4, make an entry for every outstanding check, withdrawal, and deposit. (If you don't want gaps in the register, you can go back to the oldest outstanding check, withdrawal, or deposit, and enter *every* transaction up to the current date. If you do so, be sure to add an *x* in the Clr field for every item that has cleared.)

When a bank statement arrives, the Checkbook worksheet can help with the reconciliation. Going down G (the Clr column), add an *x* for every item that has cleared. When you are through, the last figure in the Uncleared Total column will represent the total of the outstanding deposits minus the outstanding checks.

Quick Tip: Speeding Data Entry by Preselecting a Range

Although you can tab and click to move from cell to cell when you enter data, you can use a faster method to enter data into a specific section of the worksheet. Start by preselecting the range into which you will be entering data. The range might look like the one in Figure 4-28.

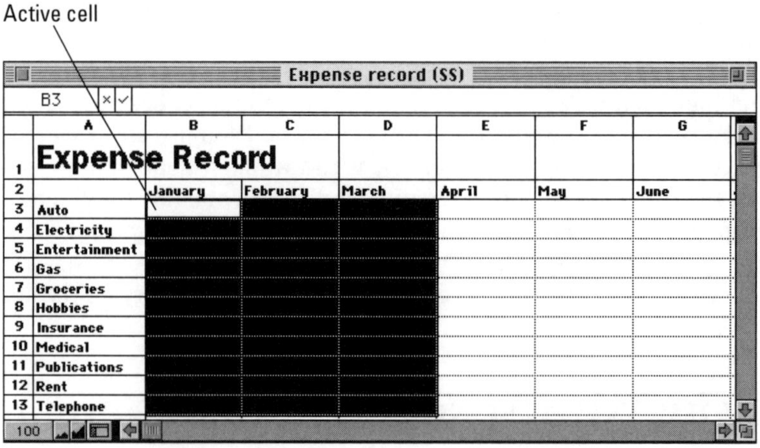

Figure 4-28: A preselected range

In a preselected range, the active cell is white, while all other cells are dark. After entering information in the first cell, press Tab. The cell to the right becomes active. If you continue to press Tab after each cell entry, the active cell shifts across each row, one cell at a time. When a row is completed, the cursor drops down to the first cell in the next row. If you press Return (rather than Tab) after each cell entry, the cursor moves down one cell at a time through each selected column.

Moving On Up

Although the ClarisWorks spreadsheet environment is sufficient for many users, as your needs become more complex you may want to check out a more full-featured spreadsheet program. Features such as a macro language, the ability to define your own functions, additional chart types and functions, and linked and three-dimensional worksheets are all commonplace in commercial spreadsheets. Currently, the leading Mac spreadsheet program is Microsoft Excel (Microsoft Corporation).

 The export capabilities of ClarisWorks make upgrading to other spreadsheets easy to do. If you save a ClarisWorks worksheet in Excel 3, Excel 4, or SYLK format, most other spreadsheet programs can interpret it correctly. Similarly, if you use a different spreadsheet program at the office and want to continue working on a worksheet at home, you can probably import the spreadsheet into ClarisWorks by using the Open command. Note, however, that macros that have been attached to the worksheet (in Excel or 1-2-3, for example) will not function in ClarisWorks.

If you're looking for additional charting capabilities, check out DeltaGraph Pro (DeltaPoint) for business charts. KaleidaGraph (Synergy Software) is excellent for scientific and statistical graphing.

Summary

- ⇒ A worksheet is a grid that is composed of numbered rows and lettered columns. A cell is the intersection of a row and a column.

- ⇒ You enter text strings, numbers, and formulas into cells. Formulas can refer to other cells, contain constants, and use any of the 100 built-in ClarisWorks functions.

- ⇒ The cell in which the cursor is positioned is known as the active cell. The location of any cell is given by its cell address.

- ➥ A group of cells is known as a range. A range is identified by its anchor points — the upper-left and lower-right cells in the range.

- ➥ Formulas are normally evaluated from left to right. The precedence levels of the operations performed within the formula can change the calculation order, however, as can the use of parentheses to enclose operations.

- ➥ You can type functions directly into formulas, or you can paste them there (along with dummy arguments) by using the Paste Function command.

- ➥ You can copy and paste formulas to other cells. You also can paste just the values contained in cells, ignoring the formulas. The Fill Down and Fill Right commands expedite copying a formula to a large range.

- ➥ The Fill Special command makes it easy to create sequences of numbers and dates. This feature is particularly useful for generating a set of ordered row or column headings.

- ➥ ClarisWorks provides many commands that make reorganizing a worksheet simple. It includes commands that insert and delete cells, columns, and rows; move ranges of cells to new locations; sort data; and transpose a range (swapping the positions of rows and columns).

- ➥ To make worksheets more attractive, you can selectively apply font, size, style, color, and alignment options to the text in cells. You can also apply colors and patterns to cells (cell shading).

- ➥ To make the contents of the cell fit inside the cell borders, you can widen column widths, change row heights, or apply a Wrap format.

- ➥ You can control the way the program displays numbers, dates, and times by choosing options in the Format Number, Date, and Time dialog box.

- ➥ The Copy Format and Paste Format commands enable you to easily apply existing cell formats to other cells.

- ➥ ClarisWorks provides a dozen different styles of charts that you can use to embellish a worksheet. Because every chart is also an object, you can copy and paste charts into other documents.

- ➥ When printing a worksheet, ClarisWorks defaults to selecting the entire active area of the worksheet. However, you can specify a particular print range, add manual page breaks, and turn off the printing of some worksheet elements, such as the cell grid and row or column headings.

- ➥ You can lock important cells to prevent them from being changed inadvertently. You can lock important information (titles, for example) at the top and left sides of the worksheet in place so that it doesn't disappear when you scroll the worksheet.

The Database Environment

■ ■

In This Chapter

- ➻ Database fundamentals
- ➻ Defining fields and modifying field definitions
- ➻ Creating calculation and summary field formulas
- ➻ Modifying field definitions
- ➻ Organizing information with layouts
- ➻ Field formatting
- ➻ Viewing, entering, and editing data
- ➻ Finding and selecting records
- ➻ Sorting records
- ➻ Creating reports
- ➻ Working with mailing labels
- ➻ Database printing
- ➻ Importing and exporting data
- ➻ Creating a custom database (Credit Card Charge Tracker)

■ ■

Overview _____

A *database* is an organized set of information — usually on one particular topic. One common example of a database is a card file that contains the names, addresses, and phone numbers of business associates, customers, or friends. Other everyday examples of databases that you can find around the office or home include employee records, inventory records, a recipe file, and a list of videotapes.

Every database is composed of *records*. In the previous examples, each record contains all the pertinent information about one friend, one employee, one inventory part, one recipe, or one videotape.

Each record is composed of *fields*. A field contains one piece of information about the employee (a social security number, for example), videotape (the name of the star), recipe (cooking time), or friend (date of birth). In an address database, you may have separate fields for each person's first name, last name, street address, city, state, and ZIP code.

Unlike a word processing document (which is free-form), a computer database has an order that comes from its use of fields. Every field holds one particular type of information (an employee identification number, for example). As you skim through the records of the database, you see that the same type of information is in that field in every record. Figure 5-1 shows the relationship between a database, records, and fields.

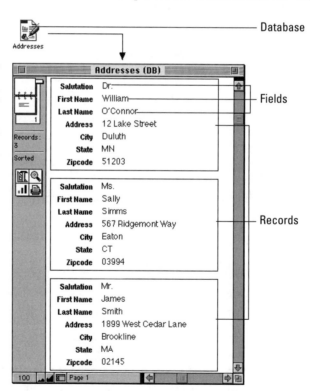

Figure 5-1:
A computer database contains a series of records; each record is composed of a set of fields.

Although you can keep database information in a word processing document, you lose the data manipulation advantages that a database provides, such as the capability to select subsets of records (for example, only employees who make between $20,000 and $30,000 per year), sort records by one or more fields (for example, by zip code, last name, years of employment, or cost of ingredients), create fields that perform calculations and computations (for example, totaling all items ordered or combining two text fields), and generate custom reports.

Another great thing about a computerized database, as compared to a paper version, is the ease with which you can modify and reorganize its contents. Early database programs required you to define every field before you started to enter data. If you later decided to add a field, delete a field, or change the type of a particular field (from text to numeric, for example), you had to execute a complex procedure to reorganize the database. Current database programs, such as the ClarisWorks database environment, make reorganizing a database remarkably easy. If you need a new field, for example, you simply define it and add it to the appropriate layouts.

Using the ClarisWorks database, you can do the following:

- ☞ Quickly identify records that match simple criteria (Name = Sam Jones) or very complex criteria (Salary <= $40,000 and Age > 45)

- ☞ Sort the records by the contents of one or more fields (by Last Name within City)

- ☞ Create multiple layouts for any database (for example, create data entry, phone directory, and label layouts for the same database)

- ☞ Set data validation criteria for some fields (such as unique data or data within a particular range)

- ☞ Specify a data type for each field (text, number, date, time, calculation, or summary)

- ☞ Automatically enter certain data (today's date or an invoice number)

- ☞ Perform calculations (totals or averages for each record, a subset of records, or the entire database)

Working with the ClarisWorks Database

You use a ClarisWorks database in four modes: Layout, Browse, Find, and List. In *Layout* mode, you arrange fields and other database objects on a screen page so that the program will display and print them the way you want. You use *Browse* or *List* mode to view, edit, add, delete, and sort records. You do all data entry in Browse or List mode. *Find* mode enables you to search for records that meet one or more criteria (Last Name = Smith, for example).

Defining Fields

Every database is composed of fields into which you enter information. In fact, you cannot begin to enter data until you have defined at least one field by specifying its name and the type of data that it will contain.

To create new fields, delete fields, or modify the definitions or options for existing fields, choose Define Fields from the Layout menu (or press Shift-⌘-D). The Define Database Fields dialog box appears, as shown in Figure 5-2. Click Done when you are finished.

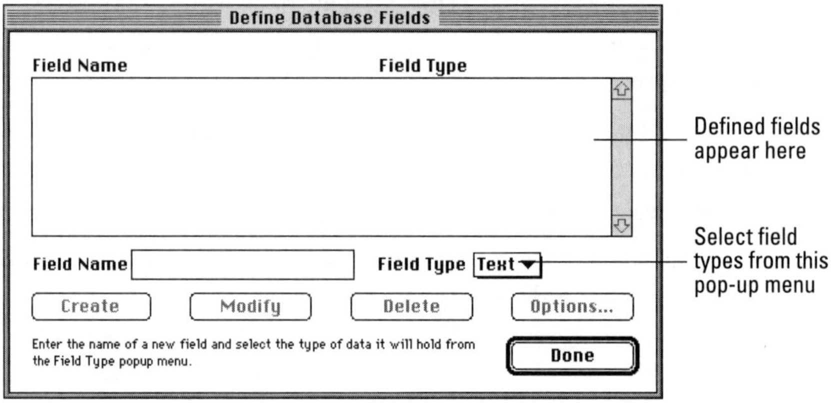

Figure 5-2: You can use the Define Database Fields dialog box to specify a name, field type, and options for every field in the database. You also can use it to modify a field definition or delete a field.

Defined fields appear here

Select field types from this pop-up menu

Although the database environment is packed with fancy features, sometimes simplest is best. You can just define the necessary fields, accept the default layout, and start entering data. The following example shows the steps for designing a basic address book database. As you progress in this chapter, you'll learn how to customize layouts and work with special data types and options.

Steps:	Creating a Simple Database

Step 1. Choose New from the File menu (or press ⌘-N). The New Document dialog box appears.

Step 2. Choose Database and click OK. A new database is created, and the Define Database Fields dialog box appears, as previously shown in Figure 5-2.

Step 3. Define the fields you want to use in the database. For the address book database, you'll define the following fields (in order): First Name, Last Name, Address, City, State, ZIP, and Birthdate. Birthdate is a Date field; all others are Text fields.

For each field, type its name in the Field Name text-edit box, choose the appropriate Field Type from the pop-up menu, and then click Create. The field is added to the list box.

When setting up any database, you should think ahead. By separating first and last name fields, for example, you'll have an easier time doing searches and sorts in the future. Try not to combine important bits of information into a single field.

The name of the field just defined is still in the text-edit box. When you begin typing a name for the *next* field, the text-edit box automatically clears.

Step 4. After you have defined all fields, click Done. A database with the default layout (field sizes, placements, fonts, and so on) appears (as shown in Figure 5-3), ready for you to enter the first record.

After completing an entry for a field, you can move to the next field by pressing the Tab key. To create additional records, choose New Record from the Edit menu (or press ⌘-R).

 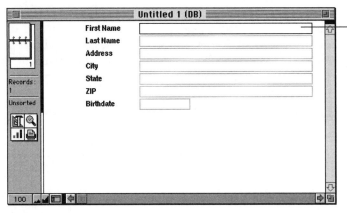

Figure 5-3:
After you
define the
fields,
ClarisWorks
displays the
first record.

The current field
is indicated by
a solid border

Field Types

ClarisWorks 4.0 offers 13 types of fields, each for a different category of data or a specific presentation format: text, number, date, time, name, pop-up menu, radio buttons, check box, serial number, value list, record info, calculation, and summary. By assigning the correct data type to each field, you can let ClarisWorks do some simple validation (for example, making sure that only dates are entered in date fields and only numbers are entered in number fields).

 Users of earlier versions of ClarisWorks should read this chapter very carefully. ClarisWorks previously supported only six field types. In ClarisWorks 4.0, however, things that were previously considered *formatting options* — pop-up menu, check boxes, and radio buttons — have been defined as separate *field types*. By selecting any of these field types, you can create more attractive databases, while making it easy for users to complete the field — *without having to type an entry!*

Although you can define every field as text, you'll miss out on some of the real power of the program if you don't take advantage of the other field types. The following sections describe how each field type works.

Text Fields

Although it's called a *text* field, you can enter any type of character into this field. Letters, numbers, punctuation marks, spaces, and so on are all legal characters. Data that you enter into a text field will word wrap, just as it does in a word processing document. You can even enter Returns to start new lines. This flexibility makes text fields ideal for notes, as well as for any type of information that contains a mixture of letters and numbers (street addresses, for example).

Options that you can set for text fields are shown in Figure 5-4.

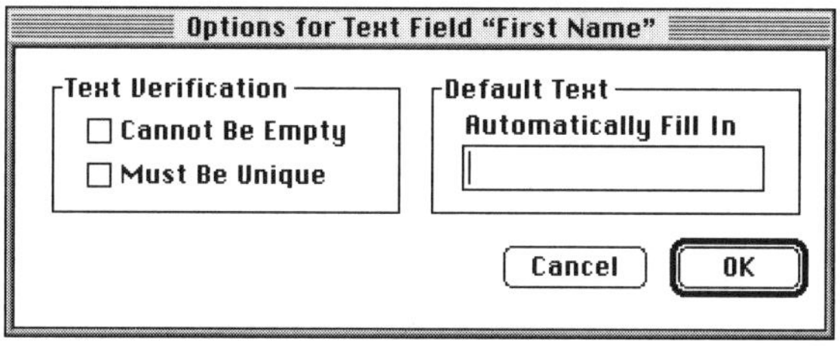

Figure 5-4:
To display this dialog
box, select a text field
in the Define Database
Fields dialog box and
click Options.

Options for Text Field "First Name"

┌─Text Verification─────┐ ┌─Default Text─────┐
☐ Cannot Be Empty   **Automatically Fill In**
☐ Must Be Unique   ┌─────────────────┐
                           └─────────────────┘

                              [Cancel] [OK]

The left side of the dialog box contains two text verification options:

- *Cannot Be Empty.* Click this check box if the field must be filled in for every record. If you attempt to change to another record, create a new record, change to another mode, or close the database without filling the field, ClarisWorks presents a warning.

- *Must Be Unique.* Click this check box if you don't want to accept duplicate values for a field. (This is a useful option for part numbers in a company catalog or an inventory database, for example.) If you attempt to enter a text string that already exists in this field in another record, ClarisWorks presents a warning.

Either warning can be overridden by clicking Yes in the warning message box.

If there is an entry that you use frequently, enter that text string in the Automatically Fill In text-edit box. All new records will automatically have that value entered in the field.

As with other fields in a ClarisWorks database, you can apply selective formatting to any portion of the text field's contents. For example, if you create a Comments field that you define as a text field, you can selectively change the font for some words or add a style such as italic to others.

The size of the bounding box for a text field does not restrict the amount of text that you can enter in the field. As you type, the bounding box expands vertically as needed to accommodate additional text. When you exit the field (by pressing the Tab key or by clicking in a different field), the bounding box returns to its normal size, obscuring any overflow text. The field expands again whenever you move the text insertion point into it.

If a text field contains overflow text, you must expand the size of the field on the layout before printing the database. Otherwise, the text in the printout will be truncated.

A ClarisWorks text field can hold a maximum of about 500 characters. If you exceed this limit, a message to that effect appears. You will have to edit the contents of the field manually by removing some of the text or style formatting before ClarisWorks will accept the entry.

Number Fields

Number fields are for numeric data only, such as prices, quantities, and so on. Legitimate numeric characters include the digits 0 through 9, parentheses or a minus sign (for negative numbers), the plus sign (+), a percent sign (%), and an *e* (for scientific notation). ClarisWorks automatically flags other characters and requests that you reenter the number. It ignores commas or dollar signs during data entry. In addition, number fields cannot contain Returns — in every number field, the entire number must be entered as a single, continuous string.

If you enter a number that exceeds the width of the field, the program converts the number to scientific notation (1.234571+e19, for example). As with overly long text entries, you have to move the text insertion point into the number field to see a number that exceeds the field width.

Like the other field types, there are several verification and default options that can be set for a number field. The Options dialog box for number fields is shown in Figure 5-5.

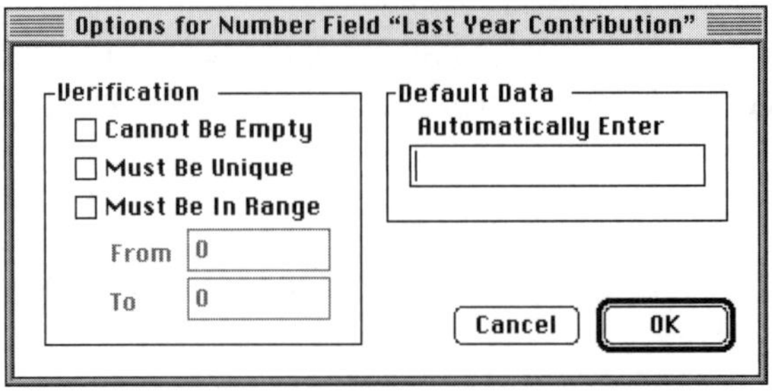

Figure 5-5:
To display this dialog box, select a number field in the Define Database Fields dialog box and click Options.

> **Options for Number Field "Last Year Contribution"**
>
> **Verification**
> ☐ Cannot Be Empty
> ☐ Must Be Unique
> ☐ Must Be In Range
>   From [0]
>   To   [0]
>
> **Default Data**
> Automatically Enter
> [   ]
>
> (Cancel)   [**OK**]

The left side of the dialog box contains three verification options.

- *Cannot Be Empty.* Click this if the field must be filled in for every record. If you attempt to change to another record, create a new record, change to another mode, or close the database without filling the field, ClarisWorks presents a warning.

- *Must Be Unique.* Click this if you don't want to accept duplicate values for a field. (This is a useful option for part numbers in a company catalog or an inventory database, for example.) If you attempt to enter a text string that already exists in this field in another record, ClarisWorks presents a warning.

∞ *Must Be In Range.* Click this and enter a pair of numbers in the From a
edit boxes if you want to specify a range of allowable numeric entries. ⊔ ⌄ ⌄
enter a number in this field that is outside of the range, a warning message appears.

All three warning messages can be overridden by clicking *Yes* in the warning
message box.

You can assign a display format (such as Currency) or a particular number of decimal
places to any field. See "Field Formatting," later in this chapter, for more information.

You should define some fields as text fields even though they are composed
entirely of numbers. Zip codes are a perfect example. Because number fields
cannot display leading zeros, a zip code of 01535 would display as *1535* in a
number field. Similarly, numbers that contain parentheses or dashes are not
allowed. Thus, Social Security numbers and phone numbers are best defined as
text fields, too.

Date Fields

You use date fields, of course, to record calendar dates, such as 7/19/95. Examples
include birth dates, the date a product was ordered, the date an employee was hired, or
the date a school project is due. You can enter dates in a number of different ways. All
of the following are acceptable:

∞ 7/19/95

∞ 7-19-95

∞ July 19, 1995

∞ Jul 19, 95

∞ 7/19

∞ Jul 19

As you can see, the methods for entering information into a date field are extremely
flexible. As long as you enter enough information to identify each portion of the date
(the first three letters of the month's name, for example), ClarisWorks will do its best to
interpret what you type. If you omit the year, as in the last two examples, ClarisWorks
assumes that you are referring to the current year and inserts it for you.

Options available for date fields are shown in Figure 5-6.

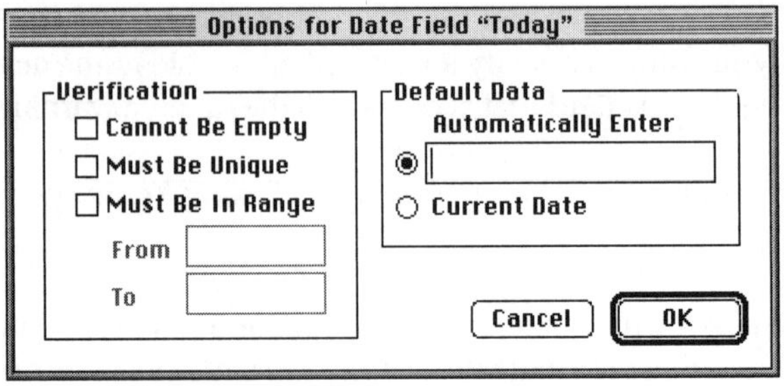

Figure 5-6:
Select a date field in the Define Database Fields dialog box and click Options to reach this dialog box.

```
═══════ Options for Date Field "Today" ═══════
┌─Uerification ──────────┐  ┌─Default Data ──────────┐
│ ☐ Cannot Be Empty      │  │    Automatically Enter  │
│ ☐ Must Be Unique       │  │ ◉ [                   ] │
│ ☐ Must Be In Range     │  │ ○ Current Date          │
│   From  [        ]     │  │                         │
│   To    [        ]     │  │      [ Cancel ] [  OK  ]│
└────────────────────────┘  └─────────────────────────┘
```

If you choose Must Be In Range as one of the verification options, you must enter valid dates in the From and To text-edit boxes. (See "Number Fields," earlier in this chapter, for more information on verification options and the ability to override verification warnings.)

In the right side of the Options dialog box, you can enter a default date, if you wish. If there's a particular date that should normally be entered, type it in the Automatically Enter text-edit box. If you want to enter the current date when each record is created, click the Current Date radio button. As with other default values, you can edit or replace them in the records, as necessary.

You can display dates within their fields in several ways. For a discussion of formatting options, see "Field Formatting" later in this chapter.

Time Fields

Time fields enable you to record times in hours, minutes, and seconds. The options for time fields are identical to those for date fields, as described previously in "Date Fields." The various time formats (discussed in "Field Formatting," later in this chapter) enable you to record times with AM and PM suffixes, as well as in 12- or 24-hour formats.

Name Fields

People's names are frequently recorded as two or more fields (First Name and Last Name, for example) because of the difficulty of sorting a complete name. Generally, you are interested in sorting by the person's last name, but — since that usually isn't an option — this means that a full name would have to be entered as Smith Bill, for example, in order to sort correctly. With the new name field type, ClarisWorks 4.0 provides a solution for gracefully handling complete names as a single field.

By default, entries in name fields are sorted by the *last* word in the field rather tha first. To force a particular name to be sorted by the first word, enter an @ symbol first character (@John Simms, for example). To force a particular name to be sorted by the next-to-last word (ignoring the final word), separate the next-to-last and the last word with an Option-space rather than a regular space. This allows a name prefix, such as Jr., to be ignored during the sort.

Name options are shown in Figure 5-7. The two verification options (Cannot Be Empty and Must Be Unique) have been explained in earlier sections of this chapter. The default options enable ClarisWorks to automatically enter a specific name (your top salesperson, for instance) or your name (User's Name) as specified in the Sharing Setup control panel.

Figure 5-7:
To access this dialog box, select a name field in the Define Database Fields dialog box and click Options.

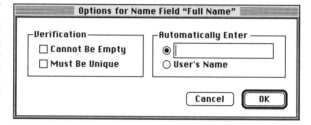

If an incorrect user name appears in the name field, check the name that appears in the Sharing Setup control panel. Change it to reflect the name that *should* be used — your name, in most cases.

Pop-up Menu Fields

Setting a field type as pop-up menu adds a menu to the field, as shown in Figure 5-8.

Figure 5-8:
A record with a pop-up menu field for State (top), and choosing a state from a pop-up menu field (bottom)

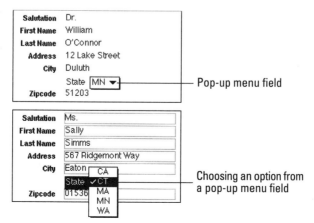

Pop-up menu field

Choosing an option from a pop-up menu field

Steps: Creating a Pop-Up Menu Field

Step 1.   Choose Define Fields from the Layout menu (or press Shift-⌘-D). The Define
Database fields dialog box appears (see Figure 5-2).

Step 2.   Enter a name for the field in the Field Name text-edit box, choose Pop-up
menu from the Field Type pop-up menu, and click Create. The Options
dialog box appears, as shown in Figure 5-9.

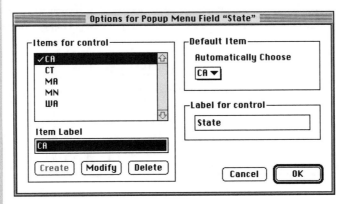

Figure 5-9: The Options dialog box for a pop-up menu field

Step 3.   To create a choice for the pop-up menu, type a name or value into the Item
Label text-edit box.

Step 4.   Click Create to add the choice to the Items for control list.

Step 5.   Repeat Steps 3 and 4 for all additional menu choices you want to create.

Step 6.   In the right side of the Options dialog box, choose a Default Item from the
Automatically Choose pop-up menu. That item will automatically be
selected when a new record is created.

Step 7.   *Optional:* Enter a new label that will be attached to the pop-up menu field.
By default, the field's name is used. You are free to change the label to
something else.

As previously illustrated in Figure 5-8, the normal field label is removed
when you display a pop-up menu field, and it is replaced by a Label for
control that is directly tied to the pop-up menu field.

Step 8. To accept the field's definition and options, click OK; to cancel the changes, click Cancel.

Step 9. Continue defining fields and editing definitions, or click Done to return to the database.

Although entries in the Items for control list reflect the order in which you created the values, you can change the positions of entries by clicking and dragging items in the list. Items can also be replaced or deleted by selecting the item and then clicking the appropriate button (Modify or Delete).

When you create a new record, the default entry is automatically chosen for any pop-up menu fields in the layout. Tabbing into a pop-up menu field does nothing; to change the default entry to a different value, you must deliberately click on the pop-up menu and drag to select another value.

Setting a field type to pop-up menu is an excellent idea when you want to restrict users' choices to a specific set of entries. Note, however, that if you or anyone else wants to enter a different, unlisted choice, it can't be done. You must choose Define Fields again and add that choice to the Items for control list.

Radio Buttons Fields

Defining a field to be a radio buttons field enables you to present a specific set of choices to the user, each with its own radio button (as shown in Figure 5-10). As in other programs, the choices are mutually exclusive — only one radio button can be selected. For help creating a radio buttons field, see "Pop-Up Menu Fields" earlier in this chapter. The options and procedures are identical.

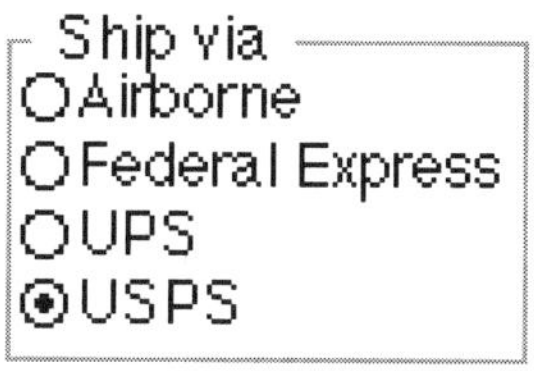

Figure 5-10:
A radio buttons field

> Ship via
> ○ Airborne
> ○ Federal Express
> ○ UPS
> ◉ USPS

You can change the size or shape of the radio button field by switching to Layout mode and dragging one of the field's handles. You can also alter the appearance of the field by choosing options from the Field Format dialog box (described in "Field Formatting," later in this chapter).

ClarisWorks provides several interesting keyboard shortcuts for choosing options in a radio buttons field (in addition to simply clicking the button of your choice). You can tab into the field and then:

- Press the spacebar repeatedly to cycle through the choices

- Press any of the arrow keys (up, down, right, or left) to cycle through the choices.

Press Tab again to leave the field, or press Enter or choose New Record from the Edit menu to complete the record.

Check Box Fields

Use a check box field to present a single label preceded by a check box, as shown in Figure 5-11. Check box fields are most appropriate for yes/no, true/false, and on/off types of data. Because of the simplicity of responding to them, they can be extremely useful as parts of data collection forms, such as surveys and business forms.

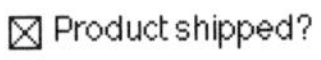

Figure 5-11:
A check box field   ☒ Product shipped?

The state of a check box can be either checked or unchecked, and you can specify either as the default state for the field. The check mark can be toggled between checked and unchecked by clicking it with the mouse, pressing the spacebar, or pressing any of the arrow keys.

Click the Options button in the Define Database Fields dialog box to set a different label for the field and to indicate whether the check box in new records should be initially checked or unchecked.

Serial Number Fields

Serial number fields are used to assign numbers to records. Each record — including every record that is already in the database — is automatically given a number that reflects the order in which it was created. Although serial numbers can be edited, deleting records or sorting them does not affect the contents of a serial number field. Serial number fields are often used to number invoices, purchase orders, statements, and checks.

For data entry and editing purposes, an entry in a serial number field is treated like any other number. Only numeric entries are permitted. This means that a serial number field cannot be used for part numbers such as 14B73, for example.

After defining a field as a serial number field, you can set options for the field by clicking the Options button in the Define Database Fields dialog box. The Options dialog box appears, as shown in Figure 5-12.

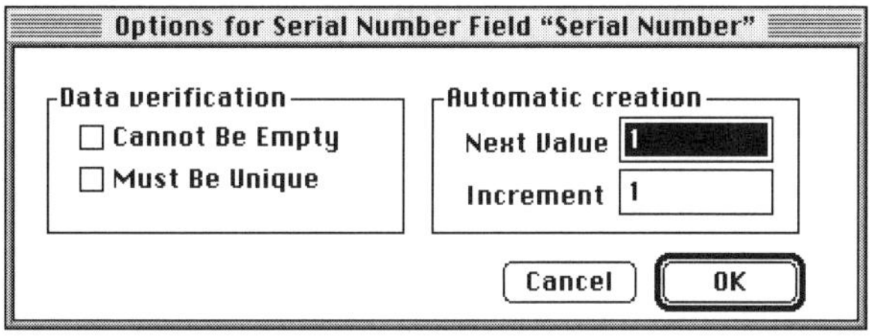

Figure 5-12:
The Options dialog box for a serial number field

> **Options for Serial Number Field "Serial Number"**
>
> ┌─Data verification─────┐ ┌─Automatic creation─────┐
> │ ☐ Cannot Be Empty   │ │ Next Value [1]   │
> │ ☐ Must Be Unique   │ │ Increment [1]   │
> └───────────────────────┘ └─────────────────────────┘
>
> (Cancel)   (**OK**)

Check Cannot Be Empty if you want ClarisWorks to present a warning if you attempt to leave or close the current record and no serial number is present. If you don't check Cannot Be Empty, you can delete serial numbers. Click Must Be Unique if you want to disallow duplicate numbers. As with the options for other field types, you can override either of these restrictions on a record-by-record basis.

In the right side of the dialog box, enter numbers for the Next Value (the serial number to be assigned to the first record in the database) and the Increment (how much you want each new serial number to increase over the previous number). When a serial number field is created, ClarisWorks offers **1** as the default Next Value.

 If there are frequent breaks in a serial number field (purchase order numbers that are skipped or checks that are voided, for example), you can go to the Options dialog box for the serial number field and reset the entry in the Next Value text-edit box to jump to the next purchase order or check number. Doing this has no effect on the numbers for existing records.

Value List Fields

 Defining a field as a value list field causes it to present a drop-down list of values from which the user can select. Unlike pop-up menu fields, the list is automatically presented whenever you tab into the field, unlisted values can be manually entered, and there are several data validation options that can be set. Figure 5-13 shows a record that contains a value list field.

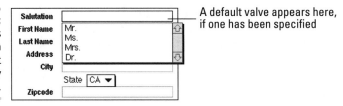

Figure 5-13:
When a user tabs into the Salutation field, this value list automatically drops down.

A default valve appears here, if one has been specified

The basic steps and options for creating a value list field are identical to those for pop-up menu fields (described earlier in this chapter). In addition to creating the list of values and optionally selecting a default value, you can also set any of the following data verification options:

- *Cannot Be Empty*: When this option is selected, ClarisWorks presents a warning if you leave the field empty and then attempt to move to another record, accept the record (by pressing Enter), or create a new record. This warning can be overridden.

- *Must Be Unique*: ClarisWorks presents a warning if your choice or manual entry for this field is already contained in another record. This warning can be overridden.

- *Alerts for Unlisted Values*: If you manually enter a value that is not contained in the value list, the warning in Figure 5-14 appears. The buttons allow you to continue editing the field's data (Continue), accept the entry as valid for this record only (Accept), or accept the entry and add it to the field's value list (Add to list). The Add to list option appends the current value to the bottom of the value list and makes the value an acceptable choice for all new and existing records.

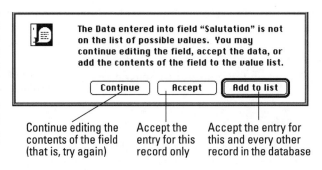

Figure 5-14:
This message appears when you manually enter a value into a field for which the Alerts for Unlisted Values option has been selected.

The Data entered into field "Salutation" is not on the list of possible values. You may continue editing the field, accept the data, or add the contents of the field to the value list.

Continue editing the contents of the field (that is, try again)

Accept the entry for this record only

Accept the entry for this and every other record in the database

When entering or editing data in a value list field, you can choose a value in several ways:

- ☞ Double-click the value with the mouse pointer
- ☞ Scroll to the value with the up- and down-arrow keys on your keyboard
- ☞ Type the first character or two of the value's text

To complete the selection, you can double-click the value, press Return, or press Enter.

When all of the following circumstances are true, ClarisWorks 4.0 ignores the default value set for a value list field:

- You are working in ClarisWorks 4.0 with a converted database (one that was created in an earlier version of the program).
- The original database contained a text field that had a value list attached to it.
- You have specified a different default value for the field (in the Options dialog box) of ClarisWorks 4.0.

When new records are created, no default value appears in the value list field.

Record Info Fields

As shown in the Options dialog box in Figure 5-15, record info fields enable you to automatically stamp each record with any of the following:

- ☞ The date or time when the record was created
- ☞ The date or time when the record was last modified
- ☞ The name of the individual who created or last modified the record

Data in a record info field is entered automatically by ClarisWorks when a record is first created (the Creation and Creator options) or edited (the Modified and Modifier options). Data in a record info field cannot be altered or deleted.

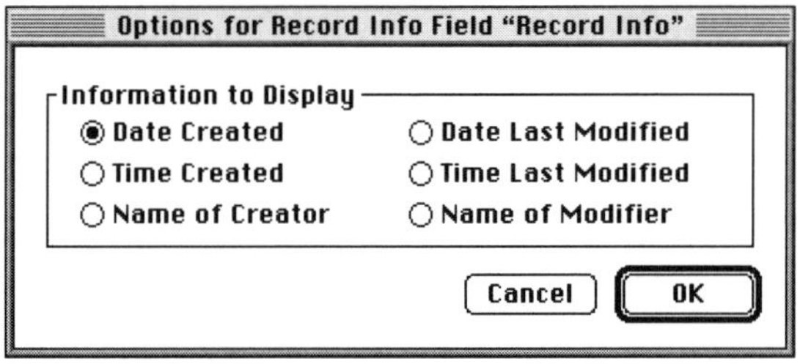

Figure 5-15:
Options that can be set for a record info field

```
Options for Record Info Field "Record Info"

┌─Information to Display─────────────────────┐
│  ⦿ Date Created        ○ Date Last Modified │
│  ○ Time Created        ○ Time Last Modified │
│  ○ Name of Creator     ○ Name of Modifier   │
└────────────────────────────────────────────┘

                        ( Cancel )  [  OK  ]
```

Calculation Fields

The availability of calculation fields sets a ClarisWorks database apart from a paper-based database or one created in a word processor.

A calculation field is based on a formula that you specify. You can use calculation fields to perform simple math, such as the computation of state sales tax ('Price'*.07), a product mark-up ('Cost'*1.5), or the sum of several fields ('Qty1'+'Qty2'+'Qty3'). Calculation fields also can incorporate any of the ClarisWorks database functions that are described in Appendix B.

When a database contains a calculation field, a separate result is computed for each record in the database. For example, in a sales database, a calculation field named Total could sum the quarterly sales data for each salesperson (as in: 'Qtr1' + 'Qtr2' + 'Qtr3' + 'Qtr4').

Steps: Defining a Calculation Field

Step 1. Choose Define Fields from the Layout menu (or press Shift-⌘-D). The Define Database Fields dialog box appears, as shown previously in Figure 5-2.

Step 2. Enter a name for the calculation field in the Field Name text-edit box and choose Calculation from the Field Type pop-up menu.

Step 3. Click Create. The Enter Formula dialog box appears, as shown in Figure 5-16.

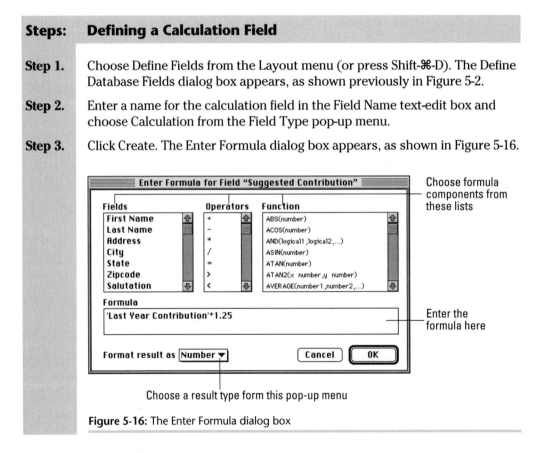

Figure 5-16: The Enter Formula dialog box

Step 4. Enter the formula in the Formula text-edit box. You can create formulas using any of the following methods:

- Type directly into the box.

- Select fields, operators, and functions from the three scrolling list boxes. (Click an option to insert it into the formula at the text insertion point.)

- Combine the first two approaches (type some parts of the formula and select others).

Step 5. Choose a result type from the Format result as pop-up menu. The choices are Text, Number, Date, and Time.

Step 6. Click OK to accept the formula. ClarisWorks notifies you if there is an error in the formula. Otherwise, you return to the Define Database Fields dialog box where you can define, modify, delete, or set options for additional fields.

You cannot enter data into a calculation field. The program fills it in automatically, based on the results of the formula for the field. Consequently, during data entry or editing, you cannot move into a calculation field by tabbing or by selecting it with the mouse. To show which fields in a database are user-modifiable and which ones are calculation fields, ClarisWorks surrounds normal fields with a light gray bounding box when you're in Browse or List mode (for data entry and editing). Calculation fields have no bounding box.

Summary Fields

Summary fields play an important role in ClarisWorks databases. They can change a database from a static collection of data to something that really works for you — providing information that cannot be gleaned from a simple scan of the records.

A calculation field makes a computation within each record (adding the total of three invoice fields, for example). Summary fields, on the other hand, make calculations *across a group of records* — either a subset of records (for a sub-summary) or all records in the database (for a grand summary).

Every summary field is based on a formula. The built-in database functions in ClarisWorks make it easy to calculate totals, averages, and counts to summarize groups of records or the entire database. *Where* a summary field is placed in the layout determines whether it summarizes each group of records (the field is in a sub-summary part) or the whole database (the field is in a leading or trailing grand summary part).

When you place a summary field in a sub-summary layout part, you have to specify a sort field for the summary field. The sort field serves to *group* the records. Suppose, for example, that you run a state-wide business and want to track total sales in different cities. You can create a summary field called Sales Total, define its formula as SUM('Sales'), and set the City field as the "sort by" field for the summary field. Then after you sort the database by City, the records for each city would form a separate group (all customers from Chicago would be listed together, for example).

At the end of every city group, the total sales for only that particular city would be shown — above or below all the individual records for that city (the location of the summary figure depends on where you place it in the layout). You should note that you can also *nest* summary fields. For example, you might use two summary fields to look at total sales within each city within each state.

When you place a summary field in a grand summary layout part, the summary field summarizes all the records in the database (or the found set of records, if you're viewing only a subset of the database). There are two types of grand summaries: leading and trailing. A *leading grand summary* appears above the data that it summarizes. A *trailing grand summary* appears below the data.

The Credit Card Charges database described later in this chapter provides additional examples of summary fields — in both sub-summary and grand summary layout parts.

 As with calculation fields, you cannot enter information into a summary field. Instead, ClarisWorks automatically calculates results for the field, based on the criteria you set. To see the results for a summary field, you need to either be in Page View or print the database. To have summary fields in a sub-summary part contain the correct information, you need to sort the database by the sort field (the one specified in the Insert Part dialog box when the sub-summary part was created). To be safe, you should always sort the database just before printing a report.

Creating a summary field requires several steps: creating a new field to hold the summary information (similar to the way you create a calculation field), adding a Summary part to the layout, placing the summary field in the Summary part, and — if the field has been added to a Sub-summary part — sorting the records.

Steps:	Creating a Summary Field
Step 1.	Choose Define Fields from the Layout menu (or press Shift-⌘-D). The Define Database Fields dialog box appears.
Step 2.	Type a name for the summary field, choose Summary from the Field Type pop-up menu, and click Create. The Enter Formula dialog box appears (the same dialog box that appears when you create a calculation field).

Step 3. Enter the formula for the summary field in the Formula text-edit box. You can create formulas by typing them directly into the box; by selecting fields, operators, and functions from the three scrolling list boxes (click an option to insert it into the formula at the text insertion point); or by combining the two approaches.

Step 4. Choose a result type from the Format result as pop-up menu. The choices are Text, Number, Date, and Time.

Step 5. Click OK to accept the formula (ClarisWorks notifies you if the formula contains an error), and click Done to exit the dialog box.

Step 6. At the bottom of the Layout menu, choose the layout to which you want to add the summary field.

Step 7. Choose Layout from the Layout menu (or press Shift-⌘-L).

If an appropriate summary part already exists in the layout, you can now skip to Step 11.

Step 8. Choose Insert Part from the Layout menu. The Insert Part dialog box shown in Figure 5-17 appears.

Figure 5-17: The Insert Part dialog box

Step 9. Choose "Leading grand summary," "Sub-summary when sorted by," or "Trailing grand summary." (You cannot use the Header or Footer parts for summary items.)

You use the Leading and Trailing grand summary options to provide a summary for the entire database. In a sales database, for example, you can use either of these choices to total or average all sales for the database.

If you choose the Sub-summary option, you have to choose a sort field from the list on the right side of the dialog box. When you sort the database by the contents of the selected field, the program groups records by the sort field and calculates a subtotal of the found set for each group. If you want to examine sales on a state-by-state basis, for example, you can create a sales sub-summary that is sorted by State.

Step 10. Click OK to leave the dialog box. (If you selected the Sub-summary option, the program asks whether you want the sub-summary part to appear above or below each record group. Choose Above, Below, or Cancel.) The program adds the summary or sub-summary part to the appropriate location in the current layout.

Step 11. Add the summary field to the layout by selecting Insert Field from the Layout menu. The Insert Field dialog box appears, as shown in Figure 5-18.

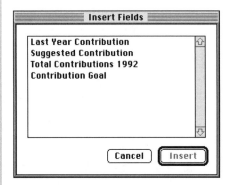

Figure 5-18: The Insert Field dialog box

Step 12. Select the summary field in the list box and click OK. (You also can double-click the summary field). In either case, the field and its label appear in the current layout. Drag the summary field and its label into the summary or sub-summary part.

Step 13. Switch to Browse mode by selecting Browse from the Layout menu (or press Shift-⌘-B).

Step 14. If the database is not in Page View, you don't see summary fields. If necessary, choose Page View from the View menu (or press Shift-⌘-P).

Step 15. If the field is a sub-summary field (rather than a grand summary), you need to sort the database by the field specified in the Insert Part dialog box. Choose Sort Records from the Organize menu (or press ⌘-J). The Sort Records dialog box appears, as shown in Figure 5-19.

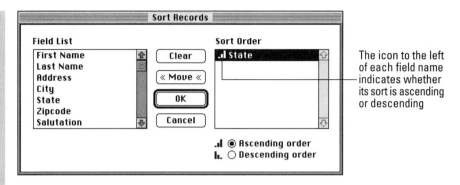

Figure 5-19: The Sort Records dialog box

Use the Move and Clear buttons, as appropriate, to select the sort field. You can sort each field in ascending or descending order, depending on which radio button you click. Click OK to conduct the sort. The sub-summary information is displayed, grouped according to the contents of the sort field.

If you want to see all of the summary data at one time or want to move it into another environment (such as the spreadsheet or word processor), change to Page View (Shift-⌘-P) and choose Copy Summaries from the Edit menu. ClarisWorks transfers the contents of summary fields to the clipboard, where they are available for pasting into other documents and applications.

Modifying Field Definitions

After you define a field, you can change its type, name, or options. You also can change the formula for a calculation or summary field.

Changing a field definition from one data type to another sometimes has unfortunate effects, and you cannot use the Undo command to undo such changes. Saving the database before you alter a field definition is a smart idea. If the transformations don't work as you intended, you can simply close the database without saving the changes.

The Fine Points of Calculation and Summary Formula Creation

You need to keep the following points in mind when creating formulas:

↩ Only calculation or summary fields can contain formulas. The program computes the results of a calculation field individually for each record in the database. Summary field formulas, on the other hand, summarize information across all or a subset of records. In a product catalog database, for example, you can use a summary field to calculate the total price of every product in the database.

↩ You need to surround field names with single quotes ('Sales') and text strings with double quotes ("Smithers").

↩ You can add extra space around operators that you manually enter (+, –, and so on) to improve readability when you are creating the formula, but ClarisWorks removes extra spaces when it checks and saves the formula.

↩ When evaluating a formula, ClarisWorks examines the elements from left to right. Different mathematical and logical operators (+, >, and so on) have different precedence, however. When you include more than one operator in a formula, the precedence of the operators determines the order in which ClarisWorks performs the calculations.

You can add parentheses to a formula to improve readability or to change the precedence for performing a calculation. If, for example, A=2 and B=3 in a given record, the formula A+B*2 gives a result of 8. Because multiplication has a higher precedence than addition, ClarisWorks evaluates the formula in this order: (B*2) equals 6, to which A is added, giving an answer of 8. By adding parentheses to the formula, as in (A+B)*2, you can change the precedence. Now the program adds A to B first (because elements that are enclosed in parentheses have a higher precedence than elements that are not enclosed in parentheses), giving a result of 5. Next, the program multiplies 5 by 2, giving an answer of 10.

Note: A common error is to have unbalanced parentheses in a formula. The number of left and right parentheses must always be equal.

Precedence levels in database formulas are as follows:

Operator	Meaning
%	percentage (divide by 100)
^	exponentiation (raise to a power, such as 'Length'^2)
+, −	change sign (for example, −'Cost')
*, /	multiplication, division
+, −	addition, subtraction
&	concatenate text strings ("Jim" & " " & "Uris" equals Jim Uris)
=,>,>=,<,<=,<>	comparison operators (equal, greater than, greater than or equal to, less than, less than or equal to, not equal)

❧ Selecting a function from the Function list inserts the function (as well as any appropriate arguments to the function) at the text insertion point. An example of a function is AVERAGE(number1,number2, . . .), where number1, number2, and . . . are the arguments to the function. The *number1, number2, . . .* means that you must replace the arguments with numbers or number fields and that you can have as many of them as you like.

Arguments are placeholders. You often replace them with field names. The fastest way to replace an argument with a field name is to double-click the argument to select it and then click a field in the Fields list.

An *ellipsis* (. . .) in an argument list means that the number of elements of the specified data type that you use is up to you. In the Average example, a completed formula may read AVERAGE('Qtr1','Qtr2','Qtr3','Qtr4'), where each of the Qtr fields contains a sales figure or a numeric grade for the quarter.

Note: You also can replace any or all number arguments with real numbers by typing them directly into the formula, as in AVERAGE('Sales',25000).

❧ Although most of the functions are available for use in both spreadsheet and database environments, database functions cannot refer to a range of fields. You must include every individual field name in a database formula, and separate the field names with commas. You can use this formula in a database:

```
SUM('QTY1','QTY2','QTY3')
```

But you cannot use this formula:

```
SUM('QTY1'..'QTY3')
```

⊷ A formula can consist entirely of a single function. You also can embed functions within a larger formula, as well as use one function to modify the result of another function. An example of the latter use is 'Due Date'–TRUNC(NOW()). This formula computes the number of days from the current date until the due date. The decimal portion of today's date and time (NOW()) is eliminated by the TRUNC function, and the result is subtracted from Due Date.

For additional information on using the ClarisWorks database and spreadsheet functions, refer to Appendix B and ClarisWorks Help.)

Steps: Changing Field Types

Step 1. Choose Define Fields from the Layout menu (or press Shift-⌘-D). The Define Database Fields dialog box appears, as shown in Figure 5-20.

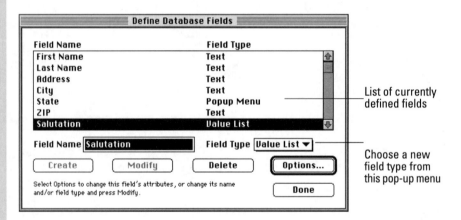

Figure 5-20: The Define Database Fields dialog box

Step 2. Select the field for which you want to set a new type. The field's name appears in the Name text-edit box.

Step 3. From the Field Type pop-up menu, choose the new type that you want to assign to the field and then click Modify.

The following warning message appears: *When modifying the field type, any data that cannot be converted will be lost.*

Step 4.   Click OK to continue or Cancel to leave the original field type unchanged.

Step 5.   Click Done to return to the database.

Renaming Fields

Once created, field names are not set in stone. To change a field name, choose Define Fields from the Layout menu, select the field name in the field list (in the Define Database Fields dialog box), type a new name, and then click the Modify button. If the field was referenced in any calculation or summary formulas, references to the old field name are automatically changed to reflect the new field name.

If you want to change a field name to make it more understandable, you can simply retype the field label in the layout. The field label has no effect on the actual field, so you could have a field called "tot sls" and label it "Total Sales," for example.

Changing Field Options

As explained in "Field Types" earlier in this chapter, every field type has options that can be set, such as setting a default value and choosing data validation measures. Field options can be altered at any time — not just when you first define the field.

Steps:	Changing Field Options
Step 1.	Choose Define Fields from the Layout menu. The Define Database Fields dialog box appears, as shown previously in Figure 5-2.
Step 2.	Select the field name in the field list, and click the Options button.
Step 3.	Change the options.
Step 4.	Click OK and then Done to dismiss the dialog boxes.

Changing a Formula for a Calculation or Summary Field

You can also change existing formulas for calculation and summary fields.

Steps:	Changing a Formula
Step 1.	Choose Define Fields from the Layout menu. The Define Database Fields dialog box appears, as shown previously in Figure 5-2.
Step 2.	Select the calculation or summary field in the field list, and then click the Modify button.
Step 3.	Make whatever changes are necessary to the formula,
Step 4.	Click OK and then Done. When you leave the Define Database Fields dialog box, the changed formula is recalculated for all database records.

Deleting Fields

Some fields outlive their usefulness, and you can easily delete them. However, deleting a field also deletes all information contained in that field *from every record in the database.*

Steps:	Deleting a Field
Step 1.	Choose Define Fields from the Layout menu (or press Shift-⌘-D). The Define Database Fields dialog box appear, as shown previously in Figure 5-20.
Step 2.	Highlight the field that you want to delete.
Step 3.	Click the Delete button. A dialog box appears with the following question: *Permanently delete this field and all of its contents?*
Step 4.	Click OK to delete the field or Cancel if you change your mind.
Step 5.	Repeat Steps 2 and 3 for any additional fields that you want to delete.
Step 6.	Click Done to exit the Define Database Fields dialog box.

To remove a field from a layout, it is not necessary to use the above procedure. Instead, change to Layout mode, select the field, and press the Delete key. Although the field is now gone from the layout, its data remains available for use in other layouts.

Adding New Fields

You can add new fields to the database at any time.

Steps:	Creating a New Field
Step 1.	Choose Define Fields from the Layout menu (or press Shift-⌘-D). The Define Database Fields dialog box appears, as previously shown in Figure 5-20.
Step 2.	Type the name of the new field in the Field Name text-edit box, choose a type for the field from the Field Type pop-up menu, and then click Create. The program adds the field to the list box.
Step 3.	Create additional fields or click Done. ClarisWorks adds the new fields and their labels to the database and to the currently selected layout.
Step 4.	Edit the layout to accommodate or omit the new fields, as you prefer (as described in the next section, "Organizing Information with Layouts").

Organizing Information with Layouts _____

In most database programs, every database has a single screen on which you do data entry, and you create reports in a separate part of the program. ClarisWorks doesn't force you to make a distinction between data-entry forms and reports. Instead, it introduces the concept of layouts.

A *layout* is a particular arrangement of fields that you've defined for a database. In each layout, you can use as many or as few of the defined fields as you like. There are no fields that you *must* use. And you can have as many layouts for each database as you need. Using an address database as an example, you can create the layouts shown in Figure 5-21.

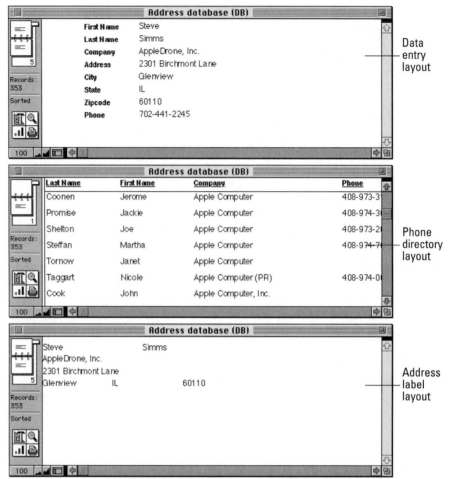

Figure 5-21:
Different
layouts
provide
different
views of the
same data.

Data entry layout

Phone directory layout

Address label layout

Steps: Creating a New Layout for a Database

Step 1. Choose New Layout from the Layout menu or the Layout pop-up in the Tool panel (see Figure 5-22). The New Layout dialog box appears, as shown in Figure 5-23.

Layout pop-up ——— Search pop-up
Sort pop-up ——— Report pop-up

Figure 5-22: These four pop-ups are shown in the Tool panel in every mode except Layout mode. Use them to work with layouts, searches, sorting, and reports.

Figure 5-23: The New Layout dialog box

Step 2. Type a name for the new layout or accept the default name that ClarisWorks presents (Layout *number*); click a radio button to choose one of the five layout formats (Standard, Duplicate, Blank, Columnar report, or Labels); and click the OK button.

Step 3. After you choose the layout type, choose fields and settings, if required. ClarisWorks creates the new layout.

The five layout formats provide the following results:

➣ If you choose a *Labels* layout, you can pick from any of the predefined label layouts in the pop-up menu or create your own layout by selecting the Custom choice. See "Working with mailing labels," later in this chapter, for a complete discussion of label options.

➣ If you choose *Standard*, ClarisWorks creates a default database layout that contains every field that you defined for the database. The fields appear one above the other in a vertical list.

➣ If you choose *Duplicate*, ClarisWorks creates an exact copy of the currently selected layout. This option is useful if you want to make a variation of the current layout — perhaps adding a few fields or rearranging the fields. You also can create a duplicate when you want to experiment with the layout. If the experiment doesn't work out, you can simply delete the layout.

➣ If you choose *Blank*, ClarisWorks creates a blank layout. You add all fields by choosing the Insert Field command from the Layout menu. (This option is useful when you want to start from scratch in designing a layout.)

☞ If you choose *Columnar report* or *Labels* (see the phone directory and label layouts in Figure 5-21 for examples), the Set Field Order dialog box appears, as shown in Figure 5-24.

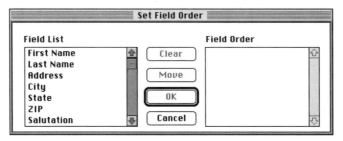

Figure 5-24:
The Set Field
Order dialog box

The purpose of the Set Field Order dialog box is to specify the fields that you want to include in the new layout and to designate their order. Choose a field from the Field List (on the left side of the dialog box) and click Move to add it to the Field Order list on the right. You can use as many or as few fields in the layout as you like.

Layout Parts

As shown in Figure 5-25, every layout is composed of labeled *parts*.

Figure 5-25:
The parts of a
database
layout

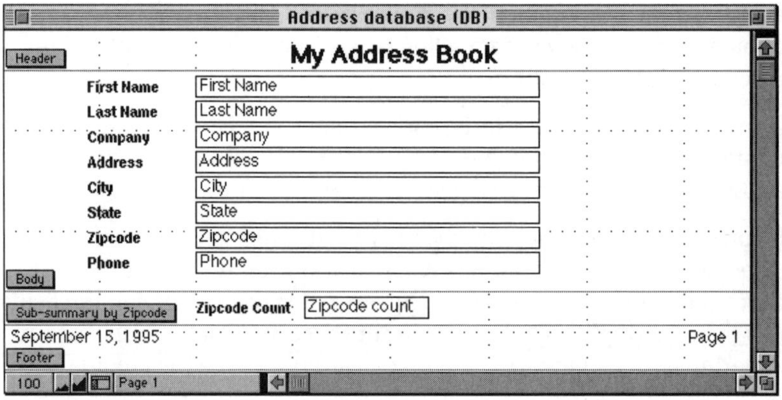

The *body* is the main part of any layout. The body holds the bulk of the data fields, mainly those into which you enter data.

All other parts of a layout are optional. The optional parts include:

- ☞ The *header* and *footer* (which hold information that repeats on every page of the layout)

- ☞ Leading or trailing *grand summaries* (which display summary data at the beginning or end of a report)

- ☞ One or more *sub-summaries* (which display summary information for groups of records — all records with the same ZIP code, for example)

You can change the size of any part by simply clicking on the dividing line for the part and dragging to make the part smaller or larger. As long as a part doesn't contain any fields or other objects, you can remove the part by dragging it up into the part immediately above it. (If the part does contain fields or other objects, you must delete the fields and objects or move them into other parts before you can remove the part.)

Although you can place any field in the body, header, or footer, you can place only summary fields in a grand summary or sub-summary part.

Arranging Fields on the Layout

Initially, ClarisWorks arranges fields on the layout according to the layout type that you selected when you created the layout (Standard, Duplicate, Blank, Columnar report, or Labels). Everything that you place on a layout — fields, field labels, text, and graphics — is considered a draw object. As such, you can do anything with items on the layout that you can do with an object. Click on any object, and you see its handles. You can drag a handle to resize a field (making it larger or smaller); drag fields to different positions; change or delete field labels; align fields with each other or the grid (using the Align commands in the Arrange menu); change the font, size, or style of text in the field or the label; place graphics on the layout; and so on. See Chapter 6 for additional information on working with objects.

Adding Graphics to a Layout

Many layouts can be made more attractive by adding a graphic or two — a logo or some clip art, for example. To add a graphic to a layout, you can do any of the following:

- ☞ Choose the Insert command from the File menu and open a graphic file.

- ☞ Copy an image from the Scrapbook, a ClarisWorks paint or draw document, or another graphics program, and then paste it into a layout.

⌖ Select an image from one of the ClarisWorks ReadyArt libraries (see Chapter 20).

⌖ Use any of the standard ClarisWorks draw tools to add lines, rectangles, and so on.

Field Formatting

The default layouts create serviceable databases, but they aren't particularly attractive. The following instructions describe how to improve a layout by changing the text attributes for field contents and labels; by setting numeric, date, and time formats for fields; and by adding a border around a field.

Steps:	Setting Text Attributes
Step 1.	At the bottom of the Layout menu, choose the layout in which you want to work.
Step 2.	Choose Layout from the Layout menu (or press Shift-⌘-L).
Step 3.	Click or Shift-click to select the fields and field labels for which you want to set new text attributes.
Step 4.	Choose options from the Font, Size, Style, Text Color, and Alignment submenus of the Format menu. The selected fields and labels change to match the new settings.

By selecting a text, name, pop-up menu, radio buttons, check box, value list, or record info field and then choosing Field Format from the Options menu (or by double-clicking one of these field types), you can summon a special Text Style dialog box in which you can simultaneously set the font, size, and text color for the field (see Figure 5-26). Additional formatting options are also presented for some of these field types.

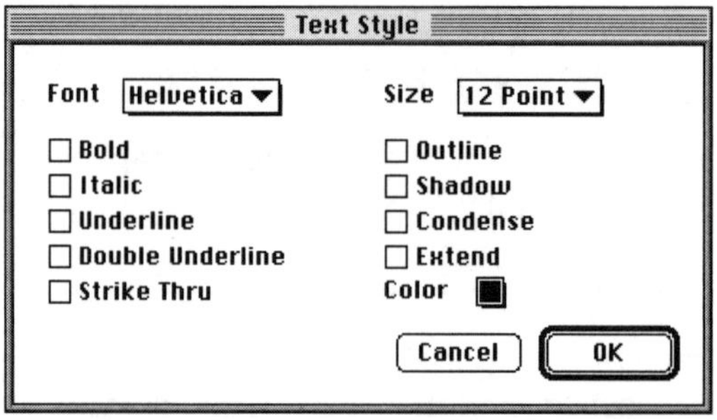

Figure 5-26:
The Text Style dialog box

```
┌──────────────────── Text Style ────────────────────┐
│                                                     │
│   Font  [Helvetica ▼]      Size  [12 Point ▼]       │
│                                                     │
│     □ Bold               □ Outline                  │
│     □ Italic             □ Shadow                    │
│     □ Underline          □ Condense                 │
│     □ Double Underline   □ Extend                   │
│     □ Strike Thru        Color  ■                   │
│                                                     │
│                      [ Cancel ]  [[ OK ]]           │
│                                                     │
└─────────────────────────────────────────────────────┘
```

If the field will contain multiple lines of data (a Comments or Notes field, for example), you can also change the field's line spacing by choosing a setting from the Spacing submenu of the Format menu.

You can change the display format for number, date, time, and serial number fields, as well as for calculation and summary fields that produce a number, date, or time result.

Steps:	Setting Number, Date, and Time Formats
Step 1.	At the bottom of the Layout menu, choose the layout in which you want to work.
Step 2.	Choose Layout from the Layout menu (or press Shift-⌘-L).
Step 3.	Click to choose a number, date, time, serial number, calculation, or summary field.
Step 4.	Choose Field Format from the Options menu (or double-click the field). Depending on the field type, one of the three dialog boxes shown in Figure 5-27 appears.

Number Format

- ⦿ General
- ○ Currency
- ○ Percent
- ○ Scientific
- ○ Fixed

☐ Commas
☐ Negatives in ()

Precision ▣ 2

[Cancel] [**OK**]

— Number formats

Date Format

- ⦿ 11/29/94
- ○ Nov 29, 1994
- ○ November 29, 1994
- ○ Tue, Nov 29, 1994
- ○ Tuesday, November 29, 1994

[Cancel] [**OK**]

— Date formats

Time Format

- ⦿ 5:20 PM
- ○ 5:20:15 PM
- ○ 17:20
- ○ 17:20:15

[Cancel] [**OK**]

— Time formats

Figure 5-27: Use these dialog boxes to set the display format for number, date, and time fields.

Step 5. Choose options in the Format dialog box and then click OK. ClarisWorks formats the field according to your selections.

Date format options include slashes, abbreviations, and day names. Time format options include AM/PM, the display of seconds, and normal versus military (24-hour) time. The various number format options produce the following results:

- *General.* Displays numbers without commas and shows the number of decimal places entered (or required by a calculation).

- *Currency.* Displays a dollar sign and two decimal places, as in $19.81. (You can change the display of commas, negative amounts, and number of decimal places with the Commas, Negatives, and Precision options.)

- *Percent.* Adds a percent sign as a suffix and multiplies the field's contents by 100 (for example, 0.1235 x 100 is 12.35%). The Precision setting determines the number of decimal places.

- *Scientific.* Uses exponential notation, as in 1.245e+3 (for 1,245), which is useful for displaying very large or small numbers.

- *Fixed.* Rounds the results to the number of decimal places that are shown in the Precision text-edit box, as in 21.433 (for a precision setting of 3).

- *Commas.* Inserts commas every three digits, as in 18,221.

- *Negatives in ().* Surrounds numbers less than zero with parentheses, as in (24), instead of using a minus sign.

- *Precision.* Sets the number of decimal places to be shown.

Steps:	Creating Field Borders

Step 1. At the bottom of the Layout menu, choose the layout in which you want to work.

Step 2. Choose Layout from the Layout menu (or press Shift-⌘-L).

Step 3. Using the pointer tool, select the fields to which you want to add a border.

Step 4. In the Tool palette, set the pen pattern to opaque. You also can select a different pen color and a line width. After you change to Browse mode (Shift-⌘-B), the fields appear with a border.

Adding and Deleting Fields from a Layout

As mentioned earlier, you can have as many or as few fields in each layout as you like. You can add fields to any layout that doesn't already display every defined field, and you can remove unnecessary fields.

Steps: **Adding a Field to a Layout**

Step 1.   At the bottom of the Layout menu, choose the layout to which you want to add a field.

Step 2.   Choose Layout from the Layout menu (or press Shift-⌘-L).

Step 3.   Choose Insert Field from the Layout menu. The Insert Field dialog box appears, as shown in Figure 5-28. Its list box contains only the defined fields that are not already in use in the current layout.

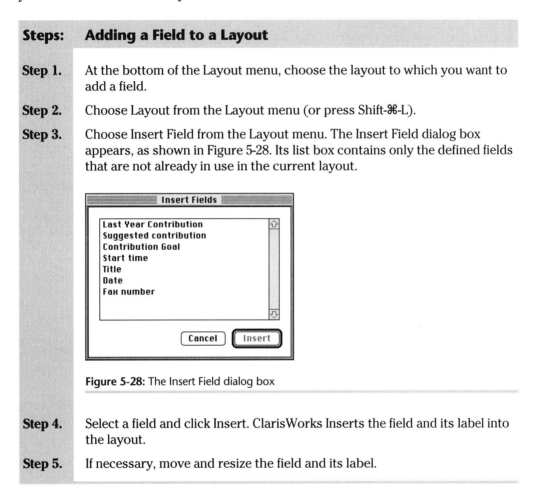

Figure 5-28: The Insert Field dialog box

Step 4.   Select a field and click Insert. ClarisWorks Inserts the field and its label into the layout.

Step 5.   If necessary, move and resize the field and its label.

Steps:	**Removing a Field from a Layout**
Step 1.	At the bottom of the Layout menu, choose the layout from which you want to remove a field.
Step 2.	Choose Layout from the Layout menu (or press Shift-⌘-L).
Step 3.	Use the pointer tool to select the fields that you want to remove from the layout.
Step 4.	Press Delete, or choose Clear or Cut (⌘-X) from the Edit menu. ClarisWorks removes the field or fields from the layout.

Removing a field from a layout is not the same as *deleting* the field. Removing a field from a layout does nothing to the data in the field. The field can still appear in other layouts with its data securely intact. And if you insert the field back into a layout, its data reappears. On the other hand, after you delete a field in the Define Database Fields dialog box (Shift-⌘-D), ClarisWorks removes the field from all layouts and permanently deletes the field's data from the database. Recreating that field will not bring back its data.

Deleting a Layout

You can delete any layout that you no longer want to use.

Steps:	**Deleting Layouts**
Step 1.	Choose Edit Layouts from the Layout menu or from the Layouts pop-up in the Tool panel. The Edit Layouts dialog box appears, as shown in Figure 5-29.

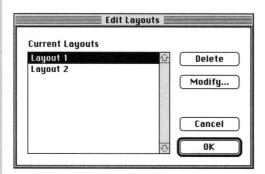

Figure 5-29: The Edit Layouts dialog box

Step 2. Choose the layout by name from the Current Layouts list.

Step 3. Click Delete. A dialog box appears and asks whether you want to *Permanently delete this layout?* Click OK to delete the layout or click Cancel to leave it intact.

A layout can only be deleted if two or more layouts are currently defined. ClarisWorks will not allow you to delete the *only* layout for a database. Thus, if you want to eliminate the original layout, you first have to create at least one additional layout.

Deleting a layout does not delete the fields that you defined for the database or any of the data that appeared in the layout. It merely eliminates one possible view or arrangement of the data. To delete a field, select the field in the Define Database Fields dialog box (Shift-⌘-D) and then click the Delete button. To delete data, remove it from the record or delete the record.

Layout Modification Options

You can assign a new name to a layout, specify the number of columns that will appear in Page View, and close up the space between fields when printing (which is particularly useful for labels).

Steps: Modifying a Layout

Step 1. Choose Edit Layouts from the Layout menu or from the Layout pop-up in the Tool panel. Select the name of the layout you want to change and click modify. The Layout Info dialog box appears, as shown in Figure 5-30.

```
┌─────────────────── Layout Info ───────────────────┐
│                                                    │
│   Name │Layout 2│      ┌─Slide Objects ─────────┐ │
│                         │ Select to remove space  │ │
│   ┌─Columns ──────────┐│ between objects when    │ │
│   │ Number of    │ 1 │ │ printing.               │ │
│   │ ○ Across first     ││                         │ │
│   │ ● Down first       ││ ☐ Slide objects left    │ │
│   └────────────────────┘│ ☐ Slide objects up      │ │
│                         └─────────────────────────┘ │
│                              ┌────────┐ ┌────────┐  │
│                              │ Cancel │ │  OK   │  │
│                              └────────┘ └────────┘  │
└────────────────────────────────────────────────────┘
```

Figure 5-30: Use the Layout Info dialog box to choose optional settings for the current layout.

Step 2. *Optional*: Enter a new name for the layout by typing it in the Name text-edit box.

Step 3. *Optional*: In the Columns section of the dialog box, set the number of columns to be displayed in reports and on-screen (in Page View only) by typing a number in the Number of text-edit box. Then click a radio button (Across first or Down first) to indicate the order in which records will be displayed in the columns.

Step 4. *Optional*: Use the Slide Objects section to close up space between fields and/or lines when printing. This option is often useful for labels. The Slide objects left check box closes up space between objects on the same line. For example, the address line

```
        Bemidji       , MN   56601
```

would print as

```
        Bemidji, MN 56601
```

The Slide objects up check box eliminates blank lines in records. When you print an address label layout that contains fields arranged in five lines (1 – name; 2 – company name; 3 – first address line; 4 – second address line; and 5 – city, state, and ZIP code), labels that contain only one address line or no company name print without blank lines in those spots.

To make sure objects slide left, they must have the tops of the fields aligned.

Step 5. Click OK to accept the layout options and return to the database.

Setting a Tab Order

You can use the Tab key to move from field to field when you are entering data. The Tab Order command enables you to set a new order for navigating between fields when you press Tab.

By default, ClarisWorks sets the tab order for a database to match the order in which you created the fields. If you have altered the default layout by rearranging fields on-screen, the tab order may cause the cursor to jump willy-nilly all over the screen. You can change the tab order so that the cursor moves more efficiently.

Steps: **Setting a New Tab Order**

Step 1. At the bottom of the Layout menu, choose the layout for which you want to specify a new tab order.

Step 2. Choose Layout from the Layout menu (or press Shift-⌘-L).

Step 3. Choose Tab Order from the Layout menu. The Tab Order dialog box shown in Figure 5-31 appears. The current (or default) tab order is shown in the Tab Order list box on the right side of the dialog box.

Figure 5-31: The Tab Order dialog box

Step 4. To create a tab order from scratch, click Clear. ClarisWorks clears the Tab Order list box.

Step 5. To specify the new order, choose a field name from the Field List and click Move (or double-click the field name). The program adds the field to the bottom of the Tab Order list. Continue selecting fields, in the order you prefer, until you have copied all of the desired fields into the Tab Order list.

 You also can Shift-Click to choose several contiguous field names simultaneously or ⌘-Click to choose several non-contiguous field names.

 If you don't want users to be able to tab into some fields, leave those fields out of the list. When a user is in Browse mode, a press of the Tab key skips right over the fields. Note, however, that users can still enter data in those fields by clicking in them (unless, of course, the fields are calculation, summary, or record info fields). Note, too, that settings in the Tab Order dialog box have no effect on a database when it is in List mode.

Browse and List Modes: Viewing, Entering, and Editing Data _____

After you have designed a database and created layouts, you will spend most of your time in Browse and List modes — entering, editing, and viewing the data.

 List mode is a new feature of ClarisWorks 4.0. It displays the database in a spreadsheet-like grid, where each row is a record and each column is a field. Unlike a normal layout — which only displays the fields that you have placed in that layout — List mode presents *every* field that has been defined for the database. Regardless of the layout you were previously viewing, when you change to List mode, the arrangement of data is always the same.

Any database can be viewed in List mode by choosing List from the Layout menu or by pressing Shift-⌘-I. You can learn about List mode later in this section.

Browse Mode

Whether you need to enter and edit data or just want to flip through records, you can use Browse mode (choose Browse from the Layout menu or press Shift-⌘-B). The advantage of using Browse mode — as opposed to List mode — is that you can display your data in any layout that you've designed for a database, so you can restrict the set of fields to only those you need at the moment. To select a layout in which to work, choose its name from the bottom of the Layout menu.

Viewing Records

When working on and viewing records in Browse mode, records can be displayed in any of three ways:

- ⇨ Continuous scrolling list (choose Show Multiple from the Layout menu)
- ⇨ One record per screen (remove the check mark from the Show Multiple command in the Layout menu)
- ⇨ Only as many records as can fit on the current page size as defined in the Page Setup dialog box (choose Page View from the View menu)

 Viewing records in Page View shows exactly how the records will appear when printed. Page View is equivalent to choosing a Print Preview command in many other Macintosh programs

Adding and Deleting Records

To create a new record for the current database, choose New Record from the Edit menu (or press ⌘-R). The new record appears with the text insertion point in the first field. The database automatically switches to Browse mode.

The following instructions describe how to delete a record.

Steps:	Deleting a Record
Step 1.	Select the record by clicking any place in the record *other than inside a field*. To show that the record is selected, ClarisWorks highlights the entire record.
Step 2.	Choose Delete Record, Cut, or Clear from the Edit menu. ClarisWorks removes the record from the database.

Entering and Editing Data

When a new record appears on-screen in Browse mode, the cursor automatically appears in the first field (or in the field which you set as first with the Tab Order command). Complete the field and then press the Tab key to move to the next field. You also can move directly to any field by clicking it with the mouse. Note, however, that you cannot click in or tab to a field that does not allow user input — namely, calculation, summary, and record info fields.

You edit data in exactly the same manner as in any other text-oriented environment. After entering Browse mode (Shift-⌘-B) and tabbing or clicking into a field, you use normal editing techniques to add to, delete, or alter the information in any field.

If a record is substantially similar to an existing record, you can save typing time by creating a duplicate of the existing record and then making the necessary editing changes to the duplicate. To create a duplicate record, select the record and then choose Duplicate Record from the Edit menu (or press ⌘-D).

Navigating Among Records

You can move among the database records in Browse mode in a number of ways. The following options are available:

∽ *To move to the next or preceding record,* click the bottom or top page of the book icon (see Figure 5-32). In normal view, this action moves to the next or previous record. In Page View, it merely scrolls the records in the appropriate direction.

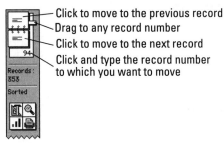

Figure 5-32:
The book icon

Click to move to the previous record
Drag to any record number
Click to move to the next record
Click and type the record number
to which you want to move

∽ *To move to the next or previous record while leaving the cursor in the same field,* press ⌘-Return or Shift-⌘-Return, respectively.

∽ *To move to a specific record (by number),* drag the tab on the right side of the book icon until you see the record number; choose Go To Record from the Organize menu (or press ⌘-G); or click once to select the record number at the bottom of the book icon, type a record number, and press Return or Enter.

∽ *To move up or down through the records*, use the scroll bar at the right side of the database window or press Page Up or Page Down (if your keyboard has these keys).

∽ *To move to a specific page of the database*, double-click the page number indicator at the bottom of the database window (you have to be in Page View). The Go to page dialog box appears. Type a page number and click OK.

∽ *To move to the beginning or end of the database*, press the Home or End keys (if your keyboard has these keys), or drag the tag on the right side of the book icon until you reach the top or the bottom.

List Mode

Everything that you can do in Browse mode can also be done in List mode, such as entering and editing data, and adding and deleting records. Working in List mode is a lot like using a spreadsheet — each row represents a single record, while each column is a single field. In normal view, fields are displayed in a continuous list that you can scroll to the right and left. In Page View (choose Page View from the View menu), columns are separated by page breaks.

As the example in Figure 5-33 shows, all field types are displayed normally in List mode. You can still choose options from pop-up menu fields and value list fields, and you can make checks in check box fields.

Currently selected field   Field names   Records

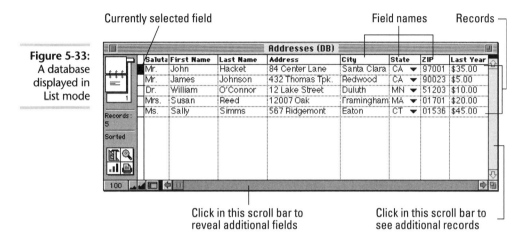

Figure 5-33:
A database
displayed in
List mode

Click in this scroll bar to   Click in this scroll bar to
reveal additional fields   see additional records

Here are some other things you can do in List mode:

∞ *Change column widths and record heights.* To change the width of a column, move the pointer into the column label area until it is over the right edge of the column whose width you want to change. The pointer changes to a tall double-arrow. Click and drag to change the column's width.

To change the height of any record, move the pointer into the area to the left of the first field for the record. The pointer changes to a tall double-arrow. When the pointer is over the bottom edge of the record of interest, click and drag to change the height of the record.

∞ *Move columns.* To move a column to a new position, move the pointer into the area just above the column of interest. The pointer changes to a short double-arrow. Click and then drag the column to a new position. Release the mouse button to complete the move.

∞ *Change the format of an entire column.* Double-click the column name. Depending on the field type of the column, the Text Style, Number Format, Date Format, or Time Format dialog box appears. Set options and click OK. Alternatively, you can select the column and then choose options from the Format menu.

You may occasionally find it necessary to select individual or multiple rows or columns. To select an individual row or column, click in the area to the left of the row or in the column label.

To select several records (in order to format, hide, or delete them all at the same time, for example), select one and then Shift-click to select the others. To select multiple non-contiguous records, hold down the ⌘ key as you click in each record. To select multiple columns (fields), Shift-click as you select the columns.

You cannot select non-contiguous columns.

Finding and Selecting Records

Flipping through a database one record at a time is the hard way to find specific information. ClarisWorks has two different commands that you can use to find and select records, based on criteria that you supply. You use the Find command to restrict displayed records to a particular subset (the program temporarily hides all other records). For example, you may want to look only at records in which State equals Ohio. The Match Records command leaves all records visible and simply selects (highlights) those records that match the criteria.

ClarisWorks 4.0. enables you to save search criteria so that you can easily re-execute the search again whenever you like. Saved searches can also be used to create reports in the new database report generator. Instructions for saving and reusing search criteria are presented later in this chapter.

Using the Find Command

To use the Find command, you type search criteria on a blank copy of a record that appears when you issue the Find command. To find an exact or partial match, you simply type the text or number that you want to search for in the appropriate field. To find all address records for people whose last name contains the string *Sch,* for example, you type **Sch** in the Last Name field. In this type of search, the program considers a record a match if it contains the string *anywhere within the field,* not just at the beginning of the field.

You also can use logical operators to specify search criteria, as described in Table 5-1.

Table 5-1
Logical Search Operators

Operator	Meaning	Examples
=	Find records that exactly match the contents of this field.	(=435; =18 Apple Street)
<	Find records that are numerically or alphabetically less than this value.	(<100; <S)
>	Find records that are numerically or alphabetically greater than this value.	(>180; >Bob)
≤ (Option-<)	Find records that are numerically or alphabetically less than or equal to this value.	(≤2000; ≤D)
≥ (Option->)	Find records that are numerically or alphabetically greater than or equal to this value.	(≥4/19/93; ≥3000)
<>	Find records that are not equal to this value.	(<>10; <>CA; <>11:15)

 You can search for blank database fields by entering only an equal sign (=) in a field.

Steps: Finding Records

Step 1. At the bottom of the Layout menu, choose the layout that you want to use as a search template. (Be sure that the fields that you intend to use as criteria appear in the layout.)

Step 2. Choose the Find command from the Layout menu (or press Shift-⌘-F). A screen with a blank record appears, as shown in Figure 5-34.

Step 3. Type the search criteria into the appropriate fields.

Step 4. *Optional*: If you want to find all records that do *not* match the search criteria, click the Omit check box.

Step 5. Click the All radio button to search the entire database or click Visible to search only records that are visible; that is, the ones that are not currently hidden. ClarisWorks conducts the search. It displays matching records and hides all others.

Search controls

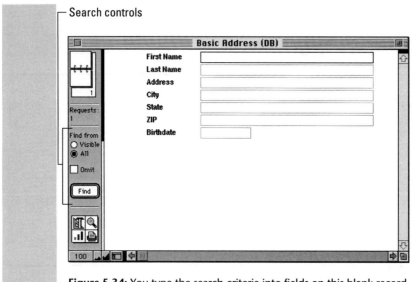

Figure 5-34: You type the search criteria into fields on this blank record.

 After you're through examining the records that match the criteria, you can make the entire database visible again by choosing Show All Records (Shift-⌘-A) from the Organize menu.

When you specify multiple criteria in a single Find request, you are conducting an *AND* search. In an AND search, ClarisWorks finds only records that satisfy all the criteria. For example, entering **Santa Clara** for the city and **CA** for the state identifies only the address records for people who come from Santa Clara, California. It does not find records for people from other California cities or from cities named Santa Clara in other states.

Sometimes, you may want to conduct an OR search — in which the program finds a record if the record matches any one of several criteria. To conduct this type of search, you have to issue multiple Find requests.

Steps: Conducting an OR Search

Step 1.   At the bottom of the Layout menu, choose the layout that you want to use as a search template. (Be sure that the fields that you intend to use as criteria appear in the layout.)

Step 2. Choose the Find command from the Layout menu (or press Shift-⌘-F). A screen with a blank record appears.

Step 3. Enter a set of search criteria in the record.

Step 4. Before clicking the All or Visible buttons, choose New Request from the Edit menu (or press ⌘-R). Another blank record appears, as shown in Figure 5-35.

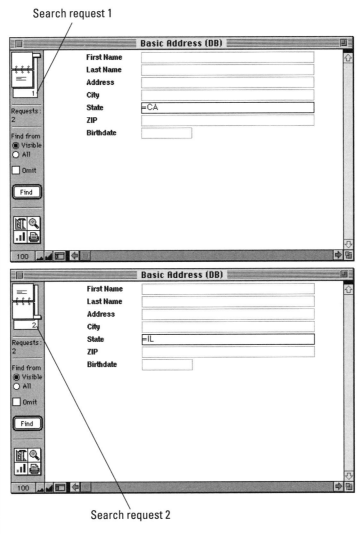

Figure 5-35: This pair of search requests identifies all records in which State equals **CA** (California) or State equals **IL** (Illinois).

Step 5.   Enter the next set of search criteria in the new record.

Step 6.   Repeat Steps 4 and 5 for each additional set of criteria that you want to impose.

Step 7.   Click All to search the entire database or click Visible to search only the records that are visible; that is, the ones that are not currently hidden.

Step 8.   Click Find. The search is conducted. Records that satisfy any of the search requests are displayed and all others are hidden.

You can issue a Find command from any layout, as long as the fields on which you want to base the search are present. Some layouts, however, are easier to search from than others. A layout that is designed to print mailing labels, for example, makes the task more difficult because the fields are not labeled. Change to a better layout by selecting a layout from the bottom of the Layout menu before initiating the search. After the program finds the records, you can change back to the original layout to view or print the records.

Creating a Named Search

Although some Find requests are issued once and then never again (when you are searching for a particular record, for example), it's not uncommon to discover that you are manually recreating many of the same Find requests over and over. Whether you are selecting important subsets of data to be used in a report or you simply want to look at all sales in a particular region of the country, ClarisWorks 4.0 has procedures for saving these Find requests and enabling you to instantly re-execute them.

Steps: Saving a Search Request

Step 1.   Choose New Search from the Search pop-up (the magnifying glass) in the Tool panel. The dialog box in Figure 5-36 appears.

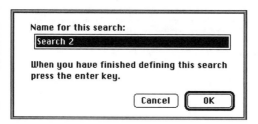

Figure 5-36: This dialog box appears when you create a new search.

Step 2.   Enter a descriptive name for the search, and click OK to continue. A Find request form appears.

Step 3.   Enter the search criteria.

Step 4.   If you need to use additional Find requests, choose New Request from the Edit menu and enter the search criteria.

Step 5.   Click the Store button in the Tool panel or press Enter. The search name is appended to the Search pop-up.

After one or more named searches has been created, there are special procedures for using and modifying the searches.

- *To execute a named search*, choose its name from the Search pop-up.

- *To rename a named search*, choose Edit Searches from the Search pop-up, choose the named search from the Edit Searches dialog box (shown in Figure 5-37), click Modify, type a new name for the search, and click OK twice to dismiss the two dialog boxes.

- *To delete a named search*, choose Edit Searches from the Search pop-up, choose the search you wish to eliminate from the Edit Searches dialog box (shown in Figure 5-37), click Delete, and then click OK.

- *To edit the Find criteria associated with a named search*, change to Find mode (choose Find from the Layout menu or press Shift-⌘-F), choose the named search from the Search pop-up, modify the search criteria, and then click Store or press Enter.

Figure 5-37:
The Edit Searches
dialog box

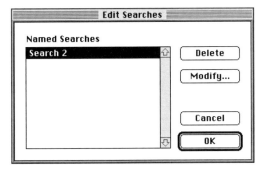

There's one general type of named search that you may want to add to every database you make — I call it the "All" search. Instead of trying to remember the command for Show All Records, just create a named search called All or All Records that finds all records in the database. In the Find request form, leave all the fields blank and click the Find from All radio button in the Tool panel.

Using the Match Records Command

The Find command is intended for simple searches. If you want to perform a more complex search, you may prefer to use the Match Records feature. A Match Records search selects (highlights) all records that meet the criteria, but it leaves the other records on-screen. Because the records are selected (highlighted), using Match Records is an ideal way to identify and delete records that you no longer need.

Steps:	**Selecting Matching Records**

Step 1. Choose Match Records from the Organize menu (or press ⌘-M). The Enter Match Records Condition dialog box appears, as shown in Figure 5-38. It is identical to the dialog box that you use to define a formula for a calculation field or a summary field.

```
╔══════════════ Enter Match Records Condition ══════════════╗

  Fields              Operators      Function
  ┌──────────────┐    ┌─────────┐    ┌──────────────────────────┐
  │ First Name ⇧ │    │ +    ⇧  │    │ ABS(number)           ⇧  │
  │ Last Name    │    │ -       │    │ ACOS(number)             │
  │ Address      │    │ *       │    │ AND(logical1,logical2,…) │
  │ City         │    │ /       │    │ ASIN(number)             │
  │ State        │    │ =       │    │ ATAN(number)             │
  │ ZIP          │    │ >       │    │ ATAN2(x number,y number) │
  │ Salutation ⇩ │    │ <    ⇩  │    │ AVERAGE(number1,number2,…)⇩│
  └──────────────┘    └─────────┘    └──────────────────────────┘

  Formula
  ┌──────────────────────────────────────────────────────────┐
  │ AND('ZIP'>80000,'ZIP'<90000)                             │
  └──────────────────────────────────────────────────────────┘

                              ( Cancel )   ║  OK  ║
╚══════════════════════════════════════════════════════════╝
```

Figure 5-38: Use this dialog box to specify the search conditions formula.

Step 2. Enter the match formula in the Formula text-edit box. You can create formulas by typing them into the box; by selecting fields, operators, and functions from the three scrolling list boxes (click an option to insert it into the formula at the text insertion point); or by combining the two approaches. Field names must be enclosed in single quotes (') and text strings in double quotes ("). The formula shown in Figure 6-36 instructs ClarisWorks to select all records with ZIP codes that are greater than 80000 and less than 90000.

Step 3. Click OK. ClarisWorks evaluates the formula. If it finds an error, it displays the message *Bad formula.* Otherwise, highlights the records that match the formula.

After using the Match Records command to select a set of records, you can use two additional commands from the Organize menu to help you focus your attention on the new record subset: Hide Selected (⌘-left parenthesis) and Hide Unselected (⌘-right parenthesis). Hide Unselected has the same effect as the normal Find command. It hides all records that do not match the Match Records formula; that is, the ones that were not selected. Hide Selected has the same effect as a Find command with the Omit check box checked — it displays only those records that were not selected.

You also can use the Hide Selected and Hide Unselected commands after you manually select records. To select a single record, click anywhere in the record except in a field. To select multiple contiguous records, hold down the Shift key as you select the records. To select non-contiguous records, hold down the ⌘ key as you select the records.

Perhaps the most important reason for using the Match Records command is because you want to do something to all members of the selected (or unselected group). You can view them in context in Browse or List mode (viewing the records of all employees who have not had raises in the last two years, for example).

You can also use Match Records to help purge the database of unwanted records. For instance, you may want to eliminate all invoice records that are more than three years old. After using Match Records to identify the correct records, choose Delete Records from the Edit menu.

 Use the Delete Records command with great care. The effects of Delete Records cannot be reversed by choosing Undo. The only ways to recover from an accidental record deletion are to use the Revert command (in the File menu) to restore the database to the most recent saved version of the file or to close the file without saving your changes.

Changing the Display Order of Records

You can change the order in which records are displayed by sorting them by the contents of one or several fields. You can do an ascending (A to Z) or descending (Z to A) sort for each sort field. ClarisWorks sorts the database once for each sort field, using the order in which you selected the sort fields. Sorting changes the order of records in the database for all layouts, not just for the one that is currently displayed.

Steps:	Sorting Records

Step 1. Choose Sort Records from the Organize menu (or press ⌘-J). The Sort Records dialog box appears, as shown in Figure 5-39. (If you have sorted the database previously, the program displays the last sort instructions.)

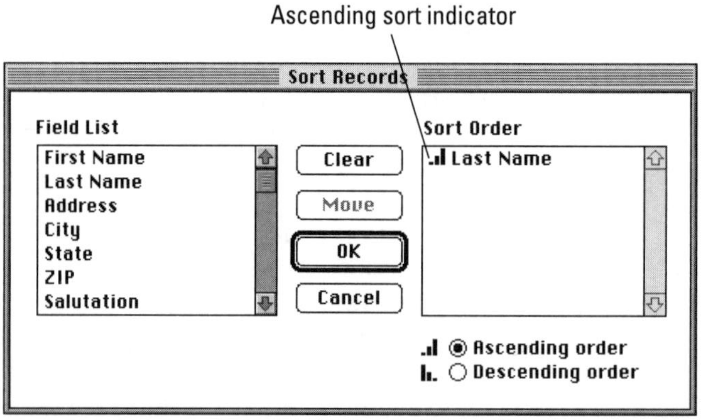

Ascending sort indicator

Sort Records

Field List
- First Name
- Last Name
- Address
- City
- State
- ZIP
- Salutation

Clear
Move
OK
Cancel

Sort Order
.ıl Last Name

.ıl ⦿ Ascending order
lı. ○ Descending order

Figure 5-39: The Sort Records dialog box

Step 2. Choose the first sort field from the list on the left. To add the field to the Sort Order list, click Move or simply double-click the field name in the Field List. ClarisWorks adds the field to the Sort Order list on the right.

If you make a mistake (choosing fields in the wrong order, for example), you can start over by clicking Clear, or you can remove individual fields by selecting them in the Sort Order list and clicking Move.

Step 3. To specify an ascending or descending sort for each chosen field, select it in the Sort Order list and then click the Ascending order or Descending order radio button.

Alternatively, you can specify an ascending or descending order sort by clicking the appropriate radio button *before* moving the field into the Sort Order list.

Step 4. Choose additional sort fields by repeating Steps 2 and 3, as required.

Step 5. Click OK to execute the sort instructions. The program displays the records in the new order.

If the layout has sub-summary fields, you have to sort the database by the designated sort field if you want the summary information to be displayed. For example, if you have created a sub-summary when sorted by Last Name, you must sort by Last Name. See "Summary Fields," earlier in this chapter, for more information.

ClarisWorks 4.0. enables you to save sort criteria so that you can easily re-execute the sort whenever you like. Named (saved) sorts also can be used to create reports in the new report generator (discussed in "Creating and Using Named Reports," later in this chapter).

Steps: Creating Named Sorts

Step 1. Choose New Sort from the Sort pop-up (the three rising bars) in the Tool panel. The Sort Records dialog box appears, as shown in Figure 5-40.

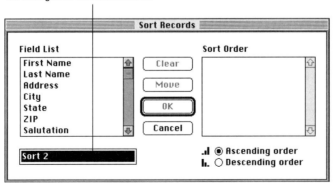

Figure **5-40:** This Sort Records dialog box differs from the normal one only in that it has a text-edit box at the bottom in which you can name the sort.

Step 2.	Enter a descriptive name for the sort.
Step 3.	Select the sort fields and set ascending or descending order for each one.
Step 4.	Click OK. The sort name is appended to the Sort pop-up's menu.

After one or more named sorts has been created, there are special procedures for using and modifying the sorts.

- *To execute a named sort*, choose its name from the Sort pop-up.

- *To rename or edit a named sort*, choose Edit Sorts from the Sort pop-up, choose the sort from the Edit sorts dialog box (shown in Figure 5-41), and click Modify. The Sort Records dialog box appears (previously shown in Figure 5-40). Type a new name for the sort and/or modify the sort instructions, and then click OK twice to dismiss the two dialog boxes.

- *To delete a named sort*, choose Edit Sorts from the Sort pop-up, select the name of the sort you wish to eliminate from the Edit Sorts dialog box (shown in Figure 5-41), click Delete, and then click OK.

Figure 5-41:
The Edit Sorts
dialog box

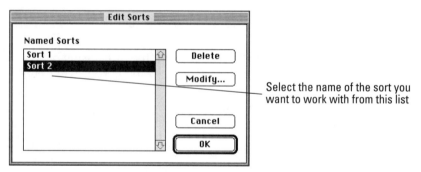

Select the name of the sort you
want to work with from this list

Creating Reports

One of the main reasons for building a database is the ease with which you can create custom reports and mailing labels. Although you can print any layout, creating special layouts for reports often makes more sense, especially if you create layouts that show the particular fields and summary information that you require, organized in a manner that makes sense for a report.

In ClarisWorks 4.0, you can select report elements — including sort instructions, record selection criteria, and the appropriate layout — and save them as a custom report. Details are provided later in this chapter.

Adding Headers and Footers

You can add a header and a footer to a database layout. A header or footer appears in every report page and can be used to include a title or page numbers, for example.

Steps:	Creating a Header or a Footer
Step 1.	At the bottom of the Layout menu, choose the layout to which you want to add a header or footer.
Step 2.	Choose Layout from the Layout menu (or press Shift-⌘-L).
Step 3.	Choose Insert Part from the Layout menu. The Insert Part dialog box appears.
Step 4.	Click the Header or Footer radio button and then click OK. A header or footer area is inserted at the top (header) or bottom (footer) of the current layout.
Step 5.	Add graphics or text in the header or footer area. Whatever you insert will appear in that position at the top or bottom of every page. To see how the header or footer will look when printed, change to Browse mode (Shift-⌘-B) and choose Page View (Shift-⌘-P) from the View menu.

Headers and footers frequently include a report date and page numbers. To add automatic page numbering (so that page numbers increment by one for each new page) and date- or time-stamping, select the appropriate layout, change to Layout mode, select the text tool, click the spot in the header or footer where you want to place the element, and then choose Insert Page #, Insert Date, or Insert Time from the Edit menu. You should note, however, that every time you open the database, the date or time change to match the current date or time. If you want to insert today's date or the current time and make sure that it does not change, press the Option key when you choose Insert Date or Insert Time.

Calculating Summary and Sub-Summary Information

By creating summary fields and adding them to a layout, you can calculate statistics that span the entire database or that summarize data based on record groupings (generating subtotals for each type of household expense, for example). Summary information can come at the beginning or end of a report or be displayed at the break between each group of records. And you aren't restricted to just totals. You can use any formula that you like, as well as take advantage of the dozens of database functions that ClarisWorks offers. For instructions for adding summary and sub-summary fields to a database, see "Summary Fields," earlier in this chapter.

Creating and Using Named Reports

Using the Report pop-up in the Tool panel, you can save reporting options and later reuse them to quickly produce complex reports.

To create a named report, choose New Report from the Report pop-up in the Tool panel. The New Report dialog box appears, as shown in Figure 5-42.

Figure 5-42:
The New Report dialog box

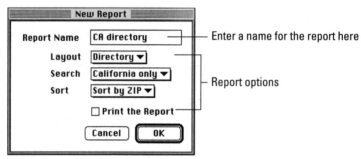

As you can see in the figure, creating a report consists of the following tasks:

- ∞ Naming the report (in the Report Name text-edit box)
- ∞ Choosing a layout for the report, search criteria, and sort instructions
- ∞ Deciding whether or not the report should automatically be printed

Layout choices are restricted to the names of existing layouts, List mode, and None. Search and sort criteria are limited to None or existing named searches and sorts that have been saved for the database. After making your choices, click OK. The name of the new report is added to the Report pop-up for the database.

To produce a named report, choose its name from the Report pop-up in the Tool panel. The database instantly changes to the selected layout and executes the designated search and sort instructions, if any. If you also clicked the Print the Report check box in the New Report dialog box, a standard Print dialog box appears. Turn on your printer, change options in the dialog box (if necessary), and click the Print button.

To modify any of the elements of the report, choose Edit Reports from the Report pop-up, select the name of the report in the Named Reports dialog box that appears, click Modify, make the changes, and then click OK twice to dismiss the dialog boxes.

To delete a report, choose Edit Reports from the Report pop-up, select the name of the report in the Named Reports dialog box that appears, click Delete, and then click OK.

Working with Mailing Labels

Although you can design your own layouts for printing labels, ClarisWorks comes with more than 50 predefined layouts for popular Avery label formats. And if you don't find a layout to match the size of labels that you use, you can easily create a custom layout.

Steps:	Using a Predefined Label Layout
Step 1.	Choose New Layout from the Layout menu or the Layout pop-up in the Tool panel. The New Layout dialog box appears.
Step 2.	Click the Labels radio button and then click its pop-up menu. A list of the supported label formats pops up. (If you aren't using an Avery label, measure your label and match it to the equivalent Avery label format or create a custom label layout by following the instructions in "Steps: Creating a Custom Label Layout.")
Step 3.	Choose a label format and click OK. The Set Field Order dialog box appears, as shown in Figure 5-43.

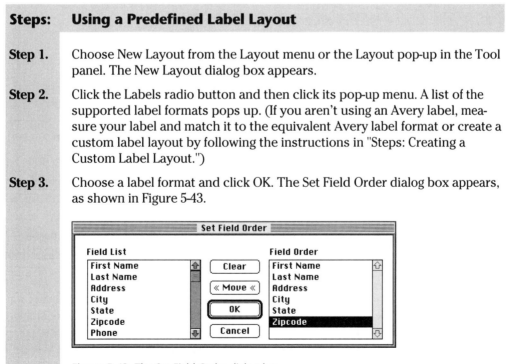

Figure 5-43: The Set Field Order dialog box

Step 4. Select fields in the order in which you want them to appear in the labels and click Move to transfer each field to the Field Order list box.

Step 5. Click OK. The label layout appears.

In Step 1, if you chose New Layout from the Layout pop-up rather than choosing this command from the Layout menu, you will now be in Browse mode. Change to Layout mode by choosing Layout from the Layout menu.

Step 6. Resize and move the fields to correspond with the way they should appear on the labels. Figure 5-44 shows a typical layout after editing.

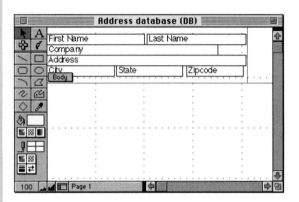

Figure 5-44: A sample label layout

Step 7. If you want an idea of how the labels will look, choose Browse from the Layout menu (or press Shift-⌘-B). Make sure that Page View (Shift-⌘-P) is also in effect. (Note that the space between fields, as well as blank lines, will be closed up when you print the labels but not when you view them on-screen.)

As an alternative, you can create a new view, tile windows, and have one view in Layout mode and one in Browse mode — giving instant feedback.

ClarisWorks has unusual requirements that you need to adhere to when you are attempting to close up space during printing. These requirements apply not only to labels but also to any other type of database layout:

↪ *Objects do not slide toward other objects that are smaller than they are.* In order for a field to slide left, therefore, the field to the left must be exactly the same size or larger than the sliding field. Also, the top edges must be aligned if the fields are on the same line. The left edges must be aligned if fields are stacked one above the other (on different lines).

To check the dimensions of each field, choose Object Info from the Options menu and then click each field. The Info palette lists each field's distance from the margins, as well as its height and width. See Chapter 6 for information on using the Info palette to set the dimensions of an object.

↝ Fields will not slide at all if their edges are touching on the layout.

Also, if you are using a laser printer, you should note that the printer cannot print on the entire page. Most laser printers require a minimum margin of 0.2 to 0.25 inches all around the page. To ensure that you can print as close to the edges as possible, choose Page Setup from the File menu, click Options, and then click the check box for Larger Print Area (Fewer Downloadable Fonts).

Finally, because of the difficulty of getting text to align perfectly on labels, you're well advised to print a test page on standard paper and then place the test printout over a page of labels to see how they align. Continue to adjust the fields and make test printouts until the alignment is correct.

If you don't see a predefined label format that matches the labels you want to use, you can create a custom label layout.

Steps:	Creating a Custom Label Layout

Step 1. Choose New Layout from the Layout menu or the Layout pop-up in the Tool panel. The New Layout dialog box appears.

Step 2. Click the Labels radio button and be sure that the Custom option is selected.

Step 3. Enter a descriptive name for the label layout in the Name text-edit box and click OK. The Label Layout dialog box appears, as shown in Figure 5-45.

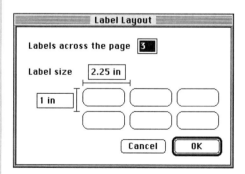

Figure 5-45: The Label Layout dialog box

Step 4.   Enter the number of labels across (enter 3 for a page with three labels across it, for example) and the dimensions for a single label, and then click OK. The Set Field Order dialog box appears (see Figure 5-43).

You measure the width of a label from the left edge of the first label to the left edge of the next label. Similarly, you measure label height from the top of one label to the top of the label below it. That is, the gaps that follow each label to the right and below are considered part of the label's size.

Step 5.   Select the fields that you want to appear on the labels, click the Move button to transfer them to the Field Order list, and click OK. The new layout appears.

In Step 1, if you chose New Layout from the Layout pop-up rather than choosing this command from the Layout menu, you will now be in Browse mode. Change to Layout mode by choosing Layout from the Layout menu.

Step 6.   Resize and move the fields to correspond with the way they should appear on the labels. The initial placement of the Body dividing line is correct for the size of label that is specified. Do not move it and be sure that all fields stay within its boundaries.

Step 7.   If you want an idea of how the labels will look, choose Browse from the Layout menu (or press Shift-⌘-B). Make sure that Page View (Shift-⌘-P) is also in effect. (Note that the space between fields, as well as blank lines, will be closed up when you print the labels but not when you view them on-screen.)

If you want to eliminate some of fuss and muss of creating mailing labels, you may want to use the new Create Labels Assistant. From any appropriate database, choose ClarisWorks Assistants from the Balloon Help menu, and then choose Create Labels. Follow the steps in the series of dialog boxes that are presented. When you are finished, the Assistant generates a new label layout that matches the specifications you just entered.

Creating and Saving Custom Label Definitions

All permanent label layout definitions are stored in a text file named ClarisWorks Labels. By editing this file, you can add your own custom label definitions, as well as change the names of existing layouts (Diskette Label — 3-up, rather than Avery 5096, 5196, 5896, for example). After you make the changes to the file, you can choose your own label definitions from the Labels pop-up menu in the New Layout dialog box.

To create a new label definition:

1. Locate the ClarisWorks Labels file. It is inside the Claris folder, which is inside the System Folder on the start-up hard disk.

2. Select the ClarisWorks Labels icon and choose Duplicate from the Finder's File menu (or press ⌘-D). The file is copied and named ClarisWorks Labels Copy. Making a duplicate protects the original file.

3. To protect the original ClarisWorks Labels file, change its name (to **ClarisWorks Labels.bak**, for example). Keep it as a backup copy in case you have problems with the editing.

4. Load the duplicate copy of the ClarisWorks Labels file into ClarisWorks using the Open command. The file is loaded and converted from plain text to ClarisWorks format. The figure shows the contents of the ClarisWorks Labels file.

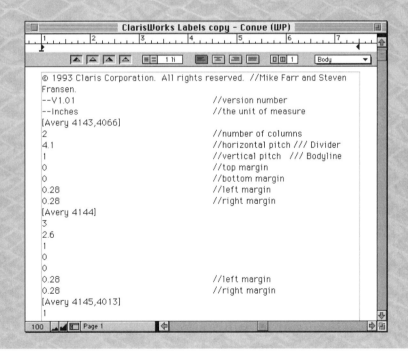

```
ClarisWorks Labels copy - Conve (WP)

© 1993 Claris Corporation. All rights reserved. //Mike Farr and Steven
Fransen.
--V1.01                        //version number
--Inches                       //the unit of measure
[Avery 4143,4066]
2                              //number of columns
4.1                            //horizontal pitch /// Divider
1                              //vertical pitch   /// Bodyline
0                              //top margin
0                              //bottom margin
0.28                           //left margin
0.28                           //right margin
[Avery 4144]
3
2.6
1
0
0
0.28                           //left margin
0.28                           //right margin
[Avery 4145,4013]
1
```

As you can see in the figure, every label definition consists of eight lines: the label name enclosed in brackets, the number of columns, the horizontal pitch (label width), the vertical pitch (label height), the top margin, the bottom margin, the left margin, and the right margin. (Ignore any information that is preceded by two or more slashes [//]; it is a comment.)

5. Use one of the existing label definitions as a template for designing a new label. Select any 8-line segment, starting with a label name and ending with its right margin data. Choose Copy from the Edit menu (or press ⌘-C).

6. Select the spot in the label list where you want to insert the new label definition. You may want to keep your own definitions together — at the end of the list, for example.

7. Place the text insertion marker at the spot where you want to insert the definition and choose Paste from the Edit menu (or press ⌘-V). Be sure that you do not break up an existing definition when you paste the template.

8. Edit the pasted text by entering your own label name within the brackets and replacing the other lines with the number of columns, width, height, top margin, bottom margin, left margin, and right margin for your label.

9. Save the file by choosing the Save As command from the File menu (or pressing Shift-⌘-S). Choose Text in the Save As pop-up menu, click the Document radio button, and type ClarisWorks Labels as the new filename.

10. Quit ClarisWorks. The next time you launch ClarisWorks, the new label layouts will be available.

Changing the name for any of the label layouts is even easier. Simply follow the preceding steps; but, instead of adding an entirely new layout, just change the text string between any pair of brackets to something more meaningful, such as [Audio Cassette — 2-up] rather than [Avery 5198]. After you change the name for a label layout and save the file, the new name appears in the Labels pop-up menu.

Database Printing

To generate a printed database report or other printout from a database, you can just select an appropriate layout and choose Print. However, you can also set other options to make reports and printouts more meaningful. (Every printout can consist of all visible [nonhidden] records or only the currently selected record.)

Steps: Printing from a Database

Step 1.   At the bottom of the Layout menu, choose the layout that you want to use to generate the printout.

Step 2.   Use the Find command (see "Finding and Selecting Records," earlier in this chapter) to select the records that you want to include. If you want to use all of the records, choose Show All Records from the Organize menu (or press Shift-⌘-A).

Step 3.   If you want the records to display in a particular order, sort the records (as described in "Changing the display order of records," earlier in this chapter).

Step 4.   Choose Print from the File menu (or press ⌘-P). The Print dialog box appears, as shown in Figure 5-46.

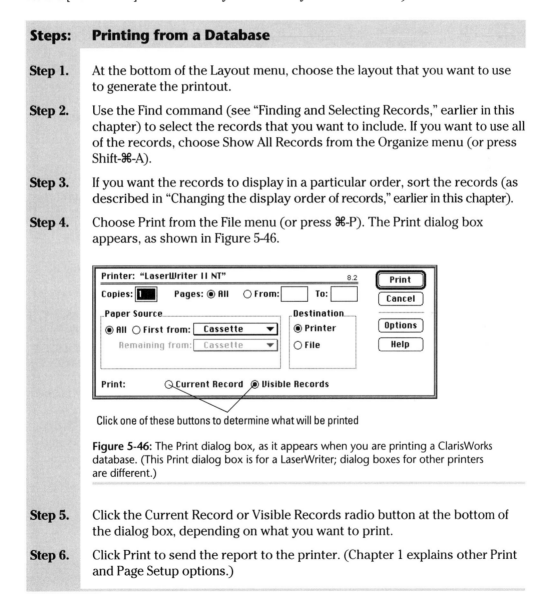

Click one of these buttons to determine what will be printed

Figure 5-46: The Print dialog box, as it appears when you are printing a ClarisWorks database. (This Print dialog box is for a LaserWriter; dialog boxes for other printers are different.)

Step 5.   Click the Current Record or Visible Records radio button at the bottom of the dialog box, depending on what you want to print.

Step 6.   Click Print to send the report to the printer. (Chapter 1 explains other Print and Page Setup options.)

Saving Changes

If you've used FileMaker Pro or any of its earlier incarnations, you've undoubtedly noticed the many features that it shares with the ClarisWorks database environment. One of the major differences, however, is the way that the two programs handle data and layout storage.

FileMaker Pro automatically saves any database changes, whether they are layout modifications or data additions, deletions, or alterations. In fact, FileMaker Pro doesn't even have a Save command. The plus side of this feature is that users never have to worry about whether their changes have been saved. The minus side is that the program saves *all* changes — both deliberate changes and unintentional or ill-advised changes. Unless you have a backup of your important FileMaker files, experimentation can be dangerous.

ClarisWorks, on the other hand, does not have an automatic save feature. You can experiment to your heart's content, secure in the knowledge that you can close the file at any time without saving changes. When you *do* want to save, on the other hand, choose the Save or Save As command from the File menu.

Importing and Exporting Data

Unless you just bought your Mac, you may already have several databases that you designed in other programs. They may be FileMaker Pro or HyperCard databases, or they may be databases that you created in an address book program, a word processor, a spreadsheet, or a desk accessory. You can easily import databases into ClarisWorks.

You use the Insert command in the File menu to add information from other databases into a ClarisWorks database. Instead of reorganizing the source database so that its fields match those of the target ClarisWorks database, you use the Import Field Order dialog box to match fields between the two databases — regardless of their order and whether the databases have the same number of fields. Thus, importing data is easier than ever.

Steps: Importing Information into a ClarisWorks Database

Step 1. In the source program, save or export the data file as a tab-delimited text file. Some programs, such as spreadsheets, may simply call this file a Text file, ASCII Text file, or Text-Only file. See the program's manual for instructions. (In a tab-delimited text file, each record is a separate paragraph. Every field in a record is separated from the next field by a tab character.)

Step 2. Open or create a ClarisWorks database to receive the imported data.

Step 3. In ClarisWorks, choose the Insert command from the File menu, choose the tab-delimited text file created in Step 1, and click Insert. The Import Field Order dialog box appears, as shown in Figure 5-47. The fields in the left side of the dialog box are from the file that you're importing (the source file). The fields on the right are in the ClarisWorks database (the destination file).

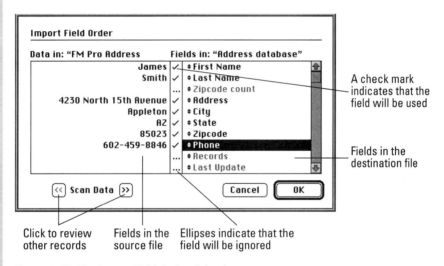

Figure 5-47: The Import Field Order dialog box

Step 4. Drag to rearrange the fields in the right side of the dialog box so that they match the appropriate fields on the left side. Fields with a counterpart that you want to import should have a check mark in front of them. Fields with no counterpart are indicated by ellipses (...) and are not imported. You can click a check mark or ellipses to toggle to the opposite state.

Not every field needs to have a counterpart. You may well have more fields in one database than in the other. No restrictions govern how many or how few fields you can import. If you find, however, that the target ClarisWorks database lacks a key field that the source file possesses, you may want to cancel the import, add the new field to the ClarisWorks database, and then proceed with the import.

Step 5. Using the Scan Data buttons, check several records of the source file to see whether the fields match correctly. If you're satisfied with the matchup, click OK to import the data. The new records are imported into the database.

As with importing data, when you export data from a ClarisWorks database to use in another program, tab-delimited ASCII text is often the best format to use. Virtually every type of Macintosh program (including word processors) can correctly handle such a file. (A tab-delimited text file contains one record per line, and each field in the record is separated from the next field by a tab character.)

Steps:	**Exporting a ClarisWorks Database File**
Step 1.	Open the ClarisWorks database by choosing Open from the File menu (or press ⌘-O).
Step 2.	Choose Save As from the File menu (or press Shift-⌘-S).
Step 3.	Choose ASCII Text from the Save As pop-up menu, click the Document radio button, and enter a new filename for the export file. (If the receiving program can read other formats, you also can choose a DBF, DIF, or SYLK format for the exported data.)
Step 4.	Click Save to save the file.
Step 5.	In the destination program, open or import the file. (See the program's manual for instructions on opening or importing foreign files.)

Using a Spreadsheet to Clean Up Import Data

Although you can use the Import Field Order dialog box to match fields as well as possible when you import data into a database, the matchup between fields isn't always as clean as it could be. When you import address data, for example, two problems are common:

∞ The address, phone number, or name fields in the import file are split into two fields (address line 1 and address line 2, area code and phone number, and first name and last name), but they are in one field in the ClarisWorks database — or vice versa.

∞ ZIP codes shorter than five digits are missing the leading zero (1276 rather than 01276).

Instead of importing the data as is and cleaning it up in the database afterward, you can use the ClarisWorks spreadsheet to make the necessary transformations to the data and do it more efficiently. Using the spreadsheet changes the steps in the ClarisWorks database import process.

To use a spreadsheet to import data:

1. Export the data from the database, spreadsheet, or address book program as a tab-delimited ASCII text file.

2. Open the ASCII text file as a ClarisWorks spreadsheet; make the transformations to the data, creating new fields as necessary; and save the revised file as an ASCII text file again.

3. Open the ClarisWorks database and use the Insert command to import the ASCII text file into the database.

The simplest way to make the transformations in the spreadsheet is to create additional columns at the right end of the spreadsheet. Each column will contain a formula that combines or converts one or more columns of the original data. After you create the appropriate formula, use the Fill Down command (⌘-D) to copy it into the remaining cells in the column. The figures illustrate three typical conversions.

In the first figure, Column A contains first names, and column B contains last names. The combination formula in the entry bar, =A2&" "&B2, takes the first name in cell A2 (*Jody*), adds a space to it (" "), and then adds the last name from cell B2 (*Privette*) to the end of the text string. The combined fields appear in column C as one name.

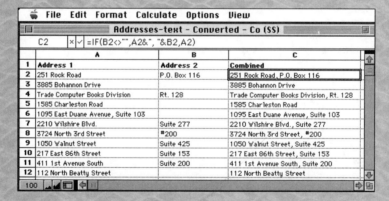

The second figure is an example of combining two address fields into a single address field. Unlike the names in the preceding example, some addresses contain only one part. The equation *=IF(B2<>"",A2&", "&B2,A2)* checks to see whether the address has a second part (*B2<>""*). If the second portion is not blank, the formula combines the two portions, separating them with a comma followed by a blank, as in *251 Rock Road, P.O. Box 116*. If the address does not have a second part, the formula simply copies the first address part (*A2*) into the cell.

In the example in the third figure, a leading zero is added to four-digit zip codes. Because zip codes are often treated as numbers, the leading zero may disappear, resulting in an improper four-digit code. The lengthy formula *=IF(LEN(A2)=4,"0"&A2, NUMTOTEXT(A2))* checks to see whether the length of the zip code is four digits (*LEN(A2)=4*). If so, a leading zero is appended to the zip code (*"0"&A2*), and the zip code is converted to text. If the zip code does not contain four digits, it is converted to text and passed through unaltered (*NUMTOTEXT(A2)*). Converting zip codes to text is necessary to display leading zeroes and to handle blank zip codes. If the formula simply ended with *A2*, rather than with *NUMTOTEXT(A2)*, a blank zip code would translate as a 0 (zero).

	File	Edit	Format	Calculate	Options	View	

Untitled 4 (SS)

B2 × ✓ =IF(LEN(A2)=4,"0"&A2,NUMTOTEXT(A2))

	A	B	C	D	E
1	Zip Code	Converted			
2	12874	12874			
3	44039	44039			
4	1759	01759			
5	2390	02390			
6	83301	83301			
7					
8	30032	30032			

Down to Business: Creating a Credit Card Charge Tracker

If all you want to do is keep track of how you're doing on your credit cards, you don't need a dedicated home finance program. You can use a simple ClarisWorks database to record charges and payments, as well as to show how you're doing overall. Figure 5-48 shows what the charge card database you're about to create looks like.

This database enables you to record the following information for every charge: the date of the transaction, the store or business where the charge was made, a description of what was charged, the amount of the charge, and the particular credit card that was used.

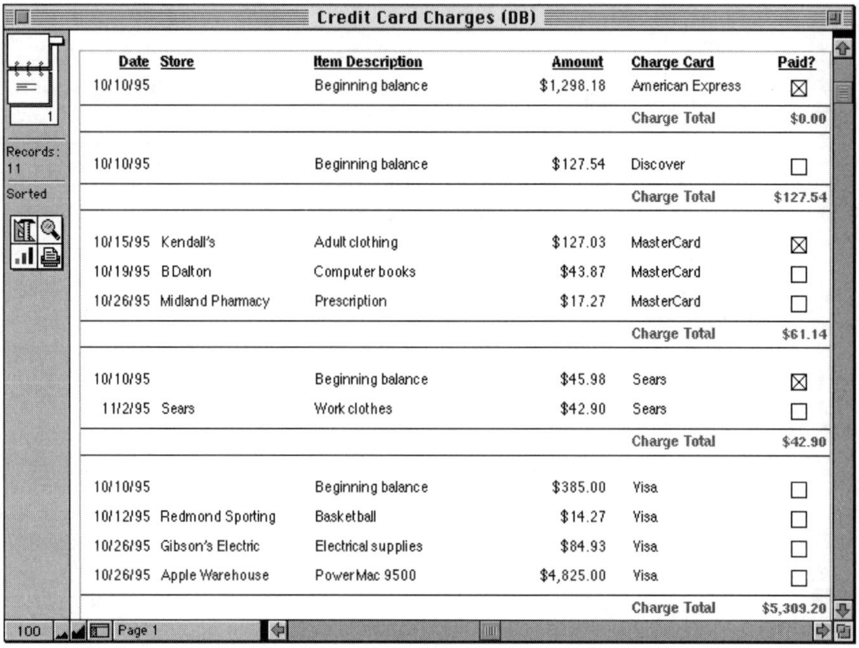

Figure 5-48:
The Credit
Card Charges
database

Defining Fields for the Database

Start by creating a new database and then define the fields listed in Table 5-2.

Table 5-2
Fields for the Credit Card Charges Database

Field Name	Type	Formula
Date	Date	
Store	Text	
Item Description	Text	
Amount	Number	
Charge Card	Value List	American Express, MasterCard, Discover, Visa, and so on
Paid?	Check Box	
Outstanding amount	Calculation	IF('Paid?'=1,0,'Amount')
Charge Total	Summary	SUM('Outstanding amount')' (Sub-summary by Charge Card)
Grand Total	Summary	SUM('Outstanding amount') (Trailing grand summary)

The first four fields (*Date, Store, Item Description,* and *Amount*) are self-explanatory. To save typing time and ensure accurate, consistent spelling, Charge Card is declared as a value list field and contains a list of the names of all charge cards you intend to track. When you select the Charge Card field in the database (by clicking the field or tabbing into it), the Charge Card field displays a pop-up list of your credit cards.

When you define *Charge Card* as a value list field, the Options dialog box automatically opens. Create a value list that consists of the names of all the credit cards that you intend to track. If you like, you can also specify a default charge card by entering its name in the Default Data section of the dialog box. Finally, click in the Cannot Be Empty and Alerts for Unlisted Values check boxes in the Data Verification section of the dialog box. This ensures that you will receive a warning if you neglect to choose a credit card for a record or if you manually enter an unlisted card. (If you later get a new credit card, you should edit this value list to include that card.) Click OK to dismiss the Options dialog box.

Paid is a check box field. After defining the Paid field, select it in the Field Name List, and click Options. In the Options dialog box, delete the text in the Label for Checkbox text-edit box, remove the check mark from Initially Checked, and click OK.

Outstanding Amount is a calculation field that is used to determine whether each charge has already been reconciled (paid). If paid (that is, there is a check in the Paid check box — which is interpreted as a 1), Outstanding Amount is set to 0 (zero). Otherwise, it is set to whatever number is currently in the Amount field for the record. Unlike the other database fields, Outstanding Amount is not displayed on the layout. It is, however, used to generate the Charge Total for each credit card, as well as the Grand Total (the total amount of all outstanding charges for all cards). Define Outstanding Amount as a calculation field, and use the formula shown in Table 5-2.

Charge Total is a summary field that calculates an individual charge total for each credit card when the database is sorted by Charge Card. To create the Charge Total field, enter its name in the Define Database Fields dialog box, choose Summary as the field type, and then click Create. A new dialog box appears in which you can enter the formula shown in Table 5-2. Indicate that you wish the result to be formatted as a number.

Define Grand Total using the same technique just used for Charge Total. As Table 5-2 shows, Grand Total uses the same formula as was entered for Charge Total.

After creating all the fields and clicking Done, a default layout appears. We won't actually use this temporary layout in the database. The next section describes how to make the *real* layout.

Making the Layout

This database requires only one layout. Not only will it serve for data entry, but you also can use it to display on-screen and printed reports.

Steps:	Designing the Layout

Step 1. Choose New Layout from the Layout menu or the Layout pop-up in the Tool panel.

Step 2. In the dialog box that appears, name the layout **Data Entry**, click the Columnar Report radio button, and then click OK.

Step 3. In the Set Field Order dialog box that appears, select every field except Outstanding amount and click Move. In order, the fields should be: Date, Store, Item Description, Amount, Charge Card, and Paid? Click OK to create the columnar layout.

Step 4. Change to Layout mode and arrange these fields (in the body) and labels (in the header) so they look like the layout in Figure 5-49.

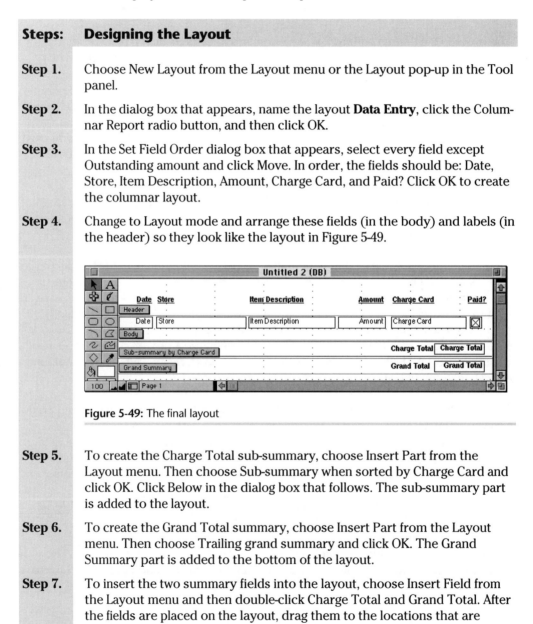

Figure 5-49: The final layout

Step 5. To create the Charge Total sub-summary, choose Insert Part from the Layout menu. Then choose Sub-summary when sorted by Charge Card and click OK. Click Below in the dialog box that follows. The sub-summary part is added to the layout.

Step 6. To create the Grand Total summary, choose Insert Part from the Layout menu. Then choose Trailing grand summary and click OK. The Grand Summary part is added to the bottom of the layout.

Step 7. To insert the two summary fields into the layout, choose Insert Field from the Layout menu and then double-click Charge Total and Grand Total. After the fields are placed on the layout, drag them to the locations that are shown in Figure 5-49.

You can add several finishing touches to pretty up the database layout:

- ⊸ Set the font and size of all text to Helvetica 10 point. (Choose Select All from the Edit menu, choose Helvetica from the Font submenu of the Format menu, and choose 10 from the Size submenu of the Format menu.)

- ⊸ Add boldface to the Charge Total and Grand Total fields by selecting the fields and choosing Bold from the Style submenu of the Format menu.

- ⊸ Set right justification as the text alignment for the Date, Amount, Charge Total, and Grand Total fields; set center justification for the Paid? field.

- ⊸ Apply the Currency format to all monetary fields (Amount, Charge Total, Grand Total) by selecting the fields and then choosing Field Format from the Options menu.

- ⊸ Change the height of all the fields in the body of the layout by selecting them, choosing Object Info from the Options menu, and typing .18 in the height text-edit box of the Info windoid. (The height text-edit box is second from the bottom of the windoid.)

- ⊸ Above and below the Charge Total field, add solid lines that extend the full width of the page.

- ⊸ Drag the Header and Body dividers up to reduce the space that they take up on the layout. (Figure 5-48 shows them with extra space so that you can see all the field names.)

Now that the real layout has been created, you can safely discard the original layout. Choose Edit Layouts from the Layout menu, select Layout 1 in the Current Layouts list, and click the Delete button.

Save the database by choosing Save As from the File menu, clicking the document radio button, entering a name, and clicking Save.

Using the Database

Using the database is fairly simple. The basic procedures include starting up, entering new records, establishing a sort order in which to display the records, reconciling the individual charges with payments made to the credit card companies, and deleting records.

Starting Up

The first time that you use the database, you are likely to have outstanding balances on some of your credit cards. If so, create a Beginning balance record for each charge card, as shown in Figure 5-48. As you pay off (or pay down) the balance, you will reduce it by your payment amounts (as described in "Reconciling the Charge Statement," later in this chapter).

Entering New Charges

Whenever you have a new charge to enter, choose New Record from the Edit menu (or press ⌘-R). A new record appears, and you can enter the charge details. Leave the Paid? field blank (unchecked).

When entering and editing data, you can work in page view (Page View is checked in the View menu) or in normal view (Page View is unchecked in the View menu). The choice is up to you.

Establishing a Sort Order

Although you can leave the records in the order in which you entered them, that order complicates reconciliation and makes finding specific records difficult. Furthermore, the Charge Total summaries won't be available to you. You can solve all of these problems by specifying a sort order for the database.

Choose Sort Records from the Organize menu (or press ⌘-J), set ascending sorts for the Charge Card and Date fields (in that order), and then click OK. ClarisWorks sorts the database by charge card and, within each charge card, by date of purchase. If the Charge Totals are still not visible, make sure that you have selected Page View from the View menu.

Each time you finish entering new records, be sure to sort the database again.

Reconciling the Charge Statement

When a charge statement arrives in the mail, you can reconcile it in one of two ways, depending on whether you pay off the entire balance or pay less than the balance due.

Steps:	Reconciling a Statement When You Pay Off the Entire Balance
Step 1.	Check each record against the statement to make sure that it contains no mistakes.
Step 2.	Click in the Paid? check box for each record that is on the statement (marking them as paid). The Charge Total for that credit card should now show as *0* (zero).

Steps:	**Reconciling a Statement When You Pay Off Less Than the Entire Balance**
Step 1.	Check each record against the statement to make sure that it contains no mistakes.
Step 2.	Subtract the amount that you intend to pay on this statement from any of the outstanding charges for that credit card.

For example, suppose that you have $500 worth of Visa charges in your database ($300 of it as the beginning balance and two other charges of $100 each). If you are paying $75 today, you can edit any of the original Amount fields for that card by subtracting the $75 payment. Thus, you may reduce the $300 beginning balance to $225.

If you are paying $100, you can simply mark one of the $100 charges as paid (which would instantly remove that amount from the Charge Total for the credit card).

Remember, the object is to show the correct outstanding amount for each card (the Charge Total). What the individual charges show is irrelevant — at least after you've verified that the credit card company has recorded them correctly.

Deleting Records

After you've paid off some charges, you can, at your option, delete their records to prevent them from cluttering up the database. (However, you may want to make a printout of the database for your permanent records first.) The simplest way to remove all of the paid records is to use the Match Records command.

Steps:	**Selecting and Deleting the Paid Records**
Step 1.	Choose Match Records from the Organize menu (or press ⌘-M). The Match Records dialog box appears.
Step 2.	Enter the formula shown in Figure 5-50 and then click OK. The records that have been paid are selected.

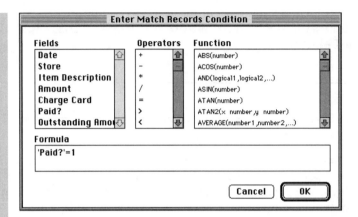

Figure 5-50: Enter the formula shown in the text-edit box to highlight all records that you've marked as paid. When Paid? = 1, the check box contains a check mark.

Instead of trying to remember this formula, you can create a ClarisWorks macro to type it for you and delete the paid records. See Chapter 13 for instructions.

Step 3. Choose Clear from the Edit menu. The paid records are removed from the database.

Quick Tips

The following Quick Tips suggest some simple ways to:

- ☞ Empty a database field for an entire database
- ☞ Perform date calculations
- ☞ Use the spelling checker, thesaurus, and the stylesheet in databases

In addition, a final Quick Tip lists several programs to consider when you're ready for a more powerful database.

Emptying a Database Field for an Entire Database

Suppose that you want to erase the contents of a single field within every record in the database. The database environment does not provide an easy way to perform this task, but you can do it if you enlist the spreadsheet to help you.

Steps:	Emptying a Database Field

Step 1.   Open the database in ClarisWorks and choose the Save As command from the File menu (or press Shift-⌘-S).

Step 2.   Save the file in ASCII text format (choose this option from the Save As Pop-up menu) and use a new filename.

Step 3.   Choose Open from the File menu (or press ⌘-O), and choose Spreadsheet from the Document Type pop-up menu. The ASCII Text file appears in the file list.

Step 4.   Choose the ASCII Text file and click Open. The text file is converted to a spreadsheet that has one database field in each column.

Step 5.   Select the column of data that corresponds to the database field that you want to empty — we'll call it "Phone" in this example. (Click the letter at the top of a column to select the column.)

Step 6.   Choose Clear from the Edit menu. The cells are cleared.

Step 7.   Save the file as text again by choosing Save As from the File menu, choosing ASCII text in the Save As pop-up menu, and changing the filename back to the one you used in Step 2. This step replaces the original ASCII text file with the modified version that you just created in the spreadsheet.

Step 8.   Switch to the database screen; choose Show All Records from the Organize menu (Shift-⌘-A), followed by Select All from the Edit menu (⌘-A). All records in the database are highlighted/selected.

Step 9.   Choose Clear from the Edit menu to remove all records simultaneously.

Step 10. Choose Insert from the File menu and choose the ASCII Text version of the spreadsheet that you saved in Step 7. Click Insert. The Import Field Order dialog box appears, as shown in Figure 5-51. This box shows you, one record at a time, how the imported data will be entered into the database fields. The match should be perfect. (Of course, the field you just emptied — Phone, in this example — should be blank.)

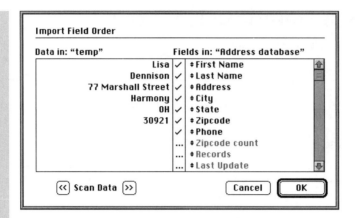

Figure 5-51: The Import Field Order dialog box

Step 11. After using the Scan Data buttons to check several records, click OK. The procedure is now complete. Figure 5-52 shows the results of clearing the Phone field for all records.

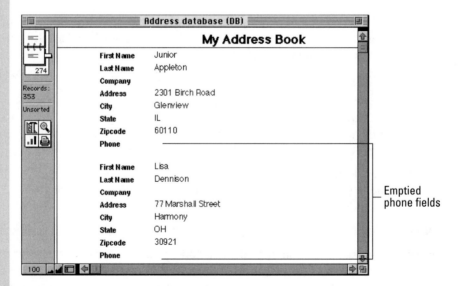

Figure 5-52: The revised database records

Date Calculations

Because the ClarisWorks database environment also enables you to create calculation fields, you may sometimes want to record two dates and then determine the number of days between them. You can calculate the number of days that completing a project required or the number of days until a special event will occur (days until your mother's birthday or payday, for example). The following steps show how to accomplish this task in your own databases.

Steps:	Calculating the Number of Days Between Two Dates
Step 1.	Choose Define Fields from the Layout menu (or press Shift-⌘-D). The Define Database Fields dialog box appears.
Step 2.	Create a pair of date fields (Start Date and End Date, for example).
Step 3.	Create a calculation field to compute the difference between the dates (Total Days, for example). The formula for the field is 'End Date'–'Start Date'. Format the result as a pop-up menu in the choose Number as the result type.

Steps:	Calculating the Number of Days Until an Upcoming Event
Step 1.	Choose Define Fields from the Layout menu (or press Shift-⌘-D). The Define Database Fields dialog box appears.
Step 2.	Create a date field (such as Due Date) in which to record the target date.
Step 3.	Create a calculation field to compute the number of days between today and the target date. The formula for the field would be 'Due Date'-TRUNC(NOW()). In Format result as pop-up menu, choose Number as the result type.
	The NOW( ) function takes the current date and time from the Mac's internal clock. When you truncate the date and time with the TRUNC function, the program discards the fractional portion of the day. Because you want to know only how many full days remain until the event, this formula produces a whole number as the result: 7 days, rather than 7.1852 days, for example.

If the Due Date has already occurred, the result of this formula is a negative number. A result of –5 indicates that the event occurred five days ago.

Formatting with Style

Although the default stylesheet doesn't contain any useful styles that can be applied to fields, labels, or static text in a database, there's nothing stopping you from creating your own!

Steps:	Creating Styles for Fields

Step 1. Select a field and format it as desired. Formatting settings can include font, size, style, alignment, text color, pen color and line width (for a border), fill color, fill pattern, gradient, and so on.

Step 2. If the stylesheet palette isn't open, choose Show Styles from the View menu (or press Shift-⌘-W).

Step 3. Click the New button at the bottom of the Stylesheet. The New Style dialog box appears, as shown in Figure 5-53.

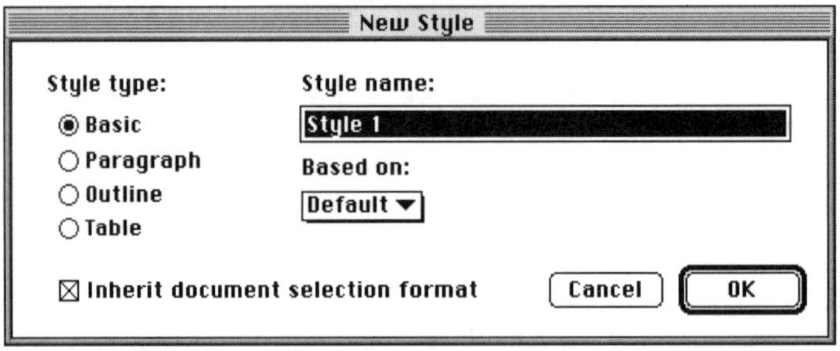

New Style

Style type:
- ⦿ Basic
- ◯ Paragraph
- ◯ Outline
- ◯ Table

Style name:
`Style 1`

Based on:
`Default ▼`

☒ Inherit document selection format [Cancel] [OK]

Figure 5-53: The New Style dialog box

Step 4. Be sure that the Basic radio button is selected and the Inherit document selection format check box is checked, and then enter a name for the style.

Step 5. Click OK to close the dialog box. The new style is added to the document's style sheet.

To format other fields, labels, or static text using this new style definition, select the items in the layout and then click on the style's name in the stylesheet. Note that the modified stylesheet is automatically saved when you save the database.

For more information about using stylesheets, see Chapter 15.

Don't Forget the Spelling Checker and Thesaurus!

The name of this section says it all. Although you normally think of the spelling checker and thesaurus in connection with word processing documents, you also can use them in other ClarisWorks environments, such as the database. You may even want to create special user dictionaries for some databases. A dictionary that contains the spellings for company and customer names would be useful for a contacts or client database, for example, and would help to ensure the accuracy of the data that you enter.

If your database includes large text fields, such as ones for notes or comments, you may want to turn on the auto-hyphenation feature. To do so, select Auto Hyphenate from the Writing Tools submenu of the Edit menu.

Moving On Up _____

If you're lusting for more database power, you'll find the transition to Claris' FileMaker Pro an easy one. The features in the ClarisWorks database environment are a subset of the features in FileMaker Pro. FileMaker Pro enables you to create powerful database scripts with a simple-to-use scripting system, add script buttons to layouts, and exercise greater control over the way that layouts display on-screen. Toward the end of 1995, Claris intends to release a version of FileMaker Pro that has relational database capabilities.

If you need programming and relational database capabilities, you might also check out 4th Dimension (ACI US Inc.), FoxBase (Microsoft), and Double Helix (Helix Technologies).

Summary

➻ A database is an organized set of information on one particular topic. Every database is composed of records, and the records are made up of fields.

➻ The ClarisWorks database has four essential modes: Layout, Browse, List, and Find. Both Browse and List modes can be used to edit, enter, and view data. List mode is layout-independent; instead of just showing the fields present in a single layout, List mode simultaneously shows all fields that have been defined for the database.

➻ ClarisWorks offers 13 types of database fields: text, number, date, time, name, pop-up menu, radio buttons, check box, serial number, value list, record info, calculation, and summary. You use different field types to allow only certain types of data to be entered into the fields and to present the data in special ways (as check boxes, radio buttons, or pop-up lists or menus, for example).

➻ Entries in calculation and summary fields are always the result of a formula that you have specified. You cannot manually enter data into a calculation or summary field. ClarisWorks also automatically fills in the data in record info fields. Like calculation and summary fields, you cannot enter or modify data in a record info field.

➻ The ClarisWorks database environment includes several data validation and auto-entry options that you can set for fields. These options can help ensure the accuracy of the data that you enter and speed up the data-entry process.

➻ For each database, you can create as many layouts (arrangements of data fields and other objects) as you need. Each layout can offer a different view of the data and use different subsets of fields.

➻ In addition to the body part of each layout (where most of the fields are), you can create header and footer parts (for placing information that you want to appear on every page of the database), as well as summary and sub-summary parts (where you can calculate statistics or formulas for the entire database or selected record groupings).

➻ By sorting the database on the contents of one or more fields, you can change the order in which the records are displayed and the way in which they are grouped.

➻ You can search for records by using two commands: Find and Match Records. The Find command displays the subset of records that match the search criteria and hides all other records. Match Records merely selects the subset without hiding the other records.

➬ Entering multiple criteria in a single Find request results in an AND search (find records that match this criterion and that criterion). You also can issue multiple Find requests to execute an OR search (find records that match this criterion or that criterion).

➬ ClarisWorks provides more than 50 layouts for Avery labels. You also can create custom label layouts.

➬ As with the other environments, the database can import and export records in a number of different formats. Importing enables you to merge records from other data files with an existing ClarisWorks database. Exporting data is useful when you want to examine or use the database data in another program (a spreadsheet or desktop publishing program, for example).

➬ ClarisWorks 4.0 includes a new set of pop-up menus in the Tool panel. By clicking them and choosing an option, you can create and switch to layouts, as well as save and execute complex searches, sorts, and reports.

Graphics: The Draw and Paint Environments

In This Chapter

- Creating objects with the drawing tools
- Editing, resizing, and smoothing objects
- Setting object attributes
- Arranging, duplicating, deleting, combining, and reshaping objects
- Designing custom colors, patterns, and gradients
- Creating paint documents and frames
- Paint modes
- Using the paint tools
- Editing paint images
- Applying special effects
- Changing the size and orientation of selected images
- Inserting clip art from the ReadyArt libraries

Overview

ClarisWorks has two graphics environments: Draw and Paint. Using the draw tools, you create *objects* — graphics that you can move, resize, and place in layers over each other. Because the graphics are objects, they maintain a separate identity from everything else on the page. You can select any draw object separately from other images. Editing, however, affects the entire object. You cannot, for example, remove a few dots from an object or cut a section away. But changing the color, pattern, or line width for an object is simple.

In paint documents or frames, on the other hand, images are composed entirely of dots (or *pixels*), and you can edit them at the dot level. This capability makes the paint environment excellent for creating detailed images, such as illustrations.

Here are the major differences between the two environments:

- Draw tools are always available (except in the communications environment). The paint tools remain hidden until you select the paintbrush tool (to work in or create a paint frame) or open a paint document.

- Draw objects are solid; you can edit them only as a whole. Paint images are composed of dots; you can edit them at the dot level.

- Selecting and manipulating draw objects is easy. Working with portions of paint images can be more difficult because they do not maintain a separate identity. (A paint image is just a mass of dots.)

- You can place draw objects in layers, with some objects obscuring portions of other objects. The objects retain their independence, enabling you to change their attributes and their position in the layers. In the paint environment, after you cover part of an image with another image, the obscured portion is gone forever (unless you immediately choose the Undo command).

- There is no such thing as a draw frame. You can place draw objects directly onto the pages of most ClarisWorks documents. Paint images, however, must be in a paint document or in a paint frame. If you copy and paste a portion of a paint image into another document, ClarisWorks automatically embeds it in a rectangular paint frame.

- You can align draw objects to each other or to the grid.

- You can rotate either type of image, flip them horizontally or vertically, and scale them to a different size.

- The paint environment enables you to apply a variety of special effects to selections. Some of the effects are invert, blend, tint, shear, distort, and perspective.

- You can alter the resolution and depth of paint documents.

Because the two environments share similar purposes and capabilities, this chapter discusses both of them.

If you have used previous versions of ClarisWorks, you should note that the Command-key equivalents for some graphics commands (the various Modify commands, for example) have been eliminated. You must now choose these commands directly from the ClarisWorks menus. Also, the names of some commands, as well as the menus in which they are located, have changed. For example, Duplicate is now the only graphics-related command that can be found in the Edit menu. The Object Size command is now Object Info. The Scale Selection command is now Scale By Percent.

The Draw Environment

The draw environment enables you to create graphics objects that you can easily move, resize, and combine. You can place these objects on any document page, copy them to other applications, and store them in the Scrapbook desk accessory.

The draw tools are available in every environment other than communications. Because everything on a draw page is treated as an object (including frames from other environments), the draw environment is excellent for laying out newsletters and ad copy.

Creating Objects with the Draw Tools

ClarisWorks provides draw tools for the following objects:

- *Lines.* A line has two endpoints. You can draw lines at any angle or restrict them to multiples of the Shift constraint angle (as set in Preferences). You can apply only pen attributes (pen color, pen pattern, line width, and arrows) to a line.

- *Rectangles.* A rectangle is an object with four sides, and every corner angle is 90 degrees. In addition to normal rectangles and squares, ClarisWorks also supports *rounded rectangles* (rectangles with rounded corners).

- *Ovals.* An oval is a closed object that is shaped as an ellipse or a circle.

- *Arcs.* An arc is a curved line. Although arcs are typically drawn as open objects, you can assign fill colors, patterns, or gradients to them.

- *Polygons.* A polygon is any figure with a fixed number of sides. Polygons can be closed or open, contain uneven sides, or have sides of equal length (regular polygons).

To create any of these draw objects, you select the appropriate drawing tool from the Tool panel (see Figure 6-1) and then click and drag in the current document. When you release the mouse button, the object is surrounded by tiny dark squares that are called *handles* (see Figure 6-2). By dragging the handles, you can change the object's size.

Figure 6-1:
The draw
tools

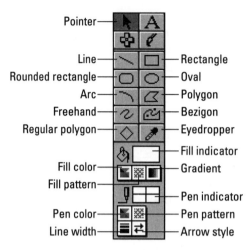

Pointer

Line — Rectangle

Rounded rectangle — Oval

Arc — Polygon

Freehand — Bezigon

Regular polygon — Eyedropper

Fill indicator

Fill color — Gradient

Fill pattern

Pen indicator

Pen color — Pen pattern

Line width — Arrow style

Figure 6-2:
A simple draw object

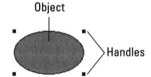

Object

Handles

After you create an object, ClarisWorks normally selects the pointer tool from the Tool panel. To keep the original drawing tool selected, double-click it when you select it, instead of single-clicking it. When you select a tool by double-clicking it, the tool's symbol in the tool panel becomes black, instead of merely darkening in the Tool panel, and you can draw multiple objects of the same type without having to select the tool each time.

Pressing Shift as you create an object constrains the effects of the following drawing tools:

- *Rectangle* or *Rounded Rectangle tool.* A square or rounded square is drawn.

- *Oval tool.* A circle is drawn.

- *Arc tool.* A quarter circle is drawn.

- *Line tool.* A straight line is drawn. Only lines that are a multiple of the Shift constraint angle (as set in the Graphics section of the Preferences dialog box) can be drawn. To find out how to change the Shift constraint, refer to Chapter 11.

Creating or Adjusting Round Corners on a Rectangle

You can adjust the roundness of the corners or add round corners to a standard rectangle.

Steps:	Creating or Adjusting Rounded Corners
Step 1.	Select a rectangle or a rounded rectangle.
Step 2.	Choose the Round Corners command from the Options menu or double-click the rectangle. The Round Corners dialog box appears, as shown in Figure 6-3.

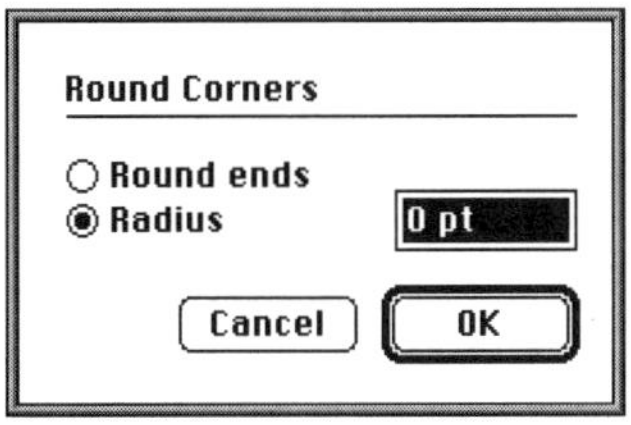

Round Corners

○ Round ends
● Radius   `0 pt`

[Cancel] [**OK**]

Figure 6-3: The Round Corners dialog box

Step 3.	To create a rectangle with semicircles at the corners, click the Round ends radio button and then click OK.
	— or —
Step 3.	Click the Radius radio button, enter a new radius (in the text-edit box) for the circle that forms the curve, and click OK.

Reshaping an Arc

The direction in which you drag when creating an arc determines the arc's curve. Normal drawing will result in a quarter ellipse. To increase or decrease an arc angle, you must modify it. You can reshape an arc in three different ways:

↪ Select a handle and drag. This changes the size (diameter) of an arc.

↪ Use the Reshape command. This allows manual resizing of the arc angle.

↪ Use the Modify Arc command. This allows precise angle adjustment and framed edges.

To reshape an arc, select the arc with the pointer tool. Choose Reshape from the Arrange menu (or press ⌘-R). A special reshape cursor appears. Click one of the arc's handles and drag to reshape the arc. The cursor is constrained to the arc's diameter. To complete the editing, select another tool or choose the Reshape command again.

To modify an arc, select the arc with the pointer tool. Choose Modify Arc from the Options menu or double-click the arc. The Modify Arc dialog box appears, as shown in Figure 6-4. Choose Normal for a normal arc or choose Frame Edges to create a *pie wedge* (closing the arc). Enter numbers for the Start angle and the Arc angle. Click OK to execute the instructions and close the dialog box.

Figure 6-4:
The Modify Arc dialog box

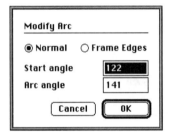

Drawing and Reshaping Polygons

The tool that you use to draw a polygon depends on whether or not it has sides of equal length.

To draw a polygon with uneven sides, select the polygon tool in the Tool panel. Click the document page once to select the starting point and then move the mouse to create the first line of the polygon. (If you press Shift as you move the mouse, the angle of the line will be restricted to an increment of the Shift constraint that is set in the Graphics Preferences.) Click once to set the endpoint for the line. Move the mouse again and click to complete the next line. Repeat this step as many times as necessary to complete the polygon. To finish the polygon, click the starting point (to create a closed polygon), double-click, or press Enter.

 To make polygons close automatically (the equivalent of clicking the starting point), choose the Graphics Preferences option for Automatic Polygon Closing. (For information on setting preferences, see Chapter 11.)

To draw a polygon that has equal sides, use the regular polygon tool. A regular polygon has three or more sides, and all sides are equal in length. The default setting is for a six-sided polygon (a hexagon).

To draw a regular polygon, select the regular polygon tool in the Tool panel. To set the number of sides for the polygon, choose Polygon Sides from the Options menu. (The Polygon Sides command is available only when the Regular Polygon tool is selected.) The Number of sides dialog box appears. Enter the number of sides desired and click OK. Click the document page once to select the starting point and then drag to create the polygon. You can rotate the polygon as you drag. When you release the mouse button, the polygon is completed.

If you press Shift as you draw the regular polygon, its angle is restricted to the Shift constraint that is set for the mouse in the Graphics section of the Preferences dialog box. By default, the angle is set to 45-degree increments.

You can use the Reshape command to change the angles between polygon sides, add anchor points, or change a straight line into a curve.

Steps:	Reshaping a Polygon
Step 1.	Select the polygon with the pointer tool.
Step 2.	Choose Reshape from the Arrange menu (or press ⌘-R). The reshape pointer appears.
Step 3.	Drag a handle to reshape the polygon.
	— or —
Step 3.	Click an anchor point and, while pressing the Option key, drag to create a curve.
	— or —
Step 3.	Click between any pair of anchor points to add a new anchor point. The new anchor point can now be dragged or Option-dragged, as described previously.
Step 4.	To complete the editing, select another tool or choose the Reshape command again.

Drawing Other Shapes

You can use the Freehand tool to create free-form objects. Unlike other objects, which are set to have a white fill, freehand objects have a transparent fill. They can, however, be made solid by assigning a fill color, pattern, or gradient to them.

By default, ClarisWorks automatically smoothes freehand shapes (removes some of the irregularities in the lines and curves). To avoid smoothing, uncheck the Automatically Smooth Freehand check box in the Graphics Preferences options. (For information on setting preferences, see Chapter 11.)

The bezigon tool enables you to draw complex shapes composed of curves and straight lines.

Steps:	Drawing with the Bezigon Tool
Step 1.	Select the bezigon tool in the Tool panel.
Step 2.	Click to select the starting point and then move to select the endpoint for the first line or curve.
Step 3.	Click to set the endpoint. To create an angular point, press Option as you click. To create a more dramatic curve, click and drag.
Step 4.	Repeat Steps 2 and 3 as required.
Step 5.	Double-click to close the shape.

To reshape any of the curves in a bezigon shape, choose Reshape from the Arrange menu (or press ⌘-R) and click the object. Select any of the hollow handles that appear and drag to reshape. To add a new anchor point, click anywhere on a line. To delete an anchor point, select it and press the Delete or Backspace key. When you've finished reshaping the object, choose the Reshape command again or select another tool.

Note that there are two types of hollow handles: circles for curved points and squares for sharp points. Pressing Option while clicking a square handle enables you to change it to a curve. Click on the handle and then drag right and/or left. Option-clicking a *Bézier handle* (one of the tiny dots that appear when creating or modifying a curve) resets the curve to a sharp point.

 The bezigon editing procedures can also be applied to freehand shapes.

Editing Objects

Drawing an object is often only the first step. You can use the different commands, procedures, and palettes to change an object's size, shape, color, pattern, and so on.

Selecting and Deselecting Objects

In order to do anything with an object (change its size, position, or attributes, for example), you must first select it. To select an object, choose the pointer tool from the Tool panel and click the object. Handles appear around the object's border to show that it is selected. (Normally, four handles appear, but you can increase the number of handles by changing the Graphics Preferences. See Chapter 11 for details.)

To select a transparent object, you have to click its border.

You also can select multiple objects. This capability is useful when you want to apply the same command or formatting to a number of objects. To select more than one object, do one of the following:

- ⌖ Select the pointer tool and press Shift as you click objects.
- ⌖ Select the pointer tool and drag a selection rectangle around the objects.
- ⌖ Select the pointer tool and press ⌘ as you drag *through* the objects.
- ⌖ Choose Select All from the Edit menu (or press ⌘-A) to select all objects on the current document page.
- ⌖ Click an object type in the Tool panel and then choose Select All from the Edit menu to select all objects of that type.

The last technique works differently with bezigons, polygons, regular polygons, and freehand shapes. If you select one of these objects from the Tool panel and issue the Select All command, objects of *all* of these types are selected.

To deselect an object, click anywhere outside the object. To deselect individual objects when several have been selected, Shift-click them.

Changing the Size of an Object

You can change the size of a selected object in three ways:

- ⌖ Dragging one of its handles
- ⌖ Using the Scale By Percent command
- ⌖ Using the Object Info command

When dragging one of an object's handles to change the size of the object, you can constrain the angle of movement by pressing Shift as you drag. You can change the Shift constraint in the Graphics Preferences. By default, the angle is set to increments of 45 degrees.

Steps: **Changing an Object's Size Using the Scale By Percent Command**

Step 1.   Select the object or objects whose size you want to change.

Step 2.   Choose Scale By Percent from the Transform submenu of the Arrange menu. The Scale By Percent dialog box appears (see Figure 6-5).

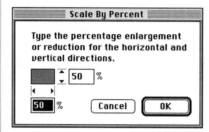

Figure 6-5: The Scale By Percent dialog box

Step 3.   Enter new figures for the vertical or horizontal dimensions of the selected object. (To change the dimensions proportionately, enter the same percentage for both dimensions.)

Step 4.   Click OK.

Steps: **Changing an Object's Size Using the Object Info Command**

Step 1.   Select the object whose size you want to change.

Step 2.   Choose Object Info from the Options menu. The Info floating windoid appears (see Figure 6-6).

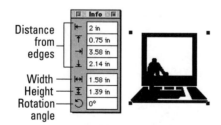

Figure 6-6: The numbers in the Info floating windoid refer to the currently selected object.

Step 3.	To change the horizontal or vertical dimensions (width or height) of the selected object, type new figures in the width and/or height text-edit boxes.
Step 4.	To change an object's orientation (rotation), type a new figure in the bottom text-edit box.

Smoothing and Unsmoothing Objects

You can smooth or unsmooth polygons, regular polygons, bezigons, and freehand shapes. *Smoothing* an object converts all angles into curves. *Unsmoothing* an object changes curves into angles. To smooth an object, select it and choose Smooth from the Transform submenu of the Arrange menu or press ⌘-(. To unsmooth an object, choose Unsmooth from the Transform submenu of the Arrange menu or press ⌘-).

When you are working with a bezigon, smoothing and unsmoothing are not necessarily opposites of each other. You may prefer to use the Undo command in the Edit menu to return to the original shape after you use either the Smooth or Unsmooth command for a bezigon.

Setting Object Attributes

You can set the following object attributes:

- ↪ Fill color
- ↪ Fill pattern
- ↪ Gradient
- ↪ Pen color
- ↪ Pen pattern
- ↪ Line width
- ↪ Arrowheads for lines

You can set these attributes before or after you create an object. To set attributes beforehand, select them from the Tool panel pop-up palettes (see Figure 6-7) and then draw the object. The object will automatically use the current attributes.

To assign or change attributes for an existing object, select the pointer tool, select the object, and then select the new attributes from the various fill and pen palettes in the Tool panel.

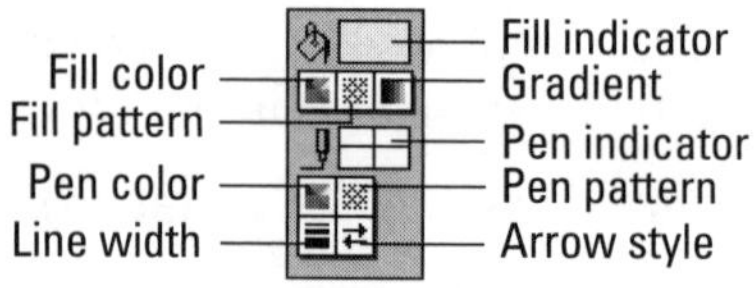

Figure 6-7:
Tool panel
pop-up palettes

Fill color — Fill indicator
Fill pattern — Gradient
Pen color — Pen indicator
Line width — Pen pattern
— Arrow style

 Although lines are normally solid, you can apply a pen pattern to a line to achieve interesting effects. For example, try different dot pen patterns to create dotted lines.

Transparent and Opaque Objects

Every object can be either transparent or opaque. An *opaque* object has a fill pattern, color, and/or gradient, and it obscures anything on the page that it covers. A *transparent* object, on the other hand, has no fill color, pattern, or gradient, and you can see anything on the page that it covers.

To make an object transparent, select the first fill pattern in the palette (the two linked blank squares). Any fill color, pattern, or gradient is temporarily removed.

If you set the default fill pattern to transparent, the transparent icon is displayed as a reminder in the pattern indicator in the Tool panel (see Figure 6-8).

Figure 6-8:
The default fill pattern
is now transparent.

 — Transparent icon

To make an object opaque (the default for all objects other than freehand shapes), select the second fill pattern in the palette (the two linked blank and black squares). Any fill color, pattern, or gradient that was previously applied to the object is restored.

 You can tear off any attribute palette and drag it onto the page as a floating windoid. After you expose the palette in this manner, you can quickly set a particular attribute for many objects without having to pop up the attribute palette again. You can manipulate floating attribute palettes in the following ways:

- To move a palette, drag it by its title bar.

- To close a palette, click its close box (in the upper-left corner).

- To shrink or expand a palette, click the box in the palette's upper-right corner.

Copying Object Attributes with the Eyedropper Tool

After setting attributes for an object, you can copy those attributes to other objects by using the eyedropper tool. To use the eyedropper tool, select the eyedropper tool from the Tool panel. Click the object whose attributes you want to copy. Select the eyedropper tool again and ⌘-click the objects to which you want to apply the attributes.

Like other draw tools, you can use the eyedropper repeatedly by double-clicking its icon in the Tool panel.

 If a destination object has a transparent fill, you need to ⌘-click its border with the eyedropper to apply the attributes.

Arranging Objects

The Arrange menu contains commands for moving, aligning, and reorienting objects. You also can move objects manually by dragging them.

Moving Objects

To reposition an object manually, select it with the pointer tool and drag the object to a new location. When you move a line, arc, rectangle, or oval, an outline of the object is visible as you drag. When you move other objects, only the bounding box is displayed as you drag.

To see the actual outline of a polygon, Bezigon, or freehand shape as you drag it (rather than a rectangular bounding box), press ⌘ as you drag . To restrict movements to the current Shift constraint angle (set in the Graphics Preferences), press Shift as you drag. (The Shift technique is particularly useful when you want to keep objects aligned with each other.)

You also can move a selected object by pressing any of the arrow keys. When Autogrid is turned off, the object moves one pixel in the direction of the arrow key. When Autogrid is turned on, the object moves one grid division (determined by the ruler type that is currently set). To turn Autogrid on or off, press ⌘-Y or choose the appropriate command from the Options menu (Autogrid On or Autogrid Off).

One other way to move an object is to use the Info palette (previously shown in Figure 6-6), which is displayed when you choose Object Info from the Options menu. To change the position of a selected object, simply type new numbers in the Info palette to set the object's distance from the left edge, top, right edge, or bottom of the page.

About the Graphics Grid and Autogrid

The dotted lines that you see on a new draw document are called the *graphics grid*. The ruler type that is in effect and the number of divisions specified for that ruler govern the spacing of the dots. (By default, the unit of measurement is inches, and each inch has eight divisions.) When you use the Rulers command on the Format menu to change the ruler or the number of divisions, you change the grid.

The grid can be shown or hidden. To hide the grid, choose Hide Graphics Grid from the Options menu. To make it visible again, choose Show Graphics Grid from the Options menu.

Only a portion of the grid is visible. You may want to think of the visible portion as being grid border markers. As Figure 6-9 illustrates, many additional grid points are inside each rectangular grid section.

Figure 6-9:
This single grid section is magnified 200 percent. The small dots inside the grid represent the grid points that you can't see.

Aligning Objects

The Autogrid feature causes objects to align with the nearest point on the grid. When Autogrid is off, you can place objects without being constrained to a grid point. Choose Turn Autogrid On or Turn Autogrid Off from the Options menu (or press ⌘-Y) to change the state of the grid.

When Autogrid is off, you can still make objects align with the grid by using the Align to Grid command.

In many cases, having a set of objects align perfectly with one another is more important than having them align with the grid.

Steps:	Aligning Objects to Each Other
Step 1.	Select the objects that you want to align to one another. (Drag or Shift-click to select multiple objects.)

Step 2. Choose Align Objects from the Arrange menu (or press Shift-⌘-K). The Align Objects dialog box appears, as shown in Figure 6-10.

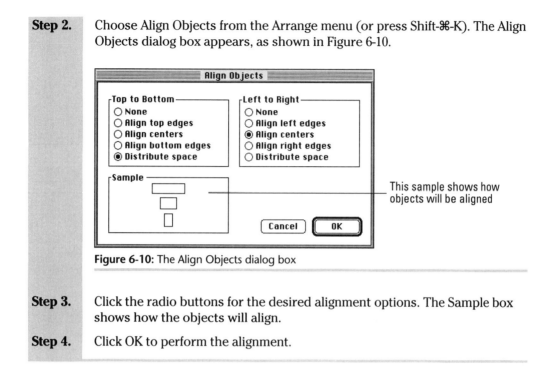

Figure 6-10: The Align Objects dialog box

Step 3. Click the radio buttons for the desired alignment options. The Sample box shows how the objects will align.

Step 4. Click OK to perform the alignment.

If the result is not what you intended, immediately choose Undo from the Edit menu and perform the steps again.

Object Layers

You can place objects over one another, creating *layers*. Using the appropriate menu command, you can move an object to the top or bottom layer of a drawing or one step up or down in the layer hierarchy. Figure 6-11 shows two different stacking orders for the same set of objects.

Figure 6-11: Bring the box in back to the top or front layer by choosing the Move to Front command.

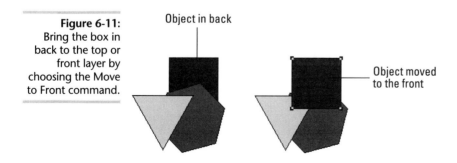

Steps:	Changing an Object's Layer
Step 1.	Select an object. Handles appear around its border.
Step 2.	To move one layer toward the front or back, choose Move Forward (Shift-⌘-+) or Move Backward (Shift-⌘- –) from the Arrange menu.
	— or —
Step 2.	To move the object directly to the top or bottom layer, choose Move to Front or Move to Back from the Arrange menu.

Flipping and Rotating Objects

The Transform submenu of the Arrange menu has three commands that you can use to change the orientation of selected objects:

- *Flip Horizontally* creates a mirror image of an object, reversing the left and right sides.

- *Flip Vertically* creates a reflection of the object (as though it were sitting on the edge of a lake), reversing the top and bottom.

- *Rotate 90°* rotates the image 90 degrees clockwise. Each time you issue the Rotate 90° command, the object is rotated an additional 90 degrees.

Figure 6-12 shows the result of applying each of these commands to an object.

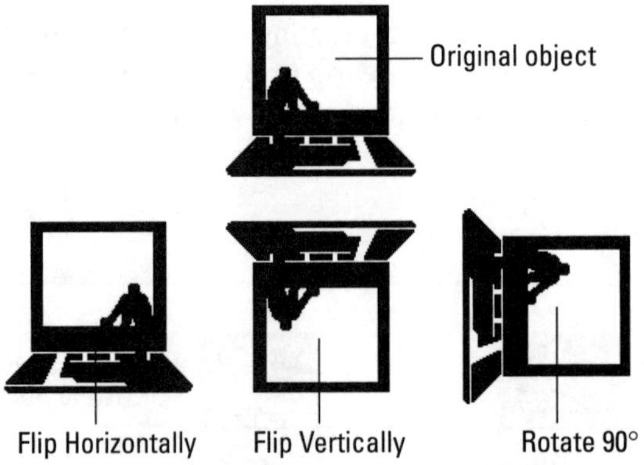

Figure 6-12:
The original object and the object after the Flip Horizontally, Flip Vertically, and Rotate 90° commands are applied to it.

Original object

Flip Horizontally   Flip Vertically   Rotate 90°

In ClarisWorks 4.0, draw objects also can be rotated manually or by typing a specific angle of rotation.

To rotate an object manually, click to select the object. Choose Free Rotate from the Arrange menu (or press Shift-⌘-R). The cursor changes to an X. Click one of the object's handles, and drag to rotate the object. When the object is correctly rotated, release the mouse button.

To rotate an object to a specific angle, click to select the object. Choose Object Info from the Options menu. The Info windoid appears (as previously shown in Figure 6-6). In the Info windoid, type a rotation angle in the bottom text-edit box. Type a positive number to rotate the object counterclockwise or a negative number to rotate it clockwise.

 When you reorient an object, working with a copy of the object is safer than working with the original, particularly if you are experimenting. Remember, too, that you can use the Undo command to undo the last change.

When *text* is rotated, it is treated as an object. You will lose some resolution as a result (text goes to 72 dpi). If you rotate the text back to its original position the original attributes will be restored.

Duplicating Objects

In addition to the normal copy-and-paste routine, you can use the Duplicate command to make a copy of an object and simultaneously paste it. To duplicate an object, select it and choose Duplicate from the Edit menu (or press ⌘-D). A copy of the object appears. If you immediately move the duplicate to its new position and then choose the Duplicate command again, the new duplicate will be offset the same distance and direction as the preceding one. Duplicate is extremely useful for quickly creating a series of parallel, equidistant lines or other objects.

 Here's a "silly tip": The duplicate changes direction if placing it would otherwise force it over a page margin. With this fact in mind, if you use the Duplicate command repeatedly with the same object, you can create interesting graphic effects — such as the 3-D tube shown in Figure 6-13.

Deleting Objects

To delete an object, select it and use one of the following methods:

- Press Delete, Backspace, or Clear.

- Choose Clear from the Edit menu.

- Choose Cut from the Edit menu (or press ⌘-X).

The Cut command places a copy of the object on the Clipboard. The other options delete the object without copying it to the Clipboard.

Figure 6-13:
Dozens of repetitions of the Duplicate command can have surprising results.

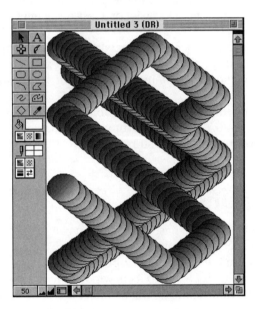

 You also can use any of these procedures to delete several objects at the same time.

Combining Objects

Sometimes, combining objects is useful. ClarisWorks provides two methods of combining objects: *grouping* (which enables you to treat several objects as a single object) and *reshaping* (which links objects end-to-end).

Combining Objects with the Group Command

After you painstakingly create a complex series of interrelated objects, dealing with the objects as a whole is often easier and safer than dealing with the individual objects. After you select all of the components of the image, you can create a single object with a single set of handles by choosing the Group command from the Arrange menu (or pressing ⌘-G). You can then, for example, move all the objects at the same time without fear of leaving a piece or two behind. You also can apply other Arrange commands to the new object to flip or rotate it, or you can choose a new color, gradient, or pattern for the object.

If you ever need to work with the component parts, simply select the object and choose Ungroup from the Arrange menu (or press Shift-⌘-G). The components reappear, and you can work with them individually again.

Combining Objects with the Reshape Command

The Group command enables you to treat several distinct objects as a united group. The Reshape command, on the other hand, enables you to physically link two or more freehand shapes, polygons, or bezigons end-to-end. This technique can be useful when you are designing repeating patterns, such as those often used in picture borders.

Steps:	Linking Freehand Shapes, Polygons, or Bezigons
Step 1.	Choose Reshape from the Arrange menu (or press ⌘-R). The reshape cursor appears.
Step 2.	Select the freehand shape, polygon, or bezigon that you want to attach to another object. Hollow handles appear around the selected object.
Step 3.	Choose Copy from the Edit menu (or press ⌘-C). A copy of the object is placed on the Clipboard.
Step 4.	Select the second object (the one to which you want to attach the first object).
Step 5.	If you want to attach the object to the second object's starting point, select the starting point. Otherwise, the object will be attached to the endpoint.
Step 6.	Choose Paste from the Edit menu (or press ⌘-V). A copy of the first object is connected to the second object.
Step 7.	If required, repeat Step 6 to attach additional copies end-to-end.
Step 8.	Choose Reshape from the Arrange menu or select another drawing tool to complete the process.

If you press Option while choosing the Paste command in Step 6, the last point (rather than the first point) of the copied object will be attached to the second object.

Locking and Unlocking Objects

If the position or attributes of a particular object are critical to a document, you can lock the object in place and keep it from being altered by selecting the object and choosing Lock from the Arrange menu (or pressing ⌘-H). If you later want to modify, delete, or move the object, choose Unlock from the Arrange menu (or press Shift-⌘-H).

Creating Custom Colors, Patterns, and Gradients

If you want to use special colors, patterns, or *gradients* (fills that blend from one color to another) that are not already in the palettes, you can create your own by replacing existing colors, patterns, or gradients with new ones.

Custom colors, patterns, and gradients are saved with the document in which they are created. To make custom patterns and gradients reusable, you can create them in a blank document and then save it as a stationery document. To create a reusable color palette, you have to use the Editable 256 Color Palette (in the Color section of the Preferences dialog box) and then save the palette as a color palette document.

You can also edit colors, patterns, and gradients in the paint environment.

Steps:	Creating a Custom Color
Step 1.	Choose Preferences from the Edit menu.
Step 2.	Click the Color icon in the left side of the Preferences dialog box, click the Editable 256 Color Palette radio button, and click OK.
Step 3.	Click the Fill color or Pen color palette and tear off the palette by dragging it onto the screen.
Step 4.	Double-click the color that you want to replace. A color wheel dialog box appears, as shown in Figure 6-14.

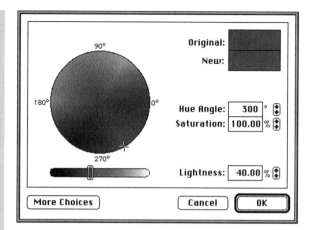

Figure 6-14: Select a new color from this color wheel. (This color wheel appears if you are running System 7.5 or 7.5.1. It looks different in earlier versions of the system software.)

Step 5. To select a replacement color, you can do any of the following (or use a combination of these approaches):

- Click a different color on the wheel.
- Drag the scroll bar to change the lightness (brightness) of the colors.
- Enter new numbers for Hue Angle, Saturation, or Lightness.

Step 6. Click OK to save the change. The new color replaces the original one in both the fill and pen color palettes. (To revert to the original color, click Cancel.)

If you want to be able to reuse the revised color palette in other documents, you can save it. To save a custom palette, choose Preferences from the Edit menu, click the Color icon in the left side of the Preferences dialog box, and click Save Palette. A standard file dialog box appears. Enter a name for the palette and click Save. When the Preferences dialog box reappears, click OK.

You can also *load* any of the color palettes that are included with ClarisWorks, as well as ones you've saved. Choose Preferences from the Edit menu, click the Color icon in the left side of the Preferences dialog box, and click Load Palette. A list of all color palettes appears. Select a palette, click Open, and then click OK.

Steps: Creating a Custom Pattern for the Current Document

Step 1.   Choose Patterns from the Options menu. The Fill pattern palette and the Pattern Editor appear (see Figure 6-15). Select the pattern to be edited by clicking it in the Fill pattern palette.

— or —

Step 1.   Tear off the Fill pattern or Pen pattern palette and double-click the pattern that you want to replace. The Pattern Editor appears (see Figure 6-15), set for the chosen pattern.

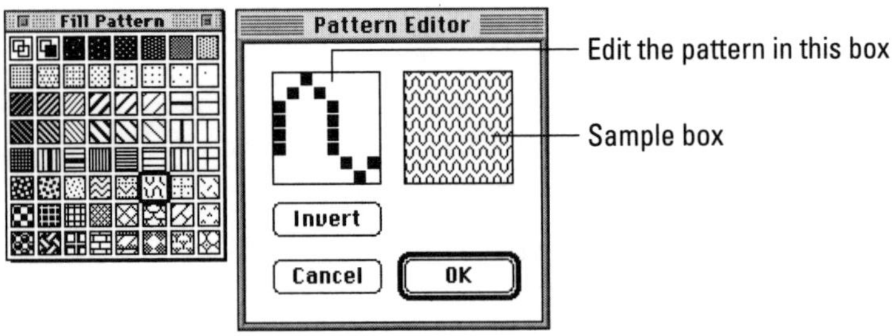

Edit the pattern in this box

Sample box

Figure 6-15: The Pattern Editor

Step 2.   In the box on the left side of the Pattern Editor, click or drag to change the pattern. White spots that are clicked turn black; black spots turn white. To reverse the pattern (swapping whites for blacks and vice versa), click Invert.

Step 3.   Click OK to accept the new pattern or Cancel to revert to the previous pattern. The edited pattern appears in both the Fill and Pen pattern palettes.

Every gradient is a sweep from one color to another and can contain two to four colors. ClarisWorks supports three types of sweeps: *directional, circular,* and *shape burst.* Every sweep has a *focus* (shown as a hollow circle in the Focus section of the Gradient Editor). In a directional sweep, the focus is the spot at which the final color appears. In a circular sweep, the focus is the point around which the gradient sweeps. A shape burst sweep is based on the shape of the object around which the gradient sweeps, and the focus is the bottom-right corner of the rectangle.

The following steps explain how to create your own gradients. When working in the Gradient Editor, you can immediately see the effects of your changes by watching the Sample box.

Steps:	**Creating a Custom Gradient for the Current Document**
Step 1.	Choose Gradients from the Options menu. The Gradient palette and the Gradient Editor appear (see Figure 6-16). Select the gradient to be edited by clicking it in the Gradient palette.

— or —

| Step 1. | Tear off the Gradient palette and double-click the gradient that you want to replace. The Gradient Editor appears (see Figure 6-16), set for the chosen gradient. |

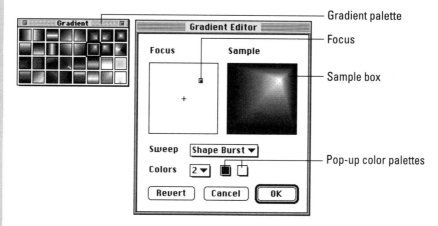

Figure 6-16: The Gradient palette and the Gradient Editor

Step 2.	Choose a sweep type from the Sweep pop-up menu.
Step 3.	Make the changes that you want. The options are as follows:

- *Directional sweep.* You can set the number of colors by choosing a number from the Colors pop-up menu. Select the specific colors for the sweep from the pop-up color palettes. To change the focus, drag the hollow circle in the Angle section of the Gradient Editor. You can set a new angle for the sweep by dragging the line or typing an angle in the Angle text-edit box.

- *Circular sweep.* You can set the number of colors by choosing a number from the Colors pop-up menu. Select the specific colors for the sweep from the pop-up color palettes. To change the focus, drag the connected pair of circles in the Angle section of the Gradient Editor. You can set a new angle for the sweep by dragging the filled circle or typing an angle in the Angle text-edit box.

- *Shape burst sweep.* You can set the number of colors by choosing a number from the Colors pop-up menu. Select the individual colors for the sweep from the pop-up color palettes. To change the size of the shape burst focus, drag the black handle of the focus box in the Focus section of the Gradient Editor. You can set the location of the focus by dragging the focus box to a new spot.

Step 4.   Click OK to save the new gradient, Cancel to ignore the changes, or Revert to change the gradient back to its ClarisWorks default.

Adding Pages to a Draw Document

By default, a graphics document contains only a single page. Adding more pages can be useful (when you are creating a slide show, for example). To add pages to a draw document, choose Document from the Format menu. The Document dialog box appears. Increase the number of Pages across and/or Pages Down in the Size section of the dialog box. Click OK. The pages you specified are added to the document.

Down to Business: Creating Border Designs

Whether you're getting ready for a presentation or just want to add some pizzazz to your document, a border frame is often a nice touch. For example, adding a border to a master page can lend consistency to slide show presentations. This task shows you how to quickly create a simple but attractive border that is composed of overlapping diamonds.

Steps: **Creating a Simple Border**

Step 1.   Launch ClarisWorks and create a new draw document.

Step 2.   Make sure that Autogrid is on. (The command in the Options menu should read Turn Autogrid Off.) Having Autogrid turned on makes aligning the shapes easy.

Step 3.   Select the Regular Polygon tool from the Tool panel. (It's shaped like a diamond.)

Step 4. Choose Polygon Sides from the Options menu, type **4** in the dialog box that appears, and click OK.

Step 5. Select a fill color from the Fill pop-up palette in the Tool panel.

Step 6. Drag to create a small diamond shape and place the shape in the upper-left corner of the page.

Step 7. With the shape still selected, choose Duplicate from the Edit menu (or press ⌘-D).

Step 8. Press the up-arrow key once. The second diamond overlaps the first one and is slightly offset to the right.

Step 9. Press ⌘-D repeatedly to create additional diamonds for the top border. Each one should overlap the previous diamond in exactly the same way as the first duplicate did. Stop when the top border is the desired width.

Step 10. Using the pointer, drag a selection rectangle around the row of diamonds.

Step 11. Choose Group from the Arrange menu (or press ⌘-G). The row of diamonds is now treated as a single object.

Step 12. With the row still selected, choose Copy from the Edit menu (or press ⌘-C).

Step 13. Choose Paste from the Edit menu (or press ⌘-V). A copy of the row is pasted over the original row.

Step 14. Choose Rotate 90° from the Transform submenu of the Arrange menu (or press Shift-⌘-R). A vertical column of diamonds appears.

Step 15. Drag the column to the left side of the page and place it so that it overlaps with the left end of the original row of diamonds.

Step 16. With the column still selected, choose Copy and then Paste from the Edit menu. A copy of the column is pasted over the original column.

Step 17. Drag the column to the right side of the page and place it so that it overlaps with the right end of the original row of diamonds. If you press Shift as you drag, the column moves in a perfectly straight line.

Step 18. Click to select the top row of diamonds and choose Copy and then Paste from the Edit menu. A copy of the row is pasted over the original row.

Step 19. Drag the copy down until it overlaps with the bottom ends of the two columns. The resulting border should look like the one shown in Figure 6-17.

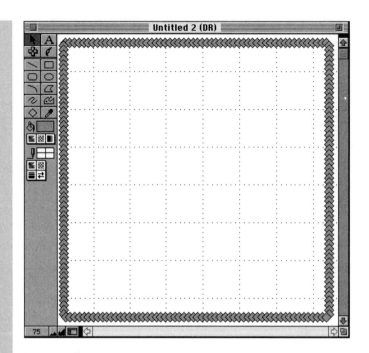

Figure 6-17: The finished diamond border

Step 20.   After the border is satisfactory, you can lock the rows and columns in place. Shift-click to select the four elements (or choose Select All from the Edit menu) and then choose Lock from the Arrange menu (or press ⌘-H).

If you plan to use this border frequently, you can save it as a ClarisWorks stationery document rather than as a normal document. (For instructions on working with stationery documents, see Chapter 10.)

The Paint Environment

The Paint environment enables you to create and edit *bitmapped images*, which are graphics composed entirely of dots. Unlike draw objects, paint images can be edited at the dot level. The precise control that this capability provides is what makes the paint environment so useful in creating complex illustrations.

Creating a New Paint Document or Frame

Although you can create draw objects in almost any document type, you must either design paint images in a paint document or place them in a paint frame in another ClarisWorks environment. To create a new paint document, choose New from the File menu (or press ⌘-N). When the New Document dialog box appears, choose Painting and then click OK.

If insufficient memory is available, you may be notified that the document size will be reduced. For instructions on increasing the available memory (and, in turn, the size of your paint documents), see the Quick Tips at the end of this chapter.

To create a paint frame in another ClarisWorks environment, click the paintbrush tool in the Tool panel and drag to draw the paint frame.

Paint frames and paint documents can contain only bitmapped graphics. Although you can place draw objects and frames from other environments into a paint frame or document, the object or frame from the other environment loses its environmental identity the instant you stop working in the frame. At that moment, the frame is converted to a paint image, which you can edit only by using the paint tools. The same is also true for text that you type or paste into a paint document or frame.

Like other frames, a paint frame is surrounded by a rectangular border. To make the border invisible (so the paint image will blend with the rest of the document), set the pen color to white or set the pen pattern to transparent.

While you are working in a paint frame or in a paint document, the normally hidden paint tools are displayed and available for use (see Figure 6-18).

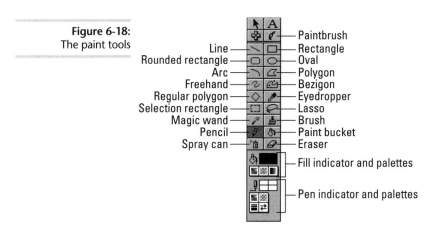

Figure 6-18:
The paint tools

Line — Paintbrush
Rounded rectangle — Rectangle
Arc — Oval
Freehand — Polygon
Regular polygon — Bezigon
Selection rectangle — Eyedropper
Magic wand — Lasso
Pencil — Brush
Spray can — Paint bucket
— Eraser

— Fill indicator and palettes

— Pen indicator and palettes

The top ten tools, which, in ordinary circumstances, produce draw objects, are now paint tools. When you use them in a paint frame or a paint document, these tools create bitmapped graphics — not objects. For instructions on using these tools in a paint frame or paint document, see "Creating Objects with the Draw Tools," earlier in this chapter. The information in that section concerning Shift constraint also applies.

Many of the object modification commands are no longer available as menu commands when you are working in the paint environment. However, you can make the following dialog boxes appear:

- *Round Corners*. Double-click the rounded rectangle tool in the Tool panel.
- *Modify Arc*. Double-click the arc tool in the Tool panel.
- *Number of sides*. Double-click the regular polygon tool in the Tool panel.

Paint Modes

ClarisWorks supports three paint modes:

- *Opaque mode*. Any color, pattern, or gradient placed on another image completely covers the image beneath.
- *Transparent pattern mode*. Any pattern that contains white areas or dots allows the image beneath to show through. A gradient or solid color placed over another image, however, is still treated as opaque (completely covering the image beneath).
- *Tint mode*. A color, pattern, or gradient placed on another image results in a blending of the colors. Depending on the colors chosen, the overlap may not show change. For best results, use colors with greater contrast.

Figure 6-19 shows examples of the three paint modes.

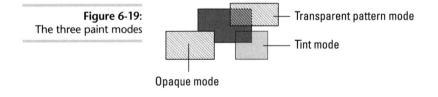

Figure 6-19:
The three paint modes

Transparent pattern mode

Tint mode

Opaque mode

To set the paint mode, choose Paint Mode from the Options menu. The Painting Mode dialog box appears. Click the radio button for Opaque, Transparent pattern, or Tint, and then click OK.

Using the Paint Tools

When you create draw objects, you can set attributes before or after you create the object. When you work in the paint environment, on the other hand, you should generally select fill and pen attributes *before* you use each tool. Except for filling closed images, assigning attributes after you create an image can be very difficult.

When you select a paint tool from the Tool panel, it automatically remains selected until you choose a different tool. You do not have to double-click the tool to keep it selected, as you do in the draw environment.

Using the Pencil

You use the pencil tool to create and edit single dots, make freehand drawings (much as you do with the freehand tool), and draw thin lines. When you first open a paint document or paint frame, the pencil is automatically selected.

Only the fill color setting affects the pencil. Other settings from the fill and pen palettes have no effect.

You can click to create single dots or click and drag to create lines. If you press Shift as you draw with the pencil, you can make straight vertical or horizontal lines.

When you click a blank or colored pixel on the screen with the pencil, a dot of the current fill color is produced. If you click a pixel that is the same color as the current fill color, on the other hand, the pixel changes to white.

Double-clicking the pencil tool zooms the document window to 800 percent, making it easy to do fine editing. To return to the 100 percent view, click the Zoom Percentage box in the lower-left corner of the document window and select 100%.

Using the Brush

Use the brush tool to paint in the current fill color and pattern. (You cannot use a gradient fill with the brush.) To change to a different brush shape, double-click the brush icon in the Tool panel or choose Brush Shape from the Options menu. The Brush Shape dialog box appears.

To choose a different brush, select it and click OK. To create a new brush (by editing one of the existing brush shapes), select a brush shape and click Edit. The Brush Editor appears.

Alter the brush shape by clicking and dragging in the box. When you click a white spot, it becomes black. When you click a black spot, it becomes white. Click OK to accept the new brush shape (for this document only), and then click OK again to close the Brush Shape dialog box.

 You can cut patterns out of images by setting the fill color to white or the fill pattern to transparent before you use the brush.

Using the Paint Bucket

The paint bucket tool's sole function is to fill a closed area with a color, pattern, or gradient. The tip of the bucket (the tiny stream of paint that is pouring over its side) is the active area of the paint bucket cursor (see Figure 6-20). It shows where the paint will be applied.

Figure 6-20:
The paint bucket is poised
to fill the pimento in this olive.

If the paint bucket is applied to an area that is currently filled with a pattern or gradient, a solid color fill will seldom be successful. The procedure for refilling an area that contains a pattern or gradient is to select it and then choose Fill from the Transform menu. (If the area is filled with a solid color, on the other hand, you can use the paint bucket to successfully fill the area with a color, pattern, or gradient.)

 If the area that you're attempting to fill is not completely closed, the fill color, pattern, or gradient may be applied to many unintended areas in the document or frame. Choose Undo immediately to remove the fill. Before filling again, zoom the screen to locate and fill in the pixels needed to close the area. If you *deliberately* apply the paint bucket to a blank area in the background, on the other hand, you can quickly add a color, pattern, or gradient to the entire background for a picture or paint frame.

Using the Spray Can

The spray can tool works like an artist's airbrush. (Set free the graffiti artist in you!) You can change both the dot size and the flow rate to achieve different effects.

To use the spray can, select a fill color, select the spray can in the Tool panel, and either click the mouse to spray or press the mouse button and drag. To spray in a straight vertical or horizontal line, press Shift as you click and drag.

Steps: Changing the Spray Can Settings

Step 1. Double-click the spray can icon in the Tool panel or choose spray can from the Options menu. The Edit Spray Can dialog box appears, as shown in Figure 6-21.

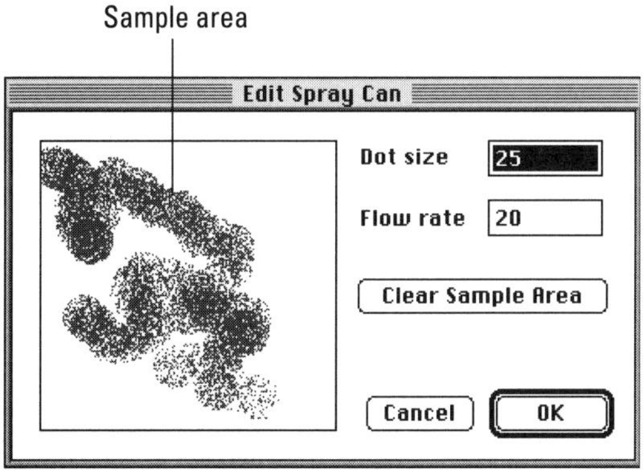

Sample area

Edit Spray Can

Dot size 25

Flow rate 20

Clear Sample Area

Cancel   OK

Figure 6-21: The Edit Spray Can dialog box

Step 2. Enter new figures for Dot size (1 to 72) and Flow rate (1 to 100).

Dot size is in pixels, and there are 72 pixels in an inch. (Dot size doesn't really vary the size of the dots; it changes the size or spread of the dot pattern.)

Flow rate governs how fast the paint flows. At the highest setting, you get splotches of color everywhere the spray pattern touches.

Step 3. To test different combinations of Dot size and Flow rate with the current fill color, click and drag in the sample area of the dialog box. (If you want to test different combinations in a clean sample area, you can click Clear Sample Area at any time.)

Step 4. Click OK when the settings are to your liking.

Editing Paint Images

As in most other graphics programs, you usually spend as much time editing an image as you do creating it. Editing tools include the eraser, the selection rectangle, the lasso, and the magic wand.

Using the Eraser

You use the eraser tool to erase portions of a paint image. Click to erase the part of the image that is beneath the eraser. You can click and drag to erase larger portions of the image. If you press Shift as you erase, you can drag the eraser in a straight horizontal or vertical line. (The first move that you make as you drag determines the direction.)

 You cannot resize the eraser. If it's too big to erase a small section of a painting, zoom the screen to a greater magnification.

If you double-click the eraser icon in the Tool panel, you erase the entire paint document or frame.

Selecting Images and Portions of Images

When you want to work with a portion of a picture — whether to cut, copy, or move it; change the fill; or add a special effect to it — you first have to select the specific portion of the picture that you want to edit. With draw objects, this task is simple. You just click the particular object that you're interested in. In a paint document or frame, on the other hand, everything is just dots. Three tools are available for selecting a portion of a picture:

➥ The selection rectangle tool enables you to make rectangular selections. Click to position one corner of the selection rectangle and then drag. When you release the mouse button, the selection is defined by the area that is enclosed in the flashing rectangle.

You can also use a selection rectangle in the following ways:

- Press ⌘ while you drag a selection rectangle around an image to make the selection snap around the image, just as the Lasso tool does.

- Double-click the selection rectangle icon in the Tool panel to select the entire paint document or frame.

- Press ⌘ while you double-click the selection rectangle icon to select only the images within the paint document or frame (ignoring blank spaces).

- Press Option while you drag a selection to make a copy of it. (For example, you can use this feature to take a picture of one car and change it into a traffic jam.)

☞ The lasso tool enables you to make irregular selections in a paint document or frame. Click and then drag around the area that you want to select. When you release the mouse button, the lasso snaps around the images that you have selected, ignoring blank background areas.

You can double-click the lasso icon in the Tool panel to select only the images within the paint document or frame. You also can press Option while you drag a selection to make a copy of it.

☞ The magic wand tool enables you to make selections that are based on color. When you position the head of the magic wand over the desired color or pattern and click the mouse button, all adjacent pixels that are the same color or pattern are selected.

To make a copy of a selection, press Option while you drag the selection.

 When you are attempting to select a pattern, dragging the magic wand through a small area of the pattern may be easier than just clicking. As you drag, a freehand-style line is displayed. When you release the mouse button, the selection is made.

To deselect an image, click outside of the selection, click any tool icon, choose Undo Select from the Edit menu, or press ⌘-Z.

Moving, Cutting, Copying, or Duplicating a Selection

When you move the cursor over a selection that you have made, the cursor changes to a pointer. If you click while the pointer is visible, you can drag the selection to a new location. If you press Shift as you drag, you drag straight horizontally or straight vertically.

You also can use the arrow keys to move the selection one pixel at a time. (If Autogrid is on, the selection moves one gridpoint at a time.)

Commands in the Edit menu become available after you select an image or a portion of an image. You can Cut (⌘-X) or Copy (⌘-C) the image to the Clipboard, Clear the image, or Duplicate it (⌘-D).

Applying Special Effects to a Selection

Special effects in the Transform menu also become available after you make a selection. These effects include *Shear, Distort,* and *Perspective*. Shear adds a vertical or horizontal slant to an image. Distort enables you to stretch an image in any direction. Perspective makes the image appear as if you are viewing it from an angle.

Steps:	Shearing, Distorting, or Adding Perspective to a Selection
Step 1.	Select a portion of the image by using one of the selection tools (selection rectangle, lasso, or magic wand).
Step 2.	Select Shear, Distort, or Perspective from the Transform menu. Blank handles appear around the selection.
Step 3.	Drag a handle to achieve the desired effect.
Step 4.	Click away from the selection to remove the handles.

Figure 6-22 shows the effects of applying Shear, Distort, and Perspective to an image.

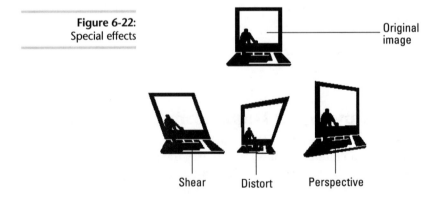

Figure 6-22:
Special effects

Original image

Shear   Distort   Perspective

You lose resolution when you modify an object by using these commands. Because you're in a 72 dpi mode and are in a bitmapped document, the pixels are modified during the transformation. Some pixels become larger, some smaller. This change is normal. If there are too many jagged edges for you, clean up by zooming in and using the tools to smooth out the image. Another trick is to use the Blend option. This option makes the edges less noticeable.

Changing the Size of a Selection

Two commands in the Transform menu enable you to change the size of a selection: Resize and Scale By Percent. To change the size manually, use the Resize command. To change the size by specifying scaling proportions, use Scale By Percent.

To use the resize command, select a portion of the image by using one of the selection tools (the selection rectangle, lasso, or magic wand). Choose Resize from the Transform menu. Blank handles appear around the selection, as shown in Figure 6-23. Drag a handle to change the size of the selection. When you release the mouse button, the selection is redrawn to the specified size. Click away from the image to eliminate the Resize handles.

Figure 6-23:
The Resize command adds handles to the selection.

 If you press Shift as you drag a handle, the original proportions of the selection rectangle are maintained.

To use the scale by percent command, select a portion of the image by using one of the selection tools (the selection rectangle, lasso, or magic wand). Choose Scale By Percent from the Transform menu. The Scale By Percent dialog box appears. Type percentages for enlargement (greater than 100%) or reduction (smaller than 100%). If you want to maintain proportions, enter the same percentage for both the horizontal and vertical dimensions. Click OK. The selection is resized.

Orientation Transformations

The same commands that are available in the draw environment for changing an object's orientation are also available in the paint environment. To change the orientation of a selection, select a portion of the image and choose Flip Horizontally, Flip Vertically, Free Rotate, or Rotate. The first three commands — Flip Horizontally, Flip Vertically, and Free Rotate — work exactly the same way as they do in the draw environment. (For additional information, see the description of these commands in "Flipping and Rotating Objects," earlier in this chapter.)

Like the Object Info command in the draw environment, the paint environment's Rotate command enables you to directly enter a rotation angle for a selection. To use the rotate command, select a portion of the image by using one of the selection tools (the selection rectangle, lasso, or magic wand). Choose Rotate from the Transform menu. The Rotate dialog box appears. Enter a number (in degrees) for the clockwise rotation that you desire. Click OK. The selection is rotated.

Color Transformations

At the bottom of the Transform menu are a number of useful color-related transformation commands. Here is what they do:

- *Fill.* This command duplicates the function of the paint bucket tool, enabling you to fill any selection with a color, pattern, or gradient. The difference is that the fill is applied only to the selected area, so it does not matter whether an image is closed or open; nor does it matter whether the selected area contains a solid color, a gradient, or a pattern.

- *Pick Up.* This command enables you to transfer the design and attributes of one image to another image. To use the command, select an image, drag it over another image, and choose Pick Up from the Transform menu.

One interesting application of Pick Up is for creating patterned text. Type the text, select it by pressing ⌘ as you drag the selection rectangle tool around it, move it over an interesting pattern, and choose the Pick Up command. Figure 6-24 shows some text with a gradient pattern that was created in this manner.

Figure 6-24:
Gradient text
created with
the Pick Up
command

——————— Original text

——————— Text with a gradient that was
picked up from the box below

⤳ *Invert.* Use this command to make a negative image of a selection. Colors in the image are reversed, but not necessarily as you might expect them to be. An inverted gray-scale gradient, for example, may show shades of yellow, green, and blue.

⤳ *Blend.* Use Blend to provide a smooth transition between colors by adding intermediate shades.

⤳ *Tint.* Choose Tint to tint a selection with the current fill color.

⤳ *Lighter* and *Darker.* Use these commands to add white or black to a selection, making it lighter or darker.

When you use any of the color transformation commands, make sure that you select only the outline of an object and not part of the background, too. Each command applies to *everything* within the selection. To select only an object without the surrounding background, use the lasso or press ⌘ while you drag the selection rectangle.

Creating Custom Colors, Patterns, and Gradients

As in the draw environment, you can replace colors, patterns, and gradients in the palettes with ones of your own choosing. Follow the instructions presented earlier in this chapter (in "Creating Custom Colors, Patterns, and Gradients" for the draw environment).

Other Paint Settings

Other menu commands that appear in the paint environment enable you to change the document size, the depth and resolution of the image, and the grid size (in conjunction with the Autogrid feature).

Steps:	Changing the Document Size
Step 1.	Choose Document from the Format menu. The Document dialog box appears, as shown in Figure 6-25.

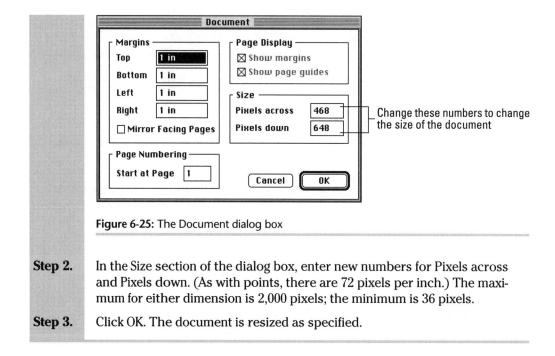

Figure 6-25: The Document dialog box

Step 2.   In the Size section of the dialog box, enter new numbers for Pixels across and Pixels down. (As with points, there are 72 pixels per inch.) The maximum for either dimension is 2,000 pixels; the minimum is 36 pixels.

Step 3.   Click OK. The document is resized as specified.

The *resolution* of a paint document is initially set to match the resolution of a typical Macintosh screen — 72 dots per inch (dpi). If you are printing on a high-resolution printer, such as an Apple LaserWriter (most versions of which print at 300 dpi), you can change the resolution to match that of the printer.

As you increase the resolution, however, the document and its contents shrink accordingly. At 300 dpi, for example, a standard paint document reduces to about 1.5 x 2.25 inches. If you have enough free memory, you can increase the size of the document by following the preceding steps. You should note, however, that the higher the resolution and the larger the document size, the more memory is required. For this reason, many users will prefer to use the default 72 dpi setting for resolution.

Depth refers to the number of colors that are available for displaying the document. Depth is initially set to match the setting in the Monitors control panel.

Steps: **Changing the Depth and Resolution of a Paint Document or Frame**

Step 1.   Choose Resolution & Depth from the Format menu. The Resolution and Depth dialog box appears, as shown in Figure 6-26.

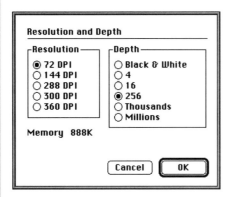

Figure 6-26: The Resolution and Depth dialog box

Step 2.   Choose a resolution by clicking its radio button. Follow these guidelines:

- Use 72 dpi for a document that you intend to display only on-screen or print on an ImageWriter printer. You also can use higher multiples of 72 (144 and 288) to maintain proportions when you print to an ImageWriter or equivalent printer.

- Use 300 dpi to match the resolution of many laser printers.

- Use 360 dpi to match the resolution of many ink-jet printers.

Step 3.   Choose a depth by clicking its radio button. The amount of memory that the new depth setting requires is shown at the bottom of the dialog box.

Step 4.   Click OK to accept the new settings or Cancel to ignore any changes.

If you are working in a paint frame, rather than in a paint document, select the frame and then choose Modify Frame from the Options menu. A similar dialog box appears that enables you to set the resolution, depth, and the *origin* (starting point) for displaying the contents of the frame. Enter values (in pixels) for the horizontal and vertical coordinates. (See Chapter 15 for additional information.)

When importing a PICT file into a paint frame or document, ClarisWorks 4.0 automatically matches the resolution of the image and uses the document's original color table.

When the Autogrid option is on (in the Options menu), the grid size determines where you can place objects and how far they will move at each step when you drag or nudge them with an arrow key. The larger the setting for grid size, the farther apart the grid locations are. You can set the grid size to 2 pixels for fine control over image placement.

To change the grid size, choose Grid Size from the Options menu. The Painting Grid Size dialog box appears. Click the radio button for the desired grid size and click OK.

Down to Business: Editing a Screen Capture

If you're new to the Mac or haven't read your system software manual, you may not be aware that the Mac has a built-in screen capture utility. By pressing Shift-⌘-3, you instruct the Mac to capture (make a copy of) the current screen image. Commercial screen capture utilities add other functions, such as the ability to capture a selected portion of the screen, capture pull-down menus, hide or display the cursor in the capture, and so on.

After you capture the screen, you'll often want to edit the capture. In this task, you learn to capture a screen that displays one of the Paint dialog boxes, edit the capture so that only the dialog box remains, and then change the image into a draw object so that you can place and resize it in any type of document.

This task demonstrates the following paint activities:

- ☞ Editing a full-screen capture at a high-zoom magnification
- ☞ Using the eraser
- ☞ Using the selection rectangle
- ☞ Using the Scrapbook to change a paint image into a resizable PICT object

Steps:	**Cleaning Up a Screen Capture**
Step 1.	In ClarisWorks, create a new paint document and add some shapes to it.
Step 2.	Choose Spray Can from the Options menu. The Edit Spray Can dialog box appears.

Step 3. Test the current spray pattern by clicking and dragging in the sample box.

Step 4. If you do not have a separate capture utility, press Shift-⌘-3. A copy of the screen is saved on disk as a new file, with the name Picture *x*.

— or —

Step 4. If you have a separate screen capture utility, you may be able to capture a specific portion of the screen, determine whether the cursor will be included in the screen shot, and choose many other useful options. Issue the utility's capture command to capture the full screen or a selection that includes the dialog box.

Step 5. Close the paint document by clicking its close box. Do not save the document.

Step 6. Choose Open from the File menu (or press ⌘-O). A file dialog box appears.

Step 7. Choose Painting from the Document Type pop-up menu at the bottom of the dialog box. (Choosing Painting restricts the file list to documents that you can open in the paint environment.)

Step 8. Navigate to the drive and folder where the screen capture is stored, select the file, and click Open. The screen capture opens as a paint document. Figure 6-27 shows what the screen may look like.

If you have performed a full-screen capture, the program may inform you that the document will be opened at a reduced size. If the entire dialog box is not visible in the document window, quit ClarisWorks and increase the memory that is available to the program. (See the Quick Tips at the end of this chapter for instructions.) Then restart ClarisWorks and return to Step 6.

Step 9. Choose the selection rectangle from the Tool panel. Drag to select the dialog box.

Step 10. Choose Cut from the Edit menu (or press ⌘-X). A copy of the dialog box is transferred to the Clipboard.

Step 11. Double-click the eraser tool. The entire painting is erased.

Step 12. Choose Paste from the Edit menu (or press ⌘-V). A copy of the dialog box is pasted onto the blank document page.

Step 13. Click the Zoom Percentage box in the lower-left corner of the document window and select 200%. This setting makes editing the image easier. (With practice and a steady hand, you also can do this kind of editing at 100%.)

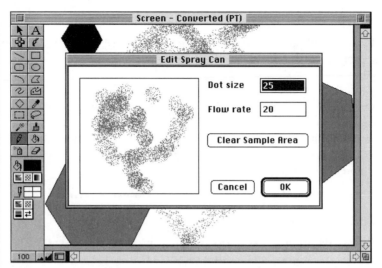

Figure 6-27: The screen capture opened as a ClarisWorks paint file

Step 14. If the eraser isn't still selected, choose it now. To remove the stray patterns and colors from around the border of the dialog box, position the eraser so that its edge is touching — but not covering — one of the sides of the dialog box. Press Shift, click the mouse button, and drag to erase the stray material along that side of the dialog box. Repeat for the other three sides.

Step 15. Click the Zoom Percentage box in the lower-left corner of the document window and select 100%. The image returns to its normal size.

Step 16. Save the edited picture of the dialog box. (In case anything goes wrong in the remaining steps, you can reopen the edited file and proceed from this step.)

Step 17. Choose the selection rectangle tool from the Tool panel. While pressing the ⌘ key, drag a selection rectangle around the dialog box. When you release the mouse button, the selection rectangle snaps around the dialog box.

Step 18. Choose Copy from the Edit menu (or press ⌘-C). A copy of the edited dialog box is transferred to the Clipboard.

Step 19. Close the paint document. If you are asked whether you want to save the document, click Don't Save.

Step 20. Open the Scrapbook desk accessory by selecting it from the Apple menu.

Using the Scrapbook to change images from painting to PICT format is also discussed in the Quick Tips at the end of this chapter.

Step 21. Press ⌘-V. A copy of the dialog box picture is added to the Scrapbook, as shown in Figure 6-28.

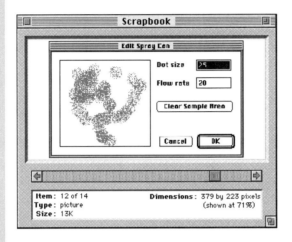

Figure 6-28: The dialog box pasted into the Scrapbook

Step 22. Press ⌘-X. The copy of the dialog box picture is removed from the Scrapbook and changed into a PICT image (an object).

Step 23. Click the close box on the Scrapbook to put it away.

Step 24. In ClarisWorks, create a new drawing or word processing document.

Step 25. Choose Paste from the Edit menu (or press ⌘-V). A copy of the dialog box is pasted into the document.

The dialog box is now an object. You can manipulate this dialog box object as you can any other object. You can, for example, change the size of the dialog box or add a border color around it.

Quick Tips _____

The following Quick Tips describe how to:

  ☞ Edit draw objects in the paint environment

  ☞ Change an edited paint image into a draw object

- ☞ Increase the memory that is available to ClarisWorks
- ☞ Create and work with a second copy of a paint document
- ☞ Preview images before opening them
- ☞ Insert graphics from the ClarisWorks ReadyArt libraries

Editing Draw Objects in the Paint Environment

Occasionally, being able to edit draw objects at the dot level is useful. To perform this task, you simply copy the object, paste it into a paint document, edit, copy again, and then paste it back into the original document.

Although this procedure works, it has an unfortunate side effect. When you paste the image back into the original document, it is a paint frame — a bitmap. It is enclosed by a border, and you can no longer resize it the way you can resize an object. Here's a better method.

Steps:	Changing a Paint Image into a Draw Object
Step 1.	After you finish editing in the paint document, select and copy the image.
Step 2.	Pull down the Apple menu and choose the Scrapbook desk accessory.
Step 3.	Press ⌘-V. The image is pasted into the Scrapbook.
Step 4.	Press ⌘-X. The image is removed from the Scrapbook and copied to the Clipboard as an object.
Step 5.	Open the target document (a draw or word processing document, for example) and choose Paste from the Edit menu (or press ⌘-V). The image is pasted into the document as an object.

Paint Memory Requirements

If you plan on working in the paint environment regularly — particularly with full-screen images — increasing the memory that is available to ClarisWorks is a good idea. Otherwise, you'll frequently see the following message: *The document size has been reduced to fit available memory.*

Steps: Increasing the Memory Available to ClarisWorks

Step 1. Quit ClarisWorks (if it is running), go to the desktop, and select the ClarisWorks program icon.

Step 2. Choose Get Info from the File menu (or press ⌘-I). The Info window for ClarisWorks appears, as shown in Figure 6-29.

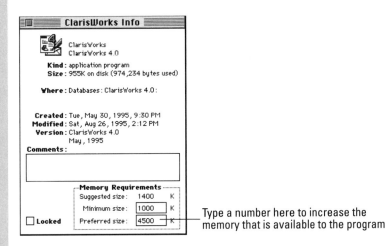

Figure 6-29: The ClarisWorks Info window

The Info window enables you to change the program's memory allocation (the amount of memory that the system will give you to run ClarisWorks and work with ClarisWorks documents).

Step 3. Type a larger number in the Preferred size text-edit box. (In the figure, I increased it to 4500K, or 4.5MB.)

Step 4. Click the Info window's close box.

You can change the memory allocation as often as necessary. To track how much memory you're using in ClarisWorks, go to the desktop and select About This Macintosh from the Apple menu. A window appears that shows how much memory the System and any open programs (ClarisWorks, for example) are currently using (see Figure 6-30).

You also can see the amount of memory that is still free for use by other programs, desk accessories, and so on. A bar for each program shows the total memory that is allocated to that program. The dark area of each bar represents memory that is currently in use. The light area is memory that you can use to open additional documents or expand the size of current documents.

Total memory in the Mac   System software version

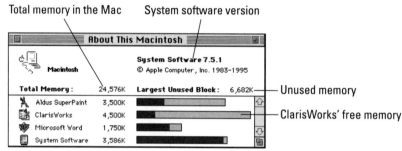

Figure 6-30: The About This Macintosh window shows how much memory the System and any open programs are currently using and how much memory is still free.

Unused memory

ClarisWorks' free memory

Painting in Two Views

When you edit a paint image at a high magnification, seeing a normal view of the image at the same time is sometimes helpful.

Steps:	Creating and Working with a Second Copy of a Paint Document
Step 1.	Choose New View from the View menu. A second copy of the document appears.
Step 2.	Choose Tile Windows from the View menu. The two copies are displayed together, one above the other.
Step 3.	Set the magnification for one of the copies to a higher level (between 200% and 800%, for example) by clicking the Zoom Percentage box in the lower-left corner of the document.

Changes made in one copy of the document are simultaneously reflected in the other copy. However, scrolling is not synchronized between the two documents. You have to scroll the copies manually to make sure that the same portions of the document are displayed in both copies.

Previewing Documents

If you load Apple's QuickTime extension at the start of your computing session, you can preview graphics files before you open them in ClarisWorks 4.0. In the Open dialog box, ClarisWorks can present a thumbnail image of every graphics file. If you have a large number of files, using the Preview feature can help you avoid opening the wrong document. (For information on creating previews, see Chapter 1.)

Inserting Art from the ReadyArt Libraries

ClarisWorks 4.0 includes dozens of clip art images that you can use in your own documents. These images are stored in *libraries* (image collections organized around a theme, such as world maps, hands, computers, and so on).

Steps:	Adding a Library Image to a Draw or Paint Document
Step 1.	Choose the library of interest from the Library submenu of the File menu. The selected library appears in its own windoid.
Step 2.	Scroll to the image that you want to use.
Step 3.	To add the image to the current document, do one of the following:
	• Drag the name of the image onto the document.
	• Drag the thumbnail picture of the image onto the document.
	• Choose the image or its name, and click the windoid's Use button.
Step 4.	The image is inserted into the document (see Figure 6-31). When added to a draw document, the graphic is inserted as a draw object; when added to a paint document or frame, the graphic is a paint (bitmapped) image.

When adding a library image to a paint *frame*, be sure that you are in paint mode. (When in paint mode, the paint tools are visible in the Tool panel.) If you are not in paint mode, the chosen image is added as a free-floating draw object rather than as a paint graphic.

You can also add your own graphics to existing libraries, as well as create new libraries. To learn more about working with libraries, see Chapter 20.

A ReadyArt library window   Preview of selected library image

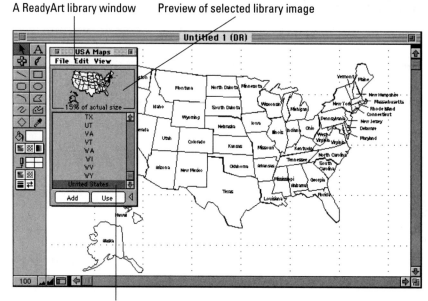

Figure 6-31:
A graphic
copied from
one of the
ReadyArt
libraries

Currently selected library image

Moving On Up

When — or if — your image creation and editing needs expand, you can choose from dozens of commercial graphics programs. They can be classified roughly according to their capabilities:

- *Draw programs*. If objects are your thing, you may prefer a capable draw program, such as ClarisDraw.

- *PostScript drawing programs*. These programs are capable of creating extremely complex and detailed PostScript images — the natural choice of illustrators and designers. The most popular of these programs are Adobe Illustrator and FreeHand (Macromedia). PostScript drawing programs tend to have a very steep learning curve, however. They're not for casual artists or users with simple graphics needs.

- *Image editors/high-end paint programs*. These programs extend paint capabilities by enabling you to create or edit 8-, 16-, 24-, or 32-bit color or gray-scale images. If you need to edit scanned images or video captures, a program such as Adobe Photoshop is a godsend.

∽ *QuickTime editors.* If you want to make your own QuickTime movies, you need software tools that make it possible. Adobe Premiere is a popular choice.

∽ *Special-purpose graphics programs.* A wide variety of graphics niche programs are also available. Some specialize in 3-D images (RayDream Designer, RayDream addDepth, and Adobe Dimensions), enable you to switch freely between paint and PICT modes or combine them in the same document (Adobe SuperPaint), or imitate an artist's brush strokes (Fractal Design Painter).

Depending on your graphics needs, you may find that you require several programs — each for a different purpose. (You may also need more memory.)

Summary

- ➥ ClarisWorks includes a pair of graphics environments. You use the draw environment to create objects and the paint environment for bitmapped images.

- ➥ Draw objects are solid; you can edit them only as a whole. Paint images are composed of dots; you can edit them at the dot level.

- ➥ The first step in editing a draw object is to select it. After you have made a selection, you can move the object, apply different fill and pen attributes to it, or choose editing commands. You also can select several objects at the same time.

- ➥ When you want to edit a paint image, three tools enable you to select a portion of a picture: the selection rectangle, the lasso, and the magic wand. After you make a selection, you can move it, resize it, or alter its attributes.

- ➥ Unlike draw objects (which you can place in almost any environment), you can use paint images only in paint documents and paint frames.

- ➥ Although you can easily add to or change the attributes of a draw object at any time, setting paint attributes is easier before you create each portion of an image than it is afterward.

- ➥ Paint documents can be memory hogs. You may have to increase the memory that is available to ClarisWorks if you regularly work with large paint documents.

- ➥ ClarisWorks 4.0 includes 20 ReadyArt libraries of clip art that you can insert into your documents.

The Communications Environment

CHAPTER 7

In This Chapter

- Understanding communications basics
- Creating communications documents for use with a modem or a direct-connect cable
- Configuring and using the scrollback pane
- Capturing incoming text and working with tables
- Using the Phone Book feature
- Using a modem to connect with an information service, another Mac, or a PC
- Sending and receiving files
- Using a direct-connect cable to transfer files between two Macs and between a Mac and a PC

Overview

Communications (also called *telecommunications*) is the process of exchanging information between computers. This chapter discusses communications by means of a device called a modem or a direct-connect cable. Another way that computers can exchange information is on a network (not discussed here).

A *modem* is a hardware device that is connected to a computer, either internally in an available NuBus slot, PDS (processor-direct slot), or a PCI slot; or externally to one of the computer's serial ports. The job of the modem is to translate outgoing data from its original digital form (ones and zeros) to an analog form (sounds) that telephone lines can carry. The modem attached to the receiving computer translates these sounds back into a digital form that the computer can understand.

The name *modem* comes from the description of what the device does. It *mod*ulates and *dem*odulates computer data. Because modems exchange data over phone lines, you can use a modem to communicate with a computer down the street or across the country.

Modems can do the following:

- Connect your computer to information services, such as CompuServe, Prodigy, GEnie, and America Online
- Connect your computer to bulletin board systems (BBSs)
- Communicate directly with computers used by your colleagues and friends
- Connect to networks and larger computers (mainframes)

Information services charge you according to the amount of time that you spend *online* (connected) each month. Some services have a flat monthly fee that provides unlimited use of basic services, and they charge separately for other parts of the system (for downloading programs and other files from their computer to your Mac, for accessing financial services, and so on). If you live in a metropolitan area, you can frequently connect to the service without incurring long-distance phone charges. The larger information services provide local phone numbers (*access nodes*) that you dial to connect with their systems. When you buy a modem, sign-up information for several information services is often included in the box.

A *BBS* is like a miniature information service and is often run by just one person. Users can typically download files and send messages to other subscribers. A BBS can be as small as a single modem and phone line, or it can contain a bank of phone lines to handle multiple subscribers simultaneously — much the same as the information services do. Fees for becoming a subscriber, if any, are usually quite reasonable.

One-to-one communications is also very popular. You can exchange documents and programs with any other person who has a modem — even if you are using different types of computers (a Mac and a PC, for example). Overnight delivery services take a full day to deliver a document, but a pair of high-speed modems can deliver an important document in a few minutes, and often at a fraction of the cost of using a delivery service.

Unlike most of the other chapters in this book, this chapter is primarily oriented to teaching by example. It contains several "Down to Business" sections that show you, step by step, how to use the ClarisWorks communications environment to perform the following tasks:

- Connect with an information service or BBS by using a modem
- Connect with another Mac by using a modem

⊶ Transfer files between a pair of Macs by using a direct-connect cable

⊶ Transfer files between a Mac and a PC by using a direct-connect cable

Choosing a Modem or Fax Modem

If your Mac didn't come with an internal or external modem (most don't), several factors can help you decide which modem is best for you.

Speed

Different modems support different maximum data transmission speeds. Speed is stated in terms of *baud* or *bps (bits per second)*. When a modem is advertised as a 14400 bps unit, for example, the ad is stating the modem's top transmission speed. Most modems can also perform at lower speeds for compatibility with older or less capable modems.

At this time, most advertised modems are either 14400 or 28800 bps units. For communicating with information services (such as CompuServe, GEnie, America Online, and Prodigy), either type of modem will serve you well. Note, however, that some information services charge a premium for connecting at any speed above 2400 bps. If that's the case with your information service, you can elect to pay the surcharge or simply instruct your modem to connect at the lower, no-surcharge speed.

If much of your communicating will be with friends or colleagues, on the other hand, the faster the modems, the better. And if this two-way communication has to occur at long-distance phone rates, the faster the transmissions occur, the lower the charges will be.

Note: Having a fast modem is particularly important if you intend to use the Internet because of its heavy use of graphics (which can take a long time to transmit).

You can increase *throughput* (the data transfer rate) in a file transfer if both modems have data compression routines in their ROMs (read-only memory). Data compression squeezes information into a smaller package, reducing the time required to transmit files. Because it is handled entirely by the modems rather than in software, the compression occurs very quickly. One standard called MNP5 (Microcom Networking Protocol) offers compression of approximately two to one. Another standard, V.42 bis, which was developed by CCITT (the Consultative Committee for International Telephone and Telegraph), offers four-to-one compression. The amount of compression varies, depending on the type of data you are transferring. Graphics and text tend to compress very well.

Computer programs compress very little. To use compression at all during a communications session, however, both modems must support the same compression features.

If two modems cannot perform compression, you can use one of the many Mac compression programs to compress files prior to going online. Examples of some of the more popular compression programs include StuffIt Deluxe (Aladdin Systems), DiskDoubler (Symantec), and Compact Pro (a shareware program from Cyclos). If the files are precompressed in this manner, however, make sure that you are not also using modem-provided compression. This causes the files to be compressed a second time, which — in most cases — will not improve the compression and can result in the files taking longer to transmit.

Tip: Although 28800 bps modems are now very common, the technology is still new. If you're outfitting different branches of your company with these modems and want to be assured of reliable high-speed connections, your best bet is to buy the same brand and model of modems for each branch. Also, because the manufacturers will tweak the instructions and algorithms in the ROMs of these modems over the next year (to improve reliability and performance), you may prefer modems that have *flash ROMs*. Flash ROMs can be updated by downloading new instructions to them, in much the same way as you download files from information services.

Data Modems versus Fax Modems

As its name implies, you use a *data modem* strictly to exchange computer data — documents, graphics, programs, and so on. A *fax modem* is a data modem that can also send and receive faxes. Most fax modems now offer the same feature set as advanced data modems, as well as providing the ability to fax documents that reside on a Mac's hard disk and to display incoming faxes on the Mac's screen.

Essentially, a fax modem is a paperless fax machine. Using a special print driver that comes with the fax software, you can issue the Print command from within almost any program. The current document is then translated into fax format and sent through the modem to the destination fax machine or fax modem. Documents that you send or receive with a fax modem are indistinguishable from documents that you send or receive with a standard fax machine. If anything, documents that you send with a fax modem tend to be a little clearer because the original document isn't scanned — it is simply converted into fax format by software. Most fax modems can send and receive faxes at speeds up to 14,400 bps. For compatibility with older fax modems and fax machines, however, they can also send and receive at 9,600 and 4,800 bps.

The one drawback of fax modems is that you cannot fax an external document, such as a lease or a photograph, unless you also have a scanner. All documents have to be resident in the Mac in order for you to fax them.

A Typical Modem

If you are new to computing or have never used a modem, choosing one can be very confusing. If you flip through the pages of any computer catalog, for example, you'll typically see many modems with a variety of features. As an example of the current crop of modems, the photo below shows a Teleport Platinum modem made by Global Village Communications.

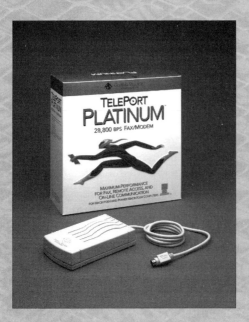

The Teleport Platinum is a 28.8 data/fax-modem that can be connected to any desktop Macintosh. With its support of the V.34 standard, the Platinum can provide throughput as high as 115,000 bps (with file compression). The current version of the Global Village software (version 2.5.5) includes software data-compression enhancements that enable 68040 Centris and Quadra Macintosh computers to transmit data at speeds above 57,600 bps. The included fax software is excellent and enables the modem to distinguish incoming fax calls from voice calls. The Platinum also has flash ROM, enabling you to update the modem by simply transmitting special

Global Village-provided data to it. (For Macintosh PowerBook computers, Global Village also offers the *PowerPort* series of modems.)

Special Features

The many useful and esoteric features that you can add to a modem are like the add-ons that a dealer offers when you buy a new car. The following features are among the available options:

∞ Advanced error correction and data compression protocols, which, because they are coded into the modem's ROM, work much faster than the same features in a communications program

∞ Voice capabilities for modems that also work as answering machines

∞ Voice/fax switching for modems that can sense what type of information is conveyed in an incoming call and automatically switch it to the appropriate device — either ringing the phone or sending a fax answer tone

Communications Terminology

Like most areas of computing, communications has its own language. The following list explains some communications terms that you need to understand:

∞ *Access number, access node.* A phone number that you can dial to reach an information service or BBS. Larger services frequently provide local access numbers for major cities. When you dial an access number, it automatically connects you with the system, and you avoid long-distance charges.

∞ *Baud, bps (bits per second).* The operating speed of a modem. Although the terms have different meanings, they're often used interchangeably. Whether the advertising says that a modem is 14400 baud or 14400 bps, it simply means that the modem's top speed (without compression) is 14,400 bits per second.

In many advertisements and catalogs, the baud/bps figure is abbreviated. If you see an ad for a "14.4 modem," it is referring to a modem with a top speed of 14,400 bps — the thousands are assumed.

∞ *Download, downloading.* Retrieving a file or program for your own use from an information service, BBS, or another user's computer.

∞ *E-mail (electronic mail).* Private messages that you leave for another user or another user leaves for you.

∞ *Log on, logging on.* Connecting with an information service or BBS. Often you have to provide a user ID and password to complete the connection and gain access to the service or BBS.

∞ *Log off, logging off.* Ending a session with an information service or BBS. Most systems have a command (such as Bye, Off, Logoff, End, or Quit) that you must type or choose to end the session.

∞ *Protocol, protocol transfer.* The computer algorithm that you've selected for assuring error-free data transfers between your computer and the other system when you are uploading or downloading files. Each protocol has its own method of making sure that each block of data is received correctly. In most cases, when an error occurs, the protocol instructs the system to resend the block. Examples of protocols include XMODEM, 1K XMODEM, Kermit, YMODEM, ZMODEM, and CompuServe B. Different information services, BBSs, and communications programs support different protocols.

∞ *Session.* The period during which you are connected to another computer, information service, or BBS.

∞ *SIG (Special Interest Group).* A section of an information service devoted to a particular topic (such as legal issues, writing, Macintosh users, game playing, or hang gliding). Information services often have many SIGS, and within each SIG, you may be able to participate in interactive discussions, read and post messages, and download files that interest you.

∞ *Upload, uploading.* Transmitting a file or program from your Mac to an information service, BBS, or another user's computer.

Communication Essentials _____

Whether you are connecting by modem to an information service, a BBS, or another computer, or transferring files between two computers by using a direct-connect cable, the two communications programs need to have matching parameters. Both modems have to transmit data at the same speed, use the same file transfer protocols, and so on. If any of the essential communication parameters do not match, you may see garbage characters on-screen, have difficulty transferring data, lose the connection inadvertently, or not be able to connect at all. Having mismatched parameters is like trying to converse with someone when each of you is speaking a different language.

After you create a standard communications document for a modem, you can use it as the starting point for any new communications session that you undertake.

Figure 7-1 shows the components of a communications document window.

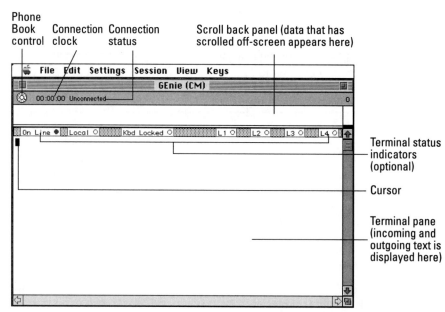

Phone Book control | Connection clock | Connection status | Scroll back panel (data that has scrolled off-screen appears here)

Figure 7-1:
A communi-
cations
document
window

Terminal status indicators (optional)

Cursor

Terminal pane (incoming and outgoing text is displayed here)

| Steps: | **Creating a General Communications Document for Use with a Modem** |

Step 1. Choose Connection from the Settings menu. The Connection Settings dialog box appears, as shown in Figure 7-2. You use this dialog box to set up the current communications document for a modem connection (Apple Modem Tool) or a direct connection (Serial Tool).

Step 2. Choose Apple Modem Tool from the Method pop-up menu. The default settings in the Port Settings section of the dialog box are 2400 bps (bits per second), no parity, 8 data bits, 1 stop bit, and no handshake. Generally, these settings are correct for a Mac with a 2400 bps modem that will be communicating with an online information service, a BBS, or a friend with a similar modem.

If you have a 9600 bps or faster modem, however, you need a special cable that is wired for a *hardware handshake.* The computer uses one line of the cable to tell the modem that data is being sent to the Mac faster than the Mac can handle it and that the modem needs to pause until the Mac catches up. If you have such a cable, choose the appropriate setting from the Handshake pop-up menu.

Step 3. In the Modem options section of the dialog box, choose your modem from the Modem pop-up menu.

Select a connection tool
from this pop-up menu

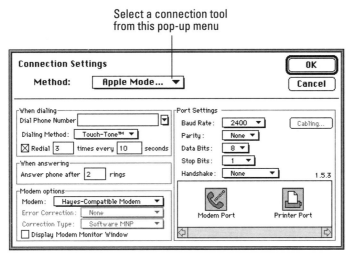

Figure 7-2: The Connection Settings dialog box

If your specific brand or model isn't listed, the Hayes-Compatible Modem choice will work for most modems. Check your modem user's guide for more details about your modem.

To choose options from the pop-up menus for Error Correction and Correction Type, you must select a modem that supports error correction. If you have a non-Apple modem, choose Custom from the Modem pop-up menu and enter the appropriate settings for your modem in the Custom Modem Definition dialog box that appears (see Figure 7-3). To fill in the settings, you'll need to have your modem manual in hand. Turning on Balloon Help also helps.

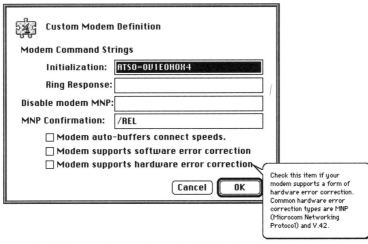

Figure 7-3: Use the Custom Modem Definition dialog box to enter settings for non-Apple modems.

If you have a non-Apple modem and need additional assistance in entering the proper strings for a Custom Modem Definition, call the modem manufacturer or contact Claris Technical Support.

Step 4. In the When dialing section, enter the telephone number of the other computer system, BBS, or information service; the type of phone service that you are using (touch-tone, pulse, or mixed); the number of times that you want the modem to redial the number if it detects a busy signal; and the number of seconds between redials. (If you don't want it to redial, remove the check from the Redial check box.)

When you type the phone number, include all digits that must be dialed. For example, if the call is long-distance, the number is usually preceded by 1. If your phone system requires you to dial 9 to get an outside line, the first digit of the phone number you enter should be **9**. You can include hyphens in the number to improve readability, although they are not required.

You also can add pauses by inserting one or more commas between numbers. Each comma normally represents a two-second pause. If you need to reach an outside line before you dial the phone number, for example, the entry may look similar to the following:

```
9,,555-8812
```

In this example, the modem dials 9, waits four seconds, and then dials the rest of the number.

Step 5. In the When answering section, set the number of rings that the modem must detect before it answers an incoming call.

The minimum allowable number of rings is 1. If you never want the modem to answer incoming calls, you can set this item to a very high number, such as 255.

Step 6. *Optional:* If you want to see the modem commands as they occur during the session, check the Display Modem Monitor Window at the bottom-left corner of the Connection Settings dialog box. A Modem Monitor window appears at the bottom of your screen.

Step 7. In the bottom-right section of the dialog box, click the icon of the port to which the modem cable is connected.

Step 8. Click OK to retain the new connection settings.

Step 9. Choose Terminal from the Settings menu. The Terminal Settings dialog box appears (see Figure 7-4).

When a Mac is connected with another computer by modem or by cable, the Mac can *emulate* (pretend to be) a number of different computer terminals. Different emulation choices provide varying degrees of control

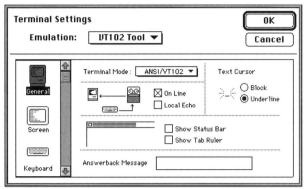

Figure 7-4: The Terminal Settings dialog box (VT102 options shown)

over how text and graphics are displayed on the Mac's screen. There are two general types of emulation provided: the VT102 Tool and the TTY tool. *VT102* provides emulation support for several varieties of intelligent terminals from Digital Equipment Corporation; *TTY* (Teletype) is for dumb terminals.

Step 10. Select the emulation type and terminal settings appropriate for your communications setup.

Table 7-1, presented after these steps, describes the VT102 terminal settings that you are most likely to use. For an explanation of the other settings, refer to ClarisWorks Help.

Click the screen icons to select Screen settings. The effects of your choices are shown in the text box on the right side of the dialog box. If you choose the TTY Tool, rather than the VT102 Tool, a single screen appears (see Figure 7-5). The screen contains options that are a subset of the options that are available for the VT102.

Step 11. Click OK to record the terminal settings.

Step 12. Choose File Transfer from the Settings menu to choose a default method for conducting file transfers. The File Transfer Settings dialog box appears. If you prefer, you can wait until you're online to make a selection. (File transfer options are discussed later in this chapter. Refer to the "Down to Business" sections for suggested protocols.)

Step 13. Save the communications document.

If you want to use the document as the basis for most communication documents, refer to the section in Chapter 10 on using stationery to set new defaults for an environment.

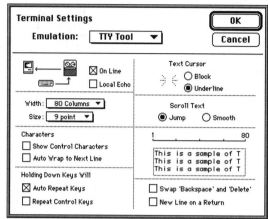

Figure 7-5: TTY Tool options

 When you save a communications document, text in the terminal and scrollback panes is also saved. If you want to use the document as a communications template, you may want to clear both panes by choosing the Clear Screen and Clear Saved Lines commands from the Session menu.

Table 7-1
VT102 Tool Settings

General

Setting	Description
Terminal mode	Terminal choices include ANSI/VT102 and VT52 (two varieties of terminals from Digital Equipment Corporation), and TTY (Teletype).
	Begin by trying the ANSI/VT102 choice, particularly if you are connecting to a PC rather than a Mac. If the information service or BBS does not respond properly to the ANSI/VT102 setting (or if you don't need the features and special keys that are defined for the VT102), try the TTY Tool setting.
On Line	When this box is checked, you can connect and communicate with the other computer system. Leaving it unchecked means that you want to work offline. Normally, you should check the On Line box.
Local Echo	When this box is checked, everything that you type is automatically displayed in the terminal window. When this box is unchecked, you are relying on the other computer to echo back to your screen whatever you just typed. After you connect with the other computer, check this box if nothing that you type appears on your screen. Remove the check mark if you see double characters for everything you type (*HHeelllllloo,* for example).
Show Status Bar	When this box is checked, informative status indicators are added to the top of the communications window (see Figure 7-1). This setting does not affect communications.

Show Tab Ruler	When this box is checked, a ruler bar is added to the top of the communications window. This setting does not affect communications.
Text Cursor	The cursor can be shown as either a flashing underline or a flashing block. Choose the one you prefer.
Answerback Message	If you want, you can enter a brief text string ("Connected with Steve's Mac," for example) that will automatically be transmitted when another computer connects with yours.

Screen

Setting	Description
Width	The text width. Terminal width options are 80 or 132 characters per line.
Size	The text size. Characters can be displayed in 9 or 12 point type.
Auto Wrap to Next Line	When this box is checked, if a line contains more characters than the number specified for the terminal width, it will automatically wrap to the next line.
Insert Characters	When this box is checked, you can insert characters in the middle of a text string that you are typing. When unchecked, characters will replace existing text.
Scroll Text	Select Jump or Smooth to determine how incoming text will be displayed on your screen.
Inverse Video	Checking this box displays white text on a black background, rather than black text on a white background.

Keyboard

Setting	Description
Keyclick Sound	When this box is checked, you hear a click whenever a key is pressed.
New Line on a Return	Click this check box if the cursor does not automatically move to a new line when you press the Return key to end a paragraph.

Making the Connection

When you are ready to connect with another computer, turn on the modem and follow one of the following procedures (depending on whether you or the other computer will initiate the connection).

Steps:	Initiating a Call to Another Computer
Step 1.	Open the ClarisWorks communications document.
Step 2.	Check the Connection, Terminal, and File Transfer settings.
Step 3.	To initiate the call, choose Open Connection from the Session menu (or press Shift-⌘-O).

The program dials the number that you entered in the Dial Phone Number text-edit box in the Connection Settings dialog box. If the text-edit box is blank (that is, you haven't entered a number), ClarisWorks prompts for the number to dial.

As an alternative, if you have created a Phone Book entry for the service, BBS, or computer (as discussed later in this chapter under "Using the Phone Book Feature"), you also can initiate the connection by choosing Phone Book from the Settings menu, pressing ⌘-B, or clicking the phone book control (the dial icon); choosing the name of the system with which you want to connect; and clicking Connect (see Figure 7-6). If you can't find the name of the system that you want to call or if you change your mind, click Done.

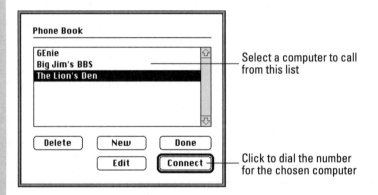

Figure 7-6: You can dial the number for the system that you want to connect with by choosing its name from the Phone Book.

Normally, you can turn on the modem just before you initiate a connection or before the other computer calls you. You don't have to leave the modem on when you don't need it. However, you need to turn on some modems, particularly some fax modems, prior to starting up the Mac. Otherwise, the software that controls the modem may not be in effect for that computing session. Check your manual to see whether your modem has any special on/off requirements.

Steps: Waiting for a Call from Another Computer

Step 1. Open the ClarisWorks communications document.

Step 2. Check the Connection, Terminal, and File Transfer settings.

Step 3. Choose Wait For Connection from the Session menu (or press Shift-⌘-W). A Modem Status window appears, as shown in Figure 7-7, and the modem is instructed to wait for and automatically answer the call. You can click Cancel at any time to reset the modem so that it will not continue to wait for an incoming call.

Figure 7-7:
The Modem Status
window when the modem
is waiting for a call

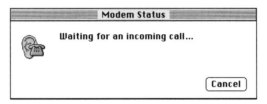

The first time that you attempt to connect with another person's computer, an information service, or a BBS, you should agree on the communication parameters beforehand. At a minimum, you need to agree on the following parameters:

- Baud rate
- Parity
- Data bits
- Stop bits
- A protocol for file transfers (if you intend to exchange files during the session)

During the initial few seconds of the connection, many modems can negotiate some of the more important settings, such as speed and protocols for error correction and compression. Unfortunately, many other modems *can't* negotiate these settings. If one of the users attempts to correct a mismatch by changing the settings while online, the connection may be lost. You can avoid potential aggravation by agreeing on settings before you try to connect.

Setting Communication Preferences

The Preferences command in the Edit menu enables you to do the following:

- Set defaults for how the scrollback pane operates
- Choose the method for capturing incoming data
- Determine what to do — if anything — when a communications document is opened
- Select a folder in which downloads will automatically be stored
- Choose tools for the connection, terminal emulation, and the file transfer protocol

You can establish different preference settings for each communications document. You can also set global defaults to be used with every new communications document (see Chapter 11 for details).

Controlling the Scrollback

Most communications programs automatically track all data that is sent or received during a session. As you type new text and information is transmitted to you, the session data scrolls off the screen. If you want to see what someone said to you earlier in the session or find the ID number of a file that has scrolled off-screen, you just drag the scroll bar back until the information reappears.

ClarisWorks, on the other hand, takes a different approach to recording session data in order to accommodate Macs that have little memory to spare. First, instead of being automatic, recording the data is an optional part of a communications session. Second, you can use the Preferences dialog box to specify how the program should handle scrollback data. Third, ClarisWorks displays the information in a separate pane at the top of the communications window.

There are two ways of looking at the ClarisWorks scrollback options:

    ⤷ The ClarisWorks scrollback options offer extensive control over how much old data is retained in memory and whether it is saved to disk when an information service or BBS sends a command to clear your screen.

    ⤷ The ClarisWorks scrollback options introduce an unnecessary set of procedures for handling something that is normally transparent to communications users.

Whichever way you choose to look at it, you're stuck with the scrollback options. The following sections describe how they work.

Viewing the Scrollback

As the terminal window fills with data, old information scrolls off the top of the window. As long as the Save Lines Off Top command (⌘-T) in the Session menu is preceded by a check mark, the old data is recorded rather than discarded. Whether the scrollback pane is displayed or hidden, the data is still being recorded.

When you first open a communications document, the scrollback pane is hidden. To view the scrollback, you can use either of the following methods:

    ⤷ Choose Show Scrollback from the Settings menu (or press ⌘-L).

    ⤷ Drag down the scrollback pane divider, as shown in Figure 7-8.

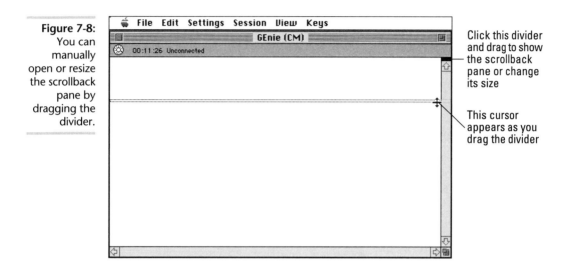

Figure 7-8:
You can manually open or resize the scrollback pane by dragging the divider.

Click this divider and drag to show the scrollback pane or change its size

This cursor appears as you drag the divider

As soon as the system has received a screenful of data, the data begins to appear in the scrollback pane.

To hide the scrollback pane, press ⌘-L again, choose Hide Scrollback from the Settings menu, or drag the scrollback pane divider upwards until it disappears.

Setting Scrollback Preferences

You set scrollback defaults in the Preferences dialog box. Choose Preferences from the Edit menu and click the Communication icon in the Preferences dialog box that appears (see Figure 7-9).

The top section of the dialog box contains the scrollback settings; Unlimited scrollback is the default setting. You can limit scrollback to a specific number of data lines, screens, or kilobytes (groups of 1,024 characters) by using the pop-up menu and text-edit box.

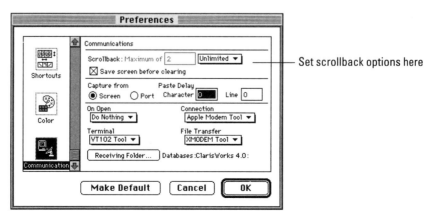

Figure 7-9:
You set communications defaults in the Preferences dialog box.

Set scrollback options here

Some information services and BBSs send information one screen at a time and send a command to clear the current screen before transmitting the next one. To avoid losing the previous screen, click the Save screen before clearing check box. For more information about setting communications preferences, see Chapter 11.

Working with the Scrollback Pane

When the scrollback pane is open, you can do several things:

- ⌚ Scroll backward and forward by using the scroll bar.

- ⌚ Copy the current screen in the terminal window into the scrollback pane by choosing Save Current Screen from the Session menu.

- ⌚ Eliminate all data in the scrollback pane by choosing Clear Saved Lines from the Session menu.

- ⌚ Copy selected data from the scrollback pane and paste it into the terminal window. The system sends information that you paste into the terminal window to the other computer or information service, just as if you had typed it manually.

 Copying information from the scrollback pane and then pasting it into the terminal window can be handy. For example, you can use this method to identify files that you want to download from an information service or a BBS. In order to download a file, you often have to identify it by its ID number. You can request a directory of new files and then, after you receive the directory, go back into the scrollback. Next, select and Copy (⌘-C) the ID number for the first file that you want to download. When the program prompts you for the file to download, use the Paste command (⌘-V) to enter the ID number.

Capturing Text

In most cases, you will want to use one of the more advanced file transfer protocols, such as XMODEM or Kermit, to transfer files from one computer to another. Regardless of whether the file is a formatted word processing document, a Macintosh program, or a simple ASCII text file, you can still use a file transfer protocol.

Occasionally, however, you may want to make a record of incoming text, such as a lengthy help message from an information service or an author's description of a program that he or she has uploaded. Because such information is normally just displayed on the screen (it doesn't have to be downloaded), a different procedure is used to capture the text. No file transfer protocol is needed.

Steps:	Capturing a Text Stream
Step 1.	Just before the information that you want to capture appears onscreen, choose Capture to File from the Session menu. A standard file dialog box appears.
Step 2.	Type the filename under which the text will be saved and click Save. All incoming data is saved to the file.
Step 3.	When you want to stop capturing incoming text, choose Stop Capture from the Session menu.

You can capture data in two different formats: Port or Screen. You select the format in the Preferences dialog box that appears when you choose Preferences from the Edit menu (see Chapter 11 for instructions).

Port format captures data exactly as it is sent, along with any tabs, line-feeds, or form-feeds that have been embedded in the text. *Screen* format, on the other hand, is straight ASCII text.

Working with Tables

You can convert some tables that you get from information services into a table format that is suitable for manipulating in a spreadsheet. Stock information is a common example.

Steps:	Copying Data in Tabular Format
Step 1.	Select the table in the terminal window.
Step 2.	Choose Copy Table from the Edit menu.
	If the table is in the middle of the terminal window, you can copy just the contents of the table and ignore information in the left and right margins by pressing the Command key as you drag to highlight the table.
Step 3.	Paste the table into a spreadsheet by clicking a destination cell and choosing Paste from the Edit menu (or pressing ⌘-V).

Using the Phone Book Feature

The Phone Book is an optional directory that you can use to record and dial the phone numbers of information services, BBSs, and other computers with which you want to connect. Every communications document can have its own Phone Book. If you use the same communication parameters for several information services or BBSs, you can create a generic communications document and add all the appropriate phone numbers to the document's Phone Book.

Steps:	Creating a Phone Book
Step 1.	Open the communications document to which you want to attach a Phone Book.
Step 2.	Choose Phone Book from the Settings menu, press ⌘-B, or click the phone book control (previously shown in Figure 7-1) and choose Edit Phone Book. The Edit Phone Book Entry dialog box appears, ready for you to create a new listing (see Figure 7-10).

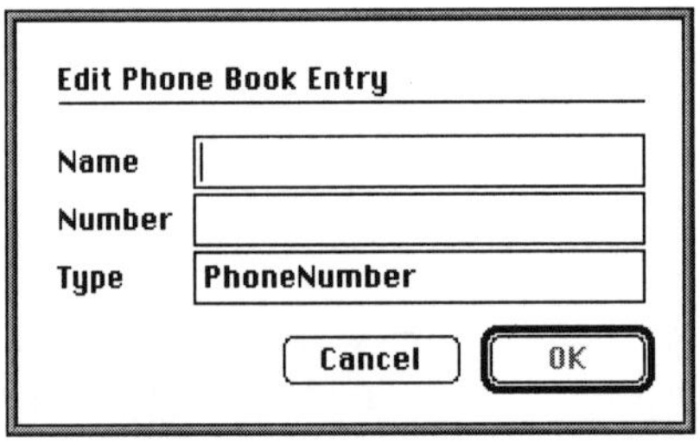

Edit Phone Book Entry

Name

Number

Type PhoneNumber

Cancel   OK

Figure 7-10: A blank page for a new Phone Book entry

Step 3.	In the appropriate text-edit boxes, enter a name for the service or computer and a complete phone number (including any required prefixes).
Step 4.	For a modem connection, leave PhoneNumber in the Type text-edit box.
Step 5.	Click OK to accept the new entry.

Steps:	**Dialing with the Phone Book**
Step 1.	Turn on the modem.
Step 2.	Open the communications document to which the Phone Book is attached.
Step 3.	Choose Phone Book from the Settings menu (or press ⌘-B). The Phone Book for the current document appears (illustrated previously in Figure 7-6), listing all of the entries that you have created.
Step 4.	Select the entry that you want to dial and click Connect. The number is dialed, and a connection is attempted, using the current communication parameters for the document.

— or —

Step 1.	Turn on the modem.
Step 2.	Click the Phone Book control (the telephone dial icon at the top right of the communications document window). A pop-up menu that lists all services, BBSs, and other computers in the current document's Phone Book appears below the control. Drag down until the correct service is selected and release the mouse button. The number for the service is dialed, and a connection is attempted, using the current communication parameters for the document.

You can edit Phone Books to add new numbers, delete unwanted numbers, and edit existing numbers. To edit the Phone Book, choose Phone Book from the Settings menu, press ⌘-B, or click the Phone Book control and choose Edit Phone Book. You can make any of the following changes:

- Click New to create a new entry.

- Select an entry and click Delete to remove it from the Phone Book.

- Select an entry and click Edit to change the name or number for an entry.

Click Done when you finish making changes.

Connecting via Modems

The most common use of communications is connecting with an information service, a BBS, or another user's computer by using a modem. This section explains how to use a modem with the ClarisWorks communications environment. After you have established the correct numbers and settings, you can save the document as a stationery document to eliminate the setup time for future sessions.

Down to Business: Connecting with an Online Information Service

Many of the larger information services, such as America Online, Prodigy, and eWorld, have their own communications software that you need to use in order to connect with their service. These services either include the cost of the software in their sign-up fee or provide it at no cost.

You can access other information services, such as CompuServe, GEnie, and most BBSs, with any standard communications program, including the ClarisWorks communications environment.

Steps:	Accessing an Online Information Service or BBS by Using ClarisWorks
Step 1.	Obtain an access number and a list of connection parameters from the service.
	Information service access numbers are often restricted to particular modem speeds. Be sure to select one that corresponds with your modem's capabilities.
Step 2.	Choose Connection and Terminal from the Settings menu, and set parameters to match the parameters that the service requires. Be sure to enter the access number for the service in the Connection Settings dialog box.
	As a starting point, you can use the communications document that you created in the section "Communication Essentials," earlier in this chapter. You also may want to select a file transfer protocol at this time, or you can select it while online, prior to initiating the first transfer.
Step 3.	Choose Open Connection from the Session menu (or press Shift-⌘-O). The number that you entered in the Connection Settings dialog box is dialed.

Step 4. When the information service or BBS responds (you may see a message saying CONNECT, for example), enter any information that is requested. Entering this information is essential to the logon process.

For example, the service may ask you to enter a user name, an ID, or your full name, address, and so on. Many services also expect you to enter a password that you've selected or that has been assigned to you.

Step 5. When you want to end the session, type or choose the command that the information service or BBS requires (Off, Bye, Quit, and Logoff are common examples). After the system responds, choose Close Connection (Shift-⌘-W) from the Session menu. The modem disconnects and releases the phone line.

 If the information service doesn't have a local access number in your city or town, don't choose one for the nearest city. Instead, pick one in a neighboring state. Out-of-state long-distance calls are usually much cheaper than in-state long-distance calls. Some services also have an 800 number that you can use to connect with them. Although such numbers are normally provided at an extra cost to you, they may be cheaper than a long-distance call.

Down to Business: Connecting with a Mac or a PC

From a communications standpoint, connecting with another PC or Mac differs little from connecting with a BBS or an information service. The main differences are

- ✎ *Speed.* Because you do not have to pay surcharges for high-speed connections, you can use the fastest baud rate that both modems can support.

- ✎ *Modem features used.* If both modems offer advanced error correction or data compression protocols in ROM, you can use those features to ensure error-free, speedy file transfers.

Steps: **Connecting with a Mac or a PC**

Step 1. Agree on a set of communication parameters to use. In particular, the parameters should include baud rate, parity, data bits, and stop bits. When you set the baud rate, select the highest speed that both modems support. When one is a 9600-baud modem and the other is a 2400-baud modem, for example, set the baud rate at 2400 for both modems.

Step 2.   In ClarisWorks, choose Connection and Terminal from the Settings menu and set parameters to match the parameters that the other computer requires. Be sure to enter the phone number for the other computer in the Connection Settings dialog box. You also may want to select a file transfer protocol at this time, or you can select it while you are online, prior to initiating the first transfer.

The other computer user should open his or her communications program and set the initial communications parameters.

Step 3.   If you are going to initiate the call, the other computer user should set the communications program to wait for your incoming call. In ClarisWorks, you then choose Open Connection from the Session menu (or press Shift-⌘-O). The number that you entered in the Connection Settings dialog box is dialed.

— or —

Step 3.   If you are going to receive the call, choose Wait for Connection from the Session menu (or press Shift-⌘-W). The other computer user then instructs the communications program to dial your computer's phone number.

The receiving computer automatically answers the phone after the predetermined number of rings. During the first few seconds of the connection, the two modems negotiate about which special features, such as data compression and error correction, to use. They also may agree on an optimal baud rate for the session.

If the connection is successful, you should now be able to type in the terminal window and have your text appear on the other user's screen (and vice verse).

Transferring Files While Online

Transferring data and program files between two computers is a bit different from transferring them with an information service or BBS. No menus appear to help you through each step or to help you choose a file transfer protocol. Setting matching protocols on the two systems is your responsibility, as is initiating the Send File and Receive File commands.

Steps:	Transmitting a File

Step 1. If you haven't already agreed on a file transfer protocol, select one now. Both programs should be set to use the same protocol.

Step 2. Type a message to the receiving system to tell it that you are about to begin sending. The other computer should choose the command to receive a file, unless it is using a protocol that is set up to receive files automatically (such as Kermit).

Step 3. In ClarisWorks, choose Send File from the Session menu, and choose the file to send.

Steps:	Receiving a File

Step 1. If you haven't already agreed on a file transfer protocol, select one now. Both programs should be set to use the same protocol.

Step 2. Choose Receive File from the Session menu when the sending system is ready to begin transmitting the file and the other user instructs you to prepare for the transmission.

You can set some protocols, such as Kermit, to automatically receive files without using a Receive File command. (See "The Kermit File Transfer Protocol" later in this chapter for more information.)

Step 3. In the sending program, the other user should choose the command to send a file and choose the file to send.

Ending the Session

When you are ready to end the session, type your intent to the other user and choose Close Connection from the Session menu (or press Shift-⌘-O).

The Direct Connection

You can transfer files between any two computers — including computers of different types, such as Macintoshes and PCs — by connecting their serial ports with a *null-modem cable.* (You don't need modems.) To connect a pair of Macs that are Mac Pluses or newer, you can use a mini DIN-8 to mini DIN-8 ImageWriter cable.

After you make the connection, all you need to do is launch a communications program on each machine, set matching communication parameters, and then use any communications protocol that they have in common — XMODEM, for example — to perform file transfers in either direction. Because you are using a cable and the Serial Tool, rather than communicating over a phone line with modems, file transfers can occur at much higher speeds.

Down to Business: Transferring Files Between a Pair of Macs

Here are some common examples of instances when you may want to transfer files between a pair of Macs that are connected by a cable:

- ☞ You have two Macs — a desktop Mac and one that you use outside the office, such as a PowerBook. You can use a direct hookup to transfer files that you've edited or created outside the office to your desktop system.

- ☞ You've prepared some important files for a presentation that you plan to give to a client. Use the direct connect method to transfer copies of the files to your PowerBook before you hit the road.

- ☞ You have purchased a new Mac and want to copy some important data files to it quickly.

- ☞ One or more of the files that you need to move between machines is too large to fit on a floppy disk.

 Another way to connect a pair of Macs without going to the bother of dealing with a communications program is to connect them with a standard AppleTalk network cable — creating a two-person network. After turning on file sharing with the appropriate system software control panels, you can easily exchange files between the two Macs.

Connecting the Cable

You can use a standard ImageWriter II printer cable to connect any pair of Macs that are Mac Pluses or newer. Each end of the cable has a round 8-pin connector called a mini DIN-8. Attach the cable to the modem or printer port on the back of each Mac. Before you connect or disconnect the cable, turn off both machines.

Configuring the Communications Document

In this section, you will create a communications document that you can use to transfer data between a pair of Macs. After you create and save the document, you make a copy of it onto a floppy disk, install it on the second Mac, and perform a typical file transfer. The first step is to configure the communications document.

Steps: Creating a Mac-to-Mac Communications Document

Step 1. Open a new communications document by choosing New from the File menu (or pressing ⌘-N).

Step 2. When the document opens, choose Connection from the Settings menu. The Connection Settings dialog box appears. Use the settings that are shown in Figure 7-11.

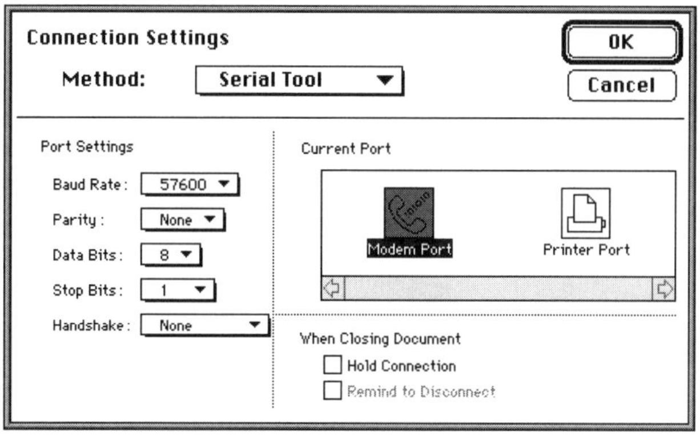

Figure 7-11: The Connection Settings dialog box

Step 3. Choose the following settings from the pop-up menus:

Method: Serial Tool

Baud Rate: 57600

Parity: None

Data Bits: 8

Stop Bits: 1

Handshake: None

Step 4. Be sure that the port to which the communications cable is connected is selected in the Current Port box.

Step 5. Click OK to accept the new settings.

If another person is going to be involved in the file transfers, you can configure the Terminal settings so that you can type back and forth to each other between transfers (Step 6). If not, skip to Step 7.

Step 6. Choose Terminal from the Settings menu. The Terminal Settings dialog box appears (illustrated previously in Figure 7-4 and described in Table 7-1). Choose the VT102 Tool from the Emulation pop-up menu and set the following options (you can leave all other settings as they were initially):

General: On Line, Local Echo

Screen: Auto Wrap to Next Line

Keyboard: New Line on a Return

After making the changes, click OK to accept the new settings.

Step 7. Choose File Transfer from the Settings menu. The File Transfer Settings dialog box appears, as shown in Figure 7-12.

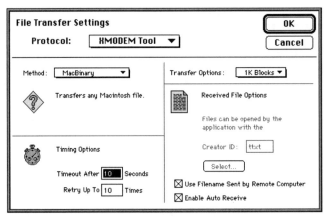

Figure 7-12: The File Transfer Settings dialog box

Step 8. Choose the following settings from the pop-up menus:

> *Protocol:* XMODEM Tool
>
> *Method:* MacBinary
>
> *Transfer Options:* 1K Blocks or CleanLink

Step 9. Check the boxes for Use Filename Sent by Remote Computer and Enable Auto Receive. Click OK to accept the new settings.

Files will be received in the folder that you specified in the Communications section of the Preferences dialog box. For information on setting preferences, see Chapter 11.

Step 10. Save the communications document (you might name it *Mac-to-Mac,* for example).

Step 11. Make a copy of the communications document on a floppy disk and copy it to the other Mac.

Next, test the file transfer process.

Steps:	**Transferring Files**
Step 1.	Launch ClarisWorks on both Macs and open the Mac-to-Mac communications document.
Step 2.	On both machines, choose Open Connection from the Session menu (or press Shift-⌘-O).
Step 3.	To test the connection, type some text on one of the Mac keyboards. It should appear simultaneously in the terminal window on both Macs.
Step 4.	Choose Send File from the Session menu on one of the Macs. A standard file dialog box appears.
Step 5.	Select a file to send and click the Send Button. The file transfer occurs automatically.

Because you selected Enable Auto Receive, file transfers can occur without requiring the recipient to choose Receive File from the Session menu. You can use this configuration to send files in either direction. When you are through transferring files, choose Close Connection from the Session menu on both Macs (or press Shift-⌘-O).

The 1K XMODEM protocol is sufficiently speedy and error free for most file transfers. If you want to send a large number of files, however, you may prefer to use the Kermit protocol. Of the protocols that are supported by ClarisWorks, Kermit is the only one that permits unattended transfers of *batches* of files. (For more information on using Kermit, see "The Kermit File Transfer Protocol" later in this chapter.)

 If you use the Kermit protocol's Overwrite Existing Files option, and you transfer a file with the same name as one that already exists in the destination folder on the receiving machine, the existing file will be replaced by the new one.

Down to Business: Transferring Files Between a Mac and a PC

With Apple's continued penetration into the business market, finding both Macs and PCs in the same office is becoming more common. In the past, sharing files between the two platforms was difficult. Disks were formatted differently, and file formats varied widely between the systems.

The inclusion of an Apple SuperDrive (the 1.4MB, 3.5-inch floppy disk drive) in all Macs that are Mac Pluses or newer has helped minimize the differences between Mac and PC data. With the older Apple File Exchange, the newly-released PC Exchange, and several other commercial programs from third-party software companies, Macs equipped with a SuperDrive can both read from and write to 3.5-inch PC floppies. Similar software is also available for the PC.

There are several translation software programs designed to handle the differences in file formats. Many programs, such as ClarisWorks, can import and export data by using file formats that are compatible with formats of other programs, so moving data between Macs and PCs is relatively easy.

This section explains how to use a direct-connect cable to shuttle files between the two systems. This approach is particularly useful in the following circumstances:

- When some files are too large to fit on a single floppy disk
- When you need to move many files
- When you frequently need to move files between the systems

Although you also can use a pair of modems (one for each computer) that are connected over a telephone line to accomplish the same thing, a direct-connect cable has one huge advantage — speed. You can move data easily and reliably across a serial cable at 57,600 baud. (In order to accomplish the same throughput with modems, you would need a pair of 14,400 bps modems that are operating with quadruple data compression (v.32 bis) and a relatively static-free phone line.)

The biggest problem with the direct-connect approach to data transfer between Macs and PCs is the difficulty in locating an off-the-shelf cable that is designed to do the job. Unless you are up to the task of building your own cable (and I'm not), you will probably need to have one built for you. Figure 7-13 shows the appropriate cable pin-outs, depending on whether the PC has a 25-pin or 9-pin serial port.

Figure 7-13:
Cable pin-outs

Cable pin-outs to connect the Macintosh serial port with an IBM PC 25-pin serial port

```
Mac (8-pin Mini DIN)              PC (DB-25 Female)
4 (Signal Ground) ——————— 7 (Signal Ground)
3 (Transmit Data) ——————— 3 (Receive Data)
5 (Receive Data) ———————— 2 (Transmit Data)
1 (DTR) ————————————————— 6 (DSR) ————————┐
                          8 (Carrier Detect) ——┘ Jumper
                          4 (RTS) ————————┐
                          5 (CTS) ————————┘ Jumper
```

Cable pin-outs to connect the Macintosh serial port with an IBM PC 9-pin serial port

```
Mac (8-pin Mini DIN)              PC (DB-9 Female)
4 (Signal Ground) ——————— 5 (Signal Ground)
3 (Transmit Data) ——————— 2 (Receive Data)
5 (Receive Data) ———————— 3 (Transmit Data)
1 (DTR) ————————————————— 6 (DSR) ————————┐
                          1 (Carrier Detect) ——┘ Jumper
                          7 (RTS) ————————┐
                          8 (CTS) ————————┘ Jumper
```

Connecting the Cable

Attach the circular 8-pin end of the cable (the mini DIN-8 connector) to the modem or printer port on the back of the Mac. Connect the other end (either 9-pin or 25-pin) to any free serial port on the back of the PC. On some PCs, the ports will be labeled (Serial 1 and Serial 2, or COM1 and COM2). The number of serial ports varies from one manufacturer to another, but PCs usually have one to three such ports.

Configuring the Communications Programs

On the Mac side, use a ClarisWorks communications document as the communications software. For the PC, almost any communications program will do. The following steps explain how to configure the two programs so that the machines can communicate with each other.

Steps: Configuring ClarisWorks for Mac-to-PC Communications

Step 1.   Open a new communications document by choosing New from the File menu (or pressing ⌘-N).

Step 2.   Choose Connection from the Settings menu. The Connection Settings dialog box appears (shown previously in Figure 7-11). Choose the following settings:

> *Method:* Serial Tool
>
> *Baud Rate:* 57600
>
> *Parity:* None
>
> *Data Bits:* 8
>
> *Stop Bits:* 1
>
> *Handshake:* None

Step 4.   Be sure that the port to which the communications cable is connected is selected in the Current Port box.

Step 5.   Click OK to accept the new settings.

Because you are only transferring files from one computer to the other, the Terminal settings are irrelevant. They control what appears on the two screens when text is typed on either keyboard; they don't affect file transfers.

Step 6.   Choose File Transfer from the Settings menu. The File Transfer Settings dialog box appears. Choose the following settings from the pop-up menus:

> *Protocol:* XMODEM Tool
>
> *Method:* Straight XMODEM
>
> *Transfer Options:* 1K Blocks or CleanLink

You can ignore the other settings.

Step 7.   Click OK to accept the new settings.

Step 8.   Choose Terminal from the Settings menu.

Step 9.   With the General icon selected in the left window, click the On Line and Local Echo check boxes, and then click OK.

Step 10.   Choose Open Connection from the Session menu (or press Shift-⌘-O).

Steps:	**Configuring the PC Communications Program**
Step 1.	Run the DOS or Windows communications program.
Step 2.	Configure the program to match the settings in ClarisWorks: *Baud Rate:* 57600 *Parity:* None *Data Bits:* 8 *Stop Bits:* 1 *Handshake:* None
Step 3.	Be sure that the port to which the communications cable is connected is selected in the program. In most cases, the port is COM1 or COM2.
Step 4.	Set Local Echo (sometimes called Half Duplex) to On.
Step 5.	If the program allows you to set a default for the file transfer protocol, choose 1K XMODEM.
Step 6.	If the program does not automatically connect to the Mac, issue the command to put the PC program online.

Testing the Connection

When both programs are running, you can test the connection by typing a string of text on the Mac's keyboard. As you type, the characters should appear on the PC's screen.

Now perform the test again by typing something on the PC's keyboard. The characters should appear on the Mac's screen.

In the tests, you don't need to be concerned if text overlaps on the same line or if you see extra blank lines between lines of text when you press Return. What's important is that the exact letters that you type on one machine appear on the screen of the other machine. If nothing appears on the other machine's screen, you can probably trace the problem to one of the following causes:

⇨ The wrong serial port is selected in either the Mac or the PC communications program.

⇨ The cable is incorrectly wired.

If you see garbled characters on the other screen, the communication parameters between the two programs are probably mismatched. Check to make sure that you have set all of the parameters correctly. If they are correct, reduce the baud rate setting in the two programs and try again.

Transferring Files

You can move document files of almost any type (word processing, spreadsheet, and graphics, for example) from one machine to the other. There is usually little point in moving programs, however. Mac programs cannot normally be run on a PC or vice versa.

Steps:	Transferring Files from the Mac to the PC
Step 1.	If necessary, save or export the Macintosh documents to a format that the destination program on the PC can read.
	If you use Microsoft Word for Windows, for example, you can save ClarisWorks word processing documents as Microsoft WinWord files. Be sure to check the import capabilities of the destination program on the PC. You may find that it can read some Macintosh files directly without any conversion.
Step 2.	In ClarisWorks, choose Send File from the Session menu. A standard file dialog box appears.
Step 3.	Select the file that you want to transmit and click Send.
Step 4.	On the PC, issue the communication program's command to receive a file. If you are prompted for a file transfer protocol, select 1K XMODEM. You may also be asked to name the file and the directory in which the file should be saved.
	During file transfers, ClarisWorks displays a window in which you can keep an eye on the progress (see Figure 7-14). Most PC communication programs display similar information.

Even though you have selected 1K XMODEM as the transfer protocol in both programs, don't be surprised if a different XMODEM protocol is used (as shown in Figure 7-14).

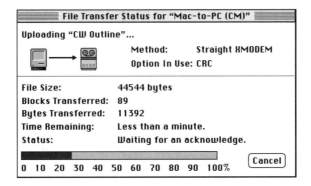

Figure 7-14:
ClarisWorks displays
this window during
file transfers.

Steps: Transferring Files from the PC to the Mac

Step 1. If necessary, save or export the PC documents to a format that the software on the Mac can read.

If you are running Microsoft Word for Windows, for example, no file conversion is necessary. The ClarisWorks word processor can read native Word documents in their original format (as Microsoft WinWord files). If you are transferring documents from a program for which ClarisWorks does not have translators, check the export capabilities of the PC program. It may offer an export or save option that ClarisWorks (or another destination program on the Mac) understands, such as RTF (Microsoft's Rich Text Format).

Step 2. On the PC, issue the communication program's command to send a file. You are asked to type the name of the file or select it from a file list. Be sure to specify the correct drive and directory in which the file is located. If you are prompted for a file transfer protocol, select 1K XMODEM.

Step 3. In ClarisWorks, choose Receive File from the Session menu. The transfer begins. After the file is received, a standard file dialog box appears, as shown in Figure 7-15.

Step 4. Select the destination drive and folder, type a filename, and then click Save.

ClarisWorks 4.0 for the Macintosh can read ClarisWorks for Windows 1.0 and 3.0 documents and can convert them for use with ClarisWorks 4.0. When ClarisWorks 4.0 for Windows is released, you will be able to exchange version 4.0 files in either direction. Until that time, you can save ClarisWorks 4.0 (Mac) files as ClarisWorks 1.0 files before transferring them to the PC. As an alternative, you can also save the files as Microsoft Word or WinWord files.

Figure 7-15:
Because the original filename is not part of the information that is sent during the file transfer, you have to enter a filename here.

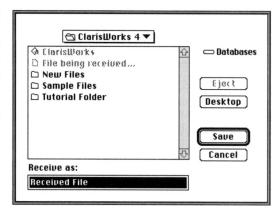

For occasional file transfers between two Macs or a Mac and a PC, the direct connect approach works fine. If you regularly make these types of transfers, however, you should check out some products that are dedicated to performing this task. Both MacLinkPlus/PC (DataViz) and LapLink Mac III (Traveling Software), for example, provide software that enables you to move files between computers effortlessly, as well as to translate them between a number of Mac and PC formats. Each product also includes an appropriate cable for connecting a Mac with another Mac or a PC.

The Kermit File Transfer Protocol _

Although XMODEM will readily handle transfers of any file type from one machine to another, it has a couple of disadvantages:

- ⮑ You can transfer only one file at a time.
- ⮑ Because the filename is not transmitted with the file, you must name each file manually as it is received.

If you're willing to put up with Kermit's slower performance, you can use the Kermit protocol to transfer batches of files with a single command. When the files are received, they can also be named automatically.

Steps: **Using Kermit to Transfer Batches of Files**

Step 1. In ClarisWorks, choose File Transfer from the Settings menu. The File Transfer Settings dialog box appears.

Step 2. Set options in the dialog box to match the settings shown in Figure 7-16.

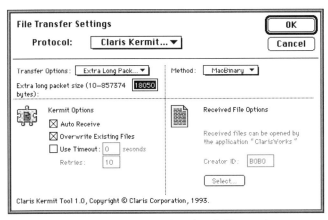

Figure 7-16: File transfer settings for a batch file transfer

When you are connecting a Mac and a non-Mac (such as a PC), select Binary as the Method. The Binary option enables you to transfer ordinary text files or formatted documents. When you are connecting two Macs, use MacBinary as the Method. MacBinary can transfer any type of Mac document, including programs.

Selecting a larger packet size (Extra Long Packets, in this example) can improve the speed of the transfer if both programs can use the larger packet size.

Step 3. On the PC, set Kermit as the new file transfer protocol. Depending on the communications program, you may be able to set a file transfer protocol as a default, or you may have to select the protocol immediately prior to issuing the send or receive command.

Step 4. On the PC or Mac, choose the command to send a file or send a group of files. (In ClarisWorks, choose Send File or Send Batch from the Session menu. If you choose Send Batch, you can specify several files to transmit together.)

Step 5. Set the other machine to receive a file. (If the PC is the receiving machine, you may have to specify the Kermit protocol at this time.) The file transfer commences.

When you are using the Kermit protocol to transfer PC files to the Mac, ClarisWorks may not recognize that the final transfer has been completed. If the transfer status window does not close by itself, click the Cancel Transfer button.

When you use Kermit, the transfer speed can be moderately or considerably slower than when you use XMODEM. But if you aren't in a rush, you can use Kermit to transfer a batch of files to either machine automatically while you occupy yourself with something more productive.

Quick Tips

The following Quick Tips tell you how to:

- Deal with a common file transfer problem
- Create an auto logon macro and macros to automate routine communications tasks
- Quickly check basic communications settings
- Issue AT commands

Choosing the Correct File Transfer Method

Whether you're connected to an online service or are simply downloading files from another computer, pay close attention to the file transfer method. MacBinary is the default and can only be used with Mac files. If you download files from a service (GEnie or CompuServe, for example), the files may not be true Mac files — they may be generic for multiple platforms — and an "Out of Memory" error message may appear, even if you have plenty of memory allocated. Switch to XMODEM if this problem occurs.

Creating an Auto Logon Macro

Although ClarisWorks 4 includes Phone Books for recording the numbers of the colleagues, friends, and information services with which you regularly connect, the Phone Book feature does not enable you to save a logon sequence along with the phone number. For most of us, memorizing IDs and passwords is a pointless exercise. With a little bit of work, you can use the ClarisWorks macro feature to create auto logon sequences that respond to a series of prompts on your favorite BBS or information service and, optionally, take you to the first area of the service that you normally visit.

Steps:	Recording an Auto Logon Macro

Step 1. Open the communications document that you have created for the information service or BBS, and choose Open Connection from the Session menu (or press Shift-⌘-O). ClarisWorks dials the number for the service.

Step 2. After the connection has been established, choose Record Macro from the Shortcuts submenu of the File menu. The Record Macro dialog box appears.

Step 3. Name the macro, choose an Option-⌘-key combination with which you will execute the macro, and click the Document Specific check box.

Step 4. Click Record to begin recording.

Step 5. Press whatever keys are necessary (if any) to complete the connection. (Some systems, for example, expect you to press Return immediately upon making the connection.)

Step 6. When the first system prompt appears (requesting a user ID, password, or both, for example), choose Macro Wait from the Shortcuts submenu of the File menu (or press Shift-⌘-J). The Macro Wait dialog box appears, as shown in Figure 7-17.

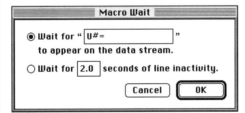

Figure 7-17: The Macro Wait dialog box offers two options: Wait for a text string, or wait for a specific number of seconds of line inactivity.

Step 7. Type the system prompt (or enough of it to uniquely identify the text string for which you are waiting) and click OK.

Step 8. After the dialog box disappears, type your normal response to the system prompt and then press Return.

Step 9. If additional actions are required to complete the logon or to move to a particular part of the information service or BBS, record them now.

Step 10. When the logon is completed, choose Stop Recording from the Shortcuts submenu of the File menu (or press Shift-⌘-J).

Step 11. Continue with the online session or issue the command to log off the system.

As an example, to log onto an information service (such as GEnie) and move to the Macintosh software library, you might use a macro that contains the following steps:

1. Macro Wait for text string: *U#=*

2. In the terminal window, type your user identification number, a comma, and your password, and then press Return.

3. Macro Wait for text string: *continue?*

4. Press Return in the terminal window.

5. Macro Wait for text string: *<H>elp?*

6. Type **Mac** in the terminal window and press Return.

7. Macro Wait for text string: *<H>elp?*

8. Type **3** in the terminal window and press Return.

To test or use your macro, choose Open Connection from the Session menu (or press Shift-⌘-O). As soon as the connection is established and before the first prompt from the service or BBS appears, execute the macro by pressing the Option-⌘-key or function key that you defined for it. In the GEnie logon example, to avoid timing problems, you may want to eliminate Step 1 (Macro Wait for text string: *U#=*) and begin with Step 2. Then you can execute the macro *after* the ID prompt appears, instead of trying to sneak it in within the few seconds between the connection and the appearance of the ID prompt.

You have to observe a few precautions whenever you are working with communications macros. First, as the preceding example shows, macros are highly dependent on an unchanging information service or BBS structure and prompt sequences. If the service alters its logon sequence, reorganizes the names or locations of SIGs that you regularly visit, or changes the wording of its prompts, the macro will fail. Then you have to rerecord each macro that is affected — you cannot edit ClarisWorks macros.

Second, although auto logon macros are convenient, anyone can use them to log onto your account with the information service or BBS. If security is a problem in your office or home, you may want to purchase one of the many available security programs to make the communications document accessible only to individuals who know its password.

Third, you don't need to type the entire text string in the Macro Wait dialog box. However, you need to be careful to type a sufficient amount of text so that the string is unique. In the GEnie example, Steps 5 and 7 wait for the text string *<H>elp?*. If the macro had been instructed to simply wait for *elp,* the next step could have been mistakenly triggered by any sentence or text string that contained *elp,* such as *helpful.* If the macro responds too early, it may fail.

Fourth, think twice before you check Play Pauses in a communications macro. Although recording the amount of time between each command that you issue (rather than using Macro Wait commands) may seem logical and easier, times can vary significantly from one session to the next. The line conditions, the number of other users accessing the BBS or information service at the same time, and so on, affect the amount of time required for prompts to appear. If your responses are sent before they are requested, the information service or BBS may ignore them and ruin the macro in the process.

 If this — or any other — macro doesn't work, you can halt its execution at any time by pressing ⌘-period.

Automating a Communications Session with Macros

Just as you can create auto logon macros, you can create macros to perform other common communication actions, such as

- ∽ Going to specific SIGs and the electronic mail section of the service

- ∽ Selecting a file transfer protocol for downloads

- ∽ Logging off the system

For complex activities that require decision capabilities (such as checking for new mail and, if found, capturing the letters to a text file), you may want to investigate a more powerful commercial macro program, such as QuicKeys (CE Software).

Checking Your Communications Settings

ClarisWorks provides an extremely handy command that lets you quickly examine basic communications settings — without having to open all those Settings dialog boxes. Choose Info from the Settings menu (or press ⌘-I). The dialog box in Figure 7-18 appears.

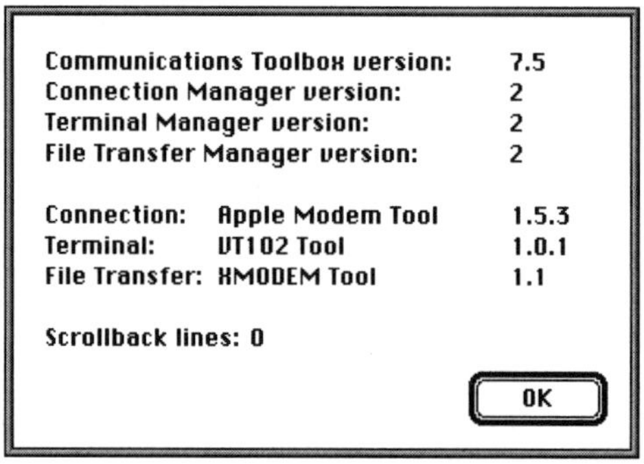

Figure 7-18:
Among other things,
the Info command tells you
the connection tool,
terminal tool, and file
transfer protocol that are
currently in effect, as well
as the number of lines
that are stored in the
scrollback pane.

Communications Toolbox version:		7.5
Connection Manager version:		2
Terminal Manager version:		2
File Transfer Manager version:		2
Connection:	Apple Modem Tool	1.5.3
Terminal:	VT102 Tool	1.0.1
File Transfer:	XMODEM Tool	1.1
Scrollback lines: 0		

OK

Those Ubiquitous AT Commands

Your communications software — in this case, the ClarisWorks communications environment in combination with Apple's Communications Toolbox — controls the modem that is attached to your Mac. The software controls the modem by sending instructions that are called *AT commands* (*AT* stands for *Attention*) to the modem.

If you want to learn more about your modem's capabilities, you can send AT commands to it. Grab your modem manual, turn to the listing of its commands, and follow the steps below for issuing AT commands.

Before you modify any of the modem's default commands, be sure that the modem has a command that you can use to reset it to its factory settings. (Often, this command is AT&F.) If you change a setting that shouldn't be changed, resetting the modem to its defaults will get you out of trouble.

Steps: Issuing AT Commands

Step 1. Create or open a new communications document.

Step 2. Choose Connection from the Settings menu. The Connection Settings dialog box appears.

Step 3. Select Serial Tool as the Method and choose a Baud Rate that is supported by the modem. Leave the other settings alone.

Step 4. Click OK to accept the new connection settings.

Step 5. Choose Terminal from the Settings menu. The Terminal Settings dialog box appears.

Step 6.	With the General icon selected (on the left side of the dialog box), enter check marks in the On Line and Local Echo check boxes. Leave the other settings alone.
Step 7.	Click OK to accept the new terminal settings.
Step 8.	Choose Open Connection from the Session menu (or press Shift-⌘-O). The modem will now respond to commands that you type in the communications document.
Step 9.	Because some commands will eventually scroll off the screen, choose Show Scrollback from the Settings menu (or press ⌘-L).

As a test, type **AT** and press Return. (You have to end every instruction that you send to the modem by pressing Return.) The modem should respond by displaying *OK* below your command.

 If you see double letters when you type commands (as in *AATT*), repeat Steps 5 through 7, but remove the check mark from the Local Echo check box.

One useful command that is supported by some modems is AT&H. On an Abaton InterFax 24/96, variations of this command list help information for controlling the modem as follows:

- ∽ AT&H or AT&H0 lists an AT Command Set Summary.

- ∽ AT&H1 lists S Register Functions (user-modifiable information stored in the modem's ROM).

- ∽ AT&H2 lists a Dialing Command Code Summary.

- ∽ AT&H3 lists the MNP Command Set Summary.

- ∽ AT&H4 lists the Evercom Proprietary Command Set Summary.

Figure 7-19 shows a sample AT&H command screen. Check your modem's manual to see if it supports this or a similar command.

The normal format for an AT command is AT, the command, an optional parameter number, and Return. An ampersand (&) or backslash (\) symbol precedes some commands. You select an option in other commands by ending them with a number (ATM0 or ATM1, for example).

Figure 7-19:
Some
modems have
built-in help
screens that
can be
displayed in
the terminal
window.

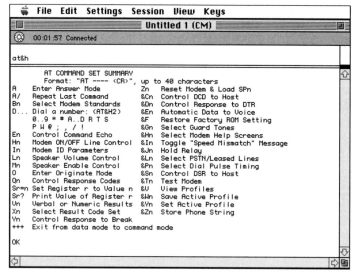

You can issue multiple AT commands on the same line, as in the following:

```
AT M1L0
```

If you like, you can add spaces between commands to improve readability. As usual, you have to end the command string by pressing Return.

You can do other useful things with AT commands (although not all modems offer these features):

- ⌐ Change the volume of the modem's speaker or turn off the speaker entirely

- ⌐ Dial a phone number through the modem, using a pulse or touch-tone phone line (ATDT*phone number*, as in ATDT555-1212)

- ⌐ Store frequently dialed numbers in the modem's memory

- ⌐ Store multiple communication setups, view them, and switch between them as needed

- ⌐ Switch between data and voice modes so that you can speak to the person on the other end of the line without having to hang up and call back

You can also use AT commands to modify the initialization string by selecting Custom from the Modem pop-up menu in the Modem Settings section of the Connection Settings dialog box. The default commands will be listed, which you can then change (to turn off the modem's speaker, for example).

If you want to learn more about the commands that your modem supports and how to issue them, refer to your modem manual. Remember, however, that unless you know what you're doing, you need to be sure to reset the modem to its factory defaults when you finish experimenting. Modern modems often include some special memory chips that retain your changes even after you turn off the modem.

Moving On Up

For basic communications, ClarisWorks serves most users very well. However, several major features are missing that you may eventually want to have, such as

- ☞ *More-advanced file transfer protocols.* In particular, the YMODEM, YMODEM-G, and ZMODEM protocols provide faster data transfers and batch transfers. When the connection is broken during a file transfer, ZMODEM can pick up automatically where the transfer left off — instead of having to restart the download from the beginning. These protocols are often available in inexpensive shareware communications programs such as ZTerm.

- ☞ *A more powerful macro or scripting language.* The ClarisWorks macro facility is crude when compared to that of stand-alone macro programs or the advanced scripting options that are provided in a dedicated communications program such as MicroPhone II and MicroPhone Pro. In particular, the inability to perform branching limits the usefulness of ClarisWorks macros.

    For example, you may want to create a macro or script that checks for new mail and, if it finds any, automatically downloads it or captures it to a text file for you. If new mail is not found, on the other hand, the macro or script could simply log off the system. You cannot use a ClarisWorks macro to perform this task.

Summary

- ➡ A communications document can connect your Mac to information services, BBSs, or other computers via a modem. With the proper Communication Toolbox settings, you can also link a pair of computers with a special direct-connect cable.

- ➡ To assure a trouble-free connection, you must set matching communication parameters in both the sending and receiving communications programs.

‣ The Connection Settings dialog box enables you to specify whether you want to make a modem connection (Apple Modem Tool) or a direct link (Serial Tool). It also enables you to select a communications port (modem or printer) and specify the port settings.

‣ You use the Terminal Settings dialog box to specify a terminal emulation and set characteristics for how text will be displayed in the terminal pane, as well as how it will be transmitted to the other computer.

‣ In the File Transfer Settings dialog box, you select a protocol to use when sending or receiving files. The purpose of a file transfer protocol is to assure that data transfers are error-free. The protocol that you choose must be supported by both the sender's and receiver's computer systems.

‣ You can store phone numbers for systems that you want to call in the Connection Settings dialog box or in the communication document's Phone Book. Every communications document can have its own Phone Book for dialing one or more information services, BBSs, or other computers.

‣ With the proper settings, you can either initiate a modem call or instruct ClarisWorks to wait for and answer an incoming modem call.

‣ Rather than storing old data in the terminal window, ClarisWorks provides a scrollback pane at the top of the window. As data is cleared from the terminal window, it is automatically transferred into the scrollback pane. You can scroll through the information in the scrollback pane, copy the information and paste it into the terminal window (or into other documents), force the current screen to be copied into the pane, and clear the contents of the pane.

‣ You can transfer files between a Mac and a non-Mac, as well as between Macs.

‣ No modems are necessary if you want to connect a pair of computers over a direct-connect cable. You must, however, have the proper cable and a communications program running on both systems. Because direct-connect file transfers between systems are not limited by modem capabilities, they can occur at very high speeds.

‣ You can use the ClarisWorks macro recorder to create auto logon macros, as well as to automate many routine communications tasks.

‣ The communications program sends commands to the modem. You can issue the same commands manually by selecting the Serial Tool and typing the commands in the terminal window.

Integrating the ClarisWorks Environments

This section offers suggestions and examples for using elements of two or more environments in the same document. You learn to put ClarisWorks "to work" and complete tasks such as generating a mail merge and using spreadsheet frames to create word processing tables.

Generating a Mail Merge

In This Chapter

- ❖ Creating merge forms
- ❖ Executing a mail merge
- ❖ Designing an envelope merge form
- ❖ Updating merge forms from earlier versions of ClarisWorks

---

Overview

A *merge* combines information from a database with a word processing document. In the most common use of a merge, a *mail merge,* you personalize form letters by inserting names from a database into a word processing document. For example, you use "Dear Mickey" or "Dear Mrs. Samuels," rather than "Dear Friend" or "Dear Customer."

Every merge has two components: a database and a merge form. The *database* contains the information that you want to insert into the merge form (names and addresses of friends, sales commission figures, or descriptions of catalog items, for example). The *merge form* is a text document, such as a form letter. You insert placeholders in the merge form, and each placeholder specifies the name of a database field («Last Name», for example). During the merge, data from the fields of each visible database record is inserted into the placeholders in the merge form. One copy of the merge document is printed for each visible (selected) database record.

 Although a merge form is usually a word processing document, you can create it within a text frame in any ClarisWorks environment. For example, you can design a party invitation in a draw document and personalize it with information that you place in a text frame. Also, even though merge forms are traditionally restricted to word processing documents, ClarisWorks can merge data into a spreadsheet document or frame, too.

Creating the Merge Database ___

You create a merge database as you do any other type of ClarisWorks database — by defining fields and creating records. (Refer to Chapter 5 for detailed information on ClarisWorks databases.)

You can also use the Name & Address List Assistant to create an address database.

Steps:	Using the Name & Address List Assistant to Create a Database
Step 1.	Choose New from the File menu. The New Document dialog box appears.
Step 2.	Click the Use Assistant or Stationary check box in the New Document dialog box, choose All Assistants from the Category pop-up menu, choose the Name & Address List Assistant, and click OK.
Step 3.	Save your new address database.

The Elements of a Merge Form ___

As discussed previously, the merge form contains placeholders for information from database fields. Each placeholder contains the name of a database field, surrounded by special bracket symbols (as in «Company»). To enter a field name and its surrounding brackets, you must select the field in the Mail Merge windoid, as explained in the step-by-step instructions for creating a merge form.

As with any other text in a word processing document or frame, you can apply different fonts, styles, colors, or other formatting options to the placeholders. You simply double-click to select the entire field name, including the brackets, and then apply formatting options.

You can use punctuation and spaces to separate merge fields from each other and from surrounding text. If the merge form contains two placeholders for the components of a name, as in «First»«Last», when the merge is performed, the result is the first name followed immediately by the last name (with no space in between), as in *TomJohnson*. To separate the two fields in the merge, add a space between the fields, as in «First» «Last».

You also can combine merge fields with normal text. For example, you can embed a merge field in a sentence:

- ∞ Just imagine your surprise when our prize van pulls up to the doorstep of the «Last Name» household.

- ∞ Because your sales were so extraordinary this quarter, «First Name», please find enclosed a commission check for «Commission» and a 15 percent bonus of «Bonus Amount».

Creating a Merge Form

To create a merge form, you type the basic text for the letter or document (that is, all the text that will be identical for each letter or document) and then, using the Mail Merge windoid, insert field placeholders at the appropriate spots in the text.

Steps:	**Inserting Fields into a Merge Form**
Step 1.	Open the merge document or create a new one. (Remember that the merge form can be a word processing document, a non–word processing document that contains a text frame, a spreadsheet document, or a spreadsheet frame.)
Step 2.	Choose Mail Merge from the File menu (or press Shift-⌘-M). A standard file dialog box appears.
Step 3.	Choose a merge database, and click Open. If the database is not already open, it now opens. The Mail Merge windoid appears, as shown in Figure 8-1.

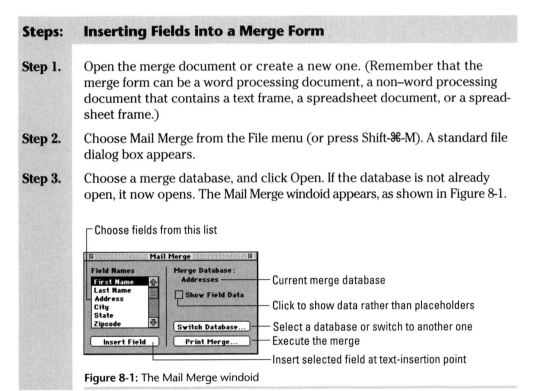

Figure 8-1: The Mail Merge windoid

If you discover that you've opened the wrong database for the merge, click Switch Database in the Mail Merge windoid, and choose another database from the file list that appears.

Step 4. In the merge document, set the text insertion point where you want to insert the first field placeholder.

Step 5. In the Field Name list box of the Mail Merge windoid, select the field that you want to insert.

Step 6. Click Insert Field to add the field name and its surrounding brackets at the current text insertion point.

Step 7. Repeat Steps 4 and 5 for additional field placeholders that you want to add to the merge form.

Step 8. Save the merge document. Saving the merge form associates the merge database with it. The next time you open the merge form and choose the Mail Merge command, the associated database will automatically open.

Figure 8-2 shows a completed merge form.

Figure 8-2:
A typical merge form. All words in brackets are merge fields.

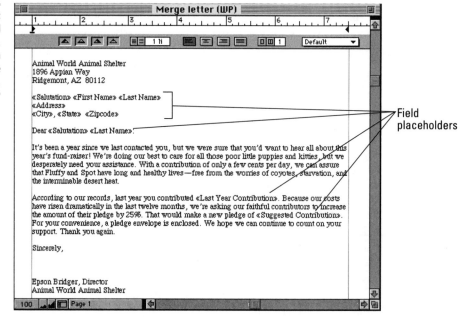

Field placeholders

Viewing Data in a Merge Form ____

When working in a ClarisWorks 4.0 merge form, you can look at either field names or actual data from the merge database. To view data, click the Show Field Data check box in the Mail Merge windoid (see Figure 8-3). The field placeholders disappear and are replaced by information from the first record of the merge database. To view other records, click the up- or down-arrow icons beside the Record text-edit box or type a specific record number in the Record text-edit box.

Click to flip through database records

Actual data is shown   Current record

Figure 8-3:
Click Show
Field Data
to show
information
from database
records in the
merge form
rather than
field name
placeholders.

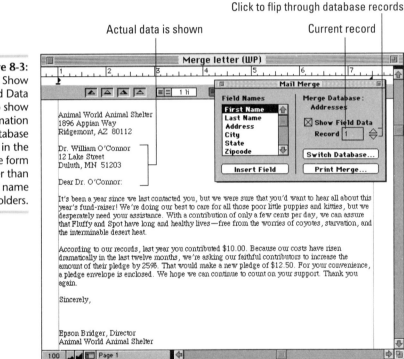

Performing a Merge _____

After the merge form is ready, the mechanics of performing the merge are straightforward.

Steps:	**Performing a Merge**

Step 1.   Open the merge database, if it is not already open.

Step 2.   To merge the entire database with the merge form, choose Show All Records from the Organize menu (or press Shift-⌘-A) and go to Step 3.

— or —

Step 2.   To merge selected records with the merge form, choose the Find command from the Layout menu (or press Shift-⌘-F). When the blank find request appears, specify criteria to find the record or records that you want to print. Click Visible to search only the visible records or All to search the entire database. Click Find to execute the search.

Step 3.   *Optional:* If you want the merge documents to print in a specific order (alphabetically by last name or in zip code order, for example), sort the records by choosing the Sort Records command from the Organize menu.

Step 4.   Open the merge document.

Step 5.   Choose Mail Merge from the File menu (or press Shift-⌘-M). The Mail Merge windoid appears.

Step 6.   Click the Print Merge button in the Mail Merge windoid. The Print dialog box appears.

Step 7.   Click Print, and the merge commences. One copy of the merge document is produced for each visible database record.

Before committing yourself to a massive merge, examine a few records on-screen by clicking the Show Field Data check box in the Mail Merge windoid and then flipping through the records. This procedure (described in "Viewing Data in a Merge Form") can save an enormous amount of paper if you have, for example, selected a wrong database field, forgotten to restrict the records to a particular subset, or incorrectly set the spacing between fields.

Down to Business:
An Envelope Merge _____

After you understand the mechanics of a merge, the process becomes routine. Rather than step you through another typical mail merge, the following instructions explain how to perform a type of merge that you may not have considered — an envelope merge. With a little experimentation, you can not only format and print envelopes from ClarisWorks, but also use a merge to automate the process by grabbing the mailing addresses from a database (an essential technique for mass mailings).

If you just want to print a single envelope, you can use ClarisWorks' Envelope or Address Envelope Assistant. See Chapter 3 for details.

Designing the Merge Form

This section explains how to create an envelope merge form as a document in the word processing environment. Figure 8-4 shows one such form that was designed for a center-feeding Apple LaserWriter IINT. The graphic rulers are displayed, rather than the normal word processing ruler, to show the approximate placement of the mailing address and return address sections.

Figure 8-4:
An envelope
merge form

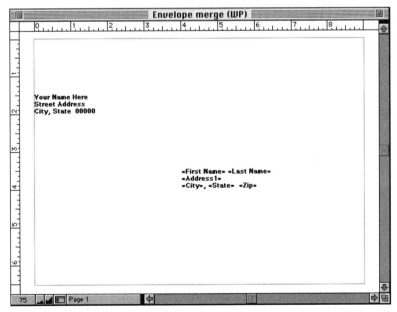

Steps: Creating the Envelope Merge Form

Step 1.   Create a new word processing document by choosing New from the File menu (or pressing ⌘-N). Choose Word Processing and then click OK.

Step 2.   Choose Page Setup from the File menu. The Page Setup dialog box appears.

Step 3.   Click the icon for landscape mode printing (the sideways icon) and select the paper option that corresponds to a #10 business envelope. Then click OK.

Step 4.   Choose Rulers from the Format menu. The Rulers dialog box appears.

Step 5.   Click the Graphics and Inches radio buttons and then click OK. The graphics rulers appear at the top and left sides of the blank word processing document (as previously shown in Figure 8-4). The outline of the document page should correspond to that of a #10 business envelope — 6.5 x 9 inches.

Step 6.   Type the return address in the position shown in Figure 8-4 or, if your envelopes are already imprinted with a return address, leave this part of the envelope blank.

These instructions assume that you are using a center-feed printer. If the printer is a right- or left-feed printer, you enter the mailing address and return address at the top or nearer the bottom of the form, respectively.

Step 7.   For the mailing address section, press Return several times until you reach the 3¹/₂- to 4-inch mark on the vertical ruler.

Step 8.   To align the lines of the address, choose the Tab command from the Format menu. The Tab dialog box appears (see Figure 8-5). Set a left tab at the 4-inch position by matching the settings shown in the figure, and then click OK. Press the Tab key once. The text insertion point is now correct for the first field of the mailing address.

Figure 8-5: To create a left tab at the 4-inch mark, match these settings.

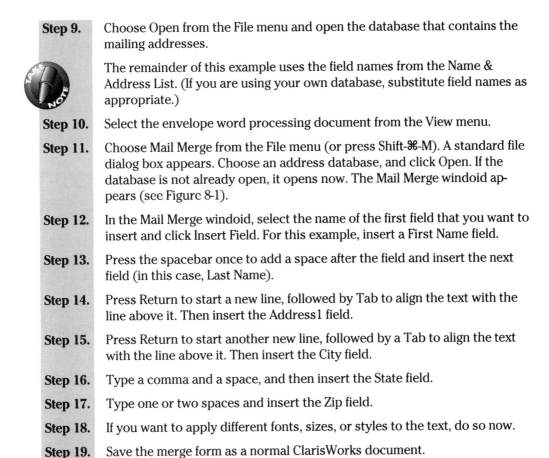

Step 9. Choose Open from the File menu and open the database that contains the mailing addresses.

The remainder of this example uses the field names from the Name & Address List. (If you are using your own database, substitute field names as appropriate.)

Step 10. Select the envelope word processing document from the View menu.

Step 11. Choose Mail Merge from the File menu (or press Shift-⌘-M). A standard file dialog box appears. Choose an address database, and click Open. If the database is not already open, it opens now. The Mail Merge windoid appears (see Figure 8-1).

Step 12. In the Mail Merge windoid, select the name of the first field that you want to insert and click Insert Field. For this example, insert a First Name field.

Step 13. Press the spacebar once to add a space after the field and insert the next field (in this case, Last Name).

Step 14. Press Return to start a new line, followed by Tab to align the text with the line above it. Then insert the Address1 field.

Step 15. Press Return to start another new line, followed by a Tab to align the text with the line above it. Then insert the City field.

Step 16. Type a comma and a space, and then insert the State field.

Step 17. Type one or two spaces and insert the Zip field.

Step 18. If you want to apply different fonts, sizes, or styles to the text, do so now.

Step 19. Save the merge form as a normal ClarisWorks document.

As mentioned in Step 6, if your envelopes have a return address printed on them, leave the return address section of the template blank. If you routinely use both kinds of envelopes — blank envelopes and envelopes with a preprinted return address — you can create *two* envelope merge forms.

Testing the Merge Form

Now comes the fun part — making sure that the mailing and return addresses print correctly. Before even thinking of printing on an envelope, however, you should do a few test printouts on standard letter paper. You do test printouts for a more important reason than to avoid wasted envelopes. If you insert an envelope into the printer and it prints outside the area of the envelope, it is printing onto the printer drum rather than onto the envelope. You won't have that problem with letter paper.

Before printing, place a small pencil mark on the paper in the upper-right corner of the page. When you issue the Print command (don't do a merge at this point), you may see a message saying that some of the printing may be clipped. Ignore it. When the printout appears, the pencil mark tells you the following:

- ☞ The side of the paper on which the printer prints (so that you know whether to insert the envelopes right side up or upside down)

- ☞ Which edge of the envelope to insert into the printer (left or right)

You can also tell from the test printout whether the printing is being clipped.

Now check the positions of the mailing and return addresses on the test printout. (You may want to lay the printout over an envelope to see how well they match up.) If necessary, adjust the positions of the mailing and return addresses and do another test. When you hold the printout sideways (so you can read it), the printing should be centered from top to bottom on a center-feed printer, near the top of the page on a right-feed printer, or near the bottom of the page on a left-feed printer. When the alignment looks correct, repeat the test with an envelope. After you print an envelope correctly, you can do the merge, as described in the next section.

Performing the Envelope Merge

Because different people have different merge needs, this section contains instructions for two types of envelope merges: printing a single envelope and printing a series of envelopes.

Steps:	Printing a Single Envelope
Step 1.	Open the merge database.
Step 2.	Choose the Find command from the Layout menu (or press Shift-⌘-F). A blank find request appears.
Step 3.	Specify criteria to find the record that you want to print. Click Visible to search only the visible records or All to search the entire database.
Step 4.	If more than one record is found, use the mouse to select the specific record that you want to print. (To select a record, click anywhere in the record other than inside a field.) Then choose Hide Unselected from the Organize menu. All records other than the one that you selected are hidden.
Step 5.	Open the envelope document.

Step 6.	Choose Mail Merge from the File menu (or press Shift-⌘-M). The Mail Merge windoid appears.
Step 7.	Click the Print Merge button. The Print dialog box appears.
Step 8.	Insert an envelope into the manual feed tray of the printer and click Print to print the envelope.

Occasionally, you may want to use the merge form to do a mass mailing, perhaps to send holiday greetings to all your friends or a business message to your clients or coworkers.

Steps:	**Printing a Set of Envelopes**
Step 1.	Open the merge database.
Step 2.	*Optional:* If you want to merge only a subset of records from the database, select the records that you want to use. To select the records, use the Find command or the Match Records and Hide Unselected commands. (Remember, the merge prints an envelope for every visible database document, so you have to hide all the records that you do not want to print.) For instructions on using the Find and Match Records commands, refer to Chapter 6.
Step 3.	*Optional:* If you want the envelopes to print in a specific order (alphabetically by last name or in zip code order), sort the records by choosing the Sort Records command from the Organize menu.
Step 4.	Open the envelope document.
Step 5.	Choose Mail Merge from the File menu (or press Shift-⌘-M). The Mail Merge windoid appears.
Step 6.	Click the Print Merge button. The Print dialog box appears.
Step 7.	Insert an envelope into the manual feed tray or paper tray for the printer, turn on the printer, and click Print to print the envelopes. As each envelope feeds into the printer, insert the next one. Continue until all of the envelopes have been printed.

If you have an envelope tray for your printer, you can print 15 to 20 envelopes at a time without having to stand and watch the process.

Envelope Feed Methods and Page Setup Dialog Boxes

Unfortunately, no one method for printing envelopes is universal to all printers. Some printers, such as the original ImageWriter, weren't designed to handle envelopes. You can use the instructions in this chapter with such printers, but I don't recommend doing so.

In general, laser and ink-jet printers (such as the StyleWriter and the HP DeskWriter) are best for printing envelopes. They have trays that assure that the envelopes are correctly aligned and that the envelopes' *paper path* (the route that paper takes after you feed it into the printer) is straight. The ImageWriters use a standard *platen* (roller bar) to feed paper. Although the platen is excellent for *tractor-feed paper* (paper with tiny holes on both sides) and reasonably good for letter paper, it's so-so for envelopes. Envelopes tend to slide around too much and can jam.

The method for feeding envelopes varies considerably among Macintosh-compatible ink-jet and laser printers. Some printers, such as the LaserWriter II series, expect you to *center-feed* envelopes (center them on the manual feed tray or in an envelope tray) and insert them facing up with the left edge of the envelope forward. Other printers require that you feed envelopes from the left or right side of the feed tray. Some printers are designed so that you have to feed paper upside down.

If you aren't sure of the printer's envelope feeding requirements, check its manual. The envelope template shown in this chapter is designed for a center-feed printer. You need to adjust the placement of the text to make it work properly with a right- or left-feed printer.

To make things more complicated, every printer also has its own version of the Page Setup dialog box. Luckily, the dialog boxes contain options that make formatting a standard #10 business envelope simple. The figure shows the settings for LaserWriter printers (note the envelope paper choice, as well as the Landscape orientation option).

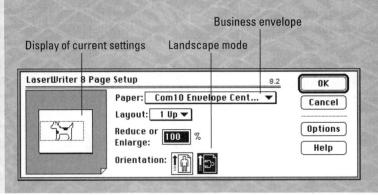

Business envelope

Display of current settings   Landscape mode

Quick Tips

The following Quick Tips explain how to

- ☞ Use a calculation field to perform a conditional merge
- ☞ Use a merge to address a form letter when you don't know the names of all of the customers
- ☞ Insert one of two different amounts in a merge
- ☞ Use a spreadsheet frame as a merge form
- ☞ Update merge forms created in older versions of the program so they work with ClarisWorks 4.0

Conditional Merges

If you're searching for the conditional merge capabilities that many of the popular stand-alone word processing programs offer, you can stop looking — ClarisWorks doesn't have them. An example of a conditional merge is: If database field X contains information that matches these criteria, do this; otherwise, do something else.

Although ClarisWorks isn't equipped for sophisticated merges, you can jury-rig a conditional test by creating a calculation field that uses the IF database function. The following examples illustrate this application.

Problem 1

You have a customer database that contains a title, first name, last name, and address for each customer. Now you want to mail a form letter to everyone to tell them about your annual fall sale. Unfortunately, through sloppy record keeping, you didn't always record the customers' names. How do you address the letters?

Steps:	Addressing a Form Letter When You Don't Know Some Customers' Names
Step 1.	In the address database, choose Define Fields from the Layout menu (or press Shift-⌘-D). The Define Fields dialog box appears.
Step 2.	Define a new calculation field called *Name Present?* using this formula (see also Figure 8-6):

```
IF('Last Name'="","Customer",'Prefix'&" "&'Last Name')
```

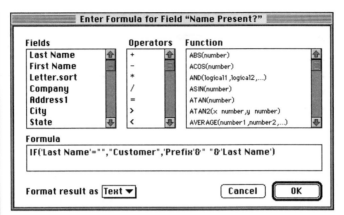

Figure 8-6: A formula to determine if a customer's last name has been recorded

The formula checks to see whether the Last Name field is blank. If it is, the word *Customer* is entered in the Name Present? field. If the Last Name field is not blank, the prefix (Mr., Dr., and so on), a blank space, and the last name are combined and copied into the Name Present? field (Ms. Smith, for example).

The field names in the formula are ones from the Name & Address File database created with the ClarisWorks Assistant. If you are using a different database, substitute the names of your fields for Last Name and Prefix.

Step 3. In the Format result as pop-up menu, choose Text.

Step 4. Use the following line as the salutation line of the form letter:

```
Dear «Name Present?»:
```

When the merge is performed, the Name Present? placeholder is evaluated separately for each record included in the merge. If a last name has been recorded for a given customer, it is combined with a prefix, producing *Dear Mrs. Johnson*, for example. If no last name is found for a record, the line becomes *Dear Customer*.

As this example illustrates, you can use any properly defined field in a database as a placeholder in a merge form. The field does not need to be visible in the layout.

Problem 2

You've volunteered as a fund-raiser for a local nonprofit organization. The amount that each patron contributed last year is accurately recorded in a ClarisWorks database. You've decided that to increase contributions this year, you will ask patrons who gave $50 or more last year to consider increasing their donation by 25 percent. If they gave less than $50, you will ask them for the same amount. How can you accomplish this task?

Steps:	Inserting One of Two Different Amounts in a Merge
Step 1.	In the address database, choose Define Fields from the Layout menu (or press Shift-⌘-D). The Define Fields dialog box appears.
Step 2.	Define a new calculation field called *Suggested Contribution*. Use the following formula for the field:

```
IF('Last Year Contribution'>=50,'Last Year
Contribution'*1.25,'Last Year Contribution')
```

The formula checks the amount in the field named Last Year Contribution. If it is greater than $50, the amount is multiplied by 1.25 to increase the amount by 25 percent. Otherwise, the Last Year Contribution field is copied directly into the Suggested Contribution field.

Step 3.	In the Format result as pop-up menu, choose Number.
Step 4.	In the form letter, insert the Suggested Contribution field in the line of text where you suggest a donation amount, as in the following example:

```
Based on your generous contribution last year,
we suggest a donation of «Suggested Contribution».
```

You do not need to place the calculation field in a database layout. As long as you have properly defined a field, you can use it in the database as a placeholder in a merge form — whether or not it is visible in a layout.

Using a Spreadsheet Frame as a Merge Form

At the beginning of this chapter, I casually mentioned that a spreadsheet or spreadsheet frame also can serve as a merge form. You might ask, "Why would you want to use a spreadsheet in this manner?" I thought for a long time and came up with an instance where this might be useful: for filling in spreadsheet tables.

As an example, suppose you've designed a letter that you want to send to all members of your company's sales force. In the word processing document, you can embed a spreadsheet table that shows each salesperson's quarterly or monthly sales and commissions earned. Because the information is merged into a spreadsheet frame rather than a text frame or document, you also can use the power of the spreadsheet to create formulas that further manipulate the merged data. Formulas could calculate each person's total annual sales or average monthly sales, for example.

Updating Old Merge Forms for ClarisWorks 4

In previous versions of ClarisWorks, there were *two* ways to insert fields into a merge form:

ം Choosing field names from the Mail Merge windoid

ം Typing the brackets and field names directly into the merge form

In ClarisWorks 4, however, you *must* select all fields from the Mail Merge windoid — typed fields and brackets are not recognized as merge fields.

If you have merge forms created in earlier versions of ClarisWorks, you can update them so they will work with ClarisWorks 4 by replacing each field with one listed in the Mail Merge dialog windoid. To do this, select the field in the merge form (including its surrounding brackets), choose a field name in the Field Names pane of the Mail Merge windoid, and click Insert Field.

Not sure which fields are old ones and which fields have already been updated or replaced? On the merge form, double-click anywhere in a field name. If it is a ClarisWorks 4.0 field name, the entire field — including the surrounding brackets — will be selected. If the field was inserted or typed in a previous version of ClarisWorks, only a portion of the field name will be selected (one word of a multiword field name, or the field name but not its surrounding brackets, for example). The important point to remember is that ClarisWorks 4.0 treats an inserted field name as a single entity, starting with the left bracket («) and ending with the right bracket (»).

Summary

➻ A merge requires two components: a database and a merge form (a word processing document, text frame, spreadsheet document, or spreadsheet frame). Information from the database fields is inserted into field placeholders in the merge document.

➻ Every merge field name is surrounded by special brackets («»). The brackets are added automatically when you select the field names from the Mail Merge windoid.

➻ Punctuation and spaces can separate merge fields from each other, as well as from surrounding text. You also can apply formatting, such as different fonts and styles, to the merge fields.

➻ In a merge, every visible database record produces its own merge document. You can restrict the number of records by using the Find or Match Records commands. You can also arrange the records in a particular order by using the Sort Records command.

➻ Merge forms designed in previous versions of ClarisWorks must be updated before you can use them with ClarisWorks 4. Field names must be reinserted by choosing them from the Mail Merge windoid.

Adding Spreadsheet Charts and Tables to Reports

9

■ ■

In This Chapter

➠ Adding spreadsheet tables to word processing documents

➠ Changing the appearance of tables

➠ Treating tables as objects and as in-line graphics

➠ Adding spreadsheet charts to word processing documents

■ ■

Overview _____

Only a few high-end word processing programs include a special feature for laying out tables. When you use a word processor without such a feature, your only recourse is to set a series of tabs and use them to format a table. Although you can use tabs to create tables in the ClarisWorks word processor, a better way to make a table is to use a spreadsheet frame. This method enables you to reap the benefits of working in an environment that can not only format text but also manipulate numbers. (For information on the spreadsheet environment's features and functions, refer to Chapter 4.)

This chapter explains how to add a spreadsheet table or chart to a word processing document. Because of the tight integration of ClarisWorks environments, however, you can apply the techniques that are described in this chapter in the other environments as well — in paint or draw documents, for example.

ClarisWorks 4 also includes a Make Table Assistant that you can use to create simple tables. See Chapter 3 for instructions.

Spreadsheet Tables

Although you can design a spreadsheet table in the spreadsheet environment, creating a spreadsheet *frame* in the word processing document is simpler. This method also enables you to tell whether the table is the correct size for the document.

Steps:	Creating a Spreadsheet Table
Step 1.	Open an existing word processing document or create a new one by choosing the appropriate command from the File menu (Open or New).
Step 2.	If the Tool panel isn't visible, click the Show/Hide Tools control at the bottom of the document window.
Step 3.	Select the spreadsheet tool (the large plus symbol near the top of the Tool panel).
Step 4.	To create the table, click where you want the upper-left corner to start and then drag down and to the right. When you release the mouse button, a new spreadsheet frame appears, as shown in Figure 9-1.

Spreadsheet tool   Spreadsheet frame

Figure 9-1:
A new
spreadsheet
frame

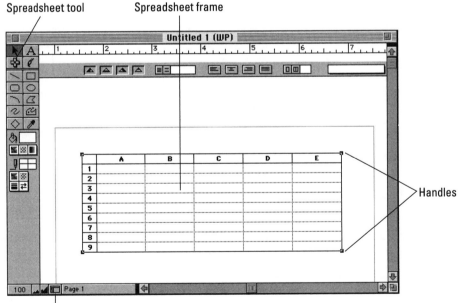

Handles

Show/Hide Tools control

Don't be overly concerned about the initial appearance or dimensions of the table. You can change its size, the number of columns and rows, column widths, and row heights as needed.

Entering Data

To enter text and data into the spreadsheet table, click the table once to select it and then click any cell in the table. The selected cell has a dark border around it. You can now enter data in that cell or anywhere else in the spreadsheet, as shown in Figure 9-2.

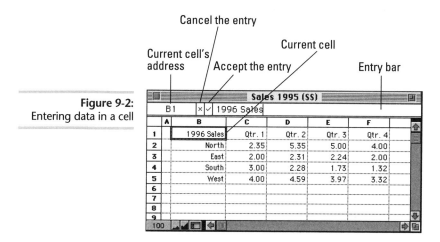

Figure 9-2:
Entering data in a cell

As you type an entry for a cell, text or numbers appear in the *entry bar,* which is shown in Figure 9-2. (Note that as you work in the spreadsheet frame, the word processing ruler is still visible but not active.) To accept the entry, do any of the following:

∞ Click the check mark (which is the *Accept* button).

∞ Press Enter or Return.

∞ Press an arrow key (or an Option-arrow key).

∞ Press Tab or Shift-Tab.

To cancel a cell entry, click the *x* button in the entry bar.

In ClarisWorks 4.0, the functions of the arrow and Option-arrow keys are defined in the spreadsheet preferences (see Chapter 11). To accept a cell entry or move to another cell, either the unmodified arrow keys *or* the Option-arrow keys can be used — depending on how you set these preferences.

Clicking the check mark or pressing Enter accepts the entry but leaves the cursor in the current cell. The other options (Return, arrow key or Option-arrow key, Tab, and Shift-Tab) accept the entry as well, but they move the cursor to a new cell, as described in Table 9-1.

Table 9-1	
Cell Navigation	
Key	**Movement**
Return	To the cell immediately below
Right arrow (or Option-right arrow) or Tab	To the cell immediately to the right
Left arrow (or Option-left arrow) or Shift-Tab	To the cell immediately to the left
Down arrow (or Option-down arrow)	To the cell immediately below
Up arrow (or Option-up arrow)	To the cell immediately above
Enter	No movement

You also can use the keys in Table 9-1 for pure cursor movements. If you are not entering data, pressing these keys simply moves the cursor in the direction stated.

You can move directly to any cell by clicking it with the mouse. In many cases, this method is the quickest way to get to any cell in the table that is not adjacent to the current cell.

You also can choose the Go To Cell command from the Options menu (or press ⌘-G) and specify the coordinates of the desired cell (A7, for example) in the dialog box that appears. Because most tables are rather small, however, clicking a cell to select it is usually easier.

For fast data entry in contiguous cells, you can select a cell range by Shift-clicking. The current cell (which is white) is in the upper-left corner of the selected range, as shown in Figure 9-3. If you press *Return* after you enter the data for each cell, the current cell automatically shifts on a column-by-column basis, as shown in the table at the top of the figure. If you press *Enter* or *Tab* as you complete each cell entry, the current cell automatically shifts on a row-by-row basis, as shown in the table at the bottom of the figure.

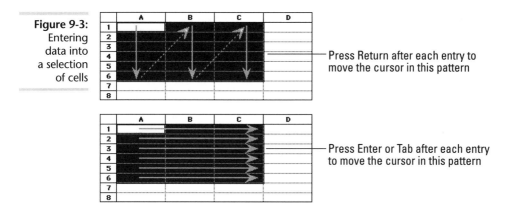

Figure 9-3:
Entering
data into
a selection
of cells

Press Return after each entry to
move the cursor in this pattern

Press Enter or Tab after each entry
to move the cursor in this pattern

Changing the Appearance of the Table

By using the mouse and menu commands, you can make any of the following changes
to the appearance of the table:

- ✏ Change the number of columns or rows that are displayed.

- ✏ Change row heights and column widths.

- ✏ Make text wrap within selected cells.

- ✏ Add shading to selected cells.

- ✏ Display or hide the cell gridlines, column letters, and row numbers.

Changing the Number of Displayed Columns or Rows

Although a spreadsheet frame is simply a window into a larger worksheet, you can
adjust the size of any spreadsheet frame and increase or reduce the number of visible
columns and rows.

Steps:	Changing the Number of Displayed Columns or Rows
Step 1.	Click the spreadsheet table once to select it. Handles appear at its four corners, and the cursor changes to a pointer.
Step 2.	Click one of the table's handles and then drag. When you release the mouse button, the table reforms and displays only the columns and rows that you have indicated.

Many finished tables look better if you hide the column and row headings (as described later in this chapter). If hiding the headings leaves an extra blank row at the bottom or a blank column at the right end of the table, you may need to resize the table again after you hide the row and column headings.

Changing Row Heights and Column Widths

ClarisWorks lets you include varying sizes of text in a worksheet. You can adjust the heights and widths of individual rows and columns to accommodate large headings (formatted as 24-point text, for example) or long text strings that spill over into adjacent cells.

Steps: **Changing Row Heights and Column Widths**

Step 1. Click the spreadsheet table once to select it. Handles appear at its four corners, and the cursor changes to a pointer.

Step 2. Select any cell in the column or row whose width or height you want to change. (Click the cell to select it.)

To change the width or height of several columns or rows simultaneously, Shift-click to select a series of contiguous columns or rows.

Step 3. From the Format menu, choose Column Width or Row Height, as appropriate. The Column width or Row height dialog box appears. Figure 9-4 shows the Column width dialog box.

Column width `72 pt`	— Enter a width (in points)
☐ Use default	
(Cancel) (OK)	— Click to reset the column width to the default (72 pts.)

Figure 9-4: The Column width dialog box

Step 4. Enter a new number for the width or height.

 Height and width numbers are shown in points rather than in characters. Points are often used for measuring type. (An inch contains 72 points.)

Step 5. Click OK. The new column width or row height is put into effect. If multiple rows or columns were selected, they all will now have the same height or width, respectively.

Changing column widths or row heights *manually* by using the mouse — as described in the following steps — is sometimes easier.

Steps:	**Changing Row Heights and Column Widths Manually**

Step 1. Click the spreadsheet table once to select it. Handles appear at the four corners, and the cursor changes to a pointer.

Step 2. Move the pointer into the heading area for the column or row whose width or height you want to change. As the cursor moves over the right edge of the column or the bottom edge of the row, a special, two-headed pointer appears, as shown in Figure 9-5.

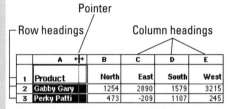

Figure 9-5: Changing the width of a column manually

To change the width or height of *several* columns or rows simultaneously, Shift-click to select a series of contiguous columns or rows.

Step 3. While pressing the mouse button, drag to change the column width or row height.

Step 4. When the width or height is correct, release the mouse button.

ClarisWorks 4.0 provides a third way to adjust rows and columns that you'll find handy. Using the following technique, you can automatically resize rows or columns so that they are the minimum height or width necessary to accommodate the largest cell in the range:

↷ To autosize a *row*, move the pointer into the row headings area of the worksheet (on the far left) and double-click the bottom of the row that you want to resize. The row height adjusts to fit the largest-point-size text in the row.

↷ To autosize a *column*, move the pointer into the column headings area of the worksheet (at the top) and double-click the right side of the column that you want to resize. The column width adjusts to fit the longest text string in the column.

This technique can also be used to simultaneously autosize a *series* of rows or columns. Select the rows or columns, and then double-click the bottom of any of the selected rows or the right side of any of the selected columns. ClarisWorks determines the minimum height or width necessary to accommodate the largest or longest text in the selected range. All selected rows or columns are resized to match that height or width.

Although there are no menu commands that you can choose to perform row and column autosizing, there *are* two shortcuts you can add to the Shortcuts palette that will accomplish the same trick: Autosize Row and Autosize Column. See Chapter 13, "Customizing the Shortcuts Palette," for information on modifying the Shortcuts palette.

Setting Text Wrap for a Cell

When a text string is too long to fit in a cell, it spills into adjacent empty cells. (The direction in which it spills depends on the original cell's Alignment setting.) To keep the entire string in its original cell, you can either widen the column (as described previously) or format the text to wrap within the cell.

Steps:	Making Text Wrap Within Selected Cells
Step 1.	Click the spreadsheet table once to select it. Handles appear at the four corners, and the cursor changes to a pointer.
Step 2.	Select the cell or cells to which you want to apply the Wrap format.
Step 3.	Choose Wrap from the Alignment submenu in the Format menu.

If the text no longer fits in the cell (some of it may be clipped at the bottom of the cell), you can change the row height by using any of the methods described previously.

Shading Cells

Previous versions of ClarisWorks had few cell-formatting features you could use to dress up a worksheet. You could set the font, size, color, alignment, borders, and a single background color. ClarisWorks 4 lets you take the next important step in worksheet design: applying shading to individual cells.

Steps:	Adding Shading to Selected Cells
Step 1.	Click the spreadsheet table once to select it. Handles appear at the four corners, and the cursor changes to a pointer.
Step 2.	If the Tool panel isn't visible, click the Show/Hide Tools control at the bottom of the document window.
Step 3.	Select the cell or cells to which you want to apply the shading.
Step 4.	Select a fill color and/or pattern from the Tool panel. The color and pattern are applied to the selected cells.

You cannot apply fill gradients, pen colors, or pen patterns to cells. Although you can select these options, ClarisWorks ignores them.

Applying Styles

The ClarisWorks 4 stylesheet contains several predefined spreadsheet styles that you may find helpful in creating attractive tables. To see the stylesheet, choose Show Styles from the View menu.

To apply a table style to a worksheet frame, click to select the worksheet frame. Then choose any of the predefined styles in the stylesheet. Figure 9-6 shows a table formatted with the 3-D Table 1 style that I easily modified by changing the text alignment and number-formatting options. (See Chapter 15, "Working with Styles" for more information on using stylesheets.)

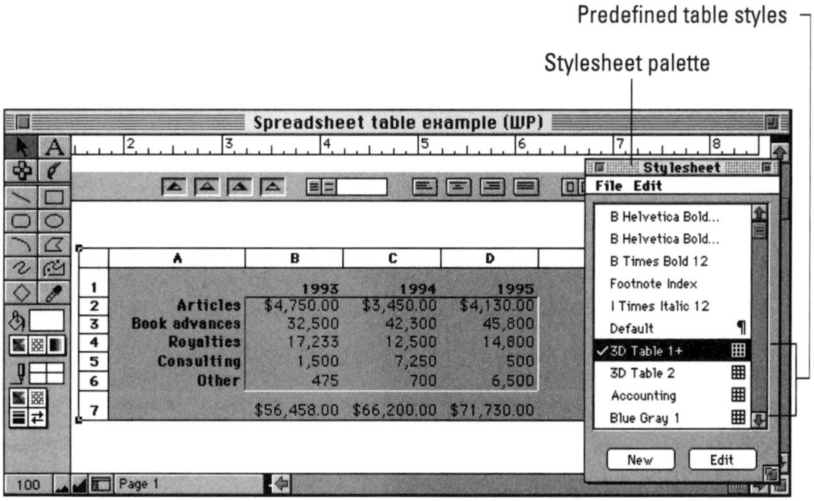

Predefined table styles

Stylesheet palette

Figure 9-6:
A table
formatted
using one of
ClarisWorks
4's new
table styles

	A	B	C	D
1		1993	1994	1995
2	Articles	$4,750.00	$3,450.00	$4,130.00
3	Book advances	32,500	42,300	45,800
4	Royalties	17,233	12,500	14,800
5	Consulting	1,500	7,250	500
6	Other	475	700	6,500
7		$56,458.00	$66,200.00	$71,730.00

Stylesheet

File Edit

B Helvetica Bold...
B Helvetica Bold...
B Times Bold 12
Footnote Index
I Times Italic 12
Default   ¶
✓3D Table 1+
3D Table 2
Accounting
Blue Gray 1

New   Edit

Spreadsheet table example (WP)

100   Page 1

Setting Display Options

By setting options in the Display dialog box, you can change the on-screen and printed look of any worksheet or table.

Steps: Displaying or Hiding the Cell Gridlines, Column Letters, and Row Numbers

Step 1. Click the spreadsheet table once to select it. Handles appear at the four corners, and the cursor changes to a pointer.

Step 2. Click in any cell of the spreadsheet. The spreadsheet menus appear in the menu bar.

Step 3. Choose Display from the Options menu. The Display dialog box appears, as shown in Figure 9-7.

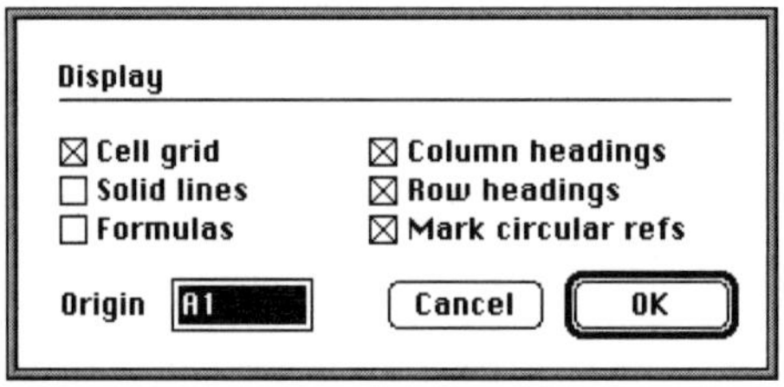

```
Display

⊠ Cell grid        ⊠ Column headings
☐ Solid lines      ⊠ Row headings
☐ Formulas         ⊠ Mark circular refs

Origin  [A1]       [ Cancel ]  [[ OK ]]
```

Figure 9-7: The Display dialog box

Step 4. Select or deselect display options by clicking the check boxes. To change the table's appearance, consider these important options:

- *Cell grid.* When this option is checked, the cell separators are dotted grid lines. When it is unchecked, lines do not appear.

- *Solid lines.* When this option is checked, the cell separators are solid grid lines.

- *Column headings* and *Row headings.* If these options are unchecked, you do not see the letters and numbers that the spreadsheet uses to label columns and rows.

Step 5. Click OK. The changes in appearance are made.

You can shorten this procedure slightly by choosing Modify Frame from the Options menu immediately after you select the spreadsheet table in Step 1. In either case, the same Display dialog box appears.

 If you have applied shading to all cells in the table, the display settings for cell grid and solid lines are irrelevant. Cell separators are not visible through cell shading.

Positioning the Table

After you finish entering data and formatting the table, you may want to change the table's position on the page. Up to this point, the spreadsheet frame has been just another object floating on the document page. You can leave it that way and, optionally, specify a text wrap for it (remember, it's an object — just like a draw graphic), or you can move it into the text as an in-line graphic. Because ClarisWorks treats in-line graphics as text, you can apply paragraph formatting commands to center the table on the page and separate it from the surrounding paragraphs. Figures 9-8 and 9-9 show the two table treatments.

Figure 9-8:
A spreadsheet table as an object

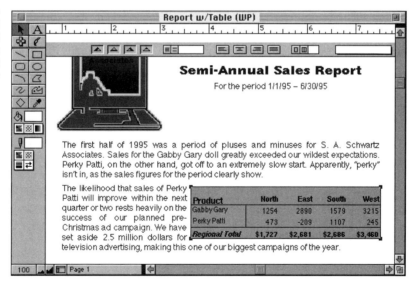

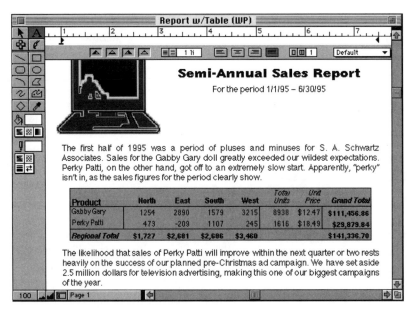

The first half of 1995 was a period of pluses and minuses for S. A. Schwartz Associates. Sales for the Gabby Gary doll greatly exceeded our wildest expectations. Perky Patti, on the other hand, got off to an extremely slow start. Apparently, "perky" isn't in, as the sales figures for the period clearly show.

Product	North	East	South	West	Total Units	Unit Price	Grand Total
Gabby Gary	1254	2890	1579	3215	8938	$12.47	$111,456.86
Perky Patti	473	-209	1107	245	1616	$18.49	$29,879.84
Regional Total	**$1,727**	**$2,681**	**$2,686**	**$3,460**			**$141,336.70**

The likelihood that sales of Perky Patti will improve within the next quarter or two rests heavily on the success of our planned pre-Christmas ad campaign. We have set aside 2.5 million dollars for television advertising, making this one of our biggest campaigns of the year.

Steps: Treating a Spreadsheet Table as an Object

Step 1. Click the spreadsheet table once to select it. Handles appear at the corners.

Step 2. Drag the table to its new position.

Step 3. Choose Text wrap from the Options menu. The Text Wrap dialog box appears.

Step 4. Click the Regular or Irregular icon to select it and then click OK. Text near the table wraps around the table.

Step 5. Continue to drag the spreadsheet until the text wraps exactly as you want.

You can fine-tune the position of the table by pressing the arrow keys.

Steps: Treating a Spreadsheet Table as an In-Line Graphic

Step 1. Click the spreadsheet table once to select it. Handles appear at the corners.

Step 2. Choose Cut from the Edit menu (or press ⌘-X). The worksheet is removed, and a copy of it is placed on the Mac's Clipboard.

Step 3. Click the text tool (the capital A) and move the text insertion point to where you want to place the table. (Because formatting is much simpler when the table is in a paragraph by itself, you may want to press Return to create a blank paragraph to receive the table.)

Step 4. Choose Paste from the Edit menu (or press ⌘-V). The table is inserted at the text insertion point.

Step 5. *Optional:* If you want to center the table in its line, place the text insertion point at the beginning or end of the paragraph that contains the table and then click the Centered Alignment control in the ruler bar (see Figure 9-10).

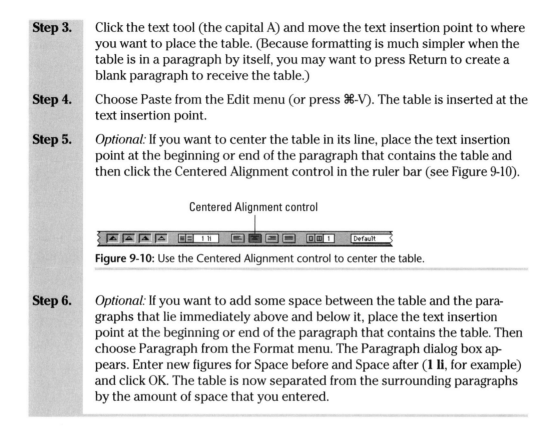

Centered Alignment control

Figure 9-10: Use the Centered Alignment control to center the table.

Step 6. *Optional:* If you want to add some space between the table and the paragraphs that lie immediately above and below it, place the text insertion point at the beginning or end of the paragraph that contains the table. Then choose Paragraph from the Format menu. The Paragraph dialog box appears. Enter new figures for Space before and Space after (**1 li**, for example) and click OK. The table is now separated from the surrounding paragraphs by the amount of space that you entered.

Deleting a Table

At some point, you may decide that you don't need a particular table after all. To delete a table, click the table once to select it and then press Delete or Backspace. If the table is an in-line graphic rather than a floating object, place the text insertion point at the end of the table and then press Delete or Backspace.

If you want to use the table on a different page or in a different document, select the table and then press ⌘-X or choose Cut from the Edit menu. You can then use the Paste command to move the table to its new location.

Spreadsheet Charts

You can also use spreadsheet charts in word processing reports. The easiest way to create a chart is to do so in a spreadsheet document rather than in a spreadsheet frame in the word processing document.

Steps:	Adding a Chart to a Word Processing Document

Step 1. Open an existing spreadsheet or create a new one by choosing Open or New from the File menu.

Step 2. Select the cell range from which the chart will be created.

Step 3. Choose Make Chart from the Options menu. The Chart Options dialog box appears, as shown in Figure 9-11. (See Chapter 4 for details on creating and modifying charts.)

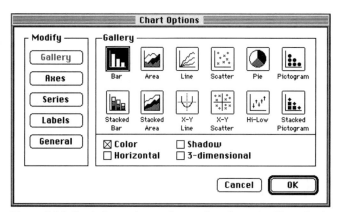

Figure 9-11: To design a chart, select options from the Chart Options dialog box.

Step 4. Select a chart size and click OK. The chart appears on the current document page and is automatically selected, as shown in Figure 9-12 (note the handles).

Step 5. Choose Copy from the Edit menu (or press ⌘-C). A copy of the chart is placed on the Mac Clipboard.

Step 6. Switch to the word processing document by selecting its name from the list at the bottom of the View menu. (If it isn't already open, choose Open from the File menu.)

Step 7. Choose Paste from the Edit menu (or press ⌘-V). The chart appears in the word processing document.

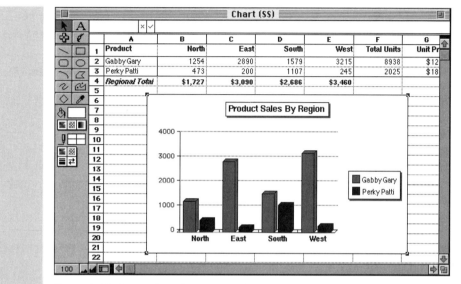

Figure 9-12: A new chart that is created in the spreadsheet environment simply floats on the page.

You can change the chart's position and size, as well as treat it as an object or an in-line graphic, by following the directions given previously for spreadsheet tables.

Any chart pasted into a document in this manner is a static entity. If you later change the chart's worksheet, the pasted chart will not reflect the changes. If you want to maintain a link between the worksheet and the chart, you can use Publish & Subscribe as described in Chapter 20.

Quick Tip: Other Table Formatting Options

As you design the table, keep in mind that you are working in a spreadsheet that happens to be embedded in a word processing document. All the power of the spreadsheet environment can be brought to bear on the table. Not only can you enter calculations and formulas, but you also can choose from additional formatting options, such as the following:

⇴ Choosing different fonts, styles, sizes, and colors for the text in selected cells

⇴ Changing the alignment of text and numbers within cells

⇴ Applying special formats for displaying numbers and dates

⇴ Sorting cells

⇴ Adding borders to cells

⇴ Embellishing the table with graphics

As an example, Figure 9-13 shows a fully dressed spreadsheet table with multiple font styles, sizes, and alignments; cell shading; selective cell borders; and graphics embellishments (an oval around a number, an arrow, and a callout that contains text).

Figure 9-13:
An example
of a formatted
spreadsheet
table

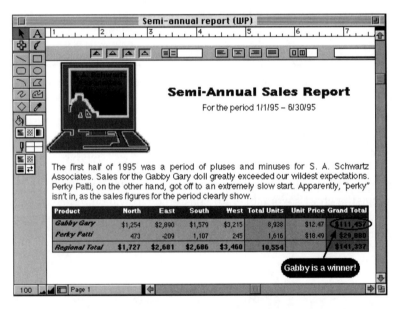

Refer to the instructions in Chapter 4 for help in formatting spreadsheet tables.

Summary

➡ Using a spreadsheet frame to create a table in a word processing environment enables you to reap the benefits of working in an environment where you can not only format text but also manipulate numbers.

➡ Some of the changes that you can make to spreadsheet tables include modifying row heights and column widths (to properly display text), changing the table's size, adding text wrap for some cells, applying cell shading, and hiding row and column headings.

➡ You can change column widths and row heights manually, or you can change them by entering numbers in a dialog box. Changing them manually is often more accurate and more direct than choosing menu commands.

➡ Like spreadsheet tables, charts can also be used to dress up a text-based report or memo.

➡ You can position tables and charts as floating objects (with text wrap) or as in-line graphics (which are subject to regular paragraph formatting commands). Both approaches work well.

Mastering ClarisWorks

IV

This sections covers material that helps you make more productive use of ClarisWorks. It isn't essential to learn about these features immediately, but you will want to tackle them after you're comfortable with the ClarisWorks basics.

Using Stationery Documents and Assistants

10

In This Chapter

➣ The differences between stationery documents and normal ClarisWorks documents

➣ Creating stationery documents

➣ Special considerations when saving stationery documents

➣ Opening a stationery document

➣ Making a new version of a stationery document

➣ Using stationery to set new environment defaults

➣ Using the ClarisWorks Assistants

Overview

When you have a document that you work with frequently but usually need to modify somewhat, the best way to save it is as a *stationery document* rather than as a normal ClarisWorks file. A stationery document is a template. It can include static text and graphics, as well as placeholders for other text elements that you intend to change each time you use the stationery document. An example of a document that would make a good stationery file is a letterhead template. In the template, you can include your return address, a date stamp (so you never have to enter the date manually), a standard salutation, and a closing. Then, whenever you want to write a new letter, you just open the stationery file, enter the addressee's name and address, and fill in the body of the text. Figure 10-1 shows a typical stationery document.

Figure 10-1:
A fax
template that
was saved as
a stationery
document

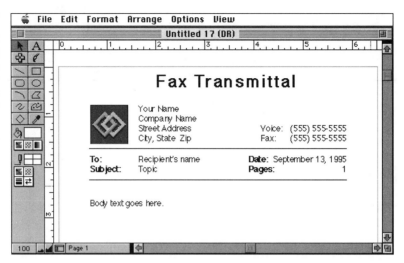

Figure 10-1:
A fax
template that
was saved as
a stationery
document

Assistants are intelligent helpers that make performing complex tasks in ClarisWorks a snap. Because you choose all stationery documents and many of the Assistants from the New Document dialog box, they are discussed together in this chapter.

Stationery Documents versus Normal ClarisWorks Documents

Of course, you don't *have* to save a template as a stationery file. You can save it as a normal ClarisWorks document. However, if you accidentally issue the Save command while you are working with a template that is not a stationery file, you will replace the template with a filled-in copy of the letterhead, fax, or whatever type of document you are working on. Bye-bye, template.

Saving the template as a stationery document protects you from this kind of mistake. When you open a ClarisWorks stationery file, you're opening a *copy* of the file, rather than the original. In fact, ClarisWorks treats the document that appears on-screen just as it treats a file that you create with the New command. It even names the file *Untitled* to remind you that it's not the original.

Creating Stationery Documents ___

You can easily create a stationery document from any ClarisWorks file. To save a document as stationery, choose Save As from the File menu. The standard Save As dialog box appears. Click the Stationery radio button. Enter a name for the document. Save the stationery document to the desired folder.

If you want to be able to choose the stationery document from the New Document dialog box, save it in the ClarisWorks Stationery folder (located inside the ClarisWorks 4.0 program folder). This folder is automatically chosen when you click the Stationery radio button in the Save As dialog box.

Any ClarisWorks stationery file that you save or move into the ClarisWorks Stationery folder is available in the file list when you issue the New command, click the Use Assistant or Stationery check box, and then choose All Stationery or an appropriate category from the Category pop-up menu.

In previous versions of ClarisWorks, the ClarisWorks Stationery folder was located inside the Claris folder within the System Folder of the startup hard disk. If you have stationery documents created with another version of ClarisWorks that you also want to use with ClarisWorks 4, simply copy or move the files into the ClarisWorks Stationery folder (located in the ClarisWorks 4.0 folder).

Of course, as with any other documents, you can save stationery files anywhere you choose. If you save them in a different location, they still function as stationery documents, but you have to load them by using the Open command from the File menu, rather than the New command.

ClarisWorks enables you to set preferences (such as the date format to use and palette options) that you can save with the current document. When you open the document, its preference settings override the normal ClarisWorks preferences. If you set preferences for a document and then save it as stationery, this rule still applies. Whenever you open a copy of the stationery document, any preferences that you have set for the document take precedence over the ClarisWorks preferences. For additional information on preferences, see Chapter 11.

Special Considerations When Saving Stationery Documents ___

When you save a ClarisWorks 4.0 document as a stationery file, it is presented in the New Document dialog box according to the information (or lack of it) that you have provided for the file in the Document Summary dialog box (see Figure 10-2). To ensure that you can easily find and promptly identify your stationery document, choose Document Summary Info from the File menu *prior to saving the file.* Be sure to fill in the following items:

- ∞ *Category.* Whatever text you enter here will be used as the category in which the stationery document is listed. To include the file in an existing category (General, Home, or Small Business, for example), type that category name. You can also create a new category (Personal, for instance), or you can simply lump the file in with all other unclassified stationery documents by not entering a category. Such a document will be assigned to the None category.

- ∞ *Description.* This descriptive text appears whenever the stationery file is high- lighted in the file list.

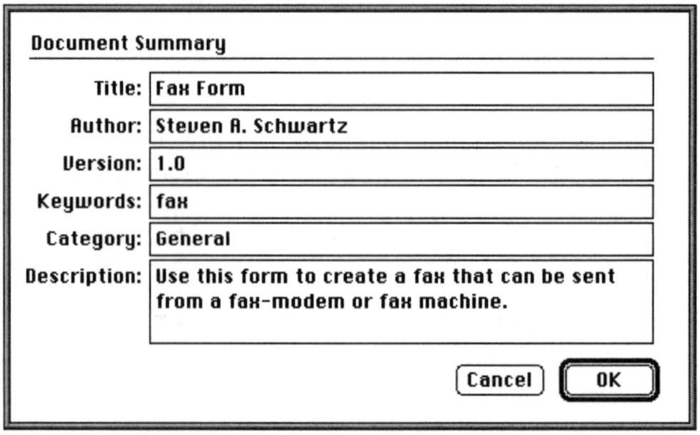

Figure 10-2:
The Document
Summary
dialog box

> **Document Summary**
>
> Title: `Fax Form`
> Author: `Steven A. Schwartz`
> Version: `1.0`
> Keywords: `fax`
> Category: `General`
> Description: `Use this form to create a fax that can be sent from a fax-modem or fax machine.`
>
> [Cancel]   [OK]

Other items in the Document Summary dialog box are optional. They do not affect the presentation of stationery files in the New Document dialog box. For additional informa- tion about the Document Summary dialog box, see "Saving New Files" in Chapter 1.

Opening a Stationery Document ___

You can open a stationery document in precisely the same way as you open any other document:

- ⮞ Select it from the file list that ClarisWorks presents when you choose Open from the File menu (or press ⌘-O).

- ⮞ Double-click the document icon on the desktop to launch ClarisWorks and open the document simultaneously.

In addition to these methods, the New Document dialog box contains a Use Assistant or Stationery check box that you can click to see several categories of stationery documents that you can open (see Figure 10-3). If the template is one that came with ClarisWorks 4.0 or one that you saved in the ClarisWorks Stationery folder, you can choose it when creating a new document or when launching the program. (The latter option assumes that the General Preferences setting for "On startup, show" is set to New Document, as described in Chapter 11.)

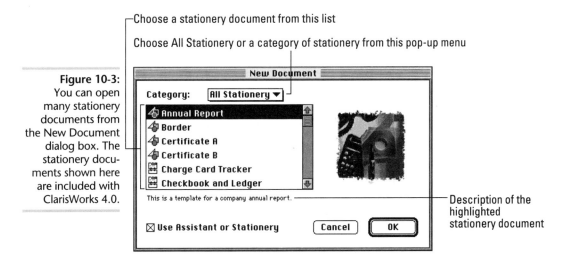

Choose a stationery document from this list

Choose All Stationery or a category of stationery from this pop-up menu

Figure 10-3:
You can open
many stationery
documents from
the New Document
dialog box. The
stationery docu-
ments shown here
are included with
ClarisWorks 4.0.

Description of the
highlighted
stationery document

Making a New Version of a Stationery Document ___

After you open a copy of a stationery document, you can edit the document and then save it under a new name, or you can simply close the file without saving it if you don't need a copy on disk. If, on the other hand, you've modified the stationery file with the intent of making a new, improved template, you can save the new file over the old one by typing the original stationery filename and clicking the Stationery radio button in the Save As dialog box. Click Replace when the program asks whether you want to replace the original file.

 If you aren't using the ClarisWorks Stationery folder for your stationery documents, be sure to save the revised stationery document in the same folder as the original. Otherwise, you could end up with multiple versions of the same file.

Using Stationery to Set New Environment Defaults

Although the Preferences command in the Edit menu enables you to set a handful of default options for several environments (see Chapter 11), you can add many more settings as defaults so that they are automatically in effect whenever you create a new document. To add settings as defaults, simply create a document that contains the new default settings and then save it as a specially named stationery document in the ClarisWorks Stationery folder. Claris refers to these special documents as *default stationery*. (In ClarisWorks 3.0, they were known as *ClarisWorks options stationery.)*

To save documents as default stationery, you need to name the files as shown in Table 10-1.

Table 10-1	
Default Stationery File-Naming Conventions	
Environment	**Name of Default Stationery Document**
Word Processing	ClarisWorks WP Options
Drawing	ClarisWorks DR Options
Painting	ClarisWorks PT Options
Spreadsheet	ClarisWorks SS Options
Database	ClarisWorks DB Options
Communications	ClarisWorks CM Options

For example, to make the word processing environment open new documents with my defaults, I created a blank stationery document, set the starting font to Times, defined four frequently used text styles, and added the styles to the stylesheet for the document.

Now every new word processing document defaults to the Times font, and the four text styles are always available.

You can create your own default stationery documents with the options that you prefer. Note, however, that you can have only one default stationery document for each environment. If you want to change an existing default stationery document, the procedure is to save the new one over the old one —in other words, replace it.

To create an environment default stationery document, choose New from the Edit menu. Choose the appropriate environment and click OK. A blank document appears. Set options for the document (and, if you want, set preferences by using the Preferences command from the Edit menu). Choose Save As from the File menu. The normal file dialog box appears. Click the Stationery radio button. The ClarisWorks Stationery folder is automatically selected for you. Name the file according to the conventions listed in Table 10-1 for saving default stationery. Click Save.

After you save a default stationery document, ClarisWorks adds it to the file list in the New Document dialog box. The default stationery document you save *replaces* the original ClarisWorks default document as the one that will be automatically used for that environment. The original default document is retained as the "Standard" document for the environment.

For example, if you created a ClarisWorks WP Options file, it will be shown in the New Document dialog box as Word Processing. If, at any time, you'd like to use the original ClarisWorks default for the environment, choose Standard Word Processing.

If you already have some options stationery files that you designed for ClarisWorks 3, you also can use them with ClarisWorks 4, if you like. Just copy or move the files into the ClarisWorks Stationery folder inside the ClarisWorks 4.0 folder. If you decide to reuse a ClarisWorks WP Options document from ClarisWorks 3.0 in ClarisWorks 4.0, styles that you added to the Styles menu automatically appear in the stylesheet.

If you are using PowerTalk messaging (refer to Chapter 19), you can create a new type of default stationery document, called a *reply stationery document,* that ClarisWorks opens automatically whenever you choose the Reply command or choose the Reply shortcut (see Figure 10-4) to answer a message. (To learn more about shortcuts, refer to Chapter 12).

Figure 10-4:
The Reply
shortcut

Create your reply stationery in a word processing document, adding graphics and text elements as desired. (Do not add a mailer to the document, however.) Then save the document as a ClarisWorks Stationery file in the ClarisWorks Stationery folder. In order to work, the stationery file must be named Reply. For additional information, see "Creating a reply stationery document" in Chapter 19.

Using the ClarisWorks Assistants

ClarisWorks 4.0 includes 13 Assistants, each designed to perform a specific task for you. You choose the majority of the Assistants in the New Document dialog box, and they create new documents. You need to invoke most of the other Assistants from within an existing document.

Each Assistant is self-explanatory. When you invoke an Assistant, you see a list on-screen of any preparatory steps that you need to perform, such as selecting a text insertion point or highlighting an address. Each Assistant is presented as a dialog box or a series of dialog boxes. You move forward (Next) and backward (Back) through the dialog boxes by clicking buttons. After you make selections from the pop-up menus, set necessary options, and type text entries, you click Create, Done, or Start (as appropriate) to make the Assistant execute.

New Document Assistants

You can choose eight Assistants from the New Document dialog box. Each of these Assistants produces a new document that is created according to your specifications.

After you click the Use Assistant or Stationery check box and choose All Assistants or a particular class of Assistants from the Category pop-up menu, you see the new document Assistants (see Figure 10-5). They include the following:

- *Name & Address List.* Creates a personal, business, or student name and address database.

- *Calendar.* Creates a single-month or multiple-month calendar. Each month is a separate ClarisWorks spreadsheet.

- *Certificate.* Creates decorative certificates, awards, and diplomas.

↪ *Envelope.* Creates a word processing document formatted as a business envelope (with an addressee and a return address).

↪ *Home Finance.* Creates worksheets that help you compute the answers to
common financial questions.

↪ *Newsletter.* Designs a newsletter or informational booklet in a variety of styles.
Placeholders for reserved for your copy.

↪ *Presentation.* Generates elaborate, multipage presentation templates that can be
displayed on-screen, shown on an overhead projector, or printed.

↪ *Register ClarisWorks.* Creates a postage-paid form that you can use to register
your copy of ClarisWorks 4.0. See "Registering ClarisWorks" in Appendix A for
instructions.

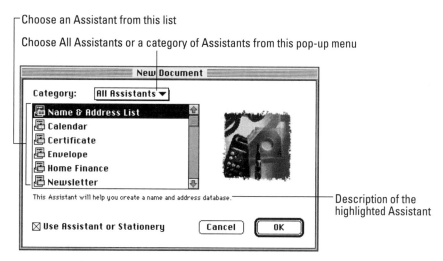

Figure 10-5:
Selecting
a new
document
Assistant

Other Assistants

You invoke four additional Assistants from within open ClarisWorks documents rather
than from the New Document dialog box:

↪ *Insert Footnote.* Adds a footnote to a word processing document, correctly
formatted in the chosen style. See Chapter 3, "Using the Word Processing
Assistants," for instructions.

↪ *Make Table.* Adds a spreadsheet table to a word processing document, a draw
document, or a database (in Layout mode only). See Chapter 3, "Using the Word
Processing Assistants," for instructions.

- ∽ *Address Envelope.* Copies the highlighted address from a word processing document and creates a new document that is formatted as a business envelope. You do not need to type the address information manually, as you do for the Envelope Assistant. Instead, the Address Envelope Assistant uses information that is already present in the document. See "Using the Word Processing Assistants," in Chapter 3 for instructions.

- ∽ *Create Labels.* Helps you design Avery or custom label layouts to be used with the current database. See "Working with Mailing Labels" in Chapter 5 for instructions.

You select these Assistants by choosing ClarisWorks Assistants from the Balloon Help menu.

The final Assistant, Find ClarisWorks Documents, helps you locate and open ClarisWorks files on your hard disk. You can invoke it regardless of whether or not a document is on-screen. To use the Find ClarisWorks Documents Assistant, choose ClarisWorks Assistants from the Balloon Help menu. After you specify the criteria, the Assistant searches the current drive and lists all matching files. You can then open found files from within the Assistant. (See Chapter 1 for a more detailed discussion of this Assistant.)

Quick Tips

The following Quick Tips suggest some practical applications for stationery documents.

Any file that you intend to reuse can be a stationery document. Keep in mind, however, that if you never intend to alter the base document, saving it as a stationery file is pointless. For example, if you have a letter that you always send without changes, you can save it as a normal ClarisWorks file and simply reprint it as often as you like.

Here are a few ideas for stationery documents:

- ∽ *Fax form or cover sheet.* Remove everything but the static information (the logo, return address, and phone number as well as the reserved areas for the date, subject, number of pages, recipient's name, and fax number) from your normal fax form or cover sheet (which is probably a word processing or draw document). Then use the Insert Date command in the Edit menu to enter the send date so that whenever you open a copy of the stationery document, the current date will be filled in automatically.

- *Letterhead.* If you have a laser or ink-jet printer, you can save money by printing your own letterhead.

- *Weekly, monthly, quarterly, or annual worksheets.* Many worksheets are reusable. (I keep my personal financial records in several of them, for example.) Open the worksheet and remove all the data, being sure to leave cells that contain labels or formulas intact. Then save the worksheet under a new name as a stationery document. Whenever the new week, month, quarter, or year begins, you can open a copy of the template and plug in the new numbers. You can use the same tactic for record-keeping database templates.

- *Business forms.* Templates are perfect for standard business forms, such as invoices, statements, petty cash vouchers, and the like.

- *Contracts.* Most legal documents, whether they are wills, leases, or terms of work-for-hire, consist largely of standard language. By saving them as stationery, you can dramatically reduce writing time on subsequent contracts.

- *Common communications settings.* You can create a general-purpose communications stationery document that contains the options you most frequently use for the baud rate, transfer protocol, and so on. Most on-line sessions will require only slight modifications to the settings in the template.

■■

Summary

➥ Save files as stationery documents when you want to use them as templates.

➥ When you open a stationery document, your template is opened as a new untitled document — protecting the original from unintentional modifications.

➥ When you launch ClarisWorks or create a new file, you can select any stationery document in the ClarisWorks Stationery folder by clicking the Use Assistant or Stationery check box, and then either choosing All Stationery or a particular class of stationery from the Category pop-up menu.

➥ You can set defaults for any environment by designing a ClarisWorks default stationery document and following a special convention for naming the document when you save it in the ClarisWorks Stationery folder.

➥ ClarisWorks includes 13 Assistants that walk you through common business and home computing tasks.

■■

Setting
Preferences

11

■ ■

In This Chapter

➡ Setting default and document-specific preferences

➡ General preferences

➡ Text preferences

➡ Graphics preferences

➡ Spreadsheet preferences

➡ Shortcuts preferences

➡ Color preferences

➡ Communications preferences

➡ Mail preferences

■ ■

Overview

By setting preferences, you can customize ClarisWorks to fit the way you work. To view
the current preferences settings or change them, choose Preferences from the Edit
menu. The Preferences dialog box appears (see Figure 11-1). The left side of the Preferences dialog box contains icons that represent the different parts of ClarisWorks that
you can customize. Each time you click an icon, a set of options for that particular
program function appears in the right side of the dialog box. The areas for which you
can set preferences in ClarisWorks 4.0 are general, text, graphics, spreadsheet, shortcuts, color, and communications.

Preference area icons   Preference options

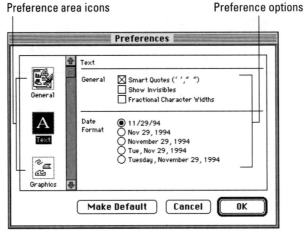

Figure 11-1:
The Preferences
dialog box with
options for text
preferences

 If you are using System 7.5, System 7 Pro, or a later version of the system software and have PowerTalk installed, electronic mail preferences also can be set.

 If you have WorldScript installed on your Mac — to enable you to work with foreign languages — you also will see a WorldScript icon when you choose Preferences from the Edit menu. For information on setting WorldScript preferences and using WorldScript with ClarisWorks, see the following topics in ClarisWorks Help: "About WorldScript," "WorldScript in ClarisWorks," and "Set WorldScript preferences."

Default and Document-Specific Preferences

In ClarisWorks, you can set preferences in two ways:

- ∞ You can create a group of *default preferences* to be used automatically for all new documents in the current session and in future sessions.

- ∞ You can set *document-specific preferences* that apply to one document and are saved with that document.

Steps:	**Setting New Default Preferences**
Step 1.	Choose Preferences from the Edit menu.
Step 2.	Click an icon on the left side of the Preferences dialog box to select the type of preferences settings that you want to modify.
Step 3.	Change the settings in the right side of the dialog box as desired.
Step 4.	Repeat Steps 2 and 3 for any other preferences that you want to change.
Step 5.	Click Make Default.

The new preferences become the default settings for all new documents that you create in this session and in future sessions.

 If you ever decide that you'd like to revert to the original preference settings for ClarisWorks 4.0, delete the file named ClarisWorks Preferences (located in the Preferences folder inside your System Folder).

Steps:	**Setting Document-Specific Preferences**
Step 1.	Select the document whose preferences you want to set, making it the active document (bringing it to the front if you have two or more open documents). You can use a document that you have just created or one that you have loaded from disk.
Step 2.	Choose Preferences from the Edit menu.
Step 3.	Click an icon on the left side of the dialog box to select the type of preferences settings that you want to modify.
Step 4.	Change the settings in the right side of the dialog box as desired.
Step 5.	Repeat Steps 3 and 4 for any other preferences that you want to change.
Step 6.	Click OK.

The new settings apply only to the current document. Other new documents that you create in the session will still use the default settings, unless you also set preferences for them. Because preferences settings are saved with each document, the next time you run ClarisWorks and open the document, the preferences will be intact.

 Preferences are also stored with files that you save as stationery documents.

General Preferences

You use general preferences to customize many of the basic options in ClarisWorks (see Figure 11-2), such as whether warnings are displayed and how graphics files are shown in Open dialog boxes and on the desktop. You can also use general preferences to set the startup action for ClarisWorks.

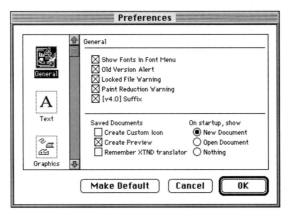

 Although you normally use the Make Default and OK buttons to modify the ClarisWorks default and document-specific preferences settings, the OK button has a different function when you use it in conjunction with general preferences. Clicking OK puts the changed settings into effect for the entire session (until you quit the program), rather than just for the current document. For example, if you click the Create Custom Icon check box and then click OK, a custom icon will automatically be created for every draw or paint document that you save during the session. In the next ClarisWorks session, however, you'll find that the Create Custom Icon setting has been turned off again. To set new general preferences as *permanent* defaults, click the Make Default button.

General preferences settings include the following:

- *Show Fonts in Font Menu.* Shows font names in their respective typefaces in the Font submenu of the Format menu.

- *Old Version Alert.* Displays a warning message whenever a file created in an earlier version of the program is opened.

- *Locked File Warning.* Displays a warning whenever a locked file is opened. (Locked files can be read but not altered.) To unlock a file, quit ClarisWorks, select the file's icon on the desktop, press ⌘-I, remove the check mark from the Locked check box, and click the close box.

⚬ *Paint Reduction Warning.* Warns when there is insufficient memory to create a full-page paint document. The document will be created at a reduced size. (See "Quick Tips" at the end of Chapter 6 for instructions on avoiding this situation by increasing the memory allocation for ClarisWorks.)

⚬ *[v4.0] Suffix.* Appends this suffix to the name of any file you open that was created with an earlier version of ClarisWorks. Because adding the suffix changes the filename, this option protects the original file from being overwritten by mistake.

⚬ *Saved Documents (options).* Click Create Custom Icon to instruct ClarisWorks to create file icons that are miniature representations of paint and draw images. This special icon is automatically created whenever a graphics file is saved.

Click Create Preview to tell ClarisWorks to save a thumbnail preview of each text, paint, or draw document. The preview will be shown in the dialog box that appears when you choose Open from the File menu.

Click Remember XTND translator to assist you in saving translated documents in their native formats. With this option chosen, whenever you edit a translated document and then save it, the Save As pop-up menu is automatically set for the program in which the translated document was created (Microsoft Word, for example). Of course, you can still select ClarisWorks or any other file type as the Save As format.

⚬ *On startup, show.* Determines what you see first each time you launch ClarisWorks. The default choice is to display the New Document dialog box. Alternatively, you can have the program display the Open dialog box (to open an existing document) or no dialog box at all (Nothing). If you normally begin each session by starting a new document or opening an existing one, you can click the New Document or Open Document radio button. If your initial action varies from one session to the next, you are better off clicking the Nothing button, which enables you to select an appropriate startup action for each session.

If you previously used ClarisWorks 3.0, you may be accustomed to seeing the Welcome dialog box at the start of each ClarisWorks session. This dialog box let you decide whether you wanted to open an existing document, create a new document, or run the guided tour. It's gone in ClarisWorks 4.0.

Text Preferences

Text preferences apply to any text that you type in a ClarisWorks document, regardless of the environment you're in. Figure 11-1 shows the options for text preferences.

Text preferences options include the following:

☞ *Smart Quotes.* With Smart Quotes enabled, ClarisWorks automatically translates your presses of the ' or " keys into curly quotes (" and "), as shown in Figure 11-3. Smart Quotes are applied intelligently. In most cases, the program can correctly determine when a right-facing or left-facing quotation mark is appropriate.

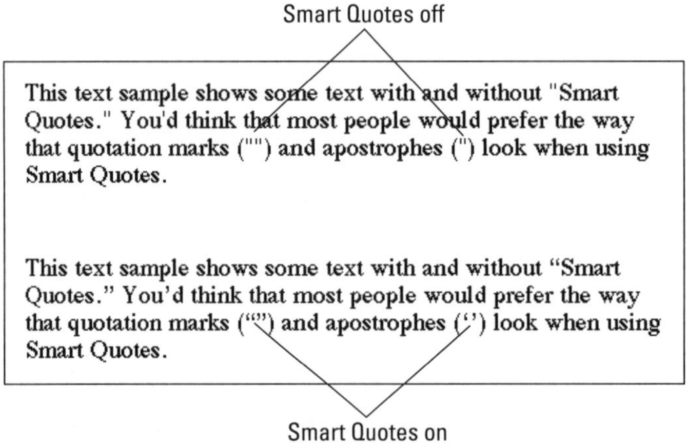

Smart Quotes off

Figure 11-3:
Examples of the
Smart Quotes
settings

This text sample shows some text with and without "Smart Quotes." You'd think that most people would prefer the way that quotation marks ("") and apostrophes (') look when using Smart Quotes.

This text sample shows some text with and without "Smart Quotes." You'd think that most people would prefer the way that quotation marks ("") and apostrophes (') look when using Smart Quotes.

Smart Quotes on

Curly quotes are preferred in modern correspondence and publications. Correct uses for straight quotes include displaying feet (') and inches (") in measurements.

To manually type curly quote characters (when Smart Quotes is off), use the keys listed in Table 11-1.

| Table 11-1 | |
Curly Quote Keys	
Character	**Key**
"	Option-[
"	Shift-Option-[
'	Option-]
'	Shift-Option-]

↪ *Show Invisibles.* When this option is checked, you can see characters that are normally invisible, such as tabs, spaces, and end-of-paragraph markers (see Figure 11-4). Turning this option on after you finish a report or letter makes clean-up editing simpler. For example, it enables you to find extra spaces between words. You also can toggle this option off and on in the Shortcuts palette.

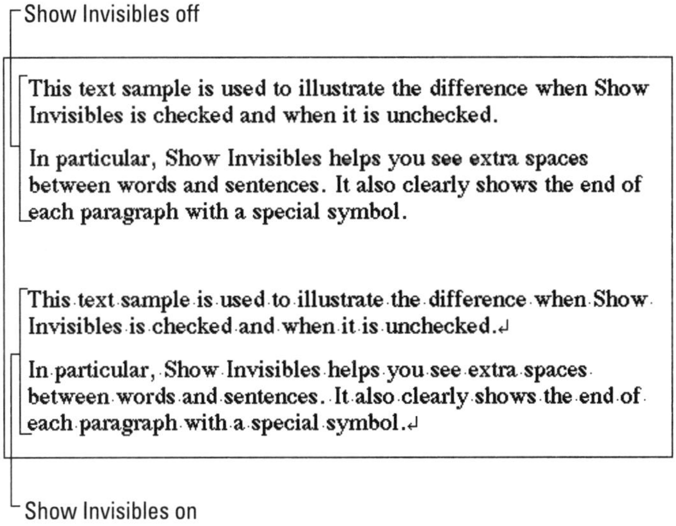

Show Invisibles off

Figure 11-4:
Examples of the
Show Invisibles
settings

This text sample is used to illustrate the difference when Show Invisibles is checked and when it is unchecked.

In particular, Show Invisibles helps you see extra spaces between words and sentences. It also clearly shows the end of each paragraph with a special symbol.

This·text·sample·is·used·to·illustrate·the·difference·when·Show· Invisibles·is·checked·and·when·it·is·unchecked.↵

In·particular,·Show·Invisibles·helps·you·see·extra·spaces· between·words·and·sentences.·It·also·clearly·shows·the·end·of· each·paragraph·with·a·special·symbol.↵

Show Invisibles on

↪ *Fractional Character Widths.* Choose this option to tighten spacing between characters (when printing to a laser printer, for example). Do not check this option if you are printing to an ImageWriter printer.

↪ *Date Format.* The format that you select is used whenever you insert the current date into a document by choosing the Insert Date command from the Edit menu.

In previous versions of ClarisWorks, the text preferences also included settings for footnotes. Those settings are now document-specific rather than preferences. To set footnote options, choose Document from the Format menu.

Graphics Preferences _____

The graphics preferences (shown in Figure 11-5) affect both draw and paint graphics, as the following explanations indicate.

Figure 11-5:
Graphics preferences
options

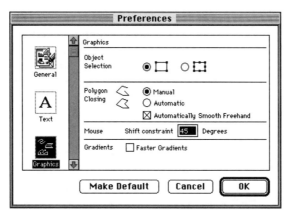

⌘ *Object Selection (draw).* When you select draw objects with the pointer, they can be displayed with four or eight handles, as shown in Figure 11-6. Note that the extra handles do not provide additional object manipulation capabilities.

Figure 11-6:
Object selection
handles

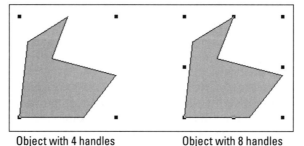

Object with 4 handles   Object with 8 handles

⌘ *Polygon Closing (draw and paint).* Polygon closing can be Manual or Automatic. When you choose the Automatic setting, you don't have to complete the final side of a draw or paint figure. You simply double-click the last point of the polygon. In Manual mode, if you want a closed polygon, you have to finish the figure by clicking its starting point. (If most of your polygons will be closed, selecting Automatic can save considerable time when compared to manually attempting to click an object's starting point.)

The Polygon Closing preference setting also affects *bezigons*.

If you check Automatically Smooth Freehand (draw), the program transforms shapes that you draw freehand into relatively smooth curves.

↝ *Mouse Shift Constraint (draw).* You use this setting to specify an angular constraint for drawing with the mouse while the Shift key is pressed. The default setting enables you to draw in increments of 45 degrees, as shown in Figure 11-7. In paint mode, the Shift key always constrains lines to 90-degree angles (straight vertical or straight horizontal).

Figure 11-7:
Lines drawn with a mouse
Shift constraint
of 45 degrees

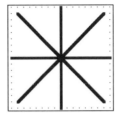

↝ *Gradients.* The Faster Gradients check box speeds up the display of gradients by temporarily showing them as rough approximations (frequently with banding lines), rather than as smooth transformations from one color to another.

Spreadsheet Preferences _____

The spreadsheet preferences enable you to customize the way that the arrow keys and Enter key are used when you are working in a spreadsheet document or frame. The spreadsheet preferences options are shown in Figure 11-8.

Figure 11-8:
Spreadsheet
preferences

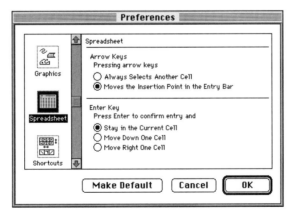

Depending on which Arrow Keys preference you choose, pressing an arrow key does one of the following:

- *Always selects another cell.* Selects the cell to the immediate right, left, above, or below the current cell when you press the right, left, up, or down arrow key, respectively.

- *Moves the insertion point in the entry bar.* Used only for entering and editing data.

Regardless of which setting you choose, you can achieve the opposite function by pressing Option in combination with an arrow key. Thus, if you elect to use the arrow keys for cell selection, you can still move to the right or left when you enter or edit data by pressing Option-right arrow or Option-left arrow.

The Enter Key preference setting enables you to set the action that occurs when you complete a cell entry by pressing the Enter key. If you've used other spreadsheet programs, you may prefer to use the default setting: Stay in the Current Cell. Other options enable the Enter key to duplicate the function of the Return key (Move Down One Cell) or the Tab key (Move Right One Cell).

Remember that, as with other preferences, you can set spreadsheet preferences either for one document or globally. Most users prefer to choose one way of doing things and then click Make Default to set preferences for all future ClarisWorks worksheets.

Shortcuts Preferences _____

Figure 11-9 shows the shortcuts preferences options.

Figure 11-9:
Shortcuts preferences
options

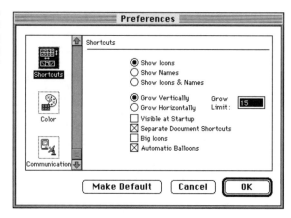

In previous versions of ClarisWorks, the shortcuts and color preferences were grouped together as the palettes preferences.

You use the shortcuts preferences options to customize the appearance of the Shortcuts palette as follows:

⌐ *Show.* The first group of options determine whether shortcuts are displayed as icons only (Show Icons), names only (Show Names), or icons and names (Show Icons & Names). If you have trouble remembering what each shortcut icon represents, you will probably prefer one of the latter options. Note, however, that choosing either Show Names or Show Icons & Names automatically displays the shortcuts in a single vertical list, as shown in Figure 11-10. The entire list may not fit on the screen, however.

Figure 11-10:
The Show Icons & Names shortcuts list

☞ *Grow...* Grow Vertically and Grow Horizontally determines how the Shortcuts palette will be displayed (in long rows or tall columns, respectively), as well as how new buttons will be added (in rows from left to right or in columns from top to bottom), as shown in Figure 11-11. The Grow Limit is the maximum number of buttons that will appear in each row or column.

Figure 11-11:
The palette on the left expands vertically (by adding new rows) when new buttons are added. The palette on the right grows horizontally (by adding new columns).

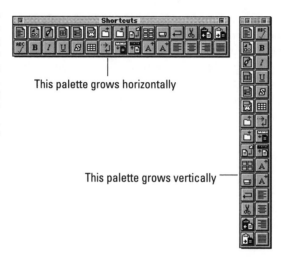

This palette grows horizontally

This palette grows vertically

☞ A check mark in the Visible at Startup check box can save you some time at the beginning of each session. The Shortcuts palette appears automatically when you launch ClarisWorks — you don't have to choose Shortcuts from the File menu and then choose Show Shortcuts in order to see it.

☞ The Separate Document Shortcuts check box enables you to save a specific set of shortcuts with a document. It also determines whether document-specific shortcuts that you've added to the palette appear with a dividing line to separate them from the application shortcuts.

If tiny icons aren't your thing, click the Big Icons check box. If the shortcuts palette contains many icons, though, you may not be able to see them all — particularly if you use this option in combination with the Show Icons & Names setting.

Automatic Balloons is a cool new feature of ClarisWorks 4.0. When this option is checked, if you rest the mouse pointer over any shortcut icon for a few seconds, a Balloon Help balloon appears that explains the purpose of the shortcut. Unlike choosing the Show Balloons command in the Balloon Help menu, choosing this option turns on Balloon Help for the Shortcuts palette only.

Color Preferences

Color preferences enable you to use the standard 81-color Drawing and Text Colors palette or load a color palette of your choice (Editable 256 Color Palette). Figure 11-12 shows the Color preferences options.

Figure 11-12:
Color preferences
options

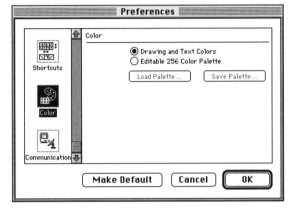

The number of colors available in the drawing and text colors palettes depends on the capabilities of your monitor and video card, as well as on the settings in the Monitors control panel. For example, if your system is currently set to display 16 colors, the color palettes will only show those 16 colors. To see the complete palette of 81 different colors, the Mac must be set for (and capable of displaying) 256 or more colors.

ClarisWorks includes a Colors and Gradients folder (stored in the Claris folder within the System Folder) that is installed when you install ClarisWorks 4.0. It contains many predefined color palettes that you can use.

To load a Color Palette, click the Editable 256 Color Palette radio button in the color Preferences dialog box. Click the Load Palette button. Select a palette from the Colors and Gradients folder.

You can also load palettes that you've created in other graphics programs (such as MacDraw Pro).

As with other preferences settings, loading a color palette affects only the active document. Thus, every document can have its own special color palette.

ClarisWorks can save and load only color palettes. You cannot save edited gradients or patterns as a new palette. However, custom gradients and patterns are saved as part of the document in which they were created. If you want to reuse a custom pattern or gradient, save the associated document as a ClarisWorks stationery file. (If *all* you want to reuse is a custom pattern or gradient — not the text or graphics in the document — strip the page of everything before saving it as stationery.)

To edit a Color Palette in ClarisWorks, tear off the Fill or Pen color palette from its location in the Tool panel. Double-click the color that you want to change. A color wheel appears. (The style of color wheel shown depends on the version of system software that's installed on your Mac.) You can switch directly to a different color by clicking the color in the wheel. Alternatively, you can enter different numerical settings in the boxes on the left or use the scroll bar (or bars) to change the wheel's color scheme. Make the desired changes and then click OK. If you think that you may want to reuse a palette that you've customized, you can save it by clicking the Save Palette button in the color Preferences dialog box.

Communications Preferences_____

At a minimum, changing the default communications preferences is useful for selecting a folder to receive electronically transmitted files and for establishing other generic communications settings. You also may want to create several different communications documents, each with its own preferences settings.

For example, you can create a document for communicating with a friend that starts by automatically instructing the modem and software to wait for the friend's call. And for logging onto a communications service, you can create a document that attempts to connect the moment you open the document. Figure 11-13 shows the communications preferences options.

Figure 11-13:
Communications
preferences options

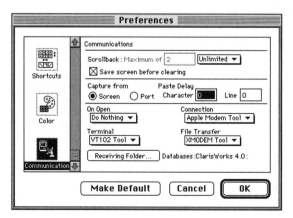

The following descriptions tell you what the communications preferences do and how they affect activity during a session:

✑ *Scrollback.* Incoming text often arrives faster than you can read it, particularly if you are using a fast modem. The scrollback setting determines how many lines or screens of text will be available for you to scroll back through. You can choose a specific number of lines, kilobytes (sets of 1024 characters), or screens; or you can choose Unlimited. Unless you find yourself running out of memory, the best choice is Unlimited.

If you choose anything other than Unlimited, ClarisWorks discards the oldest lines, kilobytes, or screens when the limit is reached. Similarly, some information services clear each screen before sending a new one. Check the "Save screen before clearing" check box if you want the program to store the old information in memory rather than discarding it.

✑ *Capture from [Screen or Port].* This setting determines whether incoming text that is captured with the Capture to File command from the Session menu is formatted or unformatted. To save the formatting (such as tabs, linefeeds, and formfeeds), choose Port. To ignore these formatting characters, choose Screen. In general, you should choose Port when you intend to use the information in a spreadsheet or database document. Choose Screen when you want to use the captured data in a word processing document that you plan to reformat anyway.

✑ *Paste Delay.* This setting instructs ClarisWorks to pause between the characters or lines of text that it transmits. This feature enables a slower computer on the other end of the line to keep up. Numbers entered in either box are in $1/60$ second. (An entry of 5, for example, represents a $5/60$ second delay.) Normally, this option can be left as is (0, for no delays).

✑ *On Open.* This setting determines the action taken, if any, when you open a communications document. The choices are Do Nothing, Automatically Connect, and Wait for Connection. In general, you rarely need to change the default setting of Do Nothing.

However, you may want to set an option for some communications documents. For example, the Automatically Connect setting is a good choice for a communications document that you use with a bulletin board service (BBS) or with an information service such as GEnie or CompuServe. Do Nothing is the best choice for documents when you initiate the connection sometimes, and a friend or colleague initiates it at other times.

✑ *Connection.* ClarisWorks ships with two connection tools: the Apple Modem Tool (for Apple and Hayes-compatible modems) and the Serial Tool (for direct communications between a pair of computers over a serial cable). Other programs may add their own connection tools that also appear in this pop-up menu.

❧ *Terminal.* This option enables your Mac to work like a Teletype (TTY) or a DEC VT-102 terminal. A TTY is a very basic scrolling terminal. Text is sent as a continuous stream of characters and lines. The VT-102 terminal is more advanced and allows the other computer to send special commands, such as one that clears your screen. Most information and bulletin board services support at least one of these terminal types.

❧ *File Transfer.* ClarisWorks supports three file transfer protocols: Text, Kermit, and XMODEM. XMODEM is the most widely used and supported protocol — especially for transferring standard Mac files. For example, you can use XMODEM to transfer ClarisWorks word processing files between two Macs. The receiving Mac will be able to open the file in ClarisWorks.

The Text option is useful for transferring text-only files between computers that don't have the same programs, as well as between different types of computers (Macs and PCs, for example).

❧ *Receiving Folder.* This setting identifies the folder that will be used to save captured text and protocol transfers (when you download files from an information service, for example). Click the button to select a folder.

Mail Preferences

If you have System 7.5, System 7 Pro, or a later version of the Macintosh system software, you can take advantage of PowerTalk, a feature that makes exchanging electronic mail easy for Mac users. The ClarisWorks mail preferences options (shown in Figure 11-14) let you customize the way certain PowerTalk mail-handling tasks are performed.

Figure 11-14:
Mail preferences
options

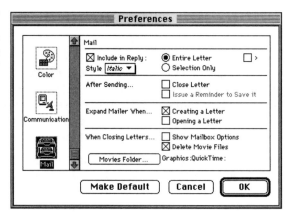

The mail preferences options give you control over the following e-mail tasks:

- *Include in Reply.* When replying to a letter, you can determine how much text from the original letter is displayed beneath your reply. Choose Entire Letter if you want the entire text from the original message included in your reply. Choose Selection Only to include only the text that you have selected. Use the Style pop-up menu to select the font style (italic or bold, for example) in which you want the text of the original letter to be displayed. If you do not want to include any text from the original letter, click the Include in Reply check box to remove the check mark.

No matter which Include in Reply option you choose, you can edit any text that you include from the original letter. For example, you can choose the Entire Letter option and then edit it to show only the key points to which you are responding.

Click the check box next to the > symbol to add a standard message that describes, in detail, the origin of the document to which you are replying. The message is in the form:

> At July 25, 1995 9:48 PM, Steven Schwartz wrote:

and is followed by the full text of the original letter or selected text from that letter, depending on the Include in Reply option you've chosen.

- *After Sending.* You can set in motion a couple of automatic actions to be performed after you send a letter. Click the Close Letter check box to automatically close a letter after you send it. Click the Issue a Reminder to Save It option (which is available only if you check Close Letter) to have ClarisWorks automatically ask you each time you send a letter whether you want to save the letter on disk.

Even if you do not save a copy of the letter to disk, you can still recall the letter from your Out Tray — as long as you haven't tossed the letter's icon into the Trash.

- *Expand Mailer When.* By clicking the small triangle to the left of the From box in any mailer, you manually expand or collapse the mailer (see Figure 11-15). You can instruct ClarisWorks to automatically expand the mailer when Creating a Letter or Opening a Letter. Just click the appropriate check boxes.

Collapsed mailer

Figure 11-15:
A collapsed
mailer and an
expanded
mailer

	Untitled 4 (WP)	
▷	**From** Steven Schwartz	**Subject** Production schedule

Untitled 4 (WP)

▽   **From**
Steven Schwartz

Subject
Production schedule

Recipients
✉ Jane Anderson   To

Enclosures

Click to collapse or expand the mailer   Expanded mailer

↪ *When Closing Letters.* You can set automatic actions to be performed when you
close a letter you've received.

If Show Mailbox Options is checked, the dialog box in Figure 11-16 appears
whenever you close a letter. The Add Tag option helps you organize your mail by
enabling you to add a key word or phrase (called a *tag*) to the letter. Every tag
that you create is automatically added to the tag pop-up list, so you can easily
assign it to other letters. Click Move to Trash if you want to delete the letter.

Figure 11-16:
Set disposi-
tion options
for a letter in
this dialog
box.

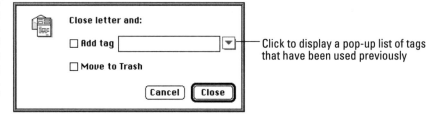

Close letter and:

☐ **Add tag** [   ] ▼ ──── Click to display a pop-up list of tags
                                            that have been used previously

☐ **Move to Trash**

(Cancel) (**Close**)

You also can add or edit tags from the desktop by selecting a letter and then
choosing Tag from the Mailbox menu. Every tag, whether created in
ClarisWorks or at the desktop, appears in all tag pop-up lists.

Delete Movie Files is checked by default and with good reason. Movies that are
attached to ClarisWorks letters are not in playable form; they must first be
converted by ClarisWorks. This conversion automatically takes place whenever
you open a letter that contains a movie. Therefore, to avoid creating duplicates
of movies, leave this option checked.

If you intend to replay movies that are enclosed in letters, click the Movies Folder button to select a folder in which to store the playable (that is, converted) versions of the movie files. After the file dialog box appears, navigate to the disk and folder in which you want to store playable movies. Highlight the desired folder (don't open it), and then click the Select "*folder name*" button to choose the highlighted folder.

To learn more about how ClarisWorks supports PowerTalk messaging, see Chapter 19.

Summary

- ClarisWorks offers two kinds of preferences settings: default and document-specific. Changing a default preference affects all new documents. Setting a document-specific preference affects only that particular document.

- Program areas for which preferences can be set include general, text, graphics, spreadsheet, shortcuts, color, communications, and mail.

- Curly quotes, which are automatic with the Smart Quotes text preferences option, help create more professional-looking documents.

- The Show Invisibles text setting is useful when you perform a cleanup edit on documents.

- The Color Preferences enables you to load and save custom color palettes that you can reuse with new documents.

- ClarisWorks can display buttons in the Shortcuts palette vertically or horizontally, and the buttons can show icons, names, or both.

- The On Open item in the communications preferences can make a communications document automatically wait for an incoming call from another modem or connect with a particular information service, computer, or BBS.

The Shortcuts Palette

CHAPTER 12

In This Chapter

- ➡ The meanings of the standard shortcuts in the Shortcuts palette
- ➡ Customizing the appearance of the Shortcuts palette
- ➡ Adding, removing, and moving shortcut icons
- ➡ Assigning custom macros to the Shortcuts palette
- ➡ Sharing your custom shortcuts with others

Overview

The Shortcuts palette (see Figure 12-1) is a floating *windoid* (a tiny window with close and collapse/expand boxes) that is covered with icons (called *shortcuts*) that you click to execute common commands, such as printing the current document or changing the style of some text. (And now for a bit of "Mac trivia": Palettes and windoids are said to *float* if you can freely change their on-screen location by dragging them to a more convenient position.)

The shortcuts on the Shortcuts palette automatically change to match the environment of the document or frame in which you are currently working. The spreadsheet shortcuts are presented when you are using a worksheet, for example.

Figure 12-1:
The Shortcuts palette for the word processing environment

In addition to the standard shortcuts, ClarisWorks provides 88 more predefined shortcuts that you can add to the palette. You also can add custom shortcuts for executing macros that you've created. Other shortcut customization options include the following:

- ☞ Removing unwanted shortcuts from the palette

- ☞ Determining whether the Shortcuts palette appears automatically when ClarisWorks is launched or appears only when you choose Show Shortcuts from the Shortcuts submenu of the File menu

- ☞ Setting the orientation of the palette (horizontal or vertical) to determine whether it will expand horizontally or vertically as new shortcuts are added

- ☞ Showing the shortcuts as icons (normal or large), as text descriptions, or as icons *and* text

The Many Faces of the Shortcuts Palette

As mentioned previously, the contents of the Shortcuts palette automatically change to match the environment in which you're currently working. Tables 12-1 through 12-8 describe the functions of the standard ClarisWorks shortcut icons in different ClarisWorks environments.

Table 12-1
The Shortcuts Palette with No Open Documents

Shortcut	Description
📄	Make a new word processing document.
📄	Make a new draw document.
📄	Make a new paint document.
📄	Make a new spreadsheet document.
📄	Make a new database document.
📄	Make a new communications document.
📄	Open a document on disk.

Table 12-2
Shortcuts Available in All Palettes (Except Communications)

Shortcut	Description
	Open a document on disk.
	Save the current document.
	Insert a file.
	Tile windows.
	Print the current document.
	Undo the last operation.
	Cut the selected text or object to the Clipboard.
	Copy the selected text or object to the Clipboard.
	Paste the contents of the Clipboard at the current cursor location.
	Check the spelling of the current document, frame, or selected text.
	Format the selected text with the boldface style.
	Format the selected text with the italic style.
	Format the selected text with the underline style.
	Show/hide the Stylesheet palette.

Table 12-3
The Word Processing Shortcuts Palette

Shortcut	Description
	Add a spreadsheet table to the document. (**Note:** If tab-delimited text is selected before the shortcut is executed, the text is converted to a spreadsheet table. A tab-delimited paragraph contains a series of items separated by tab characters.)
	Show/hide invisibles.
	Copy the current paragraph settings from the ruler.
	Use the copied ruler settings to format the current paragraph.
	Increase the size of the selected text by one point.
	Decrease the size of the selected text by one point.

(continued)

Table 12-3 *(continued)*

Shortcut	Description
	Left-align the selected paragraphs.
	Center-align the selected paragraphs.
	Right-align the selected paragraphs.
	Justify the selected paragraphs.

Table 12-4
The Draw Shortcuts Palette

Shortcut	Description
	Align objects along their top edges.
	Align objects along their left edges.
	Align objects along their bottom edges.
	Align objects along their right edges.
	Align the centers of the selected objects.
	Arrange objects in a column so they are centered between the left edge of the left-most object and the right edge of the right-most object.
	Move selected objects forward (one layer closer to the front).
	Move selected objects back (one layer closer to the back).
	Set irregular text wrap for the current object.
	Rotate the selected object 90 degrees clockwise.

Table 12-5
The Paint Shortcuts Palette

Shortcut	Description
	Rotate the selected image 90 degrees clockwise.
	Switch to opaque mode.
	Switch to transparent mode.
	Switch to tint mode.

Shortcut	Description
	Make the selected image lighter (whiter).
	Make the selected image darker (blacker).
	Tint the selected image with the current fill color.
	Fill the selected object with the current color and pattern (or gradient).
	If the current selected image has more than one color, create a smooth blend of the colors.
	Invert (reverse) the colors in the selected image.
	Pick up the selected image's attributes.

Table 12-6
The Spreadsheet Shortcuts Palette

Shortcut	Description
	Perform an ascending sort on the selected cell range.
	Perform a descending sort on the selected cell range.
	Sum the selected cell range, placing totals in the selected empty cells below and to the right.
	Apply the currency format to the selected cells.
	Apply the percentage format to the selected cells.
	Apply the comma numeric format to the selected cells.
	Toggle between showing formulas and showing values.
	Draw an outline border for the selected cells.
	Draw a left border for the selected cells.
	Draw a top border for the selected cells.
	Draw a right border for the selected cells.
	Draw a bottom border for the selected cells.
	Wrap text to fit the cell width.
	Insert selected rows or columns.
	Delete selected rows or columns.

(continued)

Table 12-6 (continued)

Shortcut	Description
	Create a bar chart based on the selected cells.
	Create a stacked bar chart based on the selected cells.
	Create a pie chart based on the selected cells.
	Create an area chart based on the selected cells.
	Create a line chart based on the selected cells.
	Create a hi-lo chart based on the selected cells.
	Create a pictogram chart based on the selected cells.

Table 12-7
The Database Shortcuts Palette

Shortcut	Description
	Perform an ascending sort of the selected records, using the current database field as the key field.
	Perform a descending sort of the selected records, using the current database field as the key field.
	Re-sort the current set of selected (found) records, using the current sort criteria.
	Select records that match (are equal to) the value in the current field.
	Select records that do not match (are not equal to) the value in the current field.
	Select records with values that are less than the value in the current field.
	Select records with values that are greater than the value in the current field.
	Add a new record.
	Select (show) all records.
	Hide the currently selected records.

Table 12-8		
The Communications Shortcuts Palette		

Shortcut	Description	
📠	Open the connection or close the connection.	
📱	Send a file.	
📱	Prepare to receive a file.	

 There are fewer standard communications shortcuts in the Shortcuts palette than there were in ClarisWorks 3. The shortcut to wait for an incoming call is no longer in the palette. See "Customizing the Shortcuts Palette" for instructions on how to add this and other shortcuts to the palette.

Hiding and Showing the Shortcuts Palette _____

If the Shortcuts palette is not on-screen, you can make it appear by choosing the Shortcuts command from the File menu and then choosing Show Shortcuts (or by pressing Shift-⌘-X).

To hide the Shortcuts palette from view, take any of the following actions:

- ➭ Choose the Shortcuts command from the File menu and then choose Hide Shortcuts.
- ➭ Press Shift-⌘-X.
- ➭ Click the close box in the upper-left corner of the Shortcuts palette.

Like other special ClarisWorks windoids, such as the tear-off fill and pattern palettes, the Shortcuts palette has another control box in its upper-right corner that is called the *collapse/expand box* (see Figure 12-2). If you click the collapse/expand box when the palette is completely displayed, the palette shrinks to show only its title bar and simultaneously moves out of the drawing area. If you click the box a second time, the palette expands to its normal size and instantly returns to its original location.

Figure 12-2:
Control boxes
appear in
ClarisWorks
windoids such as
the Shortcuts
palette.

As with other windoids, you can move the Shortcuts palette to a different position. Just Click in the Shortcuts palette's title bar, press the mouse button, and drag the palette to a new location.

Using a Shortcut

Shortcuts icons work just like buttons in other Macintosh programs. If the Shortcuts palette is not visible, choose Shortcuts from the File menu and then choose Show Shortcuts. Position the cursor or select the text or object to be modified. Then click the icon for the shortcut that you want to perform.

You must select text before you can perform some shortcuts. For example, to use the Bold or Italic shortcuts, you must first select the text to which these styles will be applied.

Customizing the Shortcuts Palette

Although the standard Shortcuts palette offers a nice selection of common commands, the fact that you can customize the palette in so many ways adds appreciably to its power. You can customize the palette to suit your needs — even create special palettes for each of the environments you work in. If you don't like the commands that the palette includes, you can remove them and, optionally, replace them with commands that are more useful to you. You can even add shortcuts that execute macros you've created. And you can use the Preferences command to control how and when the Shortcuts palette is displayed.

Setting Preferences for the Shortcuts Palette

Choose Preferences from the Edit menu to see a dialog box where you can change the appearance and start-up actions of the Shortcuts palette (see Figure 12-3). For example, you can use this dialog box to determine:

- ☞ Whether icons, shortcut names, or both will be shown
- ☞ The direction in which the palette will expand as new icons are added
- ☞ The size of the icons
- ☞ Whether the palette will automatically be displayed at start-up
- ☞ Whether document-specific shortcuts will be separated from application shortcuts
- ☞ Whether automatic help balloons will be displayed for the icons

For information on other ClarisWorks Preferences options, see Chapter 11.

Figure 12-3:
Click the Shortcuts icon in the Preferences dialog box to set options for the Shortcuts palette.

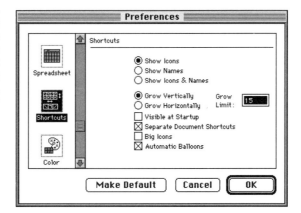

You can set any of the following Shortcuts palette options:

- ☞ Check Show Icons, Show Names, or Show Icons & Names to display the shortcut icons, names, or both, respectively (see Figure 12-4).

Figure 12-4:
Preferences
settings affect
the display of
the Shortcuts
palette.

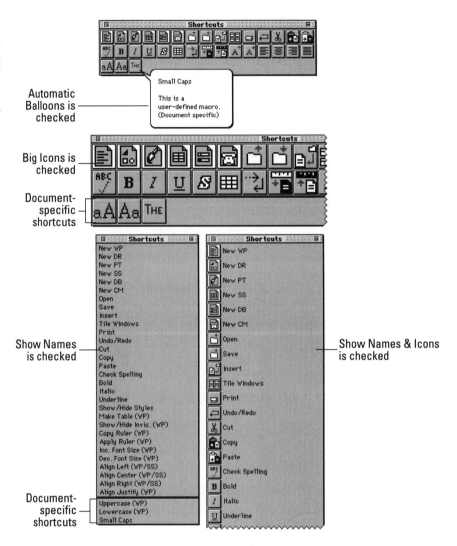

Automatic
Balloons is
checked

Big Icons is
checked

Document-
specific
shortcuts

Show Names
is checked

Document-
specific
shortcuts

Show Names & Icons
is checked

    Check Grow Vertically if you want to add new shortcuts in rows at the bottom of the palette. Check Grow Horizontally if you want to add new shortcuts in columns at the right side of the palette. The Grow Limit is the maximum number of shortcuts that will appear in each row or column. Grow Limit must be set to 30 or less.

    Check Visible at Startup if you want the palette to appear automatically at the start of each session. If you normally use the Shortcuts palette, selecting this option saves you the trouble of manually choosing Shortcuts from the File menu and then choosing Show Shortcuts.

⊙ Check Separate Document Shortcuts if you want to display document-specific shortcuts with a dividing line that separates them from the application shortcuts (see Figure 12-4). (Document-specific shortcuts are available only when the particular document in which they were saved is open.) If this option is not selected, document-specific shortcuts are added to the end of the palette, but no line separates them from the environment shortcuts.

 ⊙ Check Big Icons (see Figure 12-4) to display icons that are much larger than normal (0.5 inches square). Because of the increased size of the Shortcuts palette, Big Icons has its greatest usefulness when you have a large monitor. Note that the Big Icons setting can be combined with the Show Icons & Names setting to show big icons with descriptive names.

 ⊙ Check Automatic Balloons if you want to display Balloon Help-style messages when the cursor rests over an icon for a few seconds (see Figure 12-4). Note that these are the same balloons that appear if you select Show Balloons from the Balloon Help menu. The Automatic Balloons preference setting, however, is less intrusive.

 When setting the Grow Limit for the Shortcuts palette, be sure to take the dimensions of your monitor into account. If the Grow Limit is set to a high number, the Shortcuts palette may not fit completely on your screen. This is frequently a problem when a high Grow Limit is combined with the Big Icons preferences setting.

Adding Icons

The Shortcuts palette contains the set of icons that Claris programmers think are most useful in the various ClarisWorks environments. However, you can choose from many other predefined icons to add to the palette. And, as described in Chapter 13, you can create ClarisWorks *macros* (sequences of steps and commands), design icons to represent them, and then attach the macros to the shortcuts in their Shortcuts palette. The Small Caps icon, shown previously in Figure 12-4, is an example of a user-designed macro shortcut.

 Whether or not you think the standard Shortcuts palette could stand some modification, you'll want to check out the other predefined shortcuts. Just choose Shortcuts from the File menu and then choose Edit Shortcuts. Each icon in the Available Shortcuts list box is accompanied by a description in the box below the icons. Click a few icons to see what you're missing.

Steps: Adding Predefined Icons to the Shortcuts Palette

Step 1.   Choose Shortcuts from the File menu and then choose Edit Shortcuts. The Edit Shortcuts dialog box appears, as shown in Figure 12-5.

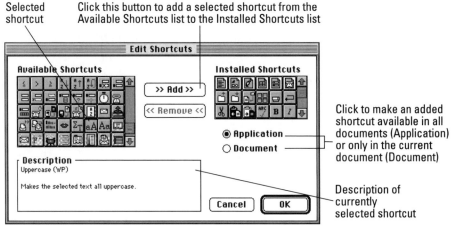

Selected shortcut

Click this button to add a selected shortcut from the Available Shortcuts list to the Installed Shortcuts list

Click to make an added shortcut available in all documents (Application) or only in the current document (Document)

Description of currently selected shortcut

Figure 12-5: The Edit Shortcuts dialog box

Step 2.   Click any shortcut in the Available Shortcuts list box (on the left). The shortcut's icon is shown as depressed. A brief description of the selected shortcut's function appears in the Description box below the list box, and the specific environment in which the shortcut is applicable (if any) is shown in parentheses at the end of the description line.

Step 3.   If you want to add a shortcut to the Shortcuts palette for every document that uses the environment shown at the end of the description line, click the Application radio button. (If no environment is shown, the shortcut will automatically be available in *every* environment.)

— or —

Step 3.   If you want to add a shortcut to the Shortcuts palette for the current document only, click Document. Document-specific shortcuts appear in the palette only when the current document is open and active.

Step 4.   Click Add.

Step 5. Repeat Steps 2 through 4 for any additional shortcuts that you want to add to the Shortcuts palette.

Step 6. Click OK to save your changes or Cancel to leave the Shortcuts palette unchanged.

You also can add user-defined shortcuts — based on macros that you've created — to the Shortcuts palette.

Steps: Adding User-Defined Icons to the Shortcuts Palette

Step 1. Create a macro and design an icon for it (as described in "Recording a Macro" in Chapter 13).

Step 2. Choose Shortcuts from the File menu and then choose Edit Shortcuts. The Edit Shortcuts dialog box shown in Figure 12-5 appears.

Step 3. Scroll to the bottom of the Available Shortcuts list box. User-defined shortcuts are stored at the bottom of the list.

Step 4. Click the icon of the macro that you want to add to the Shortcuts palette. A description of the selected shortcut's function appears below the Available Shortcuts list box.

Step 5. If you want to add the shortcut to the palettes for applicable environments, click the Application radio button.

— or —

Step 5. If you want to add the shortcut to the Shortcuts palette for the current document only, click Document.

Step 6. Click Add.

Step 7. Repeat Steps 4 through 6 for any additional shortcuts that you want to add to the Shortcuts palette.

Step 8. Click OK to save the changes or Cancel to leave the Shortcuts palette unchanged.

Application Versus Document Shortcuts

Whether you are adding a predefined shortcut that is included with ClarisWorks or a custom shortcut that represents one of your macros, you can make any shortcut application-specific or document-specific by clicking the appropriate radio button in the Edit Shortcuts dialog box. Although the default is to make all new shortcuts application-specific, give some thought to your options. If you make all of the shortcuts application shortcuts, the palette will quickly grow so large that finding the shortcut you need may become difficult, and the purpose of using a palette will be defeated.

When selecting Application or Document, think about whether you can use the shortcut in all or many of the documents that you create in the particular environment. For example, a macro for a frequently used custom text style is highly appropriate as an application shortcut. On the other hand, a shortcut that automatically types a closing for letters is more appropriate as a document shortcut (unless all that you use the word processor for is writing letters). Carrying it a step further, you may want to save the document as a stationery file that you can use for all new letters and create additional macros for several possible closings (Sincerely, Sincerely Yours, Yours Truly, Respectfully Yours, Your Obedient Servant, and so on).

Removing Icons

There's nothing sacred about the set of shortcuts that ClarisWorks initially provides in the Shortcuts palette. For example, many of the shortcuts merely correspond to menu commands that have command-key equivalents, such as Cut, Copy, Paste, Open, Save, and Print. By eliminating some of these shortcuts, you can keep the palette a manageable size. Similarly, shortcuts that you have added may no longer be necessary.

Removing a shortcut from an application or document Shortcuts palette does not delete it. It merely removes the shortcut from the Shortcuts palette. To delete the shortcut and its associated macro, choose the Shortcuts command from the File menu and then choose Delete Macros (as explained in Chapter 13).

Steps:	Removing Icons from the Shortcuts Palette
Step 1.	Choose Shortcuts from the File menu and then choose Edit Shortcuts. The Edit Shortcuts dialog box appears.

Step 2.   To remove an application-specific shortcut, click the Application radio button.

— or —

Step 2.   To remove a shortcut that has been installed in this particular document (rather than in the environment), click the Document radio button.

Step 3.   In the Installed Shortcuts list box (on the right), click the shortcut that you want to remove. The Remove button becomes active, as shown in Figure 12-6.

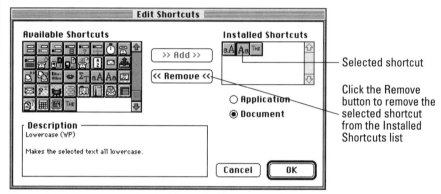

Figure 12-6: Removing a shortcut from the Shortcuts palette

Step 4.   Click the Remove button.

Step 5.   Repeat Steps 2 through 4 for any additional shortcuts that you want to remove.

Step 6.   Click OK to save the changes or Cancel to leave the Shortcuts palette unchanged.

    If you delete a macro that you also have assigned to a Shortcuts icon (by choosing the Shortcuts command in the File menu and then choosing Delete Macros), the shortcut is simultaneously removed from the Shortcuts palette.

Rearranging Icons

Another way you can customize the Shortcuts palette is by changing the order in which the icons are displayed. For example, if you constantly use a few shortcuts, you can move them to the top-right corner of the palette to make them easily accessible.

To move a shortcut to another position on the palette, hold down the Option and Command keys as you click on and drag the shortcut icon. When the shortcut is where you'd like it to be, release the mouse button.

Quick Tip: Sharing Shortcuts _____

After you have modified the Shortcuts palette, a special document is created called ClarisWorks Shortcuts. You'll find it inside the Preferences folder within the System Folder. (In previous versions of ClarisWorks, this file was stored in the Claris folder within the System Folder.)

The ClarisWorks Shortcuts file contains details of the changes you have made to the Shortcuts palette, as well as a record of any global (not document-specific) macros that you've created. (Unless you've actually changed the default shortcuts or created a global macro, you won't find the ClarisWorks Shortcuts file.) Delete the file, and you're back to square one. That is, the Shortcuts palette returns to its original, unaltered state. This feature can be very useful if you've been experimenting with macros and the Shortcuts palette and simply want to put everything back the way it was when you first installed your copy of ClarisWorks 4.0.

If you want to share your shortcuts with others, all you have to do is give them a copy of your ClarisWorks Shortcuts file. After they copy it into their Preferences folder, they'll have the same custom Shortcuts palette and global macros as you!

If the ClarisWorks Shortcuts file is copied to another user's machine, any global macros or shortcuts that the other person already has will be overwritten by the new ones.

For help with sharing document-specific macros with other users, see Chapter 13, "Using Macros."

■■

Summary

➺ The shortcuts in the Shortcuts palette automatically change to reflect the environment in which you're working.

➺ You can hide, display, move, and collapse or expand the Shortcuts palette.

➺ You can use a variety of customization options to change the appearance of the Shortcuts palette. You can determine whether the palette will display vertically or horizontally, decide whether document-specific shortcuts will be separated from application-specific shortcuts, and add and remove shortcuts.

➺ In addition to using dozens of predefined shortcuts, you can create your own macros, design custom icons for them, and add them to the Shortcuts palette.

➺ Shortcuts can be application-specific or document-specific. Application-specific shortcuts appear in the Shortcuts palette in all appropriate environments; document-specific shortcuts appear only when a particular document is open and active.

■■

Using Macros

In This Chapter

- ➡ Recording and setting options for ClarisWorks macros
- ➡ Assigning macros to the Shortcuts palette
- ➡ Playing macros
- ➡ Deleting macros
- ➡ Creating macros that execute automatically
- ➡ Transferring your macros to other users

Overview

Although the ClarisWorks macro recorder doesn't have many of the capabilities that stand-alone macro utilities have (such as repeating a macro; linking to other macros; and branching to different parts of a macro, based on certain conditions), it does provide an easier way to perform many repetitive, well-defined tasks in ClarisWorks.

The macro recorder works like a tape recorder. It simply watches the actions that you perform when you click the mouse button (such as making choices in dialog boxes and choosing commands from menus) and keeps track of the characters that you type. It does not record mouse movements, however. You cannot, for example, use the recorder to capture figures that you create with the freehand drawing tool.

Recording a Macro

ClarisWorks makes recording a macro easy.

Steps: Recording a Macro

Step 1. To start the macro recorder, choose Shortcuts from the File menu and then choose Record Macro (or press Shift-⌘-J). The Record Macro dialog box shown in Figure 13-1 appears.

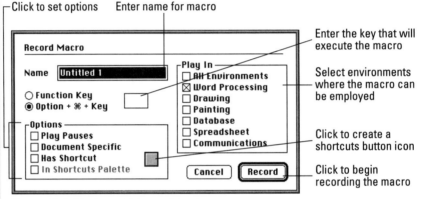

Figure 13-1: The Record Macro dialog box

Step 2. Name the macro and, optionally, specify a function key or Option-⌘-key combination that can be used to invoke the macro.

The Function Key radio button is grayed out (unselectable) if you do not have an extended keyboard.

Step 3. Set options for the macro as follows:

- Choose Play Pauses if you want the macro to record the amount of time that it takes you to perform each step. Otherwise, the macro plays back at the fastest speed possible. This option is particularly useful when you're using ClarisWorks for step-by-step demonstrations or slide shows.

- Choose Document Specific if you want the macro to be available only in this particular document, rather than in any ClarisWorks document of the appropriate type.

• If you want to add the macro to the Shortcuts palette, choose Has Shortcut to make the In Shortcuts Palette option available. Click that option to add the macro to the Shortcuts palette.

Step 4.   Click the gray box to the right of the Has Shortcut option if you've assigned the macro to a Shortcuts button and want to create a button icon for it now. The Edit Button Icon editor shown in Figure 13-2 appears. Design the button icon and then click OK to return to the Record Macro dialog box (or click Cancel if you change your mind about designing an icon at this time).

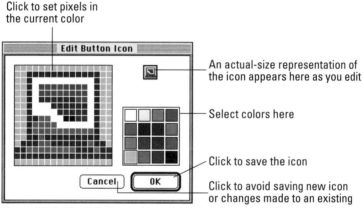

Click to set pixels in the current color

An actual-size representation of the icon appears here as you edit

Select colors here

Click to save the icon

Click to avoid saving new icon or changes made to an existing

Figure 13-2: The Edit Button Icon dialog box

Step 5.   Choose the desired Play In environments on the right side of the Record Macro dialog box. By default, ClarisWorks automatically chooses the environment that you are currently using. Check all of the environments in which you want to be able to use the macro.

Step 6.   To begin recording the macro, click Record. You return to the document. To remind you that you are recording, a flashing microphone replaces the apple at the top of the Apple menu. (If you decide not to record the macro, click Cancel in the dialog box.)

Step 7.   Perform the steps of the macro.

Step 8.   To end the macro, choose Shortcuts from the File menu and then choose Stop Recording (or press Shift-⌘-J).

A Secret Shortcut for Creating Shortcut Buttons

Designing icons for shortcuts is fine if you have some artistic skills and can work within the tiny confines of the Edit Button drawing area. If you consider yourself the reigning king or queen of ugly icons, though, there's a much simpler way to create attractive ones.

Open your Scrapbook desk accessory, a ClarisWorks draw document, or a paint document, and then use the Copy command to copy an image you like (press ⌘-C or choose Copy from the Edit menu). Go to the Edit Buttons dialog box in ClarisWorks and paste the image (press ⌘-V or choose Paste from the Edit menu). ClarisWorks automatically reduces the image so it fits on a shortcut button and remaps its colors to those of the standard 16-color palette. Simple images give the best results.

Playing a Macro

Depending on the options that you chose when you created the macro, you invoke the macro in different ways:

- ☞ Press the Option-⌘-key combination or the function key that you assigned to the macro.

- ☞ Click the Shortcuts button that you created for the macro.

- ☞ Choose Shortcuts from the File menu and then choose Play Macro. When the Play Macro dialog box appears (see Figure 13-3), choose the name of the macro and click Play.

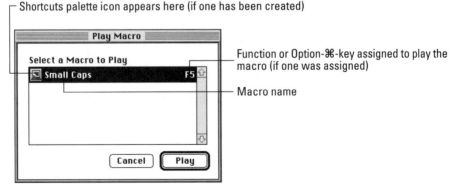

┌ Shortcuts palette icon appears here (if one has been created)

Figure 13-3: The Play Macro dialog box

Function or Option-⌘-key assigned to play the macro (if one was assigned)

Macro name

Remember to set up the conditions that are needed for the macro before you execute it. For example, if you need to select some text before you can use a word processing macro, the macro will not work properly if you have not selected the text. If the macro does not execute when you press its hot key or shortcut button, or if it is not on the list in the Play Macro dialog box, either you are in the wrong environment, or you clicked the Document Specific check box when you designed the macro and that particular document is not the active one.

Editing Macro Options

You cannot edit the steps of a macro. If you are dissatisfied with any step or need to make a change such as adding a step, you have to re-record the macro.

You cannot use the same name or key combination for two macros. If you want to reuse either component, you must delete the original macro first, as described in "Deleting a Macro" later in this chapter.

On the other hand, if you want to change some of the *options* for a macro, you can alter as many of them as you like at any time. You can even create or edit a Shortcuts button icon whenever you wish.

Steps:	**Editing Macro Options**
Step 1.	Choose Shortcuts from the File menu and then choose Edit Macros. The Edit Macros dialog box appears, as shown in Figure 13-4.

Macro pop-up menu   Name of currently selected macro

```
┌─────────────────────────────────────────────────┐
│ Edit Macros                                       │
│ ────────────────────────────                      │
│                              ┌─Play In──────────┐ │
│  Macro [Small Caps ▼]        │ ☐ All Environments│ │
│                              │ ☒ Word Processing │ │
│  Name  [Small Caps    ]      │ ☐ Drawing         │ │
│                              │ ☐ Painting        │ │
│  ◉ Function Key    ┌──┐      │ ☐ Database        │ │
│  ○ Option + ⌘ + Key│F5│      │ ☐ Spreadsheet     │ │
│                    └──┘      │ ☐ Communications  │ │
│  ┌─Options──────────────┐    └───────────────────┘ │
│  │ ☐ Play Pauses         │                         │
│  │ ☒ Document Specific   │   ┌──┐                  │
│  │ ☒ Has Shortcut        │   │▣│                   │
│  │ ☒ In Shortcuts Palette│   └──┘                  │
│  └───────────────────────┘  ( Cancel ) (( Done )) │
└─────────────────────────────────────────────────┘
```

Figure 13-4: The Edit Macros dialog box

Note: The Edit Macros dialog box is virtually identical to the Record Macros dialog box. The sole difference is that the Edit Macros dialog box contains a Macro pop-up menu that lists all installed macros.

Step 2. Choose the macro that you want to edit from the Macro pop-up menu. The selected macro's name appears in the Name text-edit box below the Macro pop-up menu.

Step 3. Change whatever options you like.

Step 4. Repeat Steps 2 and 3 for other macros that you want to change.

Step 5. To record the changes and return to ClarisWorks, click Done. (Or, to ignore all changes and leave your macros unaltered, click Cancel.)

Deleting a Macro

If you no longer want a particular macro, you can remove it from the document in which it was saved or from ClarisWorks (depending on whether or not you chose the Document Specific option). You can also delete a macro if you made a mistake in it or if it doesn't play back correctly. (Remember, you can't reuse a macro name or key combination unless you first delete the old macro.)

Steps: Deleting a Macro

Step 1. Choose Shortcuts from the File menu and then choose Delete Macros. The Delete Macros dialog box appears, as shown in Figure 13-5.

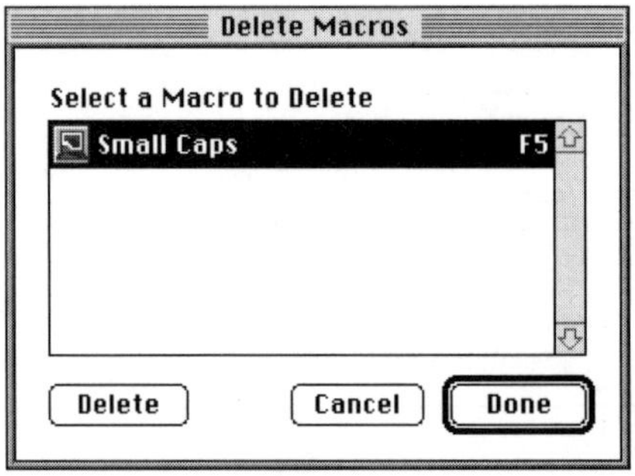

Figure 13-5: The Delete Macros dialog box

Step 2.	Choose the macro that you want to remove.
Step 3.	Click Delete.
Step 4.	Repeat Steps 2 and 3 for other macros that you want to remove at this time.
Step 5.	To record changes (deleting the macros), click Done. (Or, if you change your mind and decide to leave the macro list unaltered, click Cancel.)

Using the Macro Wait Command

In the communications environment, timing is everything. If you send your password to an information service before the service requests it, chances are excellent that the service won't receive it and you won't be able to *log on* (connect with the service) successfully.

Although you can record and play pauses in macros, often this capability isn't sufficient to ensure correct timing. Information services sometimes slow down (when they are handling large numbers of users, for example), so pauses between commands can vary dramatically from one session to the next. However, you can use a special ClarisWorks macro command — Macro Wait — to remedy this situation in macros that you create for the communications environment. The Macro Wait command has two options:

    ↩ Wait for a specific text string to be received from the other computer.

    ↩ Wait for a specific number of seconds of line inactivity.

When the condition is met, the macro continues to play. For example, in a logon macro that automatically logs you onto an information service, you can use the Macro Wait command to wait for a specific prompt (such as *Password?*) before transmitting your password.

Steps:	**Creating a Communications Macro That Uses Macro Wait**
Step 1.	Create a new communications document or open an existing document.
Step 2.	At the proper point in the communications session, start the macro recorder by choosing Shortcuts from the File menu and then choosing Record Macro (or by pressing Shift-⌘-J). The Record Macro dialog box appears.

Depending on what you want the macro to do, you may want to start the recorder (to record a logon sequence) just before you choose Open Connection from the Session menu, or you may want to start the recorder during the actual session.

Step 3. Name the macro and, optionally, specify a function key or Option-⌘-key combination that can be used to invoke the macro.

Step 4. Choose options for the macro.

Step 5. *Optional:* If you've assigned the macro to a Shortcuts button, you can create a button icon for it now by clicking in the box to the right of the Has Shortcut option and designing the button icon in the Edit Button Icon editor that appears. Click OK to return to the Record Macro dialog box (or click Cancel if you change your mind about designing an icon at this time).

If you're on-line, you may want to create the icon after the communications session is over.

Step 6. Choose Communications as the Play In environment. (Normally, this option is already selected.)

Step 7. To begin recording the macro, click Record. You return to the communications document. To remind you that you are recording, a flashing microphone replaces the apple at the top of the Apple menu. (If you decide not to record the macro, click Cancel.)

Step 8. Perform the steps of the macro. At the appropriate times, you can specify a wait period or a text string by choosing Shortcuts from the File menu and then choosing Macro Wait. The Macro Wait dialog box appears, as shown in Figure 13-6.

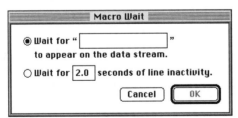

Figure 13-6: In the Macro Wait dialog box, type a text string or the number of seconds to wait.

Step 9. Choose a Macro Wait option by clicking the appropriate radio button. If you choose the first option, enter the text string for which you want to wait. The text string has to be exact — with the correct spelling, capitalization, punctuation, and spaces. If you choose the second option (Wait for x seconds of line inactivity), enter the number of seconds.

Step 10. When you're ready to end the macro, choose Shortcuts from the File menu and then choose Stop Recording (or press Shift-⌘-J).

If you want to avoid the Macro Wait command or are having difficulty getting it to work reliably, you can create a normal macro and use it at the point in the session when you might otherwise use a Macro Wait command.

Designing Automatic Macros _____

ClarisWorks provides a special type of macro capability: *automatic macros*. You can create automatic macros that play whenever:

☞ ClarisWorks is launched

☞ A new document is created in a particular environment (a new spreadsheet, for example)

☞ Any document from a selected environment is opened (a word processing file, for example)

Steps:	Creating an Automatic Macro
Step 1.	In the Record Macro dialog box (previously shown in Figure 13-1), enter one of the macro names listed in Table 13-1 (spelling, capitalization, and hyphenation must be exact).
Step 2.	Set the desired options.
Step 3.	Select the appropriate Play In environment (or deselect all environments).
Step 4.	Record the macro steps (as described in "Recording a Macro" earlier in this chapter).

Table 13-1
Automatic Macro Names and Definitions

Macro Name	Executes when...
Auto-Startup	ClarisWorks is launched
Auto-Open WP	A word processing document is opened
Auto-Open DR	A draw document is opened
Auto-Open PT	A paint document is opened
Auto-Open SS	A spreadsheet document is opened
Auto-Open DB	A database document is opened
Auto-Open CM	A communications document is opened
Auto-New WP	A new word processing document is created
Auto-New DR	A new draw document is created
Auto-New PT	A new paint document is created
Auto-New SS	A new spreadsheet document is created
Auto-New DB	A new database document is created
Auto-New CM	A new communications document is created

As you can see in the table, an automatic macro executes when one of three actions occurs: ClarisWorks launches, a particular document type is opened, or a particular document type is created. You can have only one ClarisWorks macro for each of the macro names listed in Table 13-1.

If you want to delete an automatic macro, you must go to the Delete Macros dialog box (choose Delete Macros from the Shortcuts submenu of the File menu.)

The Auto-Open Macro

Although the Auto-Open macros normally run whenever you open any document in the chosen environment, you can restrict an Auto-Open macro to a particular document by clicking the Document Specific check box when you define the macro. By linking the Auto-Open DB macro to one particular database file, for example, you can automatically sort that database and display the last record each time the file is opened. If any other database is opened, the macro will not play. If you use the Auto-Open DB macro in this manner, however, you cannot also create a similar macro for any other database; nor can you design a macro that will run when *any* database is opened. Remember, only one macro can be defined for each macro name.

Automatic Macros Versus Stationery Documents

You can easily create stationery documents or choose certain preference settings to accomplish many of the tasks that environment-specific automatic macros perform. For example, you can use a stationery or default stationery document (see Chapter 10), rather than an Auto-New WP macro, to set a particular font, display the current date, and include a Memo heading. To be truly useful, automatic macros should accomplish tasks that stationery and preferences *cannot* perform. For example, you can use an automatic macro to customize an environment by hiding or showing rulers, setting a zoom level, choosing a given tool in the Tool panel, or switching to a specific data-base layout.

Getting Down to Business: Creating a Small Caps Macro _____

Although ClarisWorks has many of the text formatting options that other word processing programs offer, it does not provide a *small caps* feature. (A phrase or text string that is formatted with small caps is completely capitalized, but the letters are slightly smaller than the surrounding text.) However, by typing text in all capital letters and choosing a smaller point size, you can create the effect of small caps in ClarisWorks.

Steps:	Manually Creating Small Caps
Step 1.	Type the text in all caps. Alternatively, you can add the Uppercase shortcut button to the Shortcuts palette, select the text, and then click the button to change the text's case.
Step 2.	Select the part of the text that you normally would have typed in lowercase letters. Ignore letters that you normally capitalize (the first letter in a proper noun or the first letter of the word at the beginning of a sentence, for example).
Step 3.	In the Size menu, choose the next smaller point size. As an alternative, you can click the Decrement Font Size shortcut a couple of times to change the font size.

Now that you know how to generate small caps, you can design a macro that will perform the small caps conversion for you.

Steps: Creating the Small Caps Macro

Step 1. Create a new word processing document or open an existing document.

Step 2. Add the Uppercase shortcut to the Shortcuts palette as follows:

- Choose Shortcuts from the File menu, and then select Edit Shortcuts. The Edit Shortcuts dialog box appears.

- Click the Application or Document radio button, depending on whether you want the macro to be available to all documents or just this one.

- Scroll to the bottom of the Available Shortcuts list, click the Uppercase shortcut icon (shown in Figure 13-7, at the end of this procedure), and click the Add button.

Step 3. If the Shortcuts palette is not visible, choose Shortcuts from the File menu and then choose Show Shortcuts (or press Shift-⌘-X).

Step 4. Type a single word (**macros**, for example).

Step 5. Position the cursor so that it's directly in front of the *m* in *macros*.

Step 6. To start the macro recorder, choose Shortcuts from the File menu and then choose Record Macro (or press Shift-⌘-J).

Step 7. Name the macro (**Small Caps**, for example) and set other options for it, such as the Option-⌘-key combination that you'll use to invoke the macro.

Because you'll want to be able to use the macro in other word processing documents, be sure that you do *not* check the Document Specific check box.

Step 8. Click Record to begin recording the steps of the macro.

Step 9. Press Shift-Option-right arrow. The entire word (*macros*) is selected.

Step 10. Click the Uppercase shortcut button. The word is changed entirely to uppercase (capital letters). Letters that are already in uppercase are unchanged.

Step 11. Click the Decrement Font Size shortcut button twice (shown in Figure 13-7, at the end of this procedure). The point size of the word is reduced by two points.

Step 12. To complete the process, choose Shortcuts from the File menu and then choose Stop Recording (or press Shift-⌘-J). The macro is saved in the document or in ClarisWorks, depending on whether you checked Document Specific when you named the macro.

Figure 13-7: The Uppercase (left) and Decrement Font Size (right) shortcuts

Steps: **Playing the Small Caps Macro**

Step 1. Position the cursor immediately in front of the first letter of the word that you want to change to small caps.

Step 2. Press the ⌘-Option keystroke or function key that you assigned to the macro.

— or —

Step 3. If you didn't assign a special keystroke to the macro, choose Shortcuts from the File menu, choose Play Macro, and then choose the macro from the list that appears.

The macro automatically converts any word to an all-caps version of the word, two points smaller than the surrounding text.

There are several advantages to the manner in which we have constructed this small caps macro:

- ☞ Because the macro works on selected text, you can use it to convert an entire word (by positioning the insertion point just before the first letter of the word) or everything except the first letter of the word (by positioning the insertion point just after the first letter of the word).

  Any word that is entirely composed of lowercase letters should be completely converted. If a word begins with a normal capital letter, on the other hand, the macro should be applied to everything but the first letter of the word.

- ☞ Using the Uppercase shortcut relieves you from having to type the original text in uppercase. ClarisWorks has no comparable menu command to change the case of text.

- ☞ Using the Decrement Font Size shortcut is a more flexible approach than selecting a specific font size from the Size menu.

  The macro always reduces the size by two points, regardless of whether the original text size was 10, 12, or 14 points, for example.

 If we had simply instructed the macro to set the selected text size to 10 points, the macro would not have worked with 10-point or smaller text, and it would have looked ridiculous when applied to large text, such as 24-point or bigger. (Admittedly, though, a 2-point reduction applied to a large text size will not have the intended effect.)

☞ Although the macro issues several commands by clicking icons on the Shortcuts palette, it runs correctly whether or not the Shortcuts palette is on-screen. (Hide the Shortcuts palette and play the macro to prove to yourself that it still works.)

Quick Tips

The following Quick Tips discuss:

☞ One-time macros

☞ Ideas for macros

☞ How to avoid keystroke conflicts

☞ Transferring macros to other users

Sometimes Once Is Enough

Most people normally think of using macros when they have a task that they will need to repeat, perhaps frequently. Sometimes, however, you have a task that may never come up again, but you need to perform it 25 times in the current document (changing every occurrence of "Ace Auto Parts" to the Helvetica Italic font, for example).

Just because you won't use a particular macro again after today doesn't mean you shouldn't make the macro. Create the macro and make it specific to the document in which you use it, or just delete it when you're done.

Macro Ideas

Having trouble coming up with reasons to create macros? Here are a few suggestions that may start those neurons firing:

☞ Create keyboard shortcuts for menu commands that don't have shortcuts.

In the word processor, for example, you can create a macro that inserts the current date, one that pops up the Paragraph dialog box from the Format menu, and another that chooses a particular font and applies it to the currently selected text.

↬ Create a series of macros that perform online communications activities for you.

For example, you can create macros that take you directly to forums or special interest groups (SIGs), such as the Mac forum, a writers' forum, or a financial forum. You can also create one macro that automatically chooses the XMODEM file transfer protocol from an information service's menus and another macro that performs a *logoff* for you (quitting from a communications session and closing the connection).

↬ Try to think in terms of many steps.

You'll get the greatest gains in productivity by automating complex, multistep procedures. For example, you can create a macro that conducts an entire online communications session — connecting ClarisWorks with GEnie or CompuServe, changing to the Macintosh forum, capturing a list of all new programs, and then logging off. After you have the list of files, you can read through it at your leisure and check off the ones you're interested in. Then log back onto the information service and download the files you want. (Why waste dollars browsing through this information online?)

↬ Think about ClarisWorks activities that you routinely perform.

Not every macro needs to have a grandiose purpose. You can, for example, assign an Option-⌘-key combination to any menu command that you frequently select. If you use a macro regularly for even small tasks such as this one, you will save a considerable amount of time.

Remember, you can also create separate Shortcuts buttons for macros so you don't have to memorize any additional commands.

Avoiding Keystroke Conflicts

You can assign ClarisWorks macros to function keys (if you have an extended keyboard) or to Option-⌘-key combinations. Because ClarisWorks uses neither of these approaches for invoking its menu commands and keyboard shortcuts, the particular key combinations that you choose should be of little consequence, right? Well, maybe.

Many desk accessories and control panels have key combinations that you can use to pop them up or to make them perform particular functions. This can cause conflicts with your ClarisWorks macros. The usual symptom of a conflict is that the ClarisWorks macro does not function and is overridden by the desk accessory or control panel (or vice versa). The solution is either to choose another key combination for the ClarisWorks macro or to choose another key combination for the desk accessory or control panel, if you can.

Transferring Macros to Other Users

Although the ClarisWorks user manual doesn't mention it, you can share macros with friends and colleagues. You simply save the macros in a document file, rather than in ClarisWorks itself. All that your friend has to do is open the file and change each macro from a document-specific macro to a ClarisWorks macro.

Steps:	Transferring Macros
Step 1.	Create a new document (choose New from the File menu) and record the macros.
Step 2.	When saving the macros, click the Document Specific check box.
Step 3.	Save the document and give a copy of it to the other user.
Step 4.	The other user launches ClarisWorks and opens the document in which you saved the macros.
Step 5.	The user chooses Shortcuts from the File menu and then chooses Edit Macros. The Edit Macros dialog box appears.
Step 6.	From the Macros pop-up menu, the user chooses a macro to add to ClarisWorks.
Step 7.	The user removes the check mark from the Document Specific check box by clicking once in the check box and then changes other options (such as the key combination used to invoke the macro) as desired.
	To add other macros to ClarisWorks, the user repeats Steps 6 and 7.
Step 8.	The user clicks Done to save the changes.

Moving On Up

The ClarisWorks macros are fine for simple tasks, but you may want to investigate one of the more powerful commercial macro programs for your more complex tasks. In addition to working with ClarisWorks, these macro programs also work in other programs and with the Finder.

QuicKeys (CE Software) and Tempo (Affinity Microsystems) are general-purpose macro utilities that are intended for the typical Macintosh user. Both programs provide a recorder function that you can use to record most macros, as well as the ability to edit macros without re-recording them.

Summary

- ◆ Macros enable you to automate ClarisWorks tasks and perform them by clicking a button or pressing an Option-⌘-key combination.

- ◆ Every macro can be a general ClarisWorks macro (available in any new document of the correct type) or be document-specific (available only when a particular document is active).

- ◆ You can assign a macro to the Shortcuts palette and display a custom icon on the macro's button.

- ◆ Although you cannot edit the steps of a macro, you can edit the options for a macro.

- ◆ You can delete macros when you no longer need them.

- ◆ The communications environment has a special macro option called Macro Wait that causes the macro to wait a specific number of seconds or for a particular incoming text string before it continues.

- ◆ You can create automatic macros that automatically run when you launch ClarisWorks, open a particular document type, or create a new file in a specific environment.

- ◆ You can share macros with another user by creating several macros in the same document and making them document specific. The recipient then opens the file and changes the macros to general ClarisWorks macros.

Working with Frames

In This Chapter

➡ Rules and exceptions for environment frames

➡ Creating and working in frames

➡ Resizing and moving frames

➡ Opening and closing spreadsheet and paint frames

➡ Linking text, spreadsheet, and paint frames

Overview

The concept of *frames* is what puts the integration into ClarisWorks. You can create a document in one environment and embed other environments in the document by adding frames. For example, in a word processing document, you can embed paint frames that contain illustrations and spreadsheet frames that contain tables and charts (see Figure 14-1).

Only the spreadsheet, word processing, and paint environments can be frames. When you work in a frame, it acts the same as a regular document created in that environment — the same menu commands and tools are available.

Unfortunately, the types of documents that enable you to use frames, the methods with which you create frames, the modes in which you can access the frames, and so on, are not consistent across environments. The next section lists the most important frame exceptions and "gotchas."

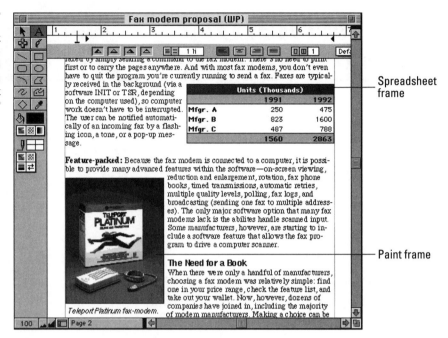

Figure 14-1:
A spreadsheet
frame within
a word
processing
document

Spreadsheet frame

Paint frame

Frame Exceptions

You should be aware of the following list of rules and exceptions when you create and work with frames. Many of them are obvious and are based on common sense (for example, there are no communications frames or frames within communications documents). Others are simply Claris design decisions — as in, that's the way it is.

Read the rules once and then go about your normal ClarisWorks business. If you don't remember whether a certain frame procedure works in a particular environment, just try it. Refer to this section only when you have problems. If you try to memorize any rules other than the most critical ones, you'll needlessly confuse yourself.

No Communications or Database Frames Allowed

☞ Communications documents cannot contain frames, nor can you embed a communications document in any other type of document.

☞ Although you can embed frames within database documents (in Layout view only), you cannot create database frames in other kinds of documents.

Draw Objects, Not Frames

ⅆ There are no draw frames. Draw objects are always drawn directly onto a document or within a frame. Draw objects can be added to the word processing, spreadsheet, database, and draw environments.

Same-Environment Frames

ⅆ You can place word processing frames into word processing documents and spreadsheet frames into spreadsheet documents. To do so, press the Option key while you draw the frame.

Adding Frames to Database Documents

ⅆ Frames can be placed and edited in database documents, but only when you're in Layout view.

Adding Frames to Paint Documents

ⅆ *The moment that you stop working in a frame that has been placed in a paint document, the contents of the frame become a regular paint image. In other words, you can no longer edit or manipulate the frame contents with its original environment tools — you can use only paint tools.*

ⅆ You cannot add draw objects to paint documents, but draw documents can contain paint frames.

Creating Text Frames

You do not have to draw an outline to place a text frame in a document (as you do with spreadsheet and paint frames). You can simply click to position the cursor and begin typing.

Opening Frames

☞ You can open spreadsheet or paint frames to display them separately in a full-sized window, but you cannot open text frames in this manner.

☞ You cannot open spreadsheet frames that are embedded in paint documents.

Linking Frames

☞ You cannot link a pair of existing frames.

☞ You cannot link frames from different environments.

☞ You cannot link frames in a paint document.

See "Linking Frames," later in this chapter, for more information on linking.

Creating Frames

Use the following procedure to create a spreadsheet, paint, or text frame within a document.

Steps:	Creating a Frame
Step 1.	Select the appropriate tool from the Tool panel (see Figure 14-2).

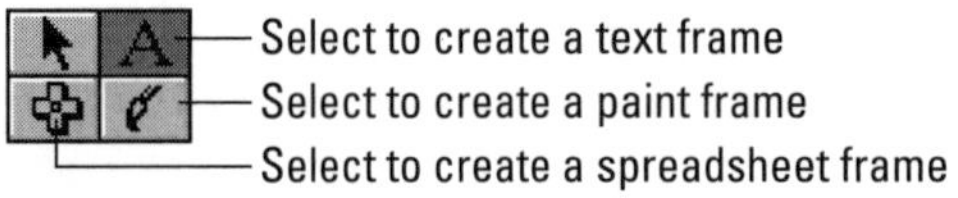

— Select to create a text frame
— Select to create a paint frame
— Select to create a spreadsheet frame

Figure 14-2: To create a frame, first select one of these tools from the Tool panel.

Step 2.	Click to position one corner of the frame, and, while pressing the mouse button, drag to complete the frame (see Figure 14-3). After you release the mouse button, the frame appears.

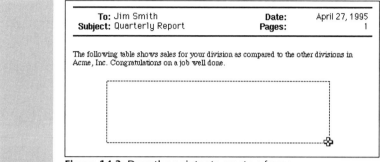

Figure 14-3: Drag the pointer to create a frame.

 If Autogrid (from the Options menu) is on, the frame aligns with the grid. (When Autogrid is on, the menu command reads Turn Autogrid Off; when it is off, the menu command reads Turn Autogrid On.)

 If frame links have not been set for the frame, a text frame will shrink to fit the text it contains. To retain a full word processing frame (as you drew it), turn on frame links.

When you are creating frames, keep the following points in mind:

- Although there is no such thing as a draw frame, you can place a draw object into word processing, spreadsheet, draw, or database documents (in Layout mode only) by choosing a draw tool and drawing.

- Spreadsheets and word processing documents can contain frames of their own type; that is, a spreadsheet can contain spreadsheet frames and a word processing document can contain text frames. To create such a frame, start by selecting the text or spreadsheet tool, as appropriate. While pressing the Option key, click the mouse button and drag to make the frame. Figure 14-4 shows a text frame in a word processing document.

Text frame

Figure 14-4:
A text frame in a
word processing
document

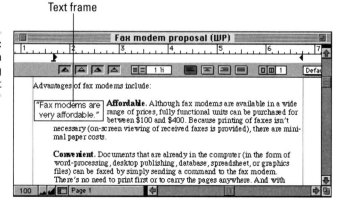

♺ You can select the text tool and drag to create a text frame, but you don't have to go to that trouble. As long as you're not in a text environment, you can click once to create a small text frame and immediately begin typing. You can later resize the frame as required (see "Resizing and Positioning Frames," later in this chapter).

Working in Frames

To work inside a frame, double-click it. The first click selects the frame; the second click moves you into the frame's environment and changes the pointer, tools, and menus to those of the new environment.

To stop working in a frame and return to the document's main environment, double-click anywhere outside the frame. If you happen to click within another frame (rather than in the main environment), the clicked frame is selected.

Resizing and Positioning Frames

After you place a frame in a document, you can treat its bounding rectangle just as you treat any other object — you use the handles to resize or reposition it.

Steps:	Changing the Size of a Frame
Step 1.	Click the frame once to select it. Handles appear at the corners of the frame.
Step 2.	Select any handle, press the mouse button and drag to change the size of the frame.
	A frame pasted into a word processing paragraph as an in-line object has only a single handle (in the lower-right corner). To resize such a frame, drag the handle.
Step 3.	Release the mouse button to set the new size. Note that this procedure changes only the size of the frame, not the size of the image or data within the frame.

If you want to make precise changes to the size of a frame, you can use the Info windoid to enter new dimensions (choose Object Info from the Options menu), or you can use the Scale By Percent command (found in the Transform submenu of the Arrange menu) to increase or decrease the horizontal and vertical dimensions by specific percentages.

Steps:	Changing the Location of a Frame
Step 1.	Click the frame once to select it. Handles appear at its corners.
Step 2.	Click anywhere inside the frame and, while pressing the mouse button, drag the frame to its new location.
Step 3.	Release the mouse button to set the new position.

Keep in mind the following points about resizing and positioning frames:

⮑ Although you can change the size of a text frame, the moment that you leave the frame, it is adjusted to the smallest height that can still contain the text. Only the new width is retained. (Note, however, that if Frame Links is turned on, the height *is* retained.)

⮑ You can drag spreadsheet frames to any size, but when you release the mouse button, the frame resizes itself to show only complete rows and columns.

⮑ After you place a frame in a paint document, it ceases to be a frame. It becomes a paint image. To move the contents of a former frame, select its contents with the marquee tool and drag to a different location. To change the size of the contents of a former frame, select it with the marquee tool and choose the Resize command from the Transform menu.

Opening and Closing Frames _____

Because spreadsheet and paint frames are merely windows on what may be much larger documents, you can open these frames in separate document windows. Changes that you make while the frame is open are automatically carried to the frame in the document.

 When you resize either a paint or spreadsheet frame by making it smaller, the rest of the image or cells don't disappear. They're simply outside the frame window — temporarily out of sight.

Steps:	Opening a Spreadsheet or Paint Frame
Step 1.	Click the spreadsheet or paint frame once to select it. Handles appear at the edges.
Step 2.	Choose Open Frame from the View menu. If a spreadsheet frame was selected, a full-screen copy of the frame opens in a new document window. If a paint frame was selected, a same-size copy of the frame opens in a new document window.

 You can also open a spreadsheet or paint frame by selecting the frame and then pressing Option while double-clicking it.

To close an opened frame, click the close box in the upper-left corner of the window. The frame disappears, and you return to your original document.

Changing the Display of Spreadsheet and Paint Frames

ClarisWorks has a Modify Frame command that you can use with either spreadsheet or paint frames:

- ↪ When you use Modify Frame with a spreadsheet frame, you can decide whether the cell grid, row headings, and column headings should be visible or hidden and whether data or formulas are displayed. You can also set a different *origin* (the upper-left corner of the worksheet frame) to display.

- ↪ When you use Modify Frame with a paint frame, you can set a different resolution and depth for the frame's contents, as well as specify a different origin.

Steps:	Modifying a Spreadsheet or Paint Frame
Step 1.	Select the frame. Handles appear around the border of the frame.
Step 2.	Choose Modify Frame from the Options menu. One of two dialog boxes appears, depending on whether a spreadsheet or paint frame is currently selected (see Figure 14-5).

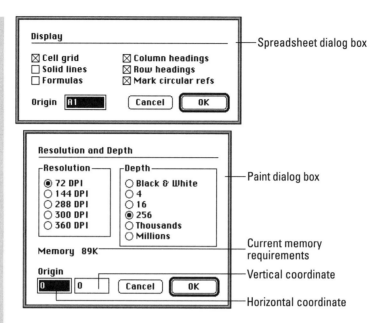

Figure 14-5: Dialog boxes for modifying spreadsheet and paint frames

In previous versions of ClarisWorks, the Modify Frame command also could be executed by pressing Shift-⌘-I. This keyboard equivalent is not supported in ClarisWorks 4.0.

Step 3. If a spreadsheet frame is selected, set options by clicking check boxes. To set a different cell origin (the cell that appears in the upper-left corner of the frame), type the new cell coordinates (**B14**, for example) in the Origin text-edit box.

— or —

Step 3. If a paint frame is selected, you can set a different resolution (the number of dots per inch) and depth (number of colors/data bits) for the images in the frame. As you click different radio buttons, the amount of memory required is shown.

Step 4. If desired, specify a different origin for displaying the image within its frame. The two Origin text-edit boxes are used to set the horizontal and vertical coordinates (in pixels). An inch contains 72 pixels. For example, to specify starting coordinates of 1 inch to the right and 1.5 inches down, you enter **72** and **108.**

Step 5. Click OK to accept the changes.

When importing a PICT file into a paint frame or document, ClarisWorks automatically matches the resolution of the image and uses the document's original color table.

 Changing the color depth of a paint frame can alter the colors in the painting. Such a change cannot be reversed with the Undo command. Thus, it's a good idea to save a copy of the document before changing the color depth.

Linking Frames

Although you can easily create multicolumn text in the word processor, ClarisWorks provides a more flexible method for creating complex layouts. You can link text frames to one another — in much the same way as you can in desktop publishing programs. A document can contain a series of linked text frames that are placed wherever you like. When text exceeds the available space in one text frame, it automatically flows into the next frame (as shown in Figure 14-6). If the linked frames do not have enough room to contain the total text, an overflow indicator (a small box with an x in it) appears in the lower-right corner of the final frame. A document can also contain combinations of linked and unlinked frames.

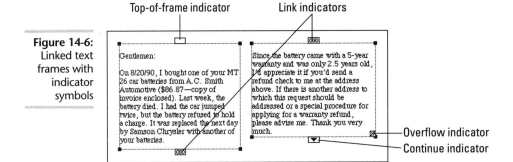

Figure 14-6:
Linked text
frames with
indicator
symbols

Steps:	**Creating Linked Text Frames**
Step 1.	Select the pointer tool in the Tool panel.
Step 2.	Choose Frame Links from the Options menu (or press ⌘-L).
Step 3.	Select the text tool from the Tool panel and draw a text frame. (If the Tool panel isn't visible, choose Show Tools from the View menu or press Shift-⌘-T.)

Step 4. Click outside the text frame. An empty text frame with top-of-frame and continue indicators appears, as shown in Figure 14-7.

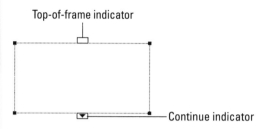

Top-of-frame indicator

Continue indicator

Figure 14-7: An empty linked text frame

Step 5. Click the continue indicator (the black triangle at the bottom of the frame) and draw a box for the next text frame.

Step 6. Repeat Steps 4 and 5 for any additional continuation frames that you want to create.

Step 7. Add text to the first frame by typing, pasting, or inserting. When the frame fills, additional text automatically flows into the other frames that are linked to it.

Step 8. If additional frames are required, click the continue indicator of the last linked frame and draw another frame. Repeat this step as necessary.

You can also start with a single frame that already contains text and then link new text frames to the first frame. Just use the pointer tool to select the first frame, choose Frame Links from the Options menu, and go to Step 5 in the preceding instructions.

You can insert a linked frame in the middle of several links — not just at the end. Simply use the pointer tool to click the link indicator on any linked frame and then draw the new frame.

Draw documents can have multiple pages, and you can link frames across pages (linking an article that starts on page 1 to a continuation on page 5, for example). To add pages to a draw document, first choose Document from the Format menu. In the Size section of the dialog box that appears, indicate the number of pages that you want. To see the breaks between pages, choose Page View from the View menu (or press Shift-⌘-P).

Why Use Linked Frames?

In a word, freedom. Unlike in a word processing document — even a multicolumn one — you can place linked text frames anywhere you like. You also can have some text frames that are linked and other text frames that stand alone. By using linked text frames, you can create layouts that are as complex as layouts designed with some desktop publishing programs. The following figure shows a simple newsletter layout in a draw document that incorporates linked text frames, stand-alone text frames, and draw objects.

Linked text frames   Independent frames

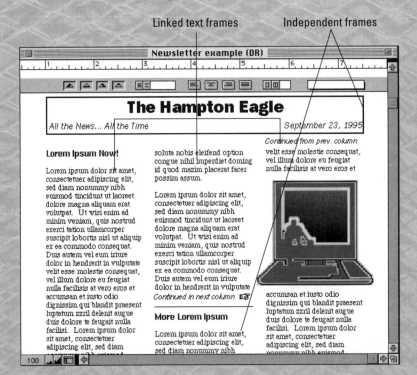

To help align the different objects and frames, you can turn on the Autogrid. After you have placed objects in position, you can select the frames and then choose the Lock command from the Arrange menu (⌘-H) to lock the frames in position. Locking the frames keeps them from moving but lets you edit the text within.

You can also create linked spreadsheet frames and linked paint frames. Unlike linked text frames, any linked spreadsheet or paint frame is merely a window into the complete spreadsheet or paint document. The purpose of creating linked spreadsheet or paint frames is to provide multiple views into the same document. You can, for example, show some pertinent raw data from a worksheet in one frame and display summary figures from the same worksheet in another frame.

You can open a spreadsheet to full-screen size for editing or open a second view of a paint frame. You can also change the origin that is used to display any spreadsheet or paint frame. For details, refer to "Opening and Closing Frames" and "Changing the Display of Spreadsheet and Paint Frames," earlier in this chapter.

Steps:	**Creating Linked Spreadsheet or Paint Frames**
Step 1.	Create a spreadsheet or paint frame and use the pointer tool to select the frame.
Step 2.	Choose Frame Links from the Options menu (or press ⌘-L).
Step 3.	Click the continue indicator at the bottom of the frame and draw a box for the continuation frame. Repeat this step for any additional continuation frames that you want to create.

Quick Tips

The following Quick Tips give some examples of things that you can do to frames and provide instructions for using spreadsheet charts that are within a frame or are free-floating.

Frames Are Objects

If it isn't apparent from the preceding discussion, I'll tell you now. Other than in the paint environment, *all frames are objects.* Anything that you can do to an object, you can do to a frame. Examples include the following:

- ✑ Changing the pen color, line width, and pattern for the border (or making the border transparent)

↪ Adding a background color

↪ Resizing the frame

↪ Placing one frame over another and sending frames forward or backward

Using Spreadsheet Charts in Frames

You can embed spreadsheet charts in a spreadsheet frame or create them as free-floating objects.

Steps:	Making a Free-Floating Chart
Step 1.	Enter the spreadsheet frame by double-clicking a cell.
Step 2.	Select the data that you want to use for the chart.
Step 3.	Choose Make Chart from the Options menu (or press ⌘-M). The Chart Options dialog box appears.
Step 4.	Choose a chart type, choose options, and click OK. The chart appears, separate from the worksheet.

Steps:	Making a Chart Within a Spreadsheet Frame
Step 1.	Enter the spreadsheet frame by double-clicking a cell.
Step 2.	Choose Open Frame from the View menu. The worksheet expands to a full-screen view.
Step 3.	Select the data that you want to use for the chart.
Step 4.	Choose Make Chart from the Options menu (or press ⌘-M). The Chart Options dialog box appears.
Step 5.	Choose a chart type, choose options, and click OK. The chart appears, embedded as an object in the worksheet.
Step 6.	Click the close box on the spreadsheet window to return to the original document.

Other objects — such as paint frames, text frames, and draw graphics — can also be embedded in a worksheet. The objects can be created or pasted when you're in the Open Frame view, or you can create them by pressing the Control key as you draw with the appropriate tool (the text tool, spreadsheet tool, paint tool, or any of the draw tools).

To select an embedded object for moving, resizing, deleting, copying, or editing, press Control while you click on the object or open the spreadsheet again with the Open Frame command. You can select *multiple* embedded objects by holding down both the Control and Shift keys as you click each object.

■■■

Summary

- ➡ Any ClarisWorks document other than a communications document can contain frames from other environments.

- ➡ When you work in a frame, the menu commands and tools change to match the environment of the frame. When you leave the frame, they change back to match the base document's environment.

- ➡ Frames are objects, and, except for frames that you create in paint documents, you can resize or move them. You can apply any attribute to a frame that you can apply to an object.

- ➡ Spreadsheet and paint frames are merely windows into larger documents, and you can expand them to full-screen size.

- ➡ You can link text, spreadsheet, and paint frames to like frames. When you link text frames, text can flow automatically from one frame to another. Linking spreadsheet or paint frames enables you to display multiple views of the same underlying spreadsheet or paint document.

■■■

Working with Styles

In This Chapter

➠ General information concerning stylesheets and how they are used

➠ Applying and removing styles

➠ Creating and editing styles

➠ Transferring styles between documents

Overview

Although ClarisWorks 3.0 supported custom text styles (enabling you to save font, size, style, and color combinations and then reapply them to other text), styles really come into their own in ClarisWorks 4.0. With the new *stylesheets* feature, you can create your own reusable text, paragraph, outline, and worksheet table styles, and apply them to any text or worksheet areas that you like. You can also design styles for objects — making it a snap to apply the same line settings, pen and fill colors, patterns, and gradients to objects. (You no longer have to guess what shade of blue you chose for text or a cell border, for example.)

By using styles instead of manually formatting text and objects, you can ensure that the appearance of elements will be consistent not only in the current document, but across an entire set of documents as well.

In addition to reusability, the real power of styles becomes apparent when you change a style that's already in use in a document. For example, if you have a paragraph style called Main Head that is defined as centered, 18-point, Times, Bold, Italic text and then change the definition so that it is left-aligned, 14-point, Helvetica, Bold, all headings to which that style has been applied are immediately reformatted to match the new definition!

To see the Stylesheet palette, choose Show Styles from the View menu or press Shift-⌘-W. To hide the palette, click its close box, choose Hide Styles from the View menu, or press Shift-⌘-W. The Stylesheet palette is shown in Figure 15-1.

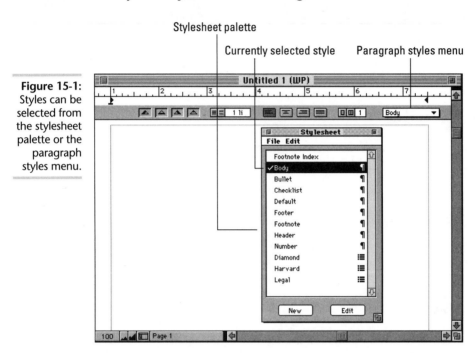

Stylesheet palette

Currently selected style   Paragraph styles menu

Figure 15-1:
Styles can be
selected from
the stylesheet
palette or the
paragraph
styles menu.

The figure shows that — when you're working in the word processing environment — some styles can also be selected from the paragraph styles menu in the ruler bar. However, only paragraph and outline styles are listed in the paragraph styles menu. A dotted line in the menu separates these two kinds of styles.

About the Stylesheet

Each document has its own stylesheet. When you save a document, you are simultaneously saving the current state of the stylesheet, too. Any changes that you have made to the stylesheet — whether you have edited any of the standard styles, deleted some styles, or created your own styles — are stored with the document. When you change from one document to another, the contents of the stylesheet changes to display the styles of the second document. Similarly, when you switch to a different environment within the same document, the *classes* of styles presented also change.

There are four classes of styles. Each corresponds to a particular type of ClarisWorks element to which it can be applied:

- ❧ *Basic*. Basic styles are for formatting text selections (applying font, size, style, and color options) and objects, such as draw graphics, spreadsheet cells, and database fields.

- ❧ *Paragraph*. Paragraph styles are applied to entire paragraphs and include indents, tabs, alignment, line spacing, and before and after spacing. Paragraph styles can also include text formatting commands (setting a font, size, style, and color for the text in the paragraph, for example).

- ❧ *Outline*. Outline styles are used to apply outline formats to paragraphs.

- ❧ *Table*. Table styles enable you to apply cell shading, borders, and other formatting options to selected worksheet ranges.

To make it simple to identify the different classes of styles in the stylesheet, each has a distinctive icon that appears to the right of the style name, as shown in Table 15-1.

Table 15-1 Style icons	
Icon	*Type of Style*
No icon (blank)	Basic style
¶	Paragraph style
≔	Outline style
⊞	Table style

Applying Styles

To apply a style, select the text, paragraph, outline topic, object, or so on to which you want to apply the style, and then choose a style from the stylesheet by clicking its name (as previously shown in Figure 15-1).

In the word processing environment, paragraph and outline styles can also be chosen from the paragraph styles menu in the ruler bar (as previously shown in Figure 15-1).

The current style — the one with the check mark in the stylesheet — is sometimes followed by a plus sign (+). This means that you have modified the selected item (text, object, paragraph, and so on) by adding formatting that is different from the style definition. For example, suppose you have defined a basic style named TB 24 that is Times, bold, 24-point text, and you have applied it to a heading. If you then reformat the heading by changing its font, size, or style, the style name is shown as TB 24+. If you then edit the style by clicking the Edit button in the stylesheet, you'll note that some properties are shown in italic at the top of the Properties list. These are the properties that you have manually changed for the selected item.

To reset any item (text, paragraph, object, and so on) to its original style (which will eliminate the manual formatting changes you have made), select the item and then click the style name again.

Removing Applied Styles _____

Styles that have been applied to text, a paragraph, an object, a spreadsheet range, and so on can be removed with the Unapply Style command.

Unapply Style is like an Undo command with an extremely long memory. You can use Unapply Style to remove any applied style whenever you like — even after hours of editing. As long as the original formatting was added by choosing options from the stylesheet or the paragraph styles menu, the formatting can be removed with Unapply Style.

The following points explain how to remove the four classes of styles:

- *Removing a basic style from some text.* Reselect the text in the word processing document or frame, spreadsheet cell, or database field. A check mark appears beside the name of the basic style that was previously applied to the text. Choose Unapply *style name* from the stylesheet's Edit menu.

- *Removing a basic style from an object* (a draw graphic or a database field in layout or list mode). Reselect the object. A check mark appears beside the name of the basic style that was previously applied to the object. Choose Unapply *style name* from the stylesheet's Edit menu.

- *Removing a paragraph or outline style from a paragraph.* Reselect the paragraph or outline topic. (It is not necessary to select an entire paragraph. As long as the text insertion point is somewhere within the paragraph, it is considered to be selected.) A check mark appears beside the name of the paragraph style that was previously applied to the paragraph. Choose Unapply *style name* from the stylesheet's Edit menu.

You can also use the Unapply Style command on a series of contiguous paragraphs, as long as they were all formatted with the same paragraph style. If you select two or more paragraphs that were assigned *different* paragraph styles, the Unapply Style command is not available.

↪ *Removing a table style from a spreadsheet table.* Reselect the entire range of the table that was previously formatted with a table style. Choose Unapply *style name* from the stylesheet's Edit menu.

Creating Styles _____

The process of creating a new style always includes the same series of initial steps.

Steps:	Creating a New Style

Step 1. Click the New button in the stylesheet. The New Style dialog box appears, as shown in Figure 15-2.

```
┌─────────────────── New Style ───────────────────┐
│                                                  │
│   Style type:       Style name:                  │
│   ⦿ Basic          ┌────────────────────────┐    │
│   ○ Paragraph      │ Style 1                │    │
│   ○ Outline        └────────────────────────┘    │
│   ○ Table           Based on:                     │
│                    ┌──────────┐                   │
│                    │ Default ▾│                   │
│                    └──────────┘                   │
│   ☐ Inherit document selection format   ┌────────┐ ┌──────┐ │
│                                         │ Cancel │ │  OK  │ │
│                                         └────────┘ └──────┘ │
└──────────────────────────────────────────────────┘
```

Figure 15-2: The New Style dialog box

Step 2. Select a class of styles by clicking one of the Style type radio buttons.

Step 3. Decide whether or not the style should be based on an existing style. If so, select the style's name from the Based on pop-up menu. Choose None if you do not want to base the new style on an existing style.

Step 4. Decide whether or not the new style should inherit format settings from the currently selected text, paragraph, cell, or object. To inherit settings, click the Inherit document selection format check box.

Step 5. Type a name for the style in the Style name text-edit box, and click OK. The new style's name is added to the stylesheet.

This ends the initial style definition process. However, the definition may not be complete yet, particularly if you chose not to base the style on an existing style or on a currently selected item (text, a paragraph, an object, and so on).

Steps: Refining a New Style Definition

Step 1. Click the Edit button at the bottom of the stylesheet. The stylesheet expands and its title changes to Edit Style. The pointer changes to the stylesheet edit pointer (a hollow S).

Step 2. Select a style by clicking its name in the left side of the stylesheet. The current *properties* for the style (the formatting options that make up the style definition) appear in the stylesheet's Properties list, as shown in Figure 15-3.

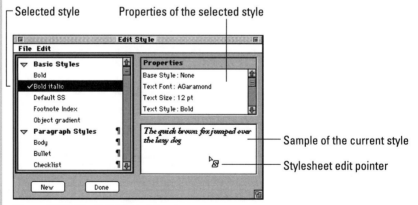

Figure 15-3: The Edit Style dialog box

You can modify the properties by choosing formatting commands from the normal ClarisWorks menus (such as Font, Size, and Style), from the ruler bar (if you're working in a word processing document or frame), and from the fill, pen, and line palettes in the Tool panel.

Step 3. When you are through making changes, click Done.

Style definitions are not universal. Each new style is only available in the document in which the style was created. If you create a new document or open another document, you'll see that the styles you've defined have disappeared from the stylesheet. They only return when you switch back to the document in which the styles were defined.

Editing Styles

As mentioned earlier, editing can be a necessary part of the initial style definition process. On the other hand, editing styles that are already in use can also be necessary. By changing a paragraph style that you previously defined for hanging indents, body text, or headings, for example, you can instantly change the formatting of those paragraphs throughout your document. Editing options for styles include renaming the style, changing the style on which the current style is based, and changing the style's properties.

 When editing styles, it is often helpful to see the cumulative effects of your edits. Choose Show Sample from the Edit menu to display style samples in the lower-right corner of the stylesheet. (Samples are visible only when you are editing styles; that is, when the stylesheet is expanded.) Repeatedly click the samples box to see how the current style affects paragraph, selected text, spreadsheet, and object formatting. To turn off the display of samples, choose Hide Samples from the stylesheet's Edit menu.

Renaming a Style or Changing the Based On Style

You can rename a style or base the style on a different style by using the Modify Style command.

Steps:	Renaming a Style or Changing the Based On Style
Step 1.	Select the style's name in the stylesheet and choose Modify Style from the stylesheet's Edit menu. The Modify Style dialog box appears, as shown in Figure 15-4.

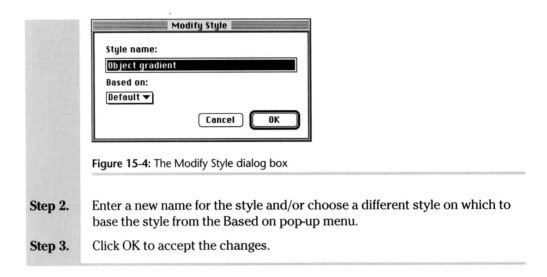

Figure 15-4: The Modify Style dialog box

Step 2. Enter a new name for the style and/or choose a different style on which to base the style from the Based on pop-up menu.

Step 3. Click OK to accept the changes.

Modifying Style Properties

Styles consist of *properties* (formatting options). To change a style, you change the properties of that style. After clicking the Edit button in the stylesheet and selecting a style to edit, you can use any of the following procedures to modify the properties of a style:

⌘ *Choose new properties* from ClarisWorks menus, the ruler bar, and the fill, pen, and line palettes. As you select them, the new properties are added to the style definition or replace components of the definition.

⌘ *Remove properties* by selecting them in the Properties section of the stylesheet and then choosing Clear Properties or Cut Properties from the stylesheet's Edit menu.

⌘ *Transfer properties* from one style to another. Select a property in the Properties section of the stylesheet and choose Copy Properties from the stylesheet's Edit menu. Select the style you want to modify, click in the Properties section, and choose Paste Properties from the stylesheet's Edit menu.

 You can copy and paste several properties simultaneously, if you like. Before copying the properties, Shift-click to select several contiguous properties or Command-click to select non-contiguous properties.

When you are through editing styles, click the Done button. The new style definitions are immediately available for use.

There is no Cancel button in the stylesheet when styles are being edited — nor can changes you make while editing a style be corrected with an Undo command. If you don't like the effects of your editing, you must either redo the editing, close the document without saving the changes, or use the Revert command to restore the document to its state as of the last Save.

If certain styles become unnecessary (or you just want to eliminate the clutter in a crowded stylesheet), you can delete selected styles (unless the style is currently in use somewhere in the document, in which case, you will *not* be allowed to remove it.)

Steps:	Deleting a Style
Step 1.	If the Stylesheet palette is not visible, choose Show Styles from the View menu (or press Shift-⌘-W).
Step 2.	Click the Edit button at the bottom of the Stylesheet palette. The palette window expands.
Step 3.	In the left side of the palette, click the name of the style you want to delete. A check mark appears beside the style name, indicating that it is now the selected style.
Step 4.	From the palette's Edit menu, choose either Cut Style or Clear Style.
	Cut Style places a copy of the style definition on the Clipboard, enabling you to paste the style definition back into this stylesheet or the stylesheet for another document. Clear Style simply deletes the style definition without placing a copy of it on the Clipboard.

Transferring Styles To and From Documents

If you've defined a style that you'd like to reuse in another document (or in *many* other documents), you can do any of the following:

- ☞ Save the document as a stationery file. (Each copy of the file that you open will contain the new styles that you have defined.) See Chapter 10 for help creating stationery documents.

⮑ Save the document as a default stationery document for an environment, such as word processing. (Every new document created in that environment will share the same initial stylesheet.) See Chapter 10 for help creating default stationery documents.

⮑ Copy the styles from the original document's stylesheet and paste them into the stylesheets of the other documents (described in the following steps).

⮑ Use the stylesheets' Import and Export commands (described later in this section).

Steps:	**Transferring a Style to Another Document via Cut-and-Paste**
Step 1.	If the Stylesheet palette is not visible, choose Show Styles from the View menu (or press Shift-⌘-W).
Step 2.	Click the name of the style you want to transfer. A check mark appears, indicating that this is now the selected style.
Step 3.	From the stylesheet's Edit menu, choose Copy Style.
Step 4.	Open or change to the ClarisWorks document that is to receive the style.
Step 5.	From the stylesheet Edit menu, choose Paste Style. The new style is added to the document's stylesheet. Repeat Steps 2 through 5 for any additional styles you wish to copy.

The stylesheet maintains its own equivalent of the Mac's Clipboard. Any style that is copied or cut (with the Copy Style or Cut Style command) remains available for pasting — *in as many documents as you like* — until you replace the Clipboard's contents by choosing Copy Style or Cut Style again.

The stylesheet's Export command enables you to save a selected set of styles to a disk file. Then, by using the Import command and choosing the new styles' file, you can quickly merge those styles with the current styles of as many documents as you like. The Export/Import procedure is the best means of moving many styles between documents, as well as the primary way of sharing your styles with other users.

Steps:	**Exporting Styles**
Step 1.	Open the document whose styles you wish to export.
Step 2.	If the Stylesheet palette is not visible, choose Show Styles from the View menu (or press Shift-⌘-W).

Step 3.   Choose Export from the stylesheet's File menu. The Select styles to export dialog box appears, as shown in Figure 15-5.

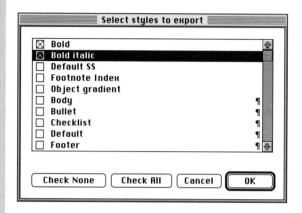

Figure 15-5: The Select styles to export dialog box

Step 4.   Click the names of the style you want to export. You can use the Check All or Check None buttons to speed the style selection process.

Step 5.   In the standard file dialog box that appears, enter a filename for the exported styles. (By default, the ClarisWorks Styles folder is selected. You can save the styles there or navigate to a different drive and/or folder.)

Style 6.   Click the Save button. The styles file is created.

Steps: Importing Styles

Step 1.   Open the ClarisWorks document into which you want to import the styles.

Step 2.   If the stylesheet palette is not visible, choose Show Styles from the View menu (or press Shift-⌘-W).

Step 3.   Choose Import from the stylesheet's File menu. A standard file dialog appears and shows the names of the stylesheets that are stored in the ClarisWorks Styles folder.

Step 4.   Choose the name of one of the style files or navigate to a different drive and/or folder and choose another file. The Select styles to import dialog box appears, as shown in Figure 15-6.

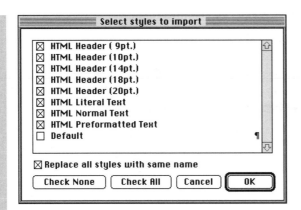

Figure 15-6: The Select styles to import dialog box

ClarisWorks 4.0 includes a style file called More Table Styles that provides additional spreadsheet table styles.

You might also want to try out HTML Styles. This style file is useful if you need to create Internet Web pages. See Chapter 23 or the "HTML Primer" in the ClarisWorks 4.0 folder for more information about using this set of style definitions.

Step 5. Click the names of the styles you want to import. You can use the Check All or Check None buttons to speed the style selection process.

Step 6. If you check the Replace All Styles With Same Name check box, imported styles with names that match those of existing styles in the document will automatically replace those styles.

If you remove the check mark, ClarisWorks will ask you how to handle each duplicate style name. You can either replace the old style with the imported style or rename the imported style.

Step 7. Click OK to import the selected styles. The imported styles appear in the document's stylesheet and can now be used.

Be careful when importing styles with names that duplicate those in the current stylesheet. If you check the Replace All Styles With Same Name check box, and both stylesheets have a style named Body, for example, any text in the document that is already formatted as Body will instantly change to match the imported style's definition. Of course, in many cases, this is exactly what you want to happen; that is, you want to make the document's formatting consistent with a company-wide stylesheet, for example.

Summary

➡ By using styles instead of manually formatting text, paragraphs, worksheet cells, and objects, you can improve consistency in your documents. You can also save considerable time.

➡ Styles are document-specific; that is, they are only available in the document in which they were created. Saving a document also saves the styles that have been defined for that document.

➡ When working in a word processing document or frame, you can also choose paragraph and outline styles from the paragraph styles menu in the ruler bar.

➡ There are four classes of styles: basic (for selected text and objects), paragraph, outline, and table (spreadsheet tables).

➡ Styles can be applied by selecting style names from the document's stylesheet or — in the case of word processing documents and frames — by choosing paragraph and outline styles from the paragraph styles menu in the ruler bar.

➡ Any style that has been applied by using the stylesheet or the paragraph styles menu can be removed by choosing Unapply *style name* from the stylesheet's Edit menu.

➡ When creating a style, it can be based on any existing style in the current document; on the currently selected text, paragraph, object, and so forth; or it can be designed from scratch.

➡ When modifying a style, you can add new or replacement properties by choosing ClarisWorks menu commands, clicking icons in the ruler bar, or choosing settings from the palettes in the Tool panel.

➡ Styles can be moved between documents by using copy-and-paste or the Export and Import commands.

Creating a Slide Show

16

In This Chapter

➡ Setting the number of slides for a slide show

➡ Arranging the order of slides, setting layering options, and selecting display options

➡ Embedding QuickTime movies in slides

➡ Running a slide show

Overview

You don't need fancy software to create and display most presentations. All you need is a program with a *slide show feature* — the capability to present a series of text charts, graphs, and other images on-screen. ClarisWorks has such a feature. You can use it from any environment except communications, and it is surprisingly flexible.

Slide Show Fundamentals

Every slide show is based on a single ClarisWorks document, and each page of the document is treated as a separate slide. Within the slide show document, you can

◌ Rearrange pages to display them in a different order

◌ Make pages opaque, transparent, or hidden

◌ Specify special effects for the presentation, such as fading out between slides and looping (for continuous, self-running demonstrations)

◌ Place QuickTime movies on slides

After you create a slide show document, you choose Slide Show from the View menu, set options, and then run the slide show. Creating an effective slide show tends to be an iterative process that consists of refining the slides, trying out different backgrounds, and experimenting with effects until you have the presentation you want.

Preparing for a Slide Show _____

Although you can take any document and instantly transform it into a serviceable slide show, a polished presentation requires that you spend some time examining different options and determining which options are best for the presentation. This chapter examines the slide show features and explains how each feature affects the presentation.

Setting the Number of Slides

In every environment except word processing, you have to set the number of slides that will appear in the slide show. Word processing is an exception because its documents are designed to accommodate multiple pages automatically. In most of the other environments, you have to add pages beyond the first one.

 Regardless of the environment that you use, be sure that ClarisWorks is set for Page View in the View menu (or press Shift-⌘-P) so that you can see where the page breaks occur. Also, unless Page View is selected, the Display options in the Document dialog box are grayed out (see Figures 16-1 through 16-3).

The instructions that follow explain how to set the number of slides in different environments.

Steps:	Setting the Number of Slides for a Draw Document
Step 1.	Choose Document from the Format menu. The Document dialog box appears, as shown in Figure 16-1.
Step 2.	In the Size section of the dialog box, enter the number of Pages across and Pages down. (When presented as a slide show, draw pages are shown across and then down.)

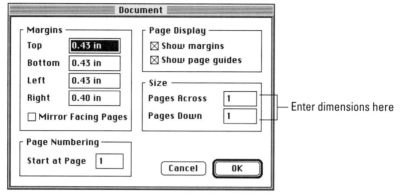

Figure 16-1: The Document dialog box for a draw document

A draw document can also have a *master page.* You use a master page to display a logo or other static objects on each slide. See Chapter 17 for more information.

Steps: **Setting the Number of Slides for a Paint Document**

Step 1. Choose Document from the Format menu. The Document dialog box appears, as shown in Figure 16-2.

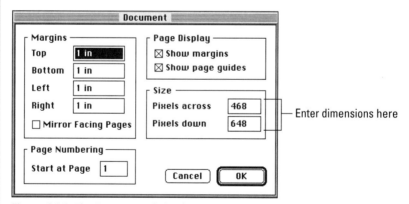

Figure 16-2: The Document dialog box for a paint document

Step 2. In the Size section of the dialog box, enter the number of Pixels across and Pixels down. (An inch contains 72 pixels.)

Large paint documents use a lot of memory, so they are not well suited for slides.

Steps: **Setting the Number of Slides for a Spreadsheet Document**

Step 1. Choose Document from the Format menu. The Document dialog box appears, as shown in Figure 16-3.

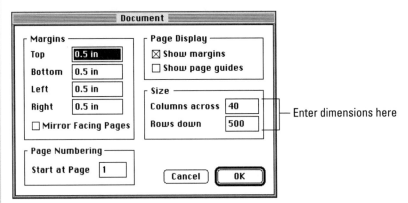

Figure 16-3: The Document dialog box for a spreadsheet document

Step 2. In the Size section of the dialog box, enter the number of Columns across and Rows down. Using the default column width and row height, a standard slide page is 7 columns wide and 50 rows high (or 9 columns wide and 37 rows high in landscape mode).

Steps: **Setting the Number of Slides for a Database Document**

Step 1. Create a layout that displays a single record per page.

Step 2. Choose Browse (Shift-⌘-B) from the Layout menu.

Step 3. Choose Slide Show from the View menu. The Slide Show dialog box appears, as shown in Figure 16-4.

Step 4. Set options and click Start.

Step 5. If more than one record appears on each slide or if the record isn't properly positioned on the slide screen, choose the Document command from the Format menu. Change the margins and then repeat Steps 3 and 4 until only a single record is displayed on each slide.

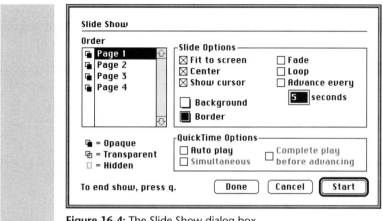

Figure 16-4: The Slide Show dialog box

 To quickly determine whether the database will show a single record on each slide, check the page numbers listed in the Order section of the Slide Show dialog box (previously shown in Figure 16-4). The number of pages listed should match the number of records you are including in the slide show.

When creating a database slide show, you can use the Find command in the Layout menu (or press Shift-⌘-F) to choose the records that you want to display as slides. If you want to display all records, choose Show All Records from the Organize menu (or press Shift-⌘-A).

Changing the Order of Slides

The slide order is displayed in the left side of the Slide Show dialog box (previously shown in Figure 16-4). To alter the order, you simply select a page with the mouse and then drag it to a new position in the list.

Setting Layering Options

Each slide can be opaque, transparent, or omitted (hidden) from the presentation. An opaque slide is solid and completely obscures any slides that you have already shown. A transparent slide, on the other hand, lets the slide beneath it show through. You can place several transparent slides on top of one another to create special effects. One common use for a series of transparent slides is to present a text chart that adds one new bullet point per slide.

To change a slide's layering in the Order list, click the icon to the left of the page number. As you click, the layering cycles through its three options: opaque, transparent, and hidden. Figure 16-5 shows examples of icons for pages that are opaque, transparent, and hidden.

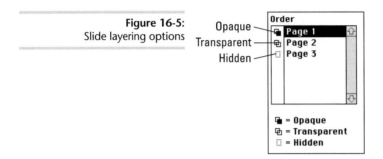

Figure 16-5:
Slide layering options

If you are using a master page as a background for a draw document, it will show through on all slides, regardless of whether they are opaque or transparent. (See Chapter 17 for more information on master pages.)

Slide Display Options

You can also use the Slide Show dialog box (previously shown in Figure 16-4) to set slide display options.

Steps:	Setting Slide Display Options
Step 1.	Open the document that you want to use for the presentation.
Step2.	Choose Slide Show from the View menu. The Slide Show dialog box appears.
Step 3.	Set the Slide and QuickTime options that you want to use in the presentation (as described in the "Slide Options" and "QuickTime Options" sections later in this chapter).
Step 4.	Click Start to see the slide show.
Step 5.	Press Q to exit the slide show (or press ⌘-period, Clear, or Esc).
Step 6.	Click Done to save the settings and return to the document or click Cancel to ignore the new settings and revert to the previous ones.

You can repeat Steps 3 through 5 as many times as necessary. If you want to record the slide show settings permanently, save the document with the Save or Save As command from the File menu.

Options in the Order section of the Slide Show dialog box are discussed earlier in this chapter. The next two sections describe how the slide options and QuickTime options affect a slide show.

Slide Options

The upper-right section of the Slide Show dialog box contains the slide options that govern the display of the slides and the manner in which they are presented. Slide options include the following:

- *Fit to screen.* This option resizes each slide to make it fit on the current screen. The slides maintain the proportions of the original document pages.

- *Center.* This option centers the slides on the screen.

- *Show cursor.* With Show cursor checked, the cursor remains on-screen as a pointer throughout the presentation. This feature is useful if you want to point at objects or text during the presentation. Leave Show cursor unchecked if the presentation is a self-running (looping) demonstration.

- *Fade.* When checked, Fade causes the screen to fade out and then fade back in between each pair of slides.

- *Loop.* Check Loop if you want the slide show to run continuously. After completing a cycle through the slides, the show starts over again from the beginning. Normally, you use Loop in conjunction with the auto-advance feature (the Advance every x seconds option). You stop a looping presentation in the same manner as you stop a normal presentation — by pressing Q, ⌘-period, Clear, or Esc.

- *Advance every x seconds.* When this option is checked, slides automatically advance at the rate that is set in the text-edit box. When it is unchecked, you have to advance pages manually by clicking the mouse or by pressing special keys (see "Running a Slide Show," later in this chapter). Note that even when the auto-advance feature is set, you can still advance any slide manually.

- *Background.* Choose from this pop-up palette to add a color to the background of a slide. The background color is in effect for the entire slide show. The default background color is white.

- *Border.* Choose from this pop-up palette to add a color to the border of a slide (the area around the outside edges of the slide page). The border color is in effect for the entire slide show. The default border color is black.

If a slide fills the screen, the border may be very thin. In this case, you may want to set the background and border to the same color.

QuickTime Options

You can set the following QuickTime options in the Slide Show dialog box:

- *Auto play.* When this option is checked, a QuickTime movie automatically runs when the slide in which it is embedded appears on-screen.

- *Simultaneous.* If you have more than one QuickTime movie on a slide, checking this option allows them to play at the same time. When this option is unchecked, the movies play in sequence from back to front according to the draw layer in which they're embedded.

- *Complete play before advancing.* This option forces the slide show to wait until the QuickTime movie has finished before moving to the next slide — even if you have set the Advance every *x* seconds option.

 The QuickTime options are selectable only if the QuickTime extension is loaded when the Mac starts up.

 In previous versions of ClarisWorks, a QuickTime movie in a slide show always played from the point at which it was last stopped. It was up to you to be sure that the movie was set to its beginning before starting the presentation. In ClarisWorks 4.0, however, a movie is automatically reset to its beginning whenever you display the slide in which it is embedded. Thus, whether you are presenting a slide show to a new audience or are simply returning to a slide that contains a QuickTime movie, the movie will play from the beginning.

There is one exception to this rule. If you have been playing a movie *manually* — outside of the slide show — the movie will start from the point at which you stopped it. You must manually reset the movie to its beginning before starting the slide show. Otherwise, it will continue to start from the point at which it was manually stopped.

Playing QuickTime Movies

QuickTime is an Apple-provided system extension that enables you to add movie clips to Macintosh documents. You can insert the clips into most ClarisWorks documents (and documents of other programs that support QuickTime), just as you add static images such as logos. Anyone else who has the QuickTime extension and the program in which you created the document can play the movie. At this writing, the current version of QuickTime is 2.0 — although new versions are released on a regular basis.

If you are successfully running ClarisWorks 4.0, you already have the necessary hardware and system software to use QuickTime. (ClarisWorks 4.0 has more stringent hardware and system software requirements than QuickTime. You must be running System 7 on a Macintosh with a 68020 or higher processor. See Appendix A for details.) If you want to play a QuickTime movie with minimal choppiness, you can improve playback by storing the movie on the fastest disk drive that you own. CD-ROM and floppy drives, for example, are extremely slow. SyQuest, Bernoulli, and optical disk cartridges are somewhat faster. A hard disk is better still.

You can incorporate QuickTime movies in a ClarisWorks word processing, spreadsheet, draw, or database document by choosing Insert from the File menu or by copying and pasting. However, if you give someone a ClarisWorks document or another type of document that contains a QuickTime movie, you need to give them a copy of the movie because QuickTime movies aren't actually stored in the documents in which they're embedded.

As with other ClarisWorks objects, you can add QuickTime movies either as in-line graphics or as objects. In-line graphics become part of the paragraph into which you paste them, enabling you to format them with standard paragraph commands. To add a movie as an in-line graphic, set the text inserion point within a word processing paragraph before choosing the Insert or Paste command.

Objects, on the other hand, are free-floating, and you can move them anywhere on the page. You also can specify a text wrap style if you place the object in a word processing document or frame. To add a movie as a floating object, select the pointer tool from the Tool panel before choosing the Insert or Paste command.

Running a Slide Show _____

To run a slide show, you choose Slide Show from the View menu, set options, and then click Start. You can also start the show without displaying the Slide Show dialog box by pressing the Option key while you choose Slide Show from the View menu.

While a slide show is running, you can use the keyboard commands and mouse actions shown in Table 16-1 to control the presentation.

Table 16-1	
Slide Show Keyboard Commands and Mouse Actions	
Command	*Key or Action*
Show next slide	Mouse click, right-arrow key, down-arrow key, Page Down, Return, Tab, or spacebar
Show previous slide	Left-arrow key, up-arrow key, Page Up, Shift-Return, Shift-Tab, or Shift-spacebar
Show final slide	End
Show first slide	Home
Play a QuickTime movie	Click in the movie frame
Pause or resume a movie	⌘-click or Option-click in the movie frame
Halt a QuickTime movie	Click in the playing movie's frame
End the slide show	Q, ⌘-period, Esc, or Clear

Quick Tips _____

The following Quick Tips tell you how to use Page Setup to make slides fit on the screen, how to create overlays and animate objects, how to create appealing bullet characters, and how to run a remote slide show.

Using Page Setup for Correct Slide Display

In most cases, monitors are considerably wider than they are tall. If you find that portions of the slides are clipped at the edges, choose Page Setup from the File menu and set the document for landscape mode by clicking the sideways icon in the lower-left corner of the Page Setup dialog box (see Figure 16-6). ClarisWorks uses the Page Setup settings when displaying documents on-screen, as well as when printing them.

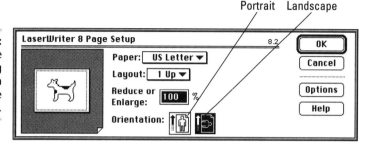

Portrait   Landscape

Figure 16-6:
The Page
Setup dialog
box for an
Apple
Laserwriter.

The dialog box will be different depending on the printer you have, as well as the version of system software you are running.

Movement in Presentations

By making several consecutive transparent slides, you can create overlays. One example is a bulleted list that adds a new bullet on each slide — enabling you to build on points as you move through the presentation.

Better Bullets for Text Charts

Items in text charts are frequently preceded by a bullet character (•). Everyone recognizes the standard bullet (Option-8), and it's available for every font. Unfortunately, it's dull. If you have the Zapf Dingbats font, on the other hand, there are dozens of interesting characters to choose from. Table 16-2 lists some Zapf Dingbat characters that you may prefer to use as bullets to add visual appeal to your slides.

The Symbol font — available on every Mac — also has characters that you can use as bullets. You can also paste a draw object (a circle with a gradient, for example) as an in-line graphic for a really unique and interesting bullet character.

Table 16-2 Zapf Dingbat Characters	
Zapf Character	*Keystroke*
✓	3
✔	4
☞	Shift-8
☆	Shift-p
●	l
○	m
■	n
❑	o
❐	p
❑	q
❐	r
▲	s
◆	u
➠	Shift-Option-7
➢	Shift-Option-0
➢	Shift-Option-W

Running a Remote Slide Show

ClarisWorks 4.0 includes an AppleScript called Remote Slide Show that lets you use one computer on your network to remotely control a ClarisWorks slide show that's running on another computer. For information on using this AppleScript, read the document named "About the AppleScripts" (found in the ClarisWorks Scripts folder).

Summary

➡ You can use documents from any environment except communications as the basis for a slide show.

➡ In environments other than the word processing environment, you need to use a special procedure to create a multipage document if you want to include more than one slide in a presentation.

➡ You can change the order in which slides are presented without affecting the contents of the underlying document. You also can specify which slides are to be shown as opaque, transparent, or hidden.

➡ If you base a slide show on a draw document, you can create a master page and use it to display static information on every slide (a company logo, for example).

➡ You use the Slide Show dialog box to set most options for the presentation, including the placement of the slides on-screen, background and border colors, special effects, and play settings for QuickTime movies.

Designing Master Pages

In This Chapter

- ➣ Creating master pages for draw documents
- ➣ Changing the layering position of a master page

Overview

Although you can use headers and footers to add graphics and other items that you want to appear at the top and bottom of every page of a document, things get a bit sticky when you want an item to appear somewhere else on every page. To handle this situation, ClarisWorks provides a feature called the *master page*.

Think of a master page as an extra layer or special page that appears on-screen — and is printed — behind every page of the document. Objects that you may want to place on a master page include *rules* (solid lines that appear at the top of each page or that separate columns of text), page borders, a solid background or gradient, company logos, and presentation instructions (for example, "Press Tab to advance to next slide; press Shift-Tab to view previous slide"). A master page lends consistency to the background elements in a document without forcing you to paste and realign the objects on every new page.

 You can create master pages only in draw documents. However, because you can place word processing, paint, and spreadsheet frames on draw documents, consider this a minor limitation, rather than a major inconvenience.

Creating Master Pages for Your Documents

You can easily create master pages to add the same background elements to all pages in a document.

Steps:	Creating a Master Page

Step 1. Open an existing draw document by pressing ⌘-O, or create a new one by pressing ⌘-N. (Alternatively, you can choose the Open or New command from the File menu.)

Step 2. Choose Edit Master Page from the Options menu. A blank master page is displayed, as shown in Figure 17-1. To remind you that you are editing a master page rather than working in the normal layer of the draw document, a check mark appears next to the Edit Master Page command in the Options menu and the page number indicator at the bottom of the document window is replaced with the text "Master Page."

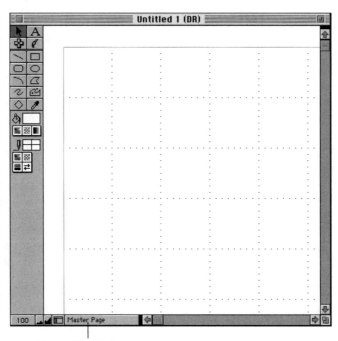

Master Page indicator

Figure 17-1: The Master Page indicator enables you to distinguish a master page from other pages of the document.

Step 3.	Add the master page elements to the page.
Step 4.	Choose Edit Master Page from the Options menu. The check mark next to the Edit Master Page command in the menu disappears, and the regular document is displayed.
Step 5.	If you are not in Page View, choose Page View from the View menu (or press Shift-⌘-P). Master page elements can only be seen when the document is in Page View.

You can edit master page elements, just as you can edit any other object, image, or text string that appears in a regular ClarisWorks document. Simply choose Edit Master Page from the Options menu and make whatever changes are necessary.

Layering Objects in Relation to a Master Page

A master page is normally assumed to be the lowest layer of a draw document; that is, its elements appear behind everything else in the document. However, by applying the Move to Back command to objects in the normal draw layer, you can effectively change the layering position of the master page elements — elevating them to the top layer, for example.

Steps:	**Altering the Layer in Which Master Page Elements Appear**
Step 1.	If you are working on the master page, switch to the draw layers of the document by choosing Edit Master Page from the Options menu. The Edit Master Page command should no longer be preceded by a check mark.
Step 2.	If you are not in Page View, choose Page View from the View menu.
Step 3.	Use the pointer tool to select the objects that are to appear behind the master page elements.
Step 4.	Choose Move to Back from the Arrange menu. All selected objects now appear behind the master page elements.

Quick Tips

The following Quick Tips tell you how to add a rotated *rubber stamp* to a master page and how to hide master page elements.

Adding a Rotated Rubber Stamp to a Master Page

Rubber stamps, such as "Confidential," "Draft," or "Paid," are excellent objects to include on a master page. Text placed over a Confidential or Draft rubber stamp, for example, is still perfectly legible, but the stamp clearly conveys that the document is not intended for general distribution.

To achieve a rubber stamp effect in earlier versions of ClarisWorks, it was necessary to create the text in a paint document or frame, rotate the text, copy it, and then paste the text into the master page of the draw document. This was the case because free rotation was only available for paint images. Objects — such as text strings — also could be rotated, but only in 90-degree increments.

ClarisWorks 4.0 has vastly superior rotation commands. Now objects of any sort — including text — can be directly rotated to any angle, not just in 90-degree increments.

Steps:	Creating Rotated Text
Step 1.	Open or create the draw document to which rotated text will be added.
Step 2.	Choose Edit Master Page from the Options menu.
Step 3.	Choose a font, size, and style from the Font, Size, and Style submenus of the Format menu.
Step 4.	Choose Text Color from the Format menu, and choose a color for the text. Because you normally want to be able to read the text in the overlying document, a light color or shade of gray is best for rubber stamp text. (A black rubber stamp would make the other text unreadable.)
Step 5.	Select the text tool (the A) from the Tool panel. Click and drag to create a text frame that is large enough to hold the rubber stamp text.
Step 6.	Type the text string for the stamp.

Step 7. Select the pointer tool, and click the text string to select it. Handles appear around the text object to show it is selected.

Step 8. Choose Free Rotate from the Transform menu (or press Shift-⌘-R). The cursor changes to a thin X. To rotate the text, click on any one of the text frame's handles and drag. When you are finished, choose the Free Rotate command again to turn the feature off.

— or —

Step 8. Choose Object Info from the Options menu. The Info palette appears (see Figure 17-2). Type an angle of rotation in the bottom box of the Info palette. Press Return, Enter, or Tab to apply the new rotation angle to the text.

Figure 17-2 shows the completed rubber stamp.

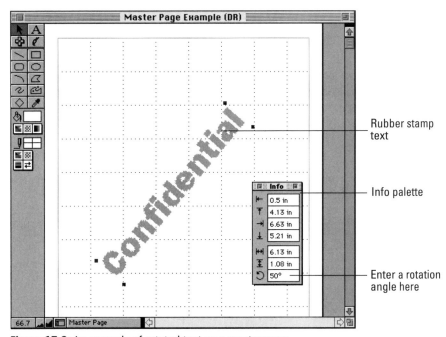

Figure 17-2: An example of rotated text on a master page

Obscuring Elements on the Master Page

Occasionally, you may want to obscure some of the elements on the master page. For example, you may want all elements to show through on every page except the first page of the document. (Perhaps you intend to use the first page as a title page.) A simple way to hide a master page element without altering the master page itself is to cover the element with an opaque white square that you place on the regular document page. The following instructions describe how to hide the "Draft" rubber stamp shown in Figure 17-3.

Figure 17-3:
The original document with two master page elements: a logo and a "Draft" rubber stamp

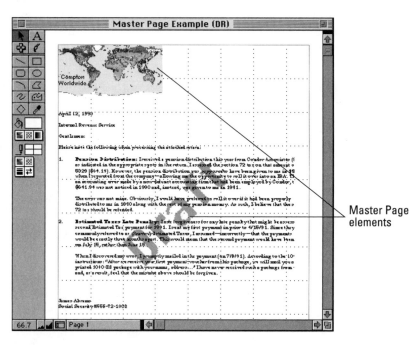

Master Page elements

Steps:	**Hiding a Master Page Element**
Step 1.	Open the draw document that contains the master page.
Step 2.	Pull down the Options menu and make sure that Edit Master Page does not have a check mark beside it. If it does, choose it again. (This action ensures that you are editing the regular document page, not the master page.)
Step 3.	If you cannot see the master page elements, choose Page View from the View menu (or press Shift-⌘-P).

Step 4. Select the rectangle tool from the Tool panel.

Step 5. Draw a rectangle that completely covers the master page element that you want to hide.

Step 6. With the rectangle still selected, set the fill and pen color to white, and set the fill and pen pattern to opaque. The document looks like the one shown in Figure 17-4.

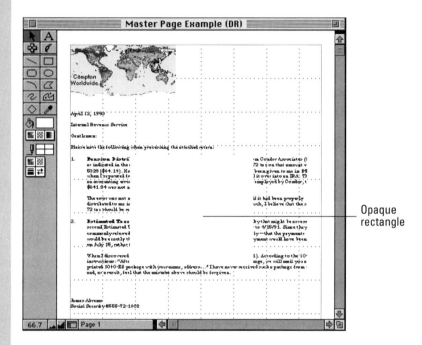

Opaque rectangle

Figure 17-4: The opaque white rectangle obscures the master page "Draft" element.

Notice that in addition to obscuring the master page "Draft" element, the white rectangle obscures much of the body text of the document. To correct this problem, you need to move the rectangle into the proper document layer.

Step 7. Choose Move Backward from the Arrange menu or press Shift-⌘- – (minus sign). The rectangle moves into the layer between the master page and the body text, as shown in Figure 17-5.

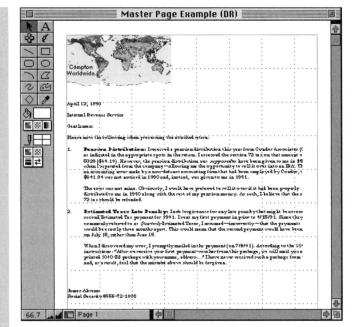

Figure 17-5: The master page element is hidden for this page only.

Dummying Up Your Document

Why would you want master page elements to obscure the normal objects and text on a page? One example is when you are designing a new layout that contains dummy or draft text. By placing a Draft or Sample rubber stamp on a master page and then forcing the master page to the top layer (causing the rubber stamp to overwrite the normal text), you can show what the layout will look like without fear that the text will be critiqued or reproduced. This is similar to adding dummy graphics to a layout and overprinting them with *For Position Only*.

■ ■

Summary

⇢ Elements that you place on a master page automatically appear in the same position on every page of the document.

⇢ Although you can create a master page only in a draw document, you can get around this limitation by placing word processing, paint, and spreadsheet frames on draw documents.

⇢ You can edit master page elements as often as you like. However, you can only see master page elements when you are editing the master page or have chosen Page View from the View menu.

■ ■

Publish & Subscribe

CHAPTER 18

In This Chapter

- ➡ Using Publish & Subscribe
- ➡ Updating an edition
- ➡ Setting subscriber and publisher options

Overview

Publish & Subscribe is a major advance that was introduced in System 7. It provides a simple way to integrate and share data among multiple programs, documents, and users without having to resort to the normal Macintosh copy-and-paste procedure. Publish & Subscribe maintains an active link between elements from two or more documents. If the published material (text or an object such as a spreadsheet chart, for example) is changed in the original document, the revised text or object can be automatically or manually updated in any document that is subscribing to the material. This feature makes Publish & Subscribe an ideal tool for coordinating the work of several individuals, as well as for linking frequently changing data and objects from different programs.

Some of the ways to use Publish & Subscribe include the following:

- ◦ Incorporating the work of several individuals on a network in a single master document (a departmental report that requires budget data from every department head, for example)

- ◦ Combining data from several different programs (adding ClarisWorks charts and Adobe Illustrator drawings to a shareholders' report created in Adobe PageMaker, for example)

- ◦ Maintaining live links between elements created in different ClarisWorks environments

Every Publish & Subscribe transaction has three components:

◦ The *publisher* is the portion of the document that is the source data — the text or object that you want to make available for use by others or in other documents.

◦ The *subscriber* is the area in a second document in which you see the published information or object.

◦ The *edition* is a special file that serves as the link between the publisher and the subscriber. It contains a copy of the publisher's contents. This intermediate file transparently notifies the subscriber whenever the publisher's data has changed and then executes whatever updates are required.

Figure 18-1 shows the relationship among these components.

Publisher document   Edition   Subscriber document

Figure 18-1:
An example
of Publish &
Subscribe

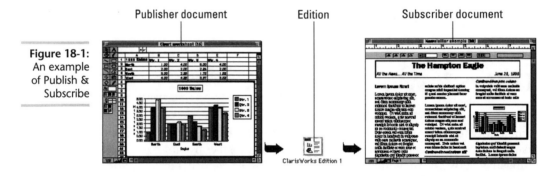

ClarisWorks Edition 1

You can publish database elements only from Layout mode, and you cannot publish or subscribe to information from the ClarisWorks communications or paint environments. Otherwise, documents from all other environments and elements, such as word processing text, worksheet sections, charts, and draw objects, are eligible for Publish & Subscribe.

At a minimum, every Publish & Subscribe transaction has a single publisher, a single subscriber, and an edition file. However, you can have multiple publishers and subscribers in any document. You can also have multiple subscribers — in different documents — to any published material.

Using Publish & Subscribe _____

Two steps create the link between the publisher and the subscriber: publishing the item and subscribing to the item's edition.

Steps:	Publishing an Item

Step 1. Open the document that contains the item you want to *publish* (make available to other users or use in other documents).

Step 2. Select the item to be published, such as a text segment, a spreadsheet chart, a range of cells, or a draw object.

Step 3. Choose Create Publisher from the Publishing submenu of the Edit menu. The dialog box shown in Figure 18-2 appears.

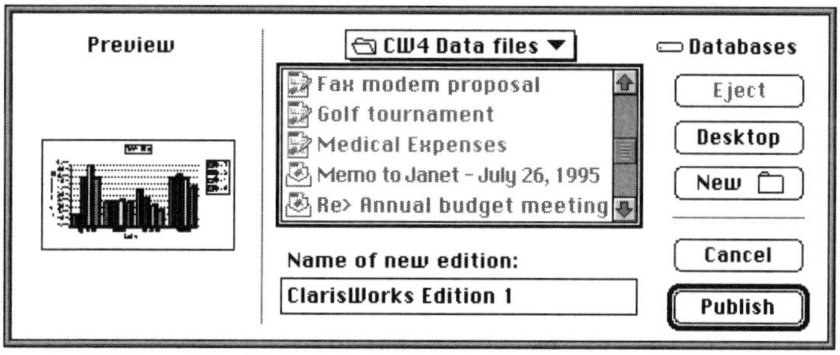

Figure 18-2: The publishing file dialog box shows a preview of the object or data that will be published.

Step 4. Navigate to the drive and folder where you want to store the edition file, type a name for the new edition, and click Publish. The edition file is created, and the selected text or object is surrounded by a border (to show and remind you that it is now a publisher).

Steps:	Subscribing to an Edition

Step 1. Open the document in which the published item will be placed.

Step 2. Select the spot in the document where you want the edition to be placed (a text insertion point in a word processing document or frame, a location in a draw document, or a range of spreadsheet cells, for example).

If the edition contains an object that you intend to place in a word processing document, you can make it a free-floating object by choosing the pointer tool. Otherwise, the object will be placed as an in-line graphic at the text insertion point.

If the edition is to be placed in a spreadsheet, be sure to choose a range that is large enough to hold the data. If the range is too small, the new data will spill over into additional cells — overwriting any data that they contain.

Step 3.   Choose Subscribe To from the Publishing submenu of the Edit menu. A dialog box similar to the one in Figure 18-2 appears.

Step 4.   Navigate to the drive and folder where the edition file is stored, select the edition's filename from the list, and click Subscribe. A copy of the edition is placed in the document.

Publish & Subscribe: An Example

The easiest way to learn more about Publish & Subscribe is to work through a simple example — one that you can do entirely within ClarisWorks. Using Publish & Subscribe, you'll create a ClarisWorks worksheet with a chart in it, publish the chart, and then subscribe to it in a report created in the ClarisWorks word processor. When a chart is simply pasted into another document, it loses all connection with the worksheet in which it was created. By using Publish & Subscribe, however, you maintain the link between the chart and the worksheet in which it was created. If you later modify the chart or the data on which it is based, the chart in the word processing report can be updated automatically.

As you read and work through this example, keep in mind that the following steps can also be done by two people on a network — one person publishing the chart and another person (the author of the report) subscribing to it. Similarly, two different programs can be used. For example, the chart can be created in and published from the ClarisWorks spreadsheet and subscribed to by a desktop publishing program or by a different word processing program.

To keep things simple, we'll use Mortgage Analyzer and Résumé A — two stationery files (a spreadsheet and a word processing document) that come with ClarisWorks 4.0.

Follow these steps to see how Publish & Subscribe works:

1. Choose New from the File menu (or press ⌘-N). In the New Document dialog box that appears, click the Use Assistant or Stationery checkbox and choose All Stationery from the Category pop-up menu. Choose Mortgage Analyzer from the file list, and then click OK.

2. The ability to update a subscribed-to object requires that the original be saved on disk. Because stationery files open as untitled temporary documents, save the Mortgage Analyzer spreadsheet by choosing Save from the File menu, naming the file (**Test**, for example), and then clicking the Save button.

3. Using the mouse, click to select the chart on the right side of the page (it begins near cell K19). Handles appear at the corners of the chart to show that it is selected. (You may want to scroll down and over in order to get a better view of the chart.)

4. Select Create Publisher from the Publishing submenu of the Edit menu. A file dialog box appears, as previously shown in Figure 18-2.

5. Type a filename for the new edition or accept the one that is presented. ClarisWorks uses the convention previously shown in Figure 18-2 to name all edition files (*ClarisWorks Edition x*). Click Publish to create the edition.

6. Choose New from the File menu (or press ⌘-N). In the New Document dialog box that appears, click the Use Assistant or Stationery checkbox and choose All Stationery from the Category pop-up menu. Choose the Résumé A word processing stationery document, and then click OK. The document opens in a new window.

7. In this example, we'll place the chart in the résumé as an in-line graphic rather than as a floating object. Click the line immediately below the "Highlights of Qualifications" bullets and press Return.

8. Select Subscribe To from the Publishing submenu of the Edit menu. A file dialog box appears similar to the one in Figure 18-2. Select the name of the edition file created in Steps 4 and 5, and then click Subscribe. A copy of the chart appears in the word processing document.

The chart is surrounded by a gray border to show that it is a subscriber object. If you like, you can turn the border off by choosing Hide Borders from the Publishing submenu of the Edit menu.

9. With the chart selected, drag the chart's handle (in its bottom-right corner) to reduce the size of the chart. Make it approximately 2 inches wide and 1.5 inches high.

10. To center the chart on the page, click the centered alignment control on the ruler bar. Figure 18-3 shows what the finished document looks like in ClarisWorks.

Figure 18-3:
The word
processing
document
now includes
a chart to
which it
subscribes.

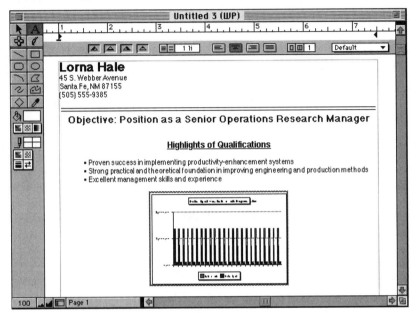

11. To see how updating works, make a change to the chart. In the worksheet, select the chart and choose Modify Chart from the Options menu. In the Chart Options dialog box, click a new chart type, such as Stacked Area, and then click OK to close the dialog box.

12. Because the published chart is updated in the edition only when its document is saved, choose the Save command from the File menu. (If you like, you can use the Save As command to save the document under a new name.)

13. Return to the word processing document. Notice that the original chart has been replaced with the revised chart. When you are done experimenting with Publish & Subscribe, close both documents.

This example demonstrates two important points. First, when you save a file that contains published material, the edition can track the file even if it has been renamed. The edition also knows when the file has been moved to a new location, and, of course, it tracks normal Saves, too. Second, the updated chart is the same size as the original rather than the size to which you previously reduced it in the word processing document. You will have to resize the chart.

In this example, I originally intended to place the chart as a floating object and then show you how to make text wrap around it. Unfortunately, ClarisWorks 4.0 contains an error that prevents text from wrapping around a subscribed-to object. If you need to wrap text around such an object, there are two workarounds:

ᐧᐧ Make all the necessary changes in the publisher, and then break the link (see "Canceling a Subscriber" later in this chapter).

ᐧᐧ Instead of using Publish & Subscribe to place the object, use the Copy and Paste commands.

Hopefully, this problem will be corrected in the next version of the program.

Updating an Edition

Until their edition is updated, subscribed-to elements remain unchanged (unless, of course, you edit them in the subscribing program). Although you can continue to edit the text or object in the original document from which they were published, the subscriber will reflect changes only when one of the following conditions is met:

ᐧᐧ The original document is saved again.

ᐧᐧ The edition is manually or automatically updated.

After the edition has been updated, changes in published material are sent to all subscribing documents.

By default, editions are automatically updated whenever a published document is saved. (It doesn't matter whether the subscribing document is open at the time the update occurs. The next time you open the subscribing document, you'll see the updated material.) However, automatic updating may not always be what you want. To control when updates occur, either the person publishing the material or the one subscribing to it can set updates to occur manually or force updates.

Steps: **Updating an Edition Manually**

Step 1. Select the published material in the publishing or the subscribing document. (If the material is an object, be sure that its outer border is selected).

Step 2. If you're working in the publishing document, choose Publisher Options from the Publishing submenu of the Edit menu. The Publisher to dialog box appears, as shown in Figure 18-4.

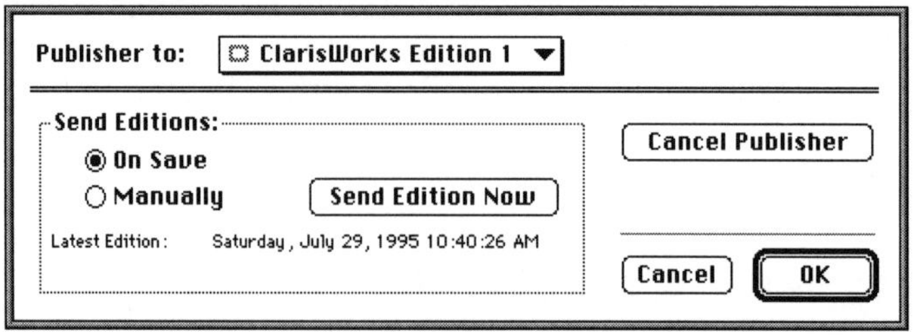

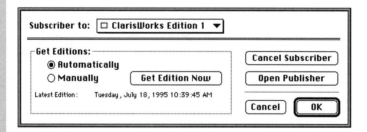

Figure 18-4: The Publisher to dialog box

Step 3. Click the Send Edition Now button. The most recently saved copy of the published material is sent from the edition to the subscribing document.

— or —

Step 2. If you're working in the subscribing document, choose Subscriber Options from the Publishing submenu of the Edit menu. The Subscriber to dialog box appears, as shown in Figure 18-5.

Figure 18-5: The Subscriber to dialog box

Step 3. Click the Get Edition Now button. The most recently saved copy of the published material is sent from the edition to the subscribing document.

When you are performing a manual update, it doesn't matter whether the Send Editions setting in the Publisher to dialog box (Figure 18-4) or the Get Editions setting in the Subscriber to dialog box (Figure 18-5) is set to be done automatically or manually. Clicking the Send Edition Now button or the Get Edition Now button forces an update to occur based on the most recently saved copy of the published material.

To ensure that *only* manual updates can occur (if you want to exercise total control over the update process), select the Manually option in either the Publisher to dialog box (Figure 18-4) or Subscriber to dialog box (Figure 18-5). When you select Automatically or On Save, on the other hand, an update occurs every time the document that contains the published material is saved.

Setting Subscriber Options _____

In addition to specifying an edition update method (automatic or manual), you can use the Subscriber Options command to find and open the publisher file, break the Publish & Subscribe link for any subscribed-to edition, and allow modification of the subscriber.

Opening a Publisher

When you are using Publish & Subscribe, you don't need to have the documents that contain the publisher and the subscriber open at the same time. If, on the other hand, the subscriber document is open and you need to view or work with the publisher, ClarisWorks provides a command to quickly locate and open the publisher file.

Steps:	Opening the Document that Contains the Publisher
Step 1.	Select the subscriber. If the subscriber is an object, select its border. If the subscriber is text or a portion of a worksheet, click anywhere inside the subscribed material.
Step 2.	Choose Subscriber Options from the Publishing submenu of the Edit menu. The Subscriber to dialog box appears, as previously shown in Figure 18-5.
	Double-clicking a subscribed-to object also makes the Subscriber to dialog box appear.
Step 3.	Click the Open Publisher button. ClarisWorks locates and opens the document that contains the publisher in a new window.

Open Publisher is a very powerful feature. You can use it to open published documents from *other* programs! For example, you can design and publish an illustration in a high-end graphics program and then subscribe to it in a ClarisWorks document. If you later find that you need to edit the graphic (to set a different background color, for example), click Open Publisher to instantly launch the graphics program and load the document for editing.

Open Publisher cannot be used to open a ClarisWorks publisher. If you try to do this, an error message appears ("Could not open the publisher document"). If you're working in a ClarisWorks document that subscribes to an object or text from another ClarisWorks document, you must use the Open command in the File menu to open the publisher.

Canceling a Subscriber

To break the link to a subscriber (so you can prevent further updates), you cancel the subscriber.

Steps:	Canceling a Subscriber
Step 1.	Select the subscriber. If the subscriber is an object, select its border. If the subscriber is text or a portion of a worksheet, click anywhere inside the subscribed material.
Step 2.	Choose Subscriber Options from the Publishing submenu of the Edit menu. The Subscriber to dialog box appears (as previously shown in Figure 18-5).
	Double-click a subscribed-to object to make the Subscriber to dialog box appear.
Step 3.	Click Cancel Subscriber.

Modifying a Subscriber

Rather than just maintaining a link to the publisher, you may also want to make your own alterations to a subscriber. However, if the subscriber is an *object* (such as a draw image), changes to the object are limited to changing its size, placement, and text wrap. To make other modifications, return to the document from which the object was published, make the changes, and then update the edition to transfer the changes to the subscriber.

Modifying a subscriber that is placed as *text*, on the other hand, is a simple procedure.

Steps:	**Modifying a Text Subscriber**
Step 1.	Select the subscriber text by clicking anywhere within it.
Step 2.	Choose Subscriber Options from the Publishing submenu of the Edit menu. The Subscriber to dialog box appears.
Step 3.	Click the Allow Modification check box. (If the box is not present, the text has probably been placed as an object rather than as text.)
Step 4.	Click OK. You can now edit the text subscriber and add formatting to it. However, if the published text is later updated, it will replace any edits that you have made to the subscriber.

The Allow Modification check box is only guaranteed to be present if the subscribed-to text originated in a ClarisWorks document. If the text originated in another word processing program, you may have to open it in the original program, make your changes, and then perform the update.

Setting Publisher Options _____

Other than specifying whether a publisher will be automatically or manually updated, there is only one publisher option: canceling the publisher. Canceling a publisher has no effect on the edition or its subscribers. It merely cuts the link between publisher and subscribers. Any additional changes that are made to the published material will not be sent as updates to the subscribers.

Steps:	**Canceling a Publisher**
Step 1.	Select the publisher. If the publisher is an object, select its border. If the publisher is text or a portion of a worksheet, click anywhere inside the published material.
Step 2.	Choose Publisher Options from the Publishing submenu of the Edit menu. The Publisher to dialog box appears (as previously shown in Figure 18-4).
Step 3.	Click Cancel Publisher.

Canceling a publisher does not eliminate its edition file (*ClarisWorks Edition 4* or whatever else you happened to name it). After you cancel a publisher, you may want to drag its edition to the Trash.

Quick Tips

The following tips explain how to deal with subscribed-to objects that are larger than the document page in which they are placed and give suggestions for using Publish & Subscribe with other programs.

Handling Large Subscribers

Finding that a subscriber in a ClarisWorks document is too wide to display completely is not unusual. And because many subscribers are objects, the resize handle (the black dot in the lower-right corner) may be off-screen. Here are two ways that you can deal with this situation:

- ☞ If the object is free-floating, click anywhere inside the object and drag to the left until the resize handle appears. You can then resize the object as needed.

- ☞ If the object has been placed as an in-line graphic (embedded in a sentence or paragraph as a "graphic character" of sorts), you can't drag it. Instead, select the object and use the Scale by Percent command from the Format menu to shrink the object to the proper size (see Figure 18-6).

Figure 18-6:
To use the Scale by Percent dialog box, enter percentages for the horizontal and vertical enlargement or reduction.

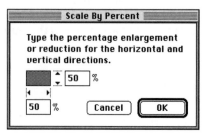

You can also apply the Scale by Percent command to free-floating objects. In this case, the command is located in the Transform submenu of the Arrange menu.

Program Differences in the Implementation of Publish & Subscribe

If you examine different programs that support Publish & Subscribe, you'll find that implementations of this feature can vary considerably. Adobe PageMaker 5.0, for example, has only Subscribe features. To determine the differences in Publish & Subscribe capabilities, options, and procedures, you need to carefully check the manuals of the programs involved. And don't be afraid to experiment. Sometimes it's the quickest way to find out how a feature works.

Summary

- Publish & Subscribe allows data to be shared by multiple users (over a network) and among multiple programs. For example, a non-Claris desktop publishing program can subscribe to a chart that was created in a ClarisWorks worksheet.

- The three components in every Publish & Subscribe transaction are a publisher, an edition, and a subscriber. If necessary, you can have multiple publishers and/or subscribers.

- Editions can be updated automatically (whenever the published material is saved) or manually (on request by either the individual who published the material or by the one who subscribed to it).

- Additional Publish & Subscribe options enable you to break the link between the publisher and the subscriber (so that future changes in the published material will not be reflected in the subscribed-to material), find and open the document that contains the published material, and modify a subscriber.

- Other programs may handle the Publish & Subscribe process differently — offering and supporting different options, for example.

Electronic Mail

In This Chapter

➥ Sending letters from ClarisWorks

➥ Saving letters

➥ Deleting mailers

➥ Handling incoming mail

Overview _____

System 7.5, System 7 Pro (also called System 7.1.1), and later versions of the system software include PowerTalk system software, a feature for creating, sending, and receiving electronic mail. If you buy the optional Direct Dialup Mail Accessory Kit from Apple Computer, you can also use a modem to exchange messages with other PowerTalk users.

 PowerTalk is not installed as part of the normal system software installation procedure; it must be installed separately. See your system software manual for instructions.

 To send PowerTalk messages from ClarisWorks, you must have System 7.5, System 7 Pro, or a later version of the system software; as well as the PowerTalk system software. If the PowerTalk software is not installed on your system, you can safely skip over this chapter. It does not apply to you.

At its simplest, PowerTalk enables you to easily exchange files of any type with individuals on a network. ClarisWorks 4.0 provides direct PowerTalk support that enables you to

- ☞ Create messages and then route them to people on the network
- ☞ Reply to messages
- ☞ Forward messages to others

Messages can be accompanied by whole documents called *enclosures*.

ClarisWorks 4.0 includes a Mail submenu (which contains message-handling functions) and special PowerTalk-specific buttons for the Shortcuts palette. (For help with installing the new buttons, see "Customizing the Shortcuts Palette" in Chapter 12.) ClarisWorks also supports PowerTalk mailers (message headers that list a letter's sender, recipient, subject, and enclosures). And ClarisWorks enables you to create a special stationery file that you can use to reply to messages.

This chapter provides the information you need to use PowerTalk to create, send, and respond to messages in ClarisWorks. It is not designed as a complete reference on PowerTalk, but rather to show you how you can use this system with ClarisWorks. Familiarity with key PowerTalk terms and concepts will help you understand and use the information in this chapter. For additional details on installing and using PowerTalk, refer to your system software's documentation.

 If you are just beginning a computing session or have locked your PowerTalk Key Chain, PowerTalk prompts you to enter your access code when you attempt to perform any mail-related task.

Sending Letters from ClarisWorks

No matter which ClarisWorks environment you're working in (except communications), you can send any document created in ClarisWorks as a *letter* — an e-mail document. A letter can be accompanied by enclosures.

Attaching a *mailer* (a message header that lists the letter's sender, recipient, subject, and enclosures) to a document changes it to a letter. You can attach mailers to new or existing documents. If you later decide to return the letter to its original form (a word processing or draw document, for example), you can remove the mailer.

Step 1.   Open or create a ClarisWorks document that you want to use as the basis of your letter. The document can exist in any environment except communications.

If you want to send a previously created letter, you can locate the file quickly by choosing Letter from the File Type pop-up menu in the Open dialog box.

Step 2.   Enter or edit the message as necessary.

Step 3.   Choose Add Mailer from the Mail submenu of the File menu. A mailer appears at the top of the document, as shown in Figure 19-1.

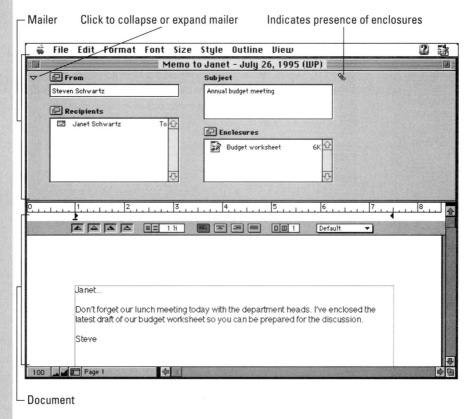

Figure 19-1: A ClarisWorks document with a mailer

Alternatively, you can click the Add/Delete Mailer button in the Shortcuts palette, as shown in Figure 19-2.

Figure 19-2: The Add/Delete Mailer button

Unlike other Shortcuts buttons, the PowerTalk-specific buttons are dynamic — they come and go as appropriate. (To read how to add buttons to the Shortcuts palette, see "Customizing the Shortcuts Palette" in Chapter 13.)

Step 4. To change the sender, click the button next to From and provide the information requested. By default, the From box initially contains the name of the owner of the machine — your name, in most cases.

Step 5. Type subject information in the Subject box. You *must* fill in this box.

Step 6. Click the button next to Recipients to select one or more recipients for the letter from the dialog box shown in Figure 19-3. (You can also drag the addresses of individuals or groups from catalogs, the desktop, or any disk into the Recipients box.)

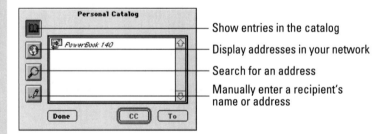

Figure 19-3: From this dialog box, you specify who should receive your letter.

Step 7. When you find a recipient, select the name in the dialog box and click the To button.

To send a copy of the letter to individuals or groups, choose the appropriate names and click CC (carbon copy). To send a blind carbon copy to someone, hold down the Option key — which changes the CC button to BCC (blind carbon copy) — and click BCC. (When you send a blind carbon copy, the recipient's name does not appear in the distribution list seen by the other recipients.)

You can add as many normal recipients, carbon copies, and blind carbon copies as you like.

If you add a recipient by mistake, you can remove him or her from the list by selecting the person's name in the Recipients box and then pressing the Delete key or dragging the person's name to the Trash.

Step 8. When you are through specifying the distribution list, click Done.

Step 9. *Optional:* If you want to attach one or more additional files to the letter (documents, data files, or programs, for example):

- Click the button next to Enclosures. A standard file dialog box appears.

- Navigate to the disk and folder that contains the file you want to enclose with the letter.

- Select the file in the file list, and click Enclose. The file is added to the Enclosures list, and a paper clip icon is added to the mailer (to the right of the Subject box).

To enclose additional files, repeat this step.

If you prefer, you also can add an enclosure by dragging file or folder icons directly into the Enclosures box.

Step 10. Select Send from the Mail submenu of the File menu. The Send document dialog box appears (see Figure 19-4).

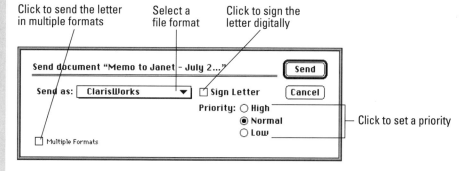

Figure 19-4: The Send document dialog box

Alternatively, you can click the Send button in the Shortcuts palette, as shown in Figure 19-5.

Figure 19-5: The Send button.

Step 11.   Set a priority for your letter by clicking the High, Normal, or Low radio button. The default setting is Normal. The priority that you set is indicated in the recipient's In Tray. (All e-mail that a user receives is automatically listed in the In Tray on the desktop.)

The priority does not affect delivery time or the method used to notify the recipient of the message's arrival.

Step 12.   *Optional:* If you want your digital signature affixed to the letter, click Sign Letter. (If you do not already have an approved digital signature, refer to your system software's documentation for details.)

Step 13.   Select a file format for the letter.

Because your letter is a ClarisWorks document, the default format is ClarisWorks. If the recipient cannot read a ClarisWorks file, select a different file format from the Send as pop-up menu.

If you don't know which formats the recipient can read, click the Multiple Formats check box. The dialog box changes its appearance, as shown in Figure 19-6. You can choose up to three formats for the document:

- *AppleMail.* The document can be read and edited in any AppleMail-compatible program.

- *Snapshot.* The letter is sent as a graphic rather than as text. This is a less-than-perfect choice if the recipient needs to edit or reuse portions of the letter. However, Snapshot works well when you want to send the document through a fax gateway or when the recipient does not have ClarisWorks.

- *A program-specific format.* You can select any format listed in the Send as pop-up menu (Microsoft Word, for example). You can choose only one program-specific format, however.

> Send document "Memo to Janet – July 2…"   [Send]
>
> Send as: ☐ AppleMail   ☐ Sign Letter   [Cancel]
>   ☐ Snapshot   Priority: ○ High
>   ☒ [ClarisWorks ▼]   ● Normal
> ☒ Multiple Formats   ○ Low

Figure 19-6: The Send document dialog box after you select the Multiple Formats option

The Send As formatting affects only the letter. Enclosures retain their native formats.

Step 14. Click the Send button. The letter and any enclosures are sent.

Step 15. *Optional:* To save the file to disk, choose the Save As command from the File menu, select Letter from the Save As pop-up menu, and click the Document or Stationery radio button (depending on whether you want to save the file as a normal letter or as a letter template). If you'd prefer to save the file as an ordinary document rather than as a letter, first choose Delete Mailer from the Mail submenu of the File menu and then choose Save As.

If you need additional help with filling in a mailer, refer to your system software's documentation.

Saving Letters

You can save any letter to disk in either of two formats: letter or letter stationery. The stationery format is useful if you want to use the letter as a template for creating other letters. For example, you can design a basic letter layout that contains a graphic or logo, has blanks for standard memo information, and uses a particular font. (For more information about creating stationery documents, see Chapter 10.)

Steps:	**Saving a Letter**
Step 1.	Choose Save As from the File menu. The Save As dialog box appears.
Step 2.	Choose Letter from the Save As pop-up menu.
Step 3.	Click the Document or Stationery radio button.
Step 4.	Enter a filename in the text-edit box.
Step 5.	Navigate to the disk and folder where you want to save the file.
Step 6.	Click Save.

Deleting Mailers

You can remove a mailer at any time; the underlying document reverts to its original form.

Steps:	**Restoring a Letter to its Original Form**
Step 1.	Open the letter in ClarisWorks.
Step 2.	Choose Delete Mailer from the Mail submenu of the File menu.
	Alternatively, click the Add/Delete Mailer button (previously shown in Figure 19-2) in the Shortcuts palette.

Handling Incoming Mail

When e-mail arrives, you can open, reply to, and/or forward the message.

 You can set the manner in which you are notified of incoming e-mail by returning to the desktop, opening your mailbox, and then choosing Preferences from the Mailbox menu. You can choose to display an alert dialog box, blink an icon in the menu bar, and/or play a particular sound when e-mail arrives.

Opening a Letter

After you're notified that a letter has arrived, choose Open Next Letter from the Mail submenu of the File menu. The letter is converted (if necessary) and opens as a ClarisWorks document. (Letters that are sent to you as Snapshots open as draw documents.)

To open an enclosure, double-click its icon (found in the Enclosures box in the mailer) or drag its icon onto the desktop and then open it with an appropriate application.

If you receive a letter that was sent by someone who used the drag-and-drop procedure described in this chapter's "Quick Tips," you cannot open the letter by using the Open Next Letter command; although the letter sits in your In Tray, it is invisible to ClarisWorks. To open the letter, you have to return to the desktop, open the In Tray, and double-click the letter's icon. If the letter is a ClarisWorks document, ClarisWorks launches and opens the letter. If the letter is in another format, a different program may open it.

You can force ClarisWorks to attempt to open almost any letter: just return to the desktop and drag the letter icon onto the ClarisWorks program icon. If ClarisWorks contains an appropriate file translator, ClarisWorks launches (if it's not already running) and automatically translates the letter into a ClarisWorks format.

Replying to a Letter

Many letters require a reply.

Steps:	Replying to a Letter
Step 1.	Open the letter in ClarisWorks (see the preceding section, "Opening a letter").
Step 2.	Choose Reply from the Mail submenu of the File menu or click the Reply button in the Shortcuts palette (see Figure 19-7). A new untitled word processing document appears (see Figure 19-8). If the received letter was also created in the word processing environment, it appears at the bottom of the reply document (unless you clicked the > check box in the mail preferences, in which case the contents of the original letter appear at the *top* of the reply document rather than at the bottom).

Figure 19-7: The Reply button

Mailer—

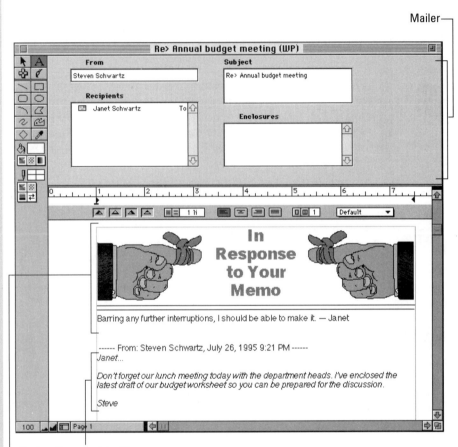

Reply   Text of original letter

Figure 19-8: The reply document already contains the appropriate mailer information and a copy of the original letter. (Clip art courtesy of T/Maker Co., ClickArt Business Cartoons.)

Step 3.   Type your reply. (The text insertion point is already placed for you.)

Step 4.   *Optional:* Add enclosures or other recipients as desired.

Step 5.   Choose Send from the Mail submenu of the File menu or click the Send button in the Shortcuts palette (see Figure 19-5). The Send document dialog box appears, as shown previously in Figure 19-4.

Step 6. Select your send options, as described earlier in this chapter.

Step 7. Click the Send button.

Creating a Reply Stationery Document

Normally, when you select the Reply command from the Mail submenu of the File menu, an ordinary blank document appears. ClarisWorks, however, supports a PowerTalk reply stationery document (much like the default stationery documents described in Chapter 10) in which you can dress up e-mail, giving your replies a more personal touch.

Steps: **Creating a Reply Stationery Document**

Step 1. Open a new, blank document in the environment where you intend to write your replies.

Step 2. Add any elements you want to appear in every reply, such as a base font and graphics (see Figure 19-9).

To ensure that your message text turns out as you expect, create a line of sample text (such as "Type your message here") at the beginning of your reply stationery that is the correct font, size, and style for your actual message.

Text

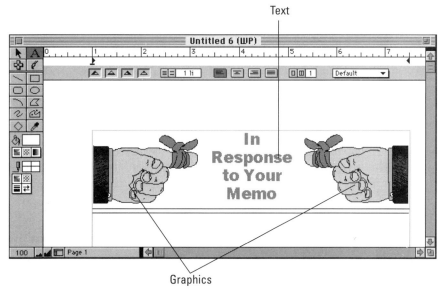

Graphics

Figure 19-9: Creating a Reply stationery document

Step 3. Choose Save or Save As from the File menu. The Save dialog box appears.

Step 4. From the Save As pop-up menu, choose ClarisWorks as the file type, and then click the Stationery radio button. Clicking the Stationery radio button automatically navigates to the ClarisWorks Stationery folder.

Step 5. Name the document Reply, and click the Save button (see Figure 19-10).

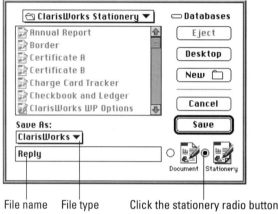

File name   File type   Click the stationery radio button

Figure 19-10: Saving the Reply stationery document

Now whenever you select the Reply command, the Reply stationery document is used.

Do not save the Reply stationary document with a mailer attached. ClarisWorks automatically adds the mailer when you choose the Reply command.

Forwarding a Letter

Occasionally, you may want to forward a received letter to someone else. For example, if you receive a letter that you think your supervisor should read, you can forward a copy of the letter.

Steps: **Forwarding a Letter**

Step 1. Open the letter and choose Forward from the Mail submenu of the File menu, or click the Forward button in the Shortcuts palette (see Figure 19-11). A new mailer is added *over* the old one, as shown in Figure 19-12.

Figure 19-11: The Forward button

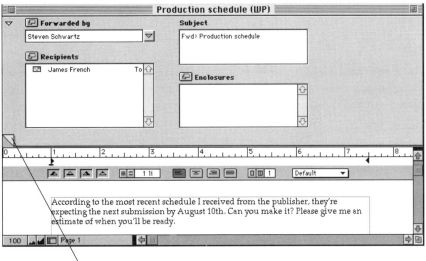

Click to view the original mailer

Figure 19-12: The new mailer

Step 2. If the mailer is collapsed, expand it.

Step 3. Select recipients for the forwarded letter.

Step 4. Choose Send from the Mail submenu of the File menu. The Send document dialog box appears.

Step 5. Select send options, as described in "Sending Letters from ClarisWorks" earlier in this chapter.

Step 6. Click the Send button. The letter is forwarded to the selected recipients.

Quick Tips

The following Quick Tips discuss the Preferences options for handling e-mail and the importance of font selection when writing letters. They also explain how to send e-mail immediately, delete old e-mail, and send documents from the desktop.

Setting Mail Preferences

As with any other major ClarisWorks component, you can set the preferred way for handling many mail-related tasks. The Mail Preferences are shown in Figure 19-13. (For details, refer to Chapter 11, "Setting Preferences.")

Figure 19-13:
Mail Preferences

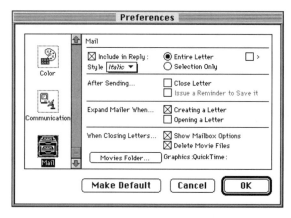

 The Mail icon appears only if PowerTalk and System 7.5, System 7 Pro, or a later version of the system software are installed.

Select Your Fonts Carefully

Be cautious about using esoteric fonts in your letters. If the recipients do not have the same fonts installed, a message to that effect appears on their screens, and every instance of a missing font is converted to a generic font — spoiling your document's look.

Handling Reluctant Mail

When checking your Out Tray on the desktop, you may see mail whose status is "Waiting." You can force PowerTalk to send a message immediately by selecting the letter in the Out Tray and then choosing Send Now from the Mailbox menu.

Discarding Mail

Old mail — sent or received — cannot be deleted from within ClarisWorks. To delete old mail, return to the desktop, open your In or Out Tray, and drag the icons of unwanted letters into the Trash.

Sending Files from the Desktop

If you want to transfer some files to another user but don't need or want to attach a message, you can use the *drag-and-drop* method.

Steps:	Sending a Document via Drag-and-Drop

Step 1. From the desktop, open the PowerShare, AppleTalk, or personal catalog that contains the address of the file's intended recipient (see Figure 19-14).

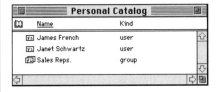

Figure 19-14: Choosing recipients via their catalog entries

If you need help locating a particular individual or group, select the Find in Catalog desk accessory from the Apple menu. In System 7.5 and 7.5.1, this desk accessory can be found within the Mail and Catalogs submenu of the Apple menu. (See your system software's documentation for additional details.)

Step 2. Click the file you want to transfer and then drag it onto the recipient's icon in the catalog. When you release the mouse button, a dialog box like the one in Figure 19-15 appears.

Figure 19-15: This dialog box changes to reflect the actual filename, the recipient's name, and the mail address (Direct AppleTalk mail or AppleShare file server, for example).

Step 3.   Click OK. A copy of the file is sent and the normal notification procedure is executed.

Summary

➻ With ClarisWorks 4.0 and System 7.5, System 7 Pro, or a later version of the system software, you can use the new PowerTalk system software to send electronic mail and documents from within ClarisWorks.

➻ ClarisWorks 4.0 provides several PowerTalk-specific buttons for the Shortcuts palette, as well as a Mail submenu for the File menu.

➻ Adding a mailer to a ClarisWorks document changes it to a PowerTalk letter.

➻ A letter created in ClarisWorks can contain non-ClarisWorks files as enclosures.

➻ To ensure that a recipient can read your letter, send the letter in any format supported by the XTND translators. (See "Opening Non-ClarisWorks Documents" in Chapter 1.) You also can send a letter in AppleMail or Snapshot format. To be sure that a recipient can read the letter, you can send it in multiple formats.

➻ Mail can be saved to disk as a letter (a document with a mailer attached) or as a normal ClarisWorks document (with the mailer removed). Letters that you want to reuse as templates can be saved as Letter Stationery documents.

➻ Letters created and sent from ClarisWorks can be opened directly from within ClarisWorks. Mail sent via drag-and-drop must be opened from the desktop.

➻ When you receive a letter, you can read it, send a reply, and/or forward the letter to others.

Working with Libraries

Overview

ClarisWorks 3.0 included an impressive collection of clip art for embellishing your documents. ClarisWorks 4.0 also includes clip art, but it is easier to use because it is in *libraries* — collections of art organized around a theme. Using any image from a ReadyArt library is as simple as dragging the image of choice into your document or frame.

Libraries also can be used to hold things other than draw and paint images. Examples include boilerplate text, spreadsheet cells, QuickTime movies, and frames of any type. Thus, in addition to using the provided clip art, you can add your own material to the Claris libraries or create new libraries.

When you open a library — regardless of whether it is a ClarisWorks-provided library or one that you created — the library appears in a palette. Like other palettes, every library palette has a title bar, a close box, and a shrink/expand box, as shown in Figure 20-1.

Close box   Title bar

Shrink/Expand box

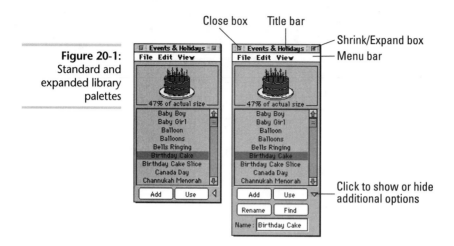

Menu bar

Figure 20-1:
Standard and
expanded library
palettes

Click to show or hide
additional options

Library palettes are different from Tool panel palettes in three ways:

℞ Library palettes can be expanded to show additional options (by clicking the tiny arrow at the bottom-right corner of the palette).

℞ A library palette contains its own menu bar.

℞ You can customize the way information in each library palette is presented (by choosing options in the palette's View menu).

You must open a document or create a new document before opening a library. If no documents are open, the Library submenu cannot be selected.

A library should be thought of as a special kind of ClarisWorks document. Although you can add and remove items, rename items, and change the viewing preferences for a library, all changes are lost unless you also *save* the library. To remind you of this, if you close a library that has been changed without choosing Save or Save As from the library's File menu, ClarisWorks presents the same dialog box that is used when you try to close a changed document without saving, as shown in Figure 20-2.

Figure 20-2:
This dialog box appears
if you close a library
palette before saving
your changes.

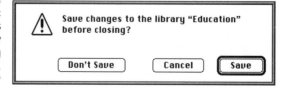

Opening and Closing Libraries

Libraries that are stored in the ClarisWorks Libraries folder (found inside the ClarisWorks 4.0 folder) are automatically listed in the Library submenu of the File menu. These libraries can be opened by selecting their names from the Library submenu.

Libraries saved in other folders or on different disks, on the other hand, can only be opened by choosing Open from the Library submenu, navigating to the appropriate disk and folder, and then clicking the Open button.

When you close all active ClarisWorks documents, any libraries that are still open automatically close. Libraries also can be closed manually by doing either of the following:

- ☞ Click the library palette's close box.
- ☞ Choose Close from the library palette's File menu.

If you have made changes to the library, ClarisWorks presents a dialog box asking if you want to save the changes (previously shown in Figure 20-2). Click Save to save the changes, Don't Save to close the library without saving changes, or Cancel if you change your mind and want to keep the library open.

You can simultaneously close *all* open library palettes by holding down the Option key as you click any library's close box.

There is no command to *delete* a library. If you want to delete an existing library, go to the desktop, open the ClarisWorks Libraries folder inside the ClarisWorks 4.0 folder (or wherever else you saved the library), click to select the library, and drag it to the Trash.

Creating New Libraries

Although you may be satisfied with using the ClarisWorks libraries as is — simply dragging the provided clip art into your documents — you also may want to create your own libraries to store logos, scanned signatures, spreadsheet formulas, and important text.

To create a new library, you must first open or create a ClarisWorks document. From the Library submenu of the File menu, choose the New command. A new, empty library palette appears, as shown in Figure 20-3. The library is given a temporary name of Library *x*, where *x* is a number.

Figure 20-3:
A new,
empty
library

Every new library is considered temporary until it has been saved. At any point before you close the library, you can choose the Save As or Save command from the library's File menu to save the library and — optionally — give it a more descriptive name.

It's not really a library until you add something. To learn how to add items to a library, see "Editing Libraries" later in this chapter. The library is saved and, if saved in the ClarisWorks Libraries folder, its name is automatically added to the Library submenu of the File menu.

Remember that if a library is saved in a folder other than the ClarisWorks Libraries folder or on a different disk, its name is *not* added to the Library submenu. To later open such a library, you must choose the Open command from the Library submenu of the File menu, and then locate the library file in the file dialog box that appears.

Inserting Library Objects into Documents

There are two ways to insert a library object into the current document:

↪ Drag the object or its name from the library palette into the document, and then release the mouse button.

↪ Select the object or its name in the library palette, and then click Use.

Depending on the type of document or frame into which the object is being inserted, it will either appear as a floating or an in-line object (see "Adding Graphics to Word Processing Documents" in Chapter 3):

- ✐ *Draw documents:* All objects are inserted as floating objects. You can specify the approximate spot where the object is placed by clicking it with the pointer tool before you click Use.

- ✐ *Paint documents or frames*: Library objects — regardless of whether they are graphics or text — are inserted as bitmapped graphics. They are surrounded by a selection rectangle enabling you to move or delete the graphic.

- ✐ *Word processing documents or frames*: If a text-insertion point is currently set in the document or frame and you click Use, a graphic object is added at the insertion point as an in-line object. If the insertion point is not currently set and you click Use, a graphic object is added as a floating object. You can also insert *text* library items into word processing documents by dragging them over or clicking Use, as described later in this chapter in "Text as Library Items."

- ✐ *Databases*: Library objects can only be inserted when you are in Layout mode. All objects are placed as floating objects.

- ✐ *Spreadsheet documents or frames*: All graphics and text strings are added as objects that float on the spreadsheet. Worksheet cell data stored in a library, on the other hand, is inserted as normal data beginning at the selected cell.

- ✐ *Communications documents*: No library objects can be inserted into communications documents. To emphasize this fact, when a communications document is active, the Library submenu is grayed out and all open libraries are temporarily hidden.

If ClarisWorks beeps when you click the Use button, it means that you must manually drag the object into the document. When insertions from libraries are not allowed (such as when you are working in a database in Browse mode), ClarisWorks grays out the library palette's buttons.

As you're dragging an object onto a document, you may notice that it's either the wrong object or the wrong document. To cancel a drag-in-progress, move the hand cursor back over the original library palette and release the mouse button.

Editing Libraries

The contents of any library can be altered in several ways. You can:

- Add items to a library
- Remove items from a library
- Reorganize the contents of a library

Adding Items to Libraries

The way in which an item is added to libraries depends on whether the item is currently selected in a ClarisWorks document or it has been copied (using the Copy command) from another program.

Steps:	Adding a ClarisWorks Object or Selection to a Library
Step 1.	Open the library to which you want to add the item.
Step 2.	In the ClarisWorks document or frame, select the object, text, spreadsheet cells, or database data of interest.
Step 3.	Click the library's Add button. The object or text is added as a new item named Object *x*, where *x* is the number of the next object in the library.

Steps:	Adding an Object or Selection from Another Program to a ClarisWorks Library
Step 1.	In the other program, select the object or text of interest, and choose the Copy command (⌘-C) from the Edit menu. A copy of the object or text is transferred to the Mac's Clipboard.
Step 2.	Launch ClarisWorks 4.0 (if it isn't already running), open an existing document or create a new one, and then choose the appropriate library from the Library submenu of the File menu.

Unless at least one ClarisWorks document is open, the Library command cannot be selected. Since libraries are not linked to particular documents, however, it doesn't matter *which* ClarisWorks document is open; any one will do.

| Step 3. | Choose Paste from the library's Edit menu. The object or text is added as a new item named Object x, where x is the number of the next object in the library. |

Text that is copied from another program and then added to a ClarisWorks library does not retain its fonts, styles, size, or formatting. It is stored as plain text. When you later insert that text into a ClarisWorks document, it is formatted using the document's default font and style. If you want the text to be stored in the library with the *original* formatting, you should paste it into a ClarisWorks document, format it as desired, select it, and *then* click the Library's Add button.

There's a simple procedure for copying an object in one library and inserting it into another library. For the sake of convenience, you might want your company logo to appear in several libraries, for example. Just select the object in any open library and then drag it into the palette of any other open library. Note that the object's original name is also transferred to the receiving library.

Adding Other Kinds of Items to Libraries

Since the supplied ClarisWorks libraries contain only clip art, many users will assume that this all that a library can hold. As the previous discussion attests, however, this is an incorrect assumption. Libraries can also store text, spreadsheet cells, and database records. However, there are some special considerations when adding and using such material as library items.

Spreadsheet Cells as Library Items

You may find it helpful to store complex spreadsheet formulas in a library so they can be easily reused. When selecting a formula to add to a library, you must be sure to select all cells that are referenced by the formula. Otherwise, when you drag the formula into another worksheet, the references will be incorrect. For example, a formula in C1 that reads =A1+B1 will only be stored correctly if you select all three cells (A1, B1, and C1) before clicking the library's Add button.

You should also note that libraries can only store a limited amount of spreadsheet data. If the selected cells contain more than 50 rows or 10 columns (columns A through J, for example), additional rows or columns are truncated from the library copy, and the dialog box in Figure 20-4 appears.

Figure 20-4:
Click OK to truncate
the cells to fit or
Cancel to abort the
library addition.

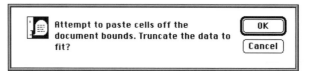

> Attempt to paste cells off the
> document bounds. Truncate the data to
> fit?
>
> OK
> Cancel

When dragged onto a worksheet, any library item that contains something other than worksheet cells (a graphic or text string, for instance) will simply float on the worksheet; it will not be entered into the selected cell or cells.

Database Records as Library Items

Database fields or records cannot be selected and then added to a library by clicking the Add button. Nor can you insert data into a database by dragging it from a library. (All library buttons are grayed out when you're working in a database in Browse mode).

To store a database record in a library, select the entire record, choose Copy from ClarisWorks' Edit menu (or press ⌘-C), and then choose the library's Paste command.

When you click Use or drag a database record object into a word processing document, it is inserted as tab-delimited text; that is, fields are separated by tab characters.

Text as Library Items

As mentioned earlier in this chapter, it's easy to add text to a library. If the text is in a ClarisWorks document, just select it and click the library's Add button. If the text is from a non-ClarisWorks document, select it, use the program's Copy command to copy it to the Clipboard, switch to ClarisWorks, and then choose the library's Paste command. (Remember, however, that non-ClarisWorks text does not retain its original fonts and formatting when pasted into a library.)

Inserting text from a library into word processing documents and frames is also simple. There are two ways to do this:

- ∞ Position the text insertion point at the spot in the word processing document where you want to add the text, select the text in the library palette, and click Use. The text is added at the insertion point.

- ∞ Drag the text into the word processing document. As you drag, a thick text-insertion bar moves to show where the insertion will appear. Release the mouse button to insert the text.

To insert library text into a draw document, paint document, or paint frame, you have to drag the text into position. (If you click the Use button, ClarisWorks just beeps.) Text inserted into a draw document is treated as an object (unless you drag the text into a word processing frame inside of the draw document). Text inserted into a paint document or frame becomes a bitmap graphic.

Saving an Edited Library

To save an existing library to which you've made changes, choose the Save command from the library's File menu. If you want to save the library using a new name or in a new location, on the other hand, choose the Save As command from the library's File menu.

Removing Items from Libraries

A library's Edit menu contains the following two commands for removing items from the library:

- ∞ *Delete*. To remove an item without transferring a copy of it to the Clipboard, select the item in the library palette and choose Delete from the library's Edit menu.

- ∞ *Cut*. To remove an item and simultaneously transfer a copy of it to the Clipboard, select the item in the library palette and choose Cut from the library's Edit menu.

The Cut command is useful for removing an item that you also intend to paste somewhere else — into a ClarisWorks document, another library, or a document in another program. Much of the time, however, all you really care about is that the item is removed from the library. In those cases, use either command.

Renaming Library Items

When you add a new item to a library, ClarisWorks assigns a generic name to the item in the form Object x. Since Object 12 isn't a very descriptive name — it's like naming a document Untitled 7 — you can use the Library palette's Rename button to assign a better name.

Steps:	**Renaming a Library Object**
Step 1.	In the library palette, select the object or its name (depending on the View options that are currently set for the palette).

Step 2.   If the bottom portion of the palette is not exposed, click the tiny triangle next to the Use button.

Step 3.   Delete the text in the Name box, type a new name, and click Rename. The new name appears in the palette's list of objects.

Reorganizing a Library

By default, library items are listed in the order in which they were added to the library. Renaming items does not change that order. If you prefer that items be listed alphabetically by their names, choose Alphabetize from the library's View menu. If you later add new objects to the library and still want the list to be alphabetical, you must choose Alphabetize again.

Setting Palette Viewing Preferences_____

Viewing preferences must be individually set for each library palette. There is no preferences command that you can use to simultaneously affect the display of *all* library palettes. Viewing preferences enable you to do the following:

∽ Show or hide the bottom part of the palette

∽ Display all objects simultaneously or one at a time

∽ Determine the number of rows, columns, and size of thumbnails in the palette

The first decision you have to make is whether to display a palette of thumbnail icons (similar to the way the Shortcuts palette is usually shown) or to list the objects by name and display only one thumbnail at a time. To show a palette of thumbnails, choose by Object from the library's View menu. To show a list of names, choose by Name from the library's View menu. Figure 20-5 shows examples of both viewing settings.

The objects or names in a library can be listed in the order in which they were added to the palette or they can be sorted alphabetically. To sort the objects, choose Alphabetize from the library's View menu.

You can also change the number of rows and columns in a palette, and the size of the thumbnails. Choose View Options from the library's View menu. In the View Options dialog box that appears (see Figure 20-6), you can make whatever changes you like.

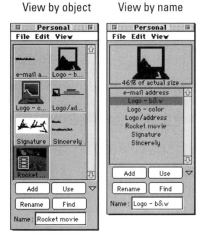

Figure 20-5:
A library palette set for
viewing by Object (left)
and by Name (right)

View by object   View by name

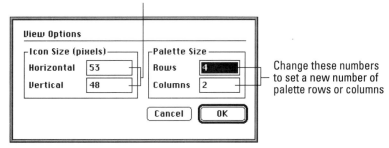

Change these numbers to change
the size of the object thumbnails

Figure 20-6:
The View Options
dialog box

Change these numbers
to set a new number of
palette rows or columns

If you select a large icon size or if you substantially increase the number of rows and columns in the palette, you may be prohibited from making the changes. ClarisWorks checks the size of the monitor on which you are working; it will not permit you to create a library palette that won't fit on-screen.

Viewing preferences are saved separately with each library. To record your new viewing preferences, you must choose the library's Save command.

Other Library Commands _____

Libraries have two other commands that you'll probably never use. You can make an exact copy of an object and add it to the current palette (select an object and choose Duplicate from the Edit menu), and you can search for objects within a library (type any part of an object name in the library's Name text-edit box and click Find).

I can't think of a good reason to duplicate an object in a library — unless you want to have the multiple copies of an object with different names. The Find command is useful only with a library that contains *many* images and when you can remember part of the object's name. (Any part will do.)

You should note, however, that since searching always begins at the top of the library, Find will locate only the *first* matching object name in the library. Thus, if a library has three objects with Office in their names, only the first one will be found — regardless of how many times you click Find.

Summary

- ClarisWorks 4.0 includes an assortment of clip art stored in 20 libraries. You also can create your own libraries.

- Before you can work with a library, you must have at least one open ClarisWorks document.

- To save changes made to a library — including newly added objects, renamed objects, deletions, and viewing preferences — you must save the library.

- Libraries that you save in the ClarisWorks Libraries folder (the default location) are automatically listed in the Library submenu of the File menu.

- To store a ClarisWorks object, text string, or set of spreadsheet cells in a library, select the object, text, or cells in the ClarisWorks document and click the library's Add button. To store non-ClarisWorks items in a library, copy them and then choose the library's Paste command.

- To insert an item stored in a library into the current document, click Use or drag the item onto the document.

- You can customize the appearance of and object presentation order for each library.

Creating Web Pages for the Internet

■ ■

In This Chapter

➥ What is the World Wide Web?

➥ What is HTML?

➥ Using the HTML stationery document to create Web pages

➥ Applying HTML styles to text and using the HTML shortcuts buttons

➥ Viewing and editing existing HTML documents

■ ■

Overview _____

The World Wide Web — a network of computers providing information and resources on the Internet — grew out of a hypertext project started at CERN, the European Laboratory for Particle Physics. As a resource for finding information and services ranging from ancient Mayan archeological digs to pizza deliveries, the World Wide Web (WWW) — or Web, for short — has become a centerpiece of the information superhighway. To access information on the Web, you use a hypertext-based browser application that leads you to the desired documents and then displays that information on your computer screen.

At the heart of the Web is a platform-independent page description language called *Hypertext Markup Language* (HTML). Based on the *Standard Generalized Markup Language* (SGML), HTML is used to prepare documents (referred to as *Web pages*) for the Web that contain embedded control codes. Different codes (commonly referred to as *tags*) are used to designate titles, headings, text formatting, and hypertext links. Figure 21-1 shows a typical ClarisWeb page.

Figure 21-1:
This HTML code
produces the
visible portion of
this cool
ClarisWeb page.

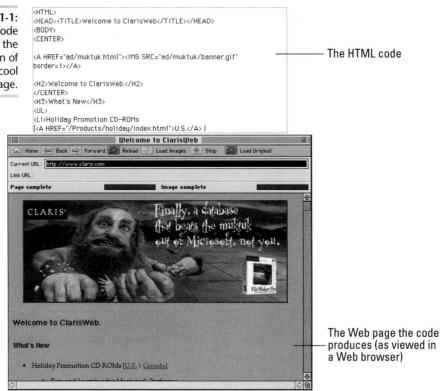

The HTML code

The Web page the code
produces (as viewed in
a Web browser)

To access the WWW and display Web pages on your computer, you must have access
to the Internet — either through an information service (such as CompuServe, Prodigy,
or America Online) or from a local Internet provider. You must also have an application
called a *Web browser*, such as Netscape Navigator or Air Mosaic. A Web browser
translates the HTML into formatted text and graphics.

If you're not content to just look at other people's Web pages and you want to create
your own Web documents, you'll need a small arsenal of software tools:

    ⇒ A word processor, text editor, or HTML editor in which you can create and edit
      your Web pages

With ClarisWorks 4.0's new HTML translator, stationery document, and shortcut
buttons, you can design basic Web pages in the word processor.

    ⇒ A browser in which to view the Web pages

Although the HTML translator shields you from working directly with HTML tags (you merely apply HTML styles to selected text by choosing the styles from the stylesheet), ClarisWorks' ability to display pages is quite limited. Graphics, for example, are shown only as hypertext links; that is, you'll see a text string like <IMG SRC="Happy_face.gif"> instead of the actual picture.

Also, the pages may resemble a browser, but only a real browser can let you test the hypertext links. (When you click on a link in a browser, the document or graphic specified in the link is loaded by the browser and then displayed.) As a result of these shortcomings, you'll be much happier if you use ClarisWorks to create the pages, but use a real browser to view them.

☞ A graphics program that supports GIF (Graphics Interchange Format) or a utility program that can convert various graphic formats to GIF files.

GIF images are the only type of viewable graphics that can be embedded in Web pages. Unfortunately, ClarisWorks doesn't support GIF. If you want to include graphics on your pages, you'll have to get a program in which to convert ClarisWorks PICT graphics into GIFs. (Shareware conversion applications such as GifConverter are widely available from on-line services and popular Macintosh FTP archives on the Internet. If you have Adobe Photoshop, you can simply use its Save As command to translate each PICT graphic into a GIF file.)

In case you didn't notice, the ClarisWorks 4.0 folder contains an important word processing document called HTML Primer. If you haven't already done so, read and print the document. It explains several additional procedures that are not discussed in this chapter, such as adding the HTML shortcuts to the Shortcuts palette for all word processing documents.

Browsing the World Wide Web

With all the current talk about the Web, you may be wondering how you can get in on the action. First, you'll need access to the Internet, either through one of the popular information services or from an Internet provider in your area. While the information services are easier to access and set up, we recommend that you choose a local provider.

The reason is money.

On the major information services, you typically get only a few hours of on-line time included in the base rate. Charges are levied for any additional on-line time that you use. Local Internet providers, on the other hand, usually charge a flat fee for a very high number of hours (150 or more hours is common). With virtually

(continued)

unlimited on-line time, you can spend all the time necessary to upload your Web pages and make sure that they look right and work correctly.

Another drawback to using an information service as an Internet gateway is that most of them require you to use *their* Web browser. Unfortunately, many browsers — including those provided by CompuServe and America Online — do not understand all of the HTML codes that might be in a Web page file. So some layouts may not look quite right, and some graphical elements (such as backgrounds) may not display at all.

Note, too, that — at this writing — information services do not provide users with space on their servers to maintain personal Web pages. If you're interested in designing Web pages for yourself or your company, you'll need an account with a local provider. (America Online has announced their intention to support personal Web pages, though, so stay tuned.)

On the other hand, using a local provider isn't always trouble-free. The provider may not include all the software you need to access all of the different Internet services, or at least not the specific programs that you want.

For example, Netscape Navigator is quickly becoming the industry standard browser. In addition to providing access to most HTML options, it's easy to use. And its ability to display and reload HTML files offline makes designing Web pages easy. (You can test your Web page creations on your own computer — even if you have no Internet access at all.) Note, however, that if you already have another browser — including one provided by an information service — chances are excellent that it can also be used to view Web pages offline.

Netscape Navigator can be downloaded from the Netscape home page at http://www.netscape.com or from the company's *file transfer protocol* (FTP) site at ftp.netscape.com. If you don't have Internet access yet, you can simply call Netscape at 415-528-2800.

What Is HTML?

If you can remember the early days of personal computing (way back in the late 1970s) and the first word processing programs, you're already familiar with the way HTML works. Back then, if you wanted to print some selected text in bold or italic, you had to embed control codes in the document — one to turn on boldface (at the beginning of the text string) and a second code to turn off boldface (at the end of the text string).

HTML works in much the same way. Most tags work in pairs; the first tag turns on the feature and a second copy of the tag that is preceded by a slash (/) turns off the feature. For instance, to mark a level one head, the text would be surrounded by a pair of tags like this:

```
<H1>HTML for Fun and Profit</H1>
```

When a browser sees this tagged text, it interprets the tags and then formats the text according to the conventions set for the browser — typically, a level one head will be displayed in a large bold font.

There is little standardization among Web browsers. Unlike PostScript (a device-independent printing language that provides the same results on a wide variety of printers), the way that HTML text is displayed is completely determined by the conventions set in the user's browser application. Thus, while a particular head may appear as 20-point Times in one browser, it may appear in a small font in all capital letters when viewed with a different browser.

Using the ClarisWorks HTML Translator and Stationery Document

When creating and editing HTML documents using the stationery file that Claris created for this purpose, ClarisWorks simultaneously functions as a word processor (or text editor) and a crude browser. Instead of manually typing tags to indicate headers, for example, you can select HTML styles from a special HTML stylesheet. You can click shortcut buttons to add other features, such as horizontal rules and hypertext links to other Web documents.

Instead of displaying the tags as part of the text (as is done by most text editors, word processors, and HTML editors), ClarisWorks presents the document as a rough approximation of what it might look like in a browser. As a result, you don't see the tags at all — unless you later open the document as a normal ClarisWorks or Text file rather than as an HTML file. Figure 21-2 shows the way ClarisWorks 4.0 displays an HTML file and how it would look if you were entering and editing the tags directly.

File opened as text   File opened as HTML

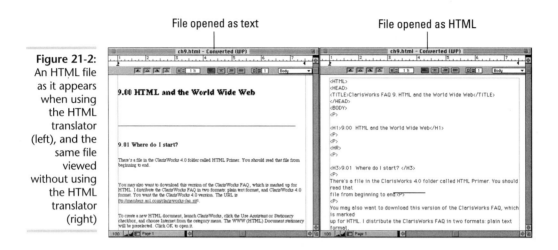

Figure 21-2:
An HTML file
as it appears
when using
the HTML
translator
(left), and the
same file
viewed
without using
the HTML
translator
(right)

Prerequisites and Caveats

The following information should be considered when deciding whether to use ClarisWorks to create HTML documents:

- ∞ You should know how to use the ClarisWorks word processing environment, as well as the Shortcuts and Stylesheet palettes. For more information on these topics, refer to Chapters 3, 12, and 15.

- ∞ You should have Internet access (through an information service or Internet provider) and a Web browser, as discussed previously in this chapter. Although you can create and view your Web pages exclusively in ClarisWorks, the point of creating HTML documents is to prepare pages that will be displayed on the World Wide Web.

- ∞ You should have a basic understanding of HTML. It is beyond the scope of this book to explain anything more than the fundamentals of HTML coding.

  In addition, there is the matter of HTML *style* to consider. The correct use of HTML only assures that your document will display properly — not that it will be attractive or make efficient use of space, for example. If you are new to HTML (as most people are), see the Quick Tips at the end of this chapter for several useful references concerning HTML definitions, coding practices, and style.

- ∞ You should understand that ClarisWorks' HTML support is very basic. Although you can certainly use ClarisWorks to create attractive text-based Web pages (complete with hypertext links to other pages), you cannot use it to design the eye-popping pages that you've seen in magazines or on corporate Web sites —

unless you're willing to work in text mode and enter the necessary tags by hand. A better approach is to use one of the many freeware, shareware, or commercial Web editors. HTML Web Weaver is a popular choice among Macintosh users.

Creating HTML Documents

The simplest way to create HTML documents in ClarisWorks 4.0 is to use the HTML stationery file. When you create your HTML document using the stationery file, you have instant access to a set of predefined HTML styles in the stylesheet, as well as three HTML-related buttons that have been added to the Shortcuts palette.

Steps: **Opening the HTML Stationery Document**

Step 1. In ClarisWorks, choose New from the File menu (or press ⌘-N). The New Document dialog box appears.

Step 2. Click the Use Assistant or Stationery check box, choose Internet from the pop-up menu, select WWW [HTML] Document (as shown in Figure 21-3), and then click OK.

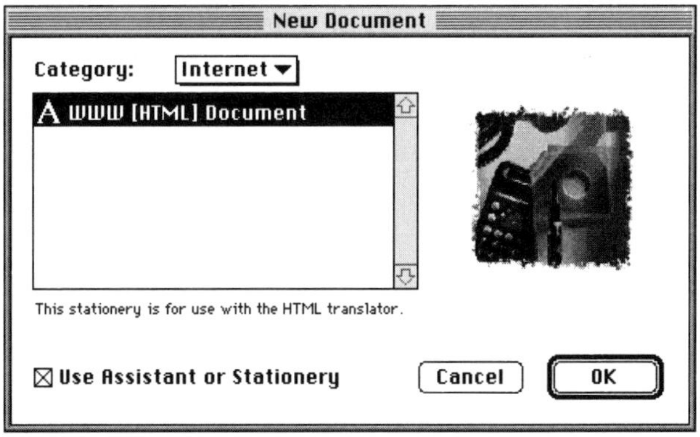

```
┌─────────────────── New Document ───────────────────┐
│                                                     │
│   Category:  │ Internet ▼ │                         │
│   ┌─────────────────────────────────┐  ┌─────────┐  │
│   │ A WWW [HTML] Document        ⇧ │  │         │  │
│   │                                 │  │         │  │
│   │                                 │  │         │  │
│   │                                 │  │         │  │
│   │                                 │  │         │  │
│   │                              ⇩ │  └─────────┘  │
│   └─────────────────────────────────┘               │
│   This stationery is for use with the HTML translator. │
│                                                     │
│   ⊠ Use Assistant or Stationery   ( Cancel )  ( OK )│
└─────────────────────────────────────────────────────┘
```

Figure 21-3: Selecting the WWW [HTML] stationery file

A blank stationery document appears.

Step 3. To open the Stylesheet palette (if it isn't already visible), choose Show Styles from the View menu. (The stylesheet includes styles for headers of various sizes, as well as for normal, literal, and preformatted text.)

Step 4. To display the Shortcuts palette (if it isn't already visible), choose Show Shortcuts from the Shortcuts submenu of the File menu. The modified Shortcuts palette appears on the stylesheet, as shown in Figure 21-4.

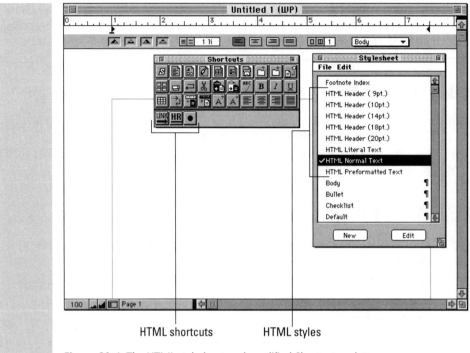

Figure 21-4: The HTML stylesheet and modified Shortcuts palette

Now that you have a copy of the stationery document on-screen and have displayed both the stylesheet and the Shortcuts palette, you're ready to begin entering the text for your Web page.

As you type, you can press Return to end a paragraph or Shift-Return to create a line break. Most browsers display paragraphs by adding white space after each one. A break, on the other hand, merely starts a new line without adding white space after it. You can also make text boldface or italic by selecting it and then choosing the appropriate option from the Style menu.

The following are some simple procedures and rules for working with HTML in ClarisWorks.

Using the Stylesheet to Apply Tags

As previously illustrated in Figure 21-4, the stylesheet contains eight HTML tags that can be applied to selected text (each style name is preceded by HTML), including the following headers (five levels), literal text, normal text, and preformatted text:

- *HTML Header (9pt.) - HTML Header (20pt.).* As when writing an outline or a report, you organize material in your Web pages via headings. The larger the heading, the more important the material. Thus, the HTML Header (20pt.) style is used to indicate a level 1 heading (a main point), and HTML Header (9pt.) is the equivalent of a level 5 heading.

When using the Header tags in a page, it is considered good style to use them in order — as you would in an outline. Don't start with a level 2 heading because you prefer the way it looks on-screen, for example.

- *HTML Normal Text.* Use this style to format normal paragraphs.

- *HTML Preformatted Text.* Use this style to format text that you want to appear exactly as typed (or you can simply apply the Monaco font to the text). Browsers display preformatted text in a monospaced font.

  When browsers see additional spaces between words in normal text, they routinely strip out the extra spaces. Spaces added to preformatted text, on the other hand, *are* displayed.

- *HTML Literal Text.* To use HTML tags other than the ones supported by ClarisWorks, apply this style to the selected text. Alternatively, you can just format the text using a shade of red (choose Text Color from the Style menu).

Unless you're typing tags by hand (that is, you're creating your HTML file in a normal ClarisWorks word processing document as an ordinary text file and are ignoring the stylesheet), it's unlikely that you'll ever use the HTML Literal Text style. If you routinely need to use tags that are not supported by the ClarisWorks HTML translator, you'll probably be better off using a different application to create your Web pages — such as a dedicated HTML editor.

To apply any HTML style to text, select the text to which the style should be applied and then click the desired HTML style in the stylesheet.

Using the HTML Shortcuts Buttons

As shown previously in Figure 21-4, three new shortcuts are added to the Shortcuts palette when you use the HTML [WWW] Document stationery file. They are used to insert horizontal rules, create hypertext links, and format unordered (bullet-point) lists.

 Horizontal rule. Horizontal rules can be used to indicate breaks between material or new sections of the document. Move to a new document line, and click the Horizontal Rule shortcut to add a line that extends across the page. The ClarisWorks stationery document displays the rule as a 1-point line. Advanced browsers often display a horizontal rule as an attractive three-dimensional line.

 Hypertext link. A hypertext link is a text string that — when clicked — typically displays another Web document or scrolls to a different spot in the current document. (Although ClarisWorks displays links, they are not clickable. You must run a real browser in order to test your links.)

To insert a link, select the text that you want to use to indicate the link (such as, "Go to IDG Books Home Page"), and click the Hypertext Link shortcut button. As shown in Figure 21-5, ClarisWorks indicates a link by formatting the text as blue and underlined, and then adds a footnote number to it. At the bottom of the current page, a footnote appears in the form:

[1]INSERT URL HERE

A hypertext link as it appears in text   Type the link information here

Figure 21-5:
This split
screen shows
what a link
looks like in
text and as a
footnote.

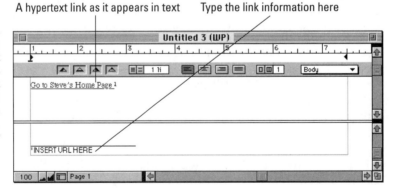

To make the link work in a browser, you must replace the footnote text with the address of the URL (Uniform Resource Locator) where the linked document can be found. A URL has the general form:

```
scheme: //host.domain [:port]/path/filename
```

Some examples of URLs are http://www.blue.aol.com (this URL points to America Online's home page on the Word Wide Web) and http://kuhttp.cc.ukans.edu/lynx_help/ HTML_quick.html (this URL points to a particular document on the Web named HTML_quick.html). Refer to the reference material listed in the Quick Tips at the end of this chapter for more information about specifying URLs.

 Unordered list item. Lists are often used to present a series of related items. Like lists in an outline, you can create a hierarchy of list items by preceding the items with different numbers of tabs. Standard HTML supports both *ordered* (numbered) and *unordered* (bullet-point) lists. The two types of lists can be nested, if you like; that is, an ordered list can contain an unordered list as a subset, for example.

To create an unordered List Item, click the Unordered list item shortcut button. A bullet-point appears, followed by a single space. Continue by typing the item, and then press Return to mark the end of the current list item. Alternatively, you can manually type an unordered list item by starting it with Option-8 (the bullet character), typing a space, and then following it with the list item.

You have to create *ordered* lists manually. Each item in an ordered list must begin with a number that is immediately followed by a period, a right parenthesis, or a hyphen; for example 1., 1), or 1.

Saving an HTML Document

You must use the Save As command in combination with the HTML translator to save an HTML file.

Steps:	Saving Documents as HTML Files
Step 1.	Choose Save As from the File menu.
Step 2.	In the Save As pop-up menu, select WWW [HTML] as the format in which to save the file.
Step 3.	Navigate to the drive and folder in which you want to save the file, type a filename (such as **Steve.html**), and click Save.

Opening an Existing HTML Document

If you want to edit an existing HTML document (whether it's one you created with the WWW [HTML] Document stationery or one that you pulled off the Web), you may run into a few problems:

⊸ Even if you created the original document using the HTML stationery file, saving it in HTML format changes the document to a foreign format. This effectively breaks the link between the document and the HTML stylesheet and modified Shortcuts palette. This is unavoidable.

⊸ HTML documents that you pull off the Web may be littered with HTML tags that are not supported by the ClarisWorks translator. They will appear in the file as embedded tags and formatting codes.

ClarisWorks supports only the tags commonly used by Mosaic, a browser created by the National Center for Supercomputing Applications (NCSA). Since Netscape is now the more popular browser, and it has greatly extended HTML by adding new tags of its own, you may find that some imported HTML documents look nothing at all like the ones you've created in ClarisWorks. In fact, when opened, they may be nothing but page after page of HTML codes.

Steps:	**Opening an HTML File in ClarisWorks**

Step 1. In ClarisWorks 4.0, choose Open from the File menu, and then navigate to the drive and folder that contains the HTML document you want to open.

Step 2. In the Document Type pop-up menu, select Word Processing. In the File Type pop-up menu, select WWW [HTML].

On the other hand, if you'd like to see what the embedded HTML tags in your text look like, select All Available or Text in the File Type pop-up menu. Refer to Figure 21-2 for examples of the two file types.

Step 3. Select the file you want to open, and click Open. The HTML document opens. You see it as it might look when viewed by an HTML browser.

Step 4. *Optional:* If you want to be able to use the optional ClarisWorks HTML styles, import the styles into your document by doing the following:

- If the stylesheet isn't visible, choose Show Styles from the View menu.

- Choose Import Styles from the Stylesheet palette's File menu.

- Select HTML Styles from the ClarisWorks Styles folder, and click Open. The Select styles to import dialog box appears.

- Click OK to import the standard, preselected HTML styles.

Summary of File Procedures

Even if you have some HTML experience or have already read the suggested reading material at the end of this chapter, if you keep the following points and procedures in mind, you'll have a much easier time using ClarisWorks to create and edit Web pages.

Creating a new HTML document: Choose New from the File menu, click Use Assistant or Stationery, choose WWW [HTML] Document, and then click OK. Choose Show Styles from the View menu, and choose Show Shortcuts from the Shortcuts submenu of the File menu.

Saving an HTML document: To maintain its identity as an HTML document, you cannot use the normal Save command to save the file. Instead, choose Save As, select WWW [HTML] from the Save As pop-up menu, and then click Save.

Opening an HTML file: To make ClarisWorks treat the HTML file correctly, you cannot simply Open the file. In the Open dialog box, you must choose Word Processing as the Document Type and WWW [HTML] as the File Type. (The only reason to use the normal Open procedure is if you want to view the actual tags in the file rather than the formatted text.) To use the HTML stylesheet with this document, open the stylesheet (if it isn't already on-screen) and import the HTML Styles file.

Quick Tips

The following Quick Tips offer methods for gaining a better understanding of HTML, as well as ways to work more productively and efficiently with it.

Learn from Others

Perhaps the fastest way to learn about HTML conventions and how to create pages with class is by examining other people's Web pages. Most browsers have a Save, Save Page, or Save Source command that enables you to save the HTML code of any page that you're currently viewing with the browser. Grab some good examples in this manner and later check out the tags they used by opening the document in ClarisWorks as a Text file.

Use a *Real* Browser

Although the ClarisWorks translator can show you an approximation of what your HTML document will look like in a Web browser, the only way to see what it will really look like — particularly if you have added pictures to the file — is to get a *real* Web browser, such as Netscape or the others mentioned in this chapter.

Load your HTML file by choosing the browser's Open, Open File, or Open Local command. When you make changes to the HTML document in ClarisWorks, you can save the document again as an HTML file and then reload it in the browser to see the effects of your edits.

More Powerful HTML Editors

If you want to move beyond the tags supported by the ClarisWorks HTML translator, you may want to check out one of the many freeware and shareware HTML editors. For example, HTML Web Weaver allows you to insert a wide variety of tags simply by choosing them from menus.

Help with HTML

If your appetite for HTML has been whetted, there are several excellent sources of in-depth HTML information — in print and on the Web itself. One of my favorite HTML books is *Teach Yourself Web Publishing with HTML in a Week* by Laura Lemay (SAMS Publishing). Two IDG books also explain how to work with HTML:

- *Macworld Creating Cool Web Pages*
- *HTML for Dummies*

In addition, some useful documents that you can find on the Web include:

- ∞ A Beginner's Guide to HTML (http://www.ncsa.uiuc.edu/General/Internet/WWW/HTMLPrimer.html)

- ∞ HTML Quick Reference (http://kuhttp.cc.ukans.edu/lynx_help/HTML_quick.html)

- ∞ Composing Good HTML (http://www.willamette.edu/html-composition/strict-html.html)

 Unlike books, the contents of Web sites change constantly. Occasionally, the particular site that contains an item of interest — like these HTML documents — also changes. (Don't blame me if they've moved.)

Summary

- ➥ ClarisWorks 4.0 provides a translator that enables you to create, edit, and save documents in HTML format — the language that is used to display pages on the World Wide Web.

- ➥ ClarisWorks also provides a special HTML stationery document that you can use as a starting point for your own HTML creations. Attached to the stationery document is a modified stylesheet that contains a set of basic HTML styles, as well as three new HTML-related shortcuts buttons.

Appendixes

Installing ClarisWorks 4.0

To install ClarisWorks 4.0, you just run the ClarisWorks installation program, select options, and watch as the appropriate files are copied to your hard disk. When the process concludes, ClarisWorks is ready to run. This appendix walks you through the installation process.

If you're upgrading from a previous version of ClarisWorks, be sure to read "Updating from a Previous Version of ClarisWorks" at the end of this appendix after you've finished installing the program.

The Installation Process

To install ClarisWorks 4.0, you need the following:

- ∞ A Macintosh with a 68020 processor or higher

  ClarisWorks 4.0 cannot run on a Macintosh 128K, 512K, Plus, SE, Classic, or PowerBook 100.

- ∞ Macintosh system software version 7.0 or later.

  You can determine the version of system software that you have by choosing About This Macintosh or About the Finder from the Apple menu. If you are still running system software version 6.x, you must upgrade to System 7 or use one of the previous versions of ClarisWorks.

- ∞ At least 4MB of memory

  If you intend to use the optional PowerTalk electronic mail feature, you need at least 5MB of memory and you must be running System 7 Pro, System 7.5, or a later version of the system software.

- ∞ An internal or external hard disk

To install ClarisWorks 4.0, you need to run a special installation program known generically as the Installer. (If you have installed any version of the system software in the past few years, you are already familiar with the Installer.) Using the Installer — rather than installing by hand — ensures that ClarisWorks and its support files are correctly installed, uncompressed, and ready to run.

Steps:	Beginning the Installation Process
Step 1.	Lock each of the ClarisWorks master disks to protect them from inadvertent changes. (To lock a floppy disk, slide the tab in the upper-right corner of the disk so that the tiny window is open.)
Step 2.	Insert Disk 1 and double-click its icon (if the disk window is not already open).
Step 3.	If Disk 1 contains a SimpleText Read Me file, double-click the file's icon to view late-breaking news about the program and installation process, as well as a summary of the new features introduced in ClarisWorks 4.0.
Step 4.	After reading and, optionally, printing the Read Me document, choose Quit from the File menu. You return to the desktop.
Step 5.	Restart your computer with the Shift key held down to turn off your extensions.

Before you run the Install ClarisWorks 4.0 program, you need to decide two things:

⌗ Whether you want to perform an easy or custom installation

⌗ The hard disk on which you want to install the software

The Easy Install option copies the program and all support files to the hard disk of your choice. The Custom Install option copies only the program components that you select. Most users should choose Easy Install and install ClarisWorks to their start-up hard disk — the one that contains the System Folder.

Performing an Easy Install

The following steps explain how to use Easy Install. If you think that you want to perform a Custom Install, read "Performing a Custom Install," later in this appendix, before proceeding with the installation.

Steps:	Installing ClarisWorks with Easy Install
Step 1.	Double-click the icon named Install ClarisWorks, as shown in Figure A-1. (This is the Installer program.) Figure A-2 shows the opening screen that appears.

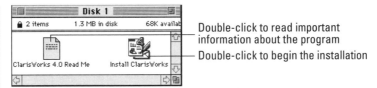

Double-click to read important information about the program
Double-click to begin the installation

Figure A-1: The Installer program icon and Read Me document icon

Click to continue

Figure A-2: The ClarisWorks Installer opening screen

Step 2.   To continue, click OK (or press Return or Enter).

Step 3.   The default procedure for the Installer is to perform an Easy Install on the start-up hard disk. Be sure that the correct hard disk is selected and then click Install, as shown in Figure A-3.

Select an installation method here

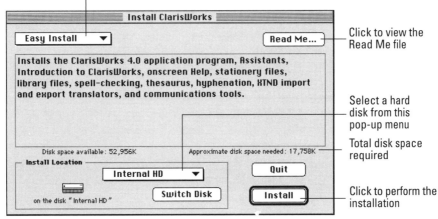

Click to view the Read Me file

Select a hard disk from this pop-up menu

Total disk space required

Click to perform the installation

Figure A-3: The main installation screen

Because you are installing ClarisWorks on the start-up hard disk, the Installer requires that any open programs, desk accessories, and control panels be shut down. If any of these items are detected, the screen shown in Figure A-4 appears.

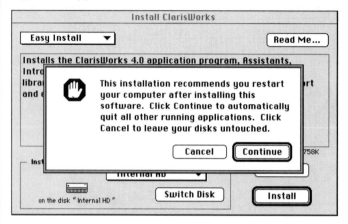

Figure A-4: This warning box is displayed if any programs, desk accessories, or control panels are open during installation.

If you want the Installer to quit any programs that are currently running, click Continue. If you have files that you want to save before continuing with the installation, click Cancel. The Installer quits, and you can save files as needed. After quitting the programs, begin again at Step 1.

Step 4. The Installer continues the installation, as shown in Figure A-5, and requests different disks as they are needed. After copying all files to the hard disk and decompressing them, the Installer asks you to restart the Macintosh. After the Mac restarts, ClarisWorks 4.0 is ready to run.

Figure A-5: The installation process

Updating from a Previous Version of ClarisWorks

ClarisWorks 1.0 through 3.0 stored many key components in the Claris folder within the System Folder of the start-up hard disk. In version 4.0, most of these important files and folders are stored in the ClarisWorks program folder. However, during the installation of ClarisWorks 4.0, the old files in the Claris folder are left untouched. If you no longer intend to use the earlier version of ClarisWorks, you can delete these old files and free some space on your hard disk.

Steps:	Deleting Old ClarisWorks Components

Step 1. Go to the desktop and open the Claris folder (found within the System Folder).

Step 2. You can delete the following folders and files:

- *ClarisWorks Assistants folder.* When you install ClarisWorks 4.0, a new copy of this folder is created for you in the ClarisWorks program folder.

- *ClarisWorks Stationery folder.* When you install ClarisWorks 4.0, a new copy of this folder is created for you in the ClarisWorks program folder. However, if you have personal stationery documents that you created in a previous version of ClarisWorks, you can use them in ClarisWorks 4.0 by dragging their icons into the new ClarisWorks Stationery folder (within the ClarisWorks program folder).

- *ClarisWorks Assistant Prefs file.* This file is not needed in ClarisWorks 4.0.

- *ClarisWorks Preferences file.* A new version of this file is created for you and stored in the Preferences folder within the System Folder.

- *ClarisWorks Shortcuts file.* A new version of this file is created for you and stored in the Preferences folder within the System Folder.

- *ClarisWorks xx Options file.* Recent versions of ClarisWorks enabled you to create default document files known as options stationery files with names like ClarisWorks WP Options and ClarisWorks SS Options. When you create a new word processing document, for example, the settings in the ClarisWorks WP Options file are used rather than the standard ClarisWorks settings for the environment. If you want to use these files to establish default settings for ClarisWorks 4.0 documents, drag their file icons into the ClarisWorks Stationery folder in your ClarisWorks program folder. (On the other hand, given the new capabilities of ClarisWorks 4.0, you may prefer to create *new* options stationery documents.)

Spreadsheet and Database Function Definitions

Appendix B is a complete reference to the spreadsheet and database functions of ClarisWorks 4.0. The functions are listed alphabetically. Each includes the format for the function (that is, how it is entered in a worksheet or database formula, along with the types of arguments that are required), a description of how the function works, and one or more examples for the spreadsheet and database environments.

Some functions are available in the spreadsheet environment only; they cannot be used in a database. They are listed with the following text: *This is a spreadsheet-only function.* Note also that some functions have optional arguments. Such arguments are surrounded by bracket symbols {}.

ABS (Absolute Value)

Format: ABS (number)

ABS is used to calculate the absolute value of a worksheet cell address, a number, or a database field, ignoring the result's sign. The result is either a positive number or zero. ABS is used when you are interested in the magnitude of a number or a difference, irrespective of the sign. Note that the absolute value of an empty cell or field returns a value of zero (0).

Spreadsheet examples: The formula =ABS (-17.35) returns 17.35; =ABS(18-A3) returns 5, where cell A3 evaluates as 23; =ABS(C7) returns 18.5, where cell C7 evaluates as either 18.5 or -18.5; =ABS(B4) returns 0, where cell B4 contains the number zero, evaluates as zero (as in the formula =5-5), or is blank.

Database examples: The formula ABS('GRADE 1'-'Grade 2') can be used to evaluate the difference between two Grade fields. The result, however, shows only the magnitude of the difference between the two grades (that is, it is a measure of change), not the direction of the change (whether the grade improved or became worse).

ACOS (Arc Cosine)

Format: ACOS (number)

ACOS calculates the arc cosine (inverse of a cosine), returning an angle in radians between 0 and π. Taking the cosine of the result produces the argument to the function.

The argument to ACOS must be a number between -1.0 and 1.0 or an operation that yields a value within that range. (**Note:** If a blank cell or blank field is used as an argument, ACOS treats the blank as though it contains a zero.)

Spreadsheet examples: =ACOS(3/4) returns 0.7227 radians; =ACOS(0) returns 1.5708; =ACOS(1) returns 0; =ACOS(-2/3) returns 2.3005 radians; =ACOS(-1) returns 3.14159 or π.

Database examples: ACOS('Field 1') returns the arc cosine of the field.

ALERT

Format: ALERT (value)

ALERT displays a dialog box with a text or numeric message of your choosing (value). You must click the OK button to dismiss the dialog box. If an alert is triggered, the contents of the ALERT message is entered into the current cell.

Because a text message is part of an ALERT, this function may be preferred to that of BEEP, which only plays the current system sound. *This is a spreadsheet-only function.*

Spreadsheet examples: =IF(C12<0,ALERT("Grade must be between 0 and 4!"),IF(C12>4,ALERT ("Grade must be between 0 and 4!"),"")) could be used to notify you that a grade entered was less than 0 or greater than 4.

AND

Format: AND (logical1, logical2, ...)

AND enables you to evaluate one or more arguments or conditions, and returns TRUE if all arguments or conditions are true; otherwise, it returns FALSE.

Spreadsheet examples: The formula =AND(A1>50000,B1<35) could be used to identify individuals with salaries of more than $50,000 who are less than 35 years old. =AND(D3) returns true if D3 contains any number other than zero.

Database examples: To determine if a customer is eligible for a special discount, you could use a formula like the following: AND('Product Total'>250,'MemberTime'>3). This equation yields a 1 (TRUE) only if the current order is for more than $250 of goods and the individual has been a member of the club or service for more than 3 years.

ASIN (Arc Sine)

Format: ASIN (number)

The ASIN function is used to calculate the inverse of a sine (the arc sine). The result is an angle in radians in the range $-\pi/2$ to $\pi/2$. The argument to ASIN must be a sine value (a number between -1.0 and 1.0) or a simple operation that yields a sine.

Spreadsheet examples: =ASIN(1) returns 1.570796; =ASIN(-1) returns -1.570796; =ASIN(0) returns 0; =ASIN(0.75) returns 0.848062.

ATAN (Arc Tangent)

Format: ATAN (number)

The ATAN function calculates the inverse of a tangent (the arc tangent). The result is an angle in radians in the range $-\pi/2$ to $\pi/2$.

Spreadsheet examples: The formula =ATAN(1) returns 0.7854.

ATAN2 (Arc Tangent 2)

Format: ATAN2 (x number, y number)

The ATAN2 function calculates the angle in radians between the positive X-axis and a line that starts at the origin (coordinates 0, 0) and passes through the specified X and Y coordinates. The result is an angle in radians, in the range $-\pi$ to π (or -3.14159 to 3.14159).

Spreadsheet examples: The formula =DEGREES(ATAN2(5,5)) returns 45, indicating that a straight diagonal line (passing through coordinate 0,0 and 5,5) is a 45-degree angle.

AVERAGE

Format: AVERAGE (number1, number2, ...)

AVERAGE calculates the arithmetic average of a set of numbers expressed as numbers, cell references, a range, or field names. The formula for an AVERAGE is the sum of the numbers divided by the number of numbers in the set.

Spreadsheet examples: =AVERAGE(7,12,5) returns 8 (that is, 24/3); =AVERAGE(A1...A5) returns 10, where cells A1, A2, A3, A4, and A5 contain 12, 4, 8, 16, and 10, respectively (that is, 50/5).

Database examples: You could use AVERAGE('SCORE 1','SCORE 2') to determine the average of the two scores for each record.

BASETONUM

Format: BASETONUM (text, base)

BASETONUM examines a text string and interprets it as a number in the specified base (between 1 and 36). The text string must be less than 256 characters long.

Spreadsheet examples: The formula =BASETONUM(10110,2) returns 22; that is, the base 2 number 10110 is 22.

BEEP

Format: BEEP ( )

BEEP plays the alert sound that is currently set in the Sound control panel. You can use BEEP to notify you of an unusual or important situation, such as a data entry error.

Spreadsheet examples: =IF(C12<0,BEEP( ),IF(C12>4,BEEP( ),"")) could be used to notify you of a numeric grade in cell C12 that was out of range; that is, less than 0 or greater than 4.

Database examples: IF('Due Date'< NOW( ),BEEP( ),"Due in "&'Due Date'- TRUNC(NOW( ))&" days.") could be used to let you know when a project is overdue. If the due date for a record has passed ('Due Date'< NOW( )), a beep is sounded. If the due date still lies ahead, on the other hand, a message is displayed in the field, as in: "Due in 10 days."

CHAR (Character)

Format: CHAR (number)

The CHAR function returns the ASCII (American Standard Code for Information Interchange) character that corresponds to the number in the specified cell or database field. If the number contains a fractional part, the fraction is discarded when the number is evaluated.

Note that ASCII codes can vary between 0 and 255. Numbers outside of that range return an error. Also, depending on the font selected, not all codes have an associated character, and codes less than 32 are control characters. In general, codes between 32 and 127 correspond to the normal typewriter letters, numbers, and symbols, while codes above 127 correspond to the foreign language characters and special symbols.

Spreadsheet examples: =CHAR(68) returns a D; =CHAR(154) returns an ö.

Database examples: CHAR('ITEMNO')

CHOOSE

Format: CHOOSE (index, value1, value2,...)

The CHOOSE function is used to select a value from an array of values. The value of the index argument (a number or numeric expression) determines which value in the array is chosen. The values in the array can contain text or numeric expressions.

Spreadsheet examples: The formula =CHOOSE(2,15,"Apple",7,"Medium",15) returns Apple; the formula =CHOOSE(4, B1, B2, B3, B4, B5) returns the contents of B4.

CODE (ASCII Code)

Format: CODE (text)

CODE returns the ASCII code (American Standard Code for Information Interchange) of the first character in the text string of a selected cell or field.

Spreadsheet examples: =CODE("a") returns 97; =CODE("Schwartz") returns 83, which corresponds to the code for a captal S; the formula =IF(OR(CODE(A1)<65, CODE(A1)>90),"Not a captal letter","Okay") could be used to check if a cell's text begins with a capital letter. Any character outside of the range A-Z results in the message: *Not a capital letter.*

Database examples: A similar formula to the error-checking formula above can be used to check that each last name begins with a capital letter, as in: IF(OR(CODE('Last Name')<65,CODE('Last Name')>90),"Error in Last Name","OK")

COLUMN

Format: COLUMN ({cell})

Returns the number of the column referenced by *cell* or the column in which the current cell is contained. *This is a spreadsheet-only function.*

Spreadsheet examples: =COLUMN(C12) returns 3, since column C is the third column; =COLUMN() returns the column in which the formula is located.

 If you want to quickly number a group of columns beginning with column A, enter the formula =COLUMN() in column A, highlight that cell as well as the appropriate cells to the right, and then choose Fill Right from the Calculate menu (or press ⌘-R).

CONCAT (Concatenation)

Format: CONCAT (text1, text2,...)

CONCAT is used to join text strings, producing a single text string as a result.

Spreadsheet examples: =CONCAT(A1," ",B1) returns *Steve Schwartz* when A1 contains "Steve" and B1 contains "Schwartz". Note that text strings also can be concatenated with the & symbol, as in: =A1 & " " & B1.

Database examples: CONCAT can be used to create a new field that combines First Name and Last Name fields into a single Name field, as in: CONCAT('First Name'," ",'Last Name'). To generate a sentence in a merge form, you could use CONCAT in the following manner: CONCAT("Your commission is $",'Commission',".").

COS (Cosine)

Format: COS (number)

COS calculates the cosine of a number, where the number is an angle in radians.

Spreadsheet examples: =COS(1) returns 0.5403.

COUNT

Format: COUNT (value1, value2,...)

Count is used to display the number of values (numbers, text, cell or range references, or formulas) in a list. Empty worksheet cells or database fields are not counted.

Spreadsheet examples: The formula =COUNT(B1, B2*3, 5) returns 2 or 3, depending on whether cell B1 is blank. Note that even if B2 is blank, the formula B2*3 still adds one to the count.

One typical use of COUNT is to determine the number of non-empty cells in a range, such as =COUNT(C1..C10). To display the number of blank cells, the previous formula could be changed to read: =10-(COUNT(C1..C10)).

Database examples: Suppose you want to calculate an average of four numeric fields, but some of the fields may be empty. If you use the AVERAGE function, the results would be erroneous because AVERAGE treats the missing fields as though they each contain zero (0) and then divides by four. To calculate a true average, you can use the COUNT function, as follows:

```
('q1'+'q2'+'q3'+'q4')/
COUNT('q1','q2','q3','q4')
```

COUNT2

Format: COUNT2 (search value, value1, value2,…)

Use COUNT2 to show the number of values in a list that match the specified search value. The values can be numbers, text, cells, or fields.

Note that when COUNT2 is used in a database formula, a separate value is returned for each record. COUNT2 does not summarize a search across all records. Note, too, that COUNT2 does not count instances in which the search value is embedded in a text string or sentence. For example, in a database, COUNT2("Macintosh",'Comments') only counts instances in which the Comments field contains only the word *Macintosh*.

Spreadsheet examples: The formula =COUNT2(4,3,7,4,-1) yields 1, since there is only a single instance of the search value (that is, 4) in the list. The formula =COUNT2(0,A1..A20) returns the number of cells in the range that contain 0. In an address book worksheet, the formula =COUNT2("CA",G2..G400) could be used to count the number of cells in the range for which CA was entered as the state (assuming that column G was used to enter state information).

Database examples: COUNT2(100,'Score1','Score2','Score3') counts the number of times 100 was achieved as a score in the three fields.

DATE

Format: DATE (year, month, day)

Use the DATE function to convert a date to a serial number that represents the number of days since January 1, 1904.

Spreadsheet examples: =DATE(1995,9,21) yields 33501. If you have spread the components of a date across cells A1 through C1 in month, day, year order, the formula =DATE(C1,A1,B1) could be used to combine them.

Database examples: If a date has been entered as three separate components, each in its own field, you could use the following formula to combine it into a single field: DATETOTEXT(DATE('Ship Year','Ship Month','Ship Day')). The DATE portion of the formula creates a serial number from the three date components; the DATETOTEXT function changes the serial number into a normal date, such as 9/21/95.

DATETOTEXT

Format: DATETOTEXT (serial number {, format number})

The DATETOTEXT function changes a serial number (the number of days that have passed since January 1, 1904) to a normal date in a particular format. Format options are as follows:

0 = 10/15/95 (the default format)

1 = Oct 15, 1995

2 = October 15, 1995

3 = Sun, Oct 15, 1995

4 = Sunday, October 15, 1995

Spreadsheet examples: =DATETOTEXT(33525,1) yields Oct 15, 1995; =DATETOTEXT(33525) yields 10/15/95, the default date format; =DATETOTEXT(A7,1) yields Nov 5, 1995 when cell A7 contains a date or serial number that represents 11/5/95.

The latter example illustrates a way to convert one date format to another — just change the format number in the formula. Of course, you could also use the spreadsheet's Format Number command to select a different date format.

DAY

Format: DAY (serial number)

For any serial number, DAY returns the day of the month.

Spreadsheet examples: =DAY(33525) yields 15, since the serial number 33525 represents October 15, 1995.

 You also can use the DAY function to extract the day number from a formatted date. The formula =DAY(A9) yields 7 when A9 contains a date, regardless of how it is formatted (e.g., 12/7/95 or Thu, Dec 7, 1995).

Database examples: DAY('DATE')

DAYNAME

Format: DAYNAME (number)

DAYNAME converts a number between 1 and 7 into the appropriate day name, as follows:

Number	Day Name
1	Sunday
2	Monday
3	Tuesday
4	Wednesday
5	Thursday
6	Friday
7	Saturday

Note that the argument to the DAYNAME function must always be, or evaluate to, a number between 1 and 7. Anything else, such as a complete date or a serial number, will result in an error.

Spreadsheet examples: =DAYNAME(5) yields Thursday.

 One use for the DAYNAME function is to create a set of worksheet headings that list the days of the week. To create them as column headings, enter the formula =DAYNAME(COLUMN( )) into column A, and then use the Fill Right command (⌘-R) to add the formula to the cells in columns B through G. To create day name row headings, enter the formula =DAYNAME(ROW( )) into row 1, and then use the Fill Down command (⌘-D) to add the formula to the cells in rows 2 through 7.

DAYOFYEAR

Format: DAYOFYEAR (serial number)

DAYOFYEAR extracts the day of the year from a serial number. Note that this function also works on formatted dates.

Spreadsheet examples: =DAYOFYEAR(33525) yields 288, where 33525 is the serial number for October 15, 1995; =DAYOFYEAR(33247) yields 10, where 33247 is the serial number for January 10, 1995.

Database examples: DAYOFYEAR('DATE')

DEGREES

Format: DEGREES (radians number)

The DEGREES function converts radians to the corresponding number of degrees.

Spreadsheet examples: =DEGREES(1.58) returns 90.5273; =DEGREES(1) returns 57.29578; =DEGREES(-3) returns -171.8873; =DEGREES(ΠI( )) returns 180; =DEGREES(-(ΠI( ))) returns -180.

ERROR

Format: ERROR ( )

The ERROR function returns *#ERROR!* It has no arguments.

Spreadsheet examples: The formula =IF(C2>2,ERROR( ),"OK") returns *#ERROR!* if the value in cell C2 is greater than 2; otherwise, it returns *OK*. If you only want the erroneous condition to return a text string, the formula could be changed to read: =IF(C2>2,ERROR( ),"").

Database examples: You can use the ERROR( ) function to report the result of a test on a field, as in:

```
IF('Hours'<0,ERROR(),"OK!")
```

EXACT

Format: EXACT (text1, text2)

EXACT compares two text strings, and returns TRUE when the two strings are identical — including case. Otherwise, it returns FALSE.

Spreadsheet examples: =EXACT(A1,A2) returns true only when the contents of cells A1 and A2 are identical. The formula =EXACT("*Minnesota*",B5) returns FALSE if cell B5 contains anything other than the string Minnesota. If B5 held *MINNESOTA*, the formula would still return FALSE, since the case of the two strings is different.

Database examples: EXACT('Last Name','First Name') returns 1 (True) when the contents of the Last Name field matches that of the First Name field; otherwise, it returns 0 (False).

EXP (Exponent)

Format: EXP (number)

EXP calculates e to the power of the argument.

Spreadsheet examples: =EXP(1) yields 2.718281; =EXP(2) yields 7.389 (or e^2).

FACT (Factorial)

Format: FACT (number)

FACT calculates the factorial of any positive whole number. Factorials of negative numbers or real numbers produce errors. Note that the factorials of 0 and 1 are both 1.

Spreadsheet examples: =FACT(3) returns 6 (or 3*2*1); FACT(4) returns 24 (or 4*3*2*1); =FACT(B7) returns 120 when cell B7 contains, or evaluates as, 5.

FIND

Format: FIND (find-text, in-text {, start-offset})

The FIND function searches the text specified in in-text and attempts to locate an occurrence of the search string (find-text). It returns the position of the first instance that it finds, if any. (A is returned if the find-text is not found.)

Optionally, you can specify a character starting position by adding the start-offset; that is, the number of characters from the beginning of the text string. Each search is case-sensitive and blanks are counted.

Spreadsheet examples: The formula =FIND("Beth","Where is Beth?") returns 10; =FIND("BETH","Where is Beth?") returns 0 because the case of the find-text does not match that of the text within the string that was searched.

Adding a start-offset, such as =FIND("Beth","Where is Beth?",5) makes the formula begin its search with the fifth character in in-text. The result is still 10, since Beth is found starting at the tenth character of in-text. On the other hand, if a start-offset of 11 was used, Beth would not be found and a result of 0 (zero) would be presented.

FRAC (Fraction)

Format: FRAC (number)

The FRAC function calculates the fractional part of a real number. The result is always a positive number.

Spreadsheet examples: The formula =FRAC(17.237) returns 0.237, the part of the number to the right of the decimal point; the formula =FRAC(-123.7) returns 0.7; and the formula =FRAC(10) returns 0 (zero).

Database examples: FRAC('Hours') returns the fractional portion of the number in the Hours field.

FV (Future Value)

Format: FV (rate, nper, pmt {, pv} {, type})

FV calculates the future value of an investment, given a particular interest rate per period (rate) and number of periods (nper). Specifying the present value of the investment (pv) and the payment type (type) are optional. The default type is 0, indicating that the payment is made at the end of the first period. A type of 1 means that the payment is made at the beginning of each period.

The rate can be entered as a percentage (9.5%) or a decimal (.095). Payment amounts and the present value should be entered as negative numbers, since they represent money paid out.

Spreadsheet examples: The formula =FV(10%,10,-500) returns $7968.71, the future value of an annual investment of $500 for 10 years at an interest rate of 10%. Because the type was not indicated, it is assumed that each yearly investment is made on the last day of the year. On the other hand, if the annual investment was made on the *first* day of each year, as shown in the revised formula =FV(10%,10,-500,0,1), the result is $8765.58 — a gain of almost $800. To calculate the future value of an initial investment of $10,000 with annual additions of $1,000 at an interest rate of 5.5% over a five-year period (with each addition made at the beginning of the year), you would use this formula:

```
=FV(5.5%,5,-1000,-10000,1)
```

returning an answer of $18,957.65.

HLOOKUP (Horizontal Lookup)

Format: HLOOKUP (lookup value, compare range, index {, method})

HLOOKUP checks the top row of the compare range for the lookup value. If the search condition is met, the row number of the found cell is increased by the amount of index and the function returns the contents of the new cell. If the search condition is not met, an error is returned.

Specifying a method is optional. When the values in the first row are arranged in increasing order, use a method of 1 to find the largest value that is less than or equal to the lookup value. When the values in the first row are arranged in decreasing order, use a method of -1 to find the smallest value that is greater than or equal to the lookup value. Use a method of 0 to accept only an exact match. *This is a spreadsheet-only function.*

Spreadsheet examples: In the grading spreadsheet shown in Figure B-1, the formula =HLOOKUP(A5,A1..F2,1,1) in cell B5 examines the numeric score that has been entered in cell A5 and then returns the letter grade to be assigned. The compare range (A1..F2) contains the possible scores in the top row (the row that the function searches), and the corresponding letter grades are listed in the second row. Note that the scores in row 1 represent the minimum score required to achieve a particular grade.

Lookup value is entered here   Lookup result appears here

Figure B-1:
A grading
worksheet that
uses the
HLOOKUP
function

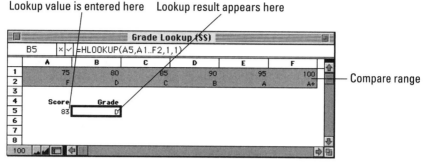

Compare range

HOUR

Format: HOUR (serial number)

The HOUR function extracts the hour from the time portion of a serial number (the numbers to the right of the decimal point). The return value is a whole number between 0 and 23.

Spreadsheet examples: The formula =HOUR(33370.80478) returns 19 (for 7 PM); =HOUR(33370.402) returns 9 (for 9 AM).

 To calculate the *current* hour, you can use the formula =HOUR(NOW( )).

Database examples: HOUR('TIME')

IF

Format: IF (logical, true value, false value)

Use IF to perform a conditional test. If the test condition is fulfilled, the true value is displayed or performed. If the test condition is not fulfilled, the false value is displayed or performed.

Spreadsheet examples: The formula =IF(A10=1053,"You're rich! You picked today's number!","Too bad. Try again.") could be used to check cell A10 for the winning number for today's lottery. If the number found is 1053, the first message (the true value) is displayed. If any other number is found, the second message (the false value) is displayed.

The formula =IF(B7,2,4) displays 2 if B7 contains any value at all, but shows 4 if the cell is blank.

Database examples: IF('Result'>0,"Positive trend","Negative trend or no change").

INDEX

Format: INDEX (range, row, column)

The INDEX function is used to reference the contents of a cell that is *x* number of rows and *y* number of columns away from the first cell in the range. The referenced cell must be within the specified range. *This is a spreadsheet-only function.*

Spreadsheet examples: =INDEX(A55..C63,7,2) returns the contents of cell B61, seven cells down in the range and in the second column of the range.

INT (Integer)

Format: INT (number)

The INT function returns the integer (whole number) closest to the value of the argument number. For any positive number, INT simply returns the integer portion of that number (the same as the TRUNC function). For negative numbers, the argument number is rounded down to the next lowest whole number.

Spreadsheet examples: =INT(4.53) returns 4; =INT(-2.33) returns -3; INT(0.321) returns 0; INT(-0.321) returns -1.

Database examples: INT('Item 1'+'Item 2').

IRR (Internal Rate of Return)

Format: IRR (range {, guess})

IRR is an approximate internal rate of return on an investment and a series of cash flows. If an optional initial *guess* for the internal rate of return is not entered, a default rate of 10% is used. If a result is not obtained within 20 iterations, the function returns a #NUM! error.

The range contains future cash flow amounts in the order that they are paid out or received. The first amount is the amount of the initial investment and is entered as a negative number. *This is a spreadsheet-only function.*

Spreadsheet examples: When formatted as a percent, the formula =IRR(B1..B5) returns 6.65% when B1..B5 contains -10000, 2000, 2500, 2500, 5000.

ISBLANK

Format: ISBLANK (value)

The ISBLANK function enables you to distinguish between blank cells or fields and those that contain an entry. If the cell is empty, ISBLANK returns TRUE. If the cell contains text or a number, ISBLANK returns FALSE. When ISBLANK is used in a ClarisWorks database, the return values are 1 and 0 rather than TRUE and FALSE, respectively.

Spreadsheet examples: =ISBLANK(5.45), =ISBLANK(0), and =ISBLANK("IDG") return FALSE. The formula =ISBLANK(B6) returns TRUE only if cell B6 is empty; otherwise, it returns FALSE.

Database examples: =ISBLANK('Last Name') returns 1 if the contents of the Last Name field is empty; otherwise, it returns 0 (zero).

ISERROR

Format: ISERROR (value {, error type})

The ISERROR function is used to check for errors in expressions. Optionally, ISERROR can check for a specific type of error, rather than errors of any type. ISERROR returns TRUE or FALSE in a worksheet, and 1 or 0 in a database.

Error types that can optionally be included are:

Error Type	Explanation
#ARG!	Incorrect number of arguments or argument type
#DATE!	Incorrect date
#DIV/0!	Divide by zero
#ERROR!	Not a true error
#N/A!	Not available
#NUM!	Incorrect number
#REF!	Reference to incorrect cell
#TIME!	Incorrect time
#USER!	User-defined error
#VALUE!	Incorrect value

Spreadsheet examples: The formula =ISERROR(F5) examines the contents of cell F5 and returns FALSE (if there is no error in cell F5) or TRUE (if there is an error in cell F5). The formula =ISERROR(F5,#DIV/0!) examines cell F5 and returns TRUE if it contains a divide by zero error. If it contains no error or an error of another type, it returns FALSE.

Database examples: The formula ISERROR('Division Result',#DIV/0!) checks the field called Division Result and displays a 1 (TRUE) if a divide by zero error is detected. Other errors or no error result in a returned value of 0 (FALSE).

ISLOGICAL

Format: ISLOGICAL (value)

The ISLOGICAL function determines whether the argument contains a Boolean expression; that is, one which can be evaluated as either TRUE or FALSE. If so, ISLOGICAL returns TRUE; otherwise, it returns FALSE.

Spreadsheet examples: The formula =ISLOGICAL(1.5>4) returns TRUE because the argument is a Boolean expression. As this example shows, it doesn't matter whether the expression is true or false; only that it is a Boolean expression. The formula =ISLOGICAL(C1) checks to see if cell C1 contains a Boolean expression.

ISNA (Is Not Available)

Format: ISNA (value)

ISNA checks for the presence of the #N/A! (Not Available) error. If that specific error is found, TRUE is returned. If no error (or an error of another type) is found, FALSE is returned. Because the MATCH, LOOKUP, VLOOKUP, and HLOOKUP functions may return an #N/A! error, ISNA can be used to check the results of formulas that include these function. *This is a spreadsheet-only function.*

Spreadsheet examples: The formula =ISNA("Happy!") returns FALSE, since "Happy!" is a text expression and not the #N/A! error. The formula =ISNA(C3) returns TRUE only if cell C3 contains the #N/A! error. The formula =ISNA(NA( )) returns TRUE because NA( ) *is* the Not Available error.

ISNUMBER

Format: ISNUMBER (value)

The ISNUMBER function enables you to check the contents of a cell or database field for the presence of a number. If the cell contains a number, ISNUMBER returns TRUE. If the cell contains text or is blank, FALSE is returned.

When ISNUMBER is used in a ClarisWorks database, the return values are 1 and 0 (rather than TRUE and FALSE, respectively). Note, however, that ISNUMBER is seldom used in ClarisWorks databases because:

- ✑ Number fields can only contain numbers, so there's no reason to check them further.

- ✑ A number found in a Text field is treated as text, so ISNUMBER always returns 0 (false).

- ✑ When importing data, text in Number fields is ignored (so there's no reason to use ISNUMBER to check for import errors).

On the other hand, ISNUMBER can be used to check for blank Number fields, much as the ISBLANK function is used. For blank fields, ISNUMBER returns 0 (false), while ISBLANK returns 1 (true).

Spreadsheet examples: The formula =ISNUMBER(17.235) returns TRUE; =ISNUMBER(Apple) returns FALSE; =ISNUMBER(D5) returns TRUE if cell D5 contains a number or a formula which results in a number, or returns FALSE if the cell contains text or is empty.

Database examples: ISNUMBER('Amount') returns 0 (false) if the Amount number field is empty; otherwise, it returns 1 (true).

ISTEXT

Format: ISTEXT (value)

The ISTEXT function is used to determine whether an expression is text, or a cell reference, function, or number that evaluates as text. ISTEXT always returns either TRUE or FALSE.

Applying the ISTEXT function to cells that contain dates or times can give confusing results. If a date or time is entered directly (as 1/12/96 or 4:43, for example), it is a number; ISTEXT returns FALSE. However, if a date or time is entered as text (="1/12/95"), ISTEXT returns TRUE. Finally, if a slash- or dash-delimited date is entered with a century (as in 12/14/1996), it is treated as text by ISTEXT and returns TRUE.

Spreadsheet examples: The formula =ISTEXT(D2) returns TRUE if the cell contains text, or a cell reference, function, or number that evaluates as text; =ISTEXT(Snakes) and =ISTEXT("24 Sapperstein Way") both return TRUE; =ISTEXT(147) and =ISTEXT(Π()) both return FALSE. The complex formula =ISTEXT(123/5 &" is the answer") returns TRUE. Although the formula contains numeric data, the result of the calculation is text (that is, *24.6 is the answer*).

LEFT

Format: LEFT (text, number of characters)

The LEFT function returns a text string that contains the number of characters specified, counting from the leftmost character in the target text string. Note that if the target text string contains fewer characters than the number specified in the LEFT function, those characters that are present are returned. Also, the LEFT function can be applied to numbers, but the returned value is text.

Spreadsheet examples: =LEFT("123 Williams Avenue",3) returns 123; =LEFT(Samuel Smith,3) returns Sam; =LEFT(47259,4) returns 4725; =LEFT(Apple,12) returns Apple, since there are fewer than 12 characters in the string.

Database examples: LEFT('ID',5) returns the leftmost five characters of the contents of the ID field.

 If you have a worksheet or database that contains 9-digit ZIP codes, you can convert them to 5-digit codes by using the LEFT function, as follows:

```
In a worksheet:  =LEFT(C1,5)
In a database:   LEFT('ZIP
Code',5)
```

Similarly, if you have a worksheet or database that holds phone numbers that are formatted as 303-772-0054, you can extract the area code with the following formulas:

```
In a worksheet:  =LEFT(F1,3)
In a database:   LEFT('Phone
Number',3)
```

LEN (Length)

Format: LEN (text)

LEN counts the number of characters in a text string. Spaces, numbers, and special characters also count toward the total.

Spreadsheet examples: =LEN(A1) returns 16, where A1 contains the string "Washington, D.C." The formula =IF(LEN(A1)>5,BEEP( ),) checks the length of the text string in cell A1, and beeps if it contains more than five characters. Otherwise, it does nothing.

Database examples: The formula LEN('Last Name') returns the number of characters in the Last Name field.

LN (Natural Log)

Format: LN (number)

LN calculates the natural logarithm of a positive number.

Spreadsheet examples: The formula =LN(5) returns 1.6094.

LOG

Format: LOG (number {, base})

The LOG function calculates the logarithm of a positive number to a base. If no base is specified, it is assumed to be base 10.

Spreadsheet examples: The formula =LOG(5) returns 0.69897; =LOG(5,2) returns 2.3219.

LOG10 (Log to Base 10)

Format: LOG10 (number)

LOG10 calculates the logarithm of a number to base 10; it is the inverse of the number e in scientific notation.

Spreadsheet examples: The formula =LOG10(1000) returns 3; =LOG10(10000) returns 4.

LOOKUP

Format: LOOKUP (lookup value, compare range, result range {, method})

The LOOKUP function searches for the lookup value row-by-row within the compare range and then returns the value of the corresponding cell in the result range. It is assumed that the values in the compare range are organized in ascending order — going from left to right

and top to bottom. If they are arranged in descending order, enter -1 for the optional method.

When the search is conducted, ClarisWorks seeks the largest number that is less than or equal to the lookup value. If no cell satisfies the search criteria, an error is returned. *This is a spreadsheet-only function.*

Spreadsheet examples: Figure B-2 contains a worksheet that can be used to calculate the amount of postage required for a specific weight of letter. The exact weight is entered in cell A2; the lookup weights and corresponding postage amounts are listed in C2..C11 and D2..D11. The LOOKUP formula presents the answer in cell B2, using the formula:

```
=LOOKUP(IF(TRUNC(A2)=A2,A2,A2+1),
C2..C11,D2..D11)
```

The IF function checks the contents of cell A2. If the value in A2 is equal to the truncated value of the same number (i.e., A2 contains a whole number), A2 is used as the lookup value. If A2 contains a fractional portion, an additional ounce (1) is added to it, so A2 +1 is used as the lookup value. (The post office requires that all fractional weights be increased to the next full ounce).

Figure B-2:
This small worksheet uses the LOOKUP function to determine the correct postage for a letter of a particular weight.

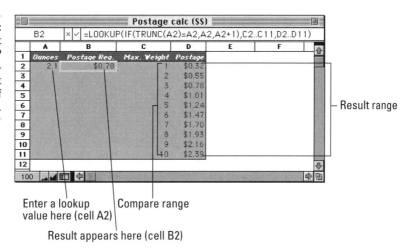

Enter a lookup value here (cell A2) Compare range

Result appears here (cell B2)

Result range

The formula then compares the lookup value to the values in column C of the worksheet and locates the largest weight value that is less than or equal to the lookup value. It then returns the appropriate postage amount from column D.

LOWER

Format: LOWER (text)

The LOWER function converts upper-case letters in text to lower-case letters.

Spreadsheet examples: =LOWER("FuNnY") returns *funny*; =LOWER("Bob lives in DC.") returns *bob lives in dc.*

Database examples: The formula LOWER('Comments') converts the entire contents of a Comments field to lower-case letters.

MACRO

Format: MACRO (text)

Use the MACRO function to execute a named macro; the macro name must be enclosed in quotation marks, spelled correctly, and have the proper capitalization.

Spreadsheet examples: The formula =IF(A1,MACRO("Chart"),0) checks cell A1 for the presence of any non-zero number and, if it finds one, the macro named Chart is played.

MATCH

Format: MATCH (lookup value, compare range {, type})

The MATCH function checks a specified range for a matching value and, if it finds one, reports the element number (the position) of that cell within the range. The compare range can contain text or numeric expressions. It is assumed that the values in the compare range are arranged in ascending or descending order, moving from left to right and top to bottom of the range. Optionally, you can enter 1 for the type to indicate an ascending range, -1 to indicate a descending range, or 0 for an exact match (range order is unimportant). *This is a spreadsheet-only function.*

Spreadsheet examples: In Figure B-3, the compare range (B1..C7) contains the numbers from 1 to 14 and is shown in gray. The formula =MATCH(5,B1..C7,1) in cell A1 instructs ClarisWorks to locate the first 5 in the compare range and specifies that the array is arranged in ascending order. The equation reports a match position at the fifth cell in the range (5).

MAX (Maximum)

Format: MAX (number1, number2,...)

The MAX function returns the largest number in a list of values. This function is often used to

Figure B-3:
An example of the
MATCH function

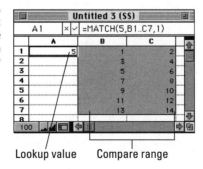

Lookup value   Compare range

identify the largest number in a worksheet column or row. Note that blank cells are ignored when calculating the MAX value for a worksheet range.

Spreadsheet examples: The formula =MAX(17,23,4,19,-111) returns 23; =MAX(5,3,6.27) returns 6.27; =MAX(C2..C25) returns the largest number in the range from cell C2 to C25.

Database examples: The formula MAX('Sale 1','Sale 2','Sale 3') identifies the largest of the three sales for each record.

MERGEFIELD

Format: MERGEFIELD (text)

As explained in Chapter 9, a worksheet can also be used as a merge form. Use the MERGEFIELD function to create merge fields in a worksheet. *This is a spreadsheet-only function.*

Spreadsheet examples: The formula =MERGEFIELD("First Name") results in «First Name» being entered in the cell. When a merge is performed with this worksheet, data from the First Name field will replace the «First Name» placeholder.

MID (Middle)

Format: MID (text, start position, number of characters)

MID examines a target text string and returns a string of a specific number of characters, based on the starting position indicated in the formula. Note that when counting character positions, a blank is also considered a character, as are all letters, numbers, and punctuation marks.

Spreadsheet examples: =MID("Steven Alan Schwartz",8,2) returns *Al*, since the starting position is the eighth character and the desired string is two characters long.

Database examples: Assuming that you have a database with a phone number field and every number is formatted as ### - ### - ####, the formula MID('Phone',5,3) could be used to extract the phone number's exchange.

MIN (Minimum)

Format: MIN (number1, number2,…)

The MIN function returns the smallest number in a list of values. The MIN function is often used to identify the smallest number in a worksheet column or row. Note that blank cells are ignored when calculating the MIN for a worksheet range.

Spreadsheet examples: The formula =MIN(17,23,4,19,-5) returns -5; =MIN(5,3,6.27) returns 3; =MIN(C2..C25) returns the smallest number in the range from cell C2 to C25.

Database examples: The formula MIN('Sale 1','Sale 2','Sale 3') identifies the smallest of the three sales for each record.

MINUTE

Format: MINUTE (serial number)

The MINUTE function calculates the minutes for a serial time or date number. Note that in a serial date, the numbers to the right of the decimal represent the time.

Spreadsheet examples: =MINUTE(33374.41288) and =MINUTE(0.41288) both return 54, since the time represented is 9:54 a.m.

MIRR (Modified Int.ernal Rate of Return)

Format: MIRR (safe, risk, values…)

The MIRR function calculates the modified internal rate of return of a series of cash flows, given particular safe and risk investment rates. *Safe* is the rate returned by the investment that finances the negative cash flows; *risk* is the rate at which positive cash flows can be reinvested; and the *values* are the future cash flows. Ranges can also be specified for the values.

Spreadsheet examples: The formula =MIRR(5%,15%,C12..C16) returns 18.65% when cells C12..C16 contain the values -5000, 2000, 4000, -2000, and 5000.

MOD (Modulo)

Format: MOD (number, divisor number)

The MOD function returns the remainder when one number is divided by another. The sign of the remainder matches that of the dividend.

Spreadsheet examples: The formula =MOD(5,2) returns 1; =MOD(-5,2) returns -1; and =MOD(5, -2) returns 1. The formula =MOD(5.75,3) returns 2.75. The formula =MOD(16,2) returns 0 because there is no remainder; that is, 2 divides evenly into 16.

MONTH

Format: MONTH (serial number)

The MONTH function converts a date serial number into the number of the corresponding month (1 through 12). MONTH also can be used to extract the month from a numeric date referenced in another cell.

 To calculate the *current* month, use the formula =MONTH(NOW( )).

Spreadsheet examples: The formula =MONTH(23140) returns 5, since this is the serial number for May 10, 1967; =MONTH(B5) returns 4 when cell B5 contains 4-15-85 or April 15, 1985, for example.

Database examples: The formula MONTH('Start Date') can be used to extract the month number from a date in Start Date field.

MONTHNAME

Format: MONTHNAME (number)

The MONTHNAME calculates the text name of a month. Acceptable arguments are the numbers from 1 to 12. Real numbers and numbers that are out of range (less than 1 or greater than 12) return errors.

Spreadsheet examples: The formula =MONTHNAME(5) returns May; =MONTHNAME(12) returns December; =MONTHNAME(B10) returns January, when B10 contains 1 or evaluates as 1.

Database examples: The formula MONTHNAME(MONTH('Start Date')) extracts the name of the month from the date in the Start Date field. (**Note:** The nested MONTH function is required in order to reduce the date in Start Date to a month number between 1 and 12 that MONTHNAME can act on.)

NA (Not Available)

Format: NA ( )

The NA( ) function takes no arguments and returns the error value #N/A!

Spreadsheet examples: An IF formula can use the NA( ) function to force an error for one condition, such as =IF(ISBLANK(E1),NA(),"Okay"). In this instance, if cell E1 is blank, it generates the #N/A! error.

NOT

Format: NOT (logical)

NOT returns the opposite result of a logical expression, in the form TRUE or FALSE. The argument must evaluate as a Boolean expression.

Spreadsheet examples: The formula NOT(C1) returns TRUE only if C1 evaluates as 0; in all other cases, the formula returns FALSE. The formula NOT(C1>D1) returns TRUE if C1 is *less than or equal to* D1; otherwise, it returns FALSE.

You can use a formula in the form =NOT(ISBLANK(D4)) to test for the presence of any value in a cell. If cell D4 contains anything (text, a number, or a formula), the formula returns TRUE; if D4 is empty, it returns FALSE.

NOW

Format: NOW ( )

The NOW function returns the current date and time (according to the Macintosh's clock), expressed as a serial number (representing the number of days since January 1, 1904). NOW takes no arguments and is written as NOW( ). You can update a =NOW( ) formula to the current date and time by choosing Calculate Now (Shift-⌘-=) from the Calculate menu.

 The result of NOW( ) is shown by default as a serial number. In most cases, though, you'll probably wish to show it as a date. NOW( ) can be displayed in any of several date formats, such as 5/12/95 or May 12, 1995, for example, by assigning a date format to the cell or field.

To set a date format in a worksheet, highlight the cell and select the Number command from the Format menu. To display NOW( ) as a date in a database field, specify Date as the result type for the calculation. Then choose a date format by changing to Layout mode (Shift-⌘-L), selecting the field, and then choosing Field Format from the Options menu.

Note that you also can express =NOW( ) as a *time* rather than a date by setting a time format for the cell or Time as the result type for the database field. The desired time format can be set as discussed above for setting a date format.

Spreadsheet examples: The formula =NOW( ) could return 33369.876875, 5/12/95, May 12, 1995, or Friday, May 12, 1995, depending on how the field was formatted. Note that the

fraction in the serial number represents the fractional portion of the day at the moment NOW( ) was calculated (that is, the number of hours, minutes, and seconds that have elapsed since midnight).

Database examples: NOW( )

NPER (Number of Periods)

Format: NPER (rate, pmt, pv {, fv} {, type})

NPER is used to calculate the number of periods required for an investment involving constant cash flows. *Rate* is the interest rate per period; *pmt* is the payment to be made each period; *pv* is the present value of the investment; *fv* is the future value of the investment after the last payment is made (fv is optional — if not included, it is assumed to be 0); and *type* represents the payment scheme (type is optional — if included, enter **0** if payments are due at the end of each period or **1** if payments are due at the beginning of each period; 0 is the default).

Spreadsheet examples: The formula =NPER(8.75%/12,-250,10000) returns 47.46 as the number of periods (payments) required to pay off a $10,000 loan at an annual rate of 8.75%, assuming that each payment is $250.

NPV (Net Present Value)

Format: NPV (interest rate, payment1, payment2,...)

Use NPV to calculate the net present value of an investment based on a series of future payments or income, assuming a fixed interest rate. *Payments* can be replaced with a range, rather than listing the individual values within the formula.

Spreadsheet examples: The formula =NPV (8%, -10000, 0, 12000, 12000, 12000) returns $17,254.08, and represents an initial investment of $10,000 with annual income of $0; $12,000; $12,000; and $12,000.

NUMTOBASE

Format: NUMTOBASE (number, base {, minimum digits})

The NUMTOBASE function converts a number in base 10 to another base and returns a string representing the converted number. *Base* can be any number between 1 and 36. *Minimum* digits is optional and represents the minimum number of digits that will be returned in the result. If the result requires fewer digits, leading zeroes will be added to the result.

Spreadsheet examples: The formula =NUMTOBASE(200,2) converts the number 200 to base 2, returning 11001000.

NUMTOTEXT

Format: NUMTOTEXT (number)

NUMTOTEXT changes a number into a text string.

Spreadsheet examples: To retain leading zeroes in a set of imported numeric ZIP codes (for example, 07146), you can change the contents of the cells from numbers to text. (Numbers cannot have leading zeroes.) To add a leading zero to any four-digit codes that are found, you could use this formula:

```
=IF(LEN(D11)<5,"0" &
NUMTOTEXT(D11),NUMTOTEXT(D11))
```

This formula examines the contents of a cell (D11, in this instance), and checks to see if it contains fewer than five characters. If there are fewer than five characters, it creates a new ZIP code by converting the numeric ZIP code to a text string and appending a zero to the string (as in 04331). If the ZIP code already contains at least five characters, it also is converted to a text string but passed through unchanged (as in 34412 or 12203-3802).

OR

Format: OR (logical1, logical2,…)

The OR function tests the logical arguments specified and returns TRUE if *any* argument is true; otherwise, it returns False.

Spreadsheet examples: The formula OR(A1, B1, C1) returns TRUE if any of cells A1, B1, or C1 evaluates as true.

Database examples: The formula OR('QTR 1','QTR 2') returns 1 (True) if either of the fields QTR 1 or QTR 2 contains a numeric entry.

PI

Format: PI ( )

PI produces the value of π (that is, 3.141592653…). Note that PI has no arguments.

Spreadsheet examples: Use PI( )*(A9^2) to calculate the area of a circle, where cell A9 contains the radius.

Database examples: PI( )*('RADIUS'^2).

PMT (Payment)

Format: PMT (rate, nper, pv {, fv} {, type})

The PMT function is used to calculate payments given a specific interest rate, number of periods, preset value, future value, and type of payment. The last two arguments are optional. The *future value* represents the value of the investment or cash value remaining after the final payment. The default value is 0. *Type* determines whether payments are due at the beginning (1) or end (0) of each period; 0 is the default.

Spreadsheet examples: To calculate monthly payments on a car loan, you could enter =PMT(8.75%/12,36,19000,-9000,1). This indicates an annual percentage rate of 8.75%, a 3-year loan (36 months), a cost (pv) of $19,000, a future value of -$9,000 (the down payment), and that payments are made at the beginning of each period.

PRODUCT

Format: PRODUCT (number1, number2,…)

Product calculates the product of the numbers in the argument list; that is, it multiplies them together.

Spreadsheet examples: The formula =PRODUCT(1.5, 4.5) returns 6.75; =PRODUCT(A1..A3) multiplies the contents of cell A1 times cell A2 times cell A3 (or A1* A2*A3).

Database examples:
PRODUCT('HEIGHT','WIDTH')

PROPER

Format: PROPER (text)

Use the PROPER function to capitalize the first letter of every word in a cell or field.

Spreadsheet examples: =PROPER("Steve's great adventure") returns *Steve's Great Adventure.*

Database examples: PROPER('Book Title').

PV (Present Value)

Format: PV (rate, nper, pmt, {, fv} {, type})

PV calculates the present value of an investment; that is, the amount of money you'd have to invest now — in addition to making fixed payments at specific periods getting a fixed interest rate — in order to have *fv* dollars at the end. *Type* is optional; the default of 0 means that payments/investments are made at the end of each period; 1 indicates that payments/investments are made at the beginning of each period.

Spreadsheet examples: The formula =PV(8%,36,-250,10000) indicates that to have $10,000 after three years (36 payments) of investing $250 per month at 8% annual return, an initial investment of $2,303.05 is required.

RADIANS

Format: RADIANS (degrees number)

Use RADIANS to convert a number of degrees to radians (standard units for trigonometric functions).

Spreadsheet examples: The formula =RADIANS(45) returns 0.785; =RADIANS(120) returns 2.094.

RAND (Random)

Format: RAND ({number})

Use the RAND function to generate random numbers. If no argument is given, as in RAND( ), the returned value is a fraction between 0 and 1. If an argument is given, an integer is returned between 1 and the argument.

Negative arguments are also allowed. For the formula =RAND(-20), an integer between -1 and -20 is returned.

 Because the RAND function gives a different answer each time it is calculated, you can instantly generate a new set of random numbers by choosing Calculate Now from the Calculate menu (or pressing Shift-⌘-=).

 If you're a lottery fan, you can use the RAND function to generate picks. For example, if your lottery is based on the numbers between 1 and 40 and you must choose six, enter the formula =RAND(40) in a cell, select the cell and the five beneath it, and then choose Fill Down from the Calculate menu (or press ⌘-D). Each time you press Shift-⌘-=, a new set of six random numbers appears. (Note, however, that you may get some duplicate numbers in a set. They *are* random, after all.)

Spreadsheet examples: =RAND( ) can return any fraction between 0 and 1, such as 0.49774; =RAND(10) returns a whole number between 1 and 10, such as 7; the range and type of random number returned for =RAND(B2) depends on the contents of cell B2.

RATE

Format: RATE (fv, pv, term)

The RATE function is used to determine the interest rate needed for a present value to grow to a given future value over a particular term, where *fv* is the future value of the investment; *pv* is the present value of the investment; and *term* is the number of payments.

Spreadsheet examples: The formula =RATE(10000,6000,5) returns 10.76%. It means that if you currently have $6,000 to invest and need it to be worth $10,000 in five years, you must find an investment paying an annual yield of 10.76% to reach your goal.

REPLACE

Format: REPLACE (old text, start number, number of characters, new text)

The REPLACE function is used to replace one text string with another string, starting from the indicated character position and continuing for *x* characters.

Spreadsheet examples: The formula =REPLACE(D32,8,4,"Yahoo!") takes the text string in cell D32, counts eight characters into the string, removes four characters (characters 8-11), and inserts the string Yahoo! at that position. Assuming that cell D32 contained *Steven Alan Schwartz*, the cell with the formula specified above would contain *Steven Yahoo! Schwartz*.

REPT (Repeat)

Format: REPT (text, number of times)

The REPT function repeats a given text string the specified number of times.

Spreadsheet examples: The formula =REPT("Hello! ",5) returns Hello! Hello! Hello! Hello! Hello!; =REPT("•",10) returns ••••••••••.

RIGHT

Format: RIGHT (text, number of characters)

The RIGHT function returns a text string that contains the number of characters specified, counting from the last character in the target text string. Note that if the target text string contains fewer characters than the number specified in the RIGHT function, those characters that are present are returned. Note, too, that the RIGHT function can be applied to numbers, but the returned value is text.

Spreadsheet examples: =RIGHT("123 Williams Avenue",6) returns Avenue; =RIGHT(Samuel Smith,5) returns Smith; =RIGHT(47259,4) returns 7259; =RIGHT(Apple,12) returns Apple, since there are fewer than 12 characters in the string.

Database examples: You could create a customer identification number by taking the final four digits of his/her phone number or Social Security number, as in RIGHT('Phone',4) or RIGHT('Soc. Sec. #',4).

ROUND

Format: ROUND (number, number of digits)

Use ROUND to specify the number of digits from the decimal point to which a number should be rounded. Note that the number of digits can be positive (to the right of the decimal) or negative (to the left of the decimal).

Spreadsheet examples: =ROUND(A3,2) rounds the contents of cell A3 to two decimal places. If A3 contains 14.33632, the result is 14.34; if A3 contains 14.333, the result is 14.33. The formula =ROUND(4235,-3) produces a result of 4000, while =ROUND(4512,-3) produces a result of 5000.

Database examples: ROUND('Grand Total',0) could be used to round a total figure to a whole dollar amount.

ROW

Format: ROW ({cell})

Returns the number of the row referenced by *cell* or the row in which the current cell is contained (when no argument is included). *This is a spreadsheet-only function.*

Spreadsheet examples: =ROW(C12) returns 12, since cell C12 is in the twelfth row; =ROW( ) returns the row in which this formula is located.

 If you want to quickly number a group of rows beginning with row 1, enter the formula =ROW( ) in row 1, highlight that cell as well as the appropriate cells below, and then choose Fill Down from the Calculate menu (or press ⌘-D).

SECOND

Format: SECOND (serial number)

The SECOND function calculates the seconds for a given serial number. It can also return the number of seconds from a normal time.

Spreadsheet examples: The formula =SECOND(NOW( )) returns the number of seconds for the current time (press Shift-⌘-= and watch the seconds change); =SECOND(D7) returns 27 when cell D7 contains 1:43:27; =SECOND(0.5003) returns 26.

Database examples: SECOND('End Time'-'Start Time').

SIGN

Format: SIGN (number)

SIGN returns the sign of a numeric value. It displays 1 for a positive number, -1 for a negative number, and 0 for zero (or for a blank cell or field).

Spreadsheet examples: =SIGN(-423.75) yields -1; =SIGN(12) yields 1; =SIGN(0) yields 0; =SIGN(A2-3) yields 0, when the contents of cell A2 evaluates as 3. A formula such as the following can use the SIGN function to test cell contents:

```
=IF(SIGN(B5),"OK","Empty or zero")
```

If the sign of the cell is non-zero (either 1 or -1), *OK* is returned. If the cell is blank or evaluates as zero, *Empty or zero* is returned.

SIN (Sine)

Format: SIN (number)

The SIN function calculates the sine of a number, where that number is an angle in radians.

Spreadsheet examples: =SIN(RADIANS(15)) yields 0.25881; =SIN(RADIANS(90)) yields 1.0.

SQRT (Square Root)

Format: SQRT (number)

SQRT calculates the square root of a number. Note that square roots can only be calculated for positive numbers.

Spreadsheet examples: =SQRT(2); =SQRT(5.73); =SQRT(A1); =SQRT(A1+(B7/5))

Database examples: SQRT('LENGTH').

STDEV (Standard Deviation)

Format: STDEV (number1, number2,...)

The standard deviation is a measure of how values are spread around the *mean* (average). The larger the standard deviation, the greater the spread. The STDEV function calculates the standard deviation of a population from the list of sample arguments provided. (Note that the standard deviation is simply the square root of the *variance*, another statistical measure of spread; see VAR.)

The formula used to calculate the standard deviation is:

$$\sqrt{\sum_{i=1}^{N} \frac{(X_i - \overline{X})^2}{N-1}}$$

Spreadsheet examples: The formula =STDEV(12,3,15,7.2,8) returns 4.616; =VAR(125,100,110,115) returns 10.408.

SUM

Format: SUM (number1, number2,...)

SUM adds the numbers in the argument list. The arguments can be numbers, cell references, or database field names. The SUM function is particularly useful for totaling worksheet columns or rows.

Spreadsheet examples: =SUM(A1..A4) adds the contents of cells A1, A2, A3, and A4; =SUM(A1,B5,17.4) adds the contents of cells A1 and B5, and then adds 17.4 to the total; =SUM(B1..B3,5.7,C5) totals the contents of the cells in the range B1..B3, and then adds 5.7 plus the contents of cell C5.

Database examples: SUM('Product Total',5,'Product Total'*.06) could be used to add a fixed shipping charge of $5 and a sales tax of 6% to a customer's order total. This same formula also could be created *without* using the SUM function, as in: 'Product Total'+5+('Product Total'*.06).

TAN (Tangent)

Format: TAN (number)

The TAN function calculates the tangent of a number, where the argument is an angle in radians.

Spreadsheet examples: The formula =TAN(RADIANS(0)) returns 0.

TEXTTODATE

Format: TEXTTODATE (date text)

The TEXTTODATE function is used to convert a date in text form to a date serial number. The date text can be in any acceptable date format.

 Although TEXTTODATE normally expects quoted date text as the argument, it also works with cell references that contain date text. The following date styles are treated as text by ClarisWorks and can be used with the TEXTTODATE function:

↪ Any date entered as a formula, such as ="3/5/95", ="5/25/1915", ="7/19/45" or ="Mar 4, 1943"

↪ Any slash- or dash-delimited date that includes the century as part of the year, such as 3/4/1927 and 4-5-1996

↪ Any date with a two-digit year between 00 and 09, such as 5/12/06, 12/18/02, and April 4, 02 (representing dates between the year 2000 and 2009)

Spreadsheet examples: The formula TEXTTODATE("12/5/96") returns 33942; =TEXTTODATE("Jan 5, 1960") returns 20458; =TEXTTODATE(C1) returns 33942, when C1 contains an acceptable date such as 12/5/1996, ="12/5/96", ="12/5/1996", or ="Dec 5, 1996".

TEXTTONUM

Format: TEXTTONUM (text)

TEXTTONUM converts a text string to its numeric equivalent. Non-numeric characters are ignored when converting the string to a number. (Note that when applied to a number rather than a text string, TEXTTONUM passes the number through unaltered.)

Spreadsheet examples: The formula =TEXTTONUM("$12,453.47") returns 12453.47; =TEXTTONUM("123 Apple Way, Apt. 4") returns 1234 (the numbers are extracted and combined); =TEXTTONUM("(602) 555-1295") returns 6025551295; =TEXTTONUM(B2) returns 477401122, when B2 contains the Social Security number 477-40-1122; =TEXTTONUM(45.67) returns 45.67 (numbers are passed through unaltered).

TEXTTOTIME

Format: TEXTTOTIME (time text)

The TEXTTOTIME function converts a time text string into a time serial number. The text time is expressed in hours, minutes, and seconds order. The seconds and an AM/PM suffix are optional.

Spreadsheet examples: The formula =TEXTTOTIME("1:15 PM") returns 0.5521; =TEXTTOTIME("1:15") returns 0.0521 (times without at AM/PM suffix are assumed to be in 24-hour format); =TEXTTOTIME("10:20:23 PM") returns 0.9308.

TIME

Format: TIME (hour, minute, second)

The TIME function converts a time (based on a 24-hour clock) into a serial number between 0 and 1, representing the fractional portion of the day from midnight.

Note that all arguments must be present; those that are not normally needed are represented by zeroes. For example, 7AM would be shown as =TIME(7,0,0); that is, 7 hours, 0 minutes, 0 seconds.

Spreadsheet examples: The formula =TIME(7,45,30) returns 0.3233 (for 7:45:30AM); =TIME(17,30,0) returns 0.7292 (for 5:30PM); =TIME(12,0,0) returns 0.5 (for noon).

Database examples:
TIME('Hours','Minutes','Seconds') returns a fraction based on the contents of three fields named Hours, Minutes, and Seconds.

TIMETOTEXT

Format: TIMETOTEXT (serial number {, format number})

Use TIMETOTEXT to convert a time serial number to text. (Note that the time portion of a serial number is found to the right of the decimal point. This function also works with a complete serial number, and simply ignores the digits to the left of the decimal point.)

Add an optional format number if you wish to specify a format for the time text. If a format number is not entered, ClarisWorks uses format 0. If you mistakenly enter a format number that is out of range (such as -3 or 4), ClarisWorks also treats it as though you requested format 0.

Format Number	Format Applied
0	Hours:Minutes AM/PM (12-hour clock)
1	Hours:Minutes:Seconds AM/PM (12-hour clock)
2	Hours:Minutes (24-hour clock)
3	Hours:Minutes:Seconds (24-hour clock)

Spreadsheet examples: The formulas =TIMETOTEXT(33373.6009375) and =TIMETOTEXT(0.6009375) both return 2:25 PM. Since a format number was not entered, format 0 is used. The formula =TIMETOTEXT(0.653,0) returns 3:40 PM; =TIMETOTEXT(0.653,1) returns 3:40:19 PM; =TIMETOTEXT(0.653,2) returns 15:40; and =TIMETOTEXT(0.653,2) returns 15:40:19.

 Applying the TIMETOTEXT function to a serial number has the same effect as selecting a time formatting option from the Number command in the Format menu.

 To display the current time, use the formula =TIMETOTEXT(NOW( )).

TRIM

Format: TRIM (text)

The TRIM function removes extra spaces from text strings. Each group of spaces is reduced to a single space. TRIM can be very useful in cleaning up text.

Spreadsheet examples: =TRIM("Woodsbridge, MD   30919") returns Woodsbridge, MD 30919.

Database examples: TRIM('Comments') can be used to remove extraneous spaces in a text field named Comments.

TRUNC (Truncate)

Format: TRUNC (number)

TRUNC discards the decimal portion of the argument number, returning only the whole number that remains.

Spreadsheet examples: =TRUNC(12.365) returns 12; =TRUNC(0.12) returns 0; =TRUNC (-5.67) returns -5.

Database examples: Assuming that Total Hours is a calculation field that sums the number of hours worked, the formula TRUNC('Total Hours') returns the number hours worked during the period, ignoring any fractional part of an hour.

TYPE

Format: TYPE (value)

The TYPE function evaluates the contents of the argument and determines its data type. Possible return values are as follows:

Data Type	Returned Value
Blank	1
Logical	2
Number	3
Text	4

Spreadsheet examples: The formula =TYPE(C7) returns 1 if cell C7 is empty; =TYPE(FALSE) and =TYPE(ISBLANK(D3)) both return 2; =TYPE(0.56) and =TYPE(-147) both return 3; =TYPE(Kenneth) and =TYPE("Empire State") both return 4.

UPPER

Format: UPPER (text)

UPPER converts lower-case text to upper-case text. Non-text characters, such as numbers and punctuation marks, are passed through unaltered.

Spreadsheet examples: =UPPER("Steve") returns STEVE; =UPPER("January 5, 1996") returns JANUARY 5, 1996.

Database examples: In a field intended for state abbreviations, UPPER('State') could be used to change all entries to upper-case, such as MN, AZ, and NY.

VAR (Variance)

Format: VAR (number1, number2,...)

Variance is a statistic that shows the distribution of values. The VAR function calculates the population variance from the sample that you provide as arguments. Arguments can include numbers, cell references, or ranges. The square root of the variance is the *standard deviation* (see STDEV).

The formula used to calculate variance is:

$$\sum_{i=1}^{N} \frac{(X_i - \overline{X})^2}{N-1}$$

Spreadsheet examples: The formula =VAR(12,3,15,7.2,8) returns 21.308; =VAR(125,100,110,115) returns 108.333.

VLOOKUP (Vertical Lookup)

Format: VLOOKUP (lookup value, compare range, index {, method})

A vertical lookup (VLOOKUP) conducts a lookup based on columns. It searches the leftmost column of the compare range for the specified lookup value. If the lookup condition is met, the column number of the found cell is offset by the amount specified in the index and the function returns the contents of that cell. An error is returned if the search condition is not satisfied.

Method is optional. Enter **1** to locate the largest value which is less than or equal to the lookup value; enter **-1** to find the smallest value which is greater than or equal to the lookup value; or enter **0** to return only an exact method. If no method is specified, a match of 1 is used. *This is a spreadsheet-only function.*

Spreadsheet examples: The worksheet shown in Figure B-4 uses VLOOKUP to choose the proper postage for any weight entered in cell A2. The formula in B2 (where the result is returned) is:

```
=VLOOKUP(IF(TRUNC(A2)=A2,A2,A2+1),
C2..D11,1,1)
```

The IF function checks the contents of cell A2. If the value in A2 is equal to the truncated value of the same number (i.e., A2 contains a whole number), A2 is used as the lookup value. If A2 contains a fractional portion, an additional ounce (1) is added to it, so A2 +1 is used as the lookup value. (The post office requires that all fractional weights be increased to the next full ounce).

The formula then compares the lookup value to the values in column C of the worksheet and locates the largest weight value which is less than or equal to the lookup value (as specified by the method entry of 1). It then uses the index value (the first 1) to return the postage amount from column D.

Figure B-4:
A VLOOKUP
example

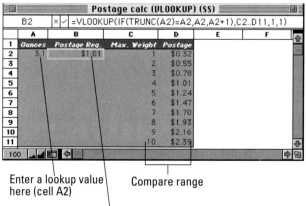

Enter a lookup value here (cell A2)

Compare range

Result appears here (cell B2)

WEEKDAY

Format: WEEKDAY (serial number)

The WEEKDAY function extracts the day of the week from any serial number (the number of days since January 1, 1904). WEEKDAY returns a value between 1 and 7, representing the days from Sunday (1) to Saturday (7).

 The WEEKDAY function can also be used to return the day of the week from a date in month/day/year format, such as =WEEKDAY(C1), where C1 contains 3/18/96.

Spreadsheet examples: The formula =WEEK-DAY(33369) returns 6, since 33369 is the serial number for May 12, 1995, which was a Friday.

Database examples: The formula DAYNAME(WEEKDAY('Important Date')) returns the name of the day of the week that corresponds with the date entered in the Important Date field. (If the DAYNAME section of this formula is removed, the number of the day of the week is returned rather than the day's name.

WEEKOFYEAR

Format: WEEKOFYEAR (serial number)

The WEEKOFYEAR function calculates the week of the year from a serial number (the number of days since January 1, 1904).

 The WEEKOFYEAR function can also be used to extract the week of the year from a date in month/day/year format, such as =WEEKOFYEAR(C1), where C1 contains 3/18/96.

Spreadsheet examples: The formula =WEEKOFYEAR(20776) returns 47. The serial number 20776 represents November 18, 1960, and November 18th falls within the 47th week of the year.)

YEAR

Format: YEAR (serial number)

The YEAR function calculates the year from a serial number (the number of days since January 1, 1904).

 The YEAR function can also be used to extract the year from a date in month/day/year format, such as =YEAR(C1), where C1 contains 3/18/96.

Spreadsheet examples: The formula =YEAR(20776) returns 1960 (20776 is the serial number for November 18, 1960).

Keyboard Shortcuts

Tables C-1 through C-17 list ClarisWorks keyboard shortcuts that will increase your productivity and make you feel at ease if you're not used to using a mouse or don't like to take your hands off the keyboard.

Table C-1
General Menu Commands (Available in Most Environments)

Command	Key Sequence	Menu
Bold	⌘-B	Style (Format)
Center	⌘-\	Alignment (Format)
Check Document Spelling	⌘-=	Writing Tools (Edit)
Check Selection Spelling	Shift-⌘-Y	Writing Tools (Edit)
Clear	Clear (Extended keyboard)	Edit
Close	⌘-W	File
Copy	⌘-C, F3 (Extended keyboard)	Edit
Cut	⌘-X, F2 (Extended keyboard)	Edit
Find Again	⌘-E	Find/Change (Edit)
Find Selection	Shift-⌘-E	Find/Change (Edit)
Find/Change	⌘-F	Find/Change (Edit)
Frame Links	⌘-L	Options
Help	⌘-?, Help (Extended keyboard)	Balloon Help
Italic	⌘-I	Style (Format)
Justify	Shift-⌘-\	Alignment (Format)
Left	⌘-[	Alignment (Format)
Mail Merge	Shift-⌘-M	File
New	⌘-N	File
Open	⌘-O	File
Other	Shift-⌘-O	Size (Format)

(continued)

Table C-1 *(continued)*

Command	Key Sequence	Menu
Page View	Shift-⌘-P	View
Paste	⌘-V, F4 (Extended keyboard)	Edit
Plain Text	⌘-T	Style (Format)
Print	⌘-P	File
Quit	⌘-Q	File
Record Macro/Stop Recording	Shift-⌘-J	Shortcuts (File)
Right	⌘-]	Alignment (Format)
Save As	Shift-⌘-S	File
Save	⌘-S	File
Select All	⌘-A	Edit
Show/Hide Rulers	Shift-⌘-U	View
Show/Hide Shortcuts	Shift-⌘-X	Shortcuts (File)
Show/Hide Styles	Shift-⌘-W	View
Show/Hide Tools	Shift-⌘-T	View
Thesaurus	Shift-⌘-Z	Writing Tools (Edit)
Underline	⌘-U	Style (Format)
Undo/Redo	⌘-Z, F1 (Extended keyboard)	Edit

Table C-2
General Navigation Commands

Command	Key Sequence
Go to beginning of document	Home (Extended keyboard)
Go to end of document	End (Extended keyboard)
Scroll down one screen	Page Down (Extended keyboard)
Scroll up one screen	Page Up (Extended keyboard)

Table C-3
Other General Commands

Command	Key Sequence
Cancel printing and most dialog boxes	⌘-.
Delete character to left of cursor	Delete/Backspace
Delete character to right of cursor	Del (Extended keyboard)
Discretionary hyphen	⌘-hyphen
First slide	Home (Extended keyboard)
End slide show	q, ⌘-., Esc, Clear
Last slide	End (Extended keyboard)
Next slide	Right-arrow, down-arrow, Page Down, Return, Tab, spacebar
Previous slide	Left-arrow, up-arrow, Page Up, Shift-Return, Shift-Tab, Shift-Spacebar

Table C-4
Communications Menu Commands

Command	Key Sequence	Menu
Info	⌘-I	Settings
Open/Close Connection	Shift-⌘-O	Session
Phone Book	⌘-B	Settings
Save Lines Off Top	⌘-T	Session
Show/Hide Scrollback	⌘-L	Settings
Wait for Connection	Shift-⌘-W	Session

Table C-5
Database Menu Commands

Command	Key Sequence	Menu
Browse	Shift-⌘-B	Layout
Define Fields	Shift-⌘-D	Layout
Duplicate Record	⌘-D	Edit
Field Format	Shift-⌘-I	Options
Find	Shift-⌘-F	Layout
Go To Record	⌘-G	Organize
Hide Selected	⌘-(	Organize
Hide Unselected	⌘-)	Organize
Layout	Shift-⌘-L	Layout
List	Shift-⌘-I	Layout
Match Records	⌘-M	Organize
New Record	⌘-R	Edit
Show All Records	Shift-⌘-A	Organize
Sort Records	⌘-J	Organize

Table C-6
Database Navigation Commands

Command	Key Sequence
Move to beginning of field	⌘-up arrow
Move to end of field	⌘-down arrow
Move to next field	Tab
Move to previous field	Shift-Tab
Move to next record (same field)	⌘-Return
Move to previous record (same field)	Shift-⌘-Return

Table C-7
Other Database Commands

Command	Key Sequence
Deselect records	Enter
Insert a tab in a text field	⌘-Tab
Paste current date, time, or record number	⌘- - (hyphen)[1]

[1]You must be in a field of the correct type (that is, a date, time, or number field).

Table C-8
Draw Menu Commands

Command	Key Sequence	Menu
Align Objects	Shift-⌘-K	Arrange
Align to Grid	⌘-K	Arrange
Duplicate	⌘-D	Edit
Free Rotate	Shift-⌘-R	Arrange
Group	⌘-G	Arrange
Lock	⌘-H	Arrange
Move Backward	Shift-⌘-- (hyphen)	Arrange
Move Forward	Shift-⌘-+	Arrange
Reshape	⌘-R	Arrange
Smooth	⌘-(	Transform (Arrange)
Turn Autogrid On/Off	⌘-Y	Options
Ungroup	Shift-⌘-G	Arrange
Unlock	Shift-⌘-H	Arrange
Unsmooth	⌘-)	Transform (Arrange)

Table C-9
Other Draw Commands

Command	Key Sequence
Complete open or closed polygon or Bezigon	Enter
Move selected image one pixel or gridpoint	Any arrow key
Select eyedropper tool	Tab

Table C-10
Paint Menu Commands

Command	Key Sequence	Menu
Duplicate	⌘-D	Edit
Free Rotate	Shift-⌘-R	Transform
Turn Autogrid On/Off	⌘-Y	Options

Table C-11
Other Paint Commands

Command	Key Sequence
Complete open or closed polygon or Bezigon	Enter
Move selected image one pixel or gridpoint	Any arrow key
Select eyedropper tool	Tab

Table C-12
Spreadsheet Menu Commands

Command	Key Sequence	Menu
Calculate Now	Shift-⌘-=	Calculate
Copy Format	Shift-⌘-C	Edit
Delete Cells	Shift-⌘-K	Calculate
Fill Down	⌘-D	Calculate
Fill Right	⌘-R	Calculate

Command	Key Sequence	Menu
Go to Cell	⌘-G	Options
Insert Cells	Shift-⌘-I	Calculate
Lock Cells	⌘-H	Options
Make Chart	⌘-M	Options
Number	Shift-⌘-N	Format
Paste Format	Shift-⌘-V	Edit
Sort	⌘-J	Calculate
Unlock Cells	Shift-⌘-H	Options

Table C-13
Spreadsheet Navigation Commands

Command	Key Sequence
Move one cell down	Return, down arrow (or Option-down arrow)[1]
Move one cell up	Shift-Return, up arrow (or Option-up arrow)[1]
Move one cell right	Tab, right arrow (or Option-right arrow)[1]
Move one cell left	Shift-Tab, left arrow (or Option-left arrow)[1]
Move one character right (in entry bar)	Option-right arrow (or right arrow)[1]
Move one character left (in entry bar)	Option-left arrow (or left arrow)[1]
Stay in current cell	Enter

[1]Whether you use an arrow key or an Option-arrow combination depends on how the spreadsheet preferences are set.

You also can use each of the commands in Table C-13 to complete a cell entry. The functions of these keys are determined by the settings in spreadsheet preferences.

Table C-14
Other Spreadsheet Commands

Command	Key Sequence
Cancel entry	Esc
Clear cell contents and format	Clear (Extended keyboard)
Delete character to left (in entry bar)	Delete/Backspace
Delete character to right (in entry bar)	Del (Extended keyboard)

Table C-15
Word Processing Menu Commands

Command	Key Sequence	Menu
Apply Ruler	Shift-⌘-V	Format
Copy Ruler	Shift-⌘-C	Format
Insert Column Break	Enter	Format
Insert Page Break	Shift-Enter	Format
Insert Footnote	Shift-⌘-F	Format
Insert Section Break	⌘-Enter	Format
Move Above	Control-up arrow	Outline
Move Below	Control-down arrow	Outline
Move Left	Shift-⌘-L/Control-left arrow	Outline
Move Right	Shift-⌘-R/Control-right arrow	Outline
New Topic Left	⌘-L	Outline
New Topic Right	⌘-R	Outline
Subscript	Shift-⌘-- (hyphen)	Style
Superscript	Shift-⌘-+	Style

Table C-16
Word Processing Navigation Commands

Command	Key Sequence
Move up one line	up arrow
Move down one line	down arrow
Move left one character	left arrow
Move right one character	right arrow
Move to beginning of document	⌘-up arrow
Move to end of document	⌘-down arrow
Move to beginning of line	⌘-left arrow
Move to end of line	⌘-right arrow
Move to beginning of paragraph	Option-up arrow
Move to end of paragraph	Option-down arrow
Move to beginning of word	Option-left arrow
Move to end of word	Option-right arrow

Table C-17
Other Word Processing Commands

Command	Key Sequence
Accept footnote entry and return to main body of document	Enter
New outline topic at same level	⌘-Return
New outline topic with same format as previous topic	Return
Select outline topic and its subtopics	Shift-Control-spacebar
Select text from insertion point to beginning of document	Shift-⌘-up arrow
Select text from insertion point to end of document	Shift-⌘-down arrow
Select text from insertion point to beginning of paragraph	Shift-Option-up arrow
Select text from insertion point to end of paragraph	Shift-Option-down arrow
Show/Hide invisible characters	⌘-;

Shortcuts for Dialog Box Buttons

With the exception of the *default button* in dialog boxes (a button surrounded by a double line that you can select by pressing Enter or Return), you normally have to use the mouse to click buttons. But some people are lazy. Dragging the mouse to the correct position just so you can click a button sometimes seems like more work than it's worth. Recognizing this fact, Claris built several keyboard shortcuts into ClarisWorks so that you can click buttons from the keyboard.

To click a dialog box button using the keyboard, press the ⌘ key while the dialog box is on-screen. Any button that has a ⌘-key equivalent will change to display the proper keystrokes inside the button (see Figure C-1).

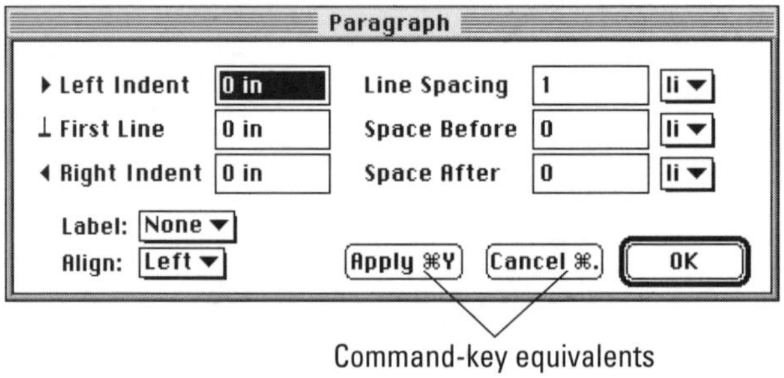

Figure C-1:
In the Paragraph dialog box, for example, the Apply and Cancel buttons have ⌘-key equivalents.

Command-key equivalents

Index

(continued)

(continued)

(continued)

The Internet For Macs® For Dummies® 2nd Edition	by Charles Seiter	ISBN: 1-56884-371-2	$19.99 USA/$26.99 Canada
The Internet For Macs® For Dummies® Starter Kit	by Charles Seiter	ISBN: 1-56884-244-9	$29.99 USA/$39.99 Canada
The Internet For Macs® For Dummies® Starter Kit Bestseller Edition	by Charles Seiter	ISBN: 1-56884-245-7	$39.99 USA/$54.99 Canada
The Internet For Windows® For Dummies® Starter Kit	by John R. Levine & Margaret Levine Young	ISBN: 1-56884-237-6	$34.99 USA/$44.99 Canada
The Internet For Windows® For Dummies® Starter Kit, Bestseller Edition	by John R. Levine & Margaret Levine Young	ISBN: 1-56884-246-5	$39.99 USA/$54.99 Canada

MACINTOSH

Mac® Programming For Dummies®	by Dan Parks Sydow	ISBN: 1-56884-173-6	$19.95 USA/$26.95 Canada
Macintosh® System 7.5 For Dummies®	by Bob LeVitus	ISBN: 1-56884-197-3	$19.95 USA/$26.95 Canada
MORE Macs® For Dummies®	by David Pogue	ISBN: 1-56884-087-X	$19.95 USA/$26.95 Canada
PageMaker 5 For Macs® For Dummies®	by Galen Gruman & Deke McClelland	ISBN: 1-56884-178-7	$19.95 USA/$26.95 Canada
QuarkXPress 3.3 For Dummies®	by Galen Gruman & Barbara Assadi	ISBN: 1-56884-217-1	$19.99 USA/$26.99 Canada
Upgrading and Fixing Macs® For Dummies®	by Kearney Rietmann & Frank Higgins	ISBN: 1-56884-189-2	$19.95 USA/$26.95 Canada

MULTIMEDIA

Multimedia & CD-ROMs For Dummies® 2nd Edition	by Andy Rathbone	ISBN: 1-56884-907-9	$19.99 USA/$26.99 Canada
Multimedia & CD-ROMs For Dummies®, Interactive Multimedia Value Pack, 2nd Edition	by Andy Rathbone	ISBN: 1-56884-909-5	$29.99 USA/$39.99 Canada

OPERATING SYSTEMS:

DOS

MORE DOS For Dummies®	by Dan Gookin	ISBN: 1-56884-046-2	$19.95 USA/$26.95 Canada
OS/2® Warp For Dummies® 2nd Edition	by Andy Rathbone	ISBN: 1-56884-205-8	$19.99 USA/$26.99 Canada

UNIX

MORE UNIX® For Dummies®	by John R. Levine & Margaret Levine Young	ISBN: 1-56884-361-5	$19.99 USA/$26.99 Canada
UNIX® For Dummies®	by John R. Levine & Margaret Levine Young	ISBN: 1-878058-58-4	$19.95 USA/$26.95 Canada

WINDOWS

MORE Windows® For Dummies® 2nd Edition	by Andy Rathbone	ISBN: 1-56884-048-9	$19.95 USA/$26.95 Canada
Windows® 95 For Dummies®	by Andy Rathbone	ISBN: 1-56884-240-6	$19.99 USA/$26.99 Canada

PCS/HARDWARE

Illustrated Computer Dictionary For Dummies® 2nd Edition	by Dan Gookin & Wallace Wang	ISBN: 1-56884-218-X	$12.95 USA/$16.95 Canada
Upgrading and Fixing PCs For Dummies® 2nd Edition	by Andy Rathbone	ISBN: 1-56884-903-6	$19.99 USA/$26.99 Canada

PRESENTATION/AUTOCAD

AutoCAD For Dummies®	by Bud Smith	ISBN: 1-56884-191-4	$19.95 USA/$26.95 Canada
PowerPoint 4 For Windows® For Dummies®	by Doug Lowe	ISBN: 1-56884-161-2	$16.99 USA/$22.99 Canada

PROGRAMMING

Borland C++ For Dummies®	by Michael Hyman	ISBN: 1-56884-162-0	$19.95 USA/$26.95 Canada
C For Dummies® Volume 1	by Dan Gookin	ISBN: 1-878058-78-9	$19.95 USA/$26.95 Canada
C++ For Dummies®	by Stephen R. Davis	ISBN: 1-56884-163-9	$19.95 USA/$26.95 Canada
Delphi Programming For Dummies®	by Neil Rubenking	ISBN: 1-56884-200-7	$19.99 USA/$26.99 Canada
Mac® Programming For Dummies®	by Dan Parks Sydow	ISBN: 1-56884-173-6	$19.95 USA/$26.95 Canada
PowerBuilder 4 Programming For Dummies®	by Ted Coombs & Jason Coombs	ISBN: 1-56884-325-9	$19.99 USA/$26.99 Canada
QBasic Programming For Dummies®	by Douglas Hergert	ISBN: 1-56884-093-4	$19.95 USA/$26.95 Canada
Visual Basic 3 For Dummies®	by Wallace Wang	ISBN: 1-56884-076-4	$19.95 USA/$26.95 Canada
Visual Basic "X" For Dummies®	by Wallace Wang	ISBN: 1-56884-230-9	$19.99 USA/$26.99 Canada
Visual C++ 2 For Dummies®	by Michael Hyman & Bob Arnson	ISBN: 1-56884-328-3	$19.99 USA/$26.99 Canada
Windows® 95 Programming For Dummies®	by S. Randy Davis	ISBN: 1-56884-327-5	$19.99 USA/$26.99 Canada

SPREADSHEET

1-2-3 For Dummies®	by Greg Harvey	ISBN: 1-878058-60-6	$16.95 USA/$22.95 Canada
1-2-3 For Windows® 5 For Dummies® 2nd Edition	by John Walkenbach	ISBN: 1-56884-216-3	$16.95 USA/$22.95 Canada
Excel 5 For Macs® For Dummies®	by Greg Harvey	ISBN: 1-56884-186-8	$19.95 USA/$26.95 Canada
Excel For Dummies® 2nd Edition	by Greg Harvey	ISBN: 1-56884-050-0	$16.95 USA/$22.95 Canada
MORE 1-2-3 For DOS For Dummies®	by John Weingarten	ISBN: 1-56884-224-4	$19.99 USA/$26.99 Canada
MORE Excel 5 For Windows® For Dummies®	by Greg Harvey	ISBN: 1-56884-207-4	$19.95 USA/$26.95 Canada
Quattro Pro 6 For Windows® For Dummies®	by John Walkenbach	ISBN: 1-56884-174-4	$19.95 USA/$26.95 Canada
Quattro Pro For DOS For Dummies®	by John Walkenbach	ISBN: 1-56884-023-3	$16.95 USA/$22.95 Canada

UTILITIES

Norton Utilities 8 For Dummies®	by Beth Slick	ISBN: 1-56884-166-3	$19.95 USA/$26.95 Canada

VCRS/CAMCORDERS

VCRs & Camcorders For Dummies™	by Gordon McComb & Andy Rathbone	ISBN: 1-56884-229-5	$14.99 USA/$20.99 Canada

WORD PROCESSING

Ami Pro For Dummies®	by Jim Meade	ISBN: 1-56884-049-7	$19.95 USA/$26.95 Canada
MORE Word For Windows® 6 For Dummies®	by Doug Lowe	ISBN: 1-56884-165-5	$19.95 USA/$26.95 Canada
MORE WordPerfect® 6 For Windows® For Dummies®	by Margaret Levine Young & David C. Kay	ISBN: 1-56884-206-6	$19.95 USA/$26.95 Canada
MORE WordPerfect® 6 For DOS For Dummies®	by Wallace Wang, edited by Dan Gookin	ISBN: 1-56884-047-1	$19.95 USA/$26.95 Canada
Word 6 For Macs® For Dummies®	by Dan Gookin	ISBN: 1-56884-190-6	$19.95 USA/$26.95 Canada
Word For Windows® 6 For Dummies®	by Dan Gookin	ISBN: 1-56884-075-6	$16.95 USA/$22.95 Canada
Word For Windows® For Dummies®	by Dan Gookin & Ray Werner	ISBN: 1-878058-86-X	$16.95 USA/$22.95 Canada
WordPerfect® 6 For DOS For Dummies®	by Dan Gookin	ISBN: 1-878058-77-0	$16.95 USA/$22.95 Canada
WordPerfect® 6.1 For Windows® For Dummies® 2nd Edition	by Margaret Levine Young & David Kay	ISBN: 1-56884-243-0	$16.95 USA/$22.95 Canada
WordPerfect® For Dummies®	by Dan Gookin	ISBN: 1-878058-52-5	$16.95 USA/$22.95 Canada

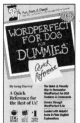

Macworld® Mac® & Power Mac SECRETS™, 2nd Edition
by David Pogue & Joseph Schorr
This is the definitive Mac reference for those who want to become power users! Includes three disks with 9MB of software!

ISBN: 1-56884-175-2
$39.95 USA/$54.95 Canada
Includes 3 disks chock full of software.

Macworld® Mac® FAQs™
by David Pogue
Written by the hottest Macintosh author around, David Pogue, *Macworld Mac FAQs* gives users the ultimate Mac reference. Hundreds of Mac questions and answers side-by-side, right at your fingertips, and organized into six easy-to-reference sections with lots of sidebars and diagrams.

ISBN: 1-56884-480-8
$19.99 USA/$26.99 Canada

Macworld® System 7.5 Bible, 3rd Edition
by Lon Poole
ISBN: 1-56884-098-5
$29.95 USA/$39.95 Canada

Macworld® ClarisWorks 3.0 Companion, 3rd Edition
by Steven A. Schwartz
ISBN: 1-56884-481-6
$24.99 USA/$34.99 Canada

Macworld® Complete Mac® Handbook Plus Interactive CD, 3rd Edition
by Jim Heid
ISBN: 1-56884-192-2
$39.95 USA/$54.95 Canada
Includes an interactive CD-ROM.

Macworld® Ultimate Mac® CD-ROM
by Jim Heid
ISBN: 1-56884-477-8
$19.99 USA/$26.99 Canada
CD-ROM includes version 2.0 of QuickTime, and over 65 MB of the best shareware, freeware, fonts, sounds, and more!

Macworld® Networking Bible, 2nd Edition
by Dave Kosiur & Joel M. Snyder
ISBN: 1-56884-194-9
$29.95 USA/$39.95 Canada

Macworld® Photoshop 3 Bible, 2nd Edition
by Deke McClelland
ISBN: 1-56884-158-2
$39.95 USA/$54.95 Canada
Includes stunning CD-ROM with add-ons, digitized photos and more.

Macworld® Photoshop 2.5 Bible
by Deke McClelland
ISBN: 1-56884-022-5
$29.95 USA/$39.95 Canada

Macworld® FreeHand 4 Bible
by Deke McClelland
ISBN: 1-56884-170-1
$29.95 USA/$39.95 Canada

Macworld® Illustrator 5.0/5.5 Bible
by Ted Alspach
ISBN: 1-56884-097-7
$39.95 USA/$54.95 Canada
Includes CD-ROM with QuickTime tutorials.

For scholastic requests & educational orders please call Educational Sales, at 1. 800. 434. 2086

FOR MORE INFO OR TO ORDER, PLEASE CALL ▶ 800. 762. 2974

For volume discounts & special orders please Tony Real, Special Sales, at 415. 655. 3048

Order Center: **(800) 762-2974** *(8 a.m.–6 p.m., EST, weekdays)*

9/19/

Quantity	ISBN	Title	Price	Total

Shipping & Handling Charges

	Description	First book	Each additional book	Total
Domestic	Normal	$4.50	$1.50	$
	Two Day Air	$8.50	$2.50	$
	Overnight	$18.00	$3.00	$
International	Surface	$8.00	$8.00	$
	Airmail	$16.00	$16.00	$
	DHL Air	$17.00	$17.00	$

*For large quantities call for shipping & handling charges.
**Prices are subject to change without notice.

Ship to:

Name _____

Company _____

Address _____

City/State/Zip _____

Daytime Phone _____

Payment: ☐ Check to IDG Books Worldwide (US Funds Only)

☐ VISA   ☐ MasterCard   ☐ American Express

Card # _____ Expires _____

Signature _____

Subtotal _____

CA residents add
applicable sales tax _____

IN, MA, and MD
residents add
5% sales tax _____

IL residents add
6.25% sales tax _____

RI residents add
7% sales tax _____

TX residents add
8.25% sales tax _____

Shipping _____

Total _____

Please send this order form to:
IDG Books Worldwide, Inc.
7260 Shadeland Station, Suite 100
Indianapolis, IN 46256

Allow up to 3 weeks for delivery.
Thank you!

IDG BOOKS WORLDWIDE REGISTRATION CARD

RETURN THIS REGISTRATION CARD FOR FREE CATALOG

Title of this book: Macworld ClarisWorks 4 Bible

My overall rating of this book: ❑ Very good [1]   ❑ Good [2]   ❑ Satisfactory [3]   ❑ Fair [4]   ❑ Poor [5]

How I first heard about this book:

❑ Found in bookstore; name: [6]

❑ Advertisement: [8]

❑ Word of mouth; heard about book from friend, co-worker, etc.: [10]

❑ Book review: [7]

❑ Catalog: [9]

❑ Other: [11]

What I liked most about this book:

What I would change, add, delete, etc., in future editions of this book:

Other comments:

Number of computer books I purchase in a year: ❑ 1 [12]   ❑ 2-5 [13]   ❑ 6-10 [14]   ❑ More than 10 [15]

I would characterize my computer skills as: ❑ Beginner [16]   ❑ Intermediate [17]   ❑ Advanced [18]   ❑ Professional [19]

I use ❑ DOS [20]   ❑ Windows [21]   ❑ OS/2 [22]   ❑ Unix [23]   ❑ Macintosh [24]   ❑ Other: [25]_____
(please specify)

I would be interested in new books on the following subjects:
(please check all that apply, and use the spaces provided to identify specific software)

❑ Word processing: [26]

❑ Data bases: [28]

❑ File Utilities: [30]

❑ Networking: [32]

❑ Other: [34]

❑ Spreadsheets: [27]

❑ Desktop publishing: [29]

❑ Money management: [31]

❑ Programming languages: [33]

I use a PC at (please check all that apply): ❑ home [35]   ❑ work [36]   ❑ school [37]   ❑ other: [38] _____

The disks I prefer to use are ❑ 5.25 [39]   ❑ 3.5 [40]   ❑ other: [41]_____

I have a CD ROM: ❑ yes [42]   ❑ no [43]

I plan to buy or upgrade computer hardware this year: ❑ yes [44]   ❑ no [45]

I plan to buy or upgrade computer software this year: ❑ yes [46]   ❑ no [47]

Name: _____   Business title: [48] _____   Type of Business: [49] _____

Address (❑ home [50] ❑ work [51]/Company name: _____)

Street/Suite# _____

City [52]/State [53]/Zipcode [54]: _____   Country [55] _____

❑ **I liked this book!** You may quote me by name in future
IDG Books Worldwide promotional materials.

My daytime phone number is _____

IDG BOOKS
®
THE WORLD OF COMPUTER KNOWLEDGE

❏ YES!

Please keep me informed about IDG's World of Computer Knowledge.
Send me the latest IDG Books catalog.